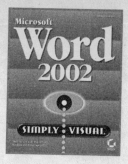

MICROSOFT WORD 2002
SIMPLY VISUAL
BY PERSPECTI

320 pages; $24
ISBN 0-7821-40

C000156396

Deciphering the ~~~~~~~~~~~~~~~~~~~~~~~~~~~~~ as-
ier, thanks to th ~~~~~~~~~~~~~~~~~~~~~~~~~~ ing.
Hands-on lessons guide you step by ~~~~, ~~~~~~~ program's fundamental tasks—from creating and customizing
document templates to adding multimedia, routing and
reviewing documents, and using Word for desktop and
web publishing.

MICROSOFT OFFICE XP
SIMPLY VISUAL
BY PERSPECTION, INC.

400 pages; $24.99
ISBN 0-7821-4004-1

This illustrated introduction to the essentials of Office XP
covers the newest features in Office, including speech and
handwriting recognition, translation tools, and improved
document recovery. You can become an expert at formatting
and enhancing Word documents, designing Excel spreadsheets, creating slide shows in PowerPoint, creating web
pages, and much more! The easy-to-read, visual format
makes learning Office XP easy.

MICROSOFT®
OFFICE XP
COMPLETE

SYBEX®

SAN FRANCISCO ▸ LONDON

Associate Publisher: Dan Brodnitz

Acquisitions and Developmental Editor: Bonnie Bills

Compilation Editor: Kate J. Chase

Editor: Ronn Jost

Production Editor: Kylie Johnston

Book Designer: Maureen Forys, Happenstance Type-O-Rama

Electronic Publishing Specialist: Maureen Forys, Happenstance Type-O-Rama

Proofreaders: Amey Garber, Dave Nash, Yariv Rabinovitch, Nancy Riddiough

Indexer: Lynnzee Elze

Cover Designer: Design Site

Cover Photograph: Photodisc

Library of Congress Card Number: 2001096249

ISBN: 0-7821-4050-5

ACKNOWLEDGMENTS

This book is the work of many, both inside and outside Sybex, including the publishing team members Cheryl Applewood, Bonnie Bills, and Dan Brodnitz, and the editorial/production team of Ronn Jost, Kylie Johnston, Maureen Forys, and Lynnzee Elze.

Kate J. Chase deserves particular thanks for making sure all of the material in this book was up-to-date, organized, and flowed in a seamless manner.

Finally, our most important thanks go to the contributors who agreed to have their work excerpted into *Microsoft Office XP Complete*: Karla Browning, Mary Burmeister, Gini Courter, Lucinda Dykes, Molly E. Holzschlag, Annette Marquis, Mark Minasi, Perspection, Inc., Deborah S. Ray, Eric J. Ray, Celeste Robinson, Alan Simpson, Ed Tittel, Denise Tyler, Chelsea Valentine, and Peter Weverka. Without their efforts, this book would not exist.

CONTENTS AT A GLANCE

CONTENTS

Part II ▸ Creating Documents with Word 2002   **91**

Chapter 3 □ Working with Word 2002 Documents   **93**

Chapter 5 □ Using Templates and Styles   **153**

Part III ▶ Working with Numbers in Excel 2002   243

Chapter 8 ▫ Basic Workbook Skills   245

Chapter 9 □ **Calculating with Functions**   **301**

Chapter 10 □ **Working with Text and Dates**   **327**

Chapter 13 □ **Managing Contacts with Outlook 2002**   **437**

Chapter 16 ◻ Creating a Slide Show with PowerPoint 2002   521

Part VII ▸ Web Publishing with Office XP 615

Appendices

INTRODUCTION

Microsoft *Office XP Complete* brings you a highly valuable reference on using the range of packages and features available within this latest release of Microsoft's ultra-popular Office productivity software.

But it's also a bit of an innovation because it compiles the work of a dozen independent Sybex texts into a single comprehensive guide that offers you all the essential information plus a good deal of value-added help and instruction. If you want just one Office XP text for your reference shelf, this was created specifically to be that one.

This book was conceived with several important goals in mind:

- ▶ Offering a knowledgeable and thorough guide at a price that works with your budget

- ▶ Helping you familiarize yourself with not just the core packages incorporated into Office XP but how you use them in a way that is relevant to the work you do

- ▶ Acquainting you with some of Sybex's best expert authors—their writing and teaching styles as well as the level of expertise they bring to their subjects and books—so that you can readily find a match for your interests as you begin to explore and work with Office XP

Thus, with this book, you get to experience and benefit from some of the best material from a whole collection of other Sybex works, most of them devoted to a specific subject, such as Word 2002 or Excel 2002. Rather than you having to handle several books at once, we've done the job of picking and choosing from several for you, to give you as much depth as you need to get started and fully into your work, and the breadth to explore beyond the boundaries of just one application or viewpoint. You, of course, have the option of choosing to add to your library one or more of the full Sybex texts on which this compilation was based.

You've likely read at least a few other computer help books, so you're probably all too aware of the different approaches (from teaching styles to language to user level and more). Because we've assembled many different authors, subjects, and book formats into one comprehensive guide, you'll see differences among the various parts and chapters. In some, you'll get a taste of the "here's what it looks like" approach of the *Simply Visual* series, while in others, you'll benefit from the in-depth explanation and analysis offered in the *Mastering* series, for example. But there's one thing you'll find they all have in common: a commitment to clarity, accuracy, and practicality.

Also, nearly every book represented here is the careful work of a single writer or a pair of writers collaborating, and so you get the benefit of each author's specific knowledge and experience.

In adapting the various source materials included here in *Microsoft Office XP Complete*, the compilers preserved these individual voices and perspectives. Chapters were edited only to minimize the duplication of content and to add updated or extended information where applicable.

WHO CAN BENEFIT FROM THIS BOOK?

Microsoft Office XP Complete was put together with the needs of a broad range of computer users in mind. Because of this, some chapters of the book may be more necessary to you than others. For example, if you're an advanced user trying to brush up on the differences between Office XP and earlier versions, you can easily skip most of the introductory material. However, if you're a novice Office XP user, you definitely want to familiarize yourself with the basics, and then explore the more advanced topics—or other, less-used applications within Office XP—when it's convenient for you.

You don't have to guess, however, since the Table of Contents and the Index can be used to help guide you through the subjects.

Beginners Introductory material in this book should make it pretty easy for you to start working with Office XP basics even if you have limited experience with Microsoft Office, Windows, or computers in general.

Intermediate users Are you more than a novice but not as experienced as a veteran? This book's core material should help you throughout the development of your skills in Office XP and beyond. In particular, you'll get a good look at the changes in this version of Office and how to perform some advanced tasks you may not have realized you could do.

Advanced users Treat this book as the strong reference it is, offering you not just the features new to Office XP, but offering you insight into other advanced options you may have not yet used.

How This Book Is Organized

Microsoft Office XP Complete has 24 chapters divided into seven chief parts, plus four appendices and an extensive Windows XP Command Reference.

Part I: Introducing Office XP   In the first two chapters which make up Part I, you are introduced to Office XP and its components, as well as to the basics for getting to work with the package.

Part II: Creating Documents in Word 2002   This section's five chapters focus in on the most frequently done work in Office: creating documents. They take you from basic use all the way through the application of templates and styles, and show you how to incorporate images into documents.

Part III: Working with Numbers in Excel 2002   Excel is the spreadsheet/worksheet component of Office XP. Part III's five chapters lead you from setting up your first workbook to calculating with functions, presenting your data graphically through charting, and creating Pivot Tables.

Part IV: Communicating with Outlook 2002   Part IV familiarizes you with the most important Outlook 2002 functions: sending and receiving E-Mail, setting up and managing contacts, and task management.

Part V: Presenting Information with PowerPoint 2001   Power-Point 2002 is the presentation software included with Office XP. The two chapters of Part V not only introduce you to creating professional-looking presentations, but also to creating and augmenting slide shows.

Part VI: Creating Databases with Access 2002   Databases are an excellent way to document, store, and retrieve sometimes vast amounts of data, but can be complex to understand, even with a package that does so much of the work for you, as Access 2002 does. The first chapter of this part helps you identify and understand key database concepts as they relate to your work with Access, and then the second chapter steps you through the creation and use of a database.

Part VII: Web Publishing with Office XP   The final four chapters of this book, making up Part VII, help you identify the many ways you can use Office XP and its packages to publish your information (documents, data, presentations, and more) to a website. They also show you how to create web pages using Word, Excel, and FrontPage 2002 and how to augment your website using Extensible Hypertext Markup Language (XHTML).

Appendix A: Installing Microsoft Office XP   Important instructions and assistance for installing Office XP are offered here.

Appendix B: Speech and Handwriting Recognition in Office XP
Two important and highly useful new features in Office XP are speech and handwriting recognition, which allow you to do more than "type" your work. Appendix B gives you an overview of these functions and how to use them.

Appendix C: Troubleshooting PC Problems   Sometimes, the problem at hand isn't with your software (Office XP) but with your hardware and/or its configuration. Appendix C gives you an overview of common problems you may see with your system, along with advice on resolving them.

Appendix D: Troubleshooting Printers   Extending the useful information presented in the previous appendix, the final appendix offers key tips for troubleshooting any difficulties you have when printing your Office XP files.

Discover Windows XP: Command and Feature Reference   This section offers you nearly 50 pages of key commands and features in Windows XP.

A Few Typographical Conventions

The ➢ symbol will appear to help you move about whenever an operation requires a series of choices from either a menu or a dialog box. An example of this may be something like: "Select Programs ➢ Settings ➢ Printers." The items that the ➢ symbol separates can be anything from menu names, to check boxes, to toolbar icons, or any other element common to the Windows interface.

TIP
Always check these out to discover quicker and savvier ways to perform a task.

NOTE

Note icons indicate some special information has been highlighted for your attention. This may relate to alternate ways to perform a particular task, or just offer you better insight into a situation.

WARNING

When you see a Warning like this, *always* read it to discover important information that may affect your work and what you're trying to do.

SIDEBARS

Sidebars elaborate on special topics that may be of interest to you.

FOR MORE INFORMATION...

See the Sybex website, www.sybex.com, to learn more about all of the books upon which *Microsoft Office XP Complete* is based. On the site's Catalog page, you'll find links to specific books of interest to you.

We hope you'll find this book extremely useful in your work with Office XP. Enjoy!

PART i
INTRODUCING OFFICE XP

Chapter 1

PRESENTING OFFICE XP

Those already familiar with earlier versions of Microsoft Office will find all their classic applications still included with the release of Office XP (*XP* stands for experience). Some of the tools, however, have undergone either a face-lift or a full revamping. Those new to the package will find a broadly featured office-function package.

Just as we have seen with recent versions of Office, this version extends the Internet connectivity and functionality available from within its applications, making the boundary between the Desktop and the Web more gray. It also further develops collaboration tools for those who work together on reports, proposals, presentations, databases, and spreadsheets.

Adapted from *Mastering Microsoft Office XP Premium Edition* by Gini Courter and Annette Marquis with Karla Browning

ISBN 0-7821-4000-9   1392 pp $49.99

EXPLORING THE OFFICE XP USER INTERFACE

The first thing you notice when you fire up one of the Office XP applications is the new *task pane* on the right side of the application window. The contents of the task pane support a range of features from opening documents to searching for clip art. Although sometimes intrusive and awkward to use, the task panes bring a lot of features to the forefront of the Office XP applications.

After you get over the surprise of the task panes, you might also notice the change in the look of Office XP's toolbars. In this section, we'll discuss what's really changed behind the scenes with the functionality of toolbars and dialog boxes. You'll also find information about the fundamental changes in the online help features in Office XP.

Task Panes Put Options at Your Fingertips

Task panes fire up and close automatically depending on your activity in the application. For example, the New Document task pane, shown in Figure 1.1, appears in place of the New dialog box whenever you start an application. If you close the New Document task pane, it reappears whenever you choose File ➤ New from the menu.

To activate the task pane manually, choose View ➤ Task Pane. You can then select the task pane you want to use from the menu at the top of the pane. The list of panes varies by application. Word's Task Pane menu appears in Figure 1.2.

After you select a task pane from the list, you can go back to previous task panes by clicking the Back button to the left of the task pane name. Use the Forward button to return to the next pane in a series of previously opened panes. To close the task pane, click the Close button to the right of the task pane name.

You may find task panes to be intrusive and annoying when you first encounter them. If you're an experienced Office user, it will even take a while to get used to using them—old habits die hard. We recommend that you give them a chance, however. They are pretty good at getting out of your way when you are ready to work, and they add some functionality that never existed in Office before—for example, Word's Reveal Formatting task pane (see Chapter 4, "Formatting Documents").

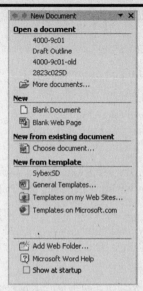

FIGURE 1.1: The New Document task pane lets you open existing documents and create new ones.

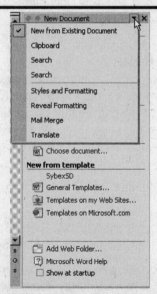

FIGURE 1.2: Choose the task pane you want to use from the Task Pane menu.

The New Document Task Pane

The New Document task pane is immediately visible when you launch Word, Excel, and PowerPoint. The task pane is divided into five sections:

Open A Document   Lists the most recently saved documents and has a More Documents link that opens the Open dialog box

New   Allows you to open a Blank Document or a Blank Web Page

New From Existing Document   Makes it easy to base a document on a previously saved document without running the risk of overwriting the saved document

New From Template   Lists recently used templates, general templates, templates saved to a web folder, and templates available from www.microsoft.com

Miscellaneous options   Allow you to add a web folder, access Word help, and disable the Show At Startup option that opens the New Document task pane when you launch the application

As soon as you select a document to open, the New Document task pane closes automatically to get out of your way while you work.

The Office Clipboard Task Pane

Microsoft introduced the Office Clipboard in Office 2000, and it quickly became one of the most exciting new features for users who create documents that cross Office applications. With the Office 2000 Clipboard, you could cut or copy more than one item and paste them individually or as a group. In Office XP, the Office Clipboard takes a giant leap forward in several significant ways:

- ▶ The number of items you can collect on the Clipboard has increased from 12 to 24.

- ▶ The Clipboard has been converted from a toolbar-based palette of icons to a task pane with larger previews of the individual items.

- ▶ The Clipboard is nearly as handy as the system clock or volume control. An icon appears in the Windows system tray from which you can control the Office Clipboard when it is not visible and that notifies you when something is being added to the Clipboard.

The Office Clipboard task pane, shown in Figure 1.3, activates automatically when you cut or copy more than one item. You can open it manually in one of three ways:

- ▶ Select Clipboard from the Task Pane menu shown earlier in Figure 1.2.

- ▶ Choose Edit ➢ Office Clipboard.

- ▶ Hold Ctrl and double-press (as in double-click) the C key.

When the Clipboard task pane is open, you can cut or copy items from your document and either paste them immediately or store them for later use. When you are ready to paste, you can choose to paste an individual item from the Clipboard task pane, or click Paste All or Clear All to paste or delete all of the items on the Clipboard.

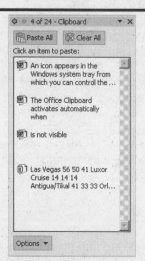

FIGURE 1.3: Use the Clipboard task pane to store up to 24 items you eventually want to paste into a document.

Setting Office Clipboard Options

The Office Clipboard has four options you can set to customize how the Clipboard task pane behaves. You can change the option settings by clicking the Options button at the bottom of the Clipboard task pane. These options are as follows:

Show Office Clipboard Automatically With this option set, the Office Clipboard task pane appears automatically after you cut or copy a second item.

Collect Without Showing Office Clipboard This option, turned off by default, allows you to collect items with the task pane closed and out of your way.

Show Office Clipboard Icon On Taskbar This great option displays the Office Clipboard icon in the Windows system tray so you can cut and copy items from non–Office XP applications and store them on the Office Clipboard for pasting into an Office document.

Show Status Near Taskbar When Copying This option displays a screen tip above the Office Clipboard icon in the system tray to indicate that an item is being copied and how many items the Clipboard currently is holding.

The Office Clipboard is one of the most welcome enhancements to Office XP. It was a great feature when it was introduced in Office 2000, and it is even more powerful now.

TIP

The Office Clipboard is not limited to use within Office. As long as the Clipboard is running in an Office application, you can cut and copy items from other applications, such as Internet Explorer or a graphics application, to the Office Clipboard for use in an Office document.

The Search Task Panes

If you've ever misplaced a document or needed to find every mention of a client's name in a group of documents, the new Basic Search and Advanced Search task panes are invaluable. These new task panes extend the search tools available in previous Office versions by searching for a specific text string in all of your documents. Although this feature has been available in Windows search tools, this is the first time you've been able to conduct your searching directly within an Office application. When you find the documents you are looking for, you can edit them in the application where they were created or copy a link to them to the Office Clipboard. Using this second choice, you can create a document directory that contains links to all the documents related to a specific topic. This is a great way to organize materials that are spread all over your drives and a key reason you may want to use Office Search instead of the traditional Windows search tools.

NOTE

To locate a text string within the open document, Find is still available in Office XP by choosing Edit ➤ Find or by clicking the Browse button on the vertical scroll bar and choosing Find.

To activate the Search pane, choose File ➤ Search, or if the task pane is open, select it from the Task Pane menu. In the Basic Search task pane, shown in Figure 1.4, you can enter text and have it search across your local computer and network drives and throughout Outlook to find what you need.

FIGURE 1.4: Use the Basic Search task pane to search through all of your files for the documents you need.

To enter a search, follow these steps:

1. Enter text in the Search Text box. Office looks through the body of documents, document properties, and keywords. Enter more words to narrow the search. Basic Search finds all word forms—for example, a search on *win* gives you *win*, *winning*, and *winner*.

2. Select the locations you would like to search from the Search In drop-down list. You can search Everywhere or limit your search to any combination of My Computer, My Network Places, and Outlook's folders.

3. Select the type of results you would like from the Results Should Be drop-down list. You can choose different types of Microsoft Office files, Outlook items, and web pages.

4. Click the Search button. The results are returned in the Search Results task pane, shown in Figure 1.5.

NOTE

When you use Office Search, you may find some surprising results. If you look closely at the results in Figure 1.5, you'll see that two of the files it returned are image files. Microsoft Office Document Imaging, a new product included with Microsoft Office XP, actually performs Optical Character Recognition (OCR) while it is generating TIFF image files. It then adds the text it recognizes to the Indexing Service, which Office also runs behind the scenes, so that even image text can be identified through a search. You can access Microsoft Office Document Imaging directly by opening the Microsoft Office Tools menu on your Programs menu.

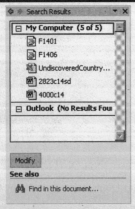

FIGURE 1.5: The search results appear in the Search Results task pane.

When you want to start a new search or narrow the existing one, click the Modify button on the Search Results task pane to return to the Basic Search task pane.

Using Advanced Search

When you need to establish more exact conditions for a search, click the Advanced Search link on the Basic Search task pane. In the Advanced Search task pane, shown in Figure 1.6, you can choose from a long list of properties and set conditions for each one. For example, you can search for only documents that were modified after a certain date and contain a certain word.

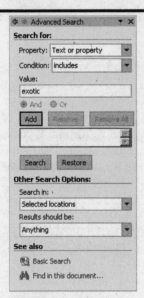

FIGURE 1.6: Use the Advanced Search task pane to conduct a more precise search of your files.

To use the Advanced Search task pane, follow these steps:

1. Select a property of the files that you want to locate from the Property drop-down list.

2. Select a condition that you want the property to meet from the Condition drop-down list.

3. Enter a value that you are looking for in the Value text box.

4. Click Add to save the search parameter.

5. Select And or Or to include another search parameter.

6. Repeat steps 1–5 until you have entered all the parameters for the search.

7. If you want to modify one of the search parameters, use the spin buttons to display the search parameter you want and then click the Remove button. Make any changes to the Property, Condition, or Value and click Add, or click Remove again to delete it.

8. Set Search In and Results Should Be search options.

9. Click Search.

Let's say, for example, you want to find all the documents created between two specific dates: 1/1/02 and 1/31/02. In the Property drop-down list, select Creation Date to search for the document creation date. In the Condition drop-down list, choose On Or After and enter **1/1/02** in the Value text box. Click Add to save the first condition. If you stop here, Office will return all the documents created on or after 1/1/02. To add the second condition, select And. Creation Date should still be selected in the Property text box. Select On Or Before as the Condition and enter **1/31/02** in the Value text box. Click Add to add the second condition. When you've finished entering your search parameters, select where you want to search in the Search In list and what kind of documents you want to see in the Results Should Be list. When all of the parameters are set, click Search to begin the search for your documents.

Cataloging Your Image, Sound, and Motion Files with the Clip Organizer

The Microsoft Clip Organizer, formerly known as the ClipArt Gallery, has been totally revamped for Office XP. It's a much more powerful tool designed to keep track of all of your media files, not just those supplied by Microsoft. Although previous versions of the gallery had this potential, very few users actually took advantage of it.

SETTING DOCUMENT PROPERTIES FOR EASY SEARCHING

If you are wondering where document properties come from in the first place, you are not alone. You would not be the first person to ask, "How does it know I created this document and why doesn't it use my full name?" Some document properties, such as Creation Date and Modified Date, are created automatically by Office when you save an Office document. Other properties, such as Author, Title, Category, Keywords, and Description, can be set by you in the document's Properties dialog box. You can access this dialog box for any open document by choosing File ➤ Properties. The first tab of the five-tab dialog box, the General tab, displays the filename, location, file size, and critical dates such as Creation Date, Modified Date, and Accessed Date—that is, after the file has been saved the first time.

The second tab, Summary, is a place for you to enter critical information about the document—its title, subject, author, manager, company, categories, keywords, and comments (description). The Author field is filled in automatically from the data entered on the User Information tab of the Options dialog box. You can change it on the Summary tab or change it permanently in the application's Options dialog box (Tools ➤ Options). If you'd like to be able to see an outline of the headings in a Word document, be sure to select the Save Preview Picture check box; the summary appears on the Contents tab.

The third tab, Statistics, displays similar data to the General tab but goes into even more detail, such as the date the document was last printed, how many revisions it has had, and the total editing time for the document (the actual time the document has been open by someone). You can also learn about the document size, from bytes to pages and everything in between.

The Contents tab displays the document's title—if the Save Picture Preview check box on the Summary tab is checked—and the headings of a Word document, the macro sheets of an Excel workbook, and the design template and slide titles of a PowerPoint presentation.

To enter even more data about a particular document, click the Custom tab. Follow these steps to set the custom properties:

1. Select a property from the list or enter your own in the Name text box.

CONTINUED ➡

2. Select a data type: Text, Date, Number, or Yes Or No.

3. Enter a value in the Value text box. The value must match the data type you set in step 2. If it doesn't match, Office changes the data type to Text.

   If you have bookmarks in Word, named ranges in Excel, or selected text in PowerPoint, you can select the Link To Content check box to link the property to the specific contents. Use this option when you want to identify a named location in a document. After selecting the check box, select the named location from the Value drop-down list.

4. Click the Add button.

You can add as many custom properties as you want, but you can enter only one value per property. Most of the time, that makes sense—you can have only one Date Completed, for example. However, you may want to use some properties, such as Reference, more than once. If you need to enter additional values, create a new property, such as Reference1, Reference2, and so on.

Because the Property dialog box is available anywhere you can see a file—the Windows Explorer, My Network Places, Office Advanced Search, the Open dialog box, to name a few—entering properties can give you critical information about a document without even having to open it. To see the properties for a document, right-click a filename and choose Properties.

If you decide properties are essential to your business and want to be prompted to enter properties each time you save a document for the first time, choose Tools ➢ Options and on the Save tab, select Prompt For Document Properties.

In Office XP, the first time you click the Insert Clip Art button on the Drawing toolbar or choose Insert ➢ Picture ➢ Clip Art, you have the option of cataloging image, sound, and motion files located on any of your local drives. Click the Options button on the message box that opens to select the folders you would like it to search to create the catalogs. It takes a few minutes to identify all your local folders and a few minutes more after you select the folders you want to actually create the catalog. However, it is worth the wait. After the cataloging is complete, you can use the Insert Clip Art task pane to search for your own images, as well as those in the Microsoft clip collection.

Part I

TIP

To take full advantage of the Clip Organizer's search power, be sure to edit the keywords on the cataloged images. When the Insert Clip Art task pane opens, click Clips Organizer in the See Also section. The Clips Organizer shows your Collections list and displays thumbnails of images in the selected collection. Right-click any media file and choose Edit Keywords.

Additional Task Panes

Each application that uses task panes—Word, Excel, PowerPoint, and Publisher—has additional task panes that are specific to that application. The task panes provide easy access to a wealth of tools and are definitely worth exploring. To learn what task panes a particular application has available, choose View ➢ Task Pane and click the Task Pane drop-down list found on the task pane header next to the Close button. You'll find additional information about the task panes in the chapters of this book pertaining to individual applications.

Personalized Menus and Toolbars Respond to the Way You Work

In Microsoft Office 2000, Microsoft introduced the personalized menus and toolbars feature. Recognizing that most users use only a small percentage of menu and toolbar options, Microsoft redesigned them to bring the tools you use to the forefront. In personalized toolbars, the Standard and Formatting toolbars share one row, and only the most frequently used tools appear on each portion of the toolbar. Personalized menus move frequently used menu items to the top of the list, and the menus themselves display only a portion of the available menu options.

This personalized menus and toolbars feature has been unequivocally either loved or hated by Office users. Microsoft heard their users' feedback and—for those in the latter category—made the feature a little easier to turn off. We consider this a blessing since we recommend that everyone turn it off before entering a single character in a document. After you have an application mastered, you might choose to make use of personalized menus and toolbars, but do not try it if you are learning an application. In our opinion, this is an invitation to indescribable aggravation.

Another less controversial change in Office XP is the new look of the toolbars and menus. When selected, toolbar buttons and menu options in Office XP turn blue with a darker blue border. Microsoft describes this as a streamlined, flatter look that is designed to take advantage of high-color displays and new Windows 2000 technologies. That may be the case, but the biggest advantage is you can look at another user's screen or a picture in a book and know at a glance which version of Office you are looking at. Beyond that, the change won't impact your use of the Office products.

Working with (or without) Personalized Menus and Toolbars

In Office XP, menu bars and toolbars adapt to the way you use the Office applications. Menus are collapsed, displaying only commonly used commands (see Figure 1.7) until you expand them to see the full list. To fully expand a collapsed menu, click the Expand arrow at the bottom of the menu, or simply hover over the menu for a moment.

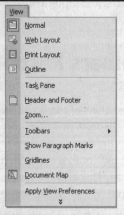

FIGURE 1.7: Menus are initially collapsed, and can be expanded to show all of the available commands.

 Personalized toolbars means that some buttons that were traditionally located on the Standard and Formatting toolbars are no longer displayed so that both toolbars can fit together on a single row. To display both these toolbars on separate rows or to access a button that is not visible, click the Toolbar Options button located at the right end of a toolbar to open the Toolbar Options menu:

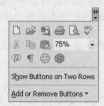

To see all of the buttons on the Standard and Formatting toolbars and display the Standard and Formatting toolbars on separate rows, choose Show Buttons On Two Rows. If you decide to keep the single-row display and have need for a button that is not currently displayed, select it from the buttons on the Toolbar Options menu.

Here's where the personalization kicks in. Unless you have unused space on your toolbar, the new button replaces some other button you haven't used in a while, and hopefully don't want to use next. Approximately 20 buttons are visible on a single toolbar—depending, of course, on the width of the buttons you have selected, the size of your monitor, and your monitor's resolution. You'll find buttons that were displaced from one of the toolbars on the Toolbar Options menu the next time you need them. Theoretically, with increased use, most of the buttons you use regularly will be displayed on your toolbars.

TIP

You can change the width of one or another of the toolbars sharing one row and consequently display more buttons from that toolbar by pointing to the vertical hash marks immediately to the right of the Toolbar Options button on the Standard portion of the toolbar. The pointer changes to a four-headed arrow, and you can drag right or left to access more buttons.

If you find that the personalized menus take more than a little getting used to and you would like to restore your application to a more predictable (Office 97–style) interface, choose Customize from the Toolbar Options menu or right-click any toolbar and choose Customize. On the Options tab of the Customize dialog box, enable two check boxes: Show Standard And Formatting Toolbars On Two Rows and Always Show Full Menus.

NOTE

If you're new to an Office application, it makes sense to turn off the personalized toolbars and menus feature, both to avoid the endless frustration of searching for buttons and so you can see all of the standard application features. When you've settled into the application, you can make an informed decision about whether you want to enable personalized toolbars.

Adding Toolbar Buttons Is a Snap

If you're looking for a button that isn't visible on either the Standard or Formatting toolbar or the Toolbar Options menu, select Add Or Remove Buttons from the Toolbar Options menu, then select Standard or Formatting to display the list of all buttons for the respective toolbar. A button that is checked is currently displayed on either the toolbar or the Toolbar Options menu. Check any button to make it visible on the toolbar.

Open and Save As Dialog Boxes Make It Easier to Work with Files

Most of us prefer to avoid filing at all costs. However, keeping electronic documents organized requires all of us to become filing pros. Anything Microsoft can do to ease this burden is a step in the right direction. In Office XP, the Open and Save As dialog boxes have been subtly modified so that they're more flexible and functional. One of the most practical and easily overlooked changes is that you can now resize the dialog boxes. Just drag an edge to make the dialog box large enough to display all of the files in a folder—definitely worth the price of admission!

The Places bar, introduced in Office 2000, is the icon list on the left side of the Open and Save As dialog boxes. Although the concept was good, users complained that it wasn't customizable—the folders you needed to access most frequently still required the navigational skills of Magellan. A couple of third-party applications sprouted up to respond to these complaints, and now Office XP rises to the challenge with an easy-to-customize Places bar.

Another addition to the Save As dialog box makes it possible to reduce file size by compressing images used in the document. This may not mean much in a Word document with two or three images, but in a PowerPoint presentation, it can make a dramatic difference in the size of your presentation file.

Adding Folders You Frequent to the Places Bar

The Places bar in the Open and Save As dialog boxes (see Figure 1.8) comes with icons for History, My Documents, Desktop, Favorites, and Web Folders.

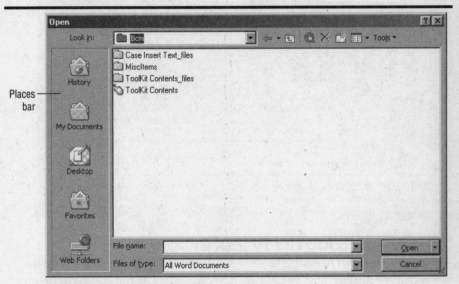

FIGURE 1.8: The Open dialog box features a customizable Places bar.

History is the list of the most recently modified or created Office documents, folders, and drives on your system. If you stored or opened an Office document, it's listed in History. The list is initially sorted in descending order based on modification date (see Figure 1.9), but you can also sort by name or type size by clicking the appropriate header on the list.

To clear the History list, choose History in the Places bar, and then select Tools ➤ Clear History from the dialog box menu.

My Documents opens the My Documents folder on your local drive. Desktop displays the files on your Desktop. Favorites opens your Favorites folder, and Web Folders displays your favorite shared folders on websites, including network drives, inside and outside of your network. These may be popular destinations in your search for the file you want to open, but chances are it takes you more than a few clicks to find the folders you frequent.

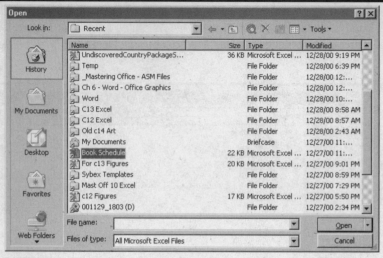

FIGURE 1.9: Choose History to open or save in a recently used folder or drive.

Customizing the Places Bar

If you are tired of navigating through the same folder structure to find the folders you use most, stay tuned—you can customize the Places bar to include frequently used folders from your computer or network. To add a folder to the Places bar, you have to navigate to the folder one last time. When you find it, select the folder, then choose Tools ➢ Add To "My Places" from the Open or Save As dialog box menu. If you can't see where the icon was added, click the More Places arrow at the bottom of the Places bar.

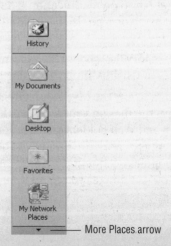

———— More Places arrow

After you've added a folder to the Places bar, you can rearrange the icons on the Places bar. Select the icon you wish to move up or down, right-click, and choose Move Up or Move Down from the shortcut menu. If you add more than a folder or two, you probably also want to switch the display to smaller icons—right-click anywhere on the Places bar and choose Small Icons from the menu.

NOTE

There's only one set of Open and Save As dialog boxes, shared by all the Office applications. Folders added to the Places bar in any application appear in all applications. When you clear the History list for one application, you're clearing it for all applications.

Compressing Pictures to Reduce File Size

Now that photographs and other high-quality images are becoming as common as stick-figure clip art used to be, documents—through no fault of their own—are getting larger. The Save As dialog box has an additional feature to address this file size issue. In Office XP, you have the option to compress pictures while saving a document. This is a great option if you are concerned about file size and not as concerned about the quality of your images. Be forewarned, though—compression may result in loss of image quality, especially if you are using high-color photographs.

To access the Compress Pictures option, choose File ➤ Save As. In the Save As dialog box, open the Tools menu and choose Compress Pictures to open the Compress Pictures dialog box.

NOTE

If you want to compress only some of the pictures in the document, select those pictures before opening the Save As dialog box.

If you have pictures selected, choose Selected Pictures. Choose the resolution you want for the pictures. If the document is for the Web or for screen viewing, such as a PowerPoint presentation, you can choose Web/Screen. This sets the resolution at 96dpi (dots per inch)—not great resolution but adequate for a lot of screen uses. If you are planning to print the document, 200dpi may be acceptable for you. If you plan to print to a high-resolution printer and want to maintain the resolution of the images in the document, choose No Change.

You are not done there, though. If you really want to maintain full image quality, you have to clear the Compress Pictures check box. If you keep the Compress Pictures check box selected, Office applies JPEG compression to high-color pictures, and a loss in image quality is the probable outcome.

The final option on this dialog box, Deleted Cropped Areas Of Pictures, may help reduce image size without a quality loss. When you crop a picture in an Office application, the cropped portion of the picture is hidden but is not actually deleted. If you are sure you don't need it, you can select this option to delete it from the image and reduce picture size as a result.

When you have the options set the way you want them, click OK and save the document. The Compress Pictures options are applied to the pictures in your document.

WARNING

After you have compressed a picture and have lost image quality, it cannot be restored. Be sure to save a copy of the image in its uncompressed form before setting the compression options.

Help Is Only a Click Away

Microsoft, like all the leading software companies, spends a great deal of effort designing help systems that will be useful for the people who use their software. This isn't altruism; good online help results in lower costs for help desk functions both at Microsoft and at the large corporations who purchase and support software. In Office 97, Microsoft introduced a social help interface: Clippit and other office assistants. In Office 2000, Clippit was redesigned as a free-floating agent, removing it from the small window that kept it contained in Office 97 applications. In both versions, however, Clippit was considered annoying to many, cute to some, and downright frustrating to everyone at some time or another. Clippit or one of its cronies was the first thing you saw when you started an application, and sooner or later, most people wanted to know how to shut it off. Clippit became the Office feature we loved to hate.

With Office XP, Microsoft has taken a different approach to our social interactions. Clippit doesn't appear until its presence is requested (Help ≻ Show The Office Assistant). In place of the social, over-eager help agent, there's an incredibly passive Ask A Question box, sharing a row with the menu bar:

Type a question for help

Type a question, and suggested avenues of inquiry are presented, ending with an offer to continue your search online at the Microsoft website:

- Adjust the value of a cell to get a specific result for another cell
- About Goal Seek
- Troubleshoot toolbars and menus
- None of the above, look for more help on the Web

The Ask A Question box maintains a history of queries, so you can search again on questions asked previously. The history is cleared at the end of the application session.

Although some people require the social interaction only the Office Assistants can provide, we're excited to see a more reserved approach to asking for help and think many of you will be too.

NEW WAYS TO LET OFFICE KNOW WHAT YOU REALLY WANT TO DO

Office XP invites your interaction and gives you more options about how you want to handle actions that you take than any other version of Office. Microsoft has made an effort to make error messages more friendly and more specific, and has added Smart Tag Options buttons that appear when you complete certain tasks. The Options buttons you will encounter most frequently are Paste Options, AutoCorrect Options, and Smart Tag Options.

More Powerful Paste Options

Cut/Copy and Paste features have been around since Windows was in its infancy, but never before have they been so flexible and so powerful. In Office XP, you can make choices about pasting that can save considerable time and effort. In Word, for example, you can choose whether you want to keep the original formatting of the text or change it to the formatting of its new location. Figure 1.10 shows an example of copying text from one Word document to another. When you paste text using any of the traditional paste methods (Paste button, Ctrl+V, Edit ➢ Paste), the Paste Options button appears next to the pasted text. If you click the button, you have options to keep the original (source) formatting, change to the formatting of the current document (destination), or insert plain text. If none of those options is sufficient, you can choose Apply Style Or Formatting and make your own choices.

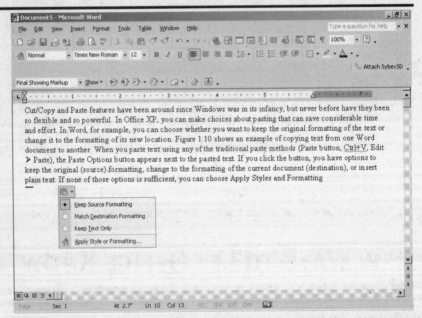

FIGURE 1.10: Paste options let you decide how text is formatted when you paste it into a document.

The paste options you have available depend on the type of pasting you are doing: Word to Excel, Word to Word, Excel to PowerPoint, and so forth. If you learn to use these options effectively, they will save you a lot of formatting hassles after the paste is completed. You can find out more about using paste options in the chapters pertaining to specific applications.

Reversing AutoCorrect

AutoCorrect, the feature that automatically corrects your mistakes and makes you think you are a better speller than your fourth-grade teacher ever dreamed possible, has gotten smarter, kinder, and more reliable in Office XP. AutoCorrect has changed in two major ways:

▶ When you correct an automatic correction by retyping the original text, AutoCorrect won't attempt to correct you again.

▶ If you point to AutoCorrected text, an AutoCorrect Options button appears that lets you reverse the current AutoCorrection, change the AutoCorrect list so that the AutoCorrection will be prevented in the future, and edit AutoCorrect options.

The AutoCorrect Options button appears as a short blue line under the word when you point to a word that AutoCorrect has already corrected. If you click the blue line, the Options menu opens.

They plan to order our product and keep it in stock at all of the Quick Stop stores.

↰	Change back to "Qwik"
	Stop Automatically Correcting "Qwik"
⌨	Control AutoCorrect Options...

If you begin to correct a word that AutoCorrect has automatically capitalized or changed using one of its other standard rules, the Options menu gives you a choice to undo the change AutoCorrect made, to turn off the rule entirely, or to not apply the rule if these circumstances reoccur.

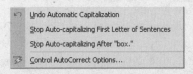

↰	Undo Automatic Capitalization
	Stop Auto-capitalizing First Letter of Sentences
	Stop Auto-capitalizing After "box."
⌨	Control AutoCorrect Options...

Data Smart Tags Make Everyday Tasks Easier

How many times have you copied and pasted someone's name and address from a Word document to an Outlook contact? How many times have you typed someone's name in a report and remembered you needed to schedule a meeting with that person? Smart Tags identify key data items, such as addresses, places, dates, and times, in your documents so you can take some action related to them. Figure 1.11 shows a Smart Tag in action. In this example, a person's name is identified as a Smart Tag—the purple dotted line underneath the name is the indicator. When you point to the name, the Smart Tags Action button appears. Click the Action button to see the Smart Tags choices available to you.

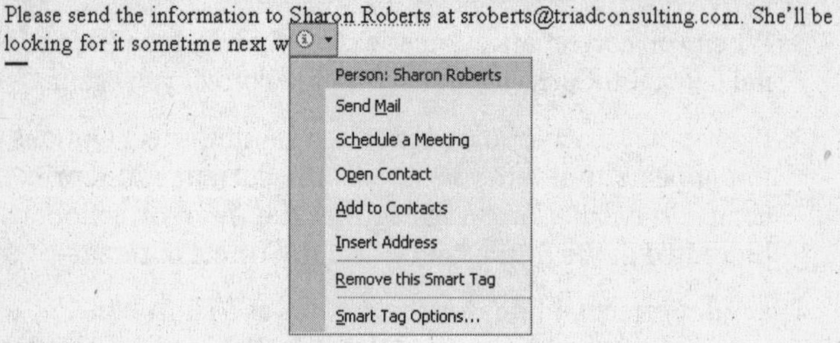

Please send the information to Sharon Roberts at sroberts@triadconsulting.com. She'll be looking for it sometime next w ⓘ ▾

| Person: Sharon Roberts |
| Send Mail |
| Schedule a Meeting |
| Open Contact |
| Add to Contacts |
| Insert Address |
| Remove this Smart Tag |
| Smart Tag Options... |

FIGURE 1.11: Smart Tags identify key data elements such as names and addresses in your documents for action.

Smart Tags options are found in the AutoCorrect dialog box. The Smart Tags tab, shown in Figure 1.12, lists the Smart Tags currently available. Notice that Person Names is not turned on by default. If you type a lot of names in your documents, you probably want to keep this option off. If you are an average name-dropper, we recommend you add names to the active list to access the options shown in Figure 1.11.

Smart Tags show a lot of promise. However, it may be a little while before Smart Tags are fully developed and show the level of consistency one would expect to see. For example, place names, including cities and states, are often ignored by Smart Tags. On a positive note, Microsoft is offering a free software development kit (SDK) so businesses can develop their own Smart Tags to include specialized uses such as product lists, inventory items, and department lists. Microsoft also plans to develop other Smart Tags that can be downloaded from their Office Update site (www.officeupdate.microsoft.com). Expect third-party vendors to follow suit.

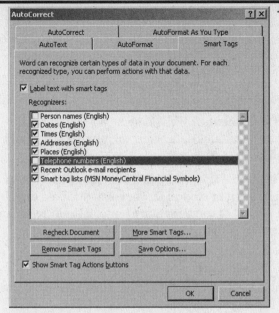

FIGURE 1.12: You can set Smart Tag options in the AutoCorrect dialog box.

NEW AND IMPROVED COLLABORATION TOOLS

Microsoft is working to improve the functionality of web pages you create in Office by providing tools that turn them from repositories of static data into living, breathing information animals. Office XP offers tools to make collaboration easier, and provides data analysis and reporting tools that can be used on active data accessible on the Web. Office XP web collaboration features include:

SharePoint team sites   Team sites are comprehensive websites with all the tools you need to collaborate with a team, including discussions, document sharing, and a host of other useful components.

Presentation broadcasts   Viewing a PowerPoint presentation across the Web can be a communal affair with real-time chat and live information sharing about the presentation's content.

Online meetings   Using Microsoft NetMeeting, users can activate a meeting across a network from any of the Office applications. Participants can use options for real-time collaboration on documents, including chat and whiteboard windows.

For teams that want to analyze live data across a network, Office XP offers three valuable tools:

Office Web Components   Web Components let you work interactively with real-time data across an intranet using pivot tables, spreadsheets, and charts.

Web Query Wizard   This wizard takes data from any site on the Web and brings it into Excel for your analysis. Data can be refreshed on request or can be set up to automatically refresh at specified intervals.

Data Access Pages   Developing live web databases is a practical possibility. If you've ever tried to create active server pages from your database, you know that it is no easy task—until now. Data Access Pages provide front-end forms in HTML format that are linked to data housed in Access. When users make changes on the forms from their browsers, the changes are immediately reflected in the database.

Working Together with a SharePoint Team Site

One of the most interesting innovations in Office XP is the ability to create SharePoint *team sites*. Team sites replace web folders previously seen in Office (and FrontPage, now a separate application again), which were locations on a web server where you could access shared documents. Expanding greatly on the web folders concept, SharePoint team sites are complete websites with a number of features designed to let you share documents, have discussions, and communicate with your team. Team site features include:

▶ Document libraries where you can post documents you want to share

▶ Discussion boards to communicate with your team about important issues (or the scores of last night's basketball games)

▶ Web document discussions where your team can add comments and make revisions to documents

- ▶ Announcements to display the latest team news

- ▶ Team events to alert team members about upcoming events

- ▶ Surveys for team members to express their opinions about important issues

- ▶ Shared favorites where members can post links to useful websites

- ▶ Custom lists where you can create a list for anything

You can create a fully working team site, like the one shown in Figure 1.13, in no time at all.

NOTE

To create a SharePoint team site, you must be able to access a server that is running SharePoint Team Services. SharePoint Team Services is available only in the Office XP Developer's Edition and for a short time in the Office XP Professional Special Edition.

After you create a team site, you can subscribe to it so you get an e-mail notice any time something has changed. You can save documents to your team site directly from Office XP programs, making it easy to keep the site up-to-date. In addition, if you are not satisfied with the team site's design, you can customize it using FrontPage 2002.

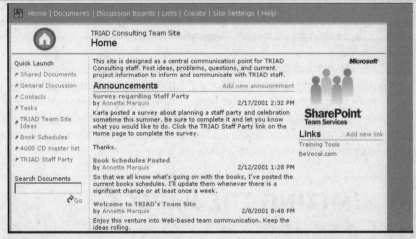

FIGURE 1.13: A SharePoint team site gives members of your team access to a wealth of information and collaboration tools.

Team sites have a ton of potential and are a welcome replacement for the less-than-reliable web folders of Office 2000. Take the time to create a site, and your team will thank you for it.

MOVING BEYOND THE KEYBOARD

Office XP incorporates two exciting new input methods: speech and handwriting. Speech recognition technology has seen major advances recently, due to software and especially hardware improvements. The Microsoft Speech Recognition System uses Lernout & Hauspie's speech recognition engine for dictation and application command and control.

Microsoft clearly admits that the speech recognition tools are not designed to be totally hands free. You still need your mouse and keyboard to use the tools effectively. We still have a way to go before we are talking to our computers a la *Star Trek*, but if you've been intrigued by this new technology, it's definitely worth exploring. Office XP's foray into speech recognition is a valid effort and beats repetitive motion strain or carpal tunnel syndrome any day—although you may find yourself getting hoarse if you are at it long enough.

NOTE

Lernout & Hauspie (L&H), based in Belgium, is the premier company in speech recognition software. With their recent purchase of Dragon Systems, L&H have control of the two most effective speech recognition systems available today: L&H Voice Express and Dragon NaturallySpeaking.

Handwriting recognition is a whole new and interesting method of inputting electronically. Office XP's handwriting tools let you draw text with your mouse or on an external drawing pad that is immediately recognized and converted to text. Although this feature works with a mouse, handwriting tablets designed for this purpose give this feature a much more natural feel and are a lot more fun.

MINIMIZING THE IMPACT OF CRASHES

Microsoft has gone all out in Office XP to protect your documents when the unexpected happens. In addition to the traditional AutoRecovery features, Office XP has a number of new options that save documents when an application crashes, recover corrupt documents, and let you choose which version of a recovered or saved document you want to use. If you have a pretty stable network and operating system environment, you may run into these features only on very rare occasions. Others who are less fortunate may get to know them intimately. Either way, it's helpful to know what to expect and what choices to make when your software or hardware crashes, and you are faced with those critical decisions about how to recover your work.

Saving When You Crash

The Document Recovery feature is relatively new to Word, Excel, and PowerPoint. (Office 2000 also offered recovery options.) After a crash occurs, Office opens a message box, like the one shown in Figure 1.14, which gives you the option of recovering your open documents and restarting the application. Clear the check box if you just want to forget it and go home.

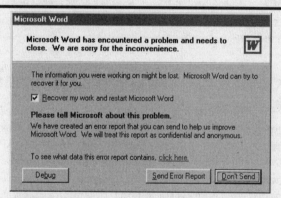

FIGURE 1.14: Office XP apologizes for your inconvenience while giving you the option of recovering your lost work.

If you are willing to stick it out, you also have the option of sending an error report to Microsoft to help them develop fixes that will avoid similar crashes in the future. You can choose to click the Send Error Report or Don't Send button. If you choose to send an error report, Office dials or connects with Microsoft and sends the report. In the meantime, if you elected to recover your data, you see this message window:

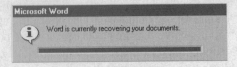

When the application restarts, you have the option of restoring this recovered version of the document (see "Recovering Documents with the Document Recovery Task Pane" later in this section).

Setting Timed Recovery Save Options

Timed Recovery Save is the traditional AutoRecovery feature. While Document Recovery will probably save a more current version of your document, Timed Recovery Save is still valuable when the power goes out and there is no time to save your work.

You can increase or decrease the frequency of AutoRecovery on the Save tab of the Options dialog box in Word, Excel, and PowerPoint or an e-mail message form in Outlook. The setting affects all four applications, so you can set it in any one of them.

Recovering Documents with the Document Recovery Task Pane

When your software or your system crashes and you restart an Office application, you are immediately presented with a Document Recovery task pane on the left side of the document window, like the one shown in Figure 1.15. It lists any documents that were open at the time of the crash and indicates whether it is the original document that was last saved by the user, a recovered document that was last saved by AutoRecovery, or a recovered document that was last saved by Document Recovery. You'll also see the time that the document was saved so you can make comparisons to determine which one might be more current. If you're still not sure, click the arrow next to the document you think you want and choose Open.

WARNING

There will occasionally be times when Recovery does not run or the recovered document is not available to you. While this should not happen frequently, it may in situations where your system reports a "blue screen" or Fatal Exception Error, or when a problem with power management (or power management and a hardware driver) locks up the Desktop. So don't forget to save regularly, just in case.

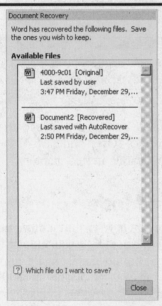

FIGURE 1.15: The Document Recovery task pane shows you any version of the document that is available to recover.

If you find the document you want to save, click the arrow next to it again and choose Save. When you've recovered the documents you want, click Close on the task pane to get it out of your way.

Microsoft Office Application Recovery

Even when an application is nonresponsive, it's possible that you can recover your document in Word, Excel, and PowerPoint. If you can open the Windows Start menu and reach Programs, find the Microsoft Office Tools group and choose Microsoft Office Application Recovery. This tool will attempt to break into the nonresponding application and save the day, or at least your documents. It's worth a try.

Corrupt Document Recovery

If a Word or Excel document becomes corrupted, the application will attempt to repair it before reopening it. You may get this dialog box when you attempt to open the document:

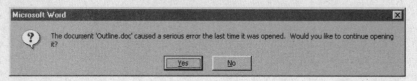

Click Yes to try to recover the document. You can also invoke this feature manually from the Open dialog box (see "Open and Save As Dialog Boxes Make It Easier to Work with Files" earlier in this chapter).

Making Use of Office Safe Mode

If an Office application fails to start and you have to shut it down using the Task Manager (press Ctrl+Alt+Del), the next time you attempt to open the application, Office gives you the option of starting the application in Safe mode. By choosing this option, you can disable any add-ins or code that may be causing the problem.

Other Recovery Features

In addition to the myriad features for users, Office XP contains a number of new features to help system administrators, help desks, and Microsoft track persistent problems. These features, including Client Logging, Crash Reporting, Hang Reporting, Corporate Tracking, and Setup Failure Reporting, make the future stability of Office even more promising. If you'd like to know about the reliability features of Office XP, refer to www.officeupdate.microsoft.com.

WHAT'S NEXT

In the next chapter, you will familiarize yourself with basic Office XP tools and methods for opening, creating, editing, saving, and closing files; selecting templates; launching and exiting an Office program; and getting help from within Office itself.

Part I

Chapter 2
GETTING TO WORK IN OFFICE XP

One of the great benefits of using an integrated office solution such as Office XP is that common elements—menus, toolbars, and various options—are available uniformly throughout all the programs you use. You will find the elements organized in a similar manner and able to interrelate in many different ways.

Understanding the basics of opening and closing Office programs and their associated files, working with those files (opening, editing, and saving), configuring Desktop options such as toolbars, and working with help as well as Office's repair utility is a big part of the job ahead as you begin to work with Office XP.

Adapted from *Microsoft Office XP Simply Visual*
by Perspection, Inc.
ISBN 0-7821-4004-1   400 pp $24.99

STARTING AN OFFICE PROGRAM

The quickest way to start an Office program is from the Start menu on the Taskbar. Office lets you customize your work area and switch from program to program with the click of a button.

NOTE
You can get Office information on the Web from within any Office program. Open the Help menu, and then choose Office On The Web. Your web browser opens, displaying the Microsoft Office Update website.

Start an Office Program from the Start Menu

1. Click the Start button on the Taskbar.

2. Point to Programs.

3. Click the Office XP program that you want to open.

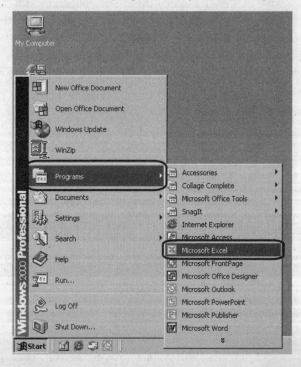

TIP

You can start an Office program and open a document from Windows Explorer. Double-click any Office document icon in Windows Explorer to open that file in its associated program.

Part i

Start an Office Program and Open a New Office Document

1. Click the Start button on the Taskbar, and then click New Office Document. The New Office Document dialog box opens.

2. Click the tab for the type of document you want to create.

3. Click a document icon, and then click the OK button to start the program and open a new document.

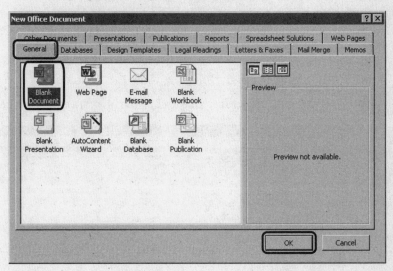

OPENING AN EXISTING FILE

Before you can begin working, you need to open a document. You can open the file (and its program) at one time, or you can start the program and then open the file from within the program.

TIP

You can reopen a recently closed file by clicking the filename at the bottom of the File menu.

NOTE

You can quickly open a copy of a file. When you open a file from the Open dialog box, click the Open button drop-down arrow, and then click Open As Copy. The Office program creates a new copy of the file in the same folder with the filename Copy of *Filename*.

Open an Existing File from the Start Menu

1. Click the Start button on the Taskbar, and then click Open Office Document.

2. Click an icon on the Places bar to open a frequently used folder.

3. If necessary, click the Look In drop-down arrow, and then choose the drive where the file is located.

4. Double-click the folder in which the file is stored.

5. Double-click a filename to start the program and open the file.

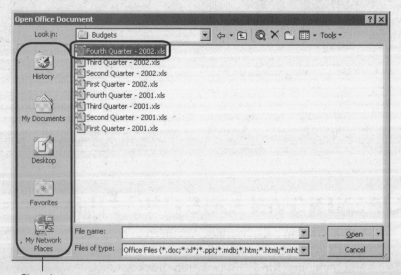

Places bar

Open an Existing File within an Office Program

1. Click the Open button on the Standard toolbar.

2. Click an icon on the Places bar to open a frequently used folder.

3. If necessary, click the Look In drop-down arrow, and then choose the drive where the file is located.

4. Double-click the folder in which the file is stored.

5. Double-click the file you want to open.

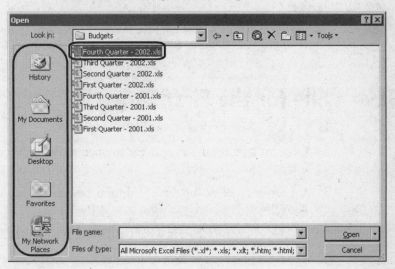

NOTE

You can delete or rename any closed file from the Open or Save As dialog box. Click the file, click the Tools drop-down arrow, and then click Delete or Rename.

SAVING A FILE

Frequently saving your files ensures that you don't lose work during an unexpected power loss. The first time you save a file, specify a filename and folder in the Save As dialog box. The next time you save the file, Office saves it with the same name in the same folder. If you want to change a file's name or location, you can use the Save As dialog box to create a copy of the original file.

TIP

What's the difference between the Save and Save As commands? The Save command saves a copy of your current document to a previously specified name and location. The Save As command creates a copy of your current document with a new name, location, or type.

NOTE

When you name a file, you do not have to type the filename extension. Each Office program automatically adds the correct filename extension to files.

Save a File for the First Time

1. Click the Save button on the Standard toolbar.

2. Click an icon on the Places bar to open a frequently used folder.

3. If necessary, click the Save In drop-down arrow, and then click the drive where you want to save the file.

4. Double-click the folder in which you want to save the file.

5. Type a name for the file, or use the suggested name that appears in the File Name box.

6. Click the Save button.

NOTE

To modify your default save settings, choose Tools ➤ Options, click the Save tab, choose the options you want, and then click the OK button.

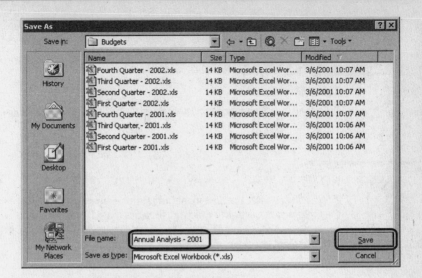

Save a File with Another Name

1. Choose File ➤ Save As. The Save As dialog box opens.

2. Click an icon on the Places bar or click the Save In drop-down arrow, and then choose the drive or folder where you want to save the file.

3. Type a new filename in the File Name box.

4. Click the Save button.

TIP

To save all your files at one time, hold down the Shift key, and then choose File ➤ Save All.

NOTE

A *file type* specifies the document format (for example, a template) as well as the program and version in which the file was created (for example, Excel 2002). You might want to change the type to an earlier version if you're not certain that your recipient has the same version of a program.

CHOOSING MENU AND DIALOG BOX OPTIONS

A *menu* is a list of related commands. For example, the Edit menu contains commands for editing a document, such as Delete and Cut. A *shortcut menu* opens when you right-click a word or object while you're working, and contains commands related to a specific object. Clicking a menu command followed by an ellipsis (...) opens a *dialog box*, which is where you choose various options and provide information for completing the command. As you switch between programs, you'll find that all Office menus and dialog boxes look similar and work in the same way.

TIP

When you first open a menu, the commands you used most recently appear first. Point to the Toolbar Options drop-down arrow to display the full menu.

Choose Menu Commands

1. Click a menu name on the menu bar, or right-click an object (such as a toolbar, spreadsheet cell, picture, or selected text).

2. If necessary, click the double arrow to expand the menu and display more commands.

3. Click the menu command you want, or point to the arrow to the right of the menu command to display a submenu of related commands, and then click the command you want.

TIP

Toolbar buttons and shortcut keys are faster than menu commands. You can learn the toolbar button equivalent of a menu command by noticing the toolbar button icon to the left of a menu command. Keyboard shortcuts appear to the right of their menu commands. To use a keyboard shortcut, hold down the first key (such as Ctrl), press the second key (such as V), and then release both keys (such as Ctrl+V).

NOTE

The most common dialog box buttons are the OK button, which confirms your selections and closes the dialog box; and the Cancel button, which closes the dialog box without accepting your selections.

Choose Dialog Box Options

All Office dialog boxes contain the same types of options, including the following:

Tabs   Click a tab to display its options. Each tab groups a related set of options.

Option buttons   Click an option button to select it. You can usually select only one.

Spin boxes   Click the up or down arrow to increase or decrease the number, or type a number in the box.

Check boxes   Click the box to turn the option on or off. A checked box means the option is selected; a cleared box means it's not.

List boxes   Click the drop-down arrow to display a list of options, and then choose the option you want.

Text boxes   Click in the box and type the requested information.

Buttons   Click a button to perform a specific action or command. A button name followed by an ellipsis (...) opens another dialog box.

Preview boxes   Many dialog boxes display an image that reflects the options you select.

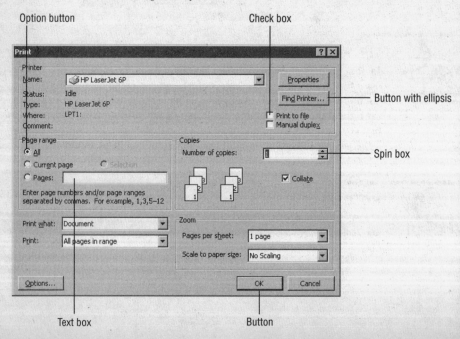

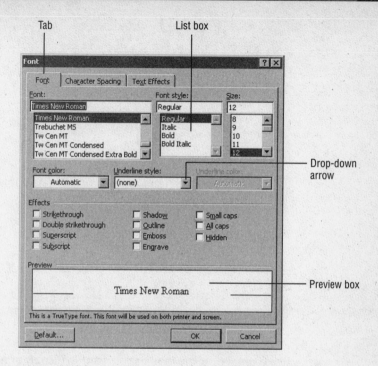

WORKING WITH TOOLBARS

Each Office toolbar contains a collection of buttons that you click to select frequently used menu commands. Most programs open by placing the Standard toolbar (which contains commands such as Save and Print) and the Formatting toolbar (which contains commands for selecting fonts and sizes) side by side. You can also display toolbars designed for specific tasks, such as drawing pictures, importing data, or creating charts. The Office program you're in will personalize the toolbars as you work, showing only the buttons you use most often. Additional toolbar buttons are available by clicking the Toolbar Options drop-down arrow at the end of the toolbar.

Display and Hide a Toolbar

1. Right-click any visible toolbar.

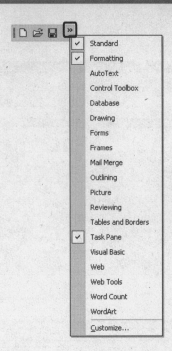

2.   Click the name of the toolbar you want to display or hide.

Move and Reshape a Toolbar

You can modify the look of a toolbar in any Office program.

▶ To move a toolbar that is *docked* (attached) or *floating* (unattached) over the window, click the gray bar on the left edge of the toolbar, and then drag it to a new location.

▶ To return a floating toolbar to its previous docked location, double-click its title bar.

▶ To change the shape of a floating toolbar, drag any border until the toolbar is the shape you want.

TIP

When you first open a toolbar, the buttons you have used most recently display. Click the Toolbar Options drop-down arrow to display any other toolbar buttons. To display the full toolbar, double-click the gray bar on the left edge of the toolbar.

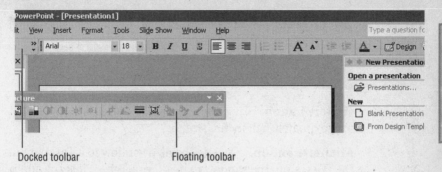

Docked toolbar   Floating toolbar

Display Toolbar Options on a Toolbar

To display more buttons on a toolbar, click the Toolbar Options drop-down arrow at the right end of the toolbar.

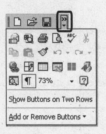

ARRANGING WINDOWS

Every Office program and document open inside a *window*, which contains all the program commands and is where you create and edit your documents. Most often, you'll probably fill the entire screen with one window. Other times, when you want to move or copy information between programs or documents, it's easier to display several windows at once. You can arrange simultaneously on the screen two or more windows from one program or from different programs. However, you must make the window active before you can work in it. You can also click the document buttons on the Taskbar to switch between open Office documents.

Resize and Move a Window

All windows contain the same sizing buttons:

Maximize button   Click to make a window fill the entire screen.

Restore button   Click to reduce a maximized window to approximately half its full size.

Minimize button   Click to shrink a window to a Taskbar button. To restore the window to its previous size, click the appropriate Taskbar button.

Close button   Click to shut a window.

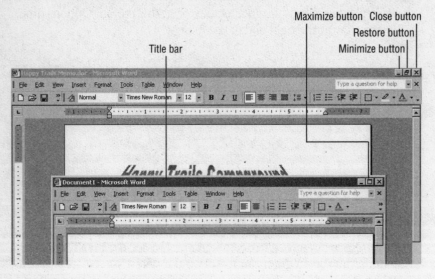

You can move a window to any location on the screen by clicking its title bar and dragging the window to a new location. Release the mouse button when the window is where you want it.

TIP
You can use shortcut keys to open and close windows, and quickly switch between windows. To close the active window, press Ctrl+W. To switch to the next window, press Ctrl+F6. And to switch to the previous window, press Ctrl+Shift+F6.

NOTE

Only one window can be active at a time. You can tell whether a window is active by the color of its title bar. By default, an active window's title bar is blue and an inactive title bar is gray. To make an inactive window active, click anywhere in the window.

Switch between Document Windows

Each open Windows file or document displays its own button on the Windows Taskbar. You can click the buttons on the Taskbar to switch between open files.

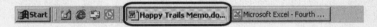

CHOOSING TEMPLATES AND WIZARDS

Office makes it easy to create many common documents based on a template or using a wizard. A *template* opens a document (such as a letter) with predefined formatting and placeholder text that specifies what information you should enter (such as your name or address). A *wizard* walks you through the steps to create a finished document tailored to your preferences. The wizard asks you for information, and then, when you click the Finish button, it creates a completely formatted document based on the options and content you entered. You use a template to add information to a designed document, and you use a wizard to add a design to information you supply.

Choose a Template

1. Click the Start button on the Taskbar and then click New Office Document, or choose File ➢ New. The New Office Document dialog box opens.

2. Click the tab for the type of document you want to create.

3. Click the template you want to use.

4. Check the Preview box to verify that the template will create the right style of document.

5. Click the OK button.

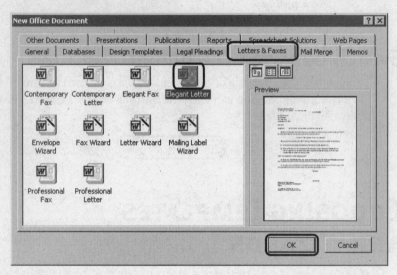

6. Type text for placeholders such as *[Click here and type your letter text]*.

TIP

If you create a Word document using a wizard, Word bases the document on the Normal document template. However, the styles Word uses in the document reflect the formatting options that you select when responding to the wizard.

Choose and Navigate a Wizard

1. Click the Start button on the Taskbar and then click New Office Document, or choose File ➤ New. The New Office Document dialog box opens.

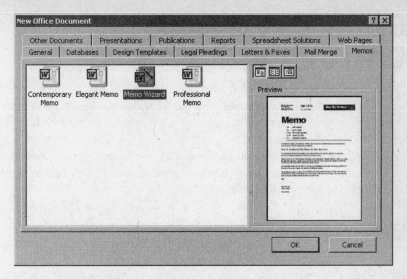

2. Click the tab for the type of document you want to create.

3. Double-click the icon for the wizard you want to use.

4. Read and select options (if necessary) in the first wizard dialog box.

5. Click the Next button to progress to the next wizard dialog box. Each wizard dialog box asks for different information.

6. Continue to select options, and then click the Next button.

7. When you reach the last wizard dialog box, click the Finish button.

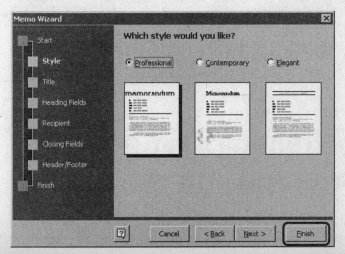

GETTING HELP IN AN OFFICE PROGRAM

At some point, you will have a question or two about the program you're using. The Office online help system provides the answers you need. Screen tips show toolbar names and short descriptions about anything you see on the screen or in a dialog box. If you need help while you work, you can use the Ask A Question box to quickly get help. You can also search an extensive catalog of help topics organized by an index or a table of contents to locate specific information.

Get a Screen Tip

1. Place the mouse pointer over a toolbar button. The name of the button, or the screen tip, appears below the button.

NOTE
To hide screen tips, choose Tools ➤ Customize ➤ Options, click the Show ScreenTips On Toolbars check box to clear it, and then click the OK button.

Get Help while You Work

1. Click the Ask A Question box on the menu bar, type a question, press the Enter key, and then click a topic.

GETTING HELP FROM THE OFFICE ASSISTANT

Often, the easiest way to learn how to accomplish a task is to ask someone who knows. Now, with Office, that knowledgeable friend is always available in the form of the Office Assistant. Tell the Office Assistant what you want to do in the same everyday language you use to ask a colleague or friend, and the Office Assistant walks you through the process step by step. If the personality of the default Office Assistant—Clippit—doesn't appeal to you, you can choose from a variety of other Office Assistants.

TIP

You can open the Office Assistant by clicking the Help button. If the Office Assistant is already turned on, you will see the Office Assistant at the top of your screen. If the Office Assistant is turned off, the Help pane appears, where you can search for help by topic.

Ask the Office Assistant for Help

1. Click the Help button on the Standard toolbar, or click the Office Assistant to activate the Office Assistant.

2. Type your question about a task with which you want help.

3. Click the Search button.

4. Click the topic in which you're interested.

5. Read and follow the directions. After you're done, click the Close button on the Help window.

6. Click the Help button on the Standard toolbar to hide the Office Assistant.

NOTE

Get useful tips from the Office Assistant. When a lightbulb appears above the Office Assistant, click the Office Assistant to see a tip for a simpler or more efficient way to accomplish a task.

Choose an Office Assistant

1. Right-click the Office Assistant and choose Options, or click the Options button in the Office Assistant window. The Office Assistant dialog box opens.

2. Click the Gallery tab.

3. Click the Next button and the Back button to preview different Office Assistants.

4. Display the Office Assistant that you want to use.

5. Click the OK button. If the Office program prompts you to insert the Office XP CD-ROM in your drive, insert the CD-ROM, and then click the OK button.

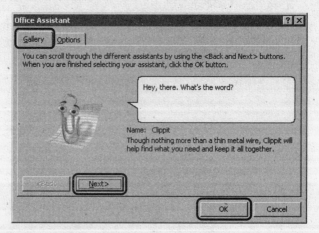

Turn Off the Office Assistant

1. Right-click the Office Assistant and choose Options, or click the Options button in the Office Assistant window.

2. Click the Options tab.

3. Click the Use The Office Assistant check box to clear it.

4. Click the OK button.

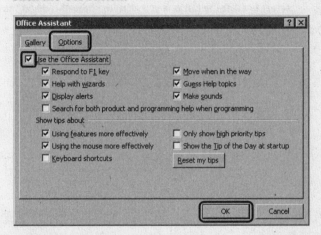

DISPLAYING THE OFFICE SHORTCUT BAR

The Office shortcut bar provides quick access to all the programs on your computer. You can display one or more toolbars and customize buttons on the Office shortcut bar. The Office shortcut bar itself can be floating (not attached to any part of your screen) or docked (attached to the left, right, or top edge of your screen).

1. Click the Start button, point to Programs, point to Microsoft Office Tools, click Microsoft Office Shortcut Bar.

2. Install the component if necessary.

3. Click Yes to start the Office shortcut bar automatically whenever Windows is started.

TIP

To customize the Office shortcut bar, right-click anywhere on the Office short-cut bar (except the title bar), choose Customize, click the Buttons tab, click to select or clear the buttons you want to show or hide on the toolbar, and then click the OK button.

Close the Office Shortcut Bar

1. Click the Office icon on the title bar.

2. Click Exit.

3. If prompted, click the Yes or No button to instruct Windows whether to display the Office shortcut bar the next time you open Windows.

CLOSING A FILE

To conserve your computer's resources, close the files and programs that you are not currently working in. You can close open documents one at a time, or you can use one command to close all open files without closing the program. Either way, if you try to close a document without saving your final changes, a dialog box appears, prompting you to do so.

TIP

When two or more documents are open in a program, the document window contains one Close button. The Close button closes the document without exiting the program. You might need to click a Word document button on the Taskbar to make it active before you click the Close button.

Close One File

1. Click the Close button in the upper-right corner of the title bar.

2. If necessary, click the Yes button to save your changes.

QUITTING AN OFFICE PROGRAM

When you decide to stop working for the day, before you shut down your computer, you must quit any running programs. All open documents close when you quit. If you haven't saved your final changes, a dialog box appears, prompting you to do so.

TIP

Access automatically compresses a database when you close the file. Choose Tools ➢ Options, click the General tab, click the Compact On Close check box to select it, and then click the OK button.

Quit an Office Program

1. Click the Close button, or choose File ➢ Exit.

2. If necessary, click the Yes button to save any changes you made to your open documents before the program quits.

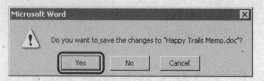

TIP

In the unlikely event the Office program has hung and refuses to close, press Ctrl+Alt+Del *once* to bring up Task Manager, select the open file, and click End Task. But be aware that this may close other Office windows that are open, depending on whether just the file in question has a problem or Office itself has crashed.

EDITING TEXT

Before you can edit text, you need to highlight, or *select*, the text you want to modify. Once you select the text, you can delete, replace, move (cut), or copy it within a document or between documents, even if they're in different programs. In either case, the steps are the same. Unlike the Windows Clipboard, which stores only a single piece of information at a time, the Office Clipboard, a temporary storage area, collects and stores up to 24 selections, any or all of which you can paste to a new location. You can also move or copy selected text without storing it on the Clipboard by using *drag-and-drop editing*.

Select and Edit Text

1. Move the mouse pointer to the left or right of the text you want to select.

2. Drag the mouse pointer to highlight the text you want to select.

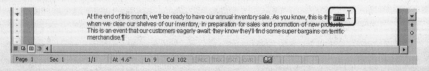

3. Type to replace the selected text, or press the Delete or Backspace key to erase the selected text.

To Delete...	Press...
One character at a time to the left of the insertion point	Backspace
One word at a time to the left of the insertion point	Ctrl+Backspace
One character at a time to the right of the insertion point	Delete
One word at a time to the right of the insertion point	Ctrl+Delete
Selected text	Backspace or Delete

Move or Copy Text

1. Select the text you want to move or copy.

2. Click the Cut button or Copy button on the Standard toolbar.

3. If you want to collect multiple selections, repeat steps 1 and 2.

4. Click in the document where you want to insert the text.

NOTE

If the Office Clipboard is not visible, choose Edit ➢ Office Clipboard to display it.

5. Click any icon on the Clipboard task pane to paste a selection, or click the Paste All button on the Clipboard task pane to paste all the selections at once.

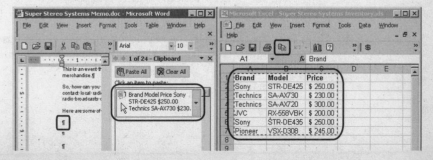

After you paste an item, the Paste Options button appears next to the item. You can click the Paste Options button to display a list of options on the shortcut menu. This button, known as a Smart Tag, allows you to immediately adjust how information is pasted or how automatic changes occur.

TIP

To turn on or off Paste Options, choose Tools ➤ Options, click the Edit tab, click the Show Paste Options Buttons check box to select or clear it, and then click the OK button.

6. When you're done, click the Close button on the Clipboard task pane.

NOTE

You can remove some or all the selections stored on the Office Clipboard. To clear all the entries, click the Clear All button on the Office Clipboard. To erase an individual entry from the Office Clipboard, click that entry's list arrow, and then choose Delete.

Move or Copy Text Using Drag-and-Drop

1. If you want to drag text between programs or documents, display both windows.

2. Select the text you want to move or copy.

3. Point to the selected text, and then hold down the mouse button. If you want to copy the text to a new location, hold down the Ctrl key and the mouse button. A plus sign (+) appears in the pointer box, indicating that you are dragging a copy of the selected text.

4. Drag the selected text to the new location, and then release the mouse button (and the Ctrl key, if necessary).

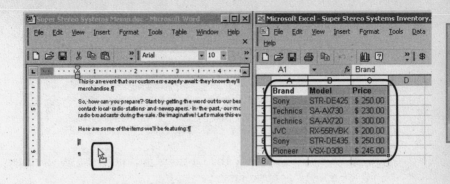

FINDING AND REPLACING TEXT

The Find and Replace commands make it easy to locate or replace specific text or formulas in a document. For example, if you're working with a long report, you might want to find each figure reference to verify that the proper graphic and caption appear. Or, you might want to replace all the references to cell A3 in your Excel formulas with the data contained in cell G3. The Find and Replace dialog boxes vary slightly from one Office program to the next, but the commands work essentially the same.

TIP

You can use wildcards to help you search. When you click the Use Wildcards check box to select it (in the Find And Replace dialog box), click the Special button to see the wildcards you can use. To enter a wildcard in the Find What or Replace With box, click Special, and then choose a wildcard. For example, enter ran* to find *ranch*, *ranger*, and so on.

Find Text

1. Click at the beginning of the document.

2. Choose Edit ➤ Find. The Find And Replace dialog box opens.

3. In the Find What box, type the text you want to locate.

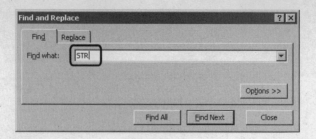

4. If necessary, click the Options button, then select other options as appropriate.

5. Click the Find Next button until you highlight the text you want to locate. You can click the Find Next button repeatedly to locate each instance of the text.

6. A message box appears when you reach the end of the document; click the OK button.

7. When you're done, click the Close button or the Cancel button.

In a Word document, you can search for and replace special characters (such as a bullet) and document elements (such as a tab character). Click the Options button, click the More button in the Find And Replace dialog box, click the Special button, and then choose the item you want from the menu.

In a Word document, you can also search for and replace text with specific formatting features, such as font and font size. Click the Options button, click the More button, click the Format button, choose the formatting option you want, and then complete the corresponding dialog box.

TIP

In a Word document, you may find yourself near the bottom of the text when you initiate a search. Sometimes, Word will check only from your initiation point to the end of the document, so you may need to rerun Find to have it search the entire document properly.

Replace Text

1. Click at the beginning of the document.

2. Choose Edit ➤ Replace. The Find And Replace dialog box opens.

3. In the Find What box, type the text for which you want to search.

4. In the Replace With box, type the text you want to substitute.

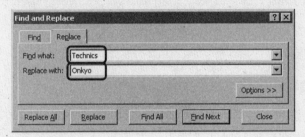

5. Select other options as appropriate. In Word, click the Options button, and then click the More button to display the additional options.

6. Click the Find Next button to begin the search and select the next instance of the search text.

7. Click the Replace button to substitute the replacement text, or click the Replace All button to substitute text throughout the document. You can click the Find Next button to locate the next instance of the search text without replacing it.

8. A message box appears when you reach the end of the document; click the OK button.

9. When you're done, click the Close button or the Cancel button.

CORRECTING TEXT AUTOMATICALLY

Since the dawn of typing with a typewriter, people have consistently mistyped certain words or letter combinations. How many times have you misspelled the word *and*, or pressed and held down the Shift key one character too long? The AutoCorrect feature fixes common misspellings and incorrect capitalization as you type. It also replaces typed characters, such as - - (two hyphens), with typographical symbols, such as — (an em dash). In addition, you can add your personal problem words to the

AutoCorrect list. In most cases, AutoCorrect fixes errors after you press the Enter key or the spacebar on the keyboard.

TIP

To reverse an AutoCorrect change, click the Undo button on the Standard toolbar as soon as AutoCorrect makes the change or point to the corrected text to display a blue box, click the AutoCorrect Options button, and then click Undo or any of the other options.

Replace Text as You Type

▶ To correct capitalization or spelling errors automatically, continue typing until AutoCorrect makes the required correction.

▶ To replace two hyphens with an em dash, turn ordinals into superscripts (such as 1st to 1st), or stack a fraction (such as ½), continue typing until AutoCorrect makes the appropriate change.

▶ To create a bulleted or numbered list, type **1.** or * (for a bullet), press the Tab key or spacebar, type any text, and then press the Enter key. AutoCorrect inserts the next number or bullet. To end the list, press the Backspace key to erase the unnecessary bullets.

TIP

You can specify abbreviations and terms that you don't want AutoCorrect to correct. In the AutoCorrect dialog box, click the Exceptions button and add these items to the list of exceptions.

NOTE

To prevent automatic corrections, choose Tools ➤ AutoCorrect, click the Replace Text As You Type check box to clear it, and then click the OK button.

Type of Correction	If You Type...	AutoCorrect Inserts...
Capitalization	cAP LOCK	Cap Lock
Capitalization	TWo INitial CAps	Two initial caps

Type of Correction	If You Type...	AutoCorrect Inserts...
Capitalization	betty Sue	Betty Sue
Capitalization	microsoft	Microsoft
Capitalization	thursday	Thursday
Common typos	acommodate	accommodate
Common typo	can;t	can't
Common typos	windoes	windows
Superscript ordinals	3rd	3rd
Smart quotes	" "	" "
Em dashes	New York--excluding its big cities--has rural communities.	New York—excluding its big cities—has rural communities.
Symbols	(c)	©
Symbols	(r)	®
Hyperlinks	www.microsoft.com	www.microsoft.com

Add or Edit AutoCorrect Entries

1. Choose Tools ➤ AutoCorrect Options. The AutoCorrect dialog box opens.

2. Click the AutoCorrect tab. To edit an AutoCorrect entry, select the entry you want to change.

3. Type the incorrect text that you want AutoCorrect to correct.

4. Type the text or symbols that you want AutoCorrect to use as a replacement.

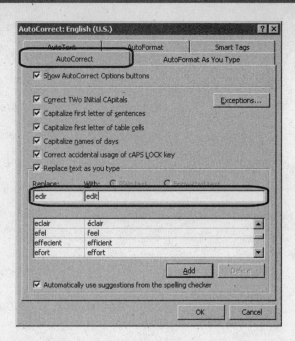

5. Click the Add button or the Replace button.

6. When you're done, click the OK button.

TIP

To delete an AutoCorrect entry, choose Tools ➤ AutoCorrect Options, click the AutoCorrect tab, select the AutoCorrect entry you want to delete, and then click the Delete button.

NOTE

You can use AutoComplete to complete your words. As you enter common text, such as your name, today's date, and some ordinary salutations and closings, Word prompts you with the rest of the text in a screen tip. Press the Enter key to accept the AutoComplete entry.

MAKING CORRECTIONS

Everyone changes their mind at some point, especially when creating or revising a document. With Office, you can instantly correct typing errors by pressing a button. You can use the Undo button to reverse more complicated actions, such as typing an entire word, formatting a paragraph, or creating a chart. If you change your mind, you can just as easily click the Redo button to restore the action you reversed.

TIP

You can use a keyboard combination to quickly undo your last action. To undo, press Ctrl+Z. To redo your undo, press Ctrl+Y.

Undo or Redo an Action

▶ Click the Undo button on the Standard toolbar to reverse your most recent action, such as typing a word, formatting a paragraph, or creating a chart.

▶ Click the Redo button on the Standard toolbar to restore the last action you reversed.

▶ Click the Undo button drop-down arrow on the Standard toolbar, and then select the consecutive actions you want to reverse.

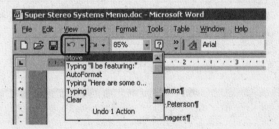

▶ Click the Redo button drop-down arrow on the Standard toolbar, and then select the consecutive actions you want to restore.

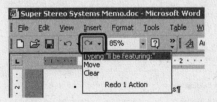

INSERTING COMMENTS

When you review an Office document, you can insert comments that will be visible to yourself—the author—or to other reviewers. *Comments* are like electronic adhesive notes tagged with your name. They appear as small yellow boxes in PowerPoint, as red triangles in Excel, or as yellow selected text in Word. You can use comments to solicit feedback or leave yourself a note.

TIP

To move to the previous or next comment, click the Previous Comment or Next Comment button on the Reviewing toolbar.

Insert a Comment

1. Click where you want to insert a comment.

2. Choose Insert ➤ Comment, or click the Insert Comment button or New Comment button on the Reviewing toolbar.

TIP

To display the Reviewing toolbar, right-click any toolbar, and then choose Reviewing.

3. Type your comment in the comment box or pane.

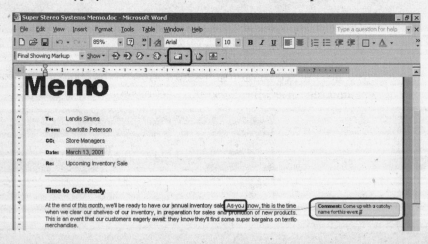

4. When you're done, click anywhere in the document.

Read a Comment

1. Point to a red triangle in Excel; read the comment in the margin in Word; position the mouse pointer over the comment indicator in PowerPoint; or click the Show/Hide Comment button on the Reviewing toolbar.

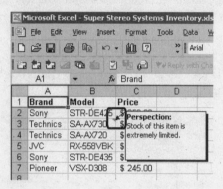

2. Read the comment.

Delete a Comment

1. Click the selected word, the cell with a red triangle, or the comment box on a slide.

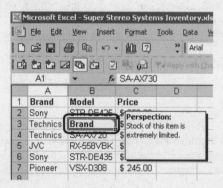

2. Click the Delete Comment button on the Reviewing toolbar; or select the comment, and then press the Delete key or the Backspace key.

USING TRACK CHANGES

When multiple people are involved in the editing and preparation of a document for publication, the Track Changes feature will note who made any particular correction and save a record of all such changes for everyone who works on the document later. Each change can be either accepted or rejected by the person who has authority over the final form of the document.

1. In Excel, choose Tools ➤ Track Changes ➤ Highlight Changes. The Highlight Changes dialog box opens. Click the Track Changes While Editing check box to select it, and then click the OK button.

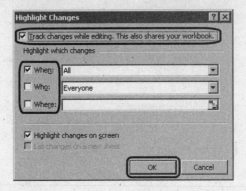

In Word, choose Tools ➤ Track Changes, or double-click TRK on the status bar to turn tracking on and off. The Track Changes button on the Reviewing toolbar is active.

2. Make changes to the document.

TIP

To see who made each change, on the Reviewing toolbar, click the Reviewing Pane button to open a new window below the main document that displays each change, the person who made it, and the time and date that the change was made. Comments (see the previous section) also appear in the Reviewing pane.

NOTE

Unless you automatically load a template that turns on the Track Changes feature, you will need to turn this feature on at the start of a work session whenever you need it.

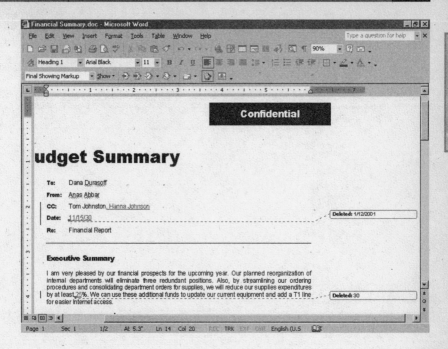

COMPARING AND MERGING DOCUMENTS

You can compare documents to graphically indicate changes between different versions of a document. The changes can be merged into one document or viewed for comparison.

1. Open an edited document (as an example, it can be any newer version of a document where the older version has also been saved and not overwritten by the updated version).

WARNING

In Excel, you need to share the workbook before you can merge it with another workbook. Choose Tools ➣ Share Workbook, click the Sharing check box to select it, and then click OK.

2. Choose Tools ➤ Compare And Merge Documents (Word) or Compare And Merge Presentations (PowerPoint) or Compare And Merge Workbooks (Excel). The Compare And Merge dialog box opens.

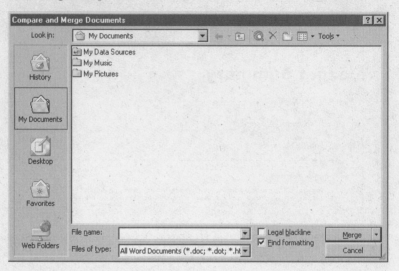

3. Select the document you want to compare and merge.

4. Click the Merge button or the OK button. In Word, you can also click the Merge button drop-down arrow, and then do one of the following:

   ▸ To display the comparison results in the original document (the unedited version), click Merge.

   ▸ To display the comparison results in the newer document that is currently open (the edited version), click Merge Into Current Document.

   ▸ To display the comparison results in a new document, click Merge Into New Document.

NOTE

When you compare or merge documents, the text that differs between the two versions will be highlighted in a different color.

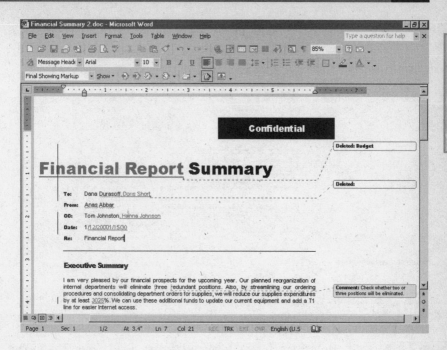

AUTOMATING YOUR WORK

Complicated keyboard sequences can be recorded and saved as a *macro*. For example, if you routinely create tables of a certain size and width, you can create the table structure once, record it as a macro, and then invoke it the next time either by using a keyboard shortcut that you assign or by clicking the Run button in the Macros dialog box.

1. Choose Tools ➤ Macro ➤ Record New Macro. The Record Macro dialog box opens.

2. In the Macro Name box, assign a name to the macro.

3. In the Store Macro In box, choose the template (or document) in which you wish to save the macro.

4. In the Description box, enter a description of the macro.

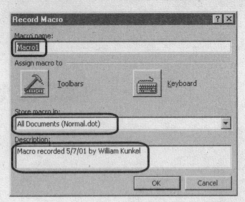

TIP

To assign macros to shortcut keys, click the Keyboard button in the Record Macro dialog box.

5. Unless you intend to assign the macro to a menu, a toolbar, or shortcut keys, click the OK button. You now begin recording the macro.

6. Perform the steps in sequence that are required to complete the action, and then click the Stop Recording button on the Macro toolbar.

TIP

Accuracy is more important than speed when recording macros.

Run a Macro

If you created a macro but did not assign it to a shortcut key, you can still invoke the macro via the Macros dialog box.

1. Click to position the insertion point in the document where you want the output of the macro to appear.

2. Choose Tools ➢ Macro ➢ Macros. The Macros dialog box opens.

3. Click the macro you want to run.

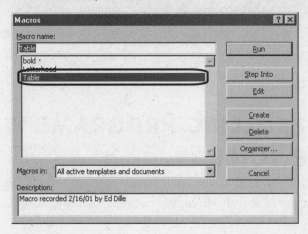

4. Click the Run button. The macro is now inserted into the document.

Delete a Macro

When a macro outlives its usefulness, it is time to delete it and make room for new macros.

1. Choose Tools ➤ Macro ➤ Macros. The Macros dialog box opens.

2. Select the macro you want to remove.

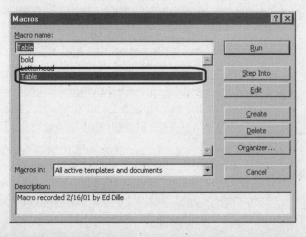

3. Click the Delete button. A dialog box appears, confirming that you wish to delete the macro.

4. Click the Yes button. The dialog box closes, and the macro is deleted.

5. Click the Close button.

CONTROLLING PROGRAMS WITH YOUR VOICE

The Office Language toolbar allows you to dictate text directly into your document and also to control buttons, menus, and toolbar functions by using the Voice Command option.

When you first install an Office XP program, the Language toolbar will appear at the top of your screen. To minimize the toolbar, click the minus sign (−) at the right end of the toolbar. The Language toolbar will dock in the Taskbar at the bottom right of the screen, near the system clock. If you are using English as the default language, the toolbar will be denoted by the letters *EN* (other languages have appropriate abbreviations as well). To restore the toolbar to the top of the screen, click the icon and select Show The Language Toolbar from the pop-up menu.

Before you can use the Language toolbar for either dictation or voice commands, you must first train your computer to recognize your voice using the Speech Recognition Wizard.

1. Click the Microphone button on the Language toolbar. The Welcome To Office Speech Recognition dialog box opens.

2. Click the Next button, read the instructions, ensure you are in a quiet environment, and then click the Next button again.

3. Read the sentence provided to automatically set the proper volume of the microphone, and then click the Next button (as shown in the top graphic on the next page).

4. Read the text with hard consonants, to help determine whether the microphone is positioned too closely to your mouth. Repeat the process, adjusting your microphone as needed until you have a clear, distinct audio playback, and then click the Next button.

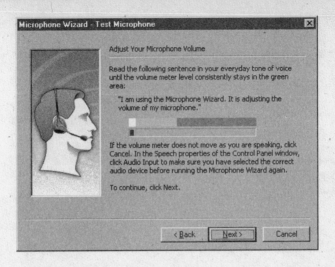

5. You are reminded to ensure that your environment is suitable for recording again; read the instructions and then click the Next button.

6. You are given a series of dialog boxes to read. As you read each paragraph, the words on-screen are highlighted as the computer recognizes them. As each dialog box is completed, the program will automatically move to the next one, and the progress meter will update accordingly.

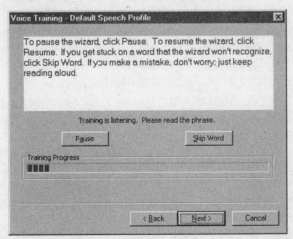

TIP

It is easier for an Office XP program to recognize complete sentences in context than individual words, so don't pause between each word and wait for the program to display it on-screen.

7. At the end of the training session, your voice profile will be updated and saved automatically.

NOTE

You are not limited to this one training session. The more that you train, the more accurately an Office XP program will recognize your voice.

TIP

If you have problems using this feature with your present microphone, verify that the microphone records properly elsewhere. This is easily accomplished using Windows Sound Recorder (in the Multimedia or Multimedia And Entertainment program group accessed by choosing Start ➤ Programs).

Execute Voice Commands

The two modes, Dictation and Voice Command, have been designed to be mutually exclusive. You do not want the word *File* typed, for example, when you are actually trying to open the File menu or, conversely, have the menu open instead of the word *File* being typed when you are in the middle of a sentence. You must manually click either mode on the Language toolbar to switch between them.

Voice Command mode allows you to talk your way through any sequence of menus or toolbar commands, simply by reading the appropriate text from them. For example, if you wanted to print the current page of the document you were working on, you would simply say **File**, **Print**, **Current Page**, **OK** (without saying the commas between the words as printed here). You need not worry about remembering every command sequence, because as you say each word in the sequence, the corresponding menu or submenu appears on-screen for your reference.

1. Click the Microphone button on the Language toolbar. The toolbar expands so that the Voice Command button becomes available on the toolbar.

2. Click the Voice Command button to shift into that mode.

3. Type the body text of your document normally. When you are ready to issue a command, simply speak the sequence just as you would click through it were you using the menus or toolbars normally.

Dictate Text

Dictating the text of a letter or other document using Office XP's speech recognition functions may be easier for some users than typing, but don't think that it is an entirely hands-free operation. For example, you must manually click the Voice Command button when you want to format anything that has been input, and then click Dictation to resume inputting text. Additionally, the Dictation function is not going to be 100 percent accurate, so you will need to clean up mistakes (such as inputting the word *noir* when you say "or") either when they occur or subsequently. Finally, although you can say punctuation marks like commas and periods to have them accurately reflected in the document, all periods are followed by double spaces (which may not be consistent with the document formatting you are using between sentences), and issues of capitalization remain as well. Nevertheless, it is fun and freeing to be able to get the first draft of any document on paper simply by speaking it.

1. Click the Microphone button on the Language toolbar. The toolbar expands so that the Dictation button becomes available on the toolbar.

2. Click to position the insertion point in the document where you want the dictated text to appear and begin speaking normally into your microphone. As you speak, the words will appear on the page.

3. When you have finished dictating your text, click the Microphone button again to make the speech recognition functions inactive.

WARNING

If you fail to turn off the Language toolbar functions while continuing to work in an Office XP program, distractions in the room, such as phone calls or even the sound of your keyboard clicking as you type, can introduce errors into your document.

RECOGNIZING HANDWRITING

Although entering information into an Office XP document through the keyboard is fast and efficient, you may find that you need to enter information in handwritten form. Office provides handwriting recognition to help you convert handwriting into text. Before you can insert handwritten text into a document, you need to have a third-party electronic stylus, handwriting tablet, or mouse attached to your computer. Although you can use the mouse, for best results, you should use a handwriting input device.

When you insert handwritten text into a document that already contains typed text, the handwritten text is converted to typed text, and then inserted in line with the existing text at the insertion point. The program recognizes the handwriting when there is enough text for it to do so, when you reach the end of the line, or if you pause for about 2 seconds. In addition, the converted text will take on the same typeface attributes as the existing text. When you insert text into a blank document, the text is placed at the beginning of the document.

NOTE

If the handwriting recognition feature is installed correctly, you'll find the Language toolbar in the upper-right corner of your Office XP program window.

Insert Handwritten Text in a Document

When you click the Handwriting button on the Language toolbar and then choose the Write Anywhere option, a dialog box similar to the Writing Pad dialog box opens, except there is no writing area within this dialog box. You use this feature just as you would the Writing Pad feature,

except that you do your "writing" right on the Word document behind
the dialog box.

1. Open the document into which you want to insert hand-
    written text.

2. Click the Handwriting button on the Language toolbar, and
    then choose Write Anywhere.

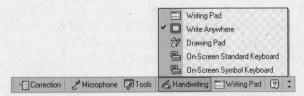

The Write Anywhere bar opens on your screen, and the Text
button is selected by default.

3. Move the mouse over a blank area of your document, and
    then write your text. The handwritten words are converted
    to text on your screen.

Insert Handwritten Text on a Writing Pad

When you click the Handwriting button on the Language toolbar and
then choose the Writing Pad option, a Writing Pad dialog box opens on
your screen. Within that dialog box is another toolbar. It has the same

options as are available through the Handwriting button on the Language toolbar. In addition, it has the following buttons: Ink, Text, Backspace, Space, directional cursors, Enter, Tab, and Recognize Now. You use these buttons to control the input into Word.

To use the basic features of the Writing Pad, click the Text button, and then move your mouse over the writing area within the dialog box. At that point, the mouse cursor turns into a pen. You then write with that pen just as you would write with a physical pen. After recognition, the characters that you write appear in the Word document open behind the dialog box. You use other buttons with the dialog box to manipulate the position of the cursor in the Word document itself.

1. Open the document into which you want to insert handwritten text.

2. Click the Handwriting button on the Language toolbar, and then choose Writing Pad. The Writing Pad dialog box opens on your screen.

3. Move the mouse cursor over the writing area of the Writing Pad dialog box to write your text. The new text is inserted into the document.

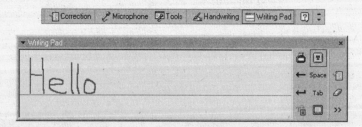

USING MULTIPLE LANGUAGES

International Microsoft Office XP users can change the language that appears on their screen by changing the default language settings. Users around the world can enter, display, and edit text in all supported languages, including European languages, Japanese, Chinese, Korean, Hebrew, and Arabic, to name a few. You'll probably be able to use Office programs in your native language. If the text in your document is written in more than one language, you can automatically detect languages or designate the language of selected text so the spell checker uses the right dictionary.

NOTE

To use dictionaries for other languages, you must have the dictionaries for the languages installed on your computer for Office programs to detect and apply their spelling and proofing tools.

Add a Language to Office XP Programs

1. Click the Start button on the Taskbar, point to Programs, point to Microsoft Office Tools, and then click Microsoft Office XP Language Settings. The Microsoft Office Language Settings dialog box opens.

2. Select the language you want to use.

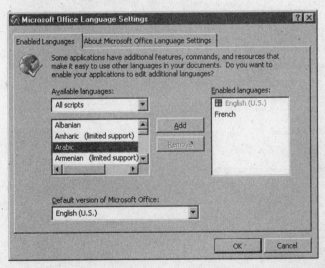

3. Click the Add button.

4. Click the OK button, and then click the Yes button to quit and restart Office.

TIP

After you enable editing for another language, you might need to install the correct keyboard so you can enter characters for that language.

Mark Text as a Particular Language

1. Start Word or PowerPoint.

2. Select the text you want to mark.

3. In Word, choose Tools ➤ Language ➤ Set Language; in PowerPoint, choose Tools ➤ Language. The Language dialog box opens.

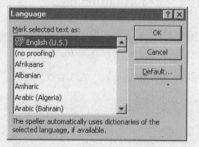

4. Choose the language you want to assign to the selected text.

5. Click the OK button.

TIP

To detect languages in Word, choose Tools ➤ Language ➤ Set Language, click the Detect Language Automatically check box to select it, and then click the OK button.

NOTE

Office XP supports an AutoCorrect list for each language to make corrections as you type in multiple languages. For example, the English AutoCorrect list capitalizes all cases of the single letter *I*, but in Swedish this is a preposition.

REPAIRING OFFICE PROGRAMS

Despite your best efforts or the quality of your computer hardware, there will be times when an Office program stops working for no apparent reason. All the Office programs are self-repairing, which means that Office checks if essential files are missing or corrupt as a program opens, and fixes the files as needed. You may never even realize there was a problem. Other times, Office starts fine but might have another problem, such as a corrupted font file or a missing template. These kinds of problems used to take hours to identify and fix. Now Office does the work for you with the Detect And Repair feature, which locates, diagnoses, and fixes any errors in the program itself. If the Office program still doesn't work properly, you can use the Microsoft Office Application Recovery program to restart or stop an Office program. If you need to add or remove features, restore the Office installation, or remove Office entirely, you can use Office Setup's maintenance feature.

Detect and Repair Problems.

1. Choose Help ➤ Detect And Repair. The Detect And Repair dialog box opens.

2. Click the Start button. Insert the Office CD in your CD-ROM drive.

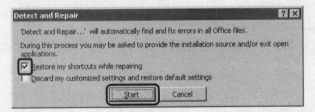

3. If necessary, click Repair Office, and then choose the Reinstall Office or Repair Errors In Your Office Installation option button.

4. Click the Finish button.

Recover an Office Program

1. Click the Start button on the Taskbar, point to Programs, point to Microsoft Office Tools, and then click Microsoft Office Application Recovery. The Microsoft Office Application Recovery dialog box opens.

2. Select the application you want to recover.

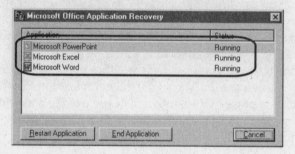

3. Click the Restart Application button or the End Application button.

TIP

In the worst-case scenario, when this option does not help (and you should try this option first), you can remove and reinstall the application.

Perform Maintenance on Office Programs

1. In Windows Explorer, double-click the Setup icon on the Office CD.

2. Click one of the following maintenance buttons:

    ▶ Add Or Remove Features to determine which features are installed or removed

    ▶ Repair Office to repair or reinstall Office

    ▶ Uninstall Office to uninstall Office

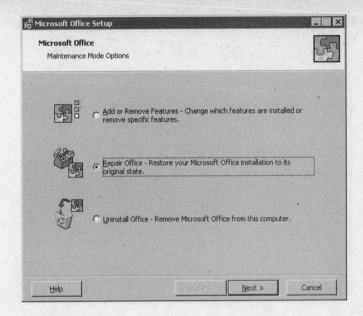

3. Follow the wizard instructions to complete the maintenance.

What's Next

Working with Word documents is by far the most commonly performed task in all versions of Office, including Office XP. Thus, the next chapter introduces you to Word 2002's features and helps you to begin working effectively. You will learn how to open existing files, create new ones, save them, and recover them in the event of a problem.

PART II
CREATING DOCUMENTS WITH WORD 2002

Chapter 3

WORKING WITH WORD 2002 DOCUMENTS

Now that you understand the Office basics presented in the first two chapters, it's time to focus on mastering the typical, day-to-day uses of the individual programs.

Of all the Office components, Word is historically the most often used, because of its versatility with different file formats and the frequency with which we tend to create documents. Thus, we start our focused discussion with Word: how to work with both existing Word 2002 documents as well as ones you create (including letters, memos, and faxes). Additional information about file recovery and the new Smart Tags option is provided, too.

Adapted from *Microsoft Word 2002 Simply Visual*
by Perspection, Inc.
ISBN 0-7821-4005-X   320 pp $24.99

OPENING AN EXISTING WORD DOCUMENT

When you create documents, they are saved, by default, in the My Documents folder. Naturally, you also have the option of saving them in other folders, and, as you build an extensive collection of documents, it is always easier to find them if you have organized them in folders that have been logically named to reflect their contents.

WARNING

The default save folder, My Documents, may not actually be the default for you if you're working with Word in an office network situation where an administrator has set up different options (such as files not being saved to a local drive but to a network drive). Check to be sure.

Open an Existing Document

1. Choose File ➤ Open. The Open dialog box opens.

2. Click the Look In drop-down arrow, and then select the drive or Internet location or click a button on the Places bar that contains the file you want to open.

3. In either the folder list or Internet location, locate the file or folder you want to open and click it. The folder containing the file appears.

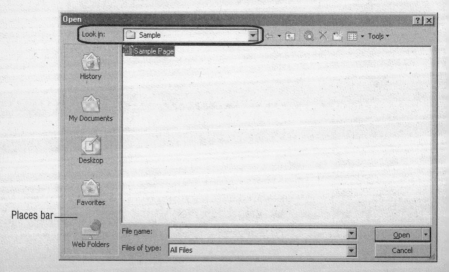

4. Click the file you want to open, and then click the Open button. The file opens and is now available.

OPENING FILES OF DIFFERENT TYPES

Word recognizes and can open for editing files created in a wide variety of other programs, including but not limited to: Lotus 1-2-3, WordPerfect, Write, Excel, Outlook, Schedule, Windows Write (included with earlier versions of Windows), and Microsoft Works. Formats for many previous versions of Word files (including ones quite old) are also supported.

Open a File in a Non-Word Format

1. Choose File ➤ Open. The Open dialog box opens.

2. Click the Files Of Type drop-down arrow, and then select the type of file that you want to open.

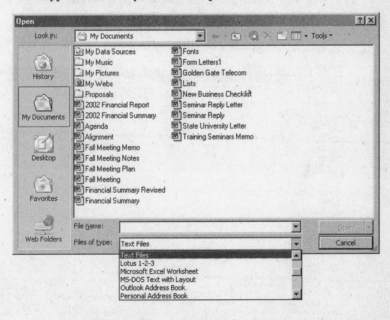

3. Click the Look In drop-down arrow, and then select the drive or Internet location or click a button on the Places bar that contains the file you want to open.

4. Double-click the file to open it.

OPENING A DOCUMENT FROM THE INTERNET

Before you can pull documents directly from the Web into Word for editing, you must first have established a shortcut to the web server or network place in question. When the shortcut has been established, you can open a document from the web server or network place in the same way you open a document from your local hard drive.

Add a New Network Place or Web Folder

If you don't see a network place or web folder for your web server, you must create a new one. The method depends on the operating system you are using.

Windows 2000 or Windows Me (or Later)

1. Choose File ➢ Open. The Open dialog box opens.

2. On the Places bar, click My Network Places.

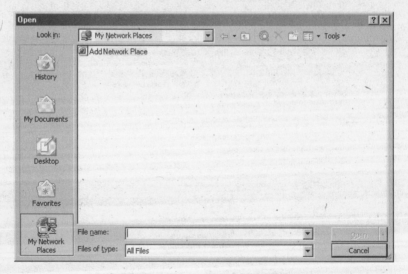

3. Double-click Add Network Place. The Add Network Place Wizard opens.

4. Choose Create A Shortcut To An Existing Network Place, and then click the Next button.

5. In the Location box, enter the server's URL.

6. In the Shortcut Name box, enter a name for the shortcut.

7. Click the Finish button. The wizard closes, and the new network place is added.

Windows NT 4 or Windows 98

1. Choose File ➢ Open. The Open dialog box opens.

2. On the Places bar, click Web Folders.

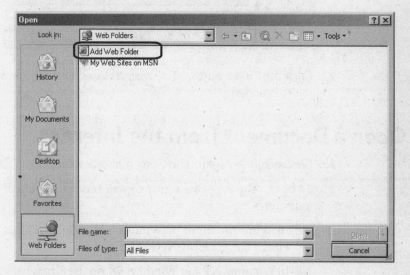

3. Double-click Add Web Folder. The Add Web Folder Wizard opens.

4. Click Create A Shortcut To An Existing Web Folder, and then click the Next button.

5. In the Location box, enter the server's URL.

6. In the Shortcut Name box, enter a name for the shortcut.

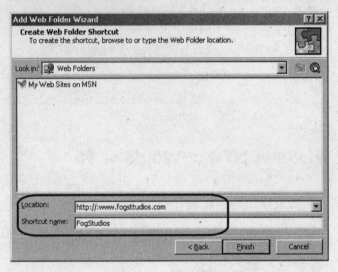

7. Click the Finish button. The wizard closes, and the new web folder is added.

Open a Document from the Internet

1. Choose File ➤ Open. The Open dialog box opens.

2. To open your list of shortcuts to web servers, do one of the following:

   ▶ In Windows 2000 or Windows Me (or later), on the Places bar, click My Network Places.

   ▶ In Windows NT 4 or Windows 98, on the Places bar, click Web Folders.

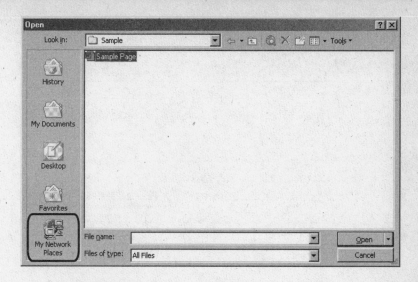

3. Double-click the network place for the web server that contains the file you want to open.

4. Double-click the file to open it.

SEARCHING FOR A WORD FILE

Perhaps you have forgotten the name of the file that you want to open, but you remember other details about the file, like the type of information that it contains. You can use Word's Search function to find the file by looking for text contained in the file, or by pulling up a list of files with names similar to the one you are searching for.

Search for a File

1. Choose File ➤ Open. The Open dialog box opens.

2. Choose Tools ➤ Search. The Search dialog box opens, displaying the Basic tab.

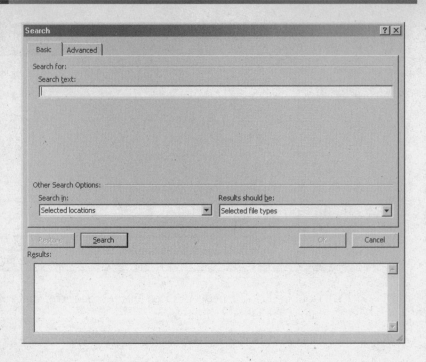

3. In the Search Text box, type some text from the file you want to find.

TIP

Wildcards can also be employed in the Search Text box. Enter a question mark (?) to match any single character you're not sure of, or type an asterisk (*) to match any number of characters you aren't sure about. For example, s?t finds *sit* and *sat*, while s*d finds *sad* as well as *standing*. *. doc pulls up a list of all Word files.

4. To limit the search, click the Search In drop-down arrow and click the check boxes to select a specific drive, folder, or website, or select Everywhere. Click the Results Should Be drop-down arrow, and then click the check boxes to select the kinds of items to locate, or select Anything.

5. Click the Search button. The results of the search appear in the Results box.

6. To open a file, double-click the document icon in the Results box.

INSERTING TEXT

In addition to the cut-and-paste techniques, you can also insert entire Word files into other files, insert text boxes, and also insert various forms of automatic text provided by Word (for example, salutations, date-time stamps, and so forth). All of these functions are available on the Insert menu on the Standard toolbar.

Insert Files

Suppose, for example, that you have previously created a document that catalogs all of the videos that you own. Now you are in the process of creating a home inventory for your insurance company to cover your belongings in the event of a loss. Rather than retyping or even cutting and pasting the list of videos into the home inventory, you can insert the entire document in its current form.

1. Click to position the insertion point where you want the inserted file to appear.

2. Choose Insert ➢ File. The Insert File dialog box opens.

3. Use the browse tools in the Insert File dialog box to locate the file that you want to insert.

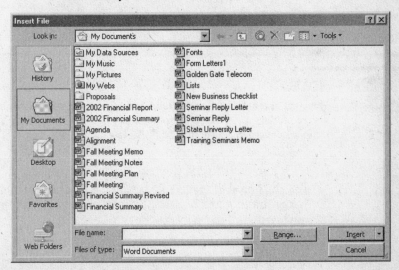

4. Double-click the file to insert it into the existing document.

Insert a Text Box

Using text boxes is a good way to offset blocks of information that are related to the body of the document, but are sufficiently different from the central thrust of the text to warrant being dealt with as a side-bar. You can also offset important quotes in text boxes, or use them to house diverse elements like your contact information or a set of related statistics.

1. Choose Insert ≻ Text Box. A text box appears in the document.

Create your drawing here.

NOTE

The smaller text box will not expand if you type text that extends beyond its visible borders. Drag the corner of the box to resize it just as you would any other window so that all of the text is displayed.

2. Click anywhere inside the text box to edit its content. The Text Box toolbar opens on the screen, as well as a smaller box within the text box frame where you can actually enter the text.

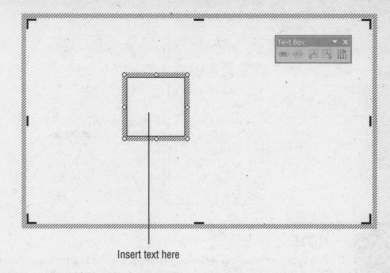

Insert text here

3. When you have completed entering text into the box, either by typing or by cutting and pasting at the insertion point, click anywhere outside the border of the text box to save the current contents and close the Text Box toolbar.

TIP

If you want to edit the contents of a text box after you have closed it, click the text box—the insertion point appears within the box, and the Text Box toolbar also returns to the screen.

Insert AutoText

AutoText elements are usually used as text fields like the greeting or closing lines in letters, headers and footers, and so forth. The most commonly used forms of AutoText are available on a submenu of the Insert menu. Additional choices are available via the AutoCorrect dialog box.

1. Position the insertion point where you want the AutoText to be inserted.

2. Choose Insert ➤ AutoText. The AutoText submenu opens.

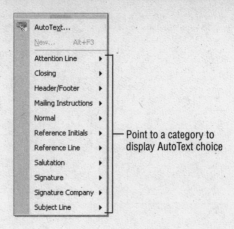

Point to a category to
display AutoText choice

NOTE

The types of AutoText include greetings, closings, attention lines, and other routinely used text. They are arranged in cascading submenus under the Insert menu. The text you see at the lowest-level submenu is the text that will appear when you click it.

3. Point to a category, and then click an entry. The text is inserted in the document.

4. To see additional choices or add your own entries, choose Insert ➤ AutoText ➤ AutoText. The AutoCorrect dialog box opens, displaying the AutoText tab.

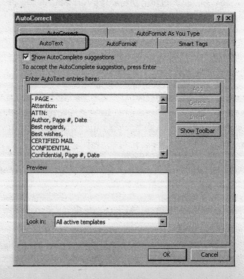

5. To add an entry to the menu, type an entry in the Enter Auto-Text Entries Here box, and then click the Add button. The entry appears on the Normal submenu.

6. Scroll down the list to find the AutoText entry you want to make, and then click the OK button.

CONTROLLING AUTOMATIC CHANGES USING SMART TAGS

You can use Smart Tags to perform actions in Word that you'd otherwise have to open other programs to accomplish. The purple dotted lines beneath text in your document indicate Smart Tags. For example, you can add a person's name and address from one of your documents to an Outlook contact folder without copying the information in Word, then opening Outlook and pasting the data. Smart Tags are created automatically when the correct parameters exist.

Set Smart Tag Parameters

By default, Word recognizes addresses, dates, times, places, and recently used Outlook addresses and tags them with Smart Tags. If you no longer want to use Smart Tags, you can turn them off at any time.

1. Choose Tools ➤ AutoCorrect Options. The AutoCorrect dialog box opens.

2. Click the Smart Tags tab.

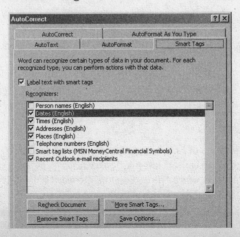

Part ii

3. To turn Smart Tags on or off, click the Label Text With Smart Tags check box to select or clear it.

4. To specify the Smart Tags you want to recognize, click the check boxes in the Recognizers box to select the ones you want.

5. Click the OK button to close the AutoCorrect dialog box.

TIP

To add Smart Tags from the Web, click the More Smart Tags button on the Smart Tags tab in the AutoCorrect dialog box. A Microsoft Office website opens in your browser where you can locate and install additional Smart Tags.

Interact with Smart Tags

When Word recognizes a text element that is applicable for one of the preset Smart Tag parameters, it underlines the next text element with a purple dotted line.

1. Position the insertion point over text underlined with a purple dotted line. The Smart Tag Actions button appears.

2. Click the Smart Tag Actions button to check the various actions you can perform, and then select one.

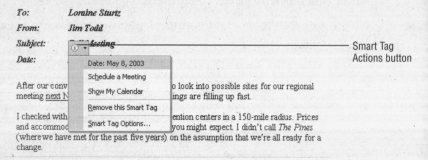

NOTE

The types of Smart Tag actions you might encounter include the ability to cut and paste contact information to Outlook, perform AutoCorrect and formatting functions, and so forth. Consult Microsoft Word help for additional information on individual options.

TIP
To remove Smart Tags in a document, click the Smart Tag Actions button, and then choose Remove This Smart Tag.

CREATING A LETTER

Creating letters is one of the most common uses of Word, both for families designing their annual Christmas update letter and businesses staying in touch with their customers. In this section, you learn how to create a basic letter from a template.

Create a Letter

1. Choose File ➤ New. The New Document task pane opens.

2. In the New Document task pane, click General Templates under the New From Template heading. The Templates dialog box opens.

3. Click the Letters & Faxes tab.

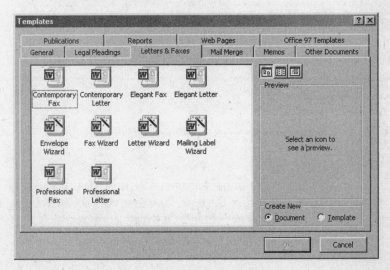

4. Double-click the Letter Wizard icon. The Letter Wizard dialog box or the Office Assistant opens.

5. Determine whether you're writing an individual letter or using a mailing list. Click the Send One Letter option or the Send Letters To A Mailing List option, and then click the OK button. The Letter Wizard – Step 1 Of 4 dialog box opens.

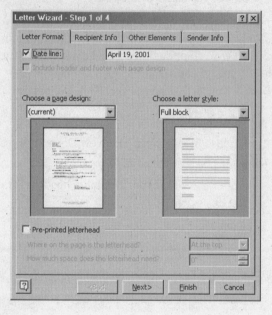

NOTE

For this example, the Send One Letter option is used.

6. Select the format for your letter, the style you want, and what date to put on the letter, and then click the Next button. The Letter Wizard – Step 2 Of 4 dialog box opens.

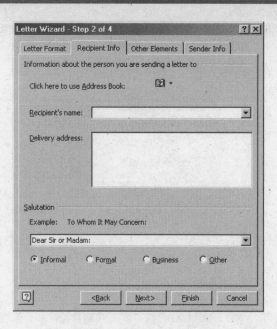

7. Enter the name and address of the recipient and what salutation you want to use, and then click the Next button. The Letter Wizard – Step 3 Of 4 dialog box opens.

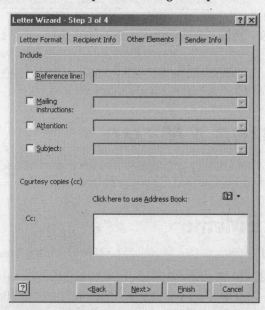

8. Enter the following optional elements: Reference Line, Mailing Instructions, Attention, and Subject, and then click the Next button. The Letter Wizard – Step 4 Of 4 dialog box opens.

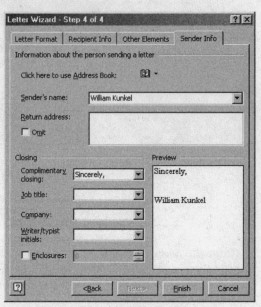

9. Enter your return address and the closing that you want to use, and then click the Finish button. The basic format of the letter is complete, and the Letter Wizard closes. You may now type the body text of the letter directly into the document.

CREATING A MEMO

Memos are another commonly used document whose creation has been simplified via the use of Word templates.

Create a Memo

1. Choose File ≻ New. The New Document task pane opens.

2. In the New Document task pane, click General Templates under the New From Template heading. The Templates dialog box opens.

3. Click the Memos tab.

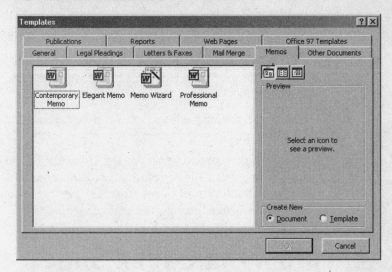

4. Double-click the Memo Wizard icon. The Memo Wizard opening screen appears.

5. Read the introduction, click the Next button, specify the style you want to use, and then click the Next button.

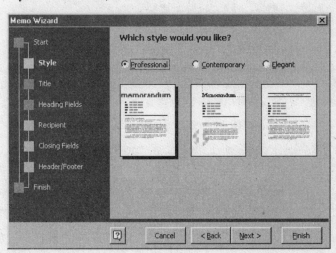

6. Specify the title you want to use, and then click the Next button.

7. Specify the heading fields you want to use, and then click the Next button.

8. Specify the recipients you want to use, and then click the Next button.

9. Specify the closing fields you want to use, and then click the Next button.

10. Specify the header and footer you want to use, and then click the Finish button. The basic format of the memo is complete, and the Memo Wizard closes. You may now type the body text of the memo directly into the document.

CREATING A FAX COVER SHEET

Word offers three varieties of basic fax cover sheets: Contemporary, Elegant, and Professional. Each of these can be edited in template form or used with the Fax Wizard.

Create a Fax Cover Sheet

1. Choose File ➤ New. The New Document task pane opens.

2. In the New Document task pane, click General Templates under the New From Template heading. The Templates dialog box opens.

3. Click the Letters & Faxes tab.

4. Double-click the Fax Wizard icon. The Fax Wizard dialog box opens.

5. Read the introduction, click the Next button, choose a cover sheet option, and then click the Next button.

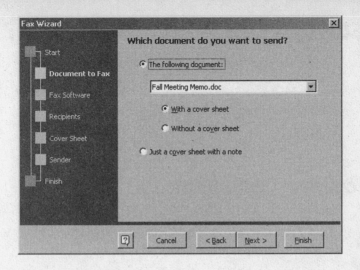

6. Select a fax program, and then click the Next button.

7. Specify the recipients' names and fax numbers to whom you want to send the fax, and then click the Next button.

8. If you selected this option, select a cover sheet style, and then click the Next button.

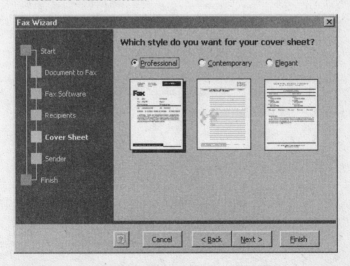

9. Specify your name, company, mailing address, phone, and fax, and then click the Next button.

10. When you complete the wizard, click the Finish button.

Part II

RECOVERING A WORD DOCUMENT

One of the best new features in the latest version of Word is the Document Recovery task pane, which simplifies the process of recovering documents if Word is closed prematurely—due to a system fault, power surge, or some other unforeseen event. If Word closes prematurely, when you reopen Word, the Document Recovery task pane opens, listing all documents that were previously open when the program closed.

Recover a Document

1. Restart the computer and open Word. All documents available for recovery appear in the Document Recovery task pane on the left side of the screen.

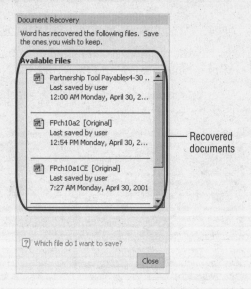

Recovered documents

2. Click the document version you want to recover in the Document Recovery task pane to open the document in the main window.

3. Choose File ➤ Save As. The Save As dialog box opens.

4. Browse to the folder where you want to save the recovered document, assign a name to the document, and then click the Save button.

5. When you have completed recovery of all the documents that you want to save, click the Close button in the Document Recovery task pane.

REPAIRING A FILE

Occasionally, a file will become corrupt, either during transmission as an e-mail attachment over the Internet or through some other means. When this happens, you can attempt to recover the data from within the file by using Word's Open And Repair command in the Open dialog box.

Recover the Text from a Damaged Document

1. Choose File ➤ Open. The Open dialog box opens.

2. Click the Look In drop-down arrow, and then choose the drive, folder, or Internet location holding the file you want to repair.

3. Click the Open button drop-down arrow to display a list of options.

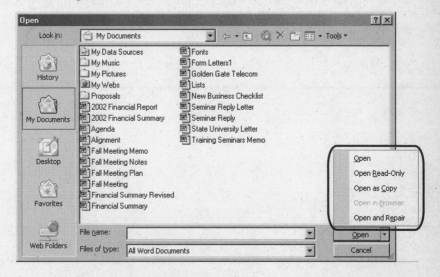

4. Choose Open And Repair. The file opens, and the necessary repairs are made.

NOTE

The repairs that Word makes do not become permanent until you save the file; you will be reminded of this fact when you issue the Save command.

In some cases, when the recovery option doesn't work, you may want to try a few other things:

▶ Take the file to another PC and try it there (in case it's a problem with your installation of Office XP).

▶ Attempt to open the file. If you can open it, choose File ➤ New to open a new document window as well. Try copying all the relevant material paragraph by paragraph (omitting any garbage or control characters you see) into the new document.

WHAT'S NEXT

In the next chapter, we take working with documents a step further by focusing closely on document formatting with Word 2002. Included are discussions of some of the trickier functions, such as working with tables (one of the issues in Word—or any other application supporting them—that generates the most questions).

Chapter 4

FORMATTING DOCUMENTS

While many documents you create or modify may contain just standard text, in many others, you will need to call particular attention to certain words or parts of the document, to alter formatting such as line spacing and paragraph indentation, and to specify organizational elements such as lists (including bulleted lists) and tables.

Such features can distinguish a long text document by helping the reader identify core topics or text, or by allowing them to quickly refer to a table or list for information they need to get quickly.

Adapted from *Microsoft Word 2002 Simply Visual* by Perspection, Inc.

ISBN 0-7821-4005-X   320 pp $24.99

ADDING EMPHASIS TO TEXT

Emphasis is added to text whenever it is displayed in something other than the basic font (defined as a collection of characters, numbers, and symbols in the same design). It might be **boldfaced**, *italicized*, underlined, superscripted (slightly raised text with a smaller point size such as is commonly used in footnote annotations), or various other emphases, each of which has one or more common applications. You can add emphasis to text by using any of the style buttons on the Formatting toolbar. The style buttons are toggle switches (on/off functions), which you click to turn the feature on and off. For special emphasis, you can combine formats, such as bold and italics. There are several techniques for adding emphasis to your characters.

Format Existing Text Quickly

1. Select the text (even entire paragraphs if you like by highlighting them) to which you want to apply emphasis.

2. Click the Bold button, Italic button, Underline button, or other style buttons on the Formatting toolbar to change font, change point size, make the character bold, or so forth.

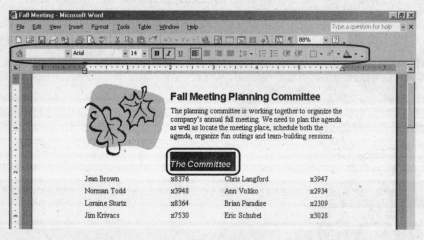

Here are the common keyboard shortcuts for manipulating text:

Ctrl+Shift+spacebar   Creates a nonbreaking space

Ctrl+- (hyphen)   Creates a nonbreaking hyphen

Ctrl+B   Makes letters bold

Ctrl+I   Makes letters italic

Ctrl+U   Makes letters underlined

Ctrl+Shift+<   Decreases font size

Ctrl+Shift+>   Increases font size

Ctrl+spacebar   Removes paragraph or character formatting

Ctrl+C   Copies the selected text or object

Ctrl+X   Cuts the selected text or object

Ctrl+V   Pastes text or an object

Ctrl+Z   Undoes the last action

Ctrl+Y   Redoes the last action

Format Existing Text

1. Select the text (even entire paragraphs if you like) to which you want to apply emphasis.

2. Choose Format ➤ Font. The Font dialog box opens, displaying the Font tab.

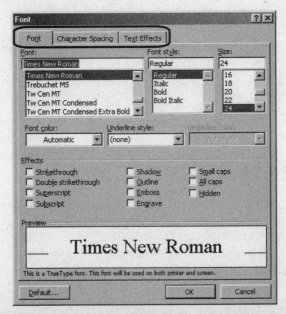

Part II

3. Set the font color and make other choices.

4. To add some flashy effects to your text, click the Text Effects tab, and then choose an animation.

5. To change character spacing, click the Character Spacing tab, and then change the settings as appropriate.

6. Click the OK button to apply them.

Highlight Text

There are many ways to accent your text and make it "pop," as they say in artistic circles. You can use an outrageous font, go to bold or italics, or even reduce or expand your text. But the best way to make your text stand out in a functional way is to use the Highlight tool to mark and locate key text within a document. Highlighting portions of a document works best when viewed electronically or when printing with a color printer. It is less effective for black-and-white print applications.

1. Click the Highlight button on the Formatting toolbar.

2. Select the text you want to highlight. Your cursor now appears as a highlighting pen, and text that you select is automatically highlighted.

   A second paragraph is also important so that we can show the differences between something being tested in one paragraph, and something being demonstrated with another.

3. To turn the feature off, click the Highlight button again or press the Esc key.

CHANGING TEXT FONTS

Although it is usually not considered good style to use numerous fonts in a document, and certainly not within paragraphs or other usually homogenous blocks of text, some designs incorporate multiple fonts. Also, you might want to globally change the font you are using after a document has been created.

Change the Font Type

1. Select the text you want to change.

2. Use one of the following methods:

   ▶ Choose Format ➤ Font. The Font dialog box opens. Select the font you want, and then click the OK button.

   ▶ Click the Font drop-down arrow on the Formatting toolbar. This opens a cascading menu of fonts, from which any font can be selected. Click the font you want, and it replaces the selected font in the original document.

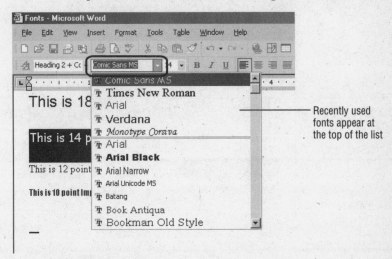

Recently used fonts appear at the top of the list

CHANGING TEXT POINT SIZES

The most commonly used text sizes for regular text (not headers or other layout elements) are 10 and 12 point type (typically abbreviated 10 pt. or 12 pt.). Again, nothing limits you from breaking with convention, and you will also want to manipulate point sizes to keep your headers from wrapping to two lines or make other aesthetic changes from time to time.

Change the Font Size

1. Select the text whose size you want to change.

2. Use one of the following methods:

   ▶ Choose Format ➤ Font. The Font dialog box opens. Select the font size you want, and then click the OK button.

   ▶ Click the Font Size drop-down arrow on the Formatting toolbar, producing a cascading menu of font sizes. Choose a size to resize the selected text.

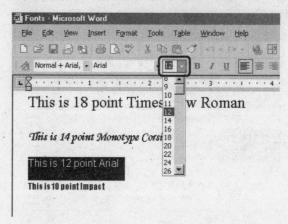

SELECTING OR CLEARING TEXT FORMATTING

If you want to change formatting for all instances of formatted text, you can use the Styles And Formatting task pane to select all instances. If you have created formatted or stylized paragraphs and subsequently want to return to the default text settings, you can remove the existing formatting.

Select or Clear Text Formatting

1. Select the text whose formatting you want to change or clear away.

2. Choose Format ➤ Reveal Formatting. The Reveal Formatting task pane opens.

3. Point to the Selected Text box, click the drop-down arrow, and then choose Select All Text With Similar Formatting or Clear Formatting.

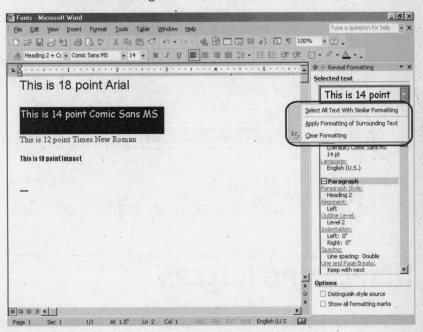

TIP

You can also press Ctrl+spacebar to remove paragraph or character formatting.

COPYING TEXT FORMATTING

The Format Painter copies and pastes formatting from one batch of selected text to another without copying the text. This is useful when you want to quickly apply multiple formatting attributes to a text block without having to create a style.

Copy Text Formatting with the Format Painter

1. Select the text with the formatting you want to copy.

2. Click the Format Painter button on the Standard toolbar.

3. Select the text you want to format with the Format Painter pointer.

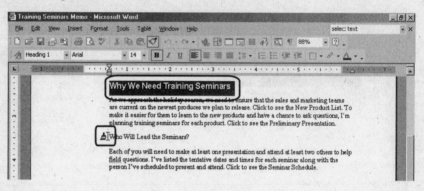

DISPLAYING RULERS

Word rulers do more than measure. The horizontal ruler above the document shows the length of the typing line, and lets you quickly adjust left and right margins and indents, set tabs, and change column widths. The vertical ruler along the left edge of the document lets you adjust top and bottom margins and change table row heights. Hide the rulers to get more room for your document.

Show and Hide the Rulers

If a horizontal ruler isn't on the screen, choose View ≻ Ruler. The ruler appears.

▶ To view the horizontal ruler, click the Normal View button or the Web Layout View button.

▶ To view the horizontal and vertical rulers, click the Print Layout View button.

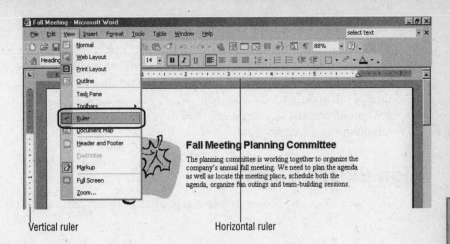

Vertical ruler   Horizontal ruler

TIP

You can change the ruler to show inches, centimeters, millimeters, points, or picas. Choose Tools ➢ Options, click the General tab, click the Measurement Units drop-down arrow, select the measurement you want, and then click the OK button.

CHANGING PARAGRAPH ALIGNMENT

Most of the documents that you create in Word will use the Normal template, which has certain preset parameters for paragraph alignment. Text starts out positioned evenly along the left margin and is uneven, or ragged, at the right margin. Left-aligned text works well for body paragraphs in most cases, but other alignments vary the look of a document and help lead the reader through the text. Right-aligned text, which is even along the right margin and ragged at the left margin, is good for adding a date to a letter. Justified text spreads text evenly between the margins, creating a clean, professional look, often used in newspapers and magazines. Centered text is best for titles and headings. To change paragraph alignment, you can use the Click-And-Type feature, alignment buttons on the Formatting toolbar, or options in the Paragraph dialog box. Use Click-And-Type to quickly center titles or set different text alignment on the same line.

Align New Text with Click-And-Type

Place the I-beam (the shape the mouse cursor takes in Word) at the left, right, or center of the line where you want to insert new text. When the I-beam shows the appropriate alignment, double-click to place the insertion point, and then type your text. When you double-click the appropriate text alignment pointer, Word adds extra lines and tabs, and sets the alignment and text wrapping as needed.

Align Existing Text

1. Place the I-beam or select at least one line in each paragraph to align.

2. Click the appropriate alignment button on the Formatting toolbar:

   ▶ Align Left button

   ▶ Center button

   ▶ Align Right button

   ▶ Justify button

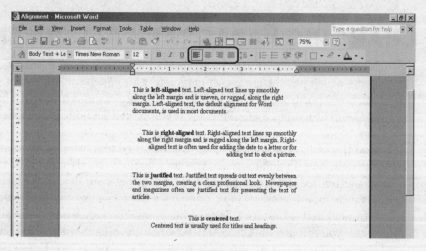

Align Text Using Custom Settings

1. Choose the paragraph(s) whose spacing you want to change.

2. Choose Format ➢ Paragraph. The Paragraph dialog box opens.

3. Click the Indents And Spacing tab.

4. In the Spacing area, enter the custom spacing parameters you want both before and after the paragraph(s).

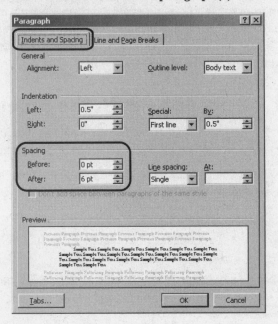

NOTE

The values in the Before and After boxes are measured in points, a common typesetting term. One point equals 1/72nd of an inch. 72 points equal 1 inch of space.

5. Click the OK button.

INDENTING PARAGRAPHS

The default setting for paragraph indentation is a half-inch (0.5"). Paragraphs can be left-aligned, centered, or right-aligned without indentation, or you can create custom indentation settings. You can quickly indent lines of text to precise locations from the left or right margin with the horizontal ruler. You can use the ruler to indent the first line of a paragraph (called a first-line indent) as books do to distinguish paragraphs; indent the second and subsequent lines of a paragraph from the left margin (called a hanging indent) to create a properly formatted bibliography; or indent the entire paragraph any amount from the left and right margin (called left indents and right indents) to separate quoted passages.

Indent Paragraphs with the Ruler

1. Select the paragraph you want to indent or just click to place your cursor within the confines of the paragraph.

2. If the horizontal ruler isn't on the screen, choose View ➤ Ruler. The ruler appears.

3. Use the markers on the ruler to set indents:

    ▶ To change the left indent of the first line, drag the First Line Indent marker.

    ▶ To change the indent of the second and subsequent lines, drag the Hanging Indent marker.

    ▶ To change the left indent for all lines, drag the Left Indent marker.

    ▶ To change the right indent for all lines, drag the Right Indent marker.

TIP

You can change the indention in increments of a half-inch. Click the paragraph or select multiple paragraphs to indent, and then click the Increase Indent button or the Decrease Indent button on the Formatting toolbar.

Left Indent marker
Hanging Indent marker
First Line Indent marker
Right Indent marker

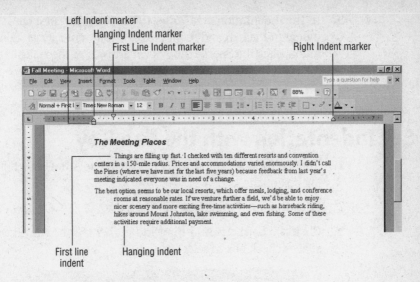

First line
indent

Hanging indent

Set a Precise Custom Indentation

Using the ruler is acceptable for draft work and altering one or two paragraphs manually; however, if you want to change the paragraph indentation throughout the document to a precise setting, you should use the Paragraph dialog box.

1. Choose Format ➤ Paragraph. The Paragraph dialog box opens.

2. Click the Indents And Spacing tab.

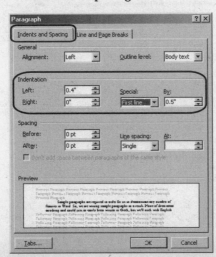

3. In the Indentation area, enter the exact space, in inches, to indent in the Left and Right boxes. If you want special indentation, click the Special drop-down arrow, and then click First Line or Hanging, and then enter the indent space in the By box.

4. Click the OK button. The new indentation is applied.

Set Indentation with the Tab Key

1. Choose Tools ➤ AutoCorrect Options. The AutoCorrect dialog box opens.

2. Click the AutoFormat As You Type tab.

3. Click the Set Left- And First-Indent With Tabs And Backspaces check box to select it.

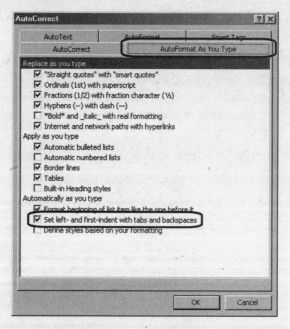

4. Click the OK button.

TIP
You can indent the first line of a paragraph by clicking the beginning of the paragraph and pressing the Tab key.

CHANGING LINE SPACING

Certain documents, particularly academic papers and draft documents, are prepared with space-and-a-half or even double spacing between lines to allow room for the reviewer of the document to handwrite comments, corrections, or critique. The lines in all Word documents are single-spaced by default, which is appropriate for letters and most documents. But you can easily change your document line spacing to double or one-and-a-half lines to allow extra space between every line. Sometimes, you'll want to add space above and below certain paragraphs, such as for headlines or indented quotations, to help set off the text.

Part ii

Change Line Spacing

1. Select the text you want to change.

2. Click the Line Spacing button drop-down arrow on the Formatting toolbar, and then choose one of the following options.

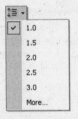

- ▶ Click the number that you want. (1.0 is single line spacing, 1.5 represents line-and-a-half, 2.0 signifies double spacing, etc.)

- ▶ To apply the setting you last used, click the Line Spacing button (not the drop-down arrow).

▶ Choose More. The Paragraph dialog box opens. The Paragraph dialog box contains single, one-and-a-half, and double line spacing as quick selections, or you can specify other modifiers in conjunction with a numeric value. Enter precise spacing parameters, and then click the OK button.

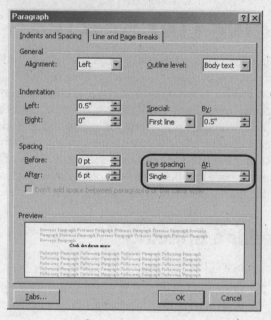

NOTE

You can also access the Paragraph dialog box directly. Choose Format ➤ Paragraph.

TIP

You can quickly change line spacing for selected text or new paragraphs by pressing Ctrl+1 for single spacing, Ctrl+5 for one-and-a-half spacing, or Ctrl+2 for double spacing.

SETTING PARAGRAPH TABS

In your document, tabs set how text or numerical data aligns in relation to the document margins. Default tab stops (predefined stopping points along the document's typing line) are set every half-inch, but you can set multiple tabs per paragraph at any location. Choose from four text tab stops: left, right, center, and decimal (for numerical data). The bar tab inserts a vertical bar at the tab stop. After tab stops are set, you can invoke them by pressing the Tab key.

Set Paragraph Tabs

1. Select one or more paragraphs in which you want to place a tab stop.

2. Click the Tab button on the horizontal ruler (left side) until it shows the type of tab stop you want. The Tab button displays the current tab stop.

3. Click the ruler where you want to set the tab stop.

4. If you want, drag the tab stop to position it.

5. To clear a tab stop, drag it off the ruler.

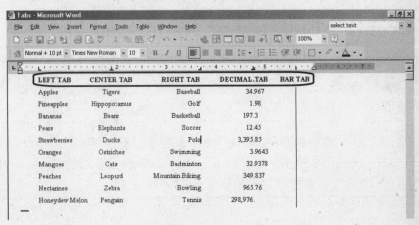

LEFT TAB	CENTER TAB	RIGHT TAB	DECIMAL.TAB	BAR TAB
Apples	Tigers	Baseball	34.967	
Pineapples	Hippopotamus	Golf	1.98	
Bananas	Bears	Basketball	197.3	
Pears	Elephants	Soccer	12.45	
Strawberries	Ducks	Polo	3,395.85	
Oranges	Ostriches	Swimming	3.9643	
Mangoes	Cats	Badminton	32.9378	
Peaches	Leopard	Mountain Biking	349.837	
Nectarines	Zebra	Bowling	965.76	
Honeydew Melon	Penguin	Tennis	298,976.	

Icon	Purpose
Left-oriented tab stop	Aligns text to the left of the tab stop
Right-oriented tab stop	Aligns text to the right of the tab stop
Center-oriented tab stop	Centers text on the tab stop
Number-oriented tab stop	Aligns numbers on the decimal point
Vertical-bar tab stop	Inserts a vertical bar at the tab stop

CREATING LISTS

The best way to draw attention to a list is to format the items with bullets or numbers. You can even create multilevel lists. For different emphasis, change any bullet or number style to one of Word's many predefined formats. For example, switch round bullets to check boxes or Roman numerals to lowercase letters. You can also customize the list style or insert a picture as a bullet. If you move, insert, or delete items in a numbered list, Word sequentially renumbers the list for you. You can also create a numbered outline. Outline numbered lists display list items at various levels rather than presenting a single level of indentation. This is useful in documents that contain one or more sublists.

Create a Bulleted or Numbered List

1. Click where you want to create a bulleted or numbered list.

2. Click the Bullets button or Numbering button on the Formatting toolbar.

3. Type the first item in your list, and then press the Enter key to insert a new bullet or the next number.

4. Type the next item, press the Enter key, and then press the Enter key again to end the list.

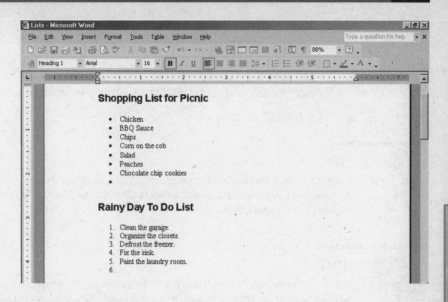

Change a List

1. Select the list you want to change.

2. Choose Format ➤ Bullets And Numbering. The Bullets And Numbering dialog box opens.

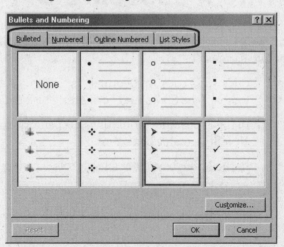

3. Click the Bulleted, Numbered, or Outline Numbered tab.

4. Choose a predefined format.

5. To add a graphic bullet, click the Customize button, click the Picture button, and then select the picture you want.

6. Click the OK button.

TIP

To create a multilevel bulleted or numbered list, press the Tab key to indent to the next level, type the item, and then press the Enter key. Press Shift+Tab to return to the previous level.

NOTE

You can move an item in a list to another indent level using buttons on the Formatting toolbar. To demote an item to a lower level, click the item in the list, and then click the Increase Indent button. The item is demoted. To promote an item to a higher level, click the item in the list, and then click the Decrease Indent button. The item is promoted.

CREATING A CUSTOM LIST

In addition to using the built-in list styles that come preconfigured with Word, you can create a custom list style, applying numbers, bullets, or other list features.

1. Click the Styles And Formatting button on the Formatting toolbar. The Styles And Formatting task pane opens.

2. In the Styles And Formatting task pane, click New Style. The New Style dialog box opens.

3. In the Name box, enter a name for your style.

4. Click the Style Type drop-down arrow, and then choose List.

5. Select the formatting options. Click the Format button to see more options.

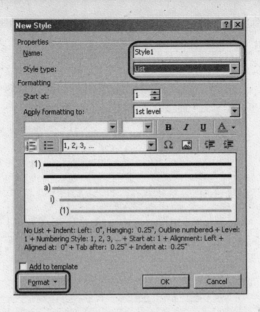

6. If you want, click the Add To Template check box to select it.

7. Click the OK button to save the custom list you have created and close the New Style dialog box.

ADDING BORDERS AND SHADING TO A PARAGRAPH

Borders are a nice way to offset important paragraphs or groups of paragraphs when you are creating a sidebar to run with an article, or calling out important quotes from the body of an article to capture the reader's attention.

Add Borders and Shading to a Paragraph

1. Select the paragraph to which you want to apply a border.

2. Choose Format ➢ Borders And Shading. The Borders And Shading dialog box opens.

3. Click the Borders tab.

4. Choose the Setting, Style, Color, and Width parameters.

5. Click the Apply To drop-down arrow, and then choose Paragraph.

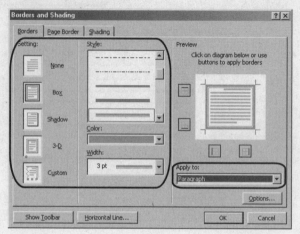

6. Click the Options button. The Borders And Shading Options dialog box opens. Set the interior spacing between the border and the text it surrounds.

7. Click the OK button to close the Borders And Shading Options dialog box.

8. Click the Shading tab, and then choose the fill color.

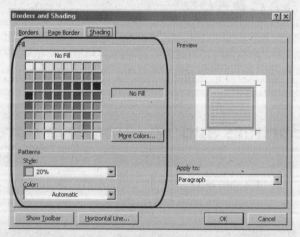

9. Click the OK button to apply the border.

CREATING A TABLE

When you need to present related information, either numerical or con-
textual, one of the common methods of doing so is to display it in table
form. A table organizes information neatly into rows and columns. The
intersection of a row and column is called a cell. You can create a table
from existing text separated by paragraphs, tabs, or commas, or you can
draw a custom table with variously sized cells and then enter text. If you
decide not to use a table, you can convert it to text.

Once you create your table, you enter text into cells just as you would
in a paragraph, except that pressing Tab moves you from cell to cell. The
first row in the table is good for column headings, whereas the leftmost
column is good for row labels. To enter text in cells, you must move
around the table. Knowing how to select the rows and columns of a table
is also essential to working with the table itself.

Create a Table

1. Position the insertion point where you want to create a table.

2. Choose Table ➤ Insert ➤ Table. The Insert Table dialog box
    opens.

3. In the Table Size area, enter the number of columns (vertical)
    and rows (horizontal) you want.

4. In the AutoFit Behavior area, select an option button to
    adjust the table size.

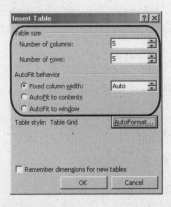

5. Click the OK button.

TIP

To quickly create a table from existing text, select the text for the table, and then choose Table ➤ Insert ➤ Table. If you want to specify options, choose Table ➤ Convert ➤ Text To Table.

Draw a Table

Rather than relying on a template, you can manually create a table layout to suit your specialized needs.

1. Position the insertion point where you want to create the table.

2. Choose Table ➤ Draw Table. The Tables And Borders toolbar opens, and your cursor becomes a pencil.

3. You can now create the cells of your table in any size, shape, and configuration. You can draw the cells one at a time; or create a large rectangle, then draw the column and row lines to divide it.

4. To enter text into your table, click any cell. At this point, you can begin typing.

TIP

To erase a table line, click the Eraser button on the Tables And Borders toolbar, and then click the lines you want to erase.

Enter Text in a Table

1. Place the insertion point in the table cell where you want to enter text.

2. After you type text in a cell, press the Enter key to start a new paragraph within that cell, press the Tab key to move to the next cell to the right, or use the arrow keys or click in a cell to move to a new location.

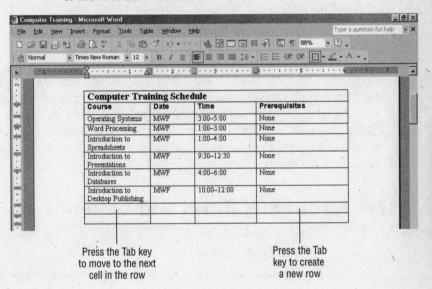

Press the Tab key to move to the next cell in the row

Press the Tab key to create a new row

TIP

You can calculate the sum of a table column. Click the Tables And Borders button on the Standard toolbar, click in the blank cell at the bottom of the column you want to total, and then click the AutoSum button on the Tables And Borders toolbar.

NOTE

Row height expands as you type. As you type in a cell, text wraps to the next line, and the height of a row expands as you enter text that extends beyond the column width.

MODIFYING A TABLE

As you begin to work on a table, you might need to modify its structure by adding more rows, columns, or cells to accommodate new text, graphics, or other tables. The table realigns as needed to accommodate the new structure. When you insert rows, columns, or cells, the existing rows shift down, the existing columns shift right, and you choose in what direction the existing cells shift. Similarly, when you delete unneeded rows, columns, or cells from a table, the table realigns itself. Moreover, you can modify the width of any column and the height of any row to better present your data.

Often, there is more to modifying a table than adding or deleting rows or columns. You may need to make cells just the right size to accommodate the text you are entering in the table. For example, a title in the first row of a table might be longer than the first cell in that row. To spread the title across the top of the table, you can *merge* (combine) the cells to form one long cell. Sometimes, to indicate a division in a topic, you need to *split* (or divide) a cell into two.

Insert Additional Rows and Columns

1. Select the row or column next to where you want the new row or column to appear.

2. Drag to select the number of rows or columns you want to insert.

3. Choose Table ➤ Insert ➤ Rows Above, Rows Below, Columns To The Left, or Columns To The Right.

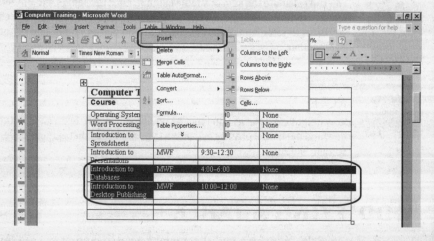

TIP

To insert additional cells, select the cells where you want the new cells to appear, choose Table ➢ Insert ➢ Cells. In the Insert Cells dialog box, select the direction in which you want the existing cells to shift, and then click the OK button.

Delete Rows, Columns, or Cells

1. Select the rows, columns, or cells you want to delete.

2. Choose Table ➢ Delete ➢ Rows, Columns, or Cells.

3. If necessary, select the direction in which you want the remaining cells to shift to fill the space, and then click the OK button.

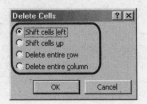

NOTE

You can quickly select elements in a table using the mouse. To select a table, place the insertion point anywhere in the table, and then click the Select Table button in the upper-right corner of the table. To select a row or column, click in the left margin next to the row or above the column you want to select. To select one or more cells, drag the cells.

Adjust Row Heights and Column Widths

1. Select the rows or columns to change.

2. Choose Table ➢ Table Properties. The Table Properties dialog box opens.

3. Click the Row tab or the Column tab.

Part ii

4. In the Specify Height box, type a row height measurement; or in the Preferred Width box, type a column width measurement.

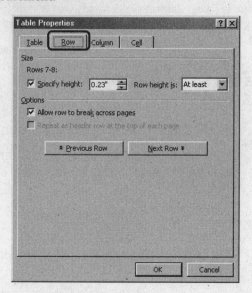

5. Click the OK button.

TIP

To quickly adjust a row height or column width, position the pointer over the boundary of the row or column you want to adjust until it changes to the resize pointer, and then drag to resize the row or column.

NOTE

To align a table in a document, click in the table; choose Table ➢ Table Properties; click the Table tab; click the Left, Center, or Right box; click the Around box to wrap text to table sides if needed; and then click the OK button.

Merge and Split Table Cells

▶ To merge two or more cells into a single cell, select the cells you want to merge, and then choose Table ➤ Merge Cells.

▶ To split a cell into multiple cells, click in the cell you want to split, and then choose Table ➤ Split Cells. The Split Cells dialog box opens. Enter the number of rows or columns (or both) you want to split the selected cell into, click the Merge Cells Before Split check box to clear it, and then click the OK button.

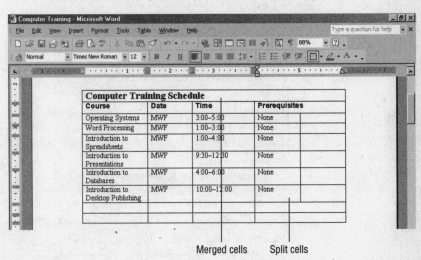

Merged cells   Split cells

FORMATTING A TABLE

Tables distinguish text from paragraphs. In turn, formatting, alignment, and text direction distinguish text in table cells. Start by applying one of Word's predesigned table formats. Then customize your table by realigning the cells' contents both horizontally and vertically, changing the direction of text within selected cells (such as the column headings), and resizing the entire table. You can also add borders and shading to make printed tables easier to read and more attractive.

Format a Table Quickly

The AutoFormat option not only provides you with a number of different default table formats to apply, it also gives you the option to add borders, shading, fonts, and colors.

1. Select the table you want to format.

2. Choose Table ➤ Table AutoFormat. The Table AutoFormat dialog box opens.

3. Choose a format.

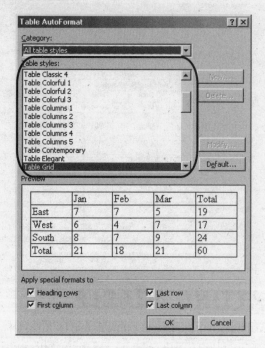

4. Click the OK button.

NOTE

You can also choose Format ➤ Borders And Shading, and then click the Borders tab or the Shading tab to format individual parts of a table.

TIP

To resize the entire table proportionally, click to place the insertion point in the table, and then drag the resize handle in the lower-right corner until the table is the appropriate size.

Align Text within Cells

1. Click the Tables And Borders button on the Standard toolbar. The Tables And Borders toolbar opens.

2. Select the cells, rows, or columns you want to align.

3. Click the Cell Alignment button drop-down arrow on the Tables And Borders toolbar.

4. Click one of the alignment buttons.

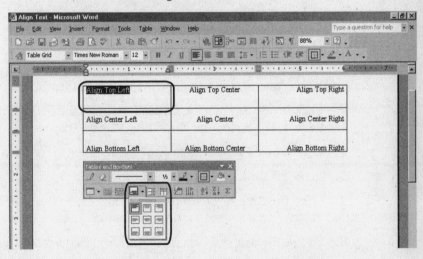

Change Text Direction within Cells

1. Click the Tables And Borders button on the Standard toolbar. The Tables And Borders toolbar opens.

2. Select the cells you want to change.

3. Click the Change Text Direction button on the Tables And Borders toolbar until the text faces the appropriate direction.

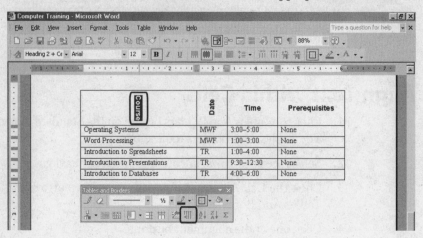

Create a New Table Style

If none of the preconfigured table styles included with Word meet your needs, you can create your own table style that you can reuse.

1. Click the Styles And Formatting button on the Formatting toolbar. The Styles And Formatting task pane opens.

2. Click the New Style button. The New Style dialog box opens.

3. In the Name box, enter a name for the style.

4. Click the Style Type drop-down arrow, and then choose Table.

5. Choose the style and formatting options in the New Style dialog box, and then click the Format button to view additional options for borders, shading, number of cells and rows, and so forth.

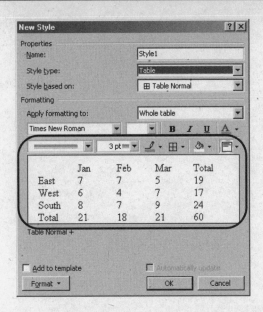

6. If you want, click the Add To Template check box to select it.

7. Click the OK button.

TIP

As with text and graphics, you can copy a table from one document to another, and then use the tips provided earlier in the chapter to modify the copied table as needed.

WHAT'S NEXT

In Chapter 5, you will finally begin to delve more deeply into the use of templates and styles to help automate the formatting of your documents, which is particularly useful when you need to duplicate a format in subsequent files.

Chapter 5

USING TEMPLATES AND STYLES

When working with Word 2002, you have probably found that there are document types you create again and again, needing similar formatting and style elements. Rather than re-create all the work each time you create a new document, you can use predesigned templates or styles (formatting characteristics that change the appearance of standard text).

In this chapter, you will learn how to work with both templates and styles, as well as how to create and use your own templates for specialized documents. You will also discover how you can take an existing template (a friend's or co-worker's) and adapt it for your own use, saving time over creating one from scratch.

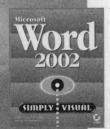

Adapted from *Microsoft Word 2002 Simply Visual* by Perspection, Inc.

ISBN 0-7821-4005-X   320 pp $24.99

CREATING A DOCUMENT FROM A TEMPLATE OR WIZARD

A template is a preconfigured document with placeholder text in each of its sections. Click any block of placeholder text to select it, and then type the correct information into the document to replace it. Templates are most commonly used with simple, one- or two-page documents like letters and faxes.

A wizard is a series of dialog boxes with steps that you must follow in sequence to prepare a more complex document, such as a report or manual, or to automate the process for simple documents like letters and faxes.

The process of beginning creation of a document with either method—using templates or wizards—is virtually identical, and significant differences occur only when you are replacing information in the particular type of document you are working with. In document creation, wizards are often used in conjunction with templates to ensure that the user replaces all of the placeholder text with the actual elements required for the finished document.

NOTE

For examples of the use of wizards to create a document, see "Creating a Letter," "Creating a Memo," or "Creating a Fax Cover Sheet" in Chapter 3, "Working with Word 2002 Documents."

Create a Document from a Template or Wizard

1. Choose File ➤ New. The New Document task pane opens.

NOTE

The New From Template list in the New Document task pane will change over time, updating itself to reflect the types of documents you most frequently create.

2. Under the New From Template heading, click General Templates. The Templates dialog box opens.

3. Select the tab that represents the type of document you'd like to create, and then click the icon that represents the type of template you want to use. (For purposes of this exercise, click the Publications tab, and then click the Manual icon.) A template for a manual opens.

4. In the Create New area, click the Document option button.

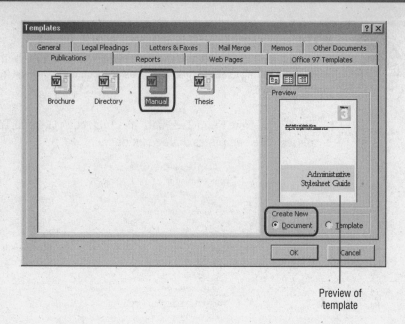

Preview of
template

5. Click the OK button.

6. Follow that template, inserting your own text and images where needed, and deleting any unnecessary original material.

CREATING YOUR OWN TEMPLATE

Although Word comes preconfigured with a wide variety of templates, you may want to create a template of your own, either to accommodate a different type of document than the ones that Word addresses or to present one of those document types in an entirely new style of your own creation.

There are several ways to create your own template. You can base a new template on an existing template, or you can base the template on an existing document that you have previously created.

Create a Template Based on an Existing Template

1. Choose File ➢ New. The New Document task pane opens.

2. Under the New From Template heading, click General Templates. The Templates dialog box opens.

3. Select a template, and then under Create New, click the Template option button.

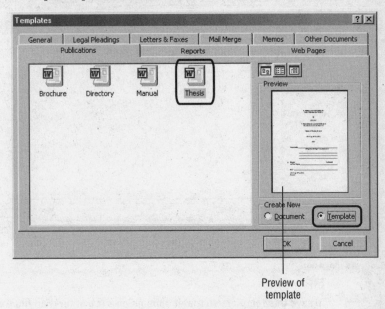

Preview of template

4. Click the OK button. The selected template opens.

[TYPE THESIS TITLE HERE]

by

[Your Name]

A thesis submitted in partial fulfillment of
the requirements for the degree of

[Name of degree]

[Name of university]

5. Choose File ➢ Save As. The Save As dialog box opens.

6. Click the Save As Type drop-down arrow, and then choose Document Template. The Templates folder appears as the

default destination for the template. When you save a template in the Templates folder, the template becomes available in the Templates dialog box on the General tab.

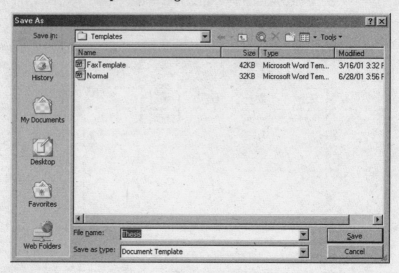

TIP
To save this template so that it appears on a tab other than the General tab, select the corresponding subfolder within the Templates folder.

7. In the File Name box, type a name for the new template, and click the Save button. A copy of the original template is saved with a new name.

8. Add the text and graphics you want in all future documents that use this template, and delete the unwanted elements. Make any additional changes in the margin settings, page size, styles, etc. using commands on the Format menu, such as Paragraph, Bullets And Numbering, and Borders And Shading.

9. Click the Save button on the Standard toolbar, and then choose File ➢ Close to close the template.

TIP

If your PC has a previous version of Windows on it, you may have a preexisting Templates folder as well as a new one created by a fresh Office installation. If this is the case, you may want to locate the old Templates folder, and using Windows Explorer, drag and drop any of its templates into your current Templates folder.

Create a Template from a Document

Suppose that you have to provide a regular memo to your company that does not fit the format of the existing Word Memo templates. There is no need to reinvent the wheel each time you have to submit the report. Any document can serve as a template after it has been created.

1. Choose File ➢ Open. The Open dialog box opens.

2. Locate and select the document you want to use as a template, and then click the Open button.

3. Adapt the existing document, making changes in the margin settings, page size, styles, and other document options. These changes can be accessed using commands on the Format menu, which gives you access to settings for all aspects of the document's visual presentation, such as Paragraph or Tab settings.

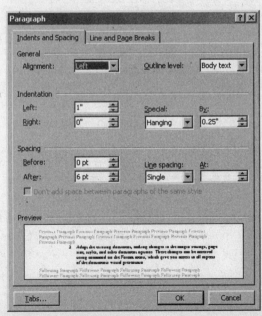

4. Choose File ➢ Save As. The Save As dialog box opens.

5. Click the Save As Type drop-down arrow, and then choose Document Template. The Templates folder appears as the default destination for the template. When you save a template in the Templates folder, the template becomes available in the Templates dialog box on the General tab.

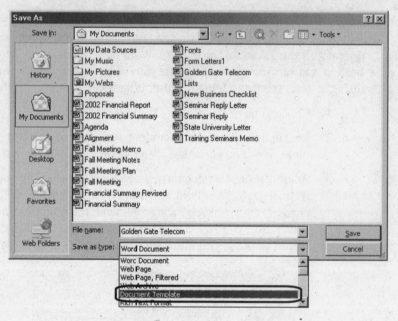

6. In the File Name box, type a name for the new template, and then click the Save button. The template is saved.

7. Choose File ➢ Close to close the template file.

CUSTOMIZING A TEMPLATE

If you find that you are consistently using a template in the same fashion, such as modifying the Contemporary Letter template to function as letterhead for your company, you do not have to use it as the basis for a new template with a different name—you can modify it once and overwrite the existing template with the changes you routinely make. The next time you open the template, the routinely used information (such as the company name, address, and so forth in the case of a letter) will already be present instead of the placeholder text.

Customize an Existing Template

1. Choose File ➤ New. The New Document task pane opens.

2. Under the New From Template heading, click General Templates. The Templates dialog box opens.

3. Select a template. Under Create New, click the Template option button, and then click the OK button. The template opens. For purposes of this example, use the Contemporary Letter template.

[Click here and type return address]

Company Name Here

May 29, 2001

[Click here and type recipient's address]

Dear Sir or Madam:

Type your letter here. For more details on modifying this letter template, double-click ✉. To return to this letter, use the Window menu.

Sincerely,

4. Customize the placeholder text that you want to modify by typing those entries that will be consistent from one document to the next.

Ed Dille
Fog Studios, Inc.
137 Fox Hollow Dr.
Langhorne, PA 19053
EdDille@aol.com

Fog Studios, Inc.

May 29, 2001

[Click here and type recipient's address]

Dear Sir or Madam:

Type your letter here. For more details on modifying this letter template, double-click ⊠. To return to this letter, use the Window menu.

Sincerely,

5. Choose File ➣ Save As. The Save As dialog box opens.

6. Click the Save As Type drop-down arrow, and then choose Document Template. The Templates folder appears as the default destination for the template.

7. Browse to the folder containing the template you have customized, and then double-click the existing template file. A Warning dialog box opens asking if you want to overwrite the existing template with the customized template.

8. Click the OK button. The customized template is saved.

COPYING BETWEEN TEMPLATES

When you create one or more custom toolbars, macros, or styles that you would like to use in multiple documents, it is much easier to copy them between the template they are currently associated with and the new one you are creating or modifying, than it is to re-create them from scratch for the new template. If you want to replace the styles from one template with another, you can attach a template to complete the replacement. You can also load and unload global templates with styles you want to use in all of your documents. Templates can be loaded either for the current session only or whenever you start Word.

Copy Functionality between Templates

1. Choose Tools ➢ Templates And Add-Ins. The Templates And Add-Ins dialog box opens.

2. Click the Organizer button. The Templates And Add-Ins dialog box closes, and the Organizer dialog box opens.

3. Click the Toolbars tab.

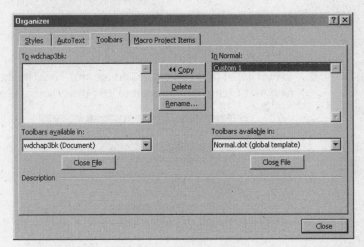

4. To copy items either to or from a different template (or file), click the Close File button. The active document and its attached template or the Normal template can then be closed.

5. Click the Open File button, and then open the template (or file) you want.

6. Click the items you want to copy in either list, and then click the Copy button.

7. Perform the same functions for the Styles and Macros tabs until all of the elements that you want to copy have been moved to the new template.

NOTE

If the Copy button is unavailable in the Organizer dialog box, check to see if the template has been password-protected against tracked changes, comments, or forms. If so, these settings must be changed before the elements can be copied to the template.

8. Click the Close button to close the Organizer dialog box.

Attach a Template

1. Choose Tools ➤ Templates And Add-Ins. The Templates And Add-Ins dialog box opens.

2. Click the Attach button, locate and select the template you want to attach, and then click the OK button. The template location and name appear in the Document Template box.

3. To add a template, click the Add button, locate and select the folder that contains the template you want to add, and then click the OK button.

4. In the Global Templates And Add-Ins area, click the check box next to the template you want to load to select it, if necessary.

5. Click the OK button.

PREVIEWING AND APPLYING STYLES

When you want to apply multiple formatting attributes to text, you can save time by creating a style. A *style* is formatting settings saved with a name within a document or template that you can apply to text at any time. If you modify a style, you make the change once, but all text tagged with that style changes to reflect the new format. If you want to change the style set that governs a document's formatting on the fly, choose Format ➤ Theme, and then open the Style Gallery. Select styles from the list on the left and preview them in the display window before making a selection.

Preview and Apply a Style Quickly

1. Drag to select any word, list, table, or other type of text block you want to see presented in another style.

2. Click the Styles And Formatting button on the Formatting toolbar. The Styles And Formatting task pane opens, displaying the styles in the document.

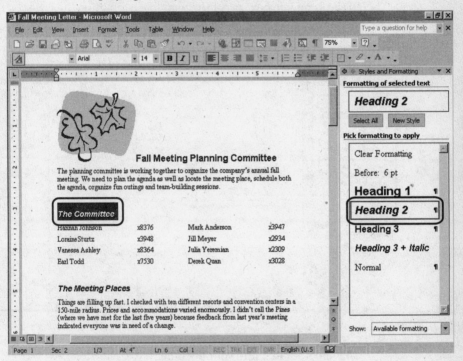

3. In the Styles And Formatting task pane, locate the style you want and click it. When you select another style in the template, or make changes to the parameters for that style, they automatically are applied to the selected text.

TIP
To show all styles in the Styles And Formatting task pane, click the Show dropdown arrow, and then choose All Styles.

Preview and Apply Styles Using the Style Gallery

1. Choose Format ➤ Theme. The Theme dialog box opens.

2. Click the Style Gallery button. The Style Gallery dialog box opens.

3. In the Template box, select the template containing the style elements you want to preview or use.

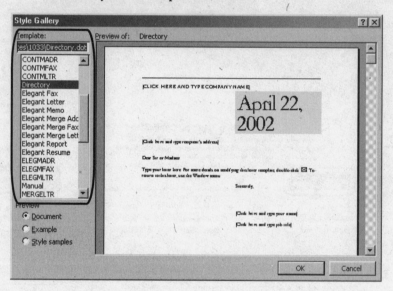

4. Click the OK button. The style elements are then automatically incorporated into your document.

CREATING STYLES

Two types of styles can be created: character and paragraph. *Character styles* apply format settings only to text that has been selected by the user, not all of the text within a paragraph. *Paragraph styles* affect all of the characters within a paragraph whenever they are applied, so less selectivity about what text will be changed is possible when using these types of styles.

NOTE
The style list on the Formatting toolbar marks character styles with an under-lined lowercase letter *a*, and paragraph styles with the ¶ symbol.

Create or Modify a Style

1. Choose Format ➤ Styles And Formatting. The Styles And Formatting task pane opens.

2. To create a style, click the New Style button in the Styles And Formatting task pane. The New Style dialog box opens.

   ▶ To modify a style, click a style's drop-down arrow in the Styles And Formatting task pane, and then click Modify. The Modify Style dialog box opens.

3. In the Name box, enter a name for the style, if necessary.

4. Click the Style Type drop-down arrow, and then choose Paragraph, Character, Table, or List.

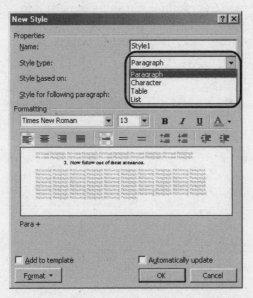

5. Click the Style Based On drop-down arrow, and then choose a style.

6. Select the formatting options that will be part of your new style, or click the Format button to see more options including the option to assign a shortcut key to the style you are creating.

7. If you want all instances of the style to be updated in the existing document, click the Automatically Update check box to select it.

8. To make the style part of the existing template set, click the Add To Template check box to select it.

9. Click the OK button.

WHAT'S NEXT

Longer documents, such as annual reports, theses, or even chapters of a book, can be more difficult to manage as well as to read without good organization (for example, breaking the text into sections or formatting it into columns) and tools (for example, page numbers and headers/footers to identify the work). Let's move to Chapter 6.

Chapter 6

DESIGNING LONGER DOCUMENTS

Word 2002 gives you a number of tools and options for working with longer documents. For example, you can divide a very long document into sections, each of which may have its own formatting. Or you can format into columns the long text in a company or organization newsletter.

By using headers and footers, you can insert special information as needed, view the working document title, and check the page numbers or creation date.

Adapted from *Mastering Microsoft Office XP Premium Edition* by Gini Courter and Annette Marquis with Karla Browning

ISBN 0-7821-4000-9   1392 pp $49.99

UNDERSTANDING SECTIONS

Word uses sections to organize documents for formatting purposes. A *section* is a contiguous portion of a document that has a specified number of columns and uses a common set of margins, page orientation, headers and footers, and sequence of page numbers. Word automatically inserts section breaks when you do the following:

- ▶ Format text as columns

- ▶ Change Page Setup options and indicate that you want the changes to apply from this point forward

You can manually insert a section break to apply a different page size or header and footer formatting within a document. For example, if you want a different header in each chapter in a document, put section breaks between the chapters before you create the headers.

To manually insert a section break:

1. Position the insertion point where you want the break to begin and choose Insert ➤ Break. The Break dialog box appears, as shown in Figure 6.1.

2. In the Section Break Types area, select one of the following options to specify where you want the new section to begin:

   Next Page   Inserts a section break and starts the new section at the beginning of the next page. You might use this type of break when you want to change page orientation.

   Continuous   Inserts a section break without inserting a page break. Any subsequent text you type directly follows the existing text. This break works well when you want to change the number of columns.

   Even Page   Inserts a section break and starts the new section at the beginning of the next even-numbered page in the document. If the section break is inserted on an even-numbered page, Word leaves the intervening page (an odd-numbered page) blank.

   Odd Page   Inserts a section break and starts the new section at the beginning of the next odd-numbered page in the document. If the section break is inserted on an odd-numbered page, Word leaves the intervening page (an even-numbered page) blank.

3. Click OK to insert the section break.

FIGURE 6.1: The options in the Break dialog box allow you to specify what type of break to insert in a document.

Section break marks can be seen in both Normal and Outline views by default. You can also see section break marks in both Web Page and Print Layout views when you display nonprinting characters in your document. To do so, use either of the following procedures:

▶ Click the Show/Hide ¶ button on the Standard toolbar.

▶ Choose Tools ➢ Options ➢ View, check the Hidden Text check box in the Formatting Marks area, and then click OK.

Section break marks appear as double dotted lines with the words *Section Break* and the type of break (*Continuous*, for example) in them, as shown below.

Section Break (Continuous)

To delete a section break, place the insertion point anywhere on the break, and press Delete.

CREATING AND MODIFYING PAGE NUMBERS

Whether or not you have inserted section breaks, you may want a simple way to automatically number the pages. Nothing could be more effortless than Word's Page Numbering feature. Follow these steps to use this feature:

1. Choose Insert ➤ Page Numbers to open the Page Numbers dialog box, shown in Figure 6.2.

2. In the Position drop-down list, select Bottom Of Page (Footer) or Top Of Page (Header) as the location for your page numbers.

3. In the Alignment drop-down list, select Left, Center, Right, Inside, or Outside to specify the location of the page number within the header or footer.

4. To prevent the page number from appearing on the first page of your document, click the Show Number On First Page check box to clear the check from it.

5. When the page numbers appear with both the position and alignment you want in the Preview area, click OK to have Word number the pages in your document.

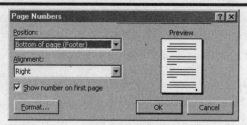

FIGURE 6.2: Use the options in the Page Numbers dialog box to place sequential page numbers in your document.

Page numbers appear on your screen in both Print Layout view and Print Preview, and they are automatically updated as you edit your document.

NOTE

You can disable Word's automatic repagination feature in both Normal and Outline views by removing the check mark in the Background Repagination check box on the General tab in the Options dialog box. With automatic repagination disabled, Word won't display the page number for the current page in the status bar. In Web Layout view, Print Layout view, and Print Preview, you cannot disable background repagination.

BOUND FOR SUCCESS: PRINTING ON BOTH SIDES OF THE PAGE

To create professional-looking business reports, contracts, proposals, or any document you want to bind along its left edge, you can combine the Inside and Outside page number alignment options with mirror margins (on the Margins tab in the Page Setup dialog box) to print a document on both sides of the paper. *Mirror margins* automatically make the margins on facing pages "mirror" each other so that the inside margins (the right margin on the left page and the left margin on the right page) are equal to each other, and so are the outside margins (the left margin on the left page and the right margin on the right page). Usually, you will want the inside margins to be larger than the outside margins to allow space for binding the document. You can specify the amount of space to add to the inside margin by adjusting the value in the Gutter text box on the Margins tab.

If you select Inside as the page number alignment, the page numbers appear on the right side of the left page and on the left side of the right page. When you select Outside as the alignment, the page numbers appear on the left side of the left page and on the right side of the right page. Each selection you make appears in the Preview area of the Page Numbers dialog box.

Changing the Page Number's Format

You can also change the format that is applied to the page numbers by applying a different numbering style and by having Word automatically insert the chapter number in front of the page number. For example, in a long document such as a proposal, it's common to number the pages of the table of contents using lowercase Roman numerals and the pages containing the text of the proposal using Arabic numerals.

To change the format of the page numbers in your document:

1. Choose Insert ➤ Page Numbers to display the Page Numbers dialog box.

2. Click the Format button to display the Page Number Format dialog box, shown in Figure 6.3.

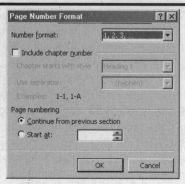

FIGURE 6.3: Display the Page Number Format dialog box to change the formatting applied to page numbers in your document.

3. Select the format for the page numbers in the Number Format drop-down list.

4. To have Word automatically place the chapter number in front of the page number, click the Include Chapter Number check box and then specify how you want the chapter number to appear using the following options:

   ▶ In the Chapter Starts With Style drop-down list, select the Heading style that you are using for each chapter in your document.

   ▶ In the Use Separator drop-down list, select the character you want to appear between the chapter number and the page number.

5. To specify the number at which you want to start numbering for the document, choose either of the following options in the Page Numbering area:

   Continue From Previous Section   Starts the page numbering in the current document section with the next number after the last number in the previous section. If this is the first section in the document, the number starts with 1.

Start At   Allows you to specify the number you want for the first page of your document. Choose this option if you want to start the page numbering at a number other than 1.

6. Click OK in the Page Number Format dialog box and again in the Page Numbers dialog box to return to the document.

If your document has more than one section, such as the proposal mentioned above, you can set up different page numbering for each section. To do this, position the insertion point on the first page of the document (in this case, the table of contents, which is the beginning of the first section of the proposal), choose Insert ➢ Page Numbers to add page numbering, and then click Format to set up the formatting for this section's numbering. Then move the insertion point to the first page of the *second* section (the proposal's chapters) and repeat the process. You will probably want to select the Start At option in the Page Numbering area of the Page Number Format dialog box to specify that the text of the proposal starts on page 1.

Repeat the process for any additional sections. If you want the page numbering to continue from the previous section, choose that option in the Page Number Format dialog box. If you want to remove page numbers, you need to edit the header or footer where the page number appears. See the following section to learn how to edit the headers and footers in your documents.

CREATING HEADERS AND FOOTERS

Page numbers are certainly useful, but you may also want to include other information on each page. For example, the current date, your name, and the name of your company are additional pieces of information that often appear on each page of a document. For this type of information, use headers and/or footers. *Headers* are placed in the top margin and *footers* in the bottom margin on each page in the current section of the document.

To place a header or footer in your document, choose View ➢ Header And Footer. The existing document text is immediately dimmed, and the Header section at the top of your document opens. A floating Header And Footer toolbar, like the one shown in Figure 6.4, also appears.

Enter the text you want to appear in the Header section. Use the Header And Footer toolbar buttons, shown in Figure 6.5, to help you edit the headers and footers.

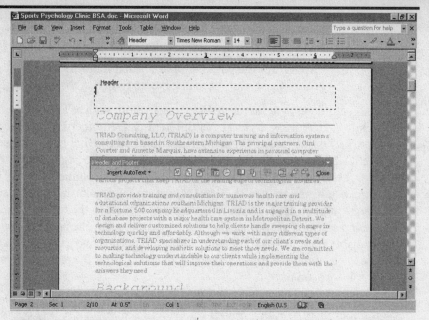

FIGURE 6.4: When you view your document's header or footer, the Header And Footer toolbar appears.

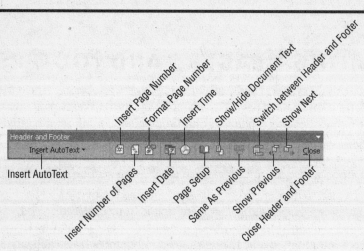

FIGURE 6.5: Use the buttons on the Header And Footer toolbar to edit the document's header and footer.

Whether you are creating headers, footers, or both, the process is the same:

1. Choose View ➤ Header And Footer to display the Header section in the active section of the document.

2. Enter text, insert graphics, and use the Header And Footer toolbar to insert AutoText, page numbers, and date and time codes.

3. To create a footer, click the Switch Between Header And Footer button on the Header And Footer toolbar to move the insertion point to the footer, and then add any necessary text or field codes.

4. To create different headers and footers in different sections, click Show Previous or Show Next to activate the footer in the previous or next section of the document, and then make any necessary changes to that footer. Click the Switch Between Header And Footer button on the Header And Footer toolbar to activate that section's header, and then edit it as necessary.

5. When you are finished editing your document's header(s) and footer(s), click Close to close the Header And Footer toolbar and return to your document.

Unless you change the header and footer in a section of a document with multiple sections, all of the headers and footers will be the same in every section.

Creating Alternate Headers and Footers

Word contains two options that allow you to further edit the position of your document's header and footer. You can choose not to display the header or footer on the first page, and you can display different headers and footers on odd and even pages. These features are particularly useful for long documents, which may contain a cover page and may be bound.

For example, you would not want the document's header and footer to appear on the title page of the sample proposal mentioned above. In addition, you might want one header and footer to appear on the left pages of the proposal and a different header and footer to appear on the right pages. To change the positions of your document's header and footer:

1. Click the Page Setup button on the Header And Footer toolbar to display the Layout tab of the Page Setup dialog box, shown in Figure 6.6.

2. Choose from the following options:

   ▶ Select the Different Odd And Even check box to create different headers and footers for even- and odd-numbered pages.

   ▶ Select the Different First Page check box to create a different header and footer for the first page.

3. Click OK in the Page Setup dialog box.

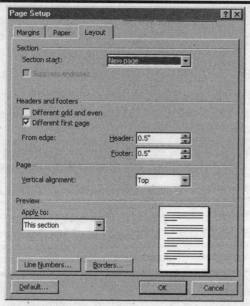

FIGURE 6.6: Display the Layout tab in the Page Setup dialog box if you want to create alternate headers and footers.

If you check the Different First Page box on the Layout tab in the Page Setup dialog box, Word provides a new section titled First Page Header. Just leave the header and footer blank on the first page to suppress its display.

If you want to create different headers or footers for odd and even pages, check the appropriate box in the Page Setup dialog box. Word provides two new sections titled Odd Page Header on the odd-numbered pages and Even Page Header on the even-numbered pages. Enter the first header or footer, and then click the Show Next button on the Header And Footer toolbar to enter the opposite page header or footer.

TIP

If part of your header or footer is cut off on the printed document, it may be situated outside of your printer's print area. To fix it, adjust the From Edge setting on the Layout tab of the Page Setup dialog box. The higher the number, the farther the header/footer is positioned from the edge of the page.

TAKING CARE OF LOOSE ENDS

Before you print the final version of a document, you should clean up dangling words, bad line and page breaks, and extra spaces that detract from the appearance of your document. There are three ways to clean up these loose ends:

- ▶ Are there spaces at the ends of lines because long words wrap to the beginning of the next line? If so, use hyphenation.

- ▶ Does the document have text strings that should be kept together but are broken over two lines? If so, use nonbreaking spaces.

- ▶ Are there paragraphs or lines of paragraphs that should be kept together but currently break across two pages? If so, use Line And Page Breaks options to specify how you want the text to flow within the document.

NOTE

Make sure you have done all of your editing and formatting before attempting any of this final cleanup. When you add, delete, or reformat text, you have to clean up the document all over again.

Using Hyphenation

Word 2002 includes options for either automatically or manually hyphenating text in your documents. With hyphenation, you can prohibit Word from hyphenating words in caps. You can also indicate the size of the *hyphenation zone*, the distance from the right margin that Word scrutinizes for words to hyphenate. Increase the area if you want more words hyphenated; decrease it if you don't mind ragged edges.

TIP

Your document may contain blocks of text that you don't want Word to hyphenate. To prevent automatic hyphenation, select the text block, choose Format ➢ Paragraph ➢ Line And Page Breaks, and turn on the Don't Hyphenate option.

When you have Word automatically hyphenate your document, hyphens are added as you type in the document. If you would like more control over how Word hyphenates your documents, you can choose to manually hyphenate your document. When you do, Word reviews your document, locates candidates for hyphenation, and then recommends a location for the hyphen.

To hyphenate your document:

1. Choose Tools ➢ Language ➢ Hyphenation to display the Hyphenation dialog box, shown in Figure 6.7.

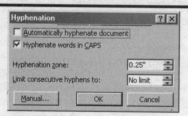

FIGURE 6.7: Display the Hyphenation dialog box when you want to place hyphens in the current document.

2. To allow hyphens to be placed in words that consist of all capital letters, leave the Hyphenate Words In CAPS box checked. Clear the check box to prevent Word from inserting a hyphen in words that appear in all capital letters.

3. If necessary, adjust the value in the Hyphenation Zone text box to specify the distance from the right margin in which Word will check for words to be hyphenated.

4. If necessary, adjust the value in the Limit Consecutive Hyphens To text box to specify the number of consecutive lines that can end in a hyphen.

5. To insert hyphens in your document, choose either of the following options:

   ▶ To have Word automatically insert hyphens in your document as you type, check the Automatically Hyphenate Document check box, and then click OK.

   ▶ Click the Manual button to display the Manual Hyphenation dialog box (shown in Figure 6.8), click in a different location for the hyphen if necessary, and then choose Yes to insert the hyphen in the document. To prevent hyphenating the selected word, choose No. Word automatically displays the next word in the document for which hyphenation is recommended.

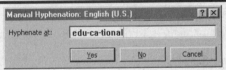

FIGURE 6.8: The Manual Hyphenation dialog box allows you to specify where you want the hyphen to appear in a recommended word.

NOTE
Word's Manual Hyphenation feature is not installed in the typical Office installation. When you click the Manual button on the Hyphenation dialog box, you may be prompted to insert the Office CD and install the feature.

When Word makes a hyphenation recommendation, it is more concerned about spacing than about proper hyphenation. It frequently leaves two characters at the end of a line, or it recommends some other awkward place for the hyphenation. Use your own judgment, and if you're not sure, refer to a dictionary or hyphenation guide.

NOTE
If you are creating a document, such as a newsletter, in which you want the right edge to be even rather than ragged, click the Justify button on the Formatting toolbar to apply that format to each paragraph.

TIP

To prevent a word or phrase that already contains a hyphen (like a phone number) from breaking at the end of a line, insert a nonbreaking hyphen by holding down Ctrl+Shift when you type the hyphen. To enter an optional hyphen, a hyphen that breaks a word or a phrase at the designated place if it occurs at the end of a line, hold down Ctrl when you type the hyphen.

Inserting Nonbreaking Spaces

Occasionally, you might have a text string, such as an address, that should not be separated at the end of a line. You can protect this string by inserting *nonbreaking spaces* instead of regular spaces within the text string. These are similar to nonbreaking hyphens; text connected with nonbreaking spaces moves to the next line rather than breaking between lines. To insert a nonbreaking space, hold down Ctrl+Shift when you press the spacebar.

Handling Page Breaks

Word 2002 offers a number of other ways to keep text together so that your document looks professionally printed. One of these options, called Widow/Orphan control, is on by default. This feature prevents the first line of a paragraph from being left alone at the bottom of the page (an orphan) or the last line of a paragraph from appearing by itself at the top of a new page (a widow).

Using the Line And Page Breaks options, you can keep selected lines of text or entire paragraphs together. In addition, you can have Word insert a page break before a paragraph when you want the entire paragraph to be placed at the top of a page.

To specify how to break document text:

1. Select the text, then choose Format ➤ Paragraph ➤ Line And Page Breaks to display the Line And Page Breaks tab in the Paragraph dialog box, shown in Figure 6.9.

2. Choose any of the following options in the Pagination area:

    ▶ Clear the Widow/Orphan Control check box to prevent Word from automatically keeping text together at the bottom and top of pages.

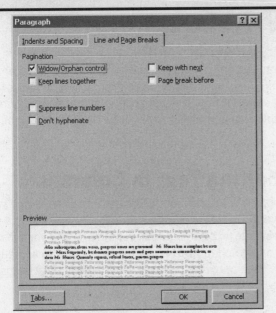

FIGURE 6.9: Choose the appropriate line or page break option for selected text on the Line And Page Breaks tab in the Paragraph dialog box.

▶ Check the Keep Lines Together box to prevent lines of the selected paragraph from being separated by a page break. The entire paragraph moves to the top of the next page.

▶ Check the Keep With Next box to keep the selected paragraph from being separated from the following paragraph by a page break (used, for example, to keep a heading with the first paragraph of text that follows).

▶ Check the Page Break Before box to insert a manual page break before the paragraph that contains the insertion point.

3. Click OK in the Paragraph dialog box.

TIP

You can also insert a manual page break before a specific paragraph by positioning the insertion point where you want to place the page break and then pressing Ctrl+Enter.

WORKING WITH COLUMNS

Some information is most effectively presented in *newspaper columns*, in which text flows from the bottom of one column to the top of the next. All Word documents consist of at least one column. If you create newsletters, flyers, reports, announcements, or other publications that contain multiple text columns, you'll probably use Word's newspaper columns feature quite a bit.

Entering and Editing Text in Columns

Working with newspaper columns requires a little advanced design work. You'll find that it is often easier to enter document text into a single column, and then convert the text into multiple columns. When you are ready to work with columns, switch to Print Layout view so you can actually see the columns as they will appear on the page. Then follow these steps:

1. Select the text you want to place in columns.

2. Perform either of the following actions to create columns of equal width:

    ▶ Click the Columns button on the Standard toolbar to open the selection palette, and then drag to select the number of columns you want.

    ▶ Choose Format ➢ Columns to display the Columns dialog box (shown in Figure 6.10), adjust the value in the Number Of Columns text box, and then click OK.

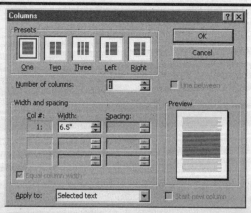

FIGURE 6.10: You can create columns using the options in the Columns dialog box.

The selected text is rearranged into columns, and column markers are visible on the horizontal ruler.

NOTE

Because of the space between the columns, a block of text poured into two or more columns takes up more room than it does in a single-column page. As a result, you may have to edit text to get it to fit on a prescribed number of pages.

Balancing Column Length

You can create *balanced* columns—that is, columns of equal length—for some documents. For example, a newsletter is a type of document that often contains multiple columns of the same length.

To create balanced columns, move the insertion point to the end of the text, choose Insert ➤ Break ➤ Continuous, and then click OK to insert a continuous section break.

TIP

If you want to begin a new page after the balanced columns, position the insertion point after the continuous page break and either press Ctrl+Enter or choose Insert ➤ Break ➤ Page Break and click OK to enter a manual page break.

Revising Column Structure

While you are creating a document with multiple newspaper columns, you may decide to change the appearance of your document by changing the number of columns in it.

To change the number of columns in a document with multiple columns, position the insertion point anywhere in the columns section and then either:

▶ Click the Columns button on the Standard toolbar, and then drag to select a new number of columns.

▶ Choose Format ➤ Columns, adjust the number in the Number Of Columns text box, and then click OK.

Part ii

TIP

To revert to a single column, specify 1 in the Number Of Columns text box, or switch to Normal or Outline view and delete the section markers.

When you create columns with the Columns button, Word makes all the columns the same width. If you want columns of differing widths, drag the Move Column marker on the horizontal ruler.

To change the amount of white space between the columns (the *gutter*), point to the right or left edge of the Move Column marker on the ruler and drag the desired distance.

Using the Columns Dialog Box

As you have already seen, you can use the options in the Columns dialog box, shown earlier in Figure 6.10, to create multiple newspaper columns and to change the number of columns in your document. Several other options in the Columns dialog box allow you to further change the appearance of columns. For example, you can use the options to establish columns of a specific width or to lock column width so that they are equal.

To specify exactly how your columns should appear, choose Format ➤ Columns, choose any of the following options in the Columns dialog box, and then click OK:

▶ Specify the number and position of the columns in the Presets area. If you choose One, Two, or Three, the Equal Column Width check box is automatically selected, so when you change the width of one column, the width of each column is automatically changed. When you choose Left, the left column is narrower than the right column. When you choose Right, the left column is wider than the right column.

▶ Create up to nine columns by adjusting the value in the Number Of Columns text box.

▶ Specify the exact width and spacing between each column by adjusting the values for each column in the appropriate Width and Spacing text boxes.

▶ Click the Line Between check box to have Word insert vertical lines between each of the columns.

Keeping Text Together in Columns

All the tools that you use to keep page text together, including nonbreaking spaces, nonbreaking hyphens, and the Line And Page Breaks options, also work within columns. Word's Columns dialog box provides you with one more option for controlling where text breaks between columns:

1. Move the insertion point to the beginning of the text you want to reposition in the next column, and then choose Format ➤ Columns to open the Columns dialog box, shown previously in Figure 6.10.

2. Change the Apply To control to This Point Forward.

3. Click the Start New Column check box.

4. Click OK to insert an End Of Section mark and move the text to the next column.

CREATING PARALLEL COLUMNS WITH TABLES

Parallel columns, such as the names and numbers in a phone book, display corresponding text in columns. Although tabs can be used to present information in parallel columns, it is far easier to use Word's powerful Tables feature. With tables, every block of text can be easily formatted, edited, deleted, and moved around without affecting the remainder of the text. Tables are one of the most versatile tools in the Word toolkit.

The handiest ways to create tables in Word are as follows:

▶ Click the Insert Table button on the Standard toolbar, and then drag to highlight the number of columns and rows you want in your table. As you drag, the number of rows and columns is displayed at the bottom of the button's menu. When the number of rows and columns is correct, release the mouse button to insert the table in your document.

▶ Click the Tables And Borders button on the Standard toolbar to display the Tables And Borders toolbar. The Draw Table button is selected by default, and the mouse pointer appears as a pencil. Drag the pencil to create a rectangle about the size of the table you want. When you release the mouse button, the outside border of the table appears in your document. Drag with the pencil again to draw in column and row borders.

NOTE

Although you can use the Draw Table feature to create a table, it's generally easiest to create the table using the Insert Table button. Use the Draw Table button to insert additional columns and rows inside an existing table. See "Modifying Table Structure" later in this chapter.

If you want to specify exact measurements and formatting for the table when you create it, you can use a third method, which is in the Insert Table dialog box:

1. Choose Table ➤ Insert ➤ Table to display the Insert Table dialog box, shown in Figure 6.11.

2. Adjust the value in the Number Of Columns text box to specify the number of columns in your table.

3. Adjust the value in the Number Of Rows text box to specify the number of rows in your table.

4. Choose one of the following options in the AutoFit Behavior area:

   Fixed Column Width   Allows you to specify the exact width of each column in the table by adjusting the value in the adjacent text box. Alternatively, choose Auto to have Word adjust the width of each column equally so the table spans from the left to the right margin.

   AutoFit To Contents   Automatically adjusts the width of each column in the table to fit the longest cell contents in that column.

   AutoFit To Window   Automatically adjusts the size of the table to fit the window of a web browser or document, even if the size of the window changes.

5. To save the settings you specified in the Insert Table dialog box so that Word displays them each time the dialog box is

displayed, click the Remember Dimensions For New Tables check box.

6. Click OK to insert the table in your document.

NOTE

See "Formatting Tables" later in this chapter to learn how to use Word's Table AutoFormat option, which is also available in the Insert Table dialog box.

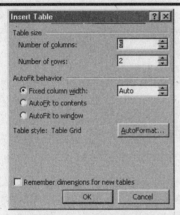

FIGURE 6.11: With the options in the Insert Table dialog box, you can simultaneously create and specify the exact size of the new table.

WARNING

When you delete a table, any data in the table is also deleted.

To delete a table, click any cell in the table and then choose Table ➤ Delete ➤ Table.

Positioning a Table

When you insert a table using the button on the Standard toolbar, or by using the Table menu, the table grid appears at the insertion point. However, you can easily move your table on the active page. To do so, position the mouse over the table until a four-headed arrow appears in a box at the upper-left corner of the table. Position the mouse pointer over the box and then drag the table. An outline of the table appears as you drag. When the outline is in the position you want, release the mouse button to drop the table in its new position on the page.

Word now supports drag-and-drop copying of tables. Hold the Ctrl key while dragging the table to make a copy. Be sure to release the mouse button *before* letting go of the Ctrl key.

Nesting Tables

One of Word's newer features now allows you to insert a table in an existing table *cell*, the rectangle formed by the intersection of a column and row. To do so, click in the cell where you want to insert a table, and then use any of the methods above to insert the table.

Working with Text in a Table

Once you have created a table, you can enter text by clicking in any cell and then typing the characters you want in that cell. You can also use any of the following keys to activate a cell so you can enter text:

- ▶ Press the Tab key or the Right arrow key on the keyboard to move to the next cell to the right.

- ▶ Hold down Shift+Tab or press the Left arrow key to move one cell to the left.

- ▶ Press the Up arrow or Down arrow key to move the insertion point to the cell above or below the current cell.

NOTE

If you created your table by drawing it, click the Draw Table button on the Tables And Borders toolbar or close the toolbar to change the pointer from a pencil back to an I-beam. Then click in the cell and begin typing.

Since pressing the Tab key takes you to the next cell in a table, you might conclude that you can't use tabs within table cells to indent text you're typing. But you can! Just press Ctrl+Tab to indent text within a table cell.

To format text in a table, you must select it just as you would any other text. Table 6.1 shows how to select portions of a table.

TABLE 6.1: Selecting in Tables

To Select...	Action
A cell	Triple-click in the cell or click the cell selection pointer by placing the mouse near the left border of the cell.
A row	Move the mouse to the left margin outside of the table, point to the row, and click.
Multiple rows	Select the first row, hold down the mouse button, and drag down the desired number of rows.
A column	Move the mouse pointer above the column until it changes to a downward arrow and click, or hold down the Alt key and click in the column.
Multiple contiguous columns	Select the first column, hold down the mouse button, and drag through the desired number of columns; or use any method to select the first column and then hold down Shift and use any method to select the last column.
Multiple noncontiguous columns	Select the first column, hold Ctrl, and select additional columns.
Entire table	Choose Table ➢ Select ➢ Table, or click the table's Move icon above the top-left corner.

Formatting Text in Tables

Each table cell can be formatted separately. You can center text in the first column, left-align it in the second column, and right-align in the third column. You can apply boldface formatting to the *header row*, the row with the column names, and italicize other rows. Whatever you can do to a paragraph, you can do to the text within a cell. Use the buttons on the Formatting toolbar or the commands on the Format menu to apply fonts, font effects, alignment, bullets and numbering, and indents and spacing to the text in a table.

 You can also change the vertical alignment of the text in the active table cell. To do so, click the Align Position drop-down button on the Tables And Borders toolbar or right-click inside the table, highlight Cell Alignment, and then click one of the text alignment options that appear.

The alignment assigned to the active cell appears on the Align Position button on the toolbar.

TIP

The Align Position button is one of several submenus that you can float as a freestanding menu. When you want to apply several different formats to a document, this saves the trouble of repeatedly opening the menu. To make the submenu float, click the Align Position drop-down arrow to open the menu. Point to the move handle (the gray bar at the top of the menu) and drag the menu into the document window.

Rotating Text in Tables

Occasionally, the best (or only) way to fit table text into the available space is to rotate the text so that it is no longer running in the traditional horizontal direction across the page. For example, you may need to rotate text if a table has many columns that require long headings. With Word's Change Text Direction feature, you can rotate text in a table so that it runs vertically, facing either right or left. To do so:

1. Select the cell or group of cells that contain the text you want to rotate.

2. Choose one of the following methods to change the text direction:

   ▶ Click the Change Text Direction button on the Tables And Borders toolbar. The first click rotates the text so that it is facing right, the second click flips it to face left, and the third click returns it to horizontal.

   ▶ Right-click inside the table, and then choose Text Direction on the shortcut menu to display the Text Direction dialog box, shown in Figure 6.12. Choose the rotation you want for the text in the Orientation area. The change appears in the Preview area. Click OK to define the direction of the text in the selected cell.

As the text rotates, so do some of the buttons on the Formatting toolbar. The alignment buttons and Numbering, Bullets, Decrease Indent, and Increase Indent buttons all rotate in the same direction as the text in the cell, as shown in Figure 6.13. The Columns button on the Standard toolbar also rotates. The Change Text Direction button on the Tables And Borders toolbar changes to display the rotation that will take place when you next click that button.

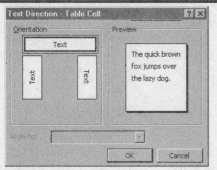

FIGURE 6.12: You can use the Text Direction dialog box to change the direction of the text in selected cells.

FIGURE 6.13: Some of the buttons on the Formatting toolbar change to reflect the rotation you've applied to the text in the active table cell.

When you rotate text, even the insertion point rotates, so editing can be a little disconcerting at first. The main thing to remember is that you have to drag the mouse vertically to select text. Once you've gotten the hang of that, you're all set.

Modifying Table Structure

One of the best reasons to use tables instead of tabs in your documents is that tables are easily modified. You can add or delete rows and columns, change column and row widths, and merge and split cells without upsetting the rest of the table text.

Further, you can set the table alignment and specify how you want document text to wrap around the table by changing the table's properties. In addition, tables can be indented a specified distance from the left margin of the page.

Adding and Deleting Rows, Columns, and Cells

You can easily adjust the number of rows in an existing table by either adding new rows or deleting existing rows. Use one of the following methods to place new rows exactly where you want them in a table:

► Select the row below where you want your new row to be and click the Insert Row button on the Standard toolbar. (It occupies the same physical space as the Insert Table button on the Standard toolbar. When you select a row, the Insert Table button becomes the Insert Row button.)

► To add a row at the end of a table, simply move to the last cell in the table and press Tab. Word adds a new row with the same formatting as the current row.

► If you want to insert several rows in the middle of the table, select the number of rows you want to insert and choose Table ➤ Insert ➤ Rows Above or Table ➤ Insert ➤ Rows Below to have Word insert rows above or below the selection. Alternatively, click the Insert Table button drop-down list on the Tables And Borders toolbar and choose Insert Rows Above or Insert Rows Below.

► To insert rows above the selected rows, right-click the table and choose Insert Rows on the shortcut menu.

NOTE

As you select different parts of the table, the Insert Table button on the Standard toolbar changes. For example, if you select a column, the Insert Table button changes to the Insert Column button. The Insert Table button on the Tables And Borders toolbar behaves similarly, but not identically—rather than changing depending on what is selected, it displays the command most recently chosen from its drop-down menu.

To delete selected rows, either choose Table ➤ Delete ➤ Rows or right-click and choose Delete Rows from the shortcut menu.

WARNING

When you delete a table row, all the data in that row is also deleted.

Inserting columns works in a way similar to inserting rows. New columns created in a table with fixed column width are the same width as the ones you select to create them, so you may have to adjust column widths if the table no longer fits into the width of the page.

Use one of the following methods to place new columns exactly where you want them in a table:

▶ Select the column to the right of where you want your new column to be and click the Insert Columns button on the Standard toolbar. (It occupies the same physical space as the Insert Table button.)

▶ To insert a column at the end of a table, click the Show/Hide ¶ button on the Standard toolbar, select the marks to the right of the last column, right-click the table, and then choose Insert Columns.

▶ Select the number of columns you want to insert and choose Table ➢ Insert ➢ Columns To The Left or Table ➢ Insert ➢ Columns To The Right to have Word insert columns to the left or right of the selection. Alternatively, click the Insert Table button drop-down list on the Tables And Borders toolbar and choose either Insert Columns To The Left or Insert Columns To The Right.

To delete selected columns, either choose Table ➢ Delete ➢ Columns or right-click the table and then choose Delete Columns.

WARNING

When you delete columns in a table, all the data in those columns is also deleted.

You can also insert new cells, rows, or columns into a table by following these steps:

1. Select the cells in the position in which you want to insert new cells.

2. Choose Table ➢ Insert ➢ Cells or click the Insert Table drop-down list button on the Tables And Borders toolbar and choose Insert Cells to display the Insert Cells dialog box, shown in Figure 6.14.

Part ii

3. Choose one of the following options to tell Word where you want the new cells to be placed in your table:

   Shift Cells Right   Inserts the new cells in the position of the selected cells, and then moves the selected cells to the right

   Shift Cells Down   Inserts the new cells in the position of the selected cells and then moves the selected cells, and every cell below the selected cells, down a number of rows equal to the number of inserted cells

   Insert Entire Row   Inserts new rows above the selected cells

   Insert Entire Column   Inserts new columns to the left of the selected cells

4. Click OK to insert the specified cells.

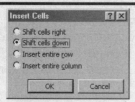

FIGURE 6.14: Display the Insert Cells dialog box when you want to insert cells in a specific location in a table.

You can also delete selected cells, rows, and columns. To do so:

1. Select the cells you want to delete, and then choose Table ➢ Delete ➢ Cells or right-click inside the table and choose Delete Cells to display the Delete Cells dialog box.

2. Choose one of the following options:

   Shift Cells Left   Deletes the cells and their contents and shifts any cells that are to the right of the selection to the left to replace the cells that were deleted

   Shift Cells Up   Deletes the cells and their contents and shifts any cells below the selection up to replace the cells that were deleted

Delete Entire Row   Deletes the row that contains the insertion point, including all the data in that row

Delete Entire Column   Deletes the column that contains the insertion point, including all the data in that column

3. Click OK in the Delete Cells dialog box.

WARNING

When you delete selected cells, rows, and columns, all the data in the selection is also deleted.

TIP

To quickly add columns or rows to a table, especially when you want them to span only a portion of the table (also referred to as *splitting cells*), click the Draw Table button and drag the pencil pointer across or down the cells you want to cross.

Changing the Column and Cell Width and the Row Height

The easiest way to make adjustments to both columns and rows is to drag their borders. To do so, just move the mouse pointer to the border between the row or column until it changes to a double-headed arrow, and then drag that border in either direction. Column borders can be dragged left (to decrease the column width) or right (to increase the column width). Row borders can be dragged up (to decrease the row height) or down (to increase the row height).

NOTE

You can't adjust row borders by dragging when you're in Normal or Outline view.

Hold down the Alt key while you drag either border to display the measurement of the row or column in the ruler. Column sizes are displayed in the horizontal ruler above the columns; row sizes appear in the vertical ruler when you are in Print Layout view.

NOTE

To increase the width of a column while simultaneously decreasing the widths of each column to its right, hold down Ctrl while dragging the column's right border. Each column's width is changed proportionately.

There may be times when you want to make all the columns the same width or all rows the same height (for example, when creating a calendar). You can have Word do the work for you. Follow these steps to do so:

▶ Select the columns you want to be the same width and click the Distribute Columns Evenly button on the Tables And Borders toolbar or choose Table ➢ AutoFit ➢ Distribute Columns Evenly.

▶ Select the rows you want to be the same height and click the Distribute Rows Evenly button on the Tables And Borders toolbar or choose Table ➢ AutoFit ➢ Distribute Rows Evenly.

There are several other ways to quickly change the row height and column width of an entire table after you have entered your data in the table. You can select the table, or click in any cell in the table, and then perform one of the following actions:

▶ To change the row height and column width simultaneously to fit the contents of each cell, choose Table ➢ AutoFit ➢ AutoFit To Contents or click the drop-down list on the Insert Table button (Tables And Border toolbar) and then choose AutoFit To Contents. The height of each row is adjusted to fit the cell with the tallest contents. The width of each column is adjusted to fit the widest contents.

▶ To adjust the width of the table to fit the window in Web Layout view, choose Table ➢ AutoFit ➢ AutoFit To Window or click the drop-down list on the Insert Table button (Tables And Borders toolbar) and then choose AutoFit To Window.

You can also specify an exact row height, column width, cell width, and vertical alignment in selected cells by using Word's Table Properties dialog box. (For more about the Table Properties dialog box, see "Changing Properties for the Entire Table" later in this chapter.) In addition, you have some row options for tables that span more than one page.

To change the properties of selected rows:

1. Select the row or rows whose properties you want to change.

2. Choose Table ➤ Table Properties ➤ Row, or right-click the table and choose Table Properties ➤ Row, to display the Row tab in the Table Properties dialog box, shown in Figure 6.15.

3. To change the height of the selected rows, click the Specify Height check box to place a check in it, adjust the value in the text box to the height you want, and then select either At Least or Exactly in the Row Height Is drop-down list.

4. To specify how you want Word to display a table that spans multiple pages, choose either of the following options:

   Allow Row To Break Across Pages Permits a selected row that contains multiple lines of text to be continued on the next page. This may be harder to read but allows you to fit more text into the available space.

   Repeat As Header Row At The Top Of Each Page Duplicates the contents of the selected top row or rows of the table on subsequent pages of the table.

5. If necessary, click Previous Row or Next Row to select that row, and then apply any necessary properties to that row as indicated in steps 2 through 4.

6. Click OK to apply the row properties you selected.

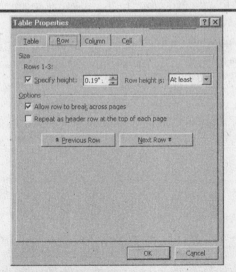

FIGURE 6.15: Change the properties of the selected row(s) on the Row tab in the Table Properties dialog box.

When you choose At Least in the Row Height Is drop-down list, you've specified that the rows will maintain a minimum height regardless of what is in them. Use Exactly when you want to designate a row height that doesn't change. This is useful when you are creating calendars, for example, where you want the row height to stay the same regardless of the contents.

TIP

If you want to break a table across two pages, you can enter a page break in the table. Select the row you want to appear on the next page, and then press Ctrl+Enter to create a manual page break.

Use the options on the Column tab in the Table Properties dialog box to specify how the width of the selected column is determined, as shown in the following steps:

1. Select the column or columns whose widths you want to change.

2. Choose Table ➢ Table Properties ➢ Column, or right-click the table and choose Table Properties ➢ Column, to display the Column tab in the Table Properties dialog box, shown in Figure 6.16.

3. Choose from the following options in the Size area to adjust the width of the selected column:

   ▶ Check the Preferred Width check box and then adjust the value in the related text box to the width you want for the column.

   ▶ In the Measure In drop-down list, choose Inches to specify an exact column width or Percent to have Word automatically adjust the column when other columns are resized.

4. Click either Previous Column or Next Column to select that column, and then choose the property options you want for that column.

5. When you have selected the options you want for each column, click OK in the Table Properties dialog box.

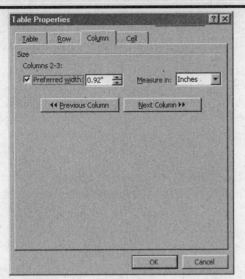

FIGURE 6.16: You can change the width of a column using the options on the Column tab in the Table Properties dialog box.

You can also choose specific properties for selected cells, such as the width of a cell, the cell's text alignment, and even the cell's margins. To do so, follow these steps:

1. Select the cell whose properties you want to change.

2. Choose Table ➢ Table Properties ➢ Cell, or right-click the table and choose Table Properties ➢ Cell, to display the Cell tab in the Table Properties dialog box, shown in Figure 6.17.

3. To change the width of the selected cell, use the following options in the Size area when appropriate:

   ▶ Check the Preferred Width check box and then adjust the value in the related text box to specify the width of the cell.

   ▶ In the Measure In drop-down list, choose Inches to define an exact cell width or Percent to define the width of the cell relative to the width of the table.

4. Choose Top, Center, or Bottom to specify the vertical alignment of the text in the cell.

Part ii

5. For additional options, click the Options button to display the Cell Options dialog box. Choose any of the following options. Then click OK to return to the Table Properties dialog box.

   Same As The Whole Table   Applies the same margins in each cell in the table. Or clear the check box and adjust the appropriate values in the Top, Bottom, Left, and Right text boxes to specify the corresponding margin for the selected cell.

   Wrap Text   Automatically wraps text to the next line in the cell when the insertion point reaches the right margin of the cell.

   Fit Text   Reduces the text so that it all appears on one line in the cell. The font size is not changed, only its appearance is.

6. Click OK in the Table Properties dialog box.

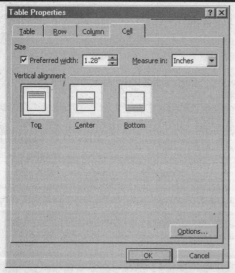

FIGURE 6.17: Use the options on the Cell tab in the Table Properties dialog box to change the width or alignment assigned to the selected cell.

Merging and Splitting Cells

It doesn't take long when working with tables to discover that you don't always want the same number of cells in every row or column. You might want to put a title in a single cell that spans the top of the table, or you might be creating a form and want fewer columns for the totals. When you want to make one cell from two or more cells, you *merge* the cells. When you want to separate a single cell into multiple cells, you *split* the cell.

Use any of the following methods to merge selected cells:

▶ Select the cells you want to merge and choose Table ➢ Merge Cells.

▶ Right-click the table and choose Merge Cells on the shortcut menu.

 ▶ Click the Merge Cells button on the Tables And Borders toolbar.

 ▶ If you prefer the visual approach, you can use the Eraser on the Tables And Borders toolbar to erase the border between cells you want to merge. Just click the Eraser button, and then click on the border you want to remove.

Follow these steps to split a selected cell:

 1. Choose Table ➢ Split Cells; right-click the table and choose Split Cells; or click the Split Cells button on the Tables And Borders toolbar to display the Split Cells dialog box, shown in Figure 6.18.

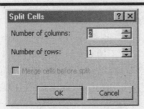

FIGURE 6.18: The Split Cells dialog box contains options that allow you to specify how you want to split selected cells.

2. Adjust the value in the Number Of Columns text box to specify the number of columns to split the cell into.

3. Adjust the value in the Number Of Rows text box to specify the number of rows to split the cell into.

4. Check the Merge Cells Before Split box if you want to merge more than one selected cell before you perform the split. This check box is not available if only one cell is selected.

5. Click OK to split the cells.

You can also click the Draw Table button on the Tables And Borders toolbar and then use the pencil to draw cell borders where you want to split cells.

The ability to define exactly how you want the cells, rows, and columns to appear in a table makes working in tables both useful and practical. You can, for example, create a table for use as an order form for your company, such as the one shown in Figure 6.19.

ORDER FORM			
Item	Price	Quantity	Total
		Total	
		Sales Tax	
		Grand Total	

FIGURE 6.19: You can create a sample order form using Word's table and text formatting features.

The Order Form table was created by inserting a table with four columns and 10 rows, merging some cells, leaving the default borders, and changing the formatting applied to text in the cells. Then, the widths of the four columns were adjusted, and the alignment of the text entered in the cells was changed. You can use any combination of these procedures to create a table to your own specifications.

Formatting Tables

Before you print your table, you might want to put some finishing touches on it to give it that polished, professional look. Word offers both automatic and manual table-formatting options to add and remove borders, change border types, and add colors and shading. Word also lets you specify some properties for your tables.

Using AutoFormat

Word's Table AutoFormat feature provides you with a variety of formats that you can apply in one easy step. Table AutoFormat applies borders, shading, fonts, and colors based on the format selection you make. In addition, you can choose AutoFit to have Word resize the table to fit its contents. Most of the formats include special formatting for the header row, last row, and first and last columns since these often contain titles or summary information.

Follow these steps to have Word automatically format your table:

1. Click anywhere in your table and choose Table ➤ Table Auto-Format, or click the AutoFormat button on the Tables And Borders toolbar, to open the Table AutoFormat dialog box, shown in Figure 6.20.

2. Select a Category of table styles to choose from.

3. Choose the name of the format to apply to the table in the Table Styles list box. A sample of the selected format appears in the Preview area.

4. If you wish to apply special formats to an area of your table, enable the Heading Rows, First Column, Last Row, and/or Last Column check boxes in the Apply Special Formats To area.

5. To adjust borders, shading, font, color, fill, and other table formats, click the Modify button to open the Modify Style dialog box. Make the formatting changes you want. (Be sure to apply the formatting to the appropriate portion of the table.) Click OK when you're through.

NOTE
Chapter 5, "Using Templates and Styles," has information about creating, modifying, and saving styles.

6. When the table in the Preview area looks the way you want your table to appear, click OK in the Table AutoFormat dialog box.

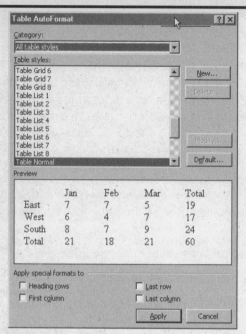

FIGURE 6.20: Display the Table AutoFormat dialog box when you want Word to apply a saved set of formatting to your table.

If you're not satisfied with the table's appearance, click the Undo button on the Standard toolbar, or open the Table AutoFormat dialog box again, and select a different format.

NOTE

It's always a good idea to save your document before applying any AutoFormatting. It's better to be safe than sorry.

Adding Your Own Borders and Shading

You don't have to settle for Word's predesigned table AutoFormats. You can adjust the table AutoFormats manually or start from scratch, whichever you prefer. Either way, you'll want to display the Tables And Borders toolbar before you begin formatting your table, so you can use the buttons and drop-down list options on the toolbar to apply formatting to selected cells.

The Line Style, Line Weight, and Border Color buttons allow you to select the formatting you want to apply to the borders of selected cells. All three buttons are dynamic, which means that your most recent choice appears on the button. Border options include the following:

▶ Click the Line Style drop-down list arrow, and then select the style of the cell's border.

▶ Click the Line Weight drop-down list arrow, and then select the size of the cell's border.

▶ Click the Border Color button to display a color menu, and then select the color for the border.

TIP
You can use the pencil pointer (Draw Table button) to draw over borders that you want to format. Make sure you draw over the entire length of the border, or the line style, weight, or color will not be applied.

Once you have selected the style, weight, and color for the border, you can then apply the border to selected cells. To do so:

1. Select the cells to which to apply the border you chose.

2. Click the Border drop-down list button on the Tables And Borders toolbar to open a menu containing 13 border choices.

3. Click the type of border you want to apply.

NOTE
Inside Border can be applied only to two or more cells. Outside Border affects the border around a single cell or a group of cells; typically, you apply outside borders to the entire table.

You can also change the background color of selected cells. To apply a background color, follow these steps:

1. Click the cell that you want to apply a background color to, or select all the cells to be formatted with the same background color.

2. Click the Shading Color drop-down list button on the Tables And Borders toolbar, and then select the background color in the color palette that appears.

The Shading Color palette contains many different shading colors, including various shades of gray. One word of warning: If you plan to make photocopies of your printed table, be aware that some shades of gray do not copy or fax well.

Borders and shading are not limited to use in tables. You can apply the same skills you just learned to any paragraph of text. Just select one or more paragraphs and click the Borders button or choose Format ➤ Borders And Shading.

TIP

To gain complete control over the borders you want to apply, choose Format ➤ Borders And Shading to display the Borders And Shading dialog box. The options for table and cell borders appear on the Borders tab, and the options for shading cells appear on the Shading tab. On the Borders tab, select the line style, color, and width you want and then click the Preview window to turn desired borders on and off.

Centering Tables Horizontally

If you've adjusted the column widths or if you've moved a table, it may no longer be centered horizontally on the page. Word lets you center the table between the left and right margins so that it appears nicely positioned when you print your document.

To center the table horizontally on the page, follow these steps:

1. Use one of the following methods to select the entire table:

    ▶ Choose Table ➤ Select ➤ Table.

    ▶ Click the Move icon that appears at the top-left corner of the table when you move your mouse pointer over the table.

    ▶ Hold Alt and double-click inside the table.

2. Click the Center button on the Formatting toolbar.

Changing Properties for the Entire Table

Word's Table Properties feature allows you to specify precisely the width and position of a table in your document. You can have regular document text wrap around a narrow table, and you can specify the distance between the table and the text.

To change the properties of a table:

1. Click in any cell in the table whose properties are to be changed.

2. Choose Table ➤ Table Properties ➤ Table to display the Table tab in the Table Properties dialog box, shown in Figure 6.21.

3. To specify an exact width for the table, check the Preferred Width check box in the Size area, and then do the following:

    ▶ Adjust the value in the Preferred Width text box to specify the table's width.

    ▶ In the Measure In drop-down list, choose either Inches, to have the value in the Preferred Width text box appear in inches, or Percent, to change the value to a percentage. If you choose Inches, the table width will be as wide as the value. If you choose Percent, the table width will be proportioned to the specified percentage in relation to the width of the page between the left and right margins.

4. Choose Left, Center, or Right in the Alignment area to specify the position of the table between the left and right margins.

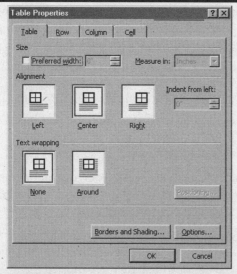

FIGURE 6.21: Display the Table tab in the Table Properties dialog box to change the size, alignment, or text-wrapping properties of the active table.

5. Adjust the value in the Indent From Left text box if you want to specify how far the table is to be indented from the left page margin.

6. Choose either of the following options in the Text Wrapping area to specify how you want the regular document text to wrap around the table:

    None   Places the table above the document text

    Around   Places the table in the document text

7. If you chose Around in step 6, click the Positioning button to display the Table Positioning dialog box (shown in Figure 6.22), and then choose any of the following options:

    ▶ In the Horizontal area, the distance from the left edge of the page to the left edge of the table is displayed. Type a different measurement if you prefer, or select Left, Right, Center, Inside, or Outside to specify the horizontal position of the table. Then choose Margin, Page, or Column in the Relative To drop-down list to specify what the Position is related to.

    ▶ In the Vertical area, the table's current distance from the previous paragraph appears in the Position drop-down list. Type a different distance or choose Top, Bottom, Center, Inside, or Outside to specify the table's vertical position. Then choose Margin, Page, or Paragraph in the Relative To drop-down list.

    ▶ In the Distance From Surrounding Text area, adjust the values in the Top, Bottom, Left, and Right text boxes to specify the distance between the table's borders and surrounding document text.

    ▶ Check the Move With Text check box in the Options area so the table can move vertically in the document when you move the paragraphs surrounding it.

    ▶ Check the Allow Overlap check box in the Options area to allow the table to be partly covered with text or pictures when you are viewing it in a web browser.

    Click OK in the Table Positioning dialog box when you have finished selecting options.

8. Click the Borders And Shading button to bring up options (previously discussed) for applying borders and shading to the table.

9. Click the Options button to change default cell margins, to add cell *spacing* (blank space between cells), or to turn on the Automatically Resize To Contents feature for the entire table.

10. Click OK in the Table Properties dialog box.

FIGURE 6.22: When document text wraps around the active table, display the Table Positioning dialog box to specify the position of the table in the document text.

Adding Calculations to Tables

Although Word supports formulas and calculation in tables, we do not recommend using Word for calculation. Unlike Excel formulas, Word table formulas do not automatically recalculate, creating a huge risk of error if numbers in the table are changed.

If you need to use calculations in a table, we suggest you create the table in Excel and paste it into Word. If the data exists in Excel, open the workbook, select the range of cells, and copy them to the Clipboard. In Word, choose Edit ➢ Paste Special to open the Paste Special dialog box. Choose Microsoft Excel Worksheet Object from the list in the dialog box and click OK to embed the selected Excel range in the Word document. When you double-click the Excel object, the Word toolbars are replaced with Excel's toolbars and menus so that you have access to Excel's tools, including automatic recalculation, in Word.

Sorting It Out

Organize your data by sorting on any field: last name, zip code, department, or anything else you find useful. Rows can be sorted in *ascending order* (A to Z, or 0 to 9) or *descending order* (Z to A, or 9 to 0).

Click in the column you wish to sort on and click the Sort Ascending or Sort Descending button to rearrange the order of the rows.

NOTE

See Chapter 9 of *Mastering Microsoft Office XP Premium Edition* by Gini Courter and Annette Marquis with Karla Browning (Sybex, 2001) for in-depth information on sorting data in tables as well as data in regular paragraphs.

WHAT'S NEXT

You now know the fundamentals of presenting, organizing, and modifying text and document appearance. What about graphics? Adding them and organizing them—the subject of the next chapter—are both handled well in Word 2002 and Office XP.

Chapter 7

MAKING THE MOST OF GRAPHICS

N ot so long ago, graphics rarely appeared in standard documents. Today, however, graphics are easier to create (from a digitizing tablet, digital camera, or scanner) or obtain from colleagues, friends, and online sources. One huge source is the Microsoft Clip Organizer, included with Office, which comes with a stock set of graphics and one-click access (with an Internet connection) to an online collection of thousands more. Read on to learn how to add, organize, and insert graphics in your Word documents.

Adapted from *Mastering Microsoft Office XP Premium Edition* by Gini Courter and Annette Marquis with Karla Browning

ISBN 0-7821-4000-9   1392 pp $49.99

ORGANIZING YOUR CLIPS WITH MICROSOFT CLIP ORGANIZER

Microsoft Clip Organizer, shared by all of the Office applications, has been dramatically revised in this version of Office. It contains an even broader selection of clips, including pictures, sounds, and motion clips. Although you can still browse the clips by category (referred to as *collections*), it is now much easier to search for the clips you want. In addition, it is even simpler to add clips from your own collection or download additional clips directly from Microsoft's online clip gallery, Microsoft Design Gallery Live. Finally, Clip Organizer is a great place to catalog and manage all of the graphics, sound files, and animated graphics files you have stored anywhere on your system.

In Office XP, the task pane offers options for searching or organizing clips. You can quickly access clips online, or look at tips for finding the perfect clip.

NOTE

Not all of the clips visible in Clip Organizer are installed in a typical Office installation. When you insert a clip that is not installed, you may be prompted to insert the Office XP CD that contains the clip.

   To access clip art, click the Insert Clip Art button on the Drawing toolbar or choose Insert ➤ Picture ➤ Clip Art to display the Insert Clip Art task pane, as shown in Figure 7.1. The first time you do this, you are prompted to catalog your media files. You'll have better luck searching for clips if you let Office do this, and it takes only a few minutes.

Searching for the Clip You Want

Microsoft assumes you are probably too busy to spend time going through hundreds of images to find the one you want. So rather than relying on luck to find the perfect graphic, the task pane gives you immediate access to Clip Organizer's built-in Search feature. Search saves time, frustration, and that inevitable feeling of hopelessness that comes from browsing through the vast clip collection. To search for a specific type of clip, follow these steps:

1. Enter a keyword or two in the Search Text box. (See Table 7.1 for tips on what to enter.)

FIGURE 7.1: The Insert Clip Art task pane allows you to search for and insert clip art from a number of sources.

2. Choose which collection(s) you wish to search by selecting from the Search In drop-down list.

3. Choose the type of file you're looking for—clip art, photographs, movies, or sound—in the Results Should Be list.

4. Click the Search button to display clips that meet your criteria. Figure 7.2 shows results of an Office Collections keyword search on *business, computer*.

TABLE 7.1: Search Tips

SEARCH FOR...	RESULTS TO EXPECT
A particular word: *school*	Clips that are cataloged with *school* as a keyword
Multiple words separated by commas: *school, teacher*	Clips that have one or both of the keywords you typed
Words in quotes: *"school teacher"*	Clips that have *school teacher* as a keyword
Multiple words without quotes or commas: *school teacher*	Clips that have both keywords you typed
Filenames with wildcards: *sc*.jpg*	Media clips with filenames such as `school.jpg` and `scooter.jpg`

Part ii

FIGURE 7.2: The task pane displays search results.

    Scroll through the search results to find the clip(s) you want to use. To see nine clips at once instead of six, click the Expand icon at the top of the pane. If you wish to search again, click the Modify button to modify search criteria.

When you move the mouse over a clip, a drop-down indicator, called the Clip Options button, appears on its right border. Click it to see a shortcut menu with options for things you can do to that clip.

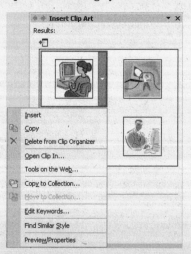

To insert a clip, click it. (You can also choose Insert from the shortcut menu if you've displayed it.) Once the clip is placed in your document, chances are you will want to adjust its size, position, and text-wrapping properties. See "Inserting Pictures into Documents," later in this chapter.

Finding Similar Clips

When you've found the perfect clip, you can instruct Clip Organizer to find additional clips that share a similar design style with the first one. Click the clip's drop-down menu and choose Find Similar Style. The results may have nothing in common with the content of the original clip, but you can use this feature when you want to incorporate a consistent look throughout your document.

Exploring Your Clip Collection

Using the new Microsoft Clip Organizer's Explorer interface, shown in Figure 7.3, you can now browse your stored clips and reorganize clips using the file management tools you already know, such as cut, copy, paste, and drag-and-drop.

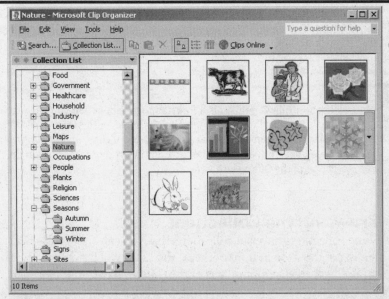

FIGURE 7.3: Microsoft Clip Organizer's Explorer interface lets you preview your clips and use file management tools to organize them into collections.

Part ii

Rather than displaying folders, Clip Organizer displays collections. You can create new collections and move and copy clips into existing collections. Clip Organizer automatically creates three collections in the My Collections folder. These are as follows:

Favorites   Your most frequently used clips, such as your company's logo or other similar clips.

Unclassified Clips   Clips that you have not added to other collections. Included in this collection are clips that Clip Organizer identifies when it reviews your system to look for media clips.

Pictures   Photographs or other clips that you want to classify as pictures.

In addition, Clip Organizer creates folders of Office Collections and Web Collections. Office Collections holds the media clips that come with Office. Click the Expand button (plus symbol) in front of Office Collections to see the list of included collections.

The Web Collections folder lets you access media clips from Microsoft's online clip gallery, Design Gallery Live. You must be connected to the Internet to access the clips in Web Collections. Expand the folder and then select a collection just like you did in the Office Collections folder. The only difference is that the clips that appear are from an ever-changing collection on the Web.

TIP
Microsoft Clip Organizer is a freestanding application you can also launch directly from the Programs menu. Look for a folder called Microsoft Office Tools and launch it from there. You can organize your clips, import clips from other sources, search and browse the clips, and insert clips into applications that are not part of the Office suite.

Browsing the Collections

Some collections have subcollections that you can also access by clicking the Expand button in front of them. You know when a collection contains some clips because thumbnails of the clips appear in the right pane.

In Thumbnails view, you can distinguish sound files by the speaker icon and filename that appear in place of an image. Movie files, or animations, are designated by the yellow star in the bottom-right corner.

j0214098...

NOTE

Animated graphics are animated only when displayed in a web browser or viewed in a PowerPoint slide show. They do not move when inserted into Word documents unless you preview the page in a browser. Refer to Chapter 19, "Creating Web Pages with Word and Excel," to learn more about using animated graphics.

Organizing the Clips You Find

After you find the perfect clips, you can save future searching time by adding them to the Favorites collection or to another collection of your choice. For either option, point to the clip and click the Clip Options button to open the shortcut menu. Choose Copy To Collection or, if it's a clip that is not part of the original Clip Organizer, choose Move To Collection. This opens the Copy To Collection dialog box, shown in Figure 7.4. Choose Favorites or select another collection from the list. After you choose the collection you want, click OK to add the clip to that category and close the dialog box.

TIP

Press and hold Ctrl to select multiple clips you want to move or copy to a collection. To select contiguous clips, press and hold Shift to select the first and last clip you want to move or copy.

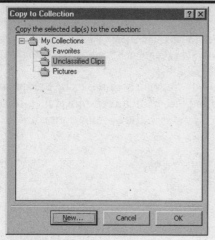

FIGURE 7.4: You can copy media clips to other collections using the Copy To Collection dialog box.

Creating a New Collection

If you would like to create a new collection, open the Copy To Collection dialog box (see previous section) and click the New button, or click any of the collections in the My Collections folder and choose File ➤ New Collection. This opens the New Collection dialog box. Enter the name of the new collection and select the folder you would like it to be a part of. When you click OK, the new collection appears in the list. In this example, we created a Logos collection in the Favorites folder.

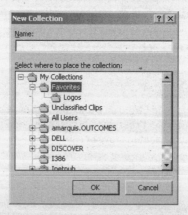

NOTE

You can't create a new collection in the Office Collections or Web Collections folders. You must select a folder in My Collections before attempting to create a new collection.

Assigning Keywords to Clips

To make it easier to find clips, clips can be assigned *keywords*, which are used by Clip Organizer's Search tool to locate the clips you are searching for. The media files that come with Office already have keywords assigned. Figure 7.5 shows a piece of clip art and the accompanying keywords that will help you find this clip.

FIGURE 7.5: Numerous keywords make it easier to find the clips you are looking for.

You can add additional keywords and delete existing keywords from any of the clips in My Collections. To add, delete, or modify keywords of individual clips, follow these steps:

1. Point to the clip you want to change.

2. Click the Clip Options button and chose Edit Keywords from the shortcut menu. This opens the Keywords dialog box, such as the one shown in Figure 7.5 above.

Part II

3. To edit the keywords of each clip individually, use the Clip By Clip tab.

4. To delete a keyword, select the keyword you want to delete and click the Delete button.

5. To add a keyword, click in the Keyword text box and enter the new keyword or, if it's a keyword you've added previously, select it from the drop-down list. Click the Add button.

6. To modify a keyword, select the keyword, make the editing changes you want to make, and click the Modify button.

7. Click the Next button to edit the keywords of the next clip, or click OK to apply the changes and close the dialog box.

To add, delete, or modify keywords of a group of clips, select the clips you want to edit: to select multiple clips, hold Ctrl and click each clip; to select multiple contiguous clips, click the first clip and hold Shift while you click the last clip. Then follow steps 2–7 above, selecting the All Clips At Once tab, shown in Figure 7.6, to make your edits.

TIP

If you are editing clips in My Collections, you might also want to add a caption to the clip. The caption appears when you point to the thumbnail of the clip in Clip Organizer. If a clip does not have a caption, the list of keywords appears when you point to the thumbnail. To add a caption, right-click the thumbnail and choose Edit Keywords. Enter the caption in the Caption text box of the Clip By Clip tab and click OK. Also remember to edit keywords if you've added clips to Clip Organizer (see "Improving Your Clip Collection" later in this chapter) or have copied clips to a new collection for use in a specific project.

NOTE

You can add and delete keywords from a clip in the Office Collections and Web Collections folders only if you've previously copied the clip to My Collections.

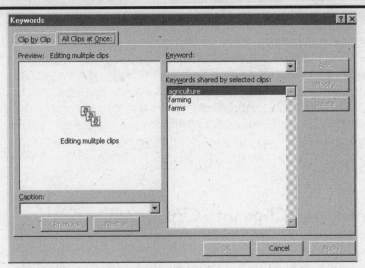

FIGURE 7.6: Use the All Clips At Once tab to add, delete, or modify keywords for multiple clips.

ORGANIZING CLIPS ACCORDING TO YOUR OWN PROJECTS

One of the best ways to gain control of your clips is to create your own collections and keywords and organize the clips according to the projects you're working on. Let's say, for example, you produce a monthly newsletter for your department or organization. You can create a collection for the newsletter and copy all the design clips that designate special sections of the newsletter to this collection. To make it even easier, you can add custom keywords and captions to help you quickly find all the clips you need through a keyword search. While you are at it, you may also want to create collections to organize photographs of your company's products, your company logos, and photos of key employees to use as the needs arise. (See "Importing Clips into Clip Organizer" later in this chapter to add your own photos to Clip Organizer.) As you are preparing for the next issue, continue to organize the artwork as you go along. When you are ready to produce the newsletter, all the art you need is right at your fingertips.

Improving Your Clip Collection

The Clip Organizer is not at all limited by the clips that come with Microsoft Office. If you really want to make it useful, add all the photographs, clip art, sound files, and motion clips you have available, even if they come with their own cataloging software. Having access to all the clips you need in one place not only makes it more convenient but improves the overall quality of your work by offering you the greatest number of choices. You can add clips you already have in your collection, and you can download clips directly from Microsoft's Design Gallery Live as you need them.

Importing Clips into Clip Organizer

When you import clips into Clip Organizer, you have three options for how you handle the import process. To access any of these options, choose File ➢ Add Clips To Organizer. From here, you can choose:

Automatically   Searches your hard drive for graphic, sound, and motion files and adds them to Clip Organizer for you. The clips are added to a collection called Unclassified Clips. Keep in mind that when you choose this option, Clip Organizer may even add clips used by applications and websites that you've accessed.

On My Own   Adds clips you select to Clip Organizer. Click the Add To button on the Add Clips To Organizer dialog box to specify which collection to add the clips to.

From Scanner Or Camera   Imports clips directly from an installed scanner or camera. If the scanner or camera you plan to use does not appear in the Device drop-down list, make sure the device is properly installed and working.

Removing Clips from Clip Organizer

With both the Automatically and On My Own options, Clip Organizer creates a shortcut to the clip files but does not change their file locations. If you delete a clip from Clip Organizer, the file is still available in its original location.

 To delete a clip from Clip Organizer, select Delete From Clip Organizer from the Clip Options shortcut menu or click the Delete From Clip

Organizer button on the Clip Organizer toolbar. This option deletes the clip from all Clip Organizer collections it is in.

To delete a clip from a specific collection, choose Delete From *Collection Name* from the Clip Options shortcut menu.

Accessing Shared Clip Organizer Catalogs

If your company's system administrator has created shared Clip Organizer catalogs and made them available on the server, you can add them to your Clip Organizer by choosing File ➤ Add Clips To Organizer ➤ On My Own, and then choosing Shared Catalogs (*.mgc) from the Files Of Type drop-down list in the Pictures – Add Clips To Catalogs dialog box. Locate the shared catalog and click Add to include the catalog in your Clip Organizer.

NOTE

To access the clips in a shared catalog, you have to be logged on to the network and have access to the file location where they are stored.

Finding New Clips on Microsoft Design Gallery Live

Microsoft has made sure that you have all the clips you need by posting a special website just for Clip Organizer users filled with over 100,000 graphic images and sounds, including clip art, photographs, sound clips, and motion files. The site is updated regularly and always has featured clips based on the season or upcoming holidays.

Clips Online   To access Microsoft Design Gallery Live, click the Clips Online button on the Clip Organizer toolbar or the link from the Insert Clip Art task pane.

In Design Gallery Live, you can browse by category or search for keywords. Searching is the best way to find what you are looking for quickly. To search, follow these steps:

1. Enter a search term in the Search For text box (see Figure 7.7). To get the best results, be descriptive but not too precise. For example, if you wanted clips of women basketball players, search for *basketball players*. *Basketball* would give

Part III

you balls, nets, and players, and *women basketball players* would return no clips.

2. Choose a category from the Search In drop-down list. If you are unsure, choose Everywhere.

3. Choose the type of results you want from the Results Should Be drop-down list: Anything, Clip Art, Photos, Sound, or Motion.

4. Choose the order you want the results to appear in from the Order By drop-down list: Newer, File Size, or Media Type.

FIGURE 7.7: Microsoft Design Gallery Live is a great place to find clip art, photos, sounds, and motion clips.

When you get results, use the page controls in the top-left corner of the page to see additional pages of clips.

 When you find the clips you want, you can download them one at a time, or you can collect them all first and then download then all at once. To download them one at a time, click the drive icon with the downward-pointing red arrow at the base of the clip.

TIP

If you access Design Gallery Live from a fast Internet connection, you may want to increase the number of clips that Design Gallery Live displays on a page. Click the Options link in the top navigation bar of Design Gallery Live and change the grid size by increasing the number of columns and rows and clicking Update. If you notice too much degradation in speed, go back to Options and choose Restore Defaults.

The clip is immediately downloaded, and Clip Organizer opens, showing only the downloaded clip. Right-click the clip to add a caption, recategorize it, and edit the keyword list. (The clip comes with keywords already assigned.) Close Clip Organizer and reopen to see all the Clip Organizer clips.

NOTE

If Microsoft Clip Organizer is not running when you download the clip, you can find your new clips by clicking the Downloaded Clips category the next time you launch Clip Organizer.

To collect clips to download once you've selected them all, click the check box under the clip. If you want all the visible clips, click the Select All link. As you add clips to the download, you will notice the counter at the top of the page increase. When you are ready to download the files, click the Download *x* Clips link. When you are ready, click Download Now.

Download 2 Clips

TIP

The Microsoft Clip Organizer maintains a database of the clips, captions, collections, keywords, and other properties. Proper maintenance of this catalog, especially if you have added or deleted clips from the catalog, makes it run faster and with fewer problems. On a routine basis, you can compact the catalog and repair any corrupted data by choosing Tools ➢ Compact from the Clip Organizer menu.

Part II

Inserting Pictures into Documents

Finding the perfect clips is more than half the battle. Positioning them in your document so they enhance rather than detract from your message is the rest. Word makes it easy to work with pictures, but knowing a few tricks will give you full control of how your clips appear in your documents.

When you insert a picture into a document, the bottom of the picture is aligned with the text at the location of the insertion point. This default text-wrapping style, In Line With Text, is rather limiting—you can only move the clip as if you were moving a block of text, one character or one line of text at a time.

For more flexibility in how the clip integrates with the text and in how easily it is to move around the document, choose a different text-wrapping option by clicking the Text Wrapping button on the Picture toolbar. You can access these options from the Picture toolbar that opens automatically when you select a picture. (For details about all of the tools on the Picture toolbar, see "Modifying Pictures with the Picture Toolbar" later in this chapter.)

You can also access text-wrapping options if you right-click the clip and choose Format Picture, or click the Format Picture button on the Picture toolbar, and then click the Layout tab of the Format Picture dialog box, shown in Figure 7.8.

When you change the clip's layout to Square, Tight, Behind Text, or In Front Of Text, you can adjust the horizontal alignment of the clip using the Horizontal Alignment options on the Layout tab of the Format Picture dialog box. Choose Other if you want to reposition the picture by dragging it with your mouse. Click OK to save the new layout changes.

NOTE
Choosing any of the alignment options does not restrict your ability to reposition a picture.

You can now reposition the picture by dragging it with the four-headed arrow pointer to a different location on the page while retaining the new text-wrapping style you set for the picture.

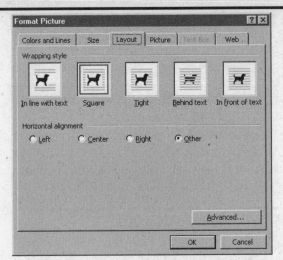

FIGURE 7.8: Display the Layout tab in the Format Picture dialog box to change the layout of the selected picture.

Resizing Clip Art

When you click a picture (or any object) to select it, eight handles appear around the outside: four at the corners and one on each side. When you point to any one of these handles, the pointer changes to a two-headed resize arrow. Drag any handle to resize the object in the desired direction. Drag one of the corner handles if you want to resize the object while maintaining the object's original proportions.

NOTE

As long as you resize a picture using a corner handle, Word 2002 automatically maintains the picture's original proportions. To turn this feature off, clear the Lock Aspect Ratio check box on the Size tab in the Format Picture dialog box (right-click the picture and choose Format Picture). You can still maintain proportions even with this option turned off by holding Shift while dragging a corner handle.

Gaining Control of Positioning and Wrapping

When you need more precise positioning of your graphics and want better control of how text wraps around the picture, click the Advanced button on the Layout tab of the Format Picture dialog box (right-click a picture and choose Format Picture).

Use the Picture Position tab, shown in Figure 7.9, to set the Horizontal and Vertical position relative to the Alignment (Left, Center, Right) or the Absolute Position. For Horizontal position, you can also choose Book Layout (position of left and right margins on opposite pages).

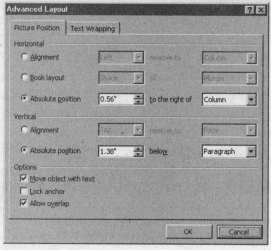

FIGURE 7.9: The Picture Position tab of the Advanced Layout dialog box lets you control the exact positioning of a picture.

The Picture Position tab also gives you these options:

Move Object With Text   Clear this check box to position the picture on the page so it does not move, even if the paragraph it is located in moves.

Lock Anchor   Click this check box so you can move a picture while anchoring it to a particular paragraph so that it always stays in the same relative position to that paragraph.

Allow Overlap   Click this check box to allow two pictures with the same text wrapping to overlap each other.

If you are not satisfied with how close the text is to the picture, click the Text Wrapping tab of the Advanced Layout dialog box, shown in Figure 7.10, to change the Distance From Text properties to increase or decrease the distance.

The Text Wrapping tab also provides options if you want the text to wrap only on one side of the picture or the other. To indicate this, choose Left Only, Right Only, or Largest Only. To wrap text on the left and right sides of the picture, select Both Sides.

For another option and even more precise control of how text wraps around the picture, click the Text Wrapping button on the Picture toolbar and select Edit Wrap Points. This adds numerous points in the picture, as you can see in Figure 7.11. Drag any one of the points to push the text away from that part of the picture.

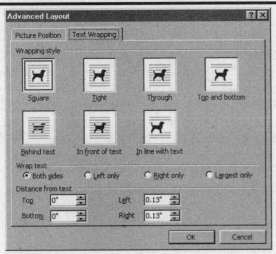

FIGURE 7.10: Use the Text Wrapping tab in the Advanced Layout dialog box to change how text wraps around a picture.

NOTE

Many of the settings you learned about in this section in relation to pictures, such as the options on the Picture toolbar and the Format Picture dialog box, can be applied to any object you insert into a Word document regardless of the source application—Excel charts, Microsoft Draw objects, WordArt objects, and so on. If the Picture toolbar does not appear automatically when you select an object, right-click any visible toolbar and choose Picture to activate it.

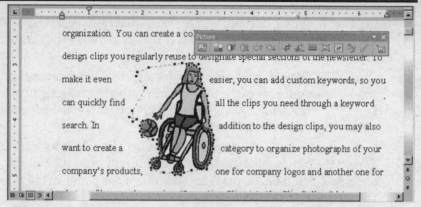

FIGURE 7.11: To change how closely text wraps around a picture, you can drag individual points to move the text further away.

Rotating Images

At the top of each picture you insert into a document is a green-filled circle above the center handle. This is the Free Rotate tool, which allows you to rotate the picture in any direction. When you point to the tool, the pointer changes to a circular arrow. When you click the arrow, the pointer changes to four circular arrows. Drag the pointer to rotate the image.

Modifying Pictures with the Picture Toolbar

Although Word does not have the features of photo-editing software such as Microsoft Photo Editor or a third-party package such as Adobe Photoshop, you still have some basic editing options available to you within Word. When you want to change a picture by adjusting the contrast or brightness, setting the transparency, or cropping it, the Picture toolbar may just have the tools you need. Table 7.2 describes the buttons you can find on the Picture toolbar.

TABLE 7.2: The Picture Toolbar Buttons

Button	Name	Use
	Insert Picture	Inserts a picture from a file
	Color	Determines the appearance of the picture: Automatic (applies the most appropriate format, usually the defaults); Grayscale (converts each color to a shade of gray); Black & White (changes each color to black or white, converting the image to line art); or Watermark (changes the picture to a bright, low-contrast format that can be placed behind document text)
	More Contrast	Increases color intensity
	Less Contrast	Decreases color intensity
	More Brightness	Adds white to lighten the colors
	Less Brightness	Adds black to darken the colors
	Crop	Trims rectangular areas from the image
	Rotate Left	Rotates the picture 90 degrees to the left with each click
	Line Style	Formats the border that surrounds the picture

Part iii

TABLE 7.2 CONTINUED: The Picture Toolbar Buttons

Button	Name	Use
	Compress Picture	Reduces the size of graphics by changing the resolution of the picture for web/screen and print uses, compressing the picture by applying JPEG compression to high-color pictures (may result in a loss of quality) and deleting cropped areas of a picture
	Text Wrapping	Determines the way document text wraps around the picture
	Format Picture/Object	Displays the Picture tab in the Format Object dialog box so you can change the format to exact specifications
	Set Transparent Color	Used like an eyedropper to make areas of JPEG pictures transparent; used extensively in web design
	Reset Picture	Returns the picture to its original format

NOTE

The Crop and Set Transparent Color buttons are used with areas of the picture. All other buttons affect the entire picture.

INSERTING PICTURES FROM OTHER SOURCES

In addition to using Clip Organizer as a source of art, you can insert pictures into your document from any file you can access. You can also format pictures inserted from a file by using the buttons on the Picture toolbar. To insert a picture that isn't in Clip Organizer, follow these steps:

1. Choose Insert ➢ Picture ➢ From File, or display the Picture toolbar and click the Insert Picture button to open the Insert Picture dialog box, shown in Figure 7.12.

2. Select the name of the file that contains the picture.

3. Click the Insert button to insert the selected picture into your document.

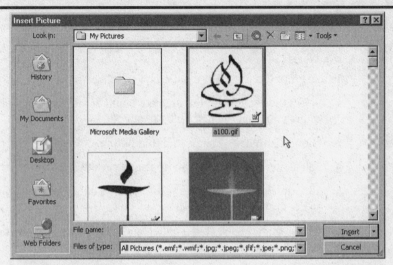

FIGURE 7.12: You can insert pictures into your documents from a variety of sources using the Insert Picture dialog box.

ADDING GRAPHICAL LINES, BULLETS, AND PAGE BORDERS

Adding clip art and photographs isn't the only way to add flair to a Word document. Word 2002 has features that allow you to insert graphical lines and bullets in place of the standard lines and bullet characters and to decorate your pages with graphical page borders. These finishing touches make your documents more interesting and more noticeable, and after all, isn't that the point?

To insert a graphical line, follow these steps:

1. Position the insertion point where you want the line to appear.

2. Choose Format ➢ Borders And Shading.

3. Click the Horizontal Line button at the bottom of the Borders tab of the Borders And Shading dialog box. This launches the Horizontal Lines dialog box, which searches your clip collections.

CONTINUED ➡

4. When you have selected a line, click OK to insert it into your document.

You can format the line by right-clicking it and choosing Format Horizontal Line.

To use graphical bullets in a bulleted list, follow these steps:

1. Select the list you want to bullet or position the insertion point where you want the first bullet to appear.

2. Choose Format ➢ Bullets And Numbering.

3. Select any bullet other than None and click Customize.

4. Click the Picture button to see the Picture Bullet dialog box with all the graphical bullets from your clip collections.

5. When you have selected a bullet, click OK to insert it into your document.

To add an artsy page border, choose Format ➢ Borders And Shading. Click the Page Borders tab and select a border from the Art drop-down list.

Inserting Scanned Graphics and Digital Photos

With today's digital cameras, scanners, and endless CDs filled with photos and clip art, it's pretty easy to capture just the right images for your documents. It may take a little legwork, but if it's out there, there is a way to turn it into a digital image. Office has built-in tools to accept images directly from scanners and digital cameras.

To import images from a digital camera, scanner, or other TWAIN device, first make sure the device is connected to your computer and the software for the device is installed through Windows. Then, follow these steps:

1. Set up the picture in the scanning device.

2. Choose Insert ➢ Picture ➢ From Scanner Or Camera.

3. Select the device you want to use from the Device drop-down list.

4. Choose the resolution you want—Web Quality or Print Quality—depending on how you plan to use the picture.

5. Click Insert, or if you are using a scanner and want to change the image settings, choose Custom Insert. If the Insert button is unavailable because your scanner doesn't support automatic scanning, you must choose Custom Insert.

You can modify, reposition, and resize scanned images and digital photos just like any other images.

WARNING

Some very old scanners and their drivers may have difficulty working directly with the Office XP interface. In these situations, you can check for an updated driver and tools package for the scanner, consider replacing your older scanner, or just scan the image through the scanner's own software and then import it as a picture into the file.

WHAT'S NEXT

In the next chapter, we turn to Excel 2002. You will learn basic workbook skills as you familiarize yourself with spreadsheet layout and fundamental functions.

As we go, you will begin to see the interfunctionality of the programs—how information from Excel can go into a Word document, and vice versa.

Part ii

PART iii

WORKING WITH
NUMBERS IN
EXCEL 2002

Chapter 8

BASIC WORKBOOK SKILLS

Now we move on to Excel 2002, the spreadsheet component of Office XP used for accounting and other numbers-based tasks, to help you understand how it is set up as well as how to use it.

In this chapter, you'll become familiar with workbooks, the fundamental work area in Excel, and how to perform basic functions in building your own workbooks.

Adapted from *Microsoft Excel 2002 Simply Visual* by Perspection, Inc.

ISBN 0-7821-4006-8   288 pp $24.99

VIEWING THE EXCEL WINDOW

When Excel opens, the program window displays a blank workbook—with the New Workbook task pane on the right—ready for you to begin working.

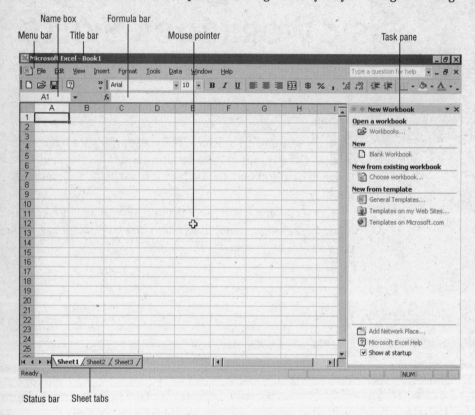

You can open more than one workbook window at a time. If you are working with one workbook and need to check or work with data in another, you don't need to close the current file. You can view open windows one at a time, or arrange all of them on the screen at the same time, and then click the window in which you want to work. You can also move and resize each window to suit your viewing needs and work habits.

Switch between Workbook Windows

1. Click the Window menu to display the list of open workbook windows.

2. Click the name of the workbook to which you want to switch.

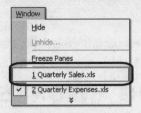

STARTING A NEW WORKBOOK

When you start Excel, the program window opens with a new workbook so that you can begin working in it. You can also start a new workbook whenever Excel is running, and you can start as many new workbooks as you want. Each new workbook displays a default name and is numbered consecutively during the current work session (Book1, Book2, and so on). When you save a workbook with a unique name, Excel's numbering scheme for the next workbook restarts from the last assigned number. Each time you start a work session, the numbering scheme restarts from 1.

Start a New Workbook from the Task Pane

1. Click the File menu, and then click the New command (File ➤ New).

2. Click Blank Workbook. Excel opens a blank workbook.

Start a New Workbook from the New Button

▶ Click the New button. Excel opens a blank workbook.

NAVIGATING A WORKSHEET

You can move around a worksheet or workbook using your mouse or the keyboard. You might find that using your mouse is most convenient when moving from cell to cell, while using various keyboard combinations is easier for covering large areas of a worksheet quickly. However, there is no one right way; whichever method feels the most comfortable is the one you should use. You can also use the arrow keys on the keyboard, but bear in mind that if you are moving across several cells, arrow keys are less effective and can cause eyestrain.

TIP

Microsoft IntelliMouse users can roll from cell to cell with IntelliMouse. If you have the new Microsoft IntelliMouse—with the wheel button between the left and right buttons—you can click the wheel button and move the mouse in any direction to move quickly around the worksheet.

Use the Keyboard to Navigate

Using the keyboard, you can navigate to one of the following:

▶ Another cell

▶ Another part of a worksheet

Refer to the following list of keyboard shortcuts for navigating around a worksheet.

Press...	To Move...
Left arrow	One cell to the left
Right arrow	One cell to the right
Up arrow	One cell up
Down arrow	One cell down

Press...	To Move...
Enter	One cell down
Tab	One cell to the right
Shift+Tab	One cell to the left
Page Up	One screen up
Page Down	One screen down
End+arrow	In the direction of the arrow key to the next cell that contains data or to the last empty cell in the current row or column
Home	To column A in the current row
Ctrl+Home	To cell A1
Ctrl+End	To the last cell in the worksheet that contains data

TIP

When you press the Enter key, Excel's default is to move the active cell down one cell. To change the default direction, choose Tools ➤ Options, click the Edit tab, click the Direction drop-down arrow, select a direction, and then click the OK button.

PREVIEWING AND PRINTING A WORKSHEET

You should always preview your work before sending it to the printer. By using *Print Preview*, you can view all or part of your worksheet as it will appear when you print it. You can print a copy of your worksheet by clicking the Print button on the Standard toolbar or on the Print Preview toolbar. You can open the Print dialog box to specify several print options, such as choosing a new printer, selecting the number of pages in the worksheet you want printed, and specifying the number of copies.

Preview a Worksheet

1. Click the Print Preview button on the Standard toolbar, or choose File ➤ Print Preview.

2. Click the Zoom button on the Print Preview toolbar, or position the Zoom pointer anywhere on the worksheet and click it to enlarge a specific area of the page.

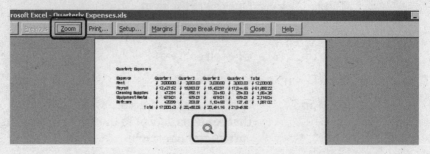

3. If you do not want to print from Print Preview, click the Close button to return to the worksheet.

4. If you want to print from Print Preview, click the Print button on the Print Preview toolbar to open the Print dialog box.

5. From the Print dialog box, specify the printing options you want, and then click the OK button, or click the Preview button to return to Print Preview.

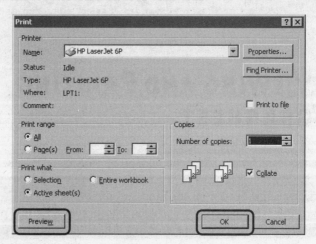

Print a Copy of a Worksheet Quickly

▶ Click the Print button on the Standard toolbar. Excel prints the selected worksheet with the current Print dialog box settings.

NOTE

To change printer properties, choose File ➤ Print, and then click Properties to change general printer properties for paper size and orientation, graphics, and fonts.

TIP

When you select the Collate check box, Excel prints multiple copies of a worksheet in complete sets. For two copies of a two-page document, the Collate option prints pages 1 and 2, and then prints pages 1 and 2 again.

Specify Print Options Using the Print Dialog Box

1. Choose File ➤ Print. The Print dialog box opens.

2. To choose another (installed) printer, click the Name drop-down arrow, and then select the printer you want to use from the list.

3. To print selected pages (rather than all pages), click the Page(s) option button, and then click the From and To up or down arrows to specify the page range you want.

4. To print more than one copy of the print range, click the Number Of Copies up or down arrow to specify the number of copies you want.

5. To change the worksheet print area, click one of the Print What option buttons that correctly identifies the area to be printed.

6. Click the OK button.

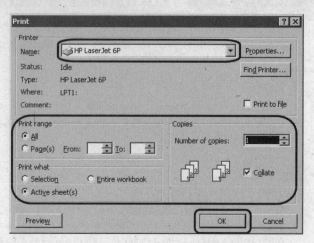

MAKING LABEL ENTRIES

Excel has three types of cell entries: labels, values, and formulas. Excel uses values and formulas to perform its calculations. A *label* is text in a cell that identifies the data on the worksheet so readers can interpret the information, such as titles or column headings. A *value* is a number you enter in a cell. To enter values easily and quickly, you can format a cell, a range of cells, or an entire column with a specific number-related format.

To perform a calculation in a worksheet, you enter a formula in a cell. A *formula* performs an operation on one or more cells. Excel calculates the formula based on cell references, values, and arithmetic operators. The result of a formula appears in the worksheet cell where you entered the formula. When you enter a formula in a cell, the contents appear on the formula bar. Entering cell references rather than actual values in a formula has distinct advantages. When you change the data in the worksheet (for example, changing the contents of cell C4 from .45 to .55) or copy the formula to other cells (copying a formula to the cell below), Excel automatically adjusts the cell references in the formula and returns the correct results.

Formula
appears here

Label   Value   Result of
Formula

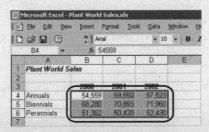

Select a Contiguous Range

In order to work with a cell—to enter data in it, edit or move it, or perform
an action—you *select* the cell so it becomes the active cell. When you
want to work with more than one cell at a time—to move or copy them,
use them in a formula, or perform any group action—you must first select
the cells as a *range*. A range can be *contiguous* (where selected cells are
adjacent to each other) or *noncontiguous* (where the cells may be in different parts of the worksheet and are not adjacent to each other). As you
select a range, you can see the range reference in the Name box. A *range
reference* contains the cell address of the top-left cell in the range, a colon
(:), and the cell address of the bottom-right cell in the range.

TIP

To deselect a range, click anywhere in the worksheet.

1. Click the first cell you want to include in the range.

2. Drag the mouse to the last cell you want to include in the range.
   When you select a range, the cell pointer surrounds the top-
   left cell, and Excel highlights the additional cells in color.

Select a Noncontiguous Range

1. Click the first cell you want to include in the range.

2. Drag the mouse to the last contiguous cell, and then release the mouse button.

3. Hold down the Ctrl key on the keyboard, and then click the next cell or drag the mouse pointer over the next group of cells you want in the range.

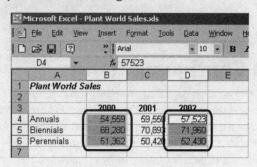

4. Repeat step 3 until you have selected the cells you want.

Enter a Text Label

Labels turn a worksheet full of numbers into a meaningful report by identifying the different types of information it contains. You use labels to describe or identify the data in worksheet cells, columns, and rows. You can enter a number as a label (for example, the year 2002), so that Excel does not use the number in its calculations. To help keep your labels consistent, you can use Excel's AutoComplete feature, which automatically completes your entries based on the format of previously entered labels.

TIP
You can accept an entry in different ways. After you've entered a value, you can click the Enter button on the formula bar to leave the insertion point in the active cell, or you can press the Enter key on the keyboard to move the insertion point down one cell on the worksheet.

1. Click the cell where you want to enter a label.

2. Type a label. A label can include uppercase and lowercase letters, spaces, punctuation, and numbers.

3. Press the Enter key on the keyboard, or click the Enter button on the formula bar.

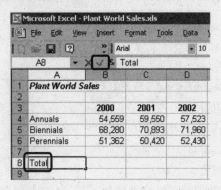

Enter a Number as a Label

1. Click the cell where you want to enter a number as a label.

2. Type ' (an apostrophe). The apostrophe is a label prefix and does not appear on the worksheet—it instructs Excel to treat the contents as text, not as a value.

3. Type a number. Examples of numbers that you might use as labels include a year, a tax form number, or a part number.

4. Press the Enter key on the keyboard, or click the Enter button on the formula bar.

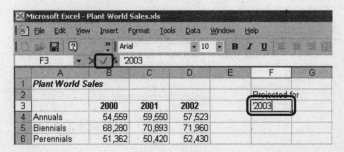

NOTE

When you enter a label that is wider than the cell it occupies, the excess text appears to spill into the next cell to the right—unless there is data in the adjacent cell. If that cell contains data, the label will appear truncated—you'll see only the portion of the label that fits in the cell's current width. Click the cell to see its entire contents displayed on the formula bar.

Enter a Label Using AutoComplete

1. Type the first few characters of a label. If Excel recognizes the entry, AutoComplete completes it.

NOTE

If you receive an error stating that Excel does not recognize the entry, verify that the AutoComplete option is turned on. To turn on the feature, choose Tools ➢ Options, and then click the Edit tab, click the Enable AutoComplete For Cell Values check box to select it, and then click the OK button.

2. To accept the suggested entry, press the Enter key on the keyboard, or click the Enter button on the formula bar.

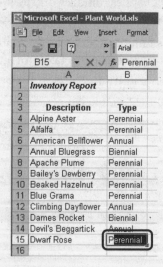

3. To reject the suggested completion, simply continue typing.

ENTERING VALUES

You can enter values as whole numbers, decimals, percentages, or dates. You can enter values using the numbers on the top row of your keyboard, or the numeric keypad on the right side of your keyboard. When you enter a date or the time of day, Excel automatically recognizes these entries (if entered in an acceptable format) as numeric values and changes the cell's format to a default date, currency, or time format.

NOTE
You can use the numeric keypad like a calculator to enter numbers on your worksheet. Before using the numeric keypad, make sure "NUM" appears in the lower-right corner of the status bar. If "NUM" is not displayed, you can turn on this feature by pressing the Num Lock key on the numeric keypad.

Enter a Value

1. Click the cell where you want to enter a value.

2. Type a value. To simplify your data entry, type the values without commas and dollar signs. You can apply a numeric format to them later.

3. Press the Enter key on the keyboard, or click the Enter button on the formula bar.

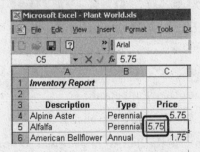

Enter a Date or Time

1. To enter a date, type the date using a slash (/) or a hyphen (-) between the month, day, and year in a cell or on the formula bar. You can enter single months or days as one numeral.

To enter a time, type the hour based on a 12-hour clock, followed by a colon (:), followed by the minute, followed by a space, and ending with an A or a P to denote AM or PM.

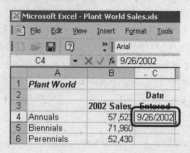

2. Press the Enter key on the keyboard, or click the Enter button on the formula bar.

TIP

You can shorten data entry time by applying a cell format to a cell. When you enter a value, you don't have to type additional formatting characters, such as periods or decimal places. For example, to enter the value *10.00*, simply type *10*. Choose Format ➢ Cells to format your cell entries with other formatting attributes such as commas, currency symbols, negative numbers, zip code + 4, or dates.

Change Date or Time Format

1. Click the cell that contains the date format you want to change.

2. Choose Format ➢ Cells. The Format Cells dialog box opens.

3. Click the Number tab.

4. In the Category list, click Date.

5. Choose the date or time format you want from the Type list.

6. Click the OK button.

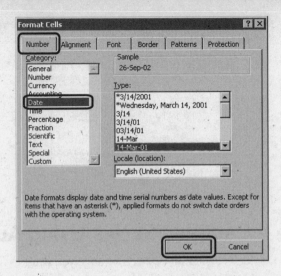

Enter Repeating Data Using AutoFill

The *AutoFill* feature automatically fills in data based on the data in adjacent cells. Using the *fill handle*, you can enter data in a series, or you can copy values or formulas to adjacent cells. The entry in a cell can create an AutoFill that repeats a value or label, or the results can be a more complex extended series, such as days of the week, months of the year, or consecutive numbering.

After you fill text or data in a worksheet, the AutoFill Options button appears. You can click the AutoFill button to display additional options, such as Copy Cells, Fill Series, Fill Formatting Only, or Fill Without Formatting.

NOTE

To select additional AutoFill commands from the Edit menu, choose Fill to select additional fill commands such as Up, Down, Left, Right, Series, or Justify.

1. Select the first cell in the range you want to fill.

2. Enter the starting value that you want to repeat.

3. Position the mouse pointer on the lower-right corner of the selected cell. The fill handle (a small black box) changes to the fill handle pointer (a black plus sign).

Part iii

4. Drag the fill handle pointer over the range where you want to repeat the value.

Fill handle
pointer

7	Annual Bluegrass	Biennial	4.50
8	Apache Plume	Perennial	5.75
9	Bailey's Dewberry		5.75
10	Beaked Hazelnut		5.75
11	Blue Grama		5.75
12	Climbing Dayflower	Annual	
13	Dames Rocket	Biennial	Perennial 4.50
14	Devil's Beggartick	Annual	1.75

Create a Complex Series Using AutoFill

1. Select the first cell in the range you want to fill.

2. Enter the starting value for the series, and then click the Enter button on the formula bar.

3. Position the mouse pointer on the lower-right corner of the selected cell, and then hold down the Ctrl key on the keyboard. The pointer changes to the fill handle pointer (a black plus sign with a smaller plus sign).

4. Drag the fill handle pointer over the range where you want the value extended. The destination value appears in a small box by the fill handle pointer.

On-Hand	Value	Item #
15	$86.25	101
10	$57.50	
6	$10.50	
12	$54.00	
24	$138.00	
15	$86.25	104

EDITING CELL CONTENTS

No matter how much you plan, you can always count on having to make changes to a worksheet. Sometimes it's because you want to correct an error or see how your worksheet results would be affected by different conditions, such as higher sales, the production of fewer units, or other variables. You can edit data just as easily as you entered it: by using the formula bar or directly editing the active cell.

TIP

To edit cell contents using the formula bar, click the cell you want to edit, click on the formula bar, and then edit the cell contents.

NOTE

To change editing options, choose Tools ➢ Options, click the Edit tab, change the appropriate editing options, and then click the OK button.

Edit Cell Contents

1. Double-click the cell you want to edit. The insertion point appears in the cell. (The status bar now displays "Edit" instead of "Ready.")

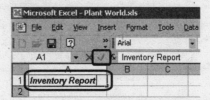

2. If necessary, use the Home, End, and arrow keys on the keyboard to position the insertion point in the cell contents.

3. Use any combination of the Backspace and Delete keys on the keyboard to erase unwanted characters, and then type new characters as needed.

4. Click the Enter button on the formula bar, or press the Enter key on the keyboard to accept the edit, or click the Cancel button to cancel it.

NOTE

You can search for a value or data in a cell and then replace it with different content. Click the cell or cells containing content you want to replace. Choose Edit ➢ Find, and then click the Replace tab for additional options.

Part iii

Clear the Contents of a Cell

You can clear a cell to remove its contents. Clearing a cell does not remove the cell from the worksheet; it just removes contents from the cell. When clearing a cell, you must specify whether to remove one, two, or all three of the various elements from the selected cell or range.

NOTE

Deleting a cell removes the cell from the worksheet. When you choose Delete from the Edit menu or from the shortcut menu, you can choose to shift the remaining cells left or up, or to remove the entire row or column.

1. Select the cell or range you want to clear.

2. Right-click the cell or range, and then choose Clear Contents, or press the Delete key on the keyboard.

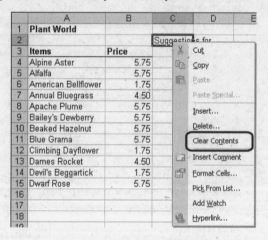

Clear Cell Contents, Formatting, and Comments

1. Select the cell or range you want to clear.

2. Choose Edit ➤ Clear ➤ All.

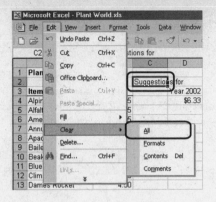

Undo an Action

We all make mistakes. Shortly after completing an action or a task, you may realize you've made a mistake. The Undo feature lets you take back one or more previous actions, including the data you entered, the edits you made, or the commands you selected. For example, instead of selecting and deleting the data or a label you just entered in a cell, you could undo the entry. A few moments later, if you decide the number or name you deleted was correct after all, you could use the Redo feature to restore it to the cell.

NOTE

If the Redo button does not appear on the toolbar, click the Toolbar Options drop-down arrow, and then click Redo. Once you use the button, it remains on the toolbar.

▶ Click the Undo button on the Standard toolbar to undo the last action you completed.

▶ Click the Undo drop-down arrow from the Standard toolbar to see a list of recent actions that can be undone. When you select an action to undo, Excel will undo that action and all actions above it.

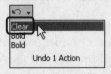

▶ Click an action. Excel reverses the selected action and all actions above it.

Part iii

Redo an Action

▶ Click the Redo button on the Standard toolbar to restore your last undone action.

▶ Click the Redo drop-down arrow to see a list of recently undone actions that can be restored. When you select an action to repeat, Excel will redo that action and all actions above it.

STORING CELL CONTENTS

Often, you might want to use data that you have already entered on your worksheet. You can cut it or copy it, and then paste it in another location. When you cut or copy data from non-Office programs, the data is placed in the Windows Clipboard. When you paste a range of cells from the Clipboard, you need to specify only the first cell in the new location. After you select the first cell in the new location and then click the Paste button on the toolbar, Excel automatically places all the selected cells in the correct order. Depending on the number of cells you select before you cut or copy, Excel pastes data in one of the following ways:

One to one   Excel pastes a single cell in the Clipboard to one cell location.

One to many   Excel pastes a single cell in the Clipboard into a selected range of cells.

Many to one   Excel pastes many cells into a range of cells, but only the first cell is identified. Excel will paste the entire contents of the Clipboard starting with the selected cell. Make sure there are enough cells for the selection; if not, the selection will copy over any previously occupied cells.

Many to many   Excel pastes many cells into a range of cells. Excel will paste the entire contents of the Clipboard into the selected cells. If the selected range is larger than the selection, the data will be repeated in the extra cells. To turn off the selection marquee and cancel your action, press the Esc key on the keyboard.

Copy Data to the Office Clipboard

1. Choose Edit ➤ Office Clipboard. The Clipboard task pane opens.

2. Select the data you want to copy.

3. Click the Copy button on the Standard toolbar. The data is copied into the first empty position on the Clipboard task pane.

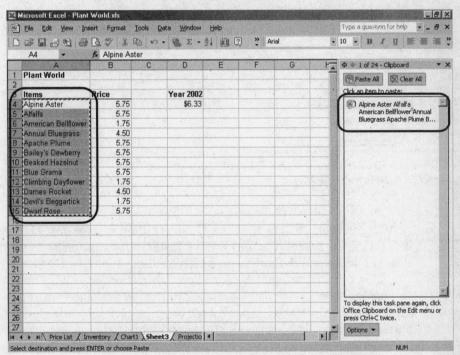

4. Click the Close button on the Clipboard task pane.

Paste Data from the Office Clipboard

1. Choose Edit ➤ Office Clipboard.

2. Click the first cell where you want to paste data.

3. On the Clipboard task pane, click the item you want to paste.

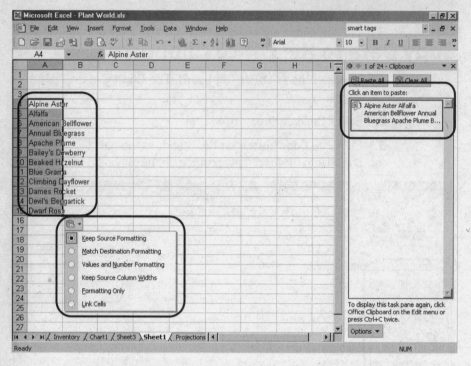

4. Click the Close button on the Clipboard task pane.

After you paste an item, the Paste Options button appears next to the item on the worksheet. You can click the Paste Options button to display a list of options on the shortcut menu. This button, known as a Smart Tag, allows you to immediately adjust how information is pasted or how automatic changes occur. For example, if you have a worksheet with specified column widths, you can paste a cell or range, click the Paste Options button, and then click Keep Source Column Widths to preserve the formatting of the column. Smart Tags and their associated choices vary depending on the operation.

TIP

To turn on or off Paste Options, choose Tools ➢ Options, click the Edit tab, click the Show Paste Options Buttons check box to select or clear it, and then click the OK button.

COPYING CELL CONTENTS

You can cancel a copy or a move while you are in the process of dragging the mouse by pressing the Esc key on the keyboard before you release the mouse button.

Copy Data Using the Standard Toolbar

You can copy and move data on a worksheet from one cell or range of cells to another location on any worksheet in your workbook. When you copy data, Excel places a duplicate of the selected cells in the Clipboard. To complete the copy or move, you must paste the data stored in the Clipboard in another location. With the Paste Special command, you can control what you want to paste and even perform mathematical operations. To copy or move data without using the Clipboard, you can use drag-and-drop. Drag-and-drop makes it easy to copy or move data short distances on your worksheet.

1. Select the cell or range that contains the data you want to copy.

2. Click the Copy button on the Standard toolbar. The data in the cells remains in its original location, and an outline of the selected cells, called a *marquee*, shows the size of the selection. If you don't want to paste this selection, press the Esc key on the keyboard to remove the marquee.

3. Click the first cell where you want to paste the data.

4. Click the Paste button on the Standard toolbar. The data remains on the Clipboard, available for further pasting until you replace it with another selection.

	Description	Type	Price	On Hand	Value	Item #
4	Alpine Aster	Perennial	5.75	15	$86.25	101
5	Alfalfa	Perennial	5.75	10	$57.50	102
6	American Bellflower	Annual	1.75	6	$10.50	103
7	Annual Bluegrass	Biennial	4.50	12	$54.00	104
8	Apache Plume	Perennial	5.75	24	$138.00	105
9	Bailey's Dewberry	Perennial	5.75	15	$86.25	106
10	Beaked Hazelnut	Perennial	5.75	10	$57.50	107
11	Blue Grama	Perennial	5.75	5	$28.75	108
12	Climbing Dayflower	Annual	1.75	6	$10.50	109
13	Dames Rocket	Biennial	4.50	2	$9.00	110
14	Devil's Beggartick	Annual	1.75	4	$7.00	111
15	Dwarf Rose	Perennial	5.75	12	$69.00	112
17	Alpine Aster	Perennial	5.75	15	$86.25	101

5. If you don't want to paste this selection anywhere else, press the Esc key on the keyboard to remove the marquee.

TIP

Use the Alt key to drag and drop to a different worksheet. Once cells are selected, hold down the Alt key, and then drag the selection to the appropriate sheet tab. Release the Alt key and drag the selection to the desired location on the new worksheet.

Copy Data Using Drag-and-Drop

1. Select the cell or range that contains the data you want to copy.

2. Move the mouse pointer to an edge of the selected cell or range until the pointer changes to an arrowhead.

3. Hold down the mouse button and the Ctrl key on the keyboard.

4. Drag the selection to the new location, and then release the mouse button and the Ctrl key.

Description	Type	Price	On-Hand	Value	Item #
Alpine Aster	Perennial	5.75	15	$86.25	101
Alfalfa	Perennial	5.75	10	$57.50	102
American Bellflower	Annual	1.75	6	$10.50	103
Annual Bluegrass	Biennial	4.50	12	$54.00	104
Apache Plume	Perennial	5.75	24	$138.00	105
Bailey's Dewberry	Perennial	5.75	15	$86.25	106
Beaked Hazelnut	Perennial	5.75	10	$57.50	107
Blue Grama	Perennial	5.75	5	$28.75	108
Climbing Dayflower	Annual	1.75	6	$10.50	109
Dames Rocket	Biennial	4.50	2	$9.00	110
Devil's Beggartick	Annual	1.75	4	$7.00	111
Dwarf Rose	Perennial	5.75	12	$69.00	112

A17:F17

Copied text appears here

Move Data Using the Clipboard

Unlike copied data, data that you move no longer remains in its original location. Perhaps you typed data in a range of cells near the top of a worksheet, but later realized it should appear near the bottom of the worksheet. Moving data lets you change its location without having to retype it. When you move data, you cut the data from its current location and paste it elsewhere. Cutting removes the selected cell or range content from the worksheet and places it in the Clipboard.

NOTE

When Excel displays the Clipboard task pane, you can move the selections that you cut into the Clipboard, and then paste them later.

1. Select the cell or range that contains the data you want to move.

2. Click the Cut button on the Standard toolbar. The marquee shows the size of the selection. If you don't want to paste this selection, press Esc on the keyboard to remove the marquee.

3. Click the top-left cell of the range where you want to paste the data.

4. Click the Paste button on the Standard toolbar. The marquee disappears. The data is still in the Clipboard; you can continue to paste it until you replace it with another selection.

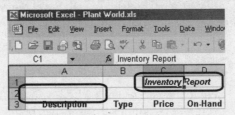

TIP

If the mouse pointer changes to a thick plus sign, reposition the pointer on the edge of the selected range until the pointer changes to an arrowhead, then drag and drop your selection.

Move Data Using Drag-and-Drop

1. Select the cell or range that contains the data you want to move.

2. Move the mouse pointer to an edge of the cell until the pointer changes to an arrowhead.

3. Hold down the mouse button while dragging the selection to its new location, and then release the mouse button.

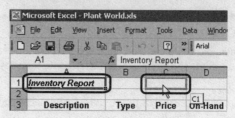

INSERTING AND DELETING CELLS

You can insert new, blank cells anywhere on the worksheet in order to enter new data or insert data that you forgot to enter earlier. Inserting cells moves the remaining cells in the column or row in the direction of your choice, and Excel adjusts any formulas so they refer to the correct cells. You can also delete cells if you find you don't need them; deleting cells shifts the remaining cells to the left or up—just the opposite of inserting cells. When you delete a cell, Excel removes the actual cell from the worksheet, not just the data it contains.

Insert a Cell

1. Select the cell or cells where you want to insert the new cell(s). For example, to insert two blank cells at the position of C10 and C11, select cells C10 and C11.

2. Choose Insert ➤ Cells. The Insert dialog box opens.

3. Choose the option you want.

    ▶ If you want the contents of cells C10 and C11 to move to cells D10 and D11, click the Shift Cells Right option button.

▸ If you want the contents of cells C10 and C11 to move to cells C12 and C13, click the Shift Cells Down option button.

By using either method, you will replace two blank cells with the data that was in cells C10 and C11.

4. Click the OK button.

Delete a Cell

Deleting a cell is different from clearing a cell: deleting removes the cells from the worksheet; clearing removes only the cell contents.

1. Select the cell or range you want to delete.

2. Choose Edit ➤ Delete. The Delete dialog box opens.

3. Choose the option you want.

▸ If you want the remaining cells to move left, click the Shift Cells Left option button.

▸ If you want the remaining cells to move up, click the Shift Cells Up option button.

4. Click the OK button.

Part iii

CHECKING YOUR SPELLING

Excel's AutoCorrect feature automatically corrects misspelled words as you type them. AutoCorrect includes hundreds of text and symbol entries you can edit or remove.

Add words and phrases that you misspell to the AutoCorrect dictionary, or add often-typed words and save time by just typing their initials. For example, you could use AutoCorrect to automatically change the initials *EPA* to *Environmental Protection Agency*. You can use the AutoCorrect Exceptions dialog box to control how Excel handles the punctuation in abbreviations and words with capital letters, and you can customize the correction of specific words.

Add an AutoCorrect Entry

1. Choose Tools ➤ AutoCorrect Options. The AutoCorrect dialog box opens.

2. In the Replace box, type a misspelled word or an abbreviation.

3. In the With box, type the replacement entry.

4. Click the Add button.

5. Repeat steps 2 through 4 for each entry you want to add.

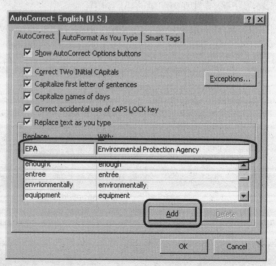

6. Click the OK button.

Edit an AutoCorrect Entry

1. Choose Tools ➤ AutoCorrect Options. The AutoCorrect dialog box opens.

2. Select the AutoCorrect entry you want to change. You can either type the first few letters of the entry to be changed in the Replace box, or scroll to the entry, and then click to select it.

3. In the With box, type the replacement entry.

4. Click the Replace button. If necessary, click the Yes button to redefine the entry.

5. Click the OK button.

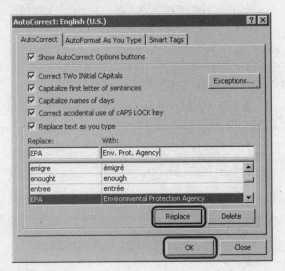

NOTE

To turn off AutoCorrect, choose Tools ➤ AutoCorrect, click the Replace Text As You Type check box to clear it, and then click the OK button.

TIP

To delete an AutoCorrect entry, choose Tools ➤ AutoCorrect, select the Auto-Correct entry you want to delete, and then click the Delete button.

Check Spelling

A worksheet's textual inaccuracies can distract the reader, so it's important that your text be error-free. Excel provides a spell checker so that you can check the spelling in an entire worksheet. You can even avoid future spelling errors on a worksheet by enabling the AutoCorrect feature to automatically correct words as you type.

1. Click the Spelling button on the Standard toolbar. The Spelling dialog box opens when it locates a word it doesn't recognize.

2. If the suggested spelling is unacceptable, or you want to use the original word, click the Ignore Once button to pass over this instance of the word, or click the Ignore All button to pass over all instances of the word.

3. If the suggested spelling is acceptable, click the Change button to change this instance, or click the Change All button to change every instance.

4. If you want to add a word to the custom dictionary, click the Add To Dictionary button.

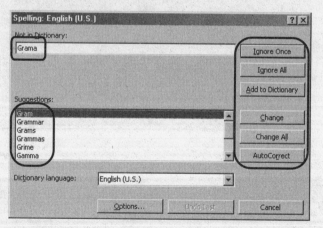

5. When the spell-check is complete, click the OK button.

TIP

To stop the spell checker at any time, click the Cancel button.

USING SMART TAGS

Smart Tags help you integrate actions typically performed in other programs directly in Excel. For example, you can insert a financial symbol to get a stock quote, add a person's name and address in a worksheet to the contacts list in Microsoft Outlook, or copy and paste information with added control. Excel analyzes the data you type in a cell and recognizes certain types that it marks with Smart Tags. The types of actions you can take depend on the type of data in the cell with the Smart Tag.

Get a Stock Quote Using a Smart Tag

1. Click a cell where you want to insert a stock quote.

2. Type a recognized financial symbol in capital letters.

3. Click outside the cell, and then point to the purple triangle in the lower-right corner of the cell to display the Smart Tag button. The purple triangle in the corner of a cell indicates a Smart Tag is available for the cell contents.

4. Point to the Smart Tag button, and then click the down arrow next to the button.

5. Click Insert Refreshable Stock Price. The Insert Stock Price dialog opens.

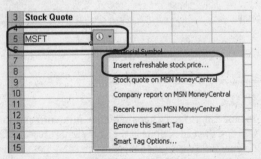

6. Click the On A New Sheet option button or the Starting At Cell option button, and then click the OK button.

Change Smart Tag Options

1. Choose Tools ➢ AutoCorrect Options. The AutoCorrect dialog box opens. Click the Smart Tags tab.

2. Click the Label Data With Smart Tags check box to select it.

3. Click the Show Smart Tags As drop-down arrow, and then click Button Only or Indicator And Button.

4. To check the worksheet for new Smart Tags, click the Check Workbook button.

5. To save all Smart Tags, click the Embed Smart Tags In This Workbook check box to select it.

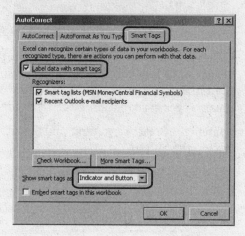

6. Click the OK button.

NOTE

To hide Smart Tags, choose Tools ➢ AutoCorrect Options, click the Smart Tags tab, and then click None in the Show Smart Tags As list. To discard Smart Tags, display the Smart Tags tab, click the Label Data With Smart Tags check box to clear it, and click the Embed Smart Tags In This Workbook check box to clear it.

TIP

Check for new Smart Tags. You can find additional Smart Tags on the Web. Choose Tools ➢ AutoCorrect, click the Smart Tags tab, and then click the More Smart Tags button to display a web page with a listing of Smart Tags.

SELECTING AND NAMING A WORKSHEET

By default, each new workbook you open contains three worksheets, although you can add additional sheets. You can easily switch among the sheets to enter or modify related information, such as budget data for separate months. Whichever sheet you are working on is the *active sheet*. Excel names each sheet consecutively—Sheet1, Sheet2, Sheet3, and so on. When you can, rename a sheet to give it a more meaningful name; the size of the sheet tab adjusts to accommodate the name's length, up to 30 characters.

TIP

Although the size of a sheet tab can expand to display a long tab name, a shorter tab name ensures that more sheet tabs will be visible. Being able to see all the sheet tabs is especially important if your workbook contains several worksheets.

Select a Worksheet

1. Move the mouse pointer over the sheet tab of the worksheet you want to make active.

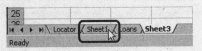

2. Click the sheet tab of the worksheet you want to make active.

Name a Worksheet

1. Double-click the sheet tab of the worksheet you want to name.

2. Type a new name. Excel automatically replaces the current name, which is selected when you begin typing.

3. Press the Enter key on the keyboard.

Color a Worksheet Tab

1. Right-click the sheet tab of the worksheet you want to color.

2. Select Tab Color from the pop-up menu. The Format Tab Color dialog box opens.

3. Click a color box.

4. Click the OK button.

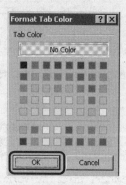

Insert a Worksheet

You can add or delete sheets in a workbook. If, for example, you are working on a project that requires more than three worksheets, you can insert additional sheets in one workbook rather than open multiple workbooks. If, on the other hand, you are using only one or two sheets in a workbook, you can delete the unused sheets to save disk space.

1. Click the sheet tab of the worksheet to the right of where you want to insert the new sheet.

2. Choose Insert ➤ Worksheet. Excel inserts a new worksheet to the left of the selected worksheet.

Delete a Worksheet

1. Click the sheet tab of the worksheet you want to delete, or click any cell on the sheet.

2. Choose Edit ➤ Delete Sheet.

3. Click the Delete button to confirm the deletion.

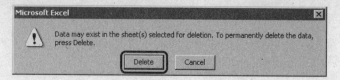

Move a Worksheet within a Workbook

After adding several sheets to a workbook, you might want to reorganize them. You can arrange sheets in chronological order or in order of their importance. You can easily move or copy a sheet within a workbook or to a different open workbook. Copying a worksheet is easier and often more convenient than reentering similar information on a new sheet.

NOTE

To insert a background image in your worksheet, click the sheet tab in which you want to insert a background, and then choose Format ➤ Sheet ➤ Background. Select the picture you want to use as a background, and then click the Insert button. The background image is visible only in that worksheet and will not print.

1. Click the sheet tab of the worksheet you want to move, and then hold down the mouse button.

2. When the mouse pointer changes to a sheet of paper, drag it to the right of the sheet tab where you want to move the worksheet.

3. Release the mouse button.

TIP

In order to copy or move a sheet to a different workbook, you must first open the other workbook, and then switch back to the workbook whose sheet you want to copy or move.

Copy a Worksheet

1. Click the sheet tab of the worksheet you want to copy.

2. Choose Edit ➤ Move Or Copy Sheet. The Move Or Copy dialog box opens.

3. If you want to copy the sheet to another open workbook, click the To Book drop-down arrow, and then select the name of that workbook. The sheets of the selected workbook appear in the Before Sheet list.

4. Click a sheet name in the Before Sheet list. Excel inserts the copy to the left of this sheet.

5. Click the Create A Copy check box to select it.

6. Click the OK button.

WORKING WITH COLUMNS OR ROWS

You can select one or more columns or rows in a worksheet in order to apply formatting attributes, insert or delete columns or rows, or perform other group actions. The *header buttons* above each column and to the left of each row indicate the letter or number of the column or row. You can select multiple columns or rows even if they are noncontiguous.

Select a Column or Row

▸ Click the column or row header button of the column or row you want to select.

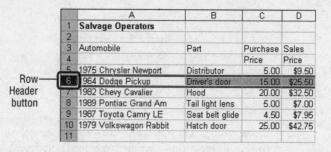

Row Header button

Select Multiple Columns or Rows

1. Drag the mouse over the header buttons of any contiguous columns or rows you want to select.

Column Header buttons

	A	B	C	D
1	Salvage Operators			
2				
3	Automobile	Part	Purchase	Sales
4			Price	Price
5	1975 Chrysler Newport	Distributor	5.00	$9.50
6	1964 Dodge Pickup	Driver's door	15.00	$25.50
7	1982 Chevy Cavalier	Hood	20.00	$32.50
8	1989 Pontiac Grand Am	Tail light lens	5.00	$7.00
9	1987 Toyota Camry LE	Seat belt glide	4.50	$7.95
10	1979 Volkswagon Rabbit	Hatch door	25.00	$42.75
11				
12				

2. To select noncontiguous columns or rows, hold down the Ctrl key on the keyboard while clicking each additional column or row header button.

Select an Entire Worksheet

▶ Click the Select All button. Excel selects all of the cells in the worksheet, including those cells that do not contain data.

Select All button

Insert a Column or Row

You can insert blank columns and rows between columns and rows on a worksheet without disturbing any existing data. Excel repositions existing cells to accommodate the new columns and rows, and adjusts any existing formulas so that they refer to the correct cells. When you insert one or more columns, Excel inserts them to the left of the selected column. When you add one or more rows, Excel inserts them above the selected row.

After you insert a column, row, or cell, the Insert Options button appears. You can click the Insert Options button to display additional formatting options, such as Format Same As Above, Format Same As Below, or Clear Formatting.

1. To insert a column, click anywhere in the column to the right of the location of the new column you want to insert. To insert a row, click anywhere in the row immediately below the location of the row you want to insert.

2. Choose Insert ➤ Columns (or Rows).

Part III

Excel inserts a new column to the left of the selected column; Excel inserts a new row above the selected row.

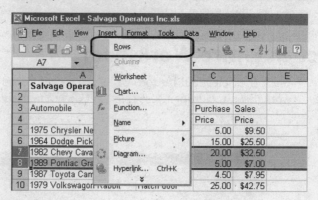

Insert Multiple Columns or Rows

1. To insert multiple columns, drag the column header buttons to the left or right for the number of columns you want to insert. To insert multiple rows, drag the row header buttons up or down for the number of rows you want to insert.

2. Choose Insert ➢ Columns (or Rows).

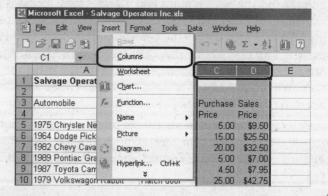

Delete a Column

At some time, you may want to remove an entire column or row from a worksheet, rather than deleting or editing individual cells. You can delete columns and rows just as easily as you insert them. You can choose whether the remaining columns and rows move to the left or move up to join the other remaining cells.

1. Click the column header button of the column(s) you want to delete.

2. Choose Edit ➢ Delete.

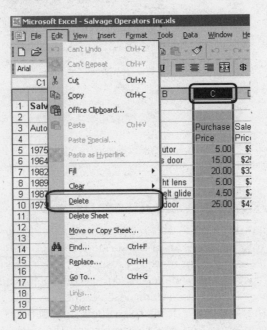

Delete a Row

1. Click the row header button of the row(s) you want to delete.

Part iii

2. Choose Edit ➤ Delete.

Hide/Unhide a Column or Row

You may not want all the data on a worksheet to be available to everyone. You can hide sensitive information without deleting it by hiding selected columns or rows. For example, you want to distribute a worksheet that includes employee information, such as addresses and phone numbers, but the main worksheet also includes their salaries. Rather than copy the worksheet, delete the column, and perhaps need to adjust formulas or formatting, you can simply hide the salary column.

Hiding columns and rows does not affect calculations in a worksheet; formulas still reference the data in hidden columns and rows. When you print the worksheet, the hidden columns and rows will not appear. When you save the workbook, the hidden rows or columns will not appear the next time you open it. You can unhide hidden data at any time.

1. Click the column or row header button of the column or row you want to hide. (Drag the mouse to select multiple header buttons to hide more than one column or row.)

2. Choose Format ➤ Column (or Row) ➤ Hide.

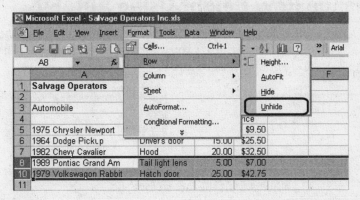

Unhide a Column or Row

1. Drag the mouse to select the column or row header buttons on either side of the hidden column or row.

2. Choose Format ➤ Column (or Row) ➤ Unhide.

Change Column Width Using AutoFit

As you build your worksheet, you'll want to change the default width of some columns or the default height of some rows to accommodate long strings of data or larger font sizes. Changing the width of a column or the height of a row will enhance the readability of your worksheet. You can manually change column widths or row heights, or you can use the Auto-Fit feature. Excel automatically adjusts column or row size to fit data you have entered.

1. Position the mouse pointer on the right edge of the header button of the column you want to adjust. The pointer changes to a double-headed arrow.

2. Double-click the mouse button. The column width automatically adjusts to fit the longest cell entry in the column.

NOTE

The Narrow Column screen tip shows you the value in a column that is too narrow to display its contents. If a value does not fit in the column, the value displays as "#####" in the cell.

Change Row Height Using AutoFit

1. Position the mouse pointer on the bottom edge of the header button of the row you want to adjust. The pointer changes to a double-headed arrow.

2. Double-click the mouse button. The row height automatically adjusts to fit the largest font size.

TIP

By default, each column in each worksheet is 8.43 points wide, and each row is 12.75 points high. A point is a unit of measurement used to size text and space on a worksheet. One inch equals 72 points.

Adjust Column Width or Row Height Using the Mouse

1. Position the mouse pointer on the right edge of the column header button or the bottom edge of the row header button for the column or row you want to change.

2. When the mouse pointer changes to a double-headed arrow, drag the pointer to a new width or height.

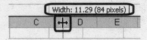

Freeze a Column or Row

Large worksheets can be difficult to work with, especially on low-resolution monitor settings or small monitor screens. When you scroll down to see the bottom of the worksheet, you can no longer see the column labels at the top of the worksheet, which makes it visually confusing to add or edit data. Instead of repeatedly scrolling up and down, you can temporarily fix, or *freeze*, your column or row headings so that you can see them no matter where you scroll in the list.

When you freeze a row or column, you are actually splitting the screen into one or more *panes* (window sections) and freezing one of the panes. You can split the screen into four panes and can freeze up to two of these panes. You can edit the data in a frozen pane just as you do any Excel data. The cells in a frozen pane remain stationary when you use the scroll bars; you can scroll only in the unfrozen portion of the screen.

1. Select the column to the right of the columns you want to freeze, or select the row below the rows you want to freeze. To freeze both the column and the row, click the cell to the right and below the column and row you want to freeze.

2. Choose Window ➢ Freeze Panes.

   ▸ When you freeze a pane horizontally, all the rows *above* the active cell freeze. When you freeze a pane vertically, all the columns to the *left* of the active cell freeze.

▶ When you freeze a pane, the printed version of your worksheet is not affected.

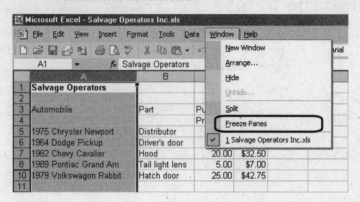

Unfreeze a Column or Row

▶ Choose Window ➢ Unfreeze Panes.

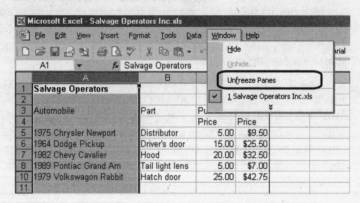

INSERTING AND MOVING PAGE BREAKS

If you want to print a worksheet that is larger than one page, Excel divides it into pages by inserting *automatic page breaks*. Excel breaks pages based on the paper size, margin settings, and scaling options you set. You can change the rows or columns that are printed on the page by inserting *horizontal* or *vertical page breaks*. In *Page Break Preview,* you can view the page breaks and move them by dragging them to a different location on the worksheet.

NOTE

To remove a page break, select the column or row next to the page break, and then choose Insert ➢ Remove Page Break.

Insert a Page Break

1. To insert a vertical page break, click the column header button to the right of the location where you want to insert a page break.

   Other page break options include a horizontal page break and a new page break.

   Horizontal page break . Click the row header button below the location where you want to insert a page break.

   New page break Click the cell below and to the right of the location where you want a new page.

2. Choose Insert ➢ Page Break.

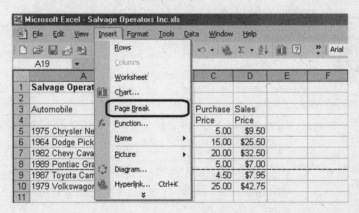

Part iii

Preview and Move a Page Break

1. Choose View ➤ Page Break Preview. Page Break Preview opens.

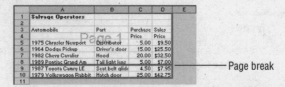
Page break

2. To move a page break to a new location, place the mouse pointer over the page break, and then drag the line to a new location.

3. Choose View ➤ Normal to return to normal editing mode.

SETTING UP THE PAGE

You can set up the worksheet page to print just the way you want. With the Page Setup dialog box, you can choose the *page orientation*, which determines whether Excel prints the worksheet data vertically or horizontally. You can also adjust the *print scaling* (to reduce or enlarge the size of printed characters), change the *paper size* (to match the size of paper in your printer), and resize or realign the left, right, top, and bottom *margins* (the blank areas along each edge of the paper).

NOTE

Changes made in the Page Setup dialog box are not reflected in the worksheet window. You can see them only when you preview or print the worksheet.

1. Choose File ➤ Page Setup. The Page Setup dialog box opens.

2. Click the Page tab.

3. Click the Portrait (8.5 × 11 inches) option button (the default) or the Landscape (11 × 8.5 inches) option button to select page orientation.

4. Click the OK button.

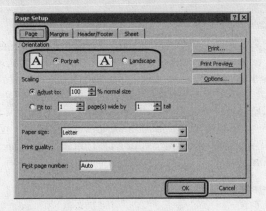

Change the Margin Settings

1. Choose File ➤ Page Setup. The Page Setup dialog box opens.

2. Click the Margins tab.

   ▶ Click the Top, Bottom, Left, and Right up or down arrows to adjust the margins.

   ▶ Click the Center On Page check boxes to automatically center data relative to the left and right margins (horizontally) or the top and bottom margins (vertically).

3. Click the OK button.

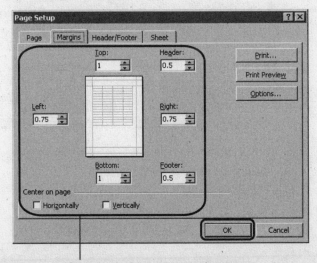

Select the check boxes to center data on page

Part iii

Change a Header or Footer

Adding a header or footer to a workbook is a convenient way to make your printout easier for readers to follow. Using the Page Setup dialog box, you can add information such as page numbers, the worksheet title, or the current date at the top and bottom of each page or section of a worksheet or workbook. Using the Custom Header and Custom Footer buttons, you can include information such as your computer's system date and time, the name of the workbook and sheet, a graphic, and other custom information.

TIP

To preview the header and footer, click the Print Preview button on the Standard toolbar.

1. Choose File ➤ Page Setup. The Page Setup dialog box opens.

2. Click the Header/Footer tab.

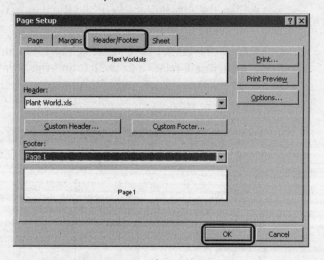

3. If the Header box doesn't contain the information you want, click the Custom Header button.

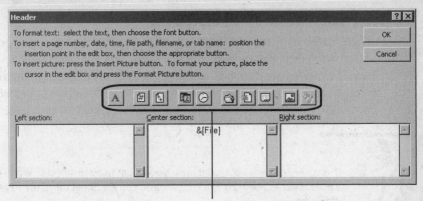

Type custom header text in a section or press an icon to insert a built-in option

4. Type the information in the Left, Center, or Right Section text boxes, or click a button to insert built-in header information. If you don't want a header to appear at all, delete the text and codes in the text boxes.

5. Select the text you want to format, and then click the Font button. The Font dialog box opens. Excel will use the default font, Arial, unless you change it.

6. Click the OK button.

7. If the Footer box doesn't contain the information you want, click the Custom Footer button.

8. Type information in the left, middle, or right text boxes, or click a button icon to insert the built-in footer information.

9. Click the OK button, then click the OK button in the Page Setup dialog box.

   ▶ To insert a picture in a header or footer, choose View ➤ Header And Footer, click the Customer Header or Custom Footer button, click the Insert Picture button, and then double-click a picture.

Print Part of a Worksheet

When you're ready to print your worksheet, you can choose several printing options. You can print all or part of any worksheet and control the appearance of many features, such as whether gridlines are displayed, whether column letters and row numbers are displayed, and whether to include *print titles*, which are the columns and rows that repeat on each page.

TIP

If you have already set a print area, you do not need to select it. When you set a print area, it appears in the Print Area box on the Sheet tab of the Page Setup dialog box.

1. Choose File ➤ Page Setup. The Page Setup dialog box opens.

2. Click the Sheet tab.

3. Click in the Print Area box, and then type the range you want to print. You can also click the Collapse Dialog button, select the cells you want to print, and then click the Expand Dialog button to restore the dialog box.

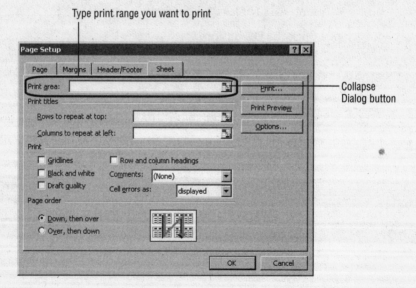

4. Click the OK button.

Print Row and Column Titles on Each Page

1. Choose File ➤ Page Setup. The Page Setup dialog box opens.

2. Click the Sheet tab.

3. Enter the number of the row or the letter of the column that contains the titles. You can also click the appropriate Collapse Dialog button, select the row or column with the mouse, and then click the Expand Dialog button to restore the dialog box.

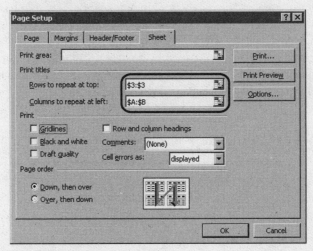

4. Click the OK button.

TIP

If you want columns or rows to print on every page, enter them in the Print Titles rows and columns text boxes. Do not include them in the cell range you enter in the Print Area box. If you enter them twice, Excel will print them twice on the first page.

NOTE

To adjust the size of printed characters, click the Adjust To up or down arrow to set the percentage size. When you click the Fit To up or down arrow to specify the number of pages on which you want the worksheet to be printed, the size of the printed characters will adjust accordingly.

Set the Print Area

The section of your worksheet that Excel prints is known as the *print area*. You can set the print area when you customize worksheet printing or any time when you are working on a worksheet. For example, you might want to print a different range in a worksheet for different people. In order to use headers and footers, you must first establish, or *set*, the print area. You can design specific headers and footers for a specific print area. The print area can consist of a single cell or a contiguous or noncontiguous range.

1. Select the range of cells you want to print.

2. Choose File ➤ Print Area ➤ Set Print Area.

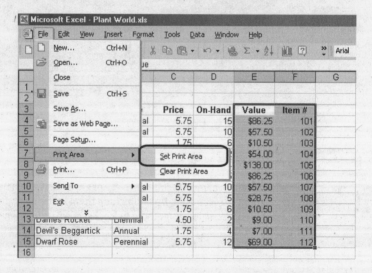

Clear the Print Area

▶ Choose File ➤ Print Area ➤ Clear Print Area.

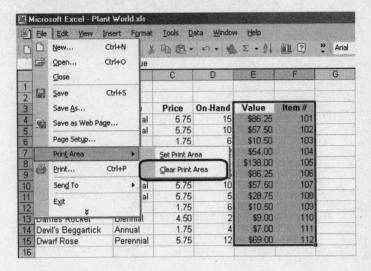

WHAT'S NEXT

In the next chapters of the book, we begin to delve deeper into the Excel workbook and functions. The next chapter tackles one of the topics that gives new workbook users the most trouble: creating and performing calculations.

Chapter 9

CALCULATING WITH FUNCTIONS

S preadsheet- and worksheet-based programs such as Excel aren't simply there to allow you to enter numbers and dollar amounts in static fashion—although you can do that, too.

Instead, these programs permit you to perform calculations and apply formulas to information you enter, so that the same calculation or function can be applied to a particular piece of data even when the actual numbers you plug in change. For example, if you always have to divide a specific sales figure by 3 and that sales figure changes each month, you can set up a cell to always divide whatever number you plug in by the number 3.

This chapter will help you familiarize yourself with the use of calculations in Excel as well as show you how to work with functions—prebuilt code that you use as part of a worksheet formula.

Adapted from *Mastering Microsoft Excel 2002*
by Gini Courter and Annette Marquis
ISBN 0-7821-4002-5   928 pp $39.99

Please note, however, that we can cover only some of over 300 built-in functions that Excel offers directly through Office XP, not to mention other specialized functions that you can buy from third-party companies.

USING FUNCTIONS

Functions—such as SUM, COUNT, AVERAGE, MIN, and MAX—are used to calculate results used in statistics, finance, engineering, math, and other fields. *Functions* are structured programs that calculate a specific result: a total, an average, the amount of a monthly loan payment, or the statistical mean of a group of numbers. Each function has a specific order, or *syntax,* that must be used for the function to work properly.

Functions are formulas, so all functions begin with the equal sign (=). The equal sign is followed by the *function name,* followed by zero, one, or more *arguments* separated by commas and enclosed in parentheses:

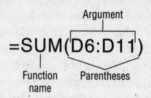

Excel's functions are grouped into the 10 categories listed in Table 9.1.

TABLE 9.1:   Excel Function Categories

CATEGORY	EXAMPLES
Financial	Calculate interest rates, loan payments, depreciation amounts, and so on; additional financial functions are included in the Analysis ToolPak add-in for Excel.
Date & Time	Return the current hour, day of week or year, time, or date from the system clock; convert text dates or strings to dates.
Math & Trig	Calculate absolute values, cosines, logarithms.
Statistical	Calculate totals, averages, and high and low numbers in a range; advanced functions for t-tests, Chi tests, and deviations.
Lookup & Reference	Search for and return values from a range; create hyperlinks to network or Internet documents.
Database	Calculate values in an Excel database table.

TABLE 9.1 CONTINUED: Excel Function Categories

CATEGORY	EXAMPLES
Text	Convert text to uppercase or lowercase, trim characters from the right or left end of a text string, concatenate text strings.
Logical	Evaluate an expression and return a value of TRUE or FALSE; used to trigger other actions or formatting.
Information	Return information from Excel or Windows about the current status of a cell, object, or the environment.
Engineering	Convert numbers from binary to hexadecimal to octal to decimal; work with complex numbers and Bessel functions; included with Excel, but must be installed separately from the Analysis ToolPak.

You don't have to learn all the functions—but you should know the common functions thoroughly and know enough about other functions that you can find them as you need them. The AutoSum functions (SUM, COUNT, AVERAGE, MIN, and MAX) are the only functions included on the Standard toolbar. You can access all the functions (including the AutoSum functions) by using the Insert Function button on the formula bar or by selecting More Functions on the drop-down menu attached to the AutoSum button.

While there are methods and shortcuts for entering functions in formulas, you'll always follow these general steps:

1. Decide which function to use.

2. Type or select the function.

3. Enter required and optional arguments for the function.

Entering Functions

 Before entering a function, click in the cell where you want the results to be displayed. When you are comfortable with the syntax of a function, you can simply type the function in the cell. For functions that you rarely use or for complex functions, use the function tools supplied by Excel. Click the Insert Function button on the formula bar to open the Insert Function dialog box, shown in Figure 9.1.

Part iii

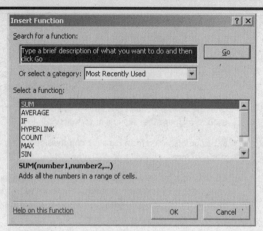

FIGURE 9.1: Locate and choose functions in the Insert Function dialog box.

Selecting and Finding Functions

If you know the category of the function you need to use, select it from the Or Select A Category drop-down list. If you know the function's name but not the category, choose the All option in the Or Select A Category drop-down list. Choose the function in the Select A Function pane, and then click OK to begin entering arguments.

If you're not sure which function to use, enter some information about what you're attempting to do in the Search For A Function text box. Click Go to search for functions, as shown in Figure 9.2.

Click the function name in the Select A Function list to display the function's syntax and description below the pane. If you need help, click the Help On This Function hyperlink to display the Excel help page on the selected function. When you've located the function you want to use, click the OK button.

Choosing a Function from the Formula Bar

If you've recently used the function you want, type = to start the formula. The Name box will change to a Function box, displaying the name of the last function that was entered from the list of functions. In Figure 9.3, IF was the last function used. Click the Function drop-down arrow to open the list of recently used functions.

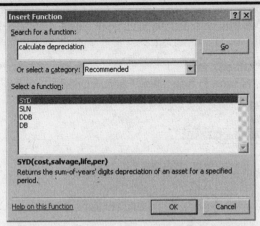

FIGURE 9.2: Enter a description of what the function needs to do, then click Go to search for functions.

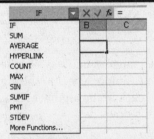

FIGURE 9.3: Click the Function drop-down arrow to display the most recently used functions.

If the function you want is on the list, select it. If the function you want is not listed in the Function box, choose More Functions at the bottom of the list to open the Insert Function dialog box (refer to Figure 9.2).

Entering Function Arguments

When you select a function, Excel moves that function to the formula bar and opens the Function Arguments dialog box. The dialog box displays a description of the function and one or more text boxes for the function's arguments, as shown in Figure 9.4. For common functions that use a single range of cells as an argument, Excel will guess which numbers you might want to use and place the range in the argument text box. Required arguments are bold, like **Number 1** in Figure 9.4. These text boxes must be filled in to successfully use the function.

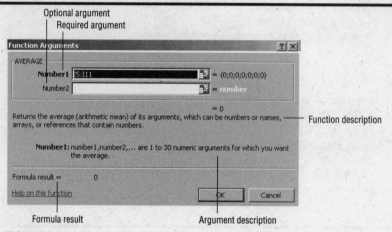

FIGURE 9.4: In the Function Arguments dialog box, the required argument for the AVERAGE function is shown in bold.

An argument for a function can be a cell range or address, another function, or a constant. To enter a constant, simply type it in the argument text box. To enter another function, click in the argument box, then choose the function from the Function drop-down list.

NOTE

When you use a function as a function argument, you create a nested function. You'll find out more about nested functions in Chapter 10, "Working with Text and Dates."

    To enter ranges as arguments, click in the argument text box and either type the range or select it in the worksheet. In Figure 9.4, you can't tell whether the range in the Number 1 text box is correct, because the Function Arguments dialog box covers the cells. Click the Collapse Dialog button to shrink the Function Arguments dialog box.

    Confirm that the correct cells are selected or use the mouse to select the correct cells before expanding the palette with the Expand Dialog button. After you have selected all the required arguments, click OK to finish the entry and close the Function Arguments dialog box.

As you enter arguments, the current value for the argument is displayed to the right of the text box. The formula result appears below the text boxes.

As with any formula, the result of the function is displayed in the active cell. The function itself is displayed on the formula bar when the cell is active.

These steps summarize how to use Excel functions:

1. Click in the cell where you want the result of the function to appear.

2. Type =. Choose a function from the Recently Used Functions list. If the function does not appear on the list, choose More Functions; or click the Insert Function button on the formula bar; or choose More Functions from the AutoSum drop-down menu to open the Insert Function dialog box.

3. Choose a category from the drop-down list and a function from the Select A Function pane. Click OK to open the Function Arguments dialog box.

4. In the Function Arguments dialog box, select the text box for the first argument. To enter cell ranges, click the Collapse Dialog button if necessary, and then select the cells you want to include in the argument. Click the Expand Dialog button to return to the Function Arguments dialog box. Type constants or open the Function box and select another function. Repeat this step for all required arguments and any optional arguments you need to use.

5. Click OK to complete the entry and close the Function Arguments dialog box.

TIP

Sometimes it's easiest to refer to an entire column or row in an argument if any entry in the column or row should be included in the formula. If, for example, you want to add every entry in column G, you don't need to specify G1:G65536. To include all cells in column G, use the range reference G:G. Likewise, use 1:1 to refer to every cell in row 1.

Relative and Absolute Cell References

When you copy a formula from one cell to another, Excel automatically adjusts each cell reference in the formula. If, for example, the formula in cell J15 is =H15+I15 and you copy the formula to J16, it is automatically adjusted to =H16+I16. In this example, H15 and I15 are *relative cell references*—references made by simply clicking in the cell or typing a cell address when creating a formula. The relative change from one row (15) to another (16) is reflected in the formula when the formula is copied: The rows in the cells are increased by one.

NOTE

When copying cells in Excel, it doesn't matter if you copy and paste, drag and drop, or drag the fill handle. Excel treats formulas the same way, regardless of the copy method you employ. You will, however, see different choices on the AutoFill Options button menu for the fill operation.

Most of the time, this is exactly what you want Excel to do. When you copy a formula from one column to another, you want Excel to adjust the column references. A copy from one row to another should result in a change in the row numbers used in the formula. However, there are exceptions.

For example, in the Undiscovered Country Travel worksheet shown in Figure 9.5, we would like to know the percentage of tickets sold for each destination city. We calculate a city's percentage by dividing the city's total into the grand total for all cities. In Figure 9.5, a formula was entered to divide the total Las Vegas package sales (217) into the grand total (633). The formula for Las Vegas is fine—but it's obviously wrong when copied to the other cities.

So what happened? The formula in F6 was =E6/E12. When the formula was filled from F6 to F7, Excel changed each cell reference, just as it did when we filled the totals in column E.

NOTE

Excel 2002 makes it easy to see what went wrong in a formula. See "Finding and Fixing Formula Errors" later in this chapter.

	A	B	C	D	E	F
1	Undiscovered Country Travel					
2	Destination Package Sales					
3						
4	Destination	April	May	June	Q2 Total	Percent of Total
5						
6	Las Vegas	102	70	45	217	34%
7	Luxor Cruise	14	14	14	42	#DIV/0!
8	Antigua/Tikal	41	33	33	107	#DIV/0!
9	Orlando Express	34	48	45	127	#DIV/0!
10	Daytona	87	34	19	140	#DIV/0!
11						
12	Totals	278	199	156	633	

Incorrect results
Correct results

FIGURE 9.5: The formula in cell F6 was correct, but yielded wrong results when copied down the column.

The formula in F7 was changed to =E7/E13, and the change from E12 to E13 created the problem. Rather than dividing the Luxor Cruise total into the total for all destinations, it divided it into the nonvalue in cell E13. The formulas for the other destinations have a similar problem.

When you fill this formula, you want E6 to change to E7 *relative* to the formula's new location, but you don't want E12 to change at all. The reference to E12 should be *absolute*—not changeable.

TIP

An Excel worksheet has two layers: a value layer, which is displayed in the worksheet window, and an underlying formula layer. When you select a worksheet cell, the cell's formula layer is displayed on the formula bar. You can toggle between the two layers by holding down the Ctrl key and pressing the accent key (`) to the left of the number 1.

Absolute Cell References

You can instruct Excel not to change the reference to E12 by making it an *absolute cell reference*. Absolute cell references are preceded with dollar signs: E12. The dollar signs lock in the cell reference so Excel doesn't change it if you fill or copy the formula to another cell.

The dollar sign in front of the E instructs Excel not to change the column; the dollar sign in front of the 12 locks in the row. So as you fill the

Part iii

formula to the other cities, E6 will change to E7, E8, and E9, but E12 will always be E12.

You create the absolute cell reference in the original formula. If you never intend to fill or copy a formula, you don't need to use absolute references, and they won't fix a formula that doesn't work correctly to begin with. (The original formula for Las Vegas in F6 worked just fine.) If you are typing the formula, just precede the column and row addresses with a $. You can also create the absolute cell reference using the F4 key, as you will see in the following steps.

TIP

Another way to handle this situation is by naming cell E12 (*QtrTotal* would be a good name) and using the name in the formula in F6. Names are always absolute, so when the formula is filled, the name will always refer to E12.

Follow these steps to create a formula that includes an absolute cell reference:

1. Place the cell pointer where you want the results of the formula to appear.

2. Begin entering the formula. After you click in the cell that should not change when the formula is copied, press the F4 key once to add $ to the row and column of the cell reference.

3. When the formula is complete, press Enter or click the green check mark on the formula bar.

When you fill the formula to the appropriate cells, the absolute cell reference will not change.

Mixed Cell References

You can also create a *mixed reference*, making part of a cell address absolute and part relative, by locking in either the column or the row. Use mixed references when you want to copy a formula down *and* across to have a reference change relatively in one direction but not in the other.

For example, E$5 will remain E$5 when copied down because the row reference is absolute, but it can change to F$5, G$5, and so on when copied across because the column reference is relative.

TIP

The Absolute key (F4) is a four-way toggle. The first time you press it, it locks both the column and row: E12. Press it again, and only the row is locked: E$12. The third time you press the Absolute key, the column is locked: $E12. Press it a fourth time, and both row and column are relative: E12.

Using Everyday Statistical Functions

Excel includes a fistful of complex statistical functions. Everyday functions that you may not think of as statistical functions are also included in the list, including all the functions on the AutoSum button:

COUNT   Returns the number of numbers in a range

COUNTA   Returns the number of entries, including text entries, in a range

AVERAGE   Sums the numbers in a range and divides the total by the number of numbers

MEDIAN   Another kind of average, returns the middle value in a range of numbers

MODE   Returns the value that occurs most frequently

MAX   Returns the largest value in a range

MIN   Returns the smallest value in a range

COUNT is used to calculate the number of cells that have values, including dates, in the specified range. If you want to count the number of entries including text entries in a range, use the COUNTA function rather than COUNT.

TIP

Subtract COUNT from COUNTA for the same range to find out how many cells are occupied with text rather than numbers.

AVERAGE returns a value called the *arithmetic mean*—the total of all the values in a range divided by the number of values in the range. When we talk about averages—bowling scores, test grades, speed on several typing tests—it's the arithmetic mean we're referring to. However, there are two other types of averages: MEDIAN and MODE. MEDIAN tells you which value is the middle value in a range, and MODE tells you which value occurs most frequently.

You can routinely use MEDIAN to test the usefulness of an AVERAGE. In a perfect bell curve, mean (AVERAGE), MEDIAN, and MODE are the same value. If MEDIAN and AVERAGE values are close to each other, then there aren't either too many incredibly high or too many incredibly low values in the range, or they offset each other. If the MEDIAN is much lower than the AVERAGE, there are some very high values that pull up the AVERAGE. A higher-than-average MEDIAN means that there are quite a few extremely low values.

NOTE

The AVERAGE function is SUM/COUNT on a range. The AVERAGEA function is SUM/COUNTA for a range, so each text value adds 1 to the divisor, but does not increase the SUM used as the dividend.

In Figure 9.6, we've used the SUM, COUNTA, COUNT, AVERAGE, AVERAGEA, MEDIAN, and MODE functions on the range of cells in D4:D18 to quickly report information about pledges for a company fundraiser:

SUM   The total in cell D20

COUNTA   The number of employees in G7

COUNT   The number of pledges in G8

AVERAGE   The average pledge in G9

AVERAGEA   The per-employee pledge in G10

MEDIAN and MODE   For the results in G11 and G12

Nonpledges are recorded as *None* in the worksheet, so the AVERAGE function returns the average of those who pledged to the fund-raising effort. If nonpledges had been recorded as zero, then the AVERAGE would include the nonpledges, dropping the average of the per-employee figure in G10, as there would be no text entries.

NOTE

The COUNTBLANK function returns the number of empty cells in a range.

	A	B	C	D	E	F	G
1	2000-2001 Gold Seal Pledges						
2							
3	Last Name	First Name	Department	Amount			
4	Adams	Abby	Admin	$ 100			
5	Benth	Greg	Production	$ 100			
6	Brown	Howard	HR	$ 50			
7	Candy	Chuck	Production	None		Employees	15
8	Fitzgerald	Elizabeth	Production	$ 100		Pledges	11
9	Griffin	Nancy	Admin	$ 250		Average	$ 145
10	Hing	Ellen	Production	None		Per employee	$ 107
11	Issacs	Helen	Production	$ 100		Median	$ 100
12	Jaimison	Mason	Admin	None		Mode	$ 100
13	Kzatz	Randall	Technical	$ 300			
14	Lieberman	Dave	Production	$ 150			
15	Main	Bill	Technical	None			
16	Stevens	John	Production	$ 100			
17	Swinzer	John	Production	$ 150			
18	Talus	Charles	Admin	$ 200			
19							
20			Total	$ 1,600			

FIGURE 9.6: The statistical functions can be used to quickly summarize results for reporting.

FINDING AND FIXING FORMULA ERRORS

Excel makes numbers look believable—even when results are so incorrect that no one should believe them. You can make two kinds of errors when creating a worksheet. One is a data entry error: typing the wrong number, misspelling a word or name, or forgetting to type both parentheses in a pair. Excel will let you know when you miss a parenthesis, but there is no software tool that can check to be sure you enter all your numbers correctly. Your experience and knowledge of historic values is the best guide.

Resolving Logical Errors

The other kind of error is a logical error: adding rather than subtracting or multiplying the wrong numbers. Some logical errors violate Excel's rules about how formulas are constructed and result in an error message in the cell or an interruption from the Office Assistant. Those errors are the easy ones to catch and correct and are discussed in the following section. But errors that don't violate Excel's internal logic are the really nasty ones, because nothing jumps out and says, "This is wrong!" If you are familiar with the data, you can check the logic yourself to make sure the results make sense. If you are not conversant with the data, find someone who is and review the worksheet with them.

Working with Error Codes

Excel has eight error codes that pop up in cells to let you know that a formula requires your attention. The first is the ###### error, which may be telling you that the data is too wide for the column or too tall for the row. This is easy to fix (hardly an error, but you get the idea). The codes, listed in Table 9.2, give you information about what caused the error.

TABLE 9.2:   Excel Error Codes

Error Code/Error Name	Causes
#####	1. Data is too wide for the cell.
	2. You subtracted one date from another, and the result is a negative number. Double-check your formula.
#DIV/0 (Divide by Zero)	The number or cell reference you divided by is either zero or blank. If you see this in cells you just filled, you needed an absolute cell reference in the original formula.
#N/A (Not Available)	1. You omitted a required argument in a function.
	2. The cell that contains the argument is blank or doesn't have the kind of entry the function requires.
#NAME	1. You misspelled the name of a range or function.
	2. You referred to a name that doesn't exist.
	3. You used text in a formula or format without putting it in quotes.
	4. You left out the colon in a range (B3:D7).
#NULL	You referred to an intersection that doesn't exist by using a space between two ranges in an argument.
#NUM	1. You used text or a blank cell in an argument that requires a number.

TABLE 9.2 CONTINUED: Excel Error Codes

ERROR CODE/ERROR NAME	CAUSES
	2. You entered a formula that creates a number too large or too small for Excel to handle.
#REF (Invalid Reference)	You deleted some cells that this formula requires, so the formula can't find the cell that it refers to. You may have deleted some cells by pasting other cells over them.
#VALUE	You entered text when a formula requires a number or a Boolean value (TRUE or FALSE).

Excel 2002 includes new tools to help you diagnose and fix errors. Let's return for a moment to the divide-by-zero error created by copying a relative formula (refer back to Figure 9.5).

Each of the four cells with errors has a green error indicator in the upper-left corner. Click any cell with an error indicator and an Error Options button appears. Select the button and open the button's menu to see the type of error, help on the error, and tools for further diagnosis:

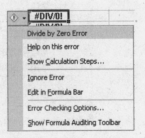

Choose Help On This Error to open the Excel help page covering divide-by-zero errors. Choose Show Calculation Steps to open the Evaluate Formula dialog box, shown in Figure 9.7. The dialog box displays the next calculation to be performed: in Figure 9.7, dividing 42 by 0. Click the Evaluate button and Excel will perform the calculation and show the result: #DIV/0!

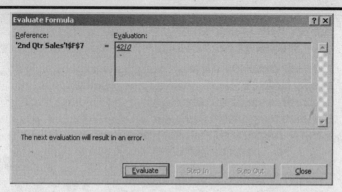

FIGURE 9.7: Use the Evaluate Formula dialog box to monitor the values as Excel steps through a calculation.

Choose Edit In Formula Bar from the Error Options button menu to open the formula for editing. In the case of a divide-by-zero error, use the Range Finder's color coding to locate the empty or zero-value cell that's used as a divisor, then drag the cell's range finder to the correct location:

Q2 Total	Percent of Total
217	34%
42	=E7/E13
107	#DIV/0!
127	#DIV/0!
140	#DIV/0!
633	

NOTE

Choose Error Checking Options to view or change the settings for error checking. For details on these options, see "Setting Error Checking Options" in the next section.

For errors that aren't as obvious, choose Show Formula Auditing Toolbar to access even more tools to help you fix your formula.

Using the Formula Auditing Toolbar

The Formula Auditing toolbar, shown in Figure 9.8, is a toolkit for formula repair. The toolbar has been greatly improved for Excel 2002 and includes features that were formerly available only in the Visual Basic Editor.

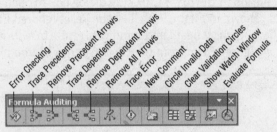

FIGURE 9.8: Use the Formula Auditing toolbar to diagnose worksheet errors.

Evaluating Errors

Click the Evaluate Formula button to open the Evaluate Formula dialog box, shown earlier in Figure 9.7.

Error Checking

Click the Error Checking button to check the worksheet for errors. If no errors are found, the following message box is displayed:

If errors are found, Excel opens the Error Checking dialog box, shown here:

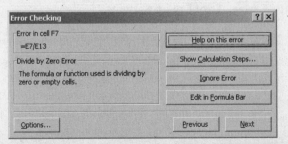

The dialog box offers the same options as the Error Options button menu, but has the advantage of Previous and Next buttons, which allow you to move through a series of errors more quickly.

Setting Error Checking Options

Click the Options button in the Error Checking dialog box to open the Options dialog box, shown in Figure 9.9. Click the Reset Ignored Errors button to check the worksheet again and reindicate errors in cells where you previously chose Ignore Error from the Error Options button menu.

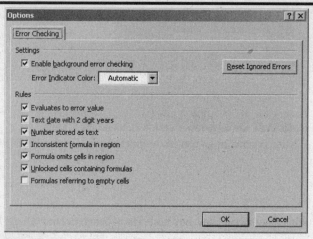

FIGURE 9.9: Use the Error Checking tab in the Options dialog box to work your way through a series of formula errors.

The dialog box settings determine the types of errors that Excel will recognize and mark with an error indicator and an Error Options button. The dialog box settings are detailed in Table 9.3.

TABLE 9.3: Error Option Settings

SETTING	DETAILS
Enable Background Error Checking	Allows Excel to check for errors automatically.
Error Indicator Color	The default is green; choose a different color from the palette if you wish.
Evaluates To Error Value	Checks for formulas that result in an error and displays error warnings.

TABLE 9.3 CONTINUED: Error Option Settings

SETTING	DETAILS
Text Date With 2 Digit Years	Checks for formulas in text-formatted cells with dates that use two-digit, rather than four-digit, years.
Number Stored As Text	Flags numbers preceded with apostrophes or formatted as text.
Inconsistent Formula In Region	Checks for formulas that differ from those that surround it; does not flag totals unless they are followed by another nontotal formula.
Formula Omits Cells In Region	Flags formulas that include most, but not all, cells in a region.
Unlocked Cells Containing Formulas	If a worksheet is protected, flags unlocked cells that contain formulas.
Formulas Referring To Empty Cells	Flags cells with formulas with precedent cells that are empty (disabled by default).

Select or clear check boxes to set the error-checking parameters. If you turn off background error checking, you can fire up error checking manually by choosing Tools ➢ Error Checking from the menu or by displaying the Formula Auditing toolbar (View ➢ Toolbars) and clicking the Error Checking button.

Tracing Errors Visually

If the source of an error isn't immediately apparent, select the cell with the error and click the Trace Error button on the Formula Auditing toolbar to show the formula's *precedents*—the cells used in the active cell's formula:

	A	B	C	D	E	F
1	Undiscovered Cou					
2	Destination Package S					
3						
4	Destination	April	May	June	Q2 Total	Percent of Total
5						
6	Las Vegas	102	70	45	217	34%
7	Luxor Cruise	14	14	14	42	#DIV/0!
8	Antigua/Tikal	41	33	33	107	#DIV/0!
9	Orlando Express	34	48	45	127	#DIV/0!
10	Daytona	87	34	19	140	#DIV/0!
11						
12	Totals	278	199	156	633	
13						

NOTE

If the Formula Auditing toolbar is not open, choose Tools ➤ Formula Auditing ➤ Trace Error to trace an error.

Dependents are cells with formulas that rely on the cell that has the error; *precedents* are the cells that are referenced, either directly or indirectly, in the error cell's formula. Click the Trace Precedents button and Excel will show you the precedent cells. Click the Trace Dependents buttons to see cells that depend on the active cell.

As you're working with precedents and dependents to diagnose an error, click the Remove Precedent Arrows or Remove Dependent Arrows button to remove one type of arrow but leave the other.

Click the Remove All Arrows button to hide both precedent and dependent arrows when you have diagnosed and corrected an error or need to clear the trace tools and start again.

Using the Watch Window

If you've worked in any of Microsoft's development environments, you'll be familiar with the Watch Window feature. The Watch Window is used to monitor the values of a cell's contents when values in precedent cells are changed; you can add multiple watches, so you can change the values in one cell and see the results in other parts of the worksheet or on other workbook sheets without scrolling or switching between worksheets. To use the Watch Window, click the Show Watch Window button on the Formula Auditing toolbar. A Watch Window with several watches is shown in Figure 9.10.

Book	Sheet	Name	Cell	Value	Formula
WellBuilt MFg.xls	F1707		E15	123,203	=E7-E13
WellBuilt MFg.xls	F1707		E13	311,094	=SUM(E10:E12)
WellBuilt MFg.xls	F1707		E7	434,297	=E5*E6

FIGURE 9.10: Use the Watch Window to monitor the results of formulas in one or more cells.

Click the Add Watch button to open the Add Watch dialog box. Select the cell you want to watch and click OK to add it to the Watch Window. The selected cell's location, current value, and formula are shown. Click Add to add the selected cell to the list in the Watch Window. When you change the value of a cell that the watched cell uses as a precedent, the value in the Watch Window changes.

To delete a watch, select the watch in the Watch Window and click the Delete Watch button. When you're finished with the Watch Window, click the window's close button.

TIP

The contents of the Watch Window are saved when the workbook is saved, so the next time you open the workbook, you can immediately check the cells you're monitoring in the window.

Resolving Circular References

Circular references are a special type of error. Circular references aren't passively flagged in the background—a circular error brings Excel to a screeching halt. A circular reference occurs when a formula refers to the cell that it is in. For example, when the formula =SUM(J15:J20) is entered in cell J20, Excel tries to add J20 to itself over and over again. Excel will iterate 100 times; then it will give up and show an error message letting you know you have a circular cell reference:

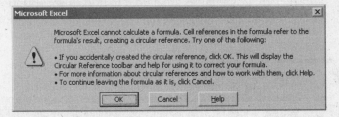

Click OK, and help opens with information about circular references. (Help opens only the first time you create a circular reference in a session.) Excel displays a blue dot next to the formula that created the circular reference and displays "Circular:" and the reference for the offending cell in the status bar. If help opened, clicking the cell with the circular reference opens the Circular Reference toolbar (or you can turn it on by choosing View ➤ Toolbars or right-clicking any toolbar).

If there's a circular cell reference anywhere in an open workbook, "CIRCULAR" appears on the status bar. Use the drop-down list on the Circular Reference toolbar to find the reference.

The drop-down list on the toolbar displays the current circular reference; clicking the drop-down arrow shows all the circular references in all open workbooks. The other three buttons on the toolbar are used to trace dependents and precedents and remove all trace arrows.

NOTE

See "Tracing Errors Visually" in the previous section for help with error tracing.

The precedent arrow shows that all the cells in the row, including the last cell, are included in the formula in the last cell. With circular errors, the problem is always a precedent—either the current cell address is included in the formula or, more indirectly, the current cell is used in a formula in one of the cells included in the current cell formula.

In the example we've used so far, the circular reference was easy to find, because the formula referred directly to the cell it was stored in. Indirect circular references are harder to find. Just continue clicking the Trace Precedents button, and you'll eventually find a formula that refers to the cell where the circular reference was reported.

TIP

If the cell with the circular reference is used explicitly in the offending formula, you can search for it using Find. Open the Find dialog box (Edit ➤ Find or Ctrl+F) and enter the cell address you're looking for: for example, J20. Find won't help if J20 is included in the middle of a range in the formula argument or if J20 is a named cell.

AUTOMATIC AND MANUAL CALCULATION

When you open a workbook, Excel automatically calculates the values for all workbook cells. When you change an entry in a worksheet, Excel automatically recalculates that cell and all of its dependents. You can continue to work while the worksheet recalculates in the background, but if your worksheet is very large with many formulas, recalculation takes a lot of Excel's attention, so it will be slower to respond to you.

You can turn off automatic recalculation in the Options dialog box. Choose Tools ➢ Options to open the Options dialog box and click the Calculation tab. The calculation options are shown in Figure 9.11.

There are three calculation modes:

▶ Automatic (the default mode)

▶ Automatic Except Tables

▶ Manual

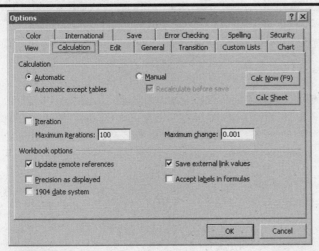

FIGURE 9.11: The calculation options determine when Excel recalculates worksheet values.

WARNING

If you choose Manual, you can turn off another automatic option, Recalculate Before Save, by disabling the check box. The calculation options affect all open workbooks.

If you choose Manual recalculation, Excel recalculates only when you force a calculation by pressing F9 or by opening the Options dialog box and clicking the Calc Now button. When you force a recalculation, Excel recalculates all open worksheets in all open workbooks. To recalculate only the current worksheet, hold Shift and press F9.

If you choose Automatic Except Tables, Excel automatically recalculates worksheets except for ranges occupied by data tables, which are used for analysis and forecasting. To recalculate data tables, force a recalculation of the current worksheet or all open worksheets as explained in the previous paragraph.

WHAT'S NEXT

Our next chapter will help you become proficient in adding and working with types of data that are not typical numbers or formulas: text and dates.

Chapter 10

WORKING WITH TEXT AND DATES

N ot all information you enter in Excel will be numbers or formulas to act on those numbers.

Text and dates, for example, are frequently added in Excel worksheets but must be treated as what they are, so that numbers contained within the text or date are not misinterpreted as numeric data.

Adapted from *Mastering Microsoft Excel 2002* by Gini Courter and Annette Marquis

ISBN 0-7821-4002-5   928 pp $39.99

WORKING WITH TEXT IN EXCEL

A chunk of text data is called a *string* or sometimes, redundantly, a *text string*. A string can be as short as a single character. Strings can include spaces, symbols, or numbers as well as uppercase and lowercase letters. Numbers formatted using the Text or Special formats in the Format Cells dialog box are text entries, as are cell contents preceded with an apostrophe.

NOTE
Excel includes more specialized functions for use with numbers and dates formatted as text. See "Converting Text to Dates" later in this chapter.

Removing Spaces and Nonprinting Characters

Spaces at the end of a text string entry are called *trailing spaces*, and those at the beginning are *leading spaces*. Trailing spaces can be accidentally added when a user hits the spacebar before moving to another column or field in any application. For a large number of extra spaces, however, nothing can compete with space-packed data exported from a mainframe database. Some mainframe programs export fixed-length fields of data and fill unused field lengths with blank spaces. For example, if the City field in a database is 15 characters wide, a 10-character city name will be followed by five spaces. If the exported data needs to be used to create mailing labels, the spaces must be removed or a large gap will appear between the city name and the state name.

Extra spaces in data are inconvenient and difficult to remove manually. You can't see them, and even if you could, manually deleting spaces is tedious work. If you use a find-and-replace operation, you risk deleting spaces within a string that shouldn't be removed. For example, if you replace all the spaces in the City column, you'll remove the space within a city (for example, the space between *Los* and *Angeles*) as well as the extra spaces (following *Angeles*). Removing leading and trailing spaces while retaining the spaces within a string is a task for the TRIM function.

The TRIM function strips only the leading or trailing spaces from a text string; the syntax is =TRIM(*string*). If, for example, cell C2 contains the text string Los Angeles followed by four spaces, the formula =TRIM(C2) will return Los Angeles without the extra spaces.

Function arguments can be constants or references to cells or, as with the SUM function, ranges of cells. For example, the string argument in the TRIM function can be a string typed in as part of the formula, =TRIM (" Los Angeles "), or a reference to a cell that contains a string, =TRIM(C2).

☐☐☐☐☐☐778☐ Nonprinting characters can't be printed or accurately represented in Excel, which displays them as empty rectangles. Nonprinting characters include printer and data instructions and are sometimes found at the beginning of imported data files. The CLEAN function, with the simple syntax =CLEAN(string), removes nonprintable characters from a string: for example, =CLEAN(C2).

COPYING THE RESULTS OF TEXT FUNCTIONS

If you create a formula with TRIM or CLEAN and then delete the cell that contains the original data (C2, in our examples), the formula will return an error. To preserve the results of the formula so you can delete the original data, you'll need to use a variation on copy-and-paste.

Begin by selecting and copying the cells with the text formulas. Click in an empty area of the worksheet where you want to paste the results of the formula, and then choose Edit ➤ Paste Special or right-click and choose Paste Special to open the Paste Special dialog box shown here:

Choose the Values option in the Paste section and click OK to paste the results of the formula beginning in the active cell. Now you can delete the cells that contain the original, untrimmed data. If you prefer, you can paste the values over top of the original, untrimmed data.

Parsing Data with LEFT, RIGHT, and MID

The LEFT and RIGHT functions return a specified number of characters from the beginning or end of a string. If, for example, you receive a mailing list with the city and two-character state abbreviation in one cell (see the sample in Figure 10.1), you can use RIGHT to list just the two-character abbreviation.

	A	B	C	D	E
1	Name	Address	City/State	MemberID	Phone
2	Olson, Diane	1414 Los Gatos Tr.	Los Angeles, CA	1977-DO1414	(213) 555-9867
3	Montgomery, Kay	459 Linwood Avenue	Detroit, MI	2001-KM0459	(313) 555-1234
4	Sinford, William	3901 Eastview St.	St. Paul, MN	1996-WS3901	(617) 555-2100
5	Spencer, Leon	2415 Williamston Dr.	Livonia, MI	1998-LS2415	(734) 555-7359

FIGURE 10.1: This spreadsheet contains useful data that can be massaged with text functions.

The syntax for the RIGHT function is =RIGHT(*string,number of characters*). To return the two-character state abbreviation from cell C5, use this formula: =RIGHT(C5,2).

This assumes, of course, that there aren't trailing spaces in the entries in column C. To strip spaces from the end of the combined City/State string in our example, first TRIM the string, then apply the RIGHT function: =RIGHT(TRIM(C5),2).

WORKING WITH NESTED FORMULAS IN EXCEL

The formula =RIGHT(TRIM(C5),2) contains a *nested function:* The results of the TRIM function are the first argument for the RIGHT function. You can easily enter nested functions in the Function Arguments dialog box. Start with the first function in the formula, the RIGHT function. Click the Insert Function (fx) button on the formula bar, then select RIGHT from the list of Text functions in the Insert Function dialog box.

When you click OK, the Function Arguments dialog box opens; in the formula bar, the function name RIGHT and the corresponding function punctuation are bold. In the Function Arguments dialog box, the text box for the first argument, Text, has focus:

CONTINUED ➡

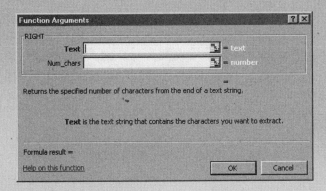

Open the drop-down list of functions (on the formula bar) and choose TRIM, or select More Functions to open the Insert Function dialog box and choose TRIM from the list of Text functions. When you close the Insert Function dialog box, the Function Arguments dialog box changes to display the arguments for the TRIM function, and the function TRIM is bold in the formula bar:

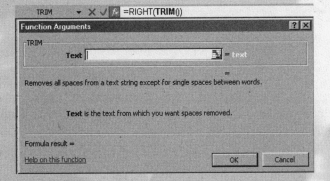

Click in cell C5 in the worksheet to enter the argument for the TRIM function. Use the formula bar to switch the function displayed in the Function Arguments dialog box. To display the arguments for the RIGHT function in the Function Arguments dialog box, click the RIGHT function name in the formula bar. Don't choose RIGHT from the drop-down list; this appends another RIGHT function. To display the argument for the TRIM function, click TRIM in the Function Arguments dialog box.

Excel supports up to nine levels of nesting in a formula.

Part iii

To return the area code (the first three characters) from a 10-digit phone number without parentheses, use =LEFT(*cell_address*,3). If the phone number includes parentheses around the area code like the numbers in column E of Figure 10.1, you have two choices. Use LEFT to retrieve five characters; the result will include the parentheses. To return the area code without parentheses, use the MID function. The syntax for the MID function is =MID(*string,starting with,number of characters*). =MID(E5,2,3) will return the second, third, and fourth characters in the telephone number in cell E5.

Using Functions to Change Case

If you're a Word user, you may miss the familiar Change Case command that appears on Word's Format menu. Excel's equivalents are the UPPER, LOWER, and PROPER functions, which convert a string to uppercase, lowercase, or proper case. Use UPPER to make a data set that contains uppercase and mixed-case entries consistent. The UPPER, LOWER, and PROPER functions use only one argument: the string you want to convert (in quotes) or the address for the cell that contains a string. If cell C2 contains the text Los angeles, CA:

▶ =UPPER(C2) returns LOS ANGELES, CA

▶ =LOWER(C2) returns los angeles, ca

▶ =PROPER(C2) returns Los Angeles, Ca

With the PROPER function, Excel converts the first letter and any letter that follows a symbol other than a letter (a space, a number, a hyphen) to uppercase. All other letters are lowercased, so the strings a and an are converted to A and An—not what you'd want in a title, but "proper" nonetheless. You can combine PROPER with RIGHT, LEFT, TRIM, MID, SEARCH (described in the next section), and other text-handling functions to apply the function to a portion of a text string.

Finding the Position of Text in a Cell

There are two functions used to locate a substring within a string: SEARCH and FIND. Both have the same basic form: =SEARCH(*substring,string to search,position to start*) and =FIND(*substring,string to search,position to start*). In both functions, the *position to start* argument is optional and is used to start searching partway into the string. FIND is the original text-searching function used in early versions of

Excel; SEARCH is a beefed-up version of FIND that supports the * and ? wildcards, described in this section.

NOTE

Because FIND can't use wildcards, you can use FIND to search for a string that contains a ? or * symbol. If the substring argument contains a question mark or asterisk symbol, but the string to search for does not, FIND returns an error.

Using SEARCH

The SEARCH function locates one string within another, so it can be used to find a single character in a string. The syntax for the function is =SEARCH (*string to find,string to search in,starting with character*); the result is the position of the string you want to find within the string you want to search. The final argument, *starting with character*, is optional. If you don't specify where Excel should start searching, it begins at the start of the string. For example, to find the comma character in the combined City/State string in cell C5 (see Figure 10.1), use =SEARCH (",",C5). Excel will return the value 8, because the comma is the eighth character in the string Livonia, MI.

TIP

The SEARCH function is not case sensitive.

SEARCH and LEFT can be combined to return only the city from the string in Figure 10.1 that includes the city name, a comma, and the state abbreviation. This is done by substituting the previously discussed SEARCH formula for the second argument in the LEFT function, which specifies how many characters to return: =LEFT(C5,SEARCH(",",C5)).

TIP

To determine the length of a text entry, use the LEN function. LEN returns the length of a string and has only one argument: the string or its cell address. An example would be =LEN(B15).

SEARCH supports wildcards, so you can use ? to search for a single character or * to search for more than one character. For example, =SEARCH ("UP?",J5) returns the starting position of the first three-character string beginning with UP that appears in J5.

If you need to search for a question mark or asterisk in a string, precede the ? or * with a tilde (~) symbol. =SEARCH("~?", J5) returns the position of the question mark symbol in the string in cell J5.

CONVERTING TEXT TO COLUMNS

Excel has another spiffy tool for massaging data: the Convert Text To Columns Wizard. The wizard is used to separate a column of data that has a delimiter—for example, a comma between the city and state or between last and first names, or a hyphen between a catalog number and an item number—or is fixed-length data.

Before invoking the Text To Columns command, save your worksheet. Insert a blank column (if needed) to hold the data you'll be splitting off. Select the column you want to split, and then choose Data ➢ Text To Columns from the menu to open the Convert Text To Columns Wizard. In the first step of the wizard, choose Delimited to split a column of data separated by a delimiter and click Next. In the second step of the wizard, shown here, choose the delimiter used in the data, or select Other and type the delimiter in the text box:

Convert Text to Columns Wizard - Step 2 of 3	? X

This screen lets you set the delimiters your data contains. You can see how your text is affected in the preview below.

Delimiters
☐ Tab   ☐ Semicolon   ☑ Comma   ☐ Treat consecutive delimiters as one
☐ Space ☐ Other: [ ]   Text qualifier: [" ▼]

Data preview

Los Angeles	CA
Detroit	MI
Cambridge	MA
Livonia	MI

Cancel   < Back   Next >   Finish

The wizard will separate your data into columns based on the delimiter you select. If, for example, you select a comma as a delimiter, Excel will place the data AAA, ,CCC into three columns, and remove the commas. The text AAA will appear in the first column, the second column will be blank, and CCC will be placed in the third column. If you enable the Treat Consecutive Delimiters As One check box,

CONTINUED ➡

the two commas will be treated as one, and CCC will be placed in the second column.

When you've set your delimiters and the check box, click the Next button. In the third step of the wizard, select a format for each column of data and a destination for the columns of separated data:

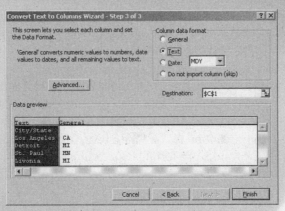

If you don't specify a destination, the first column of data is placed in the original column, and the remaining columns are placed to the right of the original column. If the columns to the right of the original column aren't empty, you'll be prompted to overwrite them. Click OK to convert the text into separate columns of data.

If the form of the data you want to convert is very consistent, you can use the Treat Consecutive Delimiters As One option to strip out spaces that follow delimiters. In column A of our sample worksheet (see Figure 10.1), which has last names followed by first names, we can set both the comma and the space as delimiters and enable the Treat Consecutive Delimiters As One check box. When Excel converts column A to text, both the comma and the space between the last and first names will be removed and the data will be placed in two columns. With the Treat Consecutive Delimiters As One option turned off, each first name in column B is preceded by a space (which can be removed with the TRIM function, but that requires an extra step or two). We can't do the same trick with the City/State data, however. Some city names include spaces (Los Angeles, St. Paul); if we treat spaces as delimiters, the data will be incorrectly separated into three, rather than two, columns.

Part iii

Putting Text Strings Together

Using the CONCATENATE function in Excel 2002, you can reassemble text strings as easily as you can tear them apart. *Concatenation* is addition for text; each string is appended to the end of the prior string. The arguments for the function are each of the strings you want to add together, separated by commas: =CONCATENATE(*string1,string2, string3*...). The strings can be cells or text entered in parentheses. To concatenate a first name in cell A10 with a last name in B10, use this formula: =CONCATENATE(A10," ",B10). The second argument, " ", puts a space between the two names.

If you're just concatenating a couple of fields, it's easier to use the symbol for concatenation: the ampersand (&). Place the ampersand in your formula between strings. This formula has the same result as the CONCATENATE formula in the previous paragraph: =A10&" "&B10.

Use concatenation to combine a text string with the contents of a cell to label the results of a formula: for example, in Figure 10.2, we've used the formula =CONCATENATE("Total Vehicle Expense: ",SUM(B5:B8)) to label the result of the SUM formula.

	A	B
4		
5	Fuel	$ 496
6	Repairs	$ 500
7	Insurance	$ 613
8	Maintenance	$ 90
9		
10	Total Vehicle Expense: 1699	

FIGURE 10.2: Use a concatenation formula to add a string to label cell contents.

Formatting Numbers in Strings

The result of the formula in cell B10 can't be used in other formulas: it's text, not a number. That also means it can't be formatted using the number-formatting tools like the Currency button on the Formatting toolbar. To format numbers within text, use the TEXT function, which has two arguments: the text you want to format and the numeric format to apply to the text, both enclosed in quotes. For example, the formula =CONCATENATE("Total Expenses: ",TEXT(SUM(B5:B8),"$#0.00") applies the custom format $#0.00 to the total of cells B5:B8.

	A	B
4		
5	Fuel	$ 496
6	Repairs	$ 500
7	Insurance	$ 613
8	Maintenance	$ 90
9		
10	Total Vehicle Expense:	$1699.00

TIP

You can use the Office Clipboard to swipe the formatting from another cell to use in the TEXT function. Before creating the formula that uses TEXT, select a cell with the format you wish to use. Open the Format Cells dialog box. On the Number page, select and copy (Ctrl+C) the contents of the Type text box. When you're creating the TEXT formula, paste (Ctrl+V) the format in the appropriate spot in the formula bar or Insert Function Argument text box.

Converting Text to Dates

When you import dates from other applications, they are often imported as text strings. You can easily tell that a date is text rather than a value by widening the column that the date appears in. Dates are numbers; therefore, dates are right-aligned by default. Text entries are left-aligned.

The DATEVALUE function converts a text string date to a serial value; the syntax of the function is =DATEVALUE(*text string date*). If the text string doesn't include a year (for example, June 8), Excel uses the current year, which is retrieved from the system clock.

NOTE

DATEVALUE converts the date to a serial value (see "Working with Dates and Times" later in this chapter), so it can be used only for dates from 1/1/1900 to 12/31/9999. If the date is outside that range, the function returns a #VALUE error.

Creating Day-of-the-Year (Julian) Dates

Another type of date, sometimes erroneously referred to as a *Julian date*, is a day-of-the-year date—a text string created by concatenating the current year with the number of days since the beginning of the year. For

Part iii

example, January 1, 2002, is represented as 2002001, where 2002 is the year and 001 is the first day of the year. The day-of-the-year date was originally used in large computer systems to provide ersatz dates that could be stored in a minimal amount of disk space, and added and subtracted more easily than text dates.

To create a day-of-the-year date, use the following formula, which assumes that the date being converted to a day-of-the-year date is in cell C2:

```
=TEXT(C2,"yyyy")&TEXT((C2-DATEVALUE
➥("1/1/"&TEXT(C2,"yy"))+1),"000")
```

NOTE

A modern Julian date (MJD) is the number of days and fractions thereof since noon on January 1, 4713 BCE. Julian dates are used in astronomy and, despite their name, have no relationship to the Julian calendar, which was used in western Europe until the 16th century, when it began being displaced by the Gregorian calendar currently used. The Julian calendar was devised, in part, by Julius Caesar; Julian dates were devised in 1582 by astronomer Joseph. J. Scaliger, who named them to honor his father, Julius Caesar Scaliger.

WORKING WITH DATES AND TIMES

When you enter dates, Excel generally recognizes them as dates. If, for example, you enter 1/31/2002, 1-31-2002, or October 31, 2002, Excel recognizes it as a date. When you enter a date, time, or date and time in a form that Excel 2002 recognizes as a date, Excel immediately does two things:

▶ Converts the entry to a serial value.

▶ Applies the Date/Time format that most closely reflects the form used to enter the cell contents. (If you've previously formatted the cell, the format you specified is applied.)

A *serial value* is the number of days since an imaginary date, January 0, 1900. January 1, 1900, is converted to serial value 1; January 2, 1900, is converted to 2. If you haven't changed Excel's default calculation settings, the serial value of 1/1/2001 is 36,892. Times are converted to fractions of a day, so 6 AM on January 2, 1900, would be converted to the serial value 2.25, one quarter of the way through the second serial day. To see the serial value for a date or time, format the cell with a non-Date/Time format like General.

NOTE

Serial values are often incorrectly assumed to be Julian dates.

Dates imported from another application may not fare as well; imported dates are often stored as text entries. Use the date and time conversion functions to convert text dates to number dates.

The fact that dates and times are numbers rather than text means you can add, subtract, and compare cells that contain dates or times. If you subtract 1/1/2002 from 1/2/2002, Excel performs a little sleight of hand and subtracts serial value 36,892 from serial value 36,893 to determine that there is one day between the two dates. The following are examples of date and time calculations you can complete in Excel:

▶ Subtracting today's date from a book's due date to see if it is overdue

▶ Adding days to a project's beginning date to calculate the date when the project should be completed

▶ Determining how many days fall between two dates

▶ Sorting dates in chronological order

▶ Subtracting the starting time for a task from the ending time to determine how long it took to complete the task

Before you can do these things, you need to make sure Excel recognizes the string you entered as a date so it can perform the serial value conversion.

NOTE

Date and time formats are applied on the Number page of the Format Cells dialog box (Format ➢ Cells).

Date/Time Forms That Excel Recognizes

Excel recognizes common date forms, including the date and time entries shown in column A in Figure 10.3. The dates and times in column C are not recognized as dates by Excel 2002.

	A	B	C
1	**Recognized as Dates**		**Not Recognized**
2	5/5/2002		May 5 2002
3	5/5		May/5/2002
4	5/5/02		Sunday, 2002
5	5-May		1 o'clock
6	37016		Sunday, May 5, 2002
7	5/5/02 1:00 PM		
8	1:00 PM		**Prompt for Recognition**
9	13:00		May-5-02

FIGURE 10.3: Excel recognizes a wide variety of date and time forms.

When you enter a date using the two-digit year format (see cell C9 in Figure 10.3), the cell is flagged with an error indicator. Select the cell and open the Error Options button's menu to convert the entry to a 1900 or 2000 date.

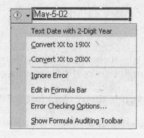

Entering Times

Use the colon symbol (:) to separate the hours, minutes, and seconds in a time entry. For times from midnight to noon, enter 0:00 through 12:00. For times after noon, either enter **PM** (1:00 PM, including a space between the time and PM) or use the 24-hour clock (13:00), or Excel assumes that they're AM times.

Not all times are clock times. Enter **3:00:30** for either 30 seconds after 3 AM or the duration 3 hours and 30 seconds. For both clock and nonclock time entries, you must enter hours, even if the number of hours is zero. For example, to enter 20 minutes, enter **0:20**, not 20 or :20. Excel treats 20 as 20 hours, and :20 as text.

Excel includes time/date conversion and mathematical functions. The conversion functions convert or extract date and time data. The mathematical functions are used for addition and subtraction.

ENTERING AND STORING DATES AND TIMES IN EXCEL 2002

If you enter a date with a two-digit year (1/1/01), Excel applies the following rule to determine which century to place the date in:

► For year values 00–29, Excel assumes the date is in the 21st century: 1/1/2000 through 12/31/2029.

► For year values 30–99, Excel assumes the date is in the 20th century: 1/1/1930 through 12/31/1999.

If your workbook includes dates prior to 1/1/1930 or after 12/31/2029, enter all four digits of the year so that Excel won't need to interpret the date. If you want to force Excel to display four-digit years, change the Short Date Style setting on the Regional Settings page of the Windows Control Panel (Start ≻ Settings ≻ Control Panel).

To ensure compliance with worksheets created on a Macintosh computer, Excel supports two date systems. In the default 1900 system used in Windows applications, January 1, 1900, has the serial value 1. In the 1904 system, used by the Macintosh operating system, 1/1/1904 is assigned serial value 1. Both systems have values for dates up to December 31, 9999. There will be a Y10K problem in Excel worksheets, but none of us will be here to worry about it.

To switch to the 1904 system, choose Tools ≻ Options to open the Options dialog box. On the Calculation tab, enable the 1904 Date System check box. (If you open a worksheet created with Excel for the Mac, Excel will automatically enable the 1904 Date System check box.) Note, however, that this will not change the serial values Excel has assigned to dates you've already entered in workbooks.

Excel stores times as decimal fractions, based on a 24-hour clock. Midnight (0:00:00) is 0; noon (12:00:00) is 0.5; and one second before midnight (23:59:59) is 0.99999999. Format the decimal fractions using the Time formats in the Format Cells dialog box.

Basic Math with Dates

Dates are stored as serial values, so you can easily add and subtract dates. For example, to add three days to the date in cell B10, use the formula =B10+3. To subtract five days, use the formula =B10-5. The result in both cases is a serial value, displayed with the date format of the formula cell or the date format used in B10 if there was no date format applied to the formula cell. You can format the results using any of the date and time formats.

Excel stores times as decimal values rather than hours, minutes, and seconds. Table 10.1 lists the decimal values for an hour, commonly used fractions of an hour, minutes, and seconds.

TABLE 10.1:   Decimal Values for Units of Time

TIME	DECIMAL VALUE
1 hour	0.0416666667
45 minutes	0.0312500000
30 minutes	0.0208333333
15 minutes	0.0104166667
10 minutes	0.0069444444
5 minutes	0.0034722222
1 minute	0.0006944444
1 second	0.0000115741

When you're creating formulas, you don't need to enter the decimal values. For example, to add one hour to a time in cell B10, instead of adding 0.0416666667, you can enter **1:00** or **1/24** (one twenty-fourth of a day). If you enter **1:00** or **1/24**, Excel converts it to a decimal value.

Table 10.2 shows the decimal equivalents for the hours of the day from midnight to 11 PM.

TABLE 10.2:   Decimal Values for Hours of the Day

TIME	DECIMAL VALUE
12:00 AM	0.0000000000
1:00 AM	0.0416666667
2:00 AM	0.0833333333
3:00 AM	0.1250000000
4:00 AM	0.1666666667
5:00 AM	0.2083333333
6:00 AM	0.2500000000
7:00 AM	0.2916666667
8:00 AM	0.3333333333
9:00 AM	0.3750000000
10:00 AM	0.4166666667
11:00 AM	0.4583333333
12:00 PM	0.5000000000
1:00 PM	0.5416666667
2:00 PM	0.5833333333
3:00 PM	0.6250000000
4:00 PM	0.6666666667
5:00 PM	0.7083333333
6:00 PM	0.7500000000
7:00 PM	0.7916666667
8:00 PM	0.8333333333
9:00 PM	0.8750000000
10:00 PM	0.9166666667
11:00 PM	0.9583333333

Part iii

If your worksheet contains hours expressed as decimals (for example, 9.5 for 9 hours and 30 minutes), divide the number by 24 to convert it to the decimal value shown in Table 10.2. Apply a time format to display the result as 9:30. Divide minutes by 1440 to convert minutes to time values.

Subtracting Dates and Times

Subtract one date or time from another as you would subtract any numbers. Figure 10.4 shows a portion of a worksheet with starting times, ending times, and total hours, calculated by subtracting the starting time from the ending time. The formula returns the hours formatted as a time (9:00 AM rather than simply 9:00). The format shown in Figure 10.4 is a custom format. In the Format Cells dialog box, delete the AM /PM portion of the default time format to leave the custom format h:mm.

	A	B.	C	D
	Date	Starting Time	Ending Time	Total Hours
1				
2	4/23/2001	10:00 AM	7:00 PM	9:00
3	4/24/2001	12:00 PM	4:30 PM	4:30
4	4/25/2001	10:00 AM	5:30 PM	7:30
5	4/26/2001	6:00 PM	1:00 AM	-17:00
6	4/27/2001	10:00 AM	6:00 PM	8:00

FIGURE 10.4: Subtract one time from another to find out how many hours elapsed between the two. The negative number in cell D5 displays an error.

There is one small problem in our worksheet. In cell D5, the result is a negative number because the shift extended past midnight into a new day. For math with times on either side of the witching hour, you need a more explicit formula that adjusts if the ending time is prior to the starting time. The formula that will produce the correct results in cell D5 and every other cell in column D is =(C5+(C5<B5)-B5).

5	4/26/2001	6:00 PM	1:00 AM	=(C5+(C5<B5)-B5)

The formula uses the conditional expression (C5<B5), which will return one of two results: TRUE or FALSE. If C5 is *not* less than B5, the expression is false and Excel subtracts B5 from C5. If C5 *is* less than B5, the expression is true and Excel subtracts a negative B5 from C5 (in effect, adding B5 to C5).

Using Date and Time Functions

Table 10.3 lists commonly used date and time conversion functions. Following the table, we'll provide some examples of how the functions are used in business settings.

TABLE 10.3: Common Date and Time Conversion Functions

FUNCTION	DESCRIPTION	SYNTAX
DATE	Creates a serial value (which you can then format) from three numbers: the year, month, and day	=DATE(*year*,*month*,*day*)
TIME	Creates a decimal (serial value) time from three numbers: hour, minute, and second	=TIME(*hour*,*minute*, *second*)
NOW	Returns the serial value for the current date and decimal fraction for the current time from your computer's system clock	=NOW()
TODAY	Returns the serial value for the current date from the computer's system clock	=TODAY()
DAY	Returns the day number (1 to 31) from a text string, date, or serial value	=DAY(*date*)
MONTH	Returns the month value (1 to 12) from a text string, date, or serial value	=MONTH(*date*)
YEAR	Returns the year value (1 to 9999) from a text string, date, or serial value	=YEAR(*date*)
HOUR	Converts a text string or decimal fraction to an hour	=HOUR(*string or fraction*)
MINUTE	Converts a text string or decimal fraction to a minute	=MINUTE(*string or fraction*)
WEEKDAY	Returns the day of the week as an integer	=WEEKDAY(*date*)
WORKDAY*	Returns the first workday (nonweekend day) based on a starting date, a number of days, and an optional list of holiday dates	=WORKDAY(*start date*,*days*,*list of holidays*)
NETWORKDAYS*	Returns the number of days (excluding weekends and, optionally, holidays) between a start date and an end date	=NETWORKDAYS(*start date*,*end date*,*list of holidays*)

* Included in the Analysis ToolPak

Installing the Analysis ToolPak

Several date and time functions require installation of the Analysis Tool-Pak. The ToolPak must be installed first on your computer, then in Excel 2002. In Excel 2002, choose Tools ➤ Add-Ins to see if the ToolPak is already fully installed. If it's not on the list of add-ins, you can check (if you wish) to see if it is on your hard drive. Click Browse in the Add-Ins dialog box to find `Analys32.xll` (generally in `Microsoft Office\Office\Library\Analysis`) or use Windows' Find feature (Start ➤ Search in Windows 2000 or Start ➤ Find in Windows 9x) to locate it.

If `Analys32.xll` is not installed, run Office Setup to install the Analysis ToolPak. After installation, choose Tools ➤ Add-Ins in Excel and click the Analysis ToolPak check box to load the installed add-in.

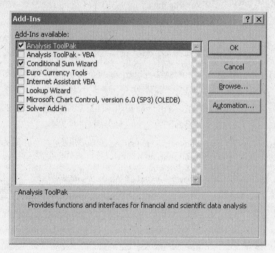

NOTE

The Add-Ins dialog box will list the Excel add-ins available on your computer.

Creating Dates with the DATE and TIME Functions

Use the DATE and TIME functions to construct dates and times when the arguments (year, month, day, hour, minute, or second) are supplied by a cell entry or another formula. For example, in the Reel World Solar Customer Sales Detail worksheet in Figure 10.5, a user enters the four-digit year in cell B4.

The formula =DATE(B4,1,1) returns the beginning date in that year; =DATE(B4,12,31) returns the last day in the year. We use the beginning and end dates as arguments in an IF function to determine if the date in column B falls between the two dates and to apply conditional formatting and totaling based on the determination.

	A	B	C	D	E	F
1	Customer Sales Detail					
2	Reel World Solar					
3						
4	Year	2000		Total Sales for 2000		1,865,880
5						
6						
7	Number	Sale Date	Name	Region	Order	Commission
8	AJ45	3/1/2001	Allison	North	361,000	18,050
9	AJ45	5/17/2000	Allison	North	379,000	18,950
10	AJ45	4/19/2001	Allison	North	250,000	12,500
11	AJ45	11/12/2000	Allison	North	519,850	25,993
12	AJ47	4/1/2001	Don	North	415,600	20,780
13	AJ47	7/5/2000	Don	North	668,950	33,448
14	AJ47	6/4/2001	Don	North	743,740	37,187
15	AJ47	6/3/2000	Don	North	298,080	14,904

FIGURE 10.5: Use the DATE function to construct a date from cell contents or formulas.

Excel can create dates from seemingly invalid data. If, for example, you ask Excel to create DATE(2000,13,1), Excel won't choke on the idea of a year with 13 months. Excel treats the "13th month" in 2000 as the first month in 2001, and returns 1/1/2001.

The TIME function uses hours, minutes, and seconds like the DATE function uses years, months, and days. For example, the formula =TIME (6,15,00) returns the time 6:15:00.

Retrieving the Current Date and Time

The NOW and TODAY functions have no arguments. Both consult the computer's system clock. TODAY returns the current date; NOW returns the current date and time.

TIP

The formula to display the current time, without the current date, is =NOW()– TODAY(). Format the cell with any of the time formats.

Part iii

Working with Date and Time Parts

Even if you need to know only the current year, you begin by retrieving the entire date with the NOW or TODAY function. Then, you can apply a DAY, MONTH, or YEAR function to extract the precise information you need. The YEAR function returns the year from a date, serial value, or text string date.

TIP

To convert the year (or any other date) to text, wrap it in a TEXT function: =TEXT(YEAR(*date*),*format as string*).

When you sort a list of birth dates or hire dates, the dates are sorted in chronological order. If you have every employee's birth date or hire date in an Excel workbook, you can use the MONTH and DAY functions to create a birthday list or anniversary list that you can sort by month and day, rather than by date. Figure 10.6 shows a list of birth dates, months, and days sorted by month first, then date. In cell E2, the formula is simply =MONTH(D2). The day formula in cell F2 is =DAY(D2).

	A	B	C	D	E	F	G
1	Last Name	First Name	Department	Birthdate	Birthmonth	Birthday	BirthText
2	Benth	Greg	Production	1/19/1957	1	19	19-Jan
3	Kzatz	Randall	Technical	2/12/1966	2	12	12-Feb
4	Talus	Charles	Admin	2/28/1946	2	28	28-Feb
5	Candy	Chuck	Production	3/8/1979	3	8	8-Mar
6	Swinzer	John	Production	3/22/1972	3	22	22-Mar
7	Adams	Abby	Admin	4/12/1969	4	12	12-Apr
8	Brown	Howard	HR	5/5/1955	5	5	5-May
9	Main	Bill	Technical	5/29/1970	5	29	29-May
10	Fitzgerald	Elizabeth	Production	7/7/1952	7	7	7-Jul
11	Griffin	Nancy	Admin	8/13/1972	8	13	13-Aug
12	Stevens	John	Production	8/15/1980	8	15	15-Aug
13	Issacs	Helen	Production	9/24/1946	9	24	24-Sep
14	Lieberman	Dave	Production	10/8/1963	10	8	8-Oct
15	Jaimison	Mason	Admin	11/11/1965	11	11	11-Nov
16	Hing	Ellen	Production	12/5/1977	12	5	5-Dec

FIGURE 10.6: Use the MONTH and DAY functions to extract birth months and days from a list of birth dates.

Adding Days, Months, and Years to a Date

If you need to increment a date by one day, you simply add one. What if you need to add a month? How many days do you add: 28, 29, 30, or 31? You could write a function to determine how many days to add based on the month of the date you're incrementing, but Excel makes it simpler because the MONTH function has a built-in calendar. Use the following formula to strip the date in C2 into a year, month, and day; increment the month by 2; then reassemble the result into a date:

```
=DATE(YEAR(C2),MONTH(C2)+2,DAY(C2))
```

Use a similar formula to increment years or, if you wish, even days.

TIP

Excel 2002 still supports the legacy function DATEDIF, which returns the number of complete years, months, or days between two dates. The syntax for the function is DATEDIF(*startdate*, *enddate*, *timeunit*). Use the following codes, enclosed in quotes, for the *timeunit* argument: y for year; m for month; d for day. For example, =DATEDIF (3/15/1999, 5/15/1999, "m") returns 2. DATEDIF isn't listed in the Paste Function dialog box, so you have to type the function name, parentheses, and commas.

Adding Hours, Minutes, and Seconds to a Time

Use the TIME function to add hours, minutes or seconds to a time. For example, if cell B20 contains the time 1:00, the formula =B10+TIME (1,30,0) adds 1 hour and 30 minutes to the starting time of 1:00 AM, and returns 2:30:00.

Functions That Exclude Weekends and Holidays

A life without weekends sounds incredibly unattractive, so Excel has two functions that take weekends into consideration. WORKDAY and NET-WORKDAYS automatically exclude weekends when calculating results, and both can be beefed up to exclude holidays.

The WORKDAY function takes a start date, adds a number of days, and produces the next workday. If you add, for example, one day to a Friday, the WORKDAY function will return the date for the following Monday. The worksheet shown in Figure 10.7 is a chart of due dates for three-day rentals. The due dates skip weekends; =WORKDAY(A4,3) takes the date in cell A4 and adds three workdays. The workbook also includes a list named Holidays of holiday dates. The range is the third argument for the function =WORKDAY(A4,3,Holidays), so Excel treats dates on the list as nonworking days.

	A	B	C
1	THREE DAY RENTAL DUE DATES		
2			
3	PICKUP DATE:	DUE BACK ON:	
4	July 1, 2001	=WORKDAY(A4,3,Holidays)	
5	July 2, 2001	July 6, 2001	
6	July 3, 2001	July 9, 2001	
7	July 4, 2001	July 9, 2001	
8	July 5, 2001	July 10, 2001	
9	July 6, 2001	July 11, 2001	
10	July 7, 2001	July 11, 2001	
11	July 8, 2001	July 11, 2001	
12	July 9, 2001	July 12, 2001	
13	July 10, 2001	July 13, 2001	
14	July 11, 2001	July 16, 2001	
15	July 12, 2001	July 17, 2001	
16	July 13, 2001	July 18, 2001	
17	July 14, 2001	July 18, 2001	
18	July 15, 2001	July 18, 2001	
19	July 16, 2001	July 19, 2001	
20	July 17, 2001	July 20, 2001	

FIGURE 10.7: The WORKDAY function skips weekends.

The NETWORKDAYS function has nothing to do with being connected to a local area network. NETWORKDAYS returns the net number of workdays between a starting date and an ending date, excluding Saturdays, Sundays, and (optionally) holidays.

Exporting a List of Holidays from Outlook

Both WORKDAY and NETWORKDAYS have an optional argument: a list of holiday dates that can also be treated as nonwork days. You need to provide the list. If your organization has a holiday list in an Office document, simply copy and paste the list in Excel, and include the list's range as the third argument in the function. If your organization uses standard holidays, you can create an Outlook Calendar view that includes holidays and their dates, formatted so that Excel will readily recognize them as dates. Using the Clipboard, you can copy these dates from the Outlook calendar into Excel for greater precision in the WORKDAY and NETWORKDAYS functions.

The Outlook view you'll create uses the Categories field to determine which dates are holidays. If you have special organizational holidays (Founder's Day, the annual staff picnic and softball game, the spring retreat) when the business is closed, add them to your Outlook calendar and include them in the Holiday category before copying the holidays to paste in Excel.

This is a multistep process, but if you save the view you create in Outlook, it will be a simple copy-and-paste operation in future years. Of course, you won't need to do it for a while unless additional holidays are added to your company's calendar, because Outlook exports six years of holidays. Follow these steps to export the list of holidays from your Outlook calendar.

1. Display the Outlook calendar, and open the Define Views For Calendar dialog box (View ➤ Current View ➤ Define Views).

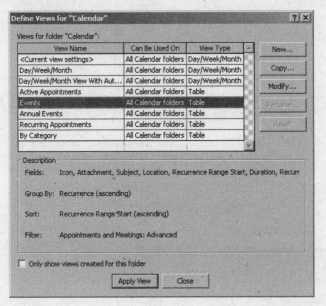

2. Select the Events view and click the Copy button in the dialog box to create a copy.

3. In the Copy View dialog box, enter a unique name for the view and click OK to open the View Summary dialog box.

4. In the View Summary dialog box, click the Filter button.

5. In the Filter dialog box, click the More Choices tab.

6. Click the Categories button to open the Categories dialog box.

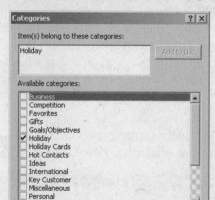

7. Enable the check box for Holiday, then click OK to close the Categories dialog box.

8. Click OK to close the Filter dialog box.

9. In the View Summary dialog box, click the Fields button to open the Show Fields dialog box.

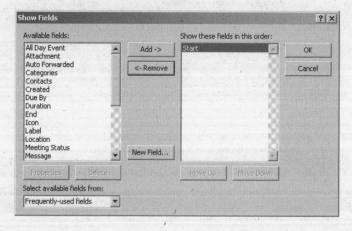

10. The completed view requires only one field: Start. Use the Add and Remove buttons to create the field list in the Show These Fields In This Order pane.

11. Click OK to close the View Summary dialog box, and click Apply View to apply the view and close the Define Views dialog box.

12. Right-click the button for the Start column in Outlook's Information Viewer and choose Format Columns from the shortcut menu.

13. Choose a short date format (4/26/2001, for example) for the Start column and click OK.

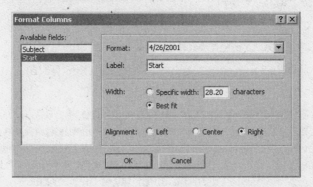

14. If the holidays are not sorted in ascending order, click the Start button to sort the Start dates in ascending order.

15. Choose Edit ➢ Select All to select all the appointments, then copy them to the Clipboard.

16. (Switch to Excel for the remaining steps.) Paste the selection into the Excel workbook where you want to use the NET-WORKDAYS or WORKDAYS function.

17. Select and delete rows that aren't required (past dates and holidays that are working days for your organization such as Groundhog Day). Add any other weekday, nonworking days that you want to exclude.

18. Select and name the range of dates imported from the Start field.

When you create formulas using the NETWORKDAYS or WORKDAYS functions, enter the named range as the third argument.

Determining the Weekday for a Date

Use the WEEKDAY function to determine what day of the week a date falls on. The function =WEEKDAY(*date*, *return type*) returns an integer to identify the weekday. The *return type* argument is optional; the default is return type 1, which returns 1 for Sunday, 2 for Monday, through 7 for Saturday. The function =WEEKDAY(4/1/2001) returns 1, as April Fools' Day fell on a Sunday in 2001. If you find it easier to work with a Monday-through-Sunday week or just want to be explicit in your formula, provide a value for the optional *return type* argument:

▶ Use 1 to use the default Sunday (1) through Saturday (7).

▶ Use 2 to return Monday (1) through Sunday (7).

▶ Use 3 to return Monday (0) through Sunday (6).

Calculating with Days of the Year

You can use the DATE and YEAR functions to determine how many days have passed since a specific date, to figure out the number of days that remain in the year, or to convert a number of days into a date to find out, for example, what date the 100th day of the year falls on. To determine the day of the year that a date represents, use the following formula, which assumes that the date is in cell C2, and format it as a number rather than a date:

```
=C2-DATE(YEAR(C2),1,0)
```

The formula subtracts the imaginary date January 0 of the year from the date (DATE(YEAR(C2),1,0), leaving only the number of days. Use a similar formula and apply a date format to subtract the date from the last day of the year to determine days remaining:

```
=DATE(YEAR(C2),12,31)-C2
```

To find the date that a specific day of the year falls on, modify the following formula, which we're using to find the 100th day of 2002:

```
=DATE(2002,1,100)
```

TIP

Another function included in the Analysis ToolPak is the little-known and barely useful function ROMAN. Give ROMAN a four-digit year, and it returns the Roman numeral: for example, =ROMAN(1957) returns MCMLVII. Alas, there is no corresponding function to convert a Roman numeral to a serial value date, but if you really want to know how old the movies are that you're renting for five nights for $1, you can quickly create a table of Roman numerals starting with a year value, a ROMAN formula, and a little fill magic.

WHAT'S NEXT

Creating charts to show data in easy-to-understand graphical representations has always been a big part of spreadsheet programs like Excel. Let's find out how it's done in Chapter 11.

Chapter 11

CREATING CHARTS

Pure numbers, percentages, and statistics can be very difficult for people to grasp as a whole. In fact, most of the experts in public presentation will tell you that if you can't help your audience picture data in a way that makes sense to them, they might not really grasp the information at all. In other words, you don't want to work hard to amass figures only to watch them slip away in a flood of information.

For this reason, the use of charts to graphically represent data has become an important part of the workplace, the media, and the marketplace.

The charting feature in Excel 2002 makes it quite easy for you to create such graphical charts for presentation of your data. They can be used to illustrate annual reports, sales reports, changes in productivity or participation, and so much more.

Adapted from *Mastering Microsoft Excel 2002*
by Gini Courter and Annette Marquis
ISBN 0-7821-4002-5   928 pp $39.99

This chapter helps you understand the fundamentals of chart creation and usage, and the types of charts you can produce depending on what you need to accomplish.

A QUICK OVERVIEW OF CHART TYPES

Excel supports a broad selection of chart types. Your data and the story you want to illustrate determine the type of chart you will plot the data on. In this chapter, we'll focus on the chart types used most frequently for business charts in North America.

Pie Charts

Use *pie charts* to show the relationships between pieces of an entity. The implication is that the pie includes *all* of something. In the simple pie chart shown in Figure 11.1, the pie shows all the packages sold in the second quarter. The pie chart type isn't appropriate for illustrating *some* of anything, so if there's not an obvious *all* in the data you're charting, don't use a pie chart.

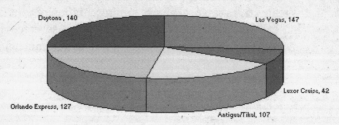

FIGURE 11.1: A pie chart from the Destination Packages sales worksheet

A pie chart can include only one data series. If you select more than one data series, Excel uses the first series and ignores all others. No error message appears, so you won't necessarily know that the chart doesn't show the data you intended to include, unless you examine the chart carefully.

Pie charts almost always show relationships at a fixed point in time—the end of the year, or a specific month, day, or week. It is possible to create a pie chart with more than one time frame; however, this kind of information would be better represented in a series chart.

When you create a pie chart, you don't need to create worksheet formulas to calculate percentages. Excel totals the data points in the series and then divides the value of each data point into the series total to determine how large each data point's pie slice should be. Don't include a total from the worksheet as a data point; this doubles the total Excel calculates, resulting in a pie chart with one large slice that represents exactly 50 percent of the pie.

Series Charts

In a *series chart*, you can chart more than one data series. Series charts let you compare the data points in the series, such as April versus June or Las Vegas compared to Orlando. Series charts are open-ended; there is no requirement that the data shown is all the data for a month or year. There are several types of series charts, so you can often improve the usefulness of a series chart simply by changing the chart type. The charts shown in Figures 11.2, 11.3, and 11.4 were created using the same data series.

Line, Ribbon, and Area Charts

The series chart in Figure 11.2 is a *line chart* showing the relationship between package sales and each city during the second quarter. The chart includes a data table that lists the values illustrated by the chart. Each data series is a city. Line charts are available in a 2D version as shown or in a 3D version called a *ribbon chart*. An *area chart* is a line chart with the area below the line filled. Line, ribbon, and area charts are typically used to show one or more variables (such as sales, income, or price) changing over time on the x-axis.

Column and Bar Charts

In Figure 11.3, the data is presented as a *bar chart*. The bars are bulkier, thus giving added substance to the chart. In the line chart (Figure 11.2), what the user notices is the trend up or down in each line and the gaps between the lines. The bar chart makes all package sales seem more substantial, but it also makes the difference between destinations even more clear. Changing the chart type shifts the focus to the difference between cities rather than the trend for each city.

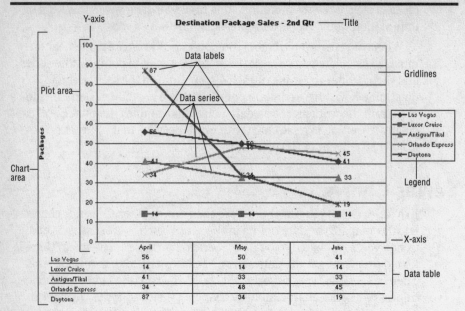

FIGURE 11.2: Line charts are typically used to illustrate changes over time.

Line and area charts share a common layout. The horizontal line is the *x-axis*, and the vertical line is the *y-axis* (the same x- and y-axes you may have learned about in algebra class). In a bar chart, however, the chart is turned 90 degrees so the x-axis is on the left side.

With a little help from Excel, you can combine columns with line or area charts and embellish line or column charts with 3D effects. You can move beyond the column/bar spectrum and use tubes, pyramids, cones, or cylinders to represent data, or you can transform regular bars into floating 3D bars.

When you need to show totals and the data points that make up the total, the natural choice is a *stacked bar chart* or a *stacked column chart*. A stacked 3D column chart is shown in Figure 11.4. Stacking adds another dimension to the chart, since it allows the user to compare sales between, as well as within, time periods—like providing a column chart and a pie chart for each time period.

In a 2D chart, the x-axis is the *category* axis and the y-axis is the *value* axis. In a 3D chart, the y-axis becomes the *series* axis, and values are plotted on the third axis, the *z-axis*, which provides the third dimension of depth in the chart. Don't worry about memorizing which axis is which in each chart type; there are ways to know which is which when you're creating or editing the chart.

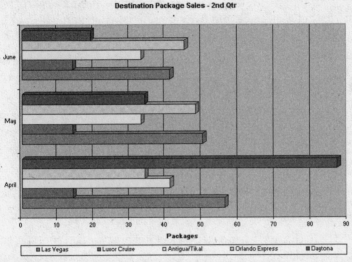

Destination Package Sales - 2nd Qtr

Packages

□ Las Vegas ■ Luxor Cruise □ Antigua/Tikal □ Orlando Express ■ Daytona

FIGURE 11.3: The bar chart focuses the user on the difference between cities.

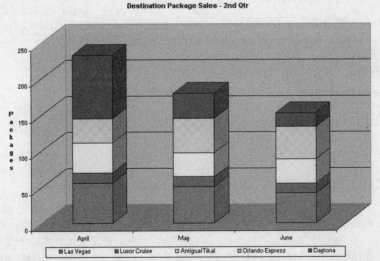

Destination Package Sales - 2nd Qtr

Packages

□ Las Vegas ■ Luxor Cruise □ Antigua/Tikal □ Orlando Express ■ Daytona

FIGURE 11.4: The stacked column chart provides total and detail information.

Excel includes other chart types suitable for presenting scientific, statistical, and financial data. *Scatter charts* are used to present experimental results. *Surface* and *contour charts* are good for presenting 3D and 2D changes in data. *Radar charts* show data values in relation to a single metric: a standard, average, or other measurement. *Stock charts* present values for between three and five series of data, including open, high, low, close, and volume trading information.

CREATING A CHART

The easiest way to create a chart is by using the Chart Wizard. In most circumstances, it's also best to use the wizard because it provides easy access to all the chart options you might need. Here's an overview of the steps for creating an Excel chart with the Chart Wizard:

1. Select the ranges you want to include in the chart.

2. Click the Chart Wizard button on the Standard toolbar.

3. In the first wizard step, select a chart type and subtype, then click Next.

4. In the second step, verify that you have selected the correct range and choose to have the series represented by rows or by columns. Click Next.

5. In the third step, set options for the chart, including titles, data labels, and legend placement. Click Next.

6. In the fourth step, select a location for the chart. Click Finish.

TIP

To quickly create a column chart, select the data, then press F11 or Alt+F1.

Selecting Data for the Chart

First, select the data that you want to include in the chart. With the exception of the chart's title, everything that appears in the chart should be selected from somewhere in the worksheet. Column and row labels provide text for the axes and legend. Make sure that the ranges you select are symmetrical: If you select four labels in rows 9–12 of column A, select data points from the other columns in rows 9–12. If you select labels in columns A–D of row 5, then the data series you select should also be in columns A–D. Figure 11.5 shows the data selected to create the charts originally shown in Figures 11.2 through 11.4.

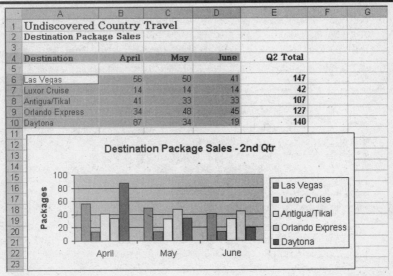

	A	B	C	D	E	F	G
1	Undiscovered Country Travel						
2	Destination Package Sales						
3							
4	Destination	April	May	June	Q2 Total		
5							
6	Las Vegas	56	50	41	147		
7	Luxor Cruise	14	14	14	42		
8	Antigua/Tikal	41	33	33	107		
9	Orlando Express	34	48	45	127		
10	Daytona	87	34	19	140		
11							

FIGURE 11.5: Select all the data required for the chart data points and text that will serve as labels.

Part iii

TIP

The selection in Figure 11.5 doesn't include the empty cells in row 5. If you include blank rows or extra empty columns in your selection, you'll have empty spaces in your chart. Remember that you can hold the Ctrl key to select non-contiguous ranges of data. If you select some cells you don't want to include, press Esc and start selecting again.

Using the Chart Wizard

With the text and numbers selected, click the Chart Wizard button on the Standard toolbar. The Chart Wizard and the Office Assistant both open. You can close the Assistant if you want to. The Chart Wizard includes a button that will reopen the Assistant if you need help.

In the first step of the Chart Wizard, choose a chart type in the Chart Type list box (see Figure 11.6). If the type of chart you want isn't listed, check out the chart types on the Custom Types page.

The wizard creates a preview so you can check the chart's general appearance using your data. After choosing a chart type in the left pane on the Standard Types page, choose a subtype in the right pane. To see a rough sample of the type and subtype using your data, use the Press And Hold To View Sample button in the Chart Wizard. When you've selected a type and a subtype, click Next to continue.

FIGURE 11.6: Choose a chart type and subtype in the first step of the wizard.

In the second step, shown in Figure 11.7, check the Data Range page to make sure the range you selected is correct. If it isn't, use the Collapse Dialog button and select the proper range before continuing. Choose Rows or Columns in the Series In option group, and the preview will change to reflect the range and series arrangement you specify. Figure 11.8 shows the preview by Rows (months on the x-axis) and Columns (destinations on the x-axis).

Click the Series tab (see Figure 11.9) to verify selected ranges and values for the series used in the chart. Select any of the items listed in the Series list box to see which cells or cell ranges in the spreadsheet correspond to the selected series and category labels. Use the Collapse Dialog button next to the Name text box, the Values text box, or the Category (X) Axis Labels text box to change the ranges used for these chart elements.

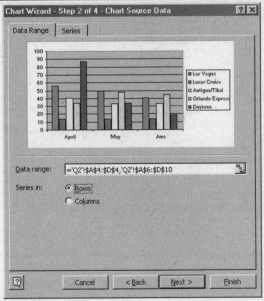

FIGURE 11.7: In the second step of the wizard, check the selected data range.

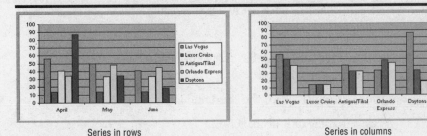

Series in rows   Series in columns

FIGURE 11.8: Indicate whether the chart's series are in rows or columns.

To remove a series, select the series in the list and click the Remove button. To add a series, click the Add button. Specify a cell reference for the label and a range for the series data.

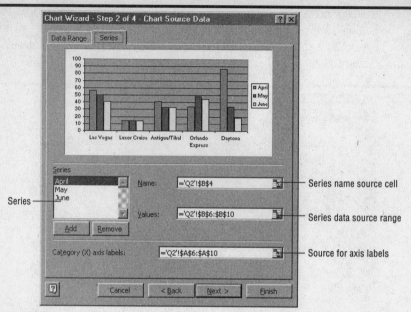

FIGURE 11.9: Verify the series data and name and axis labels on the Series page.

TIP

You don't need to use data from your worksheet as the series names. In Figure 11.9, each series' name comes from column A, the city name. To change the names (for example, to include the country name), select a series, select the cell reference in the Name box, and type the new entry: for example, **Luxor (Egypt)**. Repeat this for each series.

In the third step, use the tabs (shown in Figure 11.10) to set options for various aspects of the chart:

Titles   Enter titles for the chart and axes.

Axes   Display or hide axes.

Gridlines   Display gridlines and display or hide the third dimension of a 3D chart.

Legend   Display and place a legend.

Data Labels   Display text or values as data labels.

Data Table Show the selected range from the worksheet below the chart.

As you change options, the chart preview reflects your changes. When you've finished setting options, click Next to continue.

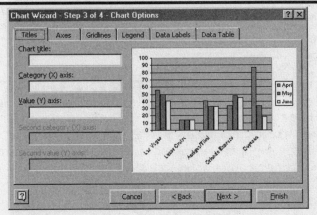

FIGURE 11.10: Set the chart's titles, labels, and display options.

Every chart needs a title. The title provides information that is not already included in the graphical portion of the chart. The chart's picture, legend, and title taken together should answer any questions about the timing, location, or contents of the chart.

In the last step of the Chart Wizard, you can choose to place the chart on the current worksheet or on a new, blank sheet in the same workbook. If the chart is placed on its own sheet, it will print as a full-size, single-page chart whenever it is printed. If you add it to the current worksheet as an object, it will print as part of the worksheet, but can also be printed separately:

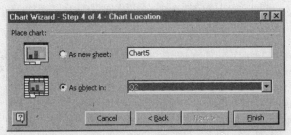

Enter a new sheet name (or choose As Object In and select the worksheet in which to place the chart), and click Finish to create and place the chart. The Office Assistant will open and offer further help with charts. The Excel Chart toolbar will open in the workbook window. You can move a chart object to its own worksheet or make a chart an object in another worksheet (like a picture that you can reposition and resize). Select the chart or chart object, right-click, and choose Location from the shortcut menu to open the Chart Location dialog box.

Editing and Formatting Charts

After you create and save your chart, use Excel's editing and formatting tools to modify it or improve its appearance. If you placed the chart as an object, you'll probably need to move and resize the chart to place it correctly in an existing report or worksheet. Moving and resizing are only the beginning. You can add, delete, and reorder data series, display error bars and data labels, or change the fill, font, and spacing of various chart elements.

Moving, Sizing, and Printing Chart Objects

If you place the chart as an object in the current worksheet, you'll inevitably need to resize and move it so it will print well with the existing data. The chart object floats on a layer above the worksheet, so it may cover part of the worksheet data or fall across a page break. Fortunately, moving a chart (or any other object) in Excel is a snap.

TIP

The Office applications handle all objects in roughly the same way as a chart object, so if you've worked with WordArt or clip art in Word or PowerPoint, you know how to move and resize chart objects.

When the Chart Wizard closes, the square handles on the corners and sides of the chart object indicate the chart is selected. If the chart isn't selected, click once on the chart to select it. To deselect the chart and return to the worksheet, click anywhere in the worksheet except on the chart object. When the chart is selected, you can move it by pointing to the chart (anywhere inside the chart frame except in the plot area or on the title or legend) and holding the mouse button down. When the pointer changes to a four-headed arrow, drag the chart to its new location. To change the chart's size, move the mouse pointer to one of the chart's handles. Hold the mouse button and drag the handle to stretch or shrink the chart. Handles on the sides of the chart change the size in one direction (width or height). To increase width and height proportionally, use a corner handle.

TIP

Turn on Page Break Preview when sizing and moving charts to make sure they remain within the boundaries of a page. The View menu doesn't include the Page Break Preview command when a chart is selected, so click anywhere in the worksheet to deselect the chart, choose View ➢ Page Break Preview, and reselect the chart. Choose View ➢ Normal to return to regular editing mode.

Printing Charts as Objects or Worksheets

If you placed your chart as an object in the current worksheet, you can still print it separately. If the chart is selected when you print, the chart will print by itself on a full page—ready to turn into an overhead or slide. If the worksheet is selected, the worksheet prints, including the chart object.

▶ To print a worksheet, including a chart object, activate any worksheet cell before printing.

▶ To print a chart object as a full-page chart, select the chart before printing.

Adding a Data Series

You can modify Excel charts quickly and easily. If you have an existing series chart, you can select and drag any excluded series to add them to the chart. Here are the steps for adding a data series to a chart:

1. In the worksheet, select the data series to be added.

2. Point to the border of the cell pointer, then drag the series and drop it in the chart.

Part iii

If you prefer a more structured approach or wish to change the label for the series, use the Chart Wizard. Select the chart object or chart worksheet and click the Chart Wizard button. Click Next to move to the second step of the Chart Wizard and add or adjust series on the Series tab. This is also a fine place to delete a data series.

Deleting a Data Series

A *chart* is a collection of graphic objects. The chart *object* contains a data series object, which contains data point objects. To access the objects, first select the chart. Then click a series to select the entire series. The series will have handles.

TIP

To select a data point, first select the chart, then the series, then the data point.

When an object is selected, you can delete or format the object. Use these steps to delete a data series from a chart:

1. In the chart, select the data series or any data point in the series.

2. Press the Delete key on the keyboard.

NOTE

Press the Delete key when the chart is selected to delete the entire chart object.

Formatting Charts

The *chart area* (see Figure 11.11) is a rectangular area within the chart window bounded by the chart border that contains all of the parts and pieces of the chart including the title, legend, and the border surrounding the chart object. Changing the size of the chart object changes the size of the chart area.

The *plot area* (see Figure 11.11) is bounded by the axes and contains the columns, lines, wedges, or other objects used to represent the data points. Objects that form the boundaries of the plot area have fixed location areas and cannot be moved or individually sized. For example, the x-axis labels must be located near the x-axis.

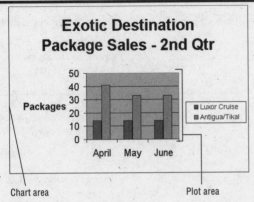

Chart area   Plot area

FIGURE 11.11: The chart area is the entire chart. The plot area is the graphical area of the chart.

Resizing and Deleting Objects in a Chart

You can resize all the objects in the plot area by increasing or decreasing the plot area itself. (There's an exception to this rule; see "Exploding Pies" later in this chapter.) Objects outside the plot area and axes can be sized or moved to other locations in the chart area. The title and legend can be placed above, below, or in the plot area.

Any object in a chart can be selected and then formatted or deleted, with the exception of individual data points. Data points can be formatted, but only data *series* can be added or deleted. To select a data point, first select the data series, and then click the data point once.

Formatting the Chart with the Chart Toolbar

Common formatting options are available on the Chart toolbar (View ➤ Toolbars ➤ Chart). The first button is used to select one of the objects in the chart; the other buttons format the entire chart or selected chart object. See Table 11.1 for descriptions of the buttons on the Chart toolbar.

TABLE 11.1:   Chart Toolbar Buttons

Button	Button Name	Function
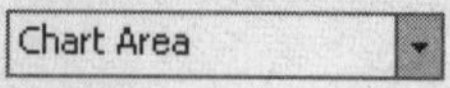 Chart Area ▼	Chart Objects	Selects the object chosen from the list.
	Format Object	Opens the Format dialog box for the selected object.
	Chart Type	The drop-down arrow opens a menu of chart types; clicking the button applies the type indicated on the button face.
	Legend	Displays or hides the legend.
	Data Table	Displays or hides the data table.
	By Row	Uses the selected worksheet row(s) as a data series.
	By Column	Uses the selected worksheet column(s) as a data series.
	Angle Clockwise	Angles selected text downward.
	Angle Counterclockwise	Angles selected text upward.

Formatting Individual Objects

The difference between a good chart and an outstanding chart is often found in a number of small, almost insignificant changes. The chart shown in Figure 11.11 is the chart as it appears right out of the wizard. Figure 11.12 shows the same chart after we've invested three minutes to format a few of the chart objects.

The following formatting changes were made:

▶ Plot area pattern set to None

▶ Plot area increased

▶ Corners on chart area rounded

▶ Legend positioned at bottom

▶ Legend text box resized

▶ Y-axis label retyped in caps and rotated

▶ Axis labels' font size decreased

▶ Title font size decreased and edited to break across lines

▶ Title font changed to match worksheet font

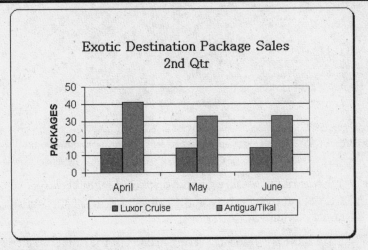

FIGURE 11.12: The chart shown in Figure 11.11 with formatting changes.

Chart Area To format chart objects such as a data series, select the object from the Chart Objects dropdown menu on the Chart toolbar. Double-click any selected object or click the Format Object button on the Chart toolbar to open the formatting dialog box for the object. For example, double-clicking any column in a data series opens the Format Data Series dialog box, shown in Figure 11.13.

There are five or six tabs in this dialog box; depending on the chart type, the dialog box may include a tab for Shape, Axis, or Y Error Bars. Each page contains a group of settings for the selected data series:

Patterns   Applies a selected color and pattern for each series.

Axis   Adds a second vertical axis at the right end of the plot area scaled to the selected series. The chart must contain two or more series.

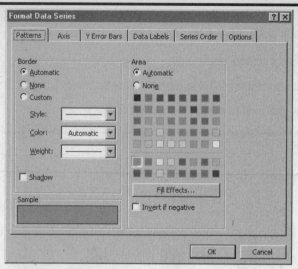

FIGURE 11.13: Double-click any object to open its formatting dialog box.

Y Error Bars   Adds a graphic display of sampling errors when the data in the chart is a statistical sample being applied to a larger population.

Data Labels   Adds a descriptive label or the numeric value for each data point in the series.

Series Order   Reorders the series in a chart; especially useful with 3D charts, where the selected range is charted in reverse order.

Options   Settings for the bar or column overlap, gap, and color variation.

For more information on a specific control within the Format Data Series dialog box, click the Help button in the title bar of the dialog box, and then click the control.

Similar options are available when you double-click a selected data point, the plot area, the chart area, or another chart object. To change font and alignment settings for axis labels (such as the April, May, and June x-axis labels in Figure 11.12), select the axis and open the Axis dialog box.

TIP

To quickly format an object, select it, right-click, then select Format from the shortcut menu. If the entire chart is selected, Chart Options appears on the menu. If you want to change the type of chart from a pie to a bar chart, for example, choose Chart Type from the shortcut menu.

Inserting and Formatting Titles

If you didn't give the chart a title while creating it, you can add one at any time. Select the chart, right-click, and open the Chart Options dialog box from the shortcut menu. On the Titles tab of the dialog box, you can edit or format existing titles (including placeholders) in a selected chart. Or you can edit directly in the chart. To change the text in a title, click once to select the title, and then edit the selected text.

TIP

To use the contents of a cell as a title or chart label, select the title text box or create a new text box using the Text Box tool on the Drawing toolbar. Select the text box. Type = (an equal sign) in the formula bar, then click in the cell you want to use as a title or label. Press Enter to insert the text into the text box.

To wrap a title into multiple lines, place the insertion point where you want the second line to begin and press Enter.

Double-click a title (or select the title, right-click, and choose Format Title from the shortcut menu) to open the Format Title dialog box. Use the controls on the Pattern, Font, and Alignment tabs to format the title as you would format other text.

TIP

To change all the fonts used in a chart, double-click in the chart area and change fonts in the Format Chart Area dialog box. If you don't like the results, click Undo to revert to the original style.

Exploding Pies

If you want to emphasize specific data points in a pie chart, you can *explode* the pie chart by moving one or more pieces of the pie farther from the center. In Figure 11.14, the Antigua/Tikal slice has been exploded. Although you can select an exploded pie in the Chart Wizard, the wizard explodes either all slices of the pie or the first slice, depending on which explosion sample you choose. It's easier to create an unexploded pie of the type you want, and then edit the chart to explode selected slices.

If you want to explode all the slices in a chart, select the chart and then select the pie in the plot area. Drag any slice away from the center to explode all the pie slices. To explode a single slice, select the chart and then click the pie to select the data series. With the series selected, click to select the slice you want to explode. Drag the slice away from the center.

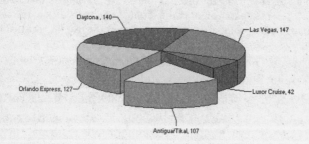

FIGURE 11.14: Explode a pie slice to emphasize a particular data point.

When you explode all slices in a pie, each slice gets smaller as you increase the space between the slices. If you explode slices individually, the other slices remain centered in the plot area, and the slices don't get smaller.

CHANGING 3D VIEWS

You can change the perspective for 3D charts using the 3D View tool on the Chart menu. With this tool, you can tilt and rotate 3D series charts and pie charts to emphasize specific data series or individual data points. For example, here's the pie from Figure 11.14 rotated and tilted so that the exploded slice is at the bottom right in the foreground where it is more noticeable. The slice also stands out better, because its lighter color is next to the darker color of the adjacent slice.

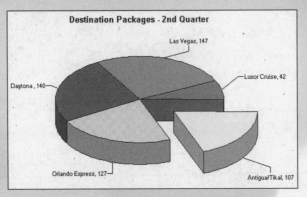

A 3D chart looks three-dimensional because objects in the foreground are larger than objects in the background. Some purists reject 3D charts because the resizing of objects to create the 3D appearance distorts the actual values represented by the objects; the slice at the bottom of a 3D pie chart is larger than it would be if it appeared at the top of the pie. Many users willingly accept the distortion created by 3D charts because they like the look or they use the distortion to exaggerate a point.

For more complex charts, optimizing the view is essential if you want to convey the data's message to viewers. Important chart objects can be obscured by other chart objects that appear closer. The larger foreground objects dominate the chart's visual impact, possibly drawing attention away from smaller elements that could be important points in a presentation or report. When a 3D column chart includes multiple series, you'll often need to change the 3D

CONTINUED ➡

Part iii

view or rearrange the series so that all the data is visible. Use these steps to change a chart's 3D view:

1. Select the chart and choose Chart ➤ 3-D View to open the 3-D View dialog box:

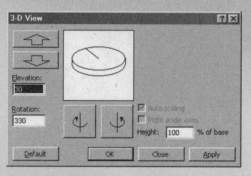

2. Click the Elevation arrows on the left to change the *elevation* (degree of tilt of the chart). The wire-frame preview changes to show the effects of your setting, as does the number in the Elevation box.

3. Use the Perspective arrows to change the ratio of the front of the chart to the back; increasing the *perspective* increases the depth of the chart. (3D pie and bar charts don't have Perspective controls.)

4. Click the clockwise or counterclockwise rotation buttons to change the chart's horizontal orientation. The Rotation setting and the preview will change to reflect your choices.

5. Type in a different percentage in the Height text box to collapse or expand the chart's height (the z-axis) relative to its width (the x-axis). A higher percentage will make the chart taller or wider, while a lower percentage will make it shorter or smaller.

6. Click OK to apply changes and close the dialog box.

To return the chart to the original settings, click the Default button and check the Auto Scaling box.

There's also an alternate way to change the 3D perspective, elevation, and rotation on 3D series charts: Choose Corners from the Chart Objects menu on the Chart toolbar and use the handles to tilt or rotate the chart.

WHAT'S NEXT

Now that you have an understanding of some of the basic skills and advanced functions in Excel, we'll move on to Part IV.

In Chapter 12, you will learn the basics of e-mail as you prepare to both send and receive it using Outlook 2002.

PART iv
COMMUNICATING WITH
OUTLOOK 2002

Chapter 12

SENDING AND RECEIVING E-MAIL WITH OUTLOOK 2002

O utlook 2002 combines many features into one package, including e-mail; office connectivity functions like Net-Meeting; scheduling; and contact information. Of Outlook's functions, e-mail is the one people use the most, as Outlook easily integrates electronic mailboxes with other work performed in Office XP.

Adapted from *Mastering Microsoft Outlook 2002* by Gini Courter and Annette Marquis

ISBN 0-7821-4001-7   752 pp $39.99

WORKING WITH E-MAIL ACCOUNTS AND FOLDERS

In Outlook 2002, you can connect to any number of POP3, IMAP, and HTTP Internet accounts, Microsoft Exchange Server networks, and other third-party networks to send and receive mail. You can also access directory services, such as those housed on LDAP servers and other address book sources. Depending on how your e-mail accounts are configured and whether you are currently logged in to a mail server, you may send and receive your mail automatically, or you may have to wait until you dial your Internet Service Provider (ISP) or your Microsoft Exchange Server network. Outlook's new e-mail options let you decide whether you want your Internet mail to sit in your Outbox until you are ready to send it or you want it to be processed as soon as you hit the Send button.

If you have used previous versions of Outlook, you may be wondering where e-mail configurations such as Internet Only and Corporate/Workgroup have gone. In Outlook 2002, all accounts are united into one configuration where you can set up Internet-only and corporate/workgroup mail services.

Outlook's E-Mail Folders

Outlook uses four folders to handle e-mail messages. When you receive a message, it's delivered to the *Inbox* folder.

If you click Save while you are creating a message (or choose Save Changes when you close a message form), a copy of the message is retained in the *Drafts* folder. When you instruct Outlook to send the message, the message is moved to the *Outbox*. If you use a dial-up connection, the message remains in the Outbox until you actually connect to your ISP and send the message (or until Outlook connects at an established time interval). If you have a continuous connection to the Internet (a cable or satellite modem, for example) or send and receive messages over your organization's network, the message has a very short stay in the Outbox.

After a message is sent from the Outbox, it is placed in the *Sent Items* folder or other folder specified in Outlook. To change the folder that stores sent items, see "Advanced Options" later in this chapter.

In addition to these four folders, items deleted from any Outlook folder are placed in the *Deleted Items* folder, Outlook's equivalent of the Recycle Bin.

TIP

You can move quickly to the Inbox or the Outbox from any Outlook module. Press Ctrl+Shift+I for the Inbox or Ctrl+Shift+O for the Outbox.

CREATING AND ADDRESSING E-MAIL

To create a message, choose File ➢ New ➢ Mail Message from the menu bar, or open the menu on the New Item button and choose Mail Message to open a message form, shown in Figure 12.1. Composing and sending a simple message is a three-step process: Address the message form, type the message in the large open text box, and send the message.

The message header includes text boxes for From, To, Cc, Bcc, and Subject. By default, the Bcc and From text boxes are not displayed. To display other text boxes, click the down arrow on the Options button and select the text box you wish to display.

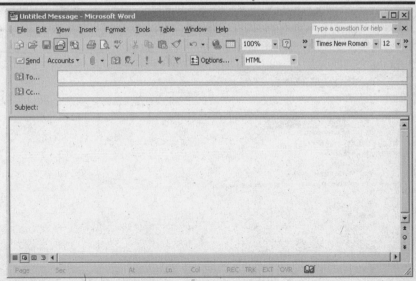

FIGURE 12.1: Open a message form to create an e-mail message.

Entering E-Mail Addresses

There are three ways to enter e-mail addresses: from your address books, by typing the address manually, or by searching for the person's e-mail address with a directory service. Enter the recipient's name or e-mail addresses in the To text box, or click the To button to open the Select Names dialog box, shown in Figure 12.2. When you open the Select Names dialog box, Outlook displays the Global Address list or an Outlook address list. Only address book entries that include either an e-mail address or a fax number are displayed.

In Outlook 2002, the names in the address list do not show the type of address next to the person's name (as you might be used to from Outlook 2000). To see if a particular listing is an e-mail address or a fax number, use the horizontal scroll bar to view additional data about the address. The fields that are available depend on the type of address book you are accessing. In the Global Address list, you can scroll to see Business Phone, Office, Title, Company, Alias, and E-Mail Type. In Outlook address books, such as Contacts folders, you can see E-Mail Address, Display Name, and E-Mail Type. These fields can help you verify that you have the right person and identify which e-mail/fax address you want to use. Unfortunately, the Select Names dialog box cannot be resized, so you are forced to follow the rows across without being able to see all the data at once (to access the Address Book dialog box where all the data is available, see "Accessing Address Books outside of a Mail Message" later in this section).

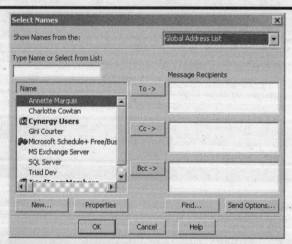

FIGURE 12.2: Select message recipients using the To, Cc, and Bcc buttons in the Select Names dialog box.

About Address Books

An *address book* is a list that, minimally, contains names, e-mail addresses, or fax numbers. You may have only one address book, or you may have several of them depending on the e-mail accounts you have set up in your Outlook profile. The major address books are as follows:

Global Address list   An address book for members of your organization stored on a server, such as a Microsoft Exchange Server; sometimes called a *post office address list*. This address book can contain additional books that contain global distribution lists, conference rooms, contacts, users, and public folders.

Outlook address book   A category of address books that includes Outlook's Contacts folder and potentially any other Contacts folders in your folder set. These address books include only contacts that have an e-mail address or fax number listed.

NOTE

If you have installed other mail services, you may also have additional address books.

Selecting an Address Book and an Address

If you have more than one address book, begin by choosing an address book from the drop-down list in the Select Names dialog box:

When the address book opens, either scroll to the person's name or begin entering the name in the Type Name text box until you find it. With the contact's name selected in the left pane, you can double-click to place it in the To box, or click the To, Cc, or Bcc button to add the name to the list of recipients. Another option is to right-click the name and select To, Cc, or Bcc from the shortcut menu. To select a contiguous list

Part iv

of names, hold Shift while you select them, or hold Ctrl to select noncontiguous names before clicking the To, Cc, or Bcc buttons. After you've added all the recipients, click OK to close the Select Names dialog box and return to the message form.

TIP

To and Cc recipients are listed in the header of the message, while recipients of blind courtesy copies (Bcc) are not. Therefore, recipients of the original message and courtesy copies won't know that the message was also sent to the Bcc recipients, while Bcc recipients won't know what other blind courtesy copies were sent. If you are responsible for sending out an e-mail newsletter or the same message to several competitors, you might consider putting everyone's name in the Bcc box. That way, no one will see who else received the correspondence, and you won't be giving away other's people's e-mail addresses without their permission.

Entering Addresses Manually

If you'd rather type than select, you can type an entire e-mail address in the To, Cc, and Bcc text boxes, or enough of the contact's name for Outlook to find the recipient. As soon as it recognizes the name, Outlook completes the recipient's display name for you automatically. For example, gcourter@triadconsulting.com is replaced with Gini Courter.

When you enter a full e-mail address, Outlook checks the address to verify that it has the proper form—two text strings separated by the @ symbol. If you are on an Exchange Server or other mail server, Outlook may also verify that the address has a mailbox on the server. When Outlook finds an Internet address in the correct format or a mail server address in the Global Address list, it verifies it by underlining it in the message header.

WARNING

Outlook is not able to verify that an Internet e-mail address is correct. It can only tell you that it's in the correct e-mail format (username followed by the @ symbol, followed by the top-level domain name, such as .com or .net).

If Outlook finds more than one possible match in your address books, if the text you enter is not a valid e-mail address, or if the name is not in the address book, Outlook marks it with the wavy red underline used in Word to mark spelling errors. Either correct the entry if you misspelled it or right-click the name and select the correct recipient from the short-cut menu.

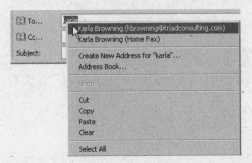

If the name does not appear on the shortcut menu, choose Address Book to open the Select Names dialog box or Create New Address For *Name* to create a new contact item for the person.

NOTE

If you find automatic name completion annoying, see "Advanced Options" later in this chapter for information about how to turn this feature off.

Determining the Order of Address Books

You can determine the order in which Outlook accesses your address books to locate a name. The order of address books determines which address list or Contacts folder Outlook searches first for an address.

To view or change the order, choose Tools ➢ Address Book from Outlook's Standard toolbar (outside of a mail message) and then choose Tools ➢ Options from the Address Book dialog box's menu. In the dialog box shown in Figure 12.3, select the address book you would like to show first when you open the Select Names or Address Book dialog boxes from the Show This Address List First drop-down list. Select the folder in which you would like to keep your personal addresses from the Keep Per-sonal Addresses In drop-down list. Finally, use the up and down arrows to the right of the open text box to change the order of the address lists in which Outlook checks names before sending mail.

Part iv

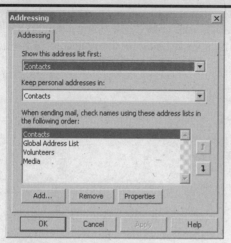

FIGURE 12.3: In the Addressing dialog box, you can change the order in which address lists appear, where your personal addresses are kept, and the order of address lists Outlook uses to process mail.

If an address book does not appear in the list of address books shown here, click the Add button to add it to the list. When you have finished setting the order, click OK and then click the Close button on the Address Book dialog box.

TIP

If a new Contacts folder does not appear in your list of available address books, you must go to the properties of the Contacts folder (select the folder in the folder list, right-click, and choose Properties) and select the Show This Folder As An E-Mail Address Book check box on the Outlook Address Book tab.

Resolving Ambiguous Names

If you don't clarify ambiguous recipients before clicking the Send button on a message, Outlook opens a dialog box so that you can select a name. For example, let's say you type **Jim** in the To text box. There are several Jims in your address book, so Outlook underlines the name. To choose the correct Jim, you can right-click the name and select the Jim you want from the shortcut menu. If you don't specify which Jim you want before you click the Send button, Outlook prompts you with a list of possible Jims.

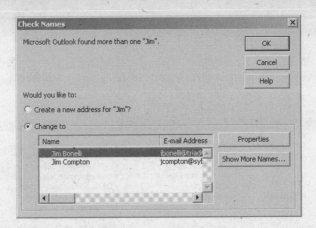

Select the Jim you want and click OK to address the message. The next time you enter **Jim** as a recipient name, Outlook automatically selects the name you chose from the menu or dialog box this time. To select a different Jim, continue typing the correct name or click the To button to select from the address book.

Accessing Address Books outside of a Mail Message

To access your address books without opening an e-mail message, click the Address Book button on Outlook's Standard toolbar. This version of the address book, shown in Figure 12.4, is resizable, and you can easily display all the available fields by dragging its bottom-right corner. You can also drag the column markers next to the column names to change column width.

When you've found the e-mail address you want to use, select it and click the New Message button to open an e-mail message form.

Using Directory Services

A *directory service* is an address book maintained in a *Lightweight Directory Access Protocol (LDAP)* directory. LDAP, developed at the University of Michigan, is an emerging Internet/intranet standard, used in many networking programs, that defines a common format for electronic directories. The directory could be on a local network server running Microsoft Exchange or on a public directory service you access via the Internet, such as Four11 or Bigfoot. The best time to use a directory service is when you know a person's name but don't have their e-mail address.

Part iv

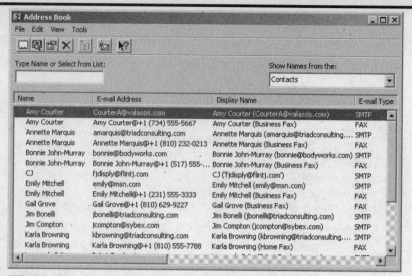

FIGURE 12.4: If you access the address book from outside an e-mail message, you can resize the dialog box and change column width to display all the data.

Public directory services may be available through your Internet Service Provider, or they may have been created or enabled by your network administrator.

If clicking the Find button doesn't open a Find People dialog box, you don't have direct access to directory services. However, if you have an Internet connection, choose Start ➢ Search ➢ For People. Internet Explorer takes you to a search engine that allows you to search for individual e-mail addresses.

Creating a Contact from an E-Mail Address

You can quickly create a contact from any verified e-mail address in the To, From, Cc, or Bcc text boxes. Right-click the underlined address and choose Add To Contacts from the shortcut menu. Outlook opens a blank Contact form with the e-mail address in both the Name and E-Mail text boxes. Correct the name, enter any additional information, and then click Save And Close to close the form and return to your e-mail message. You can also add a contact on-the-fly from e-mail you receive by right-clicking the sender's or another recipient's e-mail address and choosing Add To Contacts from the shortcut menu.

NOTE

See Chapter 13, "Managing Contacts with Outlook 2002," for information on creating contacts.

Creating and Using Distribution Lists (Groups)

When you work with a team or are a member of a committee or task force, you'll often address e-mail to the same group of people: the other members of your team. *Distribution lists* streamline this process. With a distribution list, you create a named list in your Contacts folder, and then add all the members of your team or committee to the group. When you address your next e-mail message, you can send it to the distribution list (and all its members) rather than adding each of the members as individual recipients.

To create a new distribution list in your Contacts folder, follow these steps:

1. Choose Tools ➢ Address Book to open the Address Book window, and click the New Entry button to open the New Entry dialog box.

2. Choose New Distribution List. You can store personal distribution lists in any Contacts folder—you may want to create a subfolder in your main Contacts folder to store distribution lists.

3. Choose where you would like to store this list and click OK to open the Untitled – Distribution List form, shown in Figure 12.5.

4. Enter a name for the list in the Name text box.

5. Click the Select Members button to open the Select Members dialog box.

6. Choose the address book that contains the first member you wish to add. Double-click an address to add the address to the distribution list. Continue selecting additional members.

7. When you've selected all the members of the distribution list, click OK to close the Select Members dialog box.

Part iv

8. Click Save And Close to close the Distribution List form and click the Close button to close the address book.

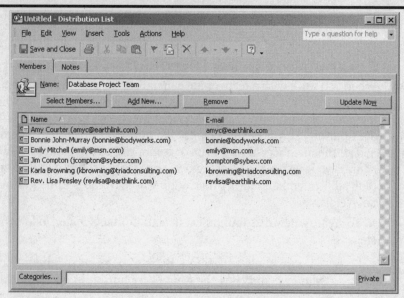

FIGURE 12.5: In the Untitled – Distribution List dialog box, enter a name for the list and select the members you want to include in the list.

NOTE

If you click the Add New button from the Distribution List form, you can enter a display name and e-mail address, and check whether you want to add this person to Contacts. If you do not add the information to Contacts, this person's address is accessible only in the distribution list.

   Figure 12.6 shows the new distribution list in the Contacts address book. Distribution lists are intermingled with contacts—look for the special group icon to tell them apart.

NOTE

If you're one of a group of users who needs the same distribution list, you can send the distribution list contact via e-mail as an attached item. See "Inserting Files and Items into Messages" later in this chapter. You might also talk with your Microsoft Exchange administrator about creating global distribution lists, which are stored in the Global Address list.

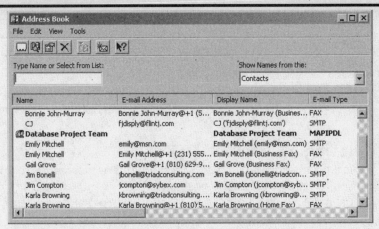

FIGURE 12.6: You can distinguish personal distribution lists in the Contacts address book by the special icon.

Addressing Mail to a Group or Distribution List

To send mail to all members of a group or distribution list, type the group name in the To, Cc, or Bcc text box on the message form, or click one of the three buttons to open the Select Names dialog box. Group names are bold in the Select Names dialog box and address books, and they are preceded by the group icon. Select the group name and click the To, Cc, or Bcc button to add the group's members as message recipients. To check the membership of a group, right-click the group name in the message's address boxes or in the Select Names dialog box and choose Properties to open the group's Properties sheet.

Adding or Removing a Name from a Group or Distribution List

The membership of a team or committee can change as members leave the team and new members are added. Follow these steps to add and remove names from a group or distribution list:

1. Choose Tools ➢ Address Book and select the address book that contains the distribution list.

2. Double-click the name of the list you want to change or right-click a distribution list name and choose Properties to open the Distribution List Properties form.

3. Click the Select Members button to add new group members.

4. To remove a member from a group, select the name you want to delete and click the Remove button in the Distribution List Properties form.

5. When you've finished adding and removing members, click Save And Close to close the Distribution List Properties form.

Deleting a Distribution List

When a team's work is complete or a committee is disbanded, you probably won't need the distribution list anymore. To remove a distribution list, open the address book (Tools ➤ Address Book) and select the group you want to remove.

Right-click the name of the distribution list and choose Delete from the shortcut menu. When you delete the distribution list, any addresses that existed *only* in the list are also deleted.

NOTE

You can also delete the distribution list by deleting the item from the Contacts folder in which it resides.

FORMATTING MESSAGES

In Outlook 2002, Microsoft Word is the default e-mail editor. If you have a computer with not quite enough memory to support Word as the e-mail editor and become uncomfortable with the speed hit you are taking, you can decide to use Outlook's built-in text editor. If you stick with Word, you compose your e-mail message in a Word document, with Word's menus and toolbars at your disposal.

In this section on formatting messages, we'll discuss the format options available to both editors and then focus on using Outlook's text editor.

To switch to Outlook's text editor, choose Tools ➤ Options from Outlook's main window and click the Mail Format tab. Clear the Use Microsoft Word To Edit E-Mail Messages check box. You have a more limited set of tools at your disposal when you make this choice.

TIP

If you like using Word to edit e-mail messages, you might like using it to read messages. On the Mail Format tab of the Options dialog box, you can choose to use Word to read messages that you receive in Rich Text format by selecting Use Microsoft Word To Read Rich-Text Messages.

In addition to selecting an e-mail editor, you may also choose from one of three e-mail formats: HTML, Rich Text, and plain text. For information about changing these options, see "Setting a Message Format" later in this chapter. To learn what these formats have to offer, continue with the next section.

Choosing a Message Format

Outlook supports three e-mail message formats:

▶ HTML is the default format in Outlook 2002. Your message is created in *Hypertext Markup Language (HTML)*, the language used to develop pages on the World Wide Web. The HTML format supports an incredibly wide range of formatting, including backgrounds, horizontal lines, numbered and bulleted lists, and any other formatting you expect to see on a web page. Most e-mail systems support HTML.

▶ With Microsoft Outlook *Rich Text,* you can format fonts, align paragraphs, and use bulleted lists in your message. Outlook Rich Text format (RTF) is understood by only Microsoft Exchange Client versions 4 and 5 and all Outlook versions.

▶ *Plain text* is created using the plain text font, Courier New, and you can't apply any formatting to the message. Plain text is understood by all e-mail systems.

HTML is the default in Outlook 2002 because it is supported by a large number of e-mail systems and if the recipient's e-mail client supports only plain text, an HTML message appears as plain, unformatted text. With the availability of HTML, RTF messages are, for the most part, a thing of the past.

NOTE

Outlook still uses RTF for special Outlook/Exchange Server messages such as meeting and task requests.

Part iv

It's important to remember, though, that while you can compose a message in any of these three formats, the appearance of the message depends on the formats supported by the recipient's e-mail software. Before you spend a long time formatting a message, you might want to check if the person receiving it will be able to see the formatting.

TIP

When you reply to a message, Outlook automatically uses the original message's format for the reply.

What format to choose and exactly what tools are available depend on which of the two e-mail editors you are using to compose your message. Table 12.1 shows what tools to expect with each text editor in each available format.

TABLE 12.1:   Outlook Editors and Formats

TEXT EDITOR	MESSAGE FORMAT	AVAILABLE TOOLS
Microsoft Word	HTML	Text formatting, numbering, bullets, alignment, horizontal lines, borders and shading, backgrounds, HTML styles, clip art, pictures, drawings, WordArt, hyperlinks, linked objects, link themes, columns, and tables. You also have access to AutoCorrect, AutoText, Spelling And Grammar, and other language tools. Almost anything you can create in Word, you can create in this format.
Outlook	HTML	Text formatting, numbering, bullets, alignment, horizontal lines, backgrounds, and HTML styles.
Microsoft Word	Rich Text	Same as Microsoft Word HTML.
Outlook	Rich Text	Text formatting, numbering, bullets, and alignment. Supported by only Exchange and Outlook clients.
Microsoft Word	Plain text	No formatting tools available—understood by all e-mail systems.
Outlook	Plain text	No formatting tools available—understood by all e-mail systems.

Setting a Message Format

You can set a message format for all messages, and you can choose a different format for a particular message. To set the default message format, follow these steps:

1. Choose Tools ➤ Options from the Outlook menu to open the Options dialog box.

2. Click the Mail Format tab, shown in Figure 12.7.

FIGURE 12.7: Choose an e-mail editor and set message format options in the Options dialog box.

3. Choose the format you want to use from the Compose In This Message Format drop-down list.

4. To set specific options related to Internet mail, click the Internet Format button to open the dialog box shown in Figure 12.8.

5. Clear the When An HTML Message Contains Pictures Located On The Internet, Send A Copy Of The Pictures Instead Of The Reference To Their Location check box if you would rather include hyperlinks in your messages rather than actual image files.

Part iv

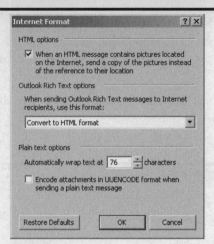

FIGURE 12.8: When sending mail across the Internet, you can set additional options about how messages are handled.

6. Choose your preferred format when you send Outlook Rich Text messages to Internet recipients from the Outlook Rich Text Options drop-down list. Unless all Internet recipients are running Outlook, chances are they will not be able to see Rich Text formatting. Convert To HTML Format is probably the best choice.

7. If you plan to use plain text, set your line-wrapping preference and check Encode Attachments In UUENCODE Format When Sending A Plain Text Message.

8. Click OK to close the Internet Format dialog box and OK again to close the Options dialog box.

Setting a Format for an Individual Message

Even if your default format is HTML, you can choose to send an individual message using Rich Text or plain text. If you are using Word as your e-mail editor, choose a format from the Message Format button in an open e-mail message form.

When you use Outlook's text editor, you cannot change directly from HTML to Rich Text or from Rich Text to HTML—you must switch to plain text first. Formatting you've already applied is lost when you make this switch, so it's best to pick a format and stick with it until you finish composing a message. To change format from HTML to plain text, choose Format ➢ Plain Text in an open e-mail message form.

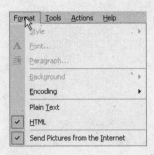

Click Yes to this warning message:

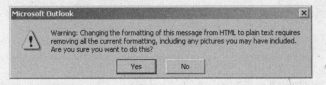

To change from plain text to Rich Text, choose Format ➢ Rich Text—all three format choices are available on the menu when you are using plain text.

Choosing Stationery

If you use an HTML editor, you can personalize your e-mail messages by choosing HTML stationery, a scheme that includes a font and a background color or picture. To select stationery, select HTML as your e-mail editor on the Mail Format tab in the Options dialog box (Tools ➢ Options from Outlook's main menu). Then choose a stationery pattern from the Use This Stationery By Default drop-down list.

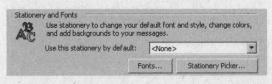

To see what the various stationery patterns look like, click the Stationery Picker button on the Mail Format tab of the dialog box to open the dialog box shown in Figure 12.9. Each stationery choice includes fonts and a background picture or color. Click OK when you've made your selection.

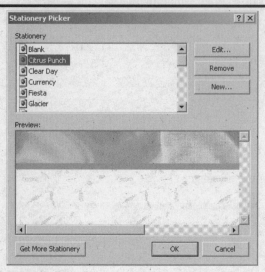

FIGURE 12.9: Select stationery from a list of choices in the Stationery Picker dialog box.

TIP

Can't find stationery to meet your needs? Just click the Get More Stationery button, and Outlook launches your browser so you can visit the Microsoft Office Download Center, where you can download more stationery patterns for free.

Editing Stationery

If you'd like to edit a stationery choice's default font, background, and colors, click the Edit button in the Stationery Picker dialog box. This opens the dialog box shown in Figure 12.10.

Click the Change Font button to change the default font used in the stationery. Choose a picture to use as the background or click Browse to apply any picture as the background. If you'd prefer a color, select Color and click the Color drop-down list to choose from a palette of background colors, or select Do Not Include A Background In This Stationery. Click OK when you have finished editing your stationery selection.

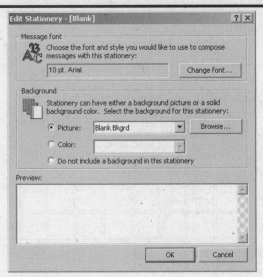

FIGURE 12.10: Edit stationery to your liking in the Edit Stationery dialog box.

TIP

If you'd like to create your own stationery from scratch, click the New button in the Stationery Picker dialog box, give your stationery a name, and then make choices for font and background just as if you were editing an existing selection.

Selecting Fonts

Because most stationery includes fonts, if you select stationery, fonts are set based on this choice. If you would like to override the stationery fonts or choose your own fonts without using stationery, click the Fonts button on the Mail Format tab of the Options dialog box (Tools ➢ Options) to open the Fonts dialog box, shown in Figure 12.11.

You can specify a font to use when composing a new message, when replying and forwarding, and when composing and reading plain text. To override the stationery fonts, be sure to choose an option in the Stationery Fonts section of the dialog box. When you have finished selecting font options, click OK and OK again to save your choices.

Part iv

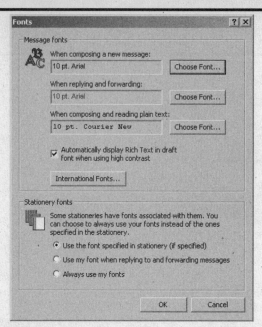

FIGURE 12.11: You can specify fonts to use in specific types of messages.

WARNING

Do not choose an obscure font that no one has. For the font to display correctly, the recipient who opens your mail must have the same font on their system.

Designing Custom Signatures

A *custom signature* is text you add to the end of a message to provide any information you want all of the recipients of your e-mail to know, such as your contact data, confidentiality information, or advertisements for your products.

With Outlook 2002, you can create multiple custom signatures and select the signature you want to use with each message you send. This lets you create a formal signature for business messages and a friendlier signature for messages to friends and family.

To create a custom signature, follow these steps:

1. Choose Tools ➤ Options from the Outlook menu to open the Options dialog box.

2. On the Mail Format tab, click the Signature button to open the Create Signature dialog box.

3. Click New and enter a name for the signature.

4. If you have existing signatures, you can choose to base this new one on one of those, or you can base it on an existing file. Make a choice of how you want to create the new signature and click Next.

5. Enter the text you want to include in your signature in the dialog box shown in Figure 12.12.

6. Click the Font and Paragraph buttons to select font, alignment, and bullets.

7. Click the Clear button if you want to start over.

8. If you want to apply additional HTML formatting, including hyperlinks and images, click the Advanced Edit button to launch an HTML editor, such as FrontPage, if it is available. (You can also insert hyperlinks and images if you are using Word as your e-mail editor and create or edit the signature in the E-Mail Options dialog box.)

9. The vCard options allow you to include your contact information as a *virtual card* in the signature. If the recipient uses Outlook or contact management software that supports the vCard standard, they can drag or copy the attached vCard to add you to their list of contacts. Select a vCard from the list of available options, or click the New vCard From Contact button to create a vCard (see Tip below).

10. When you've finished entering and formatting the text for your custom signature, click OK to return to the Create Signature dialog box and OK again to return to the Options dialog box.

The signature you just created is automatically set as the default, appearing in the text area of every new message. You can choose another default signature (or None) from the drop-down list. You can also choose a different default signature for replies and forwards.

Part iv

TIP

Before you create a new signature, create a contact for yourself (see Chapter 13) that includes your business information and excludes private information that you wouldn't routinely provide to customers or vendors (for example, your home phone number). You can then select this contact to send as a vCard with your messages in the Edit Signature dialog box.

FIGURE 12.12: Design a custom signature in the Edit Signature dialog box.

Selecting a Custom Signature

If you are using Outlook's text editor and would like to use a different signature on an individual message, select the default signature in the message and choose Insert ➤ Signature to select a different signature from the menu. If the custom signature you want to use isn't displayed on the menu, choose More to open the Signature dialog box. Select a signature, and then click OK to replace the default signature in the message.

INSERTING FILES AND ITEMS INTO MESSAGES

You can insert a file or an Outlook item into an e-mail message to send it with the message. It doesn't matter which e-mail editor or message format you use; you can attach items and files to messages in any format. You can insert a copy of the file or item, the text of the file or item, or a hyperlink to the file.

Inserting a Copy of a File

To insert a file into a message, follow these steps:

1. Choose Insert ➤ File from the message menu.

2. Click the Insert File button on the message toolbar to open the Insert File dialog box.

3. Locate the file as you would any document you want to open.

4. When you find the file, click the Insert button. The Insert File dialog box closes, and Outlook inserts an icon representing the file in a new text box labeled *Attach* in the message header.

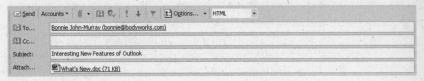

NOTE

A *file* refers exclusively to a document or object created outside of Outlook, such as a Word document, a graphic, or an Excel workbook. Something created within Outlook such as an e-mail message or a task is referred to as an *item*. See "Inserting Outlook Items into E-Mail Messages" later in this chapter.

The file you inserted retains its original formatting and is included in its entirety in the message. Use this method of inserting a file when you want the recipient to work with a copy of the file in its original format. Because the inserted file is a copy, changes your colleague makes are not reflected in the original file. To be able to open an attachment, the recipient must have an application on their system that can read the file's format. For example, to view an Excel workbook, they must have Excel or an application that opens Excel files.

Part iv

WARNING

By default, Outlook 2002 blocks attachment files (such as BAT, EXE, VBS, and JS) that can contain viruses. If you insert one of these file types, you are prompted whether you really want to send a potentially unsafe attachment. If you say Yes, Outlook does allow you to send the attachment. For more about Outlook security features, see "Grappling with Outlook's Security Features" later in this chapter.

Inserting the Text of a File

If the person you are sending the file to does not have an application with which to open it, you could insert the contents of a text-based file as text. For example, rather than attaching a Word document, you could insert the Word document as a text file. To do this, you must first save the document as a text file. Open the document in Word and choose File ➤ Save As. Change the Save As Type to Plain Text (TXT). You will lose any formatting in the document. Only the plain text is retained. To insert a file as text into a mail message, follow these steps:

1. Choose Insert ➤ File from the message menu.

2. Click the Insert File button on the message toolbar to open the Insert File dialog box.

3. Locate the file as you would any document you want to open.

4. When you find the file, click the down arrow on the Insert button to open the Insert menu. Choose Insert As Text. The Insert File dialog box closes, and Outlook inserts the text of the document in the body of the e-mail message.

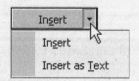

Inserting a Hyperlink to a File Using Word as Your E-Mail Editor

If the person (or people) you want to send a file to has access to a shared network drive or web server, you can insert a file shortcut as a hyperlink, rather than attaching a copy of the document. This not only saves server and mailbox space, it allows you to work on the same file rather than having multiple copies floating around. To make this work, you, first of all, need to move the file to a shared location and verify that the recipient has appropriate access to the file location. After that is taken care of, you can insert a hyperlink into an e-mail message that the recipient can use to locate the correct file. To insert a hyperlink using Word as your e-mail editor, follow these steps:

1. In an open e-mail message, click the Insert Hyperlink button or choose Insert ➢ Hyperlink from the message menu to open the Insert Hyperlink dialog box, shown in Figure 12.13.

2. Decide if you want to create a link to a web page, a document on a shared drive, or an e-mail address:

    a. If the link you want to create is a web link, click the Browse The Web button to launch your browser so you can navigate to the site you want. When you get there, click the mail message on the Windows Taskbar to bring it forward. Outlook fills in the Text To Display and the Address for you. Edit the Text To Display text box as desired and click OK to create the hyperlink.

    b. If the link you want to create is to a document on a shared network drive, navigate to the folder that contains the document and select it from the list. Outlook fills in the Text To Display and the Address for you. Edit the Text To Display text box as desired and click OK to create the hyperlink.

    c. If the link you want to create is to an e-mail address so the recipient can send an e-mail to this address (generally this would be an address other than yours, to which they could just reply), click the E-Mail Address button on the Places bar. Enter the E-Mail Address you want to use, a Subject if you want the message to contain a specific subject, and the Text To Display in the signature. Click OK to add the e-mail address link to the signature.

3. Close the Insert Hyperlink dialog box to return to the mail message and insert the link. Figure 12.14 shows an e-mail message that includes hyperlinks.

Part iv

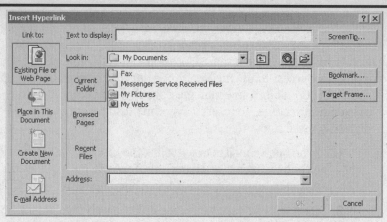

FIGURE 12.13: Use the Insert Hyperlink dialog box to insert hyperlinks in your e-mail signatures and messages.

TIP

If you know the web address, you can type it into the e-mail message and select it before clicking the Insert Hyperlink button. Outlook automatically converts the text to a hyperlink. However, you cannot use this option to insert a link to an e-mail address or file location.

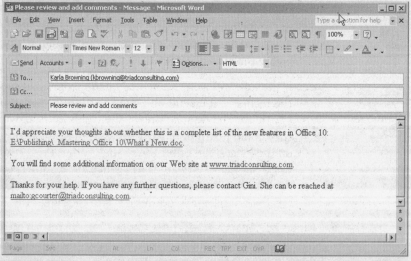

FIGURE 12.14: This e-mail message includes hyperlinks to a shared network file location, a website, and an e-mail address.

Inserting a Hyperlink Using the Outlook Editor

To insert a hyperlink into a message using Outlook as the editor, you must know the Universal Resource Locator (URL) and type it into the Hyperlink dialog box, shown here.

Follow these steps to enter a hyperlink:

1. Choose Insert ➤ Hyperlink.

2. Select the type of hyperlink you want to create: file, ftp, gopher, http, https, mailto, news, telnet, or wais.

3. Type the address in the URL text box.

4. Click OK to create the link.

Inserting Outlook Items into E-Mail Messages

Because your mail recipients do not have access to your Outlook folders, you can insert an Outlook item, such as a contact, in an e-mail message only as an attachment or as text, not as a shortcut. To insert an item as an attachment, follow these steps:

1. Create a new e-mail message.

2. Click the down arrow on the Insert button and choose Item in a Word message, or choose Insert ➤ Item from the menu in an Outlook message.

3. Select the folder that contains the item you want to insert in the Look In text box.

4. Select the item from the Items list. You can click any of the column headers to sort by that column; click the column header again to sort in reverse order. If you are inserting a

Part iv

contact, you can click the first contact in the list and start typing the contact's name to locate the contact you want.

5. If you want to insert more than one item of the same type, hold Ctrl until you have selected all the items.

6. If you are using Outlook as your editor, you can choose to insert the item as text rather than as an attachment. Select Text Only from the Insert As options.

7. Click OK to insert the items.

TIP

If you use Word as your e-mail editor, you cannot insert an Outlook item as text in Outlook 2002 like you could in previous versions of Outlook. You can, however, get around this obstacle so you can send the contents of Outlook items to people who do not run Outlook, and you can do it without changing your default editor. Before creating a new message, choose Actions ➢ New Mail Message Using ➢ Microsoft Outlook (HTML). Follow the steps above to insert the item as text. The next message you create, you'll be back to using Word.

SENDING YOUR MESSAGE

You've selected an e-mail editor, addressed your message, added and formatted text, and inserted attachments and custom signatures; now you're ready to send your message to the recipients. But first, take a moment and examine Outlook's message-handling options to make sure your message is delivered and received with the same care you took while creating it.

Setting Message Options

Unlike the message format options, such as stationery and themes, message options are set for the current message only, not for all new messages. Also, the options are the same regardless of which text editor you are using.

Click the Options button on the message form's toolbar to open the Message Options dialog box, shown in Figure 12.15. Table 12.2 explains each of the message options.

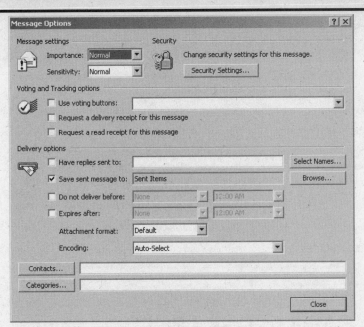

FIGURE 12.15: Message options are set for a specific message.

TABLE 12.2:   Message Options

OPTION	DESCRIPTION
Importance	Alerts the recipient about the importance of the message. Choose from Normal, Low, or High.
Sensitivity	Alerts the recipient about how sensitive the message is. Choose from Normal, Personal, Private, or Confidential.
Security Settings	A new feature of Outlook 2002 that lets you encrypt messages and attachments, and designate a digital signature to secure the message.
Use Voting Buttons	Enables use of e-mail as a voting tool (see "Using E-Mail to Take a Poll" below).
Tracking Options	Notifies you when the message has been received and/or read; depends on the capability of the recipient's mail service.
Have Replies Sent To	Allows you to designate an individual to collect replies to the message.
Save Sent Message To	Indicates which folder you want the sent message stored in; Sent Items is the default.

TABLE 12.2 CONTINUED: Message Options

OPTION	DESCRIPTION
Do Not Deliver Before	Keeps the message from being delivered before the specified date.
Expires After	Marks the message as unavailable after the specified date.
Attachment Format	Allows you to select among the three major attachment formats: MIME, UUEncode, or BinHex.
Encoding	If you have International Options set on the Mail Format tab of the Options dialog box to designate an encoding option rather than AutoSelect, you can choose a particular encoder here. Otherwise, AutoSelect is the only choice.
Contacts	Relates this message to a contact.
Categories	Assigns a category to this message.

Using E-Mail to Take a Poll

Gathering opinions, reaching agreement, and settling on a course of action are all part of working as a team. Outlook has built in a tool to help generate and then gather responses from groups of e-mail recipients. It then even tabulates the results for you, showing you a log of everyone's votes. To activate voting, click the Options tab of an open e-mail message. Click the Use Voting Buttons check box.

You can add your own text to the voting buttons that appear, and you can add additional buttons—put a semicolon between the options, or you'll get one big button. If you want to have someone else collect the results, enter their address in the Have Replies Sent To text box. When you've set up the options, click Send to distribute the ballots to the voting list.

Recipients respond by clicking one of the voting buttons below the menu bar. Their responses are sent to the Inbox like any other message. When you open the message, you can see the current vote, and you can click the information bar to open a tracking form where you can view the results, as seen in Figure 12.16. The tracking form is also available in the sent message—open the message you sent in the Sent Items folder and click the Tracking tab.

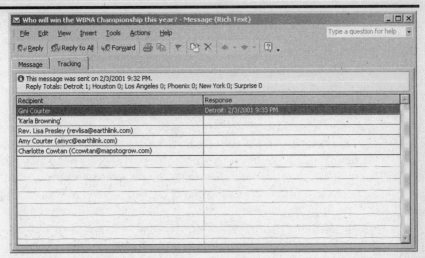

FIGURE 12.16: The Tracking page of a message with voting options lets you determine the status of the vote.

NOTE

Outlook 2002 automatically creates messages with voting buttons in Rich Text format, regardless of the default format you have set.

Using Read and Delivery Receipts

Delivery receipts are fairly reliable; most e-mail servers accurately reflect that a message has been received by the server. If, however, the recipient's e-mail address is valid, but the server can't communicate with the recipient's e-mail client, the message may never be delivered by the recipient's server, and you'll still get a receipt confirming delivery. *Read receipts* are less reliable. Some e-mail servers are restricted from sending read receipts by the server administrator to minimize the spread of viruses, and others send read receipts along with the delivery receipts. Microsoft Exchange Server handles read and delivery receipts very well; if your message leaves the Exchange environment, read receipts in particular are less reliable.

TIP

Some e-mail servers will send delivery receipts for messages sent in plain text or HTML, but not in Rich Text format. To increase the chances of reliable delivery receipts, switch to HTML.

Part iv

Sending Mail Messages

 When you're ready to send your message to its recipients, click the Send button on the message toolbar. Outlook sends the message using your default e-mail account. If you want to send it using a different e-mail account, click the Accounts button on the message toolbar and select the specific account you want to use.

As you send the message, you may be wondering how long the message will hang around in the Outbox. The answer: It depends. In most Microsoft Exchange Server or other third-party server networks, mail leaves your Inbox and goes directly to the mail server for processing. However, in Outlook 2002, you can choose to hold all of your mail in the Outbox until you choose to send it. If you have ever clicked the Send button and then said to yourself, "I really shouldn't have done that," then this feature is for you. To set this option, choose Tools ➢ Options, click the Mail Setup tab, and clear the Send Immediately When Connected check box. With this option turned off, outgoing mail stays in your Outbox until you tell it to leave.

SENDING WEB PAGES WITH OUTLOOK AND INTERNET EXPLORER

You can attach web pages, including all the hyperlinks, in an Outlook e-mail message directly from Internet Explorer. Before you jump in, you need to check a couple of settings in Outlook 2002 and Internet Explorer. In Outlook, you must be using HTML format (choose Tools ➢ Options ➢ Message Format and select HTML from the Compose In This Message Format drop-down list). To configure Internet Explorer, choose Tools ➢ Internet Options. Click the Programs tab, and make sure Microsoft Outlook is listed as the e-mail program.

You're now ready to use Outlook e-mail from Internet Explorer. Browse to find the page you want to send. Make sure you're using the live page, not a cached page, by clicking the Refresh button. (If you send a cached page, it appears as an attachment rather than as a web page in the message body.) After the page refreshes, choose File ➢ Send ➢ Page By E-Mail. If Outlook isn't running, IE launches it. In a few seconds, you see a mail message that includes the web page.

To move the message out of the Outbox and to the Internet or local mail server:

- ► Choose Tools ➢ Send/Receive and choose Send All from the Outlook menu to send, but not receive, messages to all of your e-mail accounts.

- ► Click the Send/Receive button on the toolbar or choose Tools ➢ Send/Receive and choose Send And Receive ➢ All to send and receive messages to all of your e-mail accounts.

- ► Choose Tools ➢ Send/Receive and select a specific account to send and receive messages from only one e-mail account.

CREATING AND USING SEND/RECEIVE GROUPS

If you have more than one e-mail account, you can create *send/receive groups* designating different send/receive options for each group. A group can contain one e-mail account or several. You decide what makes sense for your situation. Send/receive groups are particularly valuable when you are working offline because you can control how often you send and receive mail, the size of attachments you download, and whether you download headers or full messages. See Chapter 13 of *Mastering Microsoft Outlook 2002* by Gini Courter and Annette Marquis (Sybex, 2001) to learn how to create send/receive groups that you can use online and offline.

REVIEWING MAIL MESSAGES

When you are using another application and Outlook is running in the background, an envelope icon appears in the Windows system tray to notify you that you have received a message. Double-click the icon to activate Outlook and review your messages. In the Inbox Information Viewer, unread messages are boldface, so they are easy to spot.

Select a message, and the beginning of the message appears in the preview pane below the messages. If the preview pane is not open, choose View ➢ Preview Pane from the Outlook menu to display it. The previews usually let you see enough of a message to gauge its urgency. You can change the size of the preview pane by adjusting the bar at the top of the pane up or down with the mouse pointer. You cannot preview messages that have been encrypted for security by the sender.

WARNING

Viewing a message in the preview pane triggers some e-mail viruses, just as they would be if you opened the message that contains the attached virus. For increased security, turn off the preview pane (View ➤ Preview Pane turns the pane display on or off).

The first four columns of the default Inbox view show the message's Importance, Message Icon, Flag Status, and Attachment information. If the sender set the importance of the message, it is displayed in the first column; high importance is marked with a red exclamation point, low importance with a blue arrow. Table 12.3 shows the major icons used in the Inbox.

TABLE 12.3:   Inbox Message Icons

ICON	MESSAGE
!	High importance
↓	Low importance
✉	Unread
✉	Digitally signed message
✉	Read
✉	Forwarded
✉	Replied to
⚑	Flagged for follow-up
⚑	Flagged; follow-up completed
📎	Includes an attachment
📧	Meeting request
📧	Task request
📧	Digitally signed

OPENING MAIL MESSAGES

To open a message, double-click the closed-envelope icon in front of the message—the same symbol that announced the message's arrival in the system tray. Outlook opens the message in a separate window. An information bar above the message header indicates if the message was flagged or has importance or sensitivity settings other than Normal. In Figure 12.17, the message header indicates that this message has high importance and was replied to.

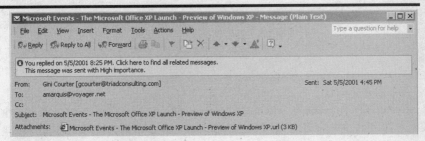

FIGURE 12.17: The message header contains important information about the message.

TIP

To open multiple messages, each in its own window, hold Ctrl and click to select each message in the list; then right-click and choose Open Selected Items.

To close a message, click the Close button on the message's title bar, choose File ➤ Close from the message's menu, or press Alt+F4. When you close a message, it remains in the Inbox but is no longer bold.

TIP

The To, From, and Subject fields in a received message have a gray background, which indicates that they can't be edited. In the case of the Subject field, this isn't true. You can change the subject of a message, including keywords in the subject to make it easier to find later. For example, a message with the subject *RE: Inquiry* that contains a quote you requested might be better titled *Design Quote*. To change the subject, select the subject text and start typing. When you close the message, you'll be prompted to save changes.

SENDING AND RECEIVING DIGITALLY SIGNED MESSAGES

When you need to send or receive secure data over the Internet, a digitally signed message can give you confidence that the message has not been altered. To send or receive a digitally signed message, you must receive a digital ID or certificate from a certified security authority, such as VeriSign, Inc. Your Microsoft Exchange Server administrator may also be able to issue a digital ID. You can use your digital ID to verify your signature and encrypt your message so only the intended recipient (who must also have a valid digital ID) can read it.

A secured message has a Certificate button just above the message box.

To view the signature or encryption used with the message, click the Certificate button to open the Digital Signature dialog box. Outlook validates certificates by ensuring that:

▶ The contents of the message didn't change after the message was signed.

▶ The certificate is not revoked or expired.

▶ The e-mail address on the certificate matches the address on the message.

▶ There is a check mark in front of each item to indicate that it is valid.

By default, Outlook notifies you before you open a message with an invalid certificate. You can check the Digital Signature dialog box to find the item that is not valid; it will be marked with a red X rather than a check mark.

If the certificate has expired, you can e-mail a message to the sender and let them know. Otherwise, it may be that the certificate is not from a certifying organization that Outlook already recognizes. If you know the certificate is acceptable, click the Edit Trust button in the Certificate Or Digital Signature dialog box and choose Explicitly Trust This Certificate to accept this certificate in the future.

To find out more about digital signatures, visit www.thawte.com/, www.verisign.com, or www.globalsign.net.

Opening Messages with Attachments

Outlook 2002 displays attachments in the message header, as shown in Figure 12.18. To open the attachment, double-click the icon.

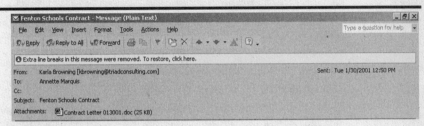

FIGURE 12.18: Icons in the message header represent attachments.

The first time you double-click an attachment created using certain applications, an Opening Mail Attachment dialog box warns you that this type of file may include a virus. This is just a standard precaution and does not indicate that there is anything unusual about this particular file. Choose whether you want to open the file or save it to disk, and click OK. If the file isn't from a trusted source and you'd rather not open it, click Cancel.

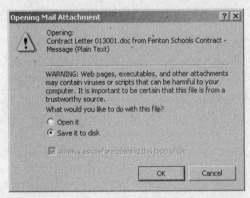

With some file types, you can disable the Always Ask Before Opening This Type Of File check box, and Outlook will quit prompting you about the particular file type.

After you select Open It and click OK, Windows searches for the application needed to open the attachment, launches the application, and opens the file. If you don't have the required application, or if the file extension isn't properly registered in the Windows Registry, you're notified that the file can't be opened and told what action you could take to open the file.

Part iv

TROUBLESHOOTING ATTACHMENTS AND ENCODED MESSAGES

If you send and receive a lot of attachments to and from people who use different e-mail systems and applications than you do, you have probably had some occasional trouble opening an attachment or even receiving a message. Here are a few pointers that might come in handy.

Attachments

If you receive a file created with an application that you do not have on your computer, you may be able to associate the file with another application. For example, you don't have Adobe Illustrator but know that CorelDRAW will open Illustrator files. You can associate files with the Illustrator extension to CorelDRAW using Windows Explorer (View ➤ Folder Options ➤ File Types).

If you are uncertain whether you have a suitable application, look at the icon used to display the attachment. When the familiar Windows icon is displayed, there is no application associated with the file on your computer:

If you are not sure about whether the file type is supported by the application you choose, be sure to clear the Always Use This Program To Open These Files check box until you've verified that it works. If the file can't be opened directly in any application, associating the file won't solve the problem. If you don't have success and still don't know which program an attachment was created in, ask the sender before you give up. You may need to request that the sender convert the file to a format you can open.

Encoded Messages

Messages sent over the Internet are often encoded to preserve formatting and maintain the integrity of attachments. The most common encoding schemes are the Unix-to-Unix encoding format (UUEncode) and the Multipurpose Internet Mail Extensions format (MIME).

CONTINUED ➡

Outlook automatically decodes messages encoded in both of these formats. The only way you can know that the message was encoded is by looking at the text at the beginning of the message. If you receive a message encoded with a scheme other than UUEncode or MIME, the text of the message appears to be garbled.

The sender may have chosen to encode the message using some other coding scheme. You can let them know that they need to choose to encode messages in MIME or UUEncode so that Outlook can decode them for you.

Often, however, the sender's mail program automatically encoded the message, so the sender doesn't know that the message was encoded. They may be able to change a mail format or delivery option and switch to UUEncode or MIME, or they may not have this option. If you regularly receive encoded mail from users with other formats (like Mac users who use BinHex), consider a separate decoding program. You can find out more about decoding e-mail attachments in an excellent article by Michael Santovec at http://pages.prodigy.net/michael_santovec/.

Grappling with Outlook's Security Features

If you receive a lot of attachments, one of the first things you may notice is that Microsoft has significantly beefed up Outlook's security and warnings in Office XP. When you try to open an attachment with one of the file types that provide excellent containers for viruses, you don't have the option to open it. As a matter of fact, you can never open it—access to it is completely blocked. This should have a positive impact on the spread of many e-mail viruses, but it also creates havoc when you need to have a certain file. The file types that Outlook blocks completely include some commonly used files such as Internet shortcuts, executables, and Microsoft Access databases. Table 12.4 shows you the file attachment extensions that Outlook blocks from access.

Part iv

TABLE 12.4:   Blocked File Extensions—Level-One File Types

FILE EXTENSION	FILE TYPE
ADE; ADP; MDA; MDB; MDE; MDZ	Microsoft Access files
BAS; VB; VBE; VBS	Microsoft Visual Basic and Visual Basic Script files
BAT; COM; PIF	Batch files and Microsoft MS-DOS programs
CHM; HTA; INS; ISP	HTML and Internet files
CMD; MSI; MSP	Microsoft Windows NT Command Script and Windows Installer files
CRT	Security certificates
EXE	Programs
JS; JSE	JScript files
LNK; URL	Shortcuts
MSC; MST; PCD	Microsoft Common Console documents
CPL; HLP; INF; REG; SCR; SHS	Miscellaneous files
SCT; WSC; WSF; WSH	Windows Script files

If you receive an e-mail message with one of these attachments, you still see the paper clip icon to indicate that the message has an attachment. When you open the message, however, the attachment is not there. In its place, you see the following message in the information area of the message.

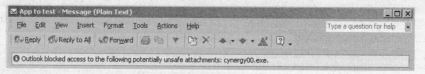

The only thing you can do about it is ask the sender to send the attachment to you in a different format. For example, you could ask them to zip an Access database or copy a URL for a website into the message text instead of sending the link as an attachment.

NOTE

If you are unfamiliar with zipping files, we recommend downloading Winzip from www.winzip.com. It's shareware, so you can buy it up front or pay after you've tried it. It's well worth the investment.

Preventing File Blocking

If you regularly receive e-mail messages of a certain type and want to be able to continue to do so, you or, if you are on a Microsoft Exchange Server, your server administrator can prevent Outlook from blocking particular file types. Before you do this, though, make sure you have excellent, up-to-date virus protection software. Use big-name software such as Norton or McAfee that stays on top of all the latest viruses and provides you with updates on a regular basis either for free or on a subscription basis. When you are confident that your e-mail protection is working properly and plan to keep it working properly, then, and only then, consider lessening these security restrictions.

If you are on a Microsoft Exchange Server network, the Exchange Server administrator can customize the security settings by installing a special Outlook custom form in a public folder and then configuring the security options for both individual users and groups of users. You can get information on Outlook 2002 e-mail security and links to the downloadable files on the Office Update website—`http://office.microsoft.com/assistance`.

If you are not on an Exchange Server network, you can control your own settings, but you have to be willing to edit the Windows Registry to do it. Follow these steps to safely edit the Registry using Windows 2000:

1. Choose Start ➢ Run.

2. Type **regedit** in the Open text box and click OK.

3. Before you make any changes to the Registry, it's always a good idea to back it up first. To do that, choose Registry ➢ Export Registry Files. Identify the file location where you'd like to save the backup and give it a name such as *Before Security Changes*. Click Save to save the Registry file.

4. Click the folders to open this key: `HKEY_CURRENT_USER\Software\Microsoft\Office\10.0\Outlook\Security`.

5. Choose Edit ➢ New ➢ String Value.

6. Enter **Level1Remove** as the name of the string value.

7. Right-click the new string value and choose Modify.

8. Enter the file extensions separated by semicolons that you do not want Outlook to block. For example, if you would like to receive URL and MDB files, enter **url;mdb**.

9. Click OK to save the new string value and then close the Registry.

10. Close Outlook and reboot before testing the new settings. You can send yourself a file with one of the newly unblocked extensions to test the changes.

If you decide at a later time to remove the new string value, you can reopen the Registry and delete the string value.

TIP

Microsoft suggests that the safest way to share potentially dangerous files is to post them to a shared network location or web server. If you don't have access to a web server of your own, you may want to check out some of the free web services that allow you to upload and download files. Some provide as much as 200MB of free storage space and offer a good option for safe file exchange. Whalemail at www.whalemail.com provides 75MB, and it even allows you to send pickup notifications to the people you want to receive the file. Other similar services include www.visto.com and www.bigvault.com.

REPLYING TO MAIL

`Reply` After you read a message, you can reply to the sender or everyone who received the message, including those who received courtesy copies of the message. Select or open the message you want to reply to; then click the Reply button to address a reply only to the sender.

`Reply to All` Select the Reply To All button to send a reply to the sender and all the other recipients of the message you received. Outlook opens a message form and enters the recipients' addresses in the To text box. You can add other recipients using the To, Cc, and Bcc buttons on the message form. Keep in mind that when you reply to a message, Outlook uses the same format as the original message to ensure that the recipient can read the reply. If the Bcc text box is not visible, click the Options button's drop-down list and select Bcc.

NOTE

Reply To All does not reply to individuals who received a blind courtesy copy (Bcc) of the original message.

TIP

When you click the Reply or Reply To All button, Outlook opens and addresses the new message form, but the original message remains open. To have Outlook automatically close the original message when you click Reply, Reply To All, or Forward, enable the Close Original Message On Reply Or Forward check box in the Options dialog box (Tools ➢ Options ➢ Preferences ➢ E-Mail Options).

FORWARDING MESSAGES

Forwarding sends the entire message and any text you add to another recipient. To forward an open message, click the Forward button or choose Actions ➢ Forward from the message menu. If the message is not open, right-click the message in the Information Viewer and choose Forward from the shortcut menu.

Formatting Options for Forwarded Messages

To indicate how the original text and text you add should appear in the forwarded message, follow these steps:

1. Choose Tools ➢ Options on the Outlook menu to open the Options dialog box.

2. On the Preferences tab, click the E-Mail Options button to open the E-Mail Options dialog box.

3. Choose a format from the When Forwarding A Message drop-down list:

   ▶ Attach Original Message

   ▶ Include Original Message Text (the default)

   ▶ Include And Indent Original Message Text

   ▶ Prefix Each Line Of The Original Message

4. To add comments to replies and forwarded messages, enable the Mark My Comments With check box and enter your name, initials, or other text in the text box.

5. Click OK to close the E-Mail Options dialog box.

6. Click OK to close the Options dialog box.

Part iv

FLAGGING MESSAGES FOR FURTHER ACTION

You can't always reply to, forward, or even fully read and review a message when you receive it. *Flagging* messages ensures a message doesn't get lost and helps you stay organized. When you flag a message, you note the type of action that's required. You can even set a reminder so you don't forget to follow up on the message.

TIP

You can flag messages you're sending or forwarding as well as those you receive. Flagging is a quick way to let the recipient know that they need to act on a message by a particular date.

 To flag an open message, choose Actions ➤ Follow Up from the message menu, or click the Follow Up button on the message toolbar. If the message is not open, right-click it in the Information Viewer and choose Follow Up from the shortcut menu. Choose a flag description from the list of choices, or enter your own description in the Flag To text box, as shown in Figure 12.19.

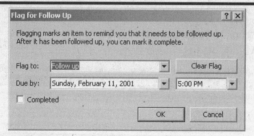

FIGURE 12.19: In the Flag For Follow Up dialog box, you can set the type of flag, and the date and time you want the flag to notify you.

Choose a date on which to be reminded about the message using the Due By calendar control. If you want, edit the reminder time. When you're finished entering flag information, click OK to close the dialog box.

When you've completed follow-up with the message, you can either clear the flag or mark the action complete. You can sort by the Flag Status column in table views, so if you want to be able to sort or group messages that you've flagged as complete, change the flag status to *Completed*. To clear the flag, open the Flag For Follow Up dialog box, click the Clear Flag button, and click OK. To mark a flag as complete, open the Flag For Follow Up dialog box and enable the Completed check box, then click OK to close the dialog box.

TIP

You can right-click a flag in any table view and choose Flag Complete or Clear Flag from the shortcut menu.

SETTING E-MAIL OPTIONS

Outlook is an options-rich application. Everywhere you turn, you find options for customizing how Outlook handles whatever it is you want to do. Outlook e-mail options include settings for how messages are handled, what to do with replies and forwards, and how to format messages, and a whole range of Advanced options.

Options related to e-mail fall into three major categories:

▶ General options including Advanced and Tracking options

▶ Mail Setup options

▶ Mail Format options—covered earlier in this chapter—including message formats, stationery, fonts, and signature

In this last section, we'll review the key General, Advanced, and Tracking options available in Outlook.

General Options

You can find the General options by clicking the E-Mail Options button in the Options dialog box (Tools ➤ Options). Here you'll find options related to message handling and replies and forwards. You'll also find the only access to the Advanced and Tracking options.

Message Handling Options

Message Handling options, shown in Figure 12.20, are the options that control how your messages and your Inbox behave. Using these options, you can determine if, when you move or delete a message, you are returned to the Inbox or to the previous or next message in your Inbox. You can decide what happens when you reply to or forward a message and whether the messages you send are saved in the Sent Items folder.

Some people like to have a notification box pop up when they are working to let them know that they've received new mail. If you like that kind of interruption or if your job requires that you respond to e-mail immediately, select the Display A Notification Message When New Mail Arrives check box.

Be sure to select the Automatically Save Unsent Messages check box to save messages you aren't finished with to the Drafts folder.

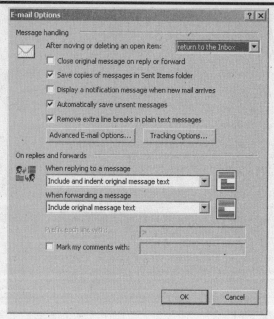

FIGURE 12.20: You can change the behavior of your Inbox using the Message Handling options.

Reply and Forward Options

For some people and some organizations, it's more important to save server space and network speed than it is to provide message recipients with a copy of their original message in a reply. Others prefer the more convenient approach of including the original message when replying. Whatever your choice, Outlook has an option for you. In the On Replies And Forwards options on the E-Mail Options page of the Options dialog box (see Figure 12.20), you can choose from the following about how replies are handled:

- ▶ Do Not Include Original Message
- ▶ Attach Original Message
- ▶ Include Original Message Text
- ▶ Include And Indent Original Message Text
- ▶ Prefix Each Line Of The Original Message

The options for forwarding messages are the same except that you cannot choose to not include the original message—that kind of defeats the purpose, wouldn't you say?

If you choose the Prefix Each Line Of The Original Message option, you can choose the character you'd like to prefix the lines with. If you are using HTML or Rich Text as your message format, you can also choose to mark your comments with text such as your initials or name.

WARNING

If you choose to prefix each line of a reply or forward, for some strange reason, Outlook cannot resist spell-checking the entire message. That means you'll be correcting the sender's spelling as well as your own.

When you have set the options in the E-Mail Options dialog box, click the Advanced E-Mail Options button to set options related to saving messages, receiving new items, and sending messages.

Advanced Options

The Advanced options, shown in Figure 12.21, are really not all that advanced, so don't worry that you might be over your head. Nothing in here is going to make Outlook blow up, your computer crash, or a nuclear holocaust happen. In fact, some of these options are pretty useful.

In the Save Messages group of options, you can choose where you want your unsent messages saved and how often you'd like Outlook to save them there. If you have rules set up that deliver mail directly to folders, you may want to select the In Folders Other Than The Inbox, Save Replies With Original Message check box. That keeps all your incoming and outgoing mail from particular people or on particular subjects all in one place.

Part iv

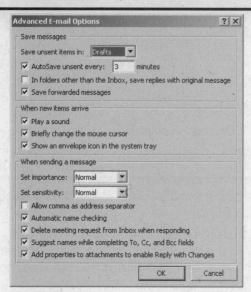

FIGURE 12.21: In the Advanced E-Mail Options dialog box, you can set options about how messages are saved, how you are alerted to new messages, and the kind of help you want when sending messages.

If you are concerned about server space, clear the Save Forwarded Messages check box. You have the original; all the forwarded message gives you is whom you forwarded it to and any other comments you added.

In the When New Items Arrive section, you can decide what you want Outlook to do to draw your attention to the fact that you have new messages. Short of tapping you on the shoulder, you have just about all the options most people need.

NOTE

Remember that the Display A Notification Message When New Mail Arrives option is in the E-Mail Options dialog box, one step back from the Advanced E-Mail Options dialog box. You won't find it here with the other types of notifications. Go figure.

The When Sending A Message group of options is the place to set the global importance and sensitivity level of your messages. However, unless you are the President or work for the CIA, you are probably better off leaving these options alone. Most people get pretty irritated if every message they receive from you has high importance.

Two new options are available in this group. Suggest Names While Completing To, Cc, And Bcc Fields is Outlook's new AutoComplete feature. If you find that it completes names incorrectly or results in sending errors, turn this feature off. It just means you'll get a Check Names dialog box from which you can pick unclear or incomplete names. If you leave Automatic Name Checking selected, you'll have to respond only when you are sending to someone that Outlook can't clearly recognize.

The other new option is Add Properties To Attachments To Enable Reply With Changes. Reply With Changes is a new feature of Office XP that allows you to send documents from any of the Office applications by choosing File ➢ Send To ➢ Mail Recipient (For Review). This option automatically activates the Reviewing toolbar and tracks changes made to the document. This option is turned on by default, and we have yet to discover a reason to turn it off.

The final set of options is the Tracking options. When you have set all the Advanced options, click OK to save them and click the Tracking Options button on the E-Mail Options dialog box to review those options.

Tracking Options

Tracking options, shown in Figure 12.22, control read and delivery receipts—those you initiate and those you receive. They also control how Outlook handles requests, such as meeting and task requests, and voting messages.

By default, requests, responses, and receipts are processed on arrival. This means, for example, if you receive a request to attend a meeting, that meeting appears on your calendar as a tentative appointment even before you respond to the meeting request.

If you have a need for a receipt for every message you send, select the Read Receipt and Delivery Receipt check boxes. Be aware, however, that many server administrators have turned off the processing of these automatic receipts as a precaution against unwanted viruses. Just because you don't receive a receipt, it doesn't mean your recipient hasn't read your message.

If you receive a message with a delivery or read receipt using Internet mail, you can determine how you'd like Outlook to handle it by selecting Always Send A Response, Never Send A Response, or Ask Me Before Sending A Response. This last choice seems the most prudent, and it's the choice we've selected.

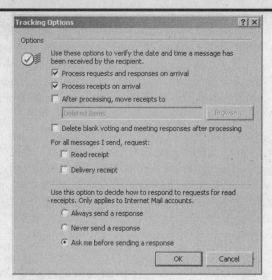

FIGURE 12.22: Tracking options can be set to track messages you send and those you receive.

When you've finished setting Tracking options, click OK three times, and you are ready to get back to work.

WHAT'S NEXT

In the next chapter, you'll discover how Outlook 2002's features make it very easy for you to receive, maintain, and use information about others—customers, co-workers, clients, and associates—by using a working database of contacts.

Chapter 13

MANAGING CONTACTS WITH OUTLOOK 2002

As you get busy using Office XP and find yourself collaborating with others and exchanging e-mail and files, it becomes vital that you develop a way to manage all that information. If you don't, it will become a sea of seemingly unrelated information.

Outlook 2002 makes it quite easy to manage your information through the use of its Contacts database, a way of consolidating information about each person you're in contact with. With Outlook, you can create new contacts to add to your database, change that contact's details, save or remove the contact to or from your list, and find a specific person when you need to do so.

Adapted from *Mastering Microsoft Outlook 2002*
by Gini Courter and Annette Marquis
ISBN 0-7821-4001-7   752 pp $39.99

CREATING A CONTACT

In Outlook, a *contact* is an individual or organization you need to maintain data about. The information can be basic, such as a name and phone number, or more detailed, including anniversary and birthday information, nicknames, and digital IDs. If you've been tracking contacts manually in a day planner or address book, you'll have some work ahead of you before the Contacts feature can be fully functional. If you have addresses in any electronic format—an Excel worksheet, contact manager software such as ACT or ECCO, or a database like Microsoft Access—you don't have to spend time reentering the data. Outlook can import data from a variety of sources.

Outlook is robust enough to manage your business and professional contacts, and don't forget to take time to add personal contacts like friends and family members so all your important names, e-mail addresses, phone numbers, and addresses are in one place.

To enter contact data, you can open a blank Contact form in several ways:

Contacts

▶ If you're going to be entering a number of contacts, click the Contacts icon on the Outlook shortcut bar to open the Contacts folder.

▶ Choose File ➢ New ➢ Contact from the menu bar.

▶ Click the New Contact button on the toolbar.

▶ If you're working in another folder (for example, Calendar), choose File ➢ New ➢ Contact from the menu bar—you'll just need to look a bit further down the menu selections to find Contact. The same list is attached to the toolbar; click the New Item button's down arrow and select Contact from the menu.

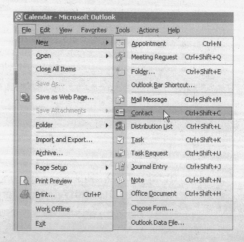

▶ If your hands are already on the keyboard, there's no need to grab the mouse—press Ctrl+Shift+C.

The Contact form is a multipage form, with tabs labeled General, Details, Activities, Certificates, and All Fields. The form opens with the General page displayed, as shown in Figure 13.1. (To move to another page, simply click the tab for the page.) In the text boxes on the General page, you can enter the kinds of information you usually store in an address or telephone book.

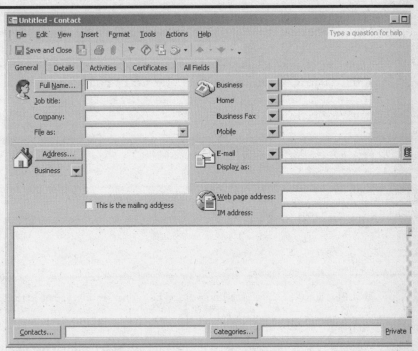

FIGURE 13.1: Use Outlook Contact forms to collect and manage information about business and personal contacts.

Entering Names, Job Titles, and Companies

Begin by entering the contact's name in the first text box on the General tab of the Contact form, next to the Full Name button. If you want to enter just the contact's first and last names, that's fine, but you can also include their title, middle name (or initial), and suffix. For example, *Mary Smith*,

Dr. Mary Smith, or *Smith, III, Mr. Richard M.* are all acceptable ways of entering names.

You don't have to fill in all the fields; however, you can't use information you don't enter. For example, Outlook provides an easy way to quickly create a letter to be sent to a contact. If you might need to send formal correspondence to your friend Bill Jones, take the time to enter Bill's title when you create the contact. You can always choose to omit the title on a specific piece of correspondence, but you can include it easily only if you've entered it in the Contact form in the first place.

When you've finished typing the contact's name, press Enter or Tab to move to the next field. Outlook parses (separates) the name into parts for storing it. If Outlook can't determine how to separate the parts of the name, or if the name you entered is incomplete (perhaps you entered only a first name in the Full Name field), the Check Full Name dialog box, shown in Figure 13.2, opens so you can verify that Outlook is storing the name correctly.

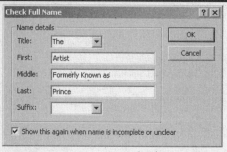

FIGURE 13.2: The Check Full Name dialog box appears when you need to verify how a name should be stored in Outlook.

Full Name... | Outlook does a fairly good job of separating names appropriately. However, it doesn't handle some names and titles perfectly. If you enter the titles Dr., Miss, Mr., Mrs., Ms., or Prof., Outlook places them in the Title field. However, if you use other titles—for example, The Rev. for a minister, The Honorable for a judge, or Fr. for a priest—Outlook does not recognize them as titles and places them in the First Name field. Names that are composed of two words, such as Jo Anne or Mary Jo, may also not be separated correctly into first, middle, and last names. You can edit these fields manually by clicking the Full Name button to open the Check Full Name dialog box.

TIP

To instruct Outlook not to check incomplete or unclear names, clear the check box in the Check Full Name dialog box before clicking OK. To turn checking back on, open a Contact form, click the Full Name button to open the dialog box, turn the option back on, and then click OK.

In the Job Title text box, enter the contact's complete job title. If you don't know the contact's job title, simply leave the field blank. Enter the name of the contact's company in the Company field. In the File As field, either select an entry from the drop-down list or type a new entry to indicate how the contact should be filed.

If you choose to file contacts with the first name first, you can still sort them by last name, so it's really a matter of personal preference. If you'll usually look up the company rather than the individual, it's a good idea to file contacts by company name. For example, ABC Graphics assigned Jim as the sales representative to your account, but it might be more useful to file the contact as *ABC Graphics (Jim)* than as just *Jim*—particularly if you have trouble remembering Jim's name.

You aren't limited to the choices in the File As drop-down list. Select the text in the File As text box, and then enter the File As text you'd like to use. This allows you to enter formal names for contacts but store them in a way that makes them easy to retrieve; you can enter *Ms. Emily Mitchell* as the contact name, but file your friend as *Emily* so you can find her quickly.

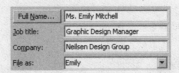

Entering Contact Addresses

Outlook allows you to store three addresses—Business, Home, and Other—for your contact and designate one of the three as the address you want to use as the contact's primary address. To choose the type of address you want to enter, click the down arrow in the Address section and select the address type from the list. The address type is displayed to the left of the arrow.

Click in the Address text box on the General page of the Contact form and type the address as you would write it on an envelope. Type the street address on the first or first and second lines, pressing Enter to move down a line. Type the city, state or province, country, and zip code or postal code on the last line. If you don't enter a country, Outlook uses the Windows default country.

NOTE

The Windows default country is set in the Windows Control Panel under Regional Settings (Windows 98) or Regional Options (Windows 2000).

When you press Tab to move to the next field, Outlook checks the address just as it did the contact name. If the address is unclear or incomplete, the Check Address dialog box opens, as shown in Figure 13.3. Make sure the information for each field is correct, and then click OK to close the dialog box.

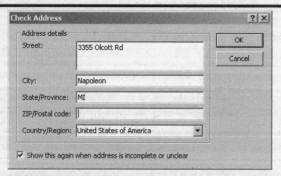

FIGURE 13.3: The Check Address dialog box opens to allow you to verify an incomplete or unclear address.

In Outlook, the primary address for a contact is called the mailing address. The mailing address is the address displayed in most views and is the address used when you merge a Word main document with your Outlook contacts. By default, the first address you enter for a contact is set as the mailing address. To change the address used as the mailing address, make sure the address you want to use (Home, Business, or Other) is displayed in the Address text box, then click the This Is The Mailing Address check box to make the displayed address the mailing address.

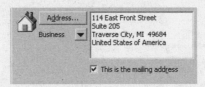

Entering Contact Telephone Numbers

This is truly the age of connectivity. While three mail addresses are sufficient for nearly everyone you know, it isn't unusual to have 5, 6, or more telephone numbers to contact one person: home phones, work phones, home and work fax numbers, mobile phones, ISDN numbers, and pager numbers. With Outlook, you can enter up to 19 different telephone numbers for a contact and display 4 numbers at a glance on the Contact form, as shown in Figure 13.4.

FIGURE 13.4: The Contact form displays 4 of the 19 phone numbers you can enter for a contact.

When you create a new contact, the four default phone number descriptions Outlook displays are Business, Home, Business Fax, and Mobile. To enter a telephone number for one of those four descriptions, simply click in or tab to the appropriate text box on the General page of the Contact form and type in the telephone number. You don't need to enter parentheses around the area code, hyphens, or spaces—just enter the digits in the telephone number, as shown here.

When you move out of the text box, Outlook automatically formats the digits, adding parentheses, spaces, and hyphens. If you enter a seven-digit telephone number, Outlook assumes the phone number is local and adds your area code to the number.

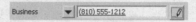

WARNING

If you include letters in your telephone numbers (like 1-800-CALLME), you won't be able to use Outlook's automated dialing program to call this contact.

To enter another telephone number, click the down arrow for any of the four text boxes to open the menu of telephone number types.

The telephone number types that have check marks are those you've already entered. Choose the type of phone number you want to enter from the menu, then enter the number in the text box.

Because Outlook displays only four numbers at a time, the numbers that are displayed in the four text boxes may not be the numbers you use most frequently. That's not a problem—just open the menu next to each text box and, from the menu, select the types you want to display.

Entering Country Codes for International Calls

To see the details of a phone number and set the country code for an international number, double-click the phone number to open the Check Phone Number dialog box.

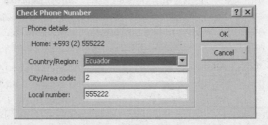

Select the country from the Country/Region drop-down list, and Outlook automatically inserts the country code into the number. Click OK to display the country code in the phone number text box.

Entering E-Mail Addresses

You can enter up to three e-mail addresses for a contact. The e-mail addresses, on the General page of the Contact form, are labeled E-Mail, E-Mail 2, and E-Mail 3, rather than Business and Home like mail addresses and telephone numbers. In many cases, the top-level domain can help you distinguish which address is for business and which is for home use.

Part iv

To enter an e-mail address, enter the entire address, including the username and the domain name. When you move out of the e-mail address text box, Outlook analyzes the address you entered to ensure that it resembles a valid e-mail address. Outlook does *not* check to make sure that the address is the correct e-mail address for this contact or that the address exists. Outlook just looks for a username, the @ symbol, and a domain name. If all the parts aren't there, Outlook opens the Check Names dialog box. If you cancel the dialog box, Outlook lets you keep the incomplete e-mail address even though it is not usable. Be sure to correct the address before continuing.

UNDERSTANDING E-MAIL ADDRESSES

Internet e-mail addresses have three parts: a username, followed by the *at* symbol (@) and a domain name. The domain name includes the host name and may include a subdomain name.

Each e-mail account has its own *username*. In Windows NT, usernames include the owner's name, such as bjones, jonesb, or billjones. Many companies and e-mail providers also add a number to the usernames, so they look like bjones1, or they include the person's middle initial so that Bill Jones and Barbara Jones don't have to fight over who gets to be the "real" bjones.

The username and domain name are separated with the @ symbol. The *domain name* begins with the host name. The *host name* is the name of the server that handles the e-mail account. For example, in the address bjones@wompus.berkeley.edu, the host name is *wompus*. (On one of the wompus server's hard drives, there's space for Bill Jones to keep his e-mail; the space is called his *mailbox*.) The *subdomain* is *berkeley*—the name or an abbreviated name of the organization that owns the server. The last part of the domain name, following the last period, is the top-level *domain*, which describes the type of organization. Prior to 2001, seven domains were available for use in the United States, with some of these being available internationally. These are as follows:

▶ com (commercial): for-profit organizations

▶ edu (educational): schools, colleges, and universities

▶ gov (governmental): federal, state, and local governmental units

CONTINUED ➡

- `mil` (military): armed services

- `net` (network): network access providers

- `org` (organization): nonprofit businesses

- `int`: international organizations

In 2000, the Internet Corporation for Assigned Names and Numbers (ICANN) approved seven additional top-level domains, which were made available in 2001. The new domains are as follows:

- `biz`: designed for business use only—not available to individuals

- `info`: for use internationally for any information site

- `name`: for individual use such as `adam.name` and `margie.adam.name`

- `pro`: restricted to attorneys, physicians, and accountants

- `museum`: restricted to accredited museums worldwide

- `coop`: restricted to business cooperatives such as credit unions and rural electric cooperatives

- `aero`: restricted for use by the airline industry

In addition to these 14 domains, each country has its own two-letter domain such as `uk` for the United Kingdom, `ca` for Canada, and `jp` for Japan. A large number of educational organizations use `us` (United States) as their domain rather than `edu`; the domain name `oak.goodrich.k12.mi.us` describes a host at Oaktree Elementary in Goodrich Public Schools, a K–12 district in Michigan. Some countries have offered their domains for sale to the general public. The people of Tuvala, for example, have formed an exclusive partnership with the dotTV Corporation and are offering `dot-tv` domain names for general use.

Some addresses used within mail systems aren't compatible with Internet mail. For example, many CompuServe addresses contain commas: 72557,1546. This is a valid e-mail address for a CompuServe member if you are also a CompuServe member and use CompuServe Mail to send your e-mail. However, it's not a valid *Internet* e-mail address. The only punctuation marks used in Internet addresses are periods and the

@ symbol. If you want to send e-mail to this CompuServe address from Outlook or any other Internet mail system, the address must be modified for use on the Internet. For CompuServe addresses, change the comma to a period and add the CompuServe domain name: 72557.1546@compuserve .com. For other addresses, talk with the person whose address you are entering and ask them for their POP3 or SMTP address.

NOTE

For the last several years, CompuServe users have had the option of adopting a username at the cs.com domain.

Viewing Display Names

When you enter an e-mail address, Outlook automatically creates a display name and inserts it into the Display As text box.

This is the name that appears on an e-mail message form addressed to this person. If you want to change the display name, just type anything you'd like to see in the Display As text box.

Entering an E-Mail Address from the Global Address List

If you are working on a Microsoft Exchange Server, your network administrator has already set up a Global Address list that includes everyone who has a mailbox on the network. In some organizations, complete contact data such as address and company information is entered when the mailbox is created. However, it is more typical to create the mailbox with nothing more than the person's name and e-mail address. In these cases, you may want to create a contact for people within your company about whom you need additional information.

If you are entering contact information for someone who is in your company's Global Address list or some other address book, you can click the Address Book button next to the e-mail text box on the General page of the Contact form to open the Select Name dialog box, shown in

Figure 13.5. Select the address you want from the list and click OK. This automatically enters the person's internal e-mail address in the text box.

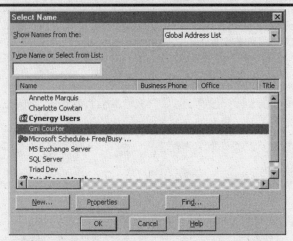

FIGURE 13.5: If the contact is already in the Global Address list, select their name from the list to enter their internal e-mail address.

TIP

If you want to see what data is already included in the Microsoft Exchange Server mailbox, select the name from the Select Name dialog box and click Properties to open the Properties dialog box.

Choosing a Format for the Message

The default format for messages created in Outlook 2002 is HTML created with Microsoft Word. If you are certain that this person's mail system does not support HTML messages (most up-to-date mail programs do), you can choose either plain text or rich text as an alternate format.

All versions of Outlook support a file format called *Rich Text format* (*RTF*). With RTF, you can format an e-mail message as you would a Word document, using boldface, italics, and different fonts and font colors to provide emphasis in the message. If you're using Outlook on a server at work, your colleagues running Outlook on the network will be able to open RTF messages and see your text in all its formatted glory.

Part iv

NOTE

If your contact's e-mail service doesn't support RTF, the formatting of the message can make it harder to decipher the actual text of the message because funny codes are inserted. At best, the formatting doesn't appear, and you've spent time formatting for no good reason. For more about selecting e-mail formats, refer to Chapter 12, "Sending and Receiving E-Mail with Outlook 2002."

To change the message format, right-click an e-mail address on the General page of a Contact form and choose Properties. This opens the E-Mail Properties dialog box.

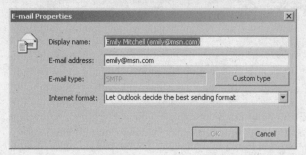

The default Internet format is Let Outlook Decide The Best Sending Format. If you are uncomfortable letting software make decisions for you, you can choose plain text or Outlook Rich Text format from the drop-down list.

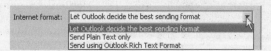

If you make a different selection, click OK to save the change or Cancel to close the dialog box without making a change.

NOTE

If you change the Internet format in the E-Mail Properties dialog box and click OK, Outlook changes the e-mail address to match the Display As address.

To access the advanced e-mail format options, right-click an e-mail address and choose Send Options. This opens the Send Options For This Recipient Properties dialog box, shown in Figure 13.6.

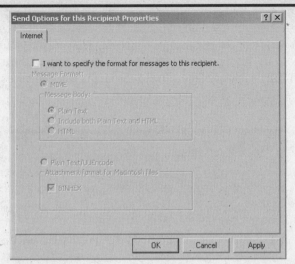

FIGURE 13.6: Use the Send Options For This Recipient Properties dialog box to set e-mail message formats for MIME and Plain Text/UUEncode.

If you would like to specify the type of encoding you want to be applied to messages you send to this e-mail address, click the I Want To Specify The Format For Messages To This Recipient check box. You can choose either MIME or UUEncode.

If you choose MIME, you can select Plain Text, Include Both Plain Text And HTML, or HTML. If you choose UUEncode and you plan to send Macintosh files, you can choose to use the encoding standard Bin-Hex for the attachments.

Click OK to apply the options you selected.

NOTE

See Chapter 12 for a discussion of these encoding standards and how they affect e-mail messages and attachments.

Entering Website Addresses

When you're preparing for a visit, telephone call, or Internet meeting with a contact, you probably have a number of information sources to check. You'll look at your Calendar to see when you met last, check your Task list to ensure that all the tasks related to the contact are complete,

Part iv

and search online for recent news about the contact's organization. The contact's website is one of the places you'll want to search. Websites often contain news about an organization, including recently announced products, promotions, legal actions, press releases, and other information of interest. By adding a *hyperlink* pointing to the URL, you can access the contact's website with one quick click of the mouse.

UNDERSTANDING URLS

An individual item you can find on the Internet is called a *resource*. Just as e-mail addresses are used to locate individuals, *Uniform Resource Locators* (*URLs*) are Internet addresses that contain all the information needed to find a website or specific document.

The URL has two parts: the resource and a *protocol* that specifies the method used for retrieving the resource. The protocol for a page on the *World Wide Web (WWW)*, the graphically based portion of the Internet, is *Hypertext Transfer Protocol (HTTP)*. Most of the URLs you'll see begin with http, but there are other protocols, including *File Transfer Protocol (FTP)*, used on sites where you download files; *Gopher*, a search and retrieve protocol used on university database sites; and *File*, used for files located on a local or network drive.

The protocol is followed by a colon and two slashes (://) and then the resource, including directions to the file you want to retrieve. The resource includes the host name and may also include a file-name and path.

Assigning a Web URL to a Contact

To assign an Internet URL to a contact, simply enter the address in the Web Page Address text box. When you enter a World Wide Web URL in the Web Page Address text box, you don't need to enter the protocol. Enter the resource name (for example, www.disney.com), and when you leave the text box, Outlook automatically adds http:// to the beginning of the URL. However, if you're entering an address for another type of protocol, such as Gopher, Telnet, or FTP, you must enter the entire URL, including the protocol and the resource. If you don't, Outlook still adds http:// to the beginning of the URL, and it will be incorrect.

NOTE

If the URL you are pointing to includes standardized elements, Outlook can handle things other than WWW links. For instance, `ftp.uunet.com` becomes `ftp://uunet.com`, and `gopher.ucla.edu` becomes `gopher://gopher.ucla.edu`. However, if an FTP site begins with a WWW prefix (this is how most ISPs allow access to personal web space), then it is still interpreted as a web address.

To visit the user's website, simply point to the URL, and the mouse pointer changes to the familiar browser-link hand shape. Click the link to launch your default browser and load the web page.

Assigning a File URL

File URLs point to addresses on a local area network. A file URL begins with the `file://` protocol, followed by the file path and filename. For example, `file://k:\Budgets\Marketing.doc` is a file on the K drive in the folder named Budgets. If there is a space anywhere in the filename or path, you must enclose the address in brackets, using the < and > symbols: For example, `<file://c:\My Documents\Marketing Budget FY01-02.doc>` is a valid URL. Without the < and > symbols, the URL is invalid. There are limitations to the usefulness of assigning URLs to files, however. You can access only files that you have network permissions for, and if another user moves or renames the files, the URL won't be correct.

Entering an Instant Messaging Address

The popularity of sending instant messages to others across the Internet has grown so dramatically that Microsoft incorporated the feature into Microsoft Exchange 2000 for use within a corporate setting. With instant messaging (IM), you can have a conversation with someone without ever picking up the telephone or waiting for an e-mail response. Because these addresses sometimes vary from the typical e-mail address, you can enter a person's IM address in the IM Address text box below the Web Page Address text box on the General page of the Contact form.

Entering Contact Comments

The large text box at the bottom of the General page of the Contact form is an open area for comments about the contact: anything from quick phrases to eloquent paragraphs. For example, if the contact is your sales

Part IV

representative, you might put your account number in the comments text box. Or you might note hobbies and favorite ice-cream flavors. If your company hands out T-shirts, it's a perfect location for shirt sizes.

TIP

An excellent use of the comments text box is to record directions to a contact's home or business. The next time you have to visit there, just click the Print button, and you have their critical phone numbers, address, and directions on one piece of paper. If you synch Outlook with a personal digital assistant (PDA), the comments also synch (as long as they are not too long), and you have everything you need in one place.

Associating Contacts with Other Contacts

Often, contacts become contacts because someone you already know introduces you. If you would like to associate one contact with another to track referrals, organize families, or just record who introduced you, you can enter a contact in the Contacts text box. Click the Contacts button at the bottom of the General page of the Contact form to open the Select Contacts dialog box, shown in Figure 13.7.

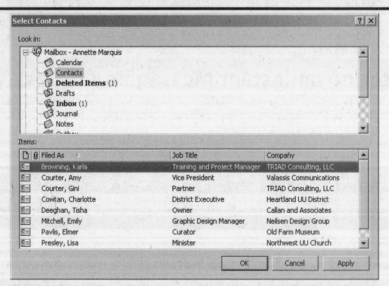

FIGURE 13.7: You can associate a contact with one or more other contacts to demonstrate relationships between them.

Select one or more contacts from the list. Hold Ctrl while clicking to select more than one associated contact. After you click OK, Outlook displays the associated contacts with links to their contact data.

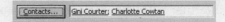

Double-click a name to open its corresponding Outlook form.

Assigning Categories

Categories are a way to organize Outlook items based on groupings you set. Outlook comes with a predefined set of categories you can use, or to make the most of categories, you can create your own. To assign categories to a contact, click the Categories button at the bottom of the General page of the Contact form. This opens the Categories dialog box, shown in Figure 13.8.

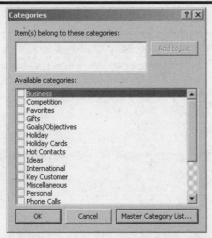

FIGURE 13.8: Assign categories to contacts in the Categories dialog box.

Click to select any of the categories listed. You can assign several categories to a single contact. Be aware, however, that some PDAs accept only a single category assignment. Click OK to assign the categories.

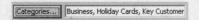

Making a Contact Private

If you're using Outlook on a network, you can give others permission to access your Contacts folder. However, you may have some contacts—your therapist or fortune teller, for example—that you prefer to keep private. In the bottom-right corner of the General page of the Contact form, there's a check box marked Private. By enabling the Private setting, you prevent other users from seeing this contact, even if they have access to your Contacts folder.

Adding Details

On the Details tab of the Contact form, shown in Figure 13.9, you can record less frequently used information about your contacts. Remember that you can sort and filter your contacts on these fields, so try to use standard entries. If, for example, you want to be able to find all the vice presidents in your Contacts folder, make sure you enter *Vice President* the same way for each contact.

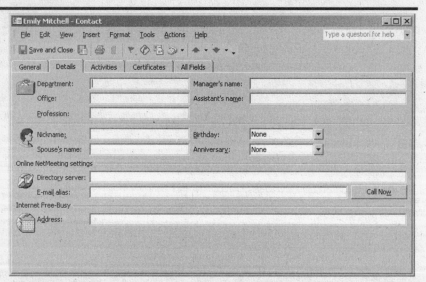

FIGURE 13.9: Use the Details tab to record other information about your contact.

The Birthday and Anniversary fields have a down arrow that opens a calendar. You can type dates directly in these fields, or you can select a date from the calendar. Click the arrow, and the calendar opens, displaying the current month.

To choose the current date, click the Today button on the bottom of the calendar. To enter a different date in the current month, just click the date. Click the arrows in the calendar's header to scroll to the prior month or the next month. This is fairly tedious if you're entering a contact's birthday (unless she was born yesterday!). To scroll more rapidly, point to the name of the month in the header and hold down your mouse button to open a list of calendar pages. Continue to hold down the mouse button and move the mouse above or below the list of months to scroll through the years. Notice the position of the mouse pointer:

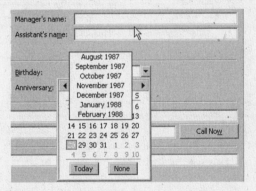

Without releasing the mouse button, select the month you want from the list. You can finally release the mouse button to select the actual date.

Entering NetMeeting Addresses

Microsoft NetMeeting is Internet-based collaboration software included with Outlook and Microsoft Exchange Server. With NetMeeting, you can work with one or more contacts "face to face" over the Internet, using video and audio as you would in a videoconference call.

NOTE

Some additional hardware is required to support NetMeeting's high-end video and audio functions.

You can use NetMeeting to send files directly to a meeting attendee, have open chat sessions for brainstorming ideas about projects, diagram ideas on a Net whiteboard, and work with other attendees in real time in shared applications.

NetMeetings are held on an Internet Locator Server (ILS); each meeting participant must log on to the server, which maintains a list of users so that other participants can find out who is available for a meeting. On the Details tab, you can enter two NetMeeting settings. Enter the ILS used for meetings with the contact in the Directory Server text box, and enter the contact's E-Mail Alias (usually their e-mail address), as shown in Figure 13.10.

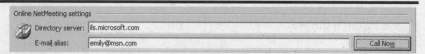

FIGURE 13.10: Enter the ILS and alias the contact uses for NetMeetings on the Details tab.

Accessing Your Contact's Schedule on the Internet

Free/busy refers to the times that a user is available (for meetings, including NetMeetings) or unavailable, according to their Outlook Calendar. With Outlook, you can publish your free/busy times in two different ways: in Exchange Server on your local area network or over the Internet using the iCalendar standard. With Exchange Server, the only people who can see your free/busy times are colleagues who can log on to your network. By publishing your free/busy times on an Internet server, you make the schedule of free time available to people outside your network.

Before users can access your free/busy schedule, you need to tell them where the file that contains the schedule is located. The file can be stored on a server, FTP site, or web page. If your contact has given you the URL for their free/busy schedule, enter it in the Internet Free/Busy text box on the Details tab of the Contact form.

Tracking Activities

The Activities tab of the Contact form, shown in Figure 13.11, displays a table of both automatic and manual entries related to the contact. The default view of the Activities tab shows an icon to designate the type of entry, the subject of the item, and the Outlook folder in which it resides.

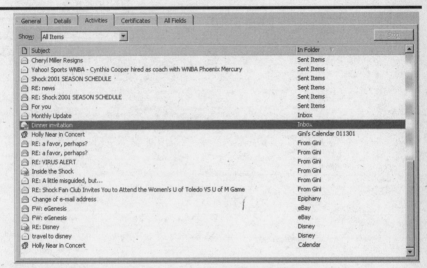

FIGURE 13.11: On the Activities tab of the Contact form, you can see all the entries related to the contact.

Previewing and Viewing Activities

If you want to see more detail about each of the entries, right-click anywhere in the activities window (except on an entry) and select the Auto-Preview option.

The first three lines of the note in each message entry are displayed, as shown in Figure 13.12. It's easy to know if the preview shows all the text in the note, because the end of the note is marked <end>. If the note is longer than the preview, the preview ends with an ellipsis (...). To turn AutoPreview off, right-click and select AutoPreview again.

To see the entire entry, double-click the entry to open it.

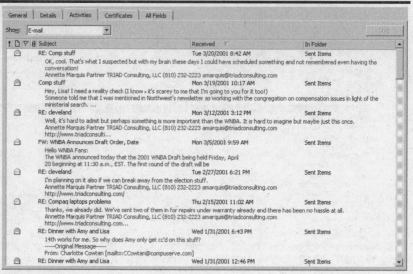

FIGURE 13.12: AutoPreview displays the first few lines of any message item.

Sorting and Grouping Activities

As with any Outlook view, you can click the heading of a column to sort the entries by the value in the column. For example, to arrange the entries by subject, click the Subject column heading.

To group items by a field, even if the field is not currently displayed, right-click in any open area of the activities list (you may have to scroll way to the bottom) and choose Group By from the shortcut menu. Choose to group the data by a field that has repetitive entries such as the In Folder field. Figure 13.13 shows data grouped by In Folder. Click the plus symbol in front of a group to expand the items in that group, and click the minus symbol to collapse it again.

To remove grouping, right-click and choose Group By again from the shortcut menu. Click Clear All and OK to remove all grouping.

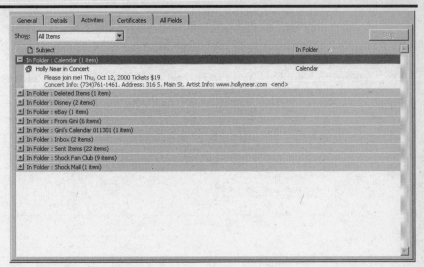

FIGURE 13.13: Grouping organizes your data to find just what you are looking for.

Viewing Certificate Information

A *certificate*, or *digital ID*, is used to verify the identity of the person who sent an e-mail message. Digital IDs have two parts: a *private key*, stored on the owner's computer, and a *public key* that others use to send messages to the owner and verify the authenticity of messages from the owner. The Certificates tab of the Contact form shows digital IDs that you've added for this contact. You can view the properties of the ID and choose which ID should be used as the default for sending encrypted messages to this contact.

NOTE

See Chapter 12 for information on adding other users' IDs to their Contact forms and sending encrypted messages.

Viewing All Fields

On the Contact form's All Fields tab, shown in Figure 13.14, you can display groups of fields in a table format. The default display on this tab is User Defined Fields. Unless you or someone else has customized your

Outlook forms and added fields, there won't be any fields displayed—but don't assume that this page is totally useless. Choose Personal Fields, for example, from the Select From drop-down list to have access to fields that are not displayed on any of the Contact form tabs, such as Children, Gender, and Hobbies. You can enter data directly into these fields and store them with the rest of the contact data.

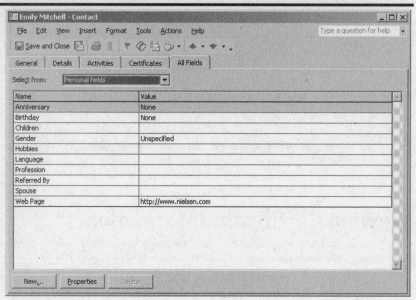

FIGURE 13.14: The All Fields tab displays fields that are not available on any of the Contact form's other tabs.

SAVING A CONTACT

 When you've finished entering information in the Contact form, click the Save And Close button, or choose File ➤ Save And Close to save this contact's information and close the form.

If you're going to be entering another contact immediately, it's faster to click the Save And New button, or choose File ➤ Save And New to save the current contact and open a blank form.

Adding a New Contact from the Same Company

Once you begin entering contacts, you'll often have several contacts from the same organization. These contacts have the same business address and the same or similar e-mail addresses and business telephone numbers. Outlook lets you create a contact based on an existing contact, so you don't have to enter the business information again. When you've finished entering the first contact, choose Actions ≻ New Contact From Same Company from the Outlook menu (if the contact is closed, select the contact first in the Information Viewer). The first contact is saved, and the business information for the contact is held over in the Contact form. Add the new contact's personal information and edit the business information as required.

DELETING A CONTACT

To delete a contact, select the contact or open the Contact form. Then choose Edit ≻ Delete from the menu, right-click and choose Delete from the shortcut menu, or press Ctrl+D. You are not prompted to confirm the deletion. However, if you immediately notice that you've deleted a contact erroneously, you can choose Edit ≻ Undo Delete to restore the contact.

FINDING CONTACT INFORMATION WHEN YOU NEED IT

When you need to find a contact in a hurry, don't worry about opening the Contacts folder and scrolling through a long list of entries. From any folder, click in the Find A Contact text box on the Standard toolbar and enter the contact you need to open.

| Type a contact to find | ▼ |

You don't even have to type their full name. Enter a first or last name, and Outlook shows you a list of possible hits.

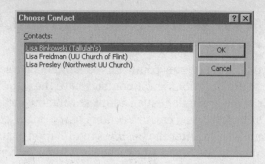

Select the contact you want to see, and Outlook opens the appropriate
Contact form.

Using Predefined Views

The Contacts folder has seven predefined views: Address Cards, Detailed
Address Cards, Phone List, By Category, By Company, By Location, and
By Follow-Up Flag. To switch to another view, choose View ➣ Current
View and select the view you want to apply.

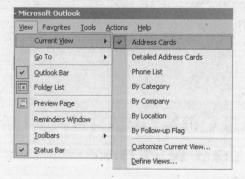

The Address Cards view, shown in Figure 13.15, is the default view in
Contacts. It displays basic information about the contact: File As name,
mailing address, e-mail address, and telephone numbers. The Detailed
Address Cards view displays additional data, including full name, job
title, company name, and categories. Card views have a handy feature: an
index on the right side that lets you quickly go to Contacts by the File As
name. Clicking the *S*, for example, takes you to contacts whose File As
name begins with the letter *S*. Many users choose either Address Cards or
Detailed Address Cards as their default view for Contacts.

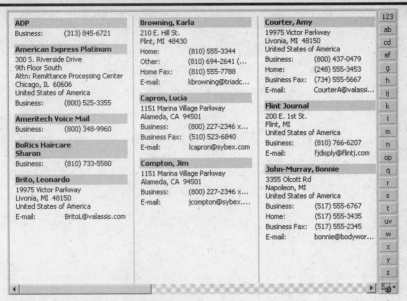

FIGURE 13.15: The Address Cards view works just like an electronic version of a Rolodex.

What's Next

In our next and final chapter focusing on Outlook 2002, you'll become acquainted with the many types of tasks that can be organized and managed directly through the program's interface.

Chapter 14

MANAGING TASKS IN OUTLOOK 2002

A key aspect of Outlook 2002—one that distinguishes it from just another e-mail program or contact organizer—is its ability to keep track of the many projects, events, and dates that come up as part of your work.

You can assign tasks to others (those in your contact list, for example), and you can check on the status of those tasks' completion. You can receive tasks from others this way, too.

Let's get started on learning how to use these options to help juggle the details of your work.

Adapted from *Mastering Microsoft Outlook 2002*
by Gini Courter and Annette Marquis
ISBN 0-7821-4001-7   752 pp $39.99

CREATING A TASK

To create a task, you simply type the name of the task and its due date. You can also enter more detailed information about the task, taking full advantage of the power that Outlook has to offer.

Tasks

To enter a task, click the Tasks icon on the Outlook bar. The default view in Tasks is the Simple List view, shown in Figure 14.1. The Simple List view has four columns:

Icon   An icon that changes if a task is assigned to someone else or was assigned by someone else

Complete   A check box indicating whether the task has been completed

Subject   A descriptive name for the task

Due Date   The date on which you expect or need to complete the task

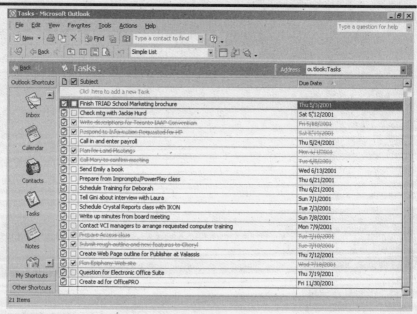

FIGURE 14.1: The Simple List view of Tasks

You can enter a task directly into the Information Viewer by clicking in the Click Here To Add A New Task text box. The row turns blue, and the box that is active for editing is white. Type a subject in the Subject field. It's helpful if you make the subject descriptive but not too long—less than 30 characters is best so you can read it all in the column.

NOTE

You must be in Simple List or Detailed List view to have the Click Here To Add A New Task text box. If you prefer to use another view, then create a new task by choosing Task from the New button's drop-down list.

Press Tab to move to the Due Date field (Shift+Tab moves you back to Subject); the text box turns white.

Because Outlook recognizes natural language dates using its AutoDate feature, you have multiple options for entering dates in this field. Just about anything you type into the field that remotely resembles a date is converted into a standard date format (Wed 8/18/99). You could type **8-18-01; aug 18; three weeks from now; a week from today; tomorrow; one month from next wed**. All are legitimate dates in Outlook (of course, they wouldn't all return the same date). Go ahead and try it—it's fun to see what AutoDate's limits are.

Click anywhere in the Task list to move the task into the list. Where the task appears in the list depends on how the list is currently sorted. Enter additional tasks the same way.

Entering Details about a Task

To take advantage of the powerful features built into Outlook, you need to add more information about the task than just the subject and due date. The most direct way to do this is to enter the data in a Task form. You can open the form for any existing task by double-clicking the task in the Information Viewer. To open a blank Task form, click the New button on the Standard toolbar (if Tasks is the active folder in the Information Viewer); or click the down arrow to the right of the New button to open the New menu, and choose Task from the list.

Part IV

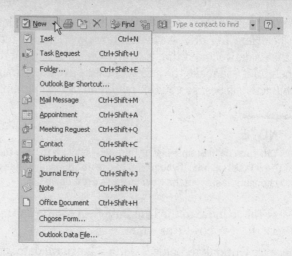

The Task form, shown in Figure 14.2, is composed of two tabs: Task and Details. The Task tab focuses on a description of the task (see "Completing a Task" later in this chapter for more information about the Details tab). Enter the subject in the Subject text box, and press Tab to move to the Due Date field. Click the down arrow to choose a date from the calendar, or enter a date in the text box. If the task is not scheduled to start right away, enter a Start Date to indicate when it should be started.

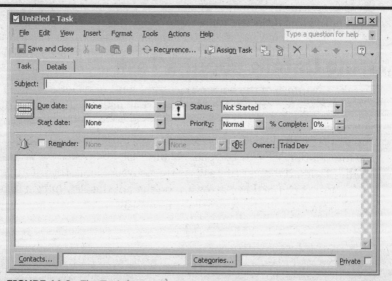

FIGURE 14.2: The Task form

Setting Reminders

Click the Reminder check box to activate a reminder that will be displayed at a specified date and time.

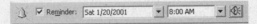

The Time drop-down list has a choice for every half hour around the clock, so be careful to select the correct AM or PM time—there's nothing like setting a reminder for 12 hours after something was supposed to be completed! You can also type an entry in this box if you need a reminder at the quarter hour.

 Reminders come with a sound by default. You have the option of disabling the sound or changing the sound file it plays. Click the Speaker icon to access the Reminder Sound options.

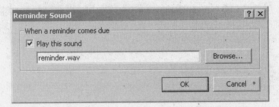

Clear the Play This Sound check box if you'd prefer your reminders to appear on your screen silently. If you would like to hear a sound but would prefer a different sound file, click the Browse button to locate the file you would like to use. Double-click the filename, and it appears in the Play This Sound text box.

TIP

If you change the sound file within a task, it will be in effect for only that specific reminder. To change the default sound file for reminders, go to Sounds in the Windows Control Panel and change the sound assigned to Microsoft Office Reminders. Sound files, or *wave files*, are designated by a WAV extension. If you would like to record your own reminder message or sound that plays when it is time to do a task, you can do so using the Windows Sound Recorder.

Updating Task Status

When you enter a task, Outlook assumes you haven't started working on the task yet. To help you manage your tasks and assess the status of

Part iv

certain projects, you have four Status options in addition to Not Started. Click the Status down arrow on the Task page of the Task form to open the list of choices:

In Progress   If a task is in progress, you might also want to indicate the percentage that is complete in the % Complete text box. Use the spin box to change the percentage, or type the actual percentage directly in the box.

Completed   In addition to marking a task as complete, you might also want to complete some additional fields on the Details page. See "Completing a Task" later in this chapter.

Waiting On Someone Else   It's helpful to set a reminder to yourself to call this person if you don't hear from them in a reasonable amount of time.

Deferred   You may want to change the start and end dates so this task doesn't show up on your list of active tasks.

Setting Priorities

By setting a priority level for a task, you can be sure that your most important tasks receive most of your attention. The default priority is Normal. You have additional options of High and Low. High-priority items are designated by a red exclamation point in the Information Viewer, and Low-priority items are designated by a blue downward-pointing arrow, as shown in Figure 14.3.

	!	⓪	Subject	Status	Due Date	% Complete	Categories
☑	!	⓪	Call Valassis Managers about custom training	Not Started	Mon 1/22/2001	0%	Valassis
☑			Plan next book project	Not Started	Wed 2/28/2001	0%	
☑			Finish TRIAD School Marketing brochure	In Progress	Thu 5/3/2001	0%	Marketing
☑	!		Check mtg with Jackie Hurd	Not Started	Sat 5/12/2001	0%	Perry Database
☑			Call in and enter payroll	Not Started	Thu 5/24/2001	0%	Admin
☑	↓		Send Emily a book	Not Started	Wed 6/13/2001	0%	
☑			Prepare from Impromptu/PowerPlay class	Not Started	Thu 6/21/2001	0%	Valassis
☑			Schedule Training for Deborah	Not Started	Thu 6/21/2001	0%	Training
☑	!		Tell Gini about interview with Laura	Not Started	Sun 7/1/2001	0%	
☑			Schedule Crystal Reports class with IKON	Not Started	Tue 7/3/2001	0%	Admin
☑	八		Write up minutes from board meeting	Not Started	Sun 7/8/2001	0%	UU
☑	!		Contact VCI managers to arrange requested co...	Not Started	Mon 7/9/2001	0%	Training
☑			Create Web Page outline for Publisher at Valassis	Not Started	Thu 7/12/2001	0%	Valassis
☑			Question for Electronic Office Suite	Not Started	Thu 7/19/2001	0%	Clients
☑			Create ad for OfficePRO	Not Started	Fri 11/30/2001	0%	Marketing

FIGURE 14.3: The Priority field, visible in Active Tasks view in the Information Viewer, indicates whether a task is High or Low priority.

Owning a Task

The task's owner is the person who created the task or the person to whom the task is currently assigned. When you create a task, you are the owner by default. To give up ownership, however, all you have to do is assign the task to someone else. As soon as that person accepts the task, they officially become the new owner.

NOTE

To learn how to assign tasks to someone else, see "Delegating Tasks" later in this chapter.

Assigning Categories to Manage a Project

Categories are user-defined values that help to organize your data throughout Outlook. Despite the fact that you have the same list of categories available to you, categories serve a slightly different purpose in Tasks than they do in Contacts or the other Outlook modules.

Categories play a vital role in tracking tasks related to a single project. When you create a task, the more specific you can be, the easier it is to complete the task. For example, if the task you enter is *Complete database for Perry*, you will have a difficult time demonstrating progress toward your goal. When is the database complete—after the application is functioning, or after the product is installed? Maybe it's not complete until employees are trained and using the product successfully.

It would be a lot more helpful to break down the various steps of the project into its logical components. In this case, you could list *Complete data analysis*, *Complete database structural design*, *Solicit feedback from client*, and so on as separate tasks in Outlook. Each could have its own description and due date. Status, priority, and percent complete could also be assigned to each task.

Categories could then pull all these individual tasks together into one project. Just click the Categories button and assign each task to the same category from the Categories dialog box. When you return to the Information Viewer, you can sort by category, group together all the tasks in the same category, or even filter out just those tasks related to a single category. Figure 14.4 shows an example of a Task list grouped by category (see "Viewing Tasks" later in this chapter).

Part iv

Categories : Admin (2 items)					
☑	Call in and enter payroll	Not Started	Thu 5/24/2001	0%	Admin
☑	Schedule Crystal Reports class with IKON	Not Started	Tue 7/3/2001	0%	Admin
Categories : Marketing (5 items)					
☑	Finish TRIAD School Marketing brochure	In Progress	Thu 5/3/2001	0%	Marketing
☑ ↓	Send Emily a book	Not Started	Wed 6/13/2001	0%	Marketing
☑ !	Tell Gini about interview with Laura	Not Started	Sun 7/1/2001	0%	Marketing
☑	Question for Electronic Office Suite	Not Started	Thu 7/19/2001	0%	Marketing
☑	Create ad for OfficePRO	Not Started	Fri 11/30/2001	0%	Marketing
Categories : Perry Database (1 item)					
☑ !	Check mtg with Jackie Hurd	Not Started	Sat 5/12/2001	0%	Perry Databa
Categories : Sybex (1 item)					
☑	Plan next book project	Not Started	Wed 2/28/2001	0%	Sybex
Categories : Training (2 items)					
☑	Schedule Training for Deborah	Not Started	Thu 6/21/2001	0%	Training
☑ !	Contact VCI managers to arrange requested c...	Not Started	Mon 7/9/2001	0%	Training
Categories : UU (1 item)					
☑ ↓	Write up minutes from board meeting	Not Started	Sun 7/8/2001	0%	UU
Categories : Valassis (3 items)					
☑ ! 📎	Call Valassis Managers about custom training	Not Started	Mon 1/22/2001	0%	Valassis
☑	Prepare from Impromptu/PowerPlay class	Not Started	Thu 6/21/2001	0%	Valassis

FIGURE 14.4: Task list grouped by category

Making a Task Private

If your Outlook folders are shared on a network, there may be times when you don't want others to see information about a task. Click the Private check box in the right-hand corner of the Task form to keep this task from being visible to others to whom you have given permission to access your Tasks folder.

SETTING UP RECURRING TASKS

A *recurring task* is a task that you must complete on a regular basis—such as a monthly report, a weekly agenda, or a quarterly tax submission. Anything that you have to do periodically qualifies. In Outlook, you can enter the task once, and then set a pattern for it to recur on your Task list. Outlook doesn't care if you've completed this month's report; when the time comes for next month's, Outlook will add another copy of the task with a new due date to your list.

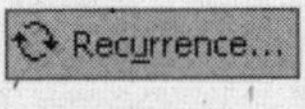

⟳ Recurrence... To set up a recurring task, enter the task as you would any other task that needs completion. When you have the data entered for the first occurrence of the task, click the Recurrence button on the Standard toolbar within the Task form. This opens the Task Recurrence dialog box, shown in Figure 14.5.

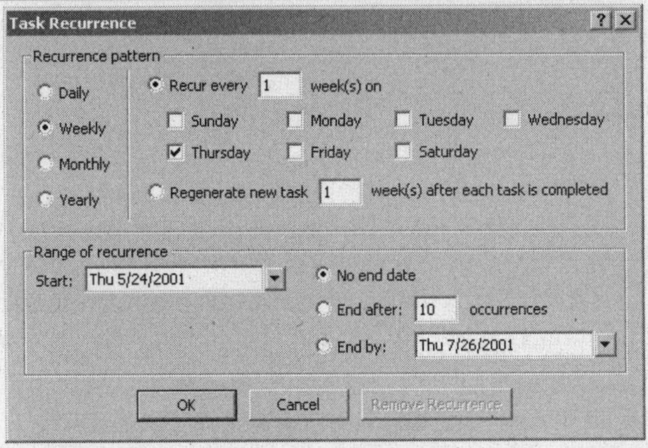

FIGURE 14.5: Task Recurrence dialog box

Here you can set the Recurrence Pattern and the Range Of Recurrence. To set the Recurrence Pattern, indicate whether the task needs to be accomplished Daily, Weekly, Monthly, or Yearly. If the task needs to be completed every three days, choose Daily; every two months, choose Monthly; and so on. Each of the four options gives you different choices for defining the actual pattern. Rather than choosing a specific date pattern, as an alternative, you can indicate how many days/weeks/months/years you want Outlook to wait after a task is marked as complete before it generates a new task.

Daily   Choose between Every *N* Days or Every Weekday.

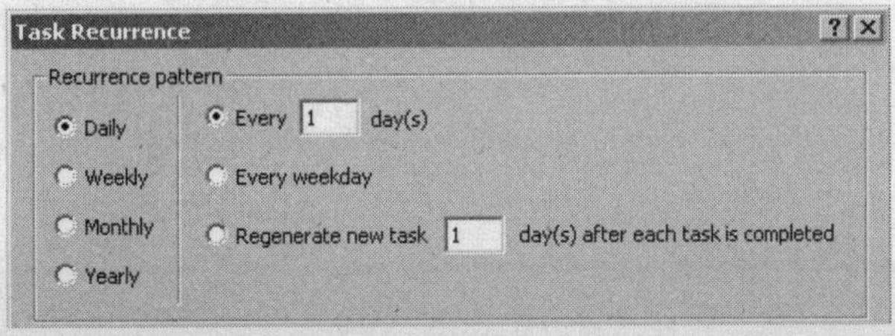

Weekly Indicate how often the task should occur: every week (1), every other week (2), every third week (3), and so on. This is the best option if the task needs to be completed every six weeks or every eight weeks (because some months have more than four weeks). Then mark on which day of the week the task needs to be accomplished.

Monthly Choose between specifying which date of each *N* month(s) or indicating the first, second, third, fourth, or last day of every *N* month(s); for example, the last Friday of every month or the third Thursday of every second month. You could also indicate the first weekday or the last weekend day of the month.

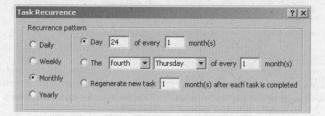

Yearly Indicate a specific date in a specific month (every May 24), or mark the first, second, third, fourth, or last day of a specific month (the first Friday in May).

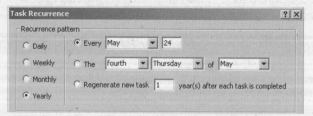

Sometimes you have to be creative to figure out how often a task really occurs. For example, if a task occurs two times a year on February 28 and August 31, do you use Monthly or Yearly? Because these dates are six months apart, you could use Monthly and indicate the last day of every six months (as long as the start date was set to one of the two dates).

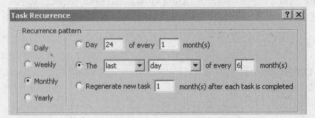

However, if this task were not so evenly spaced—May 31 and August 31, for example—you probably would have to enter two tasks: one for the May date every year and one for the August date every year.

Defining the Range of Recurrence

The *range of recurrence* refers to when the first task in the series is due and how long the task will continue.

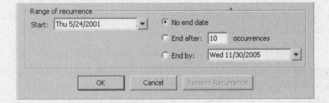

You have the following choices:

No End Date   The task will continue into eternity (or until you tell it to stop).

End After *N* Occurrences   You need to complete the task only a specific number of times, and then you are finished with it.

End By   You have to do this task only until a certain date, and then you are free.

Once you have set the range of recurrence, click OK to return to the Task form. Click Save And Close to save the task and return to the Information Viewer.

Editing Task Recurrence

To make changes to the recurrence pattern or range that you set, open the task and click the Recurrence Pattern button. Make your changes and then click Save And Close again. You may also edit the Subject of the task, but any changes you make affect only future occurrences of the task.

If you want to skip the next occurrence of a task but not interfere with the recurrence pattern, open the task and choose Actions ➤ Skip Occurrence. The due date automatically changes to the next date the task is due.

To delete the recurrence pattern without deleting the task, open the task, click the Recurrence button, and click the Remove Recurrence button on the bottom of the Task Recurrence dialog box. Close the Task Recurrence dialog box, and save and close the task. The task still appears on your list, but it is now there for one time only.

DELEGATING TASKS

If you work as a member of a team, or if you have people reporting to you, there are times when you may want to create a task for someone else to do. As long as the other person is running Outlook and you both have access to e-mail, you can assign tasks to each other.

To assign a task to someone else, create the task as you normally would; add task recurrence, if appropriate; and click the Assign Task button on the Standard toolbar of the Task form. This opens a message form with the task included, as shown in Figure 14.6.

WARNING

When sending a task to another person through Internet e-mail, make sure Properties for that person's e-mail address in Contacts are not set to Send Plain Text Only. This way, the recipient will be able to transfer the task directly into their Task list using copy-and-paste. (See Chapter 12, "Sending and Receiving E-Mail with Outlook 2002," for more information about Outlook's Send options and Internet format.)

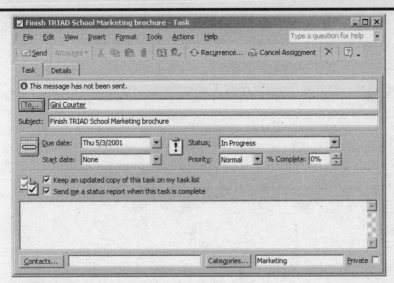

FIGURE 14.6: Assigning a task to someone else

Enter the person's e-mail address, or click the To button and choose the name from your address lists (see Chapter 12 for more information about addressing e-mail messages). You have two options related to this assignment:

Keep An Updated Copy Of This Task On My Task List   Even though you have assigned the task to someone else, you may still want to know how the task is going. Every time the new owner of the task revises the task in any way, a message is sent to you indicating that the task was updated. As soon as you open the message, the task is automatically revised in your Task list. When you close the task, the message is removed from your Inbox. This option is not available if the task is recurring.

Send Me A Status Report When This Task Is Complete
When the new owner marks the task as complete, you receive an automatic status report message informing you that the task is complete. This status report message remains in your Inbox until you move it or dispose of it. Although you can assign a task to anyone who runs Outlook, if the person is not on your network, you will not receive automatic updates when that person makes revisions to the task.

If you would like to send a message along with the task assignment, enter the text in the message box. Click Send to transfer the message to your Outbox.

Assigning a Task to More than One Person

It's possible to assign the same task to more than one person, but if you do, you cannot keep an updated copy of the task in your Task list. To assign the task to an additional person, open the task, click the Details tab, and click the Create Unassigned Copy button.

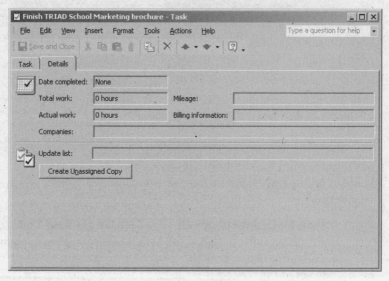

You are warned that you will become the owner again (the person you originally assigned the task to took over ownership of the task when they accepted it) and will no longer receive updates (unless you want to write them to yourself). Click OK to create the copy and assign the task.

If you really need to receive updates from more than one person about the task, create the task multiple times and assign it individually to each person. Include the person's name in the Subject so you can differentiate the tasks.

Receiving a Task Assignment

When someone sends you a task, you receive an e-mail message labeled *Task Request*.

When you open the task, you can choose to accept the task or decline the task by clicking the appropriate button on the message form.

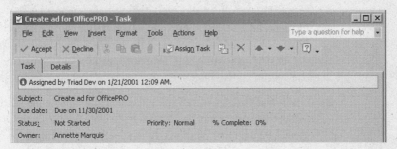

If you click Accept, the task is automatically added to your Task list, and you become the owner of the task. If you click Decline, the person who sent you the task retains ownership. Either way, the person who originated the task is sent a message indicating your response. When you click Send, you are given the option of editing the response before sending it or sending it without editing. If you want to explain why you're declining your boss's request or the conditions under which you are accepting the task, click Edit The Response Before Sending and enter your explanation in the message.

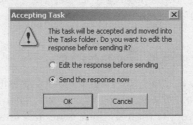

Even after you accept a task, you can change your mind and decline the task. Just open the task and choose Actions ➤ Decline Task.

Passing the Task Along

If you receive a task from someone, it's possible for you to accept the task assignment, and then turn around and assign the task to someone else (commonly referred to as *passing the buck*). When you accept the task, you become the owner of the task, and changes and updates you make are returned to the task's originator. When you reassign a task to someone else, that person becomes the owner, and future updates are returned to you and the originator of the task. To reassign a task:

1. Open the e-mail message that contains the original task request, and click the Accept button to accept the task (if you have not already done so). This sends a task update to the originator indicating you have accepted the task. You are now the owner of the task.

2. Open the task in your Task list and click the Assign button. Make sure the Keep An Updated Copy Of The Task On My Task List and the Send Me A Status Report When This Task Is Complete options are both checked so you won't lose track of the task.

3. Enter the e-mail address of the person you want to assign the task to, and click Send to send the task request to them. They are now the temporary owner of the task. When they accept the task, they become the task's owner.

4. When you receive a task update from the new owner, the originator also gets a message from you.

By following this process, you keep the task's originator informed, and you have someone else doing the work—not bad work, if you can get it!

Sending Status Reports

Even though Outlook does a great job of keeping a task's originator informed about the status of a task, you may need to incorporate more detail into a report than Outlook generates automatically. If you want to send a manual status report, choose Actions ➤ Send Status Report from the Standard toolbar of the open task. Type in (or copy and paste) your status report. Click Send to send an update to the task's originator.

VIEWING TASKS

One way to stay on top of what you have to do is to review your tasks from different perspectives. The default view for tasks in the Information Viewer is Simple List (shown back in Figure 14.1). This view shows the Subject and Due Date of both active and completed tasks. It's quite simple to switch to another view that shows only active tasks or that organizes the tasks in some other meaningful way. To change to another view, choose View ➤ Current View. This opens the list of available views displayed in Figure 14.7.

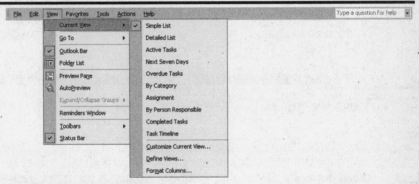

FIGURE 14.7: Available views in Tasks

Detailed List and Active Tasks are essentially the same view, except Detailed List includes completed tasks, while Active Tasks includes only those tasks yet to be completed. The Detailed List view is shown in Figure 14.8.

The Next Seven Days view displays the same fields as the Detailed List and Active Tasks views, but it filters the view to show only those tasks with due dates within the next seven calendar days.

When a task passes its due date, Outlook turns the task red to distinguish it from current tasks. You can then choose Overdue Tasks from the Current View menu to see only those tasks that require immediate attention.

The next three views allow you to examine your tasks by category, by assignment, and by person responsible. These views are especially helpful in managing the work on a particular project or managing the workloads of personnel, because they group tasks together that have something in common (see Figure 14.4 earlier in this chapter for an example of tasks grouped by category).

Part iv

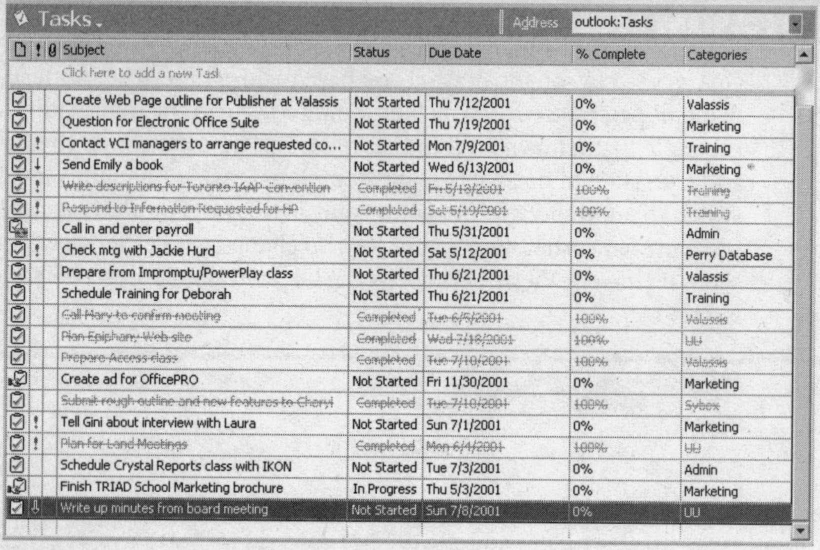

FIGURE 14.8: Detailed List view of Tasks

The final view, Task Timeline view, is designed to let you examine your tasks based on when they are due in relation to each other. Tasks are spread out along the timeline grouped together by due dates. This view, shown in Figure 14.9, can be used to plan your activities for particular days based on the tasks you have to accomplish.

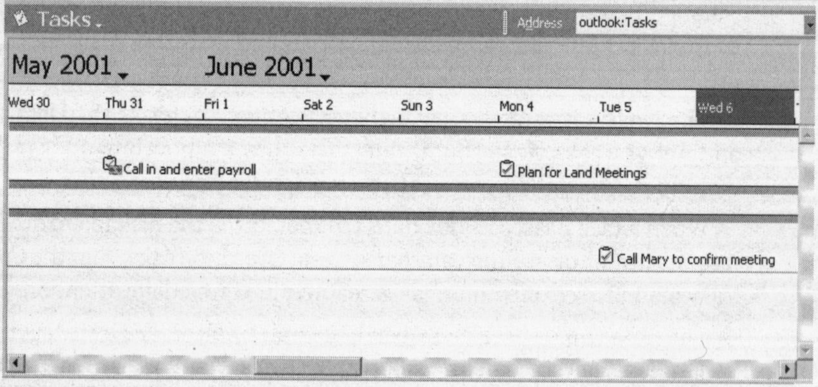

FIGURE 14.9: The Task Timeline view

CREATING TASKS FROM OTHER OUTLOOK ITEMS

Outlook's power comes from the incredible ease with which all of the components work together to make your life easier. How many times have you received an e-mail message asking you to do something? Unless you print the message, put it in the stack of papers on your desk, and hope you run across it before the task needs to get done, you may find yourself forgetting it was even asked of you. Outlook changes all that. The next time you receive an e-mail message asking you to do something, all you have to do is drag the message onto the Task icon on the Outlook bar.

Outlook automatically opens a Task form for you with the information already in it, including the actual contents of the e-mail message, as shown in Figure 14.10.

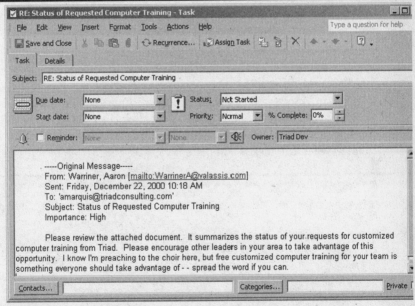

FIGURE 14.10: A Task form opens automatically from an e-mail message.

All you have to do is add due dates, assign the task to a category, and add any other details you want—and your reminder is all set. (You will, however, have to actually do the task yourself.)

Part iv

You can use this trick to create Outlook tasks with any other Outlook item, such as a Journal entry, a Calendar item, or a Note.

COMPLETING A TASK

When you've finally completed a task, there is nothing more satisfying than checking it off your list. Outlook wouldn't want you to miss out on this pleasure, so it has incorporated a check box into the Information Viewer for most of the standard views. To mark a task as complete, just click the check box, as shown in Figure 14.11.

FIGURE 14.11: Completing a task

The task is crossed off the list. If the view you are using, such as Active Tasks view, does not include completed items, the item is actually removed from the list altogether. Of course, you can always see it by switching to a view such as Simple List view, which shows all tasks. If you mistakenly check off a task as complete, just switch to Simple List view and clear the check box.

If you are interested in tracking more information about a completed task, you may want to open the task and click the Details tab of the Task form. It has several fields, shown in Figure 14.12, that are designed to be filled in when the task is completed.

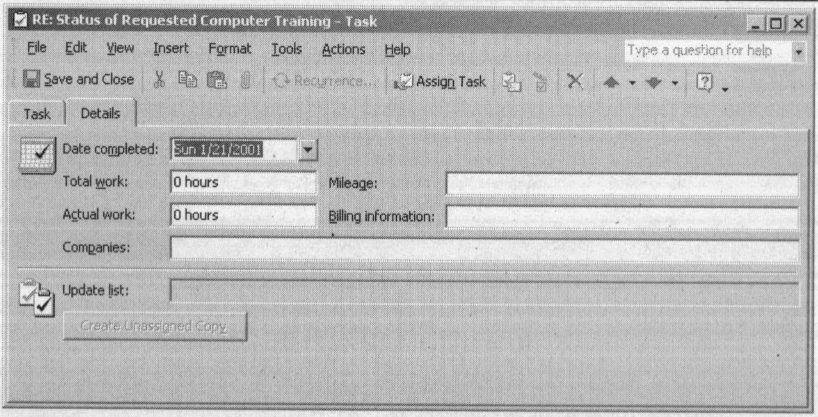

FIGURE 14.12: Tracking additional information about a completed task

On this page, you can record the date the task was completed, the planned number of hours (Outlook will translate to days), the actual number of hours, and other billing information you may want to track such as the number of miles traveled on the job. If you have to submit an expense or billing statement at the end of the month, this is a great way to track the information you need.

WHAT'S NEXT

Congratulations! By completing Part IV, you should have a good understanding of the basic as well as more sophisticated options available in Outlook 2002 for handling e-mail, contacts, and tasks.

In Part V, you'll familiarize yourself with the types of presentations that PowerPoint 2002 can help you create, including those that use information from files you have created in Office XP so far.

PART V

PRESENTING
INFORMATION WITH
POWERPOINT 2002

Chapter 15

CREATING A PRESENTATION WITH POWERPOINT 2002

PowerPoint 2002 is the professional-level presentation product packaged with Office XP to help you take the files you work with (so far, documents and workbook data) and plug them into a format suitable for presenting to others, as you might in a department meeting or a meeting with clients.

These presentations can be distributed in a number of ways: in printed form; for use with overhead projectors; by publication to a website (as you'll learn about in Part VII); or by being run from a PC or special kiosk so that an audience can watch a slide show, where different pages of the presentation are saved as individual slides and then run in sequence (more about this in Chapter 16, "Creating a Slide Show with PowerPoint 2002).

Let's begin by showing you how to create and work with a new presentation.

Adapted from *Microsoft Office XP Simply Visual* by Perspection, Inc.

ISBN 0-7821-4004-1   400 pp $24.99

CREATING A NEW PRESENTATION

When you start PowerPoint, you see a dialog box that lists your options for creating a presentation. You can use a wizard to guide you through the steps of creating a presentation. Using a wizard is the quickest way to create a presentation.

You can also select a template—a document with predefined formatting and placeholder text—that provides a structure for creating your presentation. If you want to start from scratch, you can instruct PowerPoint to provide a blank screen. PowerPoint offers two kinds of templates. *Design templates* include professionally designed colors, graphics, and other visual elements you can apply to your presentation. *Content templates* contain both design and content. *Masters*, which contain the formatting information for each slide in your presentation, are available for each part of your presentation—slides, handouts, and speaker notes. A presentation's *color scheme* is a set of eight balanced colors that coordinate your presentation's text, borders, fills, backgrounds, and so on.

Start a New Presentation

1. Start PowerPoint. The New Presentation task pane opens.

2. Click the task pane option that you want to use to begin your presentation.

3. Follow the instructions, which vary depending on the presentation option you chose.

Start a New Presentation within PowerPoint

1. Choose File ➤ New. The New Presentation task pane opens.

2. Click the task pane option that corresponds to the way you want to begin your presentation.

CREATING A PRESENTATION USING THE AUTOCONTENT WIZARD

Often, the most difficult part of creating a presentation is knowing where to start. PowerPoint solves this problem for you. You can use the AutoContent Wizard to develop presentation content on a variety of business and personal topics. An AutoContent presentation usually contains 5 to 10 logically organized slides, whose text you can edit as necessary. Many AutoContent presentations are available in Standard and Online formats.

TIP

To use the AutoContent Wizard, choose File ➤ New, click General Templates, click the General tab, click the AutoContent Wizard icon, and then click the OK button.

Create a Presentation Using the AutoContent Wizard

1. Start PowerPoint or choose File ➤ New, and then click From AutoContent Wizard in the New Presentation task pane.

2. Read the first wizard dialog box. Click the Next button to continue.

3. Click the presentation type that you want to use. If you want to focus on one particular presentation, such as a brainstorming session, click the appropriate category button, and then click the presentation type you want.

4. Click the Next button to continue.

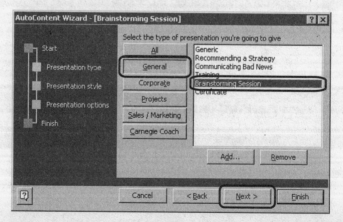

5. Click the presentation style you want to use. Click the Next button to continue.

6. Select options, including a presentation title and items you want to include on each slide. Click the Next button to continue.

7. Read the last wizard dialog box, and then click the Finish button.

CHOOSING A TEMPLATE

PowerPoint provides a collection of professionally designed templates that you can use to create effective presentations. Each template contains its own format and color scheme, so you only need to add text. You can select a new template for your presentation at any time.

TIP

You can create a new presentation with a template at any time. Choose File ➤ New, click General Templates, click the Design Templates tab, click the template you want to use, and then click the OK button.

Choose a Template for a Presentation

1. Start PowerPoint and click From Design Template on the New Presentation task pane, or click the Slide Design button on the Formatting toolbar.

2. Click a design in the Available For Use pane. PowerPoint applies the design to the new presentation.

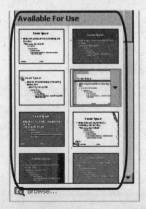

VIEWING THE POWERPOINT WINDOW

The PowerPoint workspace lets you manipulate every component of your presentation. The graphic below identifies the elements that you can manage in a presentation.

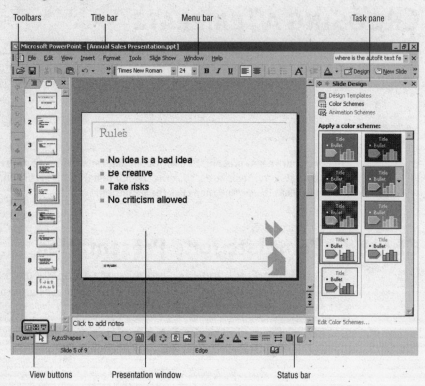

The PowerPoint Views

You can arrange the PowerPoint screen in three views: Normal, Slide Sorter, and Slide Show. You can switch from one view to another by clicking a view button located next to the horizontal scroll bar.

Normal View

Use the Normal view to work with the three underlying elements of a presentation—the outline, slide, and notes—each in their own pane. These panes provide an overview of your presentation; you can modify your presentation in each section. You can adjust the size of the panes by dragging the pane borders. You can use the outline pane to develop and organize your presentation's content—view a text outline of all the slides in your presentation or view a *thumbnail* (miniature illustration) of each slide. Use the slide pane to add text, graphics, movies, sounds, and hyperlinks to individual slides. Use the notes pane to add speaker notes or notes that you want to share with your audience.

You can preview each slide in Normal view. Click the number of the slide you want to view in the outline pane. You can also use the scroll bars or the Previous and Next Slide buttons to move from slide to slide. When you drag the scroll box up or down on the vertical scroll bar, a label appears that indicates which slide will be displayed when you release the mouse button.

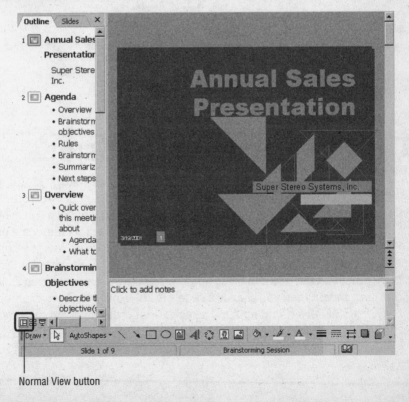

Normal View button

Slide Sorter View

Use Slide Sorter view to organize your slides, add actions between slides—called *slide transitions*—and apply other effects to your slide show. The Slide Sorter toolbar adds slide transitions and helps control the timing of your presentation. When you add a slide transition, PowerPoint inserts an icon indicating that an action will take place as one slide replaces another during the show. If you hide a slide, an icon appears indicating that the slide will not display during the presentation.

Slide Show View

Slide Show view presents your slides one at a time. Use this view when you're ready to preview, rehearse, or give your presentation. To move through the slides, right-click the navigation button on the screen to access navigation controls, or press the Enter key or spacebar on the keyboard to move through the show. To quit Slide Show view, press the Esc key on the keyboard.

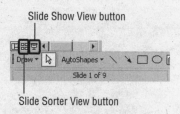

Slide Show View button

Slide Sorter View button

CREATING CONSISTENT SLIDES

You need to arrange the objects on your slides in a visually meaningful way so that others can understand your presentation. PowerPoint's *Auto-Layout* feature helps you arrange objects on your slide in a consistent manner. Choose from 27 AutoLayout designs that accommodate most common slide arrangements. When you create a new slide, you apply an AutoLayout to it. You see design elements and placeholders for text and other objects. You can also apply an AutoLayout to an existing slide at any time. When you change a slide's AutoLayout, you keep existing information. PowerPoint applies the new AutoLayout, and you can arrange the placeholders the way you want them.

Insert a New Slide

1. Click the slide where you want to place the new slide.

2. Click the New Slide button on the Formatting toolbar. Power-Point inserts a new slide following the slide you selected.

3. Click the AutoLayout you want to use.

Apply an AutoLayout to an Existing Slide

1. In Normal view, display the slide you want to change.

2. Choose Format ➤ Slide Layout. The Slide Layout task pane opens.

3. Click the AutoLayout you want to use.

Entering Information in a Placeholder

When you apply an AutoLayout to a slide, an arranged group of place-holders appears—one placeholder for each object on the slide. The placeholders include instructions for entering object contents.

▶ For text placeholders, click the placeholder, and then type the text.

▶ For other objects, double-click the placeholder, and then use the tools for the accessory that PowerPoint starts.

Entering Text

In Normal or Slide view, you type text directly into the text placeholders. A *text placeholder* is an empty text box. If you type more text than can fit in the placeholder, PowerPoint automatically resizes the text to fit in the text box. The *AutoFit Text* feature changes the line spacing—or paragraph spacing—between lines of text and then changes the font size to ensure that the text fits. You can also manually increase or decrease the line spacing or font size of the text. The insertion point indicates where the text will appear when you type. To place the insertion point into your text, move the pointer arrow over the text. The pointer changes to an I-beam to indicate that you can click and then type.

Enter Text into a Placeholder

1. In Normal view, click the text placeholder (if it isn't already selected).

2. Type the text that you want to enter.

3. Click outside the text object to deselect the object.

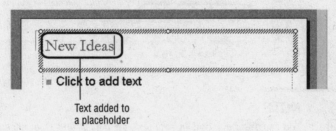

Text added to
a placeholder

Placeholder	Description
Bulleted List	Displays a short list of related items
Clip Art	Inserts a picture
Chart	Inserts a chart
Organization Chart	Inserts an organizational chart
Table	Inserts a table from Microsoft Word
Media Clip	Inserts a music, sound, or video clip
Object	Inserts an object created in another program, such as an Excel spreadsheet or a WordArt object

Insert Text

1. Click to place the insertion point where you want to insert text.

2. Type the text. When you enter bulleted text, make sure that the insertion point is at the beginning of the line, and then press the Tab key on the keyboard to indent a level or hold down the Shift+Tab keys on the keyboard to move back out a level.

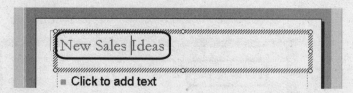

NOTE

You can enter symbols in your text, such as © and ®, or accented characters, such as ô, depending on the fonts installed on your computer. Choose Insert ➢ Symbol, click the Font drop-down arrow, click the font that contains the symbol you want, click the symbol, click the Insert button, and then click the Close button when you're done.

TIP

When you decrease paragraph spacing, make sure you leave enough space for the height of each entire letter, including extenders such as the bottom of *p* and the top of *b*.

Enter Text in a Bulleted List

1. In Normal view, click the bulleted text placeholder.

2. Type the first bulleted item.

3. Press the Enter key on the keyboard.

4. Type the next bulleted item.

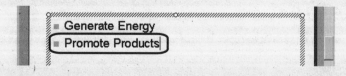

5. Repeat steps 3 and 4 until you complete the list.

Adjust Paragraph Line Spacing

1. Click anywhere in the paragraph you want to adjust.

2. Choose Format ➢ Line Spacing. The Line Spacing dialog box opens.

3. Set the spacing options that you want.

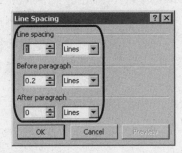

4. Click the OK button.

DEVELOPING AN OUTLINE

If you create your presentation using an AutoContent Wizard, PowerPoint generates an outline. If you prefer, you can develop your own outline from a blank presentation. As you develop an outline, you can add new slides and duplicate existing slides in your presentation. You can also insert an outline you created in another program, such as Microsoft Word. Make sure that the document that contains the outline is set up using outline heading styles. When you insert the outline in PowerPoint, it creates slide titles, subtitles, and bulleted lists based on those styles.

TIP

If the Outlining toolbar is not visible, right-click a visible toolbar, and then click Outlining.

NOTE

To change the display view size, click the Zoom drop-down arrow on the Standard toolbar, and then select a view size.

Enter Text in Outline View

1. On the Outline tab of Normal view, click to position the insertion point where you want the text to appear.

2. Type the text you want to enter, pressing the Enter key on the keyboard after each line. If you want to show or hide formatting, click the Show Formatting button on the Outlining toolbar.

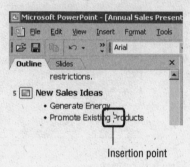

Insertion point

Add a Slide in Outline View

1. On the Outline tab of Normal view, click at the end of the slide text where you want to insert a new slide.

2. Click the New Slide button on the Formatting toolbar and then double-click a layout, or hold down the Ctrl+Enter keys on the keyboard to insert a slide using the existing slide layout.

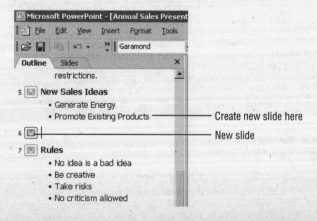

Create new slide here

New slide

TIP

You can delete a slide in several ways. On the Outline tab or in Slide Sorter view, select the slide you want to delete, and then press the Delete key on the keyboard. In Slide view, select the slide you want to delete, and then choose Edit ➢ Delete Slide.

NOTE

To open an outline from another program in PowerPoint, click the Open button on the Standard toolbar, click the Files Of Type drop-down arrow, click All Outlines, and then double-click the outline file you want to open.

REARRANGING SLIDES

You can instantly rearrange slides in an outline or in Slide Sorter view. You can use the drag-and-drop method or the Cut and Paste buttons to move slides to a new location. On the Outline tab of Normal view, you can use the Move Up and Move Down buttons to move selected slides within the outline. You can also collapse the outline to its major points to easily see its structure.

NOTE

To select an entire slide, click the slide icon on the Outline tab or the slide miniature in Slide Sorter view. To select more than one slide, hold down the Shift key on the keyboard while you click each slide.

Rearrange a Slide in Slide Sorter View

1. Click the Slide Sorter View button.

2. Click to select the slide that you want to move.

3. Drag the selected slide to a new location. A vertical bar appears next to the slide where the slides will be moved when you release the mouse button.

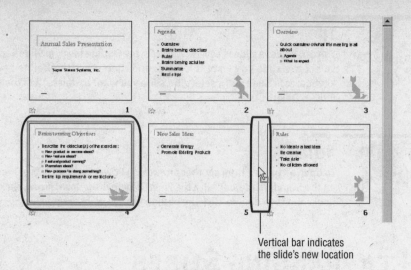

Vertical bar indicates
the slide's new location

Rearrange a Slide in an Outline

1. Click the Normal View button.

2. If necessary, choose View ➢ Toolbars ➢ Outlining to display the Outlining toolbar.

3. Click the slide icon of the slide you want to move.

4. Click the Move Up button to move the slide up, or click the Move Down button to move the slide down. Repeat until the slide is where you want it.

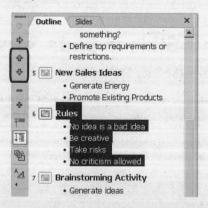

NOTE

To change the indent level, in Normal view or Slide view, or on the Outline tab, click in the line of the body of text you want to indent, then click the Demote button to move the line in one level or click the Promote button to move the line out one level.

TIP

If you are in Slide Sorter view and you want to open a slide in Slide view, double-click the slide.

Collapse and Expand Slides in an Outline

1. In an outline, select the slide, and then click the appropriate button. You can expand or collapse your view of a slide—the content is unaffected. On the Outline tab of Normal view, double-click a collapsed slide to expand and show all bullets on that slide; or double-click an expanded slide to collapse the content and show only the title.

   ▶ To collapse the selected slides, click the Collapse button. A horizontal line appears below a collapsed slide in Outline view.

   ▶ To expand the selected slides, click the Expand button.

   ▶ To collapse all slides, click the Collapse All button.

   ▶ To expand all slides, click the Expand All button.

Move a Slide with Cut-and-Paste

1. In an outline or in Slide Sorter view, select the slides you want to move.

2. Click the Cut button on the Standard toolbar.

3. Click the new location.

4. Click the Paste button on the Standard toolbar.

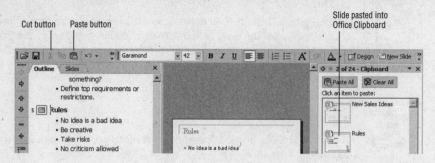

Cut button   Paste button

Slide pasted into
Office Clipboard

CONTROLLING SLIDE APPEARANCE WITH MASTERS

If you want an object, such as a company logo or clip art, to appear on every slide in your presentation (except the title slide), place it on the slide master. You can also select the slides in which you do not want the object to appear, or you can create unique slides that do not contain any formatting from the masters. If you change your mind, you can easily reapply a master format to a slide that you altered. As you view the master, you can use the Slide Miniature window to view a sample miniature of the slide.

TIP

To view a master quickly, hold down the Shift key on the keyboard, point to a view button to determine the master, and then click a view button to go to a master view.

Include an Object on Every Slide

1. Choose View ➤ Master ➤ Slide Master. To display the Master toolbar while in master view, choose View ➤ Toolbars ➤ Master.

2. Add the object you want and modify its size and placement.

3. Click the Close Master View button on the Master toolbar.

TIP

Click the vertical scroll arrows to switch between the slide master and the title master. An object that you place on the slide master does not appear on the title slide unless you also place it on the title master.

NOTE

The Handout Master toolbar has buttons for displaying two, three, four, six, and nine slides per page, and for setting how the outline appears.

WORKING WITH COLOR SCHEMES

You can apply a color scheme to one slide or all of the slides in a presentation. You can choose from one or more standard color schemes in each template. You can also create and save your own color scheme, which you can apply to other slides and other presentations.

TIP

To view a presentation in black and white, click the Color/Grayscale button on the Standard toolbar. Click the button again to view the presentation in color.

NOTE

You can change the background color or fill effect. Display the slide you want to change, choose Format ➢ Background, click the Background Fill drop-down arrow, and then select a color; or click Fill Effects and the gradient, texture, pattern, or picture effect you want, and then click the Apply To All button or the Apply button.

Choose a Color Scheme

1. Click the Design button on the Formatting toolbar.

2. Click Color Schemes in the Slide Design task pane.

3. Click the color scheme you want.

Delete a Color Scheme

1. Click the Design button on the Formatting toolbar.

2. Click Edit Color Schemes in the Slide Design task pane. The Edit Color Scheme dialog box opens.

3. Click the Standard tab to view the available color schemes.

4. Click the scheme that you want to delete.

5. Click the Delete Scheme button.

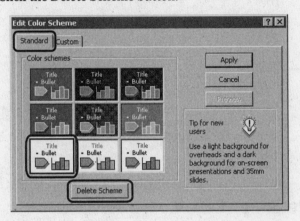

NOTE

You can change a color in a standard color scheme. In Slide view, right-click a blank area of the slide whose color scheme you want to change, and then click Slide Color Scheme. Click the Custom tab, click the element you want to change in the Scheme Colors list, click Change Color, click a color on the Standard tab, click the OK button, and then click the Apply button or the Apply To All button.

TIP

To save a changed color scheme, choose Format ➤ Slide Color Scheme, and then click the Custom tab. Alter the eight colors that comprise the color scheme as you wish, and then click the Add As Standard Scheme button.

CREATING A TEXT BOX

Usually you use the title, subtitle, and bulleted list placeholders to place text on a slide. However, when you want to add text outside one of the standard placeholders, you can create a text box. Your text box doesn't have to be rectangular—you can also use one of PowerPoint's *AutoShapes*, a collection of shapes that range from rectangles and circles to arrows and stars. When you place text in an AutoShape, the text becomes part of the AutoShape.

NOTE

Text boxes appear in the slide pane of Normal view or in Slide view, but not on the Outline tab.

TIP

You can orient text in text boxes, table cells, and AutoShapes vertically. Select the object with the text you want to change, choose Format ➢ Text Box, click the Rotate Text Within AutoShape By 90° check box to select it, and then click the OK button.

Create a Text Box

1. In Normal view, choose View ➢ Toolbars ➢ Drawing to display the toolbar, if necessary.

2. Click the Text Box button on the Drawing toolbar.

3. To add text that wraps, drag to create a box and then start typing. To add text that doesn't wrap, click and then start typing.

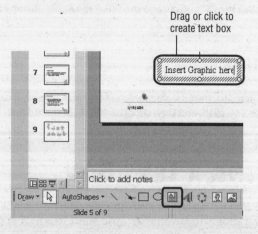

Drag or click to create text box

Insert Graphic here

4. Click outside the text box to deselect it.

Add Text to an AutoShape

1. Click the AutoShapes button on the Drawing toolbar.

2. Point to the shape category you want to use.

3. Click the shape you want.

4. Drag to draw the shape on the slide.

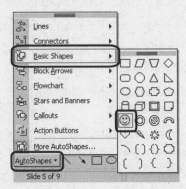

5. Type the text.

INSERTING SLIDES FROM OTHER PRESENTATIONS

To insert slides from other presentations in a slide show, you can open the presentation and then copy and paste the slides you want, or you can use the *Slide Finder* feature. With Slide Finder, you don't have to open the presentation first; instead, you view a miniature of each of the slides, and then insert only the ones you select. With Slide Finder, you can also create a list of favorite presentations that you can use for future slide shows.

TIP

You can add or remove a slide presentation from your list of favorites. Choose Insert ➢ Slides From Files, locate the presentation you want to add, and then click the Add To Favorites button. To remove a presentation, click the List Of Favorites tab, select a presentation, and then click the Remove button.

Insert Slides Using the Slide Finder

1. Choose Insert ➤ Slides From Files. The Slide Finder dialog box opens.

2. Click the Find Presentation tab.

3. Click the Browse button, locate and select the file you want, and then click the Open button.

4. If necessary, click the Display button to display a miniature of each slide.

5. Select the slides you want to insert.

   ▶ To insert just one slide, click the slide and then click the Insert button.

   ▶ To insert multiple slides, click each slide you want to insert, and then click the Insert button.

   ▶ To insert all the slides in the presentation, click the Insert All button.

6. Click the Close button.

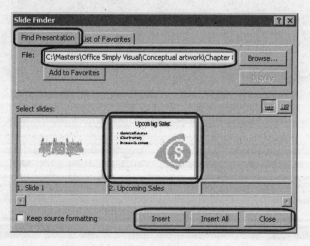

ADDING A HEADER AND FOOTER

You can add a header and a footer that will appear on each slide. Headers and footers often include information such as the presentation title, slide number, date, and name of the presenter. Use the masters to place header and footer information on your slides, handouts, or notes pages. Be sure to keep the text in your header and footer brief and uncomplicated so that they do not clutter your slide.

TIP

To remove the header or footer from the title slide only, choose View ➤ Header And Footer, click the Slide tab, click the Don't Show On Title Slide check box to select it, and then click the Apply To All button.

Add a Header and Footer

1. Choose View ➤ Header And Footer. The Header And Footer dialog box opens.

2. Click the Slide or Notes And Handouts tab.

3. Enter or select the information you want to include on your slide or your notes and handouts.

4. Click the Apply button to apply your selections to the current slide, or click the Apply To All button to apply the selections to all slides.

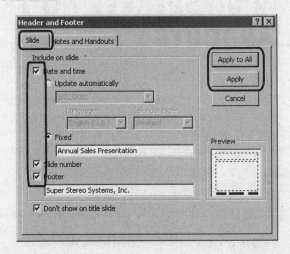

Change the Look of a Header or Footer

1. Choose View ➢ Master.

2. Click the master you want to change.

3. Make the necessary changes to the header and footer place-holders. You can move or resize them or change their text attributes.

4. Click the Close Master View button on the Master toolbar.

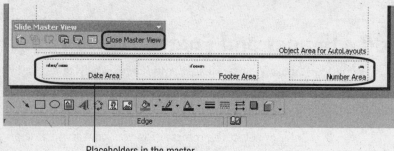

Placeholders in the master
are dotted rectangles

PREPARING SPEAKER NOTES AND HANDOUTS

You can add speaker notes to a slide in Normal view using the notes pane. Every slide has a corresponding *notes page* that displays a reduced image of the slide and a text placeholder where you can enter speaker notes. Once you have created speaker notes, you can reference them as you give your presentation, either from a printed copy or from your computer. You can enhance your notes by including objects on the notes master.

TIP

To change the size of the notes pane in Normal view, point to the top border of the notes pane until the pointer changes to a double-headed arrow, and then drag the border until the pane is the size you want.

Enter Notes in Normal View

1. Switch to the slide in which you want to enter notes.

2. Click in the notes pane and type your notes.

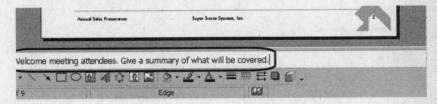

Enter Notes in Notes Page View

1. Switch to the slide for which you want to enter notes.

2. Choose View ➤ Notes Page. Notes Page view appears.

3. If necessary, click the Zoom drop-down arrow, and then increase the zoom percentage to better see the text as you type it.

4. Click the text placeholder.

5. Type your notes.

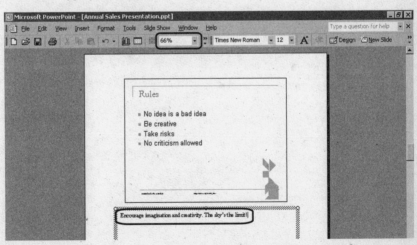

TIP

Objects on the notes master don't appear in the notes pane in Normal view or when you save your presentation as a web page. They will appear when you print the notes pages.

NOTE

You can insert the date and time on the current slide. Click to place the insertion point where you want the date and time, choose Insert ➤ Date And Time, select the date and time format you want, and then click the OK button.

WHAT'S NEXT

Now that you've started to work with PowerPoint and begun your first presentation, it's time to leap ahead.

In the next chapter, you'll go through the steps of refining a presentation for use with a slide show—where action buttons, animations, and audio can be added, and timing and transitioning of the presentation can be set and tweaked for best results.

Chapter 16
CREATING A SLIDE SHOW WITH POWERPOINT 2002

F or the majority of users working in PowerPoint, the ability
to create a presentation and then put it together as a slide
show is their very reason for using the package.

Having access to a tool such as this lets you focus your attention less on the functional details needed to pull off a professional-
looking slide show, and more on putting your time where it
really counts: the creative organization of content.

In this chapter, you can build on the fundamentals of Power-
Point 2002 learned in the previous chapter, by implementing
control over how the slide show will be presented. Coverage will
include the use of action buttons and animations on slides;
good transitioning between slides in a presentation; and how to
both time your presentation and run your slide show.

Let's get started.

Adapted from *Microsoft Office XP Simply Visual*
by Perspection, Inc.

ISBN 0-7821-4004-1   400 pp $24.99

ADDING ACTION BUTTONS

When you create a self-running presentation to show at a conference kiosk, you might want a user to be able to move easily to specific slides or to view a different presentation altogether. You can insert *action buttons* to give this capability to your users. By clicking an action button, your users activate a *hyperlink*, a connection between two locations in the same document or in different documents.

TIP

To insert an action button using the Drawing toolbar, click the AutoShapes button, point to Action Buttons, and then click the action button you want to insert on your slide.

Insert an Action Button

1. Choose Slide Show ➤ Action Buttons.

2. Choose the action button you want to insert.

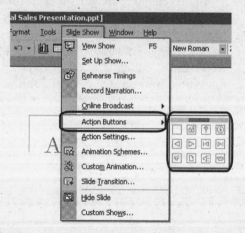

3. Drag the pointer to insert the action button, and then release the mouse button when the action button is the size you want. To create a square action button, hold down the Shift key on the keyboard as you drag. The Action Settings dialog box opens.

TIP
You can initiate an action button with a mouse click or mouseover in a slide show. In the Action Settings dialog box, click the Mouse Click tab or the Mouse Over tab, and then select an action.

4. If necessary, fill out the Action Settings dialog box, and then click the OK button.

Test an Action Button

1. Click the Slide Show View button. The slide show starts.

2. Display the slide containing the action button.

3. Click the action button.

Annual Sales Presentation

NOTE
Insert the Return action button to return to the slide you were previously viewing, regardless of its location in the presentation.

TIP
To edit a hyperlink, right-click the object with the hyperlink and then click Edit Hyperlink.

Create an Action Button to Go to a Specific Slide

1. Choose Slide Show ➢ Action Buttons ➢ Custom Button.

2. Drag the pointer to insert the action button on the slide. The Action Settings dialog box opens.

3. Click the Hyperlink To option button, click the drop-down
   arrow, and then click Slide from the list of hyperlink destinations. The Hyperlink To Slide dialog box opens.

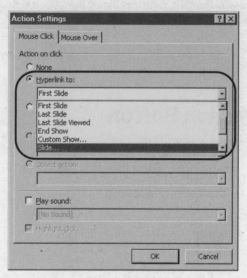

4. Select the slide to which you want the action button to jump.

5. Click the OK button.

6. Right-click the action button, and then click Add Text.

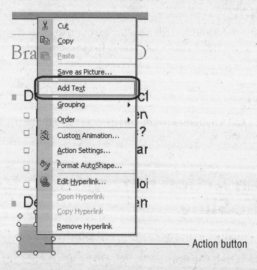

Action button

7. Type the name for the action button.

8. Click outside the action button to deselect it.

9. Run the slide show and test the action button.

CREATING SLIDE TRANSITIONS

If you want to maintain your viewers' attention at all times in your presentation, you can add transitions between slides. For example, you can create a fade-out effect so that one slide becomes lighter as it is replaced by a new slide, or you can have one slide appear to push another slide out of the way. You can also add sound effects to your transitions, although you need a sound card and speakers to play them.

TIP

When you add a transition effect to a slide, the effect takes place between the previous slide and the selected slide.

Specify a Transition

1. Click the Slide Sorter View button.

2. Click the slide to which you want to add a transition effect.

3. Click the Slide Transition button to display the Slide Transition task pane.

4. Click the transition effect you want.

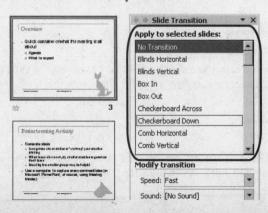

Apply a Transition to All Slides in a Presentation

1. Choose Slide Show ➤ Slide Transition. The Slide Transition task pane opens.

2. In the Apply To Selected Slides list, click the transition you want.

3. Click the Apply To All Slides button.

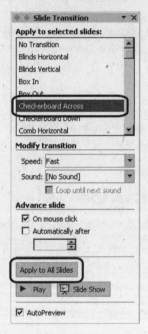

NOTE
You can view a slide's transition by clicking the slide's transition icon in Slide Sorter view, or by playing the slide show in Slide Show view.

TIP
In Slide Sorter view, click the Slide Transition button on the Slide Sorter toolbar to quickly open the Slide Transition dialog box.

Set Transition Effect Speeds

1. In Normal or Slide Sorter view, click or display the slide whose transition effect you want to edit.

2. Choose Slide Show ➤ Slide Transition. The Slide Transition task pane opens.

3. Click the Speed drop-down arrow, and then click the speed you want.

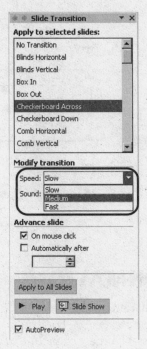

Add Sound to a Transition

1. In Normal or Slide Sorter view, click or display the slide to which you want to add a transition sound.

2. Choose Slide Show ➤ Slide Transition. The Slide Transition task pane opens.

3. Click the Sound drop-down arrow, and then click the sound you want.

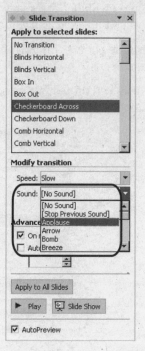

ADDING ANIMATION

You can use animation to introduce objects onto a slide one at a time or with special animation effects. For example, a bulleted list can appear one bulleted item at a time, or a picture or chart can fade gradually into the slide's foreground. You can use many kinds of animations with Power-Point. Some are called *animation schemes*—effects that PowerPoint has designed for you. Many of the preset animations contain sounds. You can also design your own *customized animations*, including those with your own special effects and sound elements.

TIP

In Slide Sorter view, click a slide's animation icon to quickly view the animation.

Use Animation Schemes

1. Select the slide or object that you want to animate.

2. Choose Slide Show ➤ Animation Schemes. The Slide Design task pane opens.

3. In the Apply To Selected Slides list, click the animation you want.

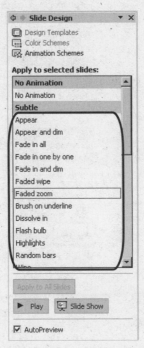

Preview an Animation

1. Click the Normal View button or the Slide Sorter View button, and then display the slide containing the animation you want to preview.

2. Click the Design button, and then click Animation Schemes.

3. Click the Play button.

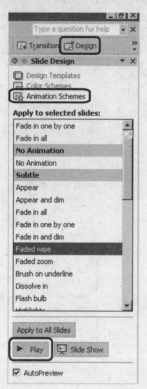

TIP

To remove an animation, view the slide in Normal view, click the Design button, and then click Animation Schemes. Click the slide from which you want to remove the animation, and then click the No Animation option.

Apply a Customized Animation

1. In Normal view, right-click the object, and then click Custom Animation. The Custom Animation task pane opens.

2. Click the Add Effect button, point to an effect category, and then click the effect you want.

USING SPECIALIZED ANIMATIONS

Using specialized animations, you can apply animations to particular objects. For example, for a text object, you can introduce the text on your slide all at once or by word or letter. Similarly, you can introduce bulleted lists one bullet item at a time and apply different effects to older items, such as graying out the existing items in a list as PowerPoint inserts new ones. You can animate charts by introducing chart series or chart categories one at a time.

NOTE

Set times between animations. Display the slide in Normal view, click the Slide Show menu, click Custom Animation, and then click the list item you want to change. Choose one of the animations from the Animation Order list, and then click the Automatically option button. Enter the number of seconds between this animation and the previous event, and then click the OK button.

TIP

Animate the attached shape with text. In the Custom Animation task pane, select the text object you want to animate, click the Add Effect button, hold down the Shift key on the keyboard, click the Effects drop-down arrow, and then select an effects option.

Animate Text

1.   In Normal view, right-click the selected text object, and then click Custom Animation. The Custom Animation task pane opens.

2. Click the Add Effect button, point to an effect category, and then click the effect you want.

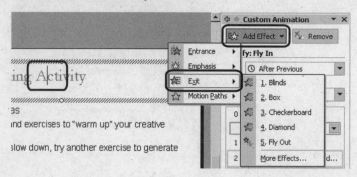

Animate Bulleted Lists

1. In Normal view, right-click the selected bulleted text object, and then click Custom Animation.

2. Click the Add Effect button, point to an effect category, and then click the effect you want to add.

3. Click the Animation drop-down arrow for the bulleted text object, and then click Effect Options. The Box dialog box opens.

4. Click the Text Animation tab (if necessary), click the Group Text drop-down arrow, and then click an option.

5. Click the OK button.

TIP

You can change the order of bullets from the last bulleted list item to the first. In the Custom Animation task pane, select the object with the text you want to reverse, click the Effects drop-down arrow, click the Text Animation tab in the Box dialog box, click the In Reverse Order check box to select it, and then click the OK button.

Part v

Fade Text after It Is Animated

1. In Normal view, right-click the text, and then click Custom Animation.

2. In the Custom Animation task pane, click the Add Effect button, and then click the effect you want to add.

3. Click the Modify: Fade (Start) drop-down arrow, and then click an option for when you want the fade to start.

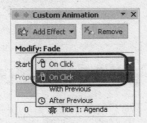

Modify the Animation Order

1. In Normal view, display the slide with the animation, and then choose Slide Show ➤ Custom Animation. The Custom Animation task pane opens.

2. Click the slide object whose animation order you want to change.

3. Click the Re-Order up arrow button or the Re-Order down arrow button.

TIMING A PRESENTATION

If you have a time limit for presenting your slide show, you can use Power-
Point's timing features to make sure that your presentation is not dragging
on too long or going too fast. You can specify the amount of time allotted
to each slide and test yourself during rehearsal using the *slide meter*, which
ensures that your timings are workable. By rehearsing timings, you can
vary the amount of time each slide appears on the screen. If you want the
timings to take effect, make sure the slide show is set to use timings in the
Set Up Show dialog box (choose Slide Show ➢ Set Up Show).

TIP

You can record a narration that accompanies your slides. Choose Slide Show ➢
Record Narration, set the microphone level and sound quality, click the OK button, click the Link Narrations In check box to select it, click the OK button, click
Current Slide or First Slide, record your narration, and then click the Yes button
to save the slide timings.

Set Timings between All Slides

1. Choose Slide Show ➤ Slide Transition. The Slide Transition task pane opens.

2. Click the Automatically After check box to select it.

3. Enter the time (in seconds) before the presentation automatically advances to the next slide after displaying the entire slide.

4. Click the Apply To All Slides button.

Create Timings through Rehearsal

1. Choose Slide Show ➤ Rehearse Timings. The slide show starts, and the Rehearsal toolbar opens.

2. As the slide show runs, rehearse your presentation by pressing the Enter key or spacebar on the keyboard to advance to the next slide, or by clicking the Next button.

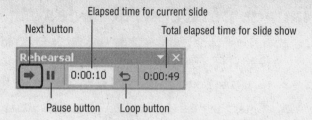

3. When you're finished, click the Yes button to accept the timings you just recorded.

4. Review the timings in Slide Sorter view.

SETTING UP A SLIDE SHOW

PowerPoint offers several types of slide shows appropriate for a variety of presentation situations, from a traditional full-screen slide show to a show that runs automatically on a computer screen at a conference kiosk. When you don't want to show all of the slides in a PowerPoint presentation to a particular audience, you can hide individual slides or specify the range of slides to show.

NOTE

If you want a presentation file to open directly to a slide show rather than in a document window, choose File ➢ Save As, click the Save As Type drop-down arrow, and then click PowerPoint Show.

TIP

To hide a slide, click the Slide Sorter View button, select the slides you want to hide, and then click the Hide Slide button on the Slide Sorter toolbar.

Set Up a Slide Show

1. Choose Slide Show ➢ Set Up Show. The Set Up Show dialog box opens.

2. Choose the show type you want:

    ▶ Click the Presented By A Speaker option button to run a traditional full-screen slide show, where you can advance the slides manually or automatically.

    ▶ Click the Browsed By An Individual option button to run a slide show in a window and allow access to some Power-Point commands.

    ▶ Click the Browsed At A Kiosk option button to create a self-running, unattended slide show for a booth or kiosk. The slides will advance automatically, or a user can advance the slides or activate hyperlinks.

3. Change additional slide show settings as appropriate:

    ▶ Loop Continuously

    ▶ Show Without Narration

    ▶ Show Without Animation

4. Click the OK button.

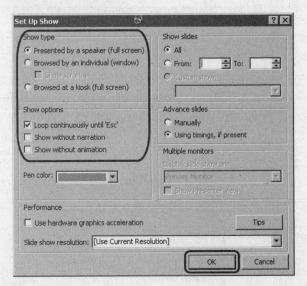

CREATING A CUSTOM SLIDE SHOW

If you plan to present a slide show to more than one audience, you don't have to create a separate slide show for each audience. Instead, you can create a *custom slide show* that allows you to specify which slides from the presentation you will use and the order in which they will appear.

NOTE

You can use the Set Up Show dialog box to display a custom slide show. Choose Slide Show ➤ Set Up Show, click the Custom Show option button, click the Custom Show drop-down arrow, select the custom slide show, and then click the OK button.

TIP

To delete a custom slide show, choose Slide Show ➤ Custom Shows, click the show you want to delete, click the Remove button, and then click the Close button.

Create a Custom Slide Show

1. Choose Slide Show ➤ Custom Shows. The Custom Shows dialog box opens.

2. Click the New button.

3. Type a name for the show.

4. Double-click the slides you want to include in the show in the order you want to present them. You can change their order using the up arrow button and the down arrow button.

5. Click the OK button.

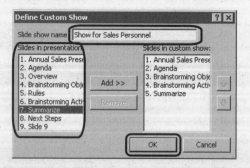

6. Click the Close button.

Show a Custom Slide Show

1. Choose Slide Show ➤ Custom Shows. The Custom Shows dialog box opens.

2. Click the custom slide show that you want to run.

3. Click the Show button.

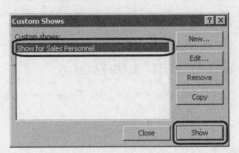

STARTING A SLIDE SHOW

Once you have set up your slide show, you can start the show at any time. As you run your slide show, you can use the Slide Show view pop-up menu to access certain PowerPoint commands without leaving Slide Show view. If your show is running at a kiosk, you might want to disable this feature.

TIP
To start a slide show quickly from the current slide, click the Slide Show button.

NOTE
You can open the pop-up menu quickly in Slide Show view by right-clicking the screen.

Start a Slide Show and Display the Pop-Up Menu

1. Choose Slide Show ➤ View Show. The slide show starts.

2. Move the mouse pointer to display the pop-up menu button.

3. Click the pop-up menu button in the lower-left corner of the slide to display the pop-up menu.

Click to display pop-up menu

Set Pop-Up Menu Options

1. Choose Tools ➤ Options. The Options dialog box opens.

2. Click the View tab.

3. Click to select the pop-up menu options you want.

4. Click the OK button.

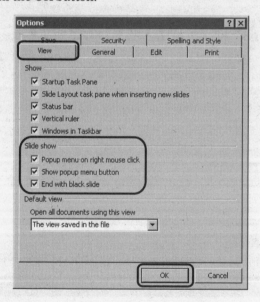

NAVIGATING A SLIDE SHOW

In Slide Show view, you advance to the next slide by clicking the mouse button or by pressing the Enter key or spacebar on the keyboard. In addition to those basic navigational techniques, PowerPoint provides keyboard short-cuts that can take you to the beginning, end, or any particular slide in your presentation. You can also use the navigation commands on the shortcut menu to access slides in custom slide shows.

TIP

After a period of inactivity during a normal full-screen slide show, PowerPoint automatically hides the pointer and the slide show icon. Move the mouse to display them again.

NOTE

You can use a light pen during a slide show. In Slide Show view, press Ctrl+P to change the pointer to the shape of a pen. Simply drag to draw on the screen. Press the E key to erase the drawing. To change the pen color, right-click the screen in Slide Show view, point to Pointer Options, point to Pen Color, and then select a color.

Go to a Specific Slide

1. In Slide Show view, right-click a slide.

2. Point to Go, and then point to By Title.

3. Click the title of the slide to which you want to go.

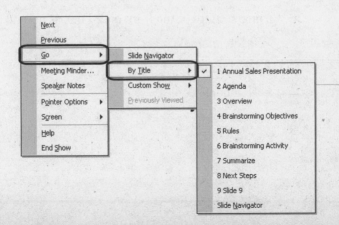

NOTE

You can quickly navigate in a slide show using keyboard shortcuts. Press the Left arrow or P key to go to the previous slide, press the Right arrow or N key to go to the next slide, or press the slide number and Enter to go to a specific slide.

PRINTING A PRESENTATION

You can print all the elements of your presentation—the slides, outline, notes, and handouts—in color or in black and white. The Print dialog box offers standard Windows features, giving you the option to print multiple copies, specify ranges, access printer properties, and print to a file.

When you print an outline, PowerPoint prints the presentation outline shown on the Outline tab.

TIP

Use the Print button on the Standard toolbar only when you want to bypass the Print dialog box. If you need to select options in the Print dialog box, choose File ➢ Print.

Print a Presentation

1. Choose File ➢ Print. The Print dialog box opens.

2. Click the Print What drop-down arrow, and then click what you want to print.

3. Change settings in the Print dialog box as necessary:

   ▸ Printer name

   ▸ Print range

   ▸ Number of copies

   ▸ Handouts

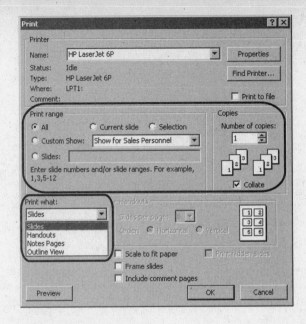

4. Click the OK button.

WHAT'S NEXT

You have now developed your first presentation and slide show. Consider it one more tool in your Office XP skills arsenal.

In Part VI, you will be introduced to the basic concepts behind an Access 2002 database and its organization.

PART VI
CREATING DATABASES WITH ACCESS 2002

Chapter 17

UNDERSTANDING DATABASES

Information, we are frequently told, is the most valuable product of today's economy. However, we're all swimming up to our necks in bits and pieces of information.

Large collections of data are only as useful as our ability to summarize and retrieve information when we want it. To do this best, we need specialized and powerful data organization tools such as databases, the focus of this chapter.

Most people are accustomed to working with *information*, which is *data* that's organized into some meaningful form. You probably can recognize the information shown in Figure 17.1 as an invoice. You can find the customer's name and address, the products that person ordered, and just about any other information you might want simply by looking at the invoice. The invoice as a whole presents business information—namely, what happened in a transaction—by meaningfully drawing together various related items of data.

· ·

Adapted from *Mastering Access 2002 Premium Edition* by Celeste Robinson and Alan Simpson

ISBN 0-7821-4008-4   1224 pp $49.99

Invoice

E & K Sporting Goods
1337 West 47th Street
Fridley, NC 28228
USA

Invoice Date	2/5/2001	*Contact Name*	Andy Adams		*Customer ID*	1
Order ID	1	*PO Number*	52		*Ship Date*	2/5/2001
Order Date	2/3/2001				*Shipping Method*	Federal Express

Ship To:

ABC Corporation
87 Polk St.
San Francisco, CA 94117
USA

Bill To:

ABC Corporation
87 Polk St.
San Francisco, CA 94117
USA

Product ID	Product Name	Quantity	Unit Price	Discount	Line Total
9	Tether ball	5	$9.65	0.00%	$48.25
1	Basketball	2	$4.95	0.00%	$9.90
2	Football	2	$5.65	0.00%	$11.30
10	Foosball	4	$17.85	0.00%	$71.40
6	Crystal ball	2	$45.55	0.00%	$91.10

Subtotal	$231.95
Freight Charge	$2.00
Sales Tax	$11.60
Order Total	$245.55

FIGURE 17.1: A sample printed invoice. You probably can find whatever information you need about the transaction on this sheet of paper because you recognize different types of information (name, address, products, order total) based on their context.

Suppose you want to store all of your invoices on the computer. You might consider buying a scanner and scanning each invoice into a computer file. Later, you could display a copy of the invoice on the screen and print it. You wouldn't even need a database management system; all you would need is a scanner and a simple graphics program.

WHY STORE DATA?

The problem with the scanner approach is that all you can do is retrieve, view, and print the invoices. You can't analyze or reformat the data on the invoice. For instance, you can't print mailing labels, envelopes, or form letters for all your customers. You can't analyze your orders to view overall sales. Why not? Because the computer doesn't have the eyes or brains it takes to look into the invoice and pull out certain types of information. Only you can do that job because *you* have eyes and a brain.

FLEXIBILITY IS THE GOAL

If you want the flexibility to display, print, and analyze your information in whatever format you want, you first need to break down that information into small units of data. For example, a person's last name is one unit of data. That person's zip code is another. The name of a product the customer purchased is another unit of data, and so forth.

After breaking the information into discrete units of data, you can use a database management system, such as Access, to analyze and present that data any way you want. If each person's surname is a discrete unit of data, for example, you can tell Access to alphabetize your customers by name or to find the order that Smith placed yesterday.

You can put the individual units of data into any format you want—for example, mailing labels, envelopes, or invoices.

YOU USE TABLES TO STORE DATA

In Access, you must break all your information into data that's stored in tables. A table is just a collection of data that's organized into rows and columns. You can put any information that's available to you into a table.

Let's forget about invoices for a moment and focus on storing information about customers. Suppose you have a Rolodex or card file containing customer names and addresses, as shown next. For each customer, you maintain the same pieces of information—name, address, and so on.

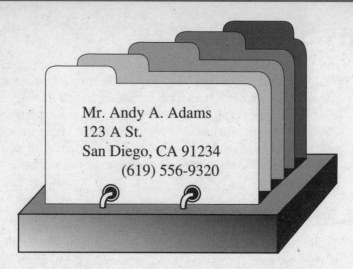

How can you break down the information on this Rolodex into raw data that's neatly organized as a table? Easy. Just make a column for each data element, such as last name or state, and then list the corresponding data elements for each customer in rows, as shown in Figure 17.2.

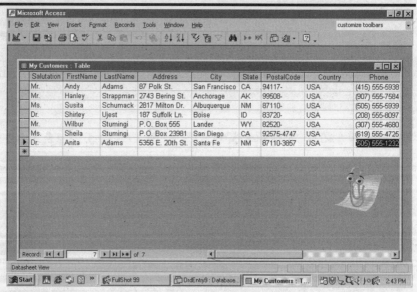

FIGURE 17.2 : Names and addresses, which might once have been on Rolodex cards, organized and typed into an Access table

TERMINOLOGY TIME

Now is as good a time as any to get some terminology out of the way so we can talk about tables and databases more precisely. Here are four terms you'll see often:

Table   A collection of data organized into rows and columns.

Field   A single unit (or column) of information in a table. The sample table in Figure 17.2 consists of fields named Salutation, FirstName, LastName, Address, City, State, PostalCode, Country, and Phone, as you can see by looking across the top of the table.

Record   The set of all data fields for one row of the table. The sample table in Figure 17.2 contains seven filled records: one for a customer named Wilbur Stumingi, another for Shirley Ujest, and so forth.

Database   Contrary to what some people think, a database is not a table. A database is a collection of *all* the tables and other objects (such as forms and reports) that you use to manage data.

We'll tell you more about why a database might contain several tables later in this chapter.

THE MORE FIELDS, THE BETTER

Looking back at Figure 17.2, you may be wondering why we bothered to break the information into so many different fields. Isn't using the three fields Salutation, LastName, and FirstName a little excessive?

Not really, because organizing the data into separate fields now will make it easier to arrange the data in a meaningful form later. Here are some ways to arrange the data in one of the records of the table shown in Figure 17.2:

- ▶ Mr. Wilbur Stumingi
- ▶ Mr. Stumingi
- ▶ Stumingi, Wilbur
- ▶ Dear Wilbur:
- ▶ Wilbur Stumingi
- ▶ Yo, Wilbur!

You can rearrange the table columns in any order you want, and you can use forms and reports to organize table data into any format.

WHY USE MULTIPLE TABLES?

Earlier we said that a database can contain many tables. So now you may be wondering why you'd want to put more than one table into a database. The simple reason is that it's easier to manage data if all the information about a particular subject is in its own table. For example, if you're designing a database to track membership in an organization, you might create separate tables, such as these:

- ▶ All Members
- ▶ Committees
- ▶ Payments Made
- ▶ Company Or Organization
- ▶ Membership Types And Dues
- ▶ Committee Members
- ▶ Payment Methods

If you're using Access to manage orders for your company's products, you might use these tables:

- ▶ Customers
- ▶ Order Details
- ▶ Payment Methods
- ▶ Products
- ▶ Employees
- ▶ Orders
- ▶ Payments
- ▶ Shipping Methods

Remember that these tables are suggestions only. Access really doesn't care *what* type of data you put into tables. All that matters is that you find a way to break the information you need to manage into the tabular fields-and-records format.

TIP

The Database Wizard and Table Wizard can create many types of tables for you automatically. These wizards organize your database into tables and divide your tables into separate fields with only a small amount of guidance from you. The process is so fast and painless that you'll be creating complete databases in no time. You can learn more about these wizards by using the Office Assistant.

When to Use One Table

Until you get the hang of how to structure a database, deciding whether data should go into one table or several tables is a bit difficult. But this general rule of thumb always applies: If a one-to-one correspondence exists between two fields, put those fields into the same table.

For example, it makes sense to put all of the My Customers information in one table because there's an exact one-to-one relationship between fields. That is, for every one customer, there's one customer name, one address, one city, and so forth.

When to Use More than One Table

Just because you put all your customer information into a single table doesn't mean you should put all the information for an entire business in one table. After all, you wouldn't put all the information for your customers, orders, products, and so forth on one Rolodex card. Likewise, you wouldn't put all that information into a single table.

A better plan is to put customer data in one table, product data in another, and order data in yet another because no one-to-one correspondence exists among these categories of information. Any one customer might place many orders, and any order might be for many products. So here we have some natural one-to-many relationships among the subjects of your tables.

The One-to-Many Relationship

The *one-to-many relationship* describes a situation in which each record in a table may be related to many records in another table. For example, each one of your customers might place many orders (at least you hope so!). Therefore, it makes sense to put all of your customer data in one table and data about the orders they place in another table, as shown in Figure 17.3. (In the figure, only the first few fields from each table are shown. Additional information about customers and orders is scrolled off the screen.)

If we do use more than one table, however, we also need a way to determine exactly *which* customer goes with each order. And that's where the primary key field comes in.

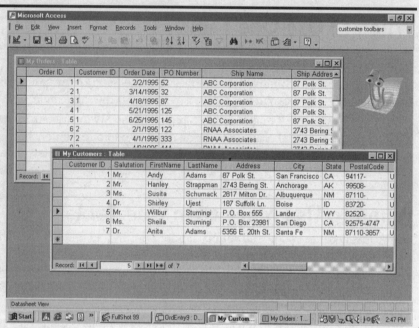

FIGURE 17.3: A one-to-many relationship between orders and customers. (Any one customer might place many orders.) The Customer ID field in the My Orders table identifies which customer placed each order.

The Primary Key Field

The *primary key field* in a table uniquely identifies each record in that table. In the My Customers table shown in Figure 17.3, only one customer has Customer ID 7. Even if that table has other people named Dr. Anita Adams from other cities, only one customer has Customer ID 7. When we added the Customer ID field to the My Customers table, we made it the primary key so that Access would make sure that no two people were given the same Customer ID number.

TIP

Your social security number is an example of a primary key field because it uniquely identifies you in the government's databases. Even though other people in the country may have the same first, last, and even middle names as you, nobody else in the country has the same social security number.

Notice, too, that the information in the My Orders table is compact. For example, the customer's honorific, first name, and last name aren't repeated in the My Orders table. All the My Orders table needs in order to get that information is the customer's unique ID number (Customer ID). Access can then dig up any information about that customer just by looking up the corresponding record in the My Customers table.

It's Easier than It Looks

This business of breaking down information into data in separate tables confuses many beginners, and it has been known to end the careers of many budding database designers. But there's no need to throw in the towel if you're feeling uneasy. Access will help you figure out how to break your information into related tables, and it will help you define primary key fields for the tables. So all you really need to understand now is the following:

▶ Your database is likely to contain several tables.

▶ Your tables will use a primary key field to uniquely identify records.

WHAT'S NEXT

In the next chapter, it's time to get started creating your own databases so that you can practice developing and organizing data as you read about here. You will learn how to present that data through either a report or a special kind of web page that can interact with your database.

Eight lessons will take you all the way through.

Part VI

Chapter 18

CREATING A DATABASE WITH ACCESS 2002

Databases are logical beasts, and they require those who work with them to exercise some logic as well in creating and customizing them, as you may have concluded from the previous chapter. Thankfully, however, Access 2002 automates a lot of the detail work, giving you the basics of a database, which you can then modify to fit your specific situation and needs.

A series of lessons in this chapter will take you through the process of creating a database, then customizing it by choosing optional fields for the table making up the database, by creating forms, and by selecting how reports generated from the database's output will look. You'll also learn how to work with Access to create special web pages to report data results. By the time you reach the final lesson, you should feel comfortable with the design, tools, and functions within this package.

Adapted from *Mastering Access 2002 Premium Edition* by Celeste Robinson and Alan Simpson

ISBN 0-7821-4008-4   1224 pp $49.99

BEFORE YOU START THESE LESSONS

Before you start these lessons, you already should have your basic Windows skills down pat—using a mouse; sizing, moving, opening, and closing windows; using dialog boxes; and so on.

For best results, give yourself 15 to 30 *uninterrupted* minutes to finish each lesson. If you need to pause after a lesson, see "Taking a Break" at the end of Lesson 1. To resume with the next lesson, see "Returning from a Break."

NOTE

If you will be using an Access project to work with SQL Server tables, instead of an Access database that holds its own tables, you can still benefit from going through the lessons in this chapter. The way you work with forms, data access pages, and reports is the same for databases and projects.

LESSON 1: CREATING A DATABASE AND TABLES AUTOMATICALLY

The first step to using Access is to start the program. You should see the New File task pane or an empty Microsoft Access window. If you don't know how to start Access or other Office XP programs, see Chapter 2, "Getting to Work in Office XP," for help.

Creating an Instant Database

During these hands-on lessons, you'll create a new database (named Contact Management Lessons) that can help you manage information about your contacts. You'll use the Database Wizard to create this database. Here goes:

1. If you're starting from an empty Microsoft Access window, choose File ➤ New from the menu bar. If the New File task pane is already visible, go to step 2.

2. On the New File task pane, click General Templates under New From Template.

3. When the Templates dialog box opens, click the Databases tab (if it's not already active) and then double-click the Contact Management icon.

4. Type **Contact Management Lessons** in the File Name text box of the File New Database dialog box, and then click Create or press Enter.

NOTE

Access normally looks for and stores your databases in a folder named My Documents on the disk drive where Access is installed. To change this default location, open any database and choose Tools ➤ Options, click the General tab, and specify a folder name in the Default Database Folder text box. To return to the default setting, change the folder name in the Default Database Folder text box back to . (a period).

You'll see an empty Database window titled Contact Management Lessons: Database. After a brief delay, the first Database Wizard dialog box will appear on top of the Database window, as shown in Figure 18.1. This dialog box tells you something about the database you're about to create.

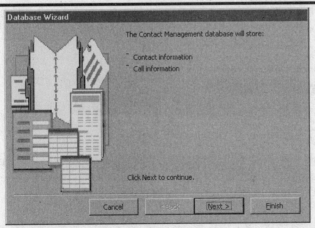

FIGURE 18.1: The first Database Wizard dialog box appears on top of the Contact Management Lessons: Database window.

Understanding the Wizards

The Database Wizard will ask you a few questions and then use your answers to build tables, forms, and reports automatically. Read the first

Database Wizard dialog box and then click Next. The second dialog box, shown in Figure 18.2, asks which fields to include in each table.

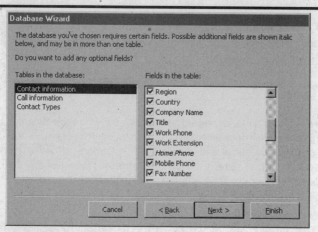

FIGURE 18.2: The second Database Wizard dialog box lets you choose optional fields for tables in the new database.

All the Access wizards work in similar ways, and they have the same buttons at the bottom of each dialog box (see Figure 18.2). Just follow the directions, answer questions, and use the buttons described below to navigate until you finish using the wizard:

Cancel   Cancels the wizard and returns to wherever you were before you started the wizard.

Back   Returns you to the previous wizard dialog box.

Next   Continues to the next dialog box.

Finish   Goes straight to the last wizard dialog box. The wizard will use default settings for any dialog boxes that it skips. The Finish button is available only when the wizard has enough information to complete its job.

Choosing Optional Fields for Your Tables

A *field* is a single unit of information stored in a table—for example, a person's name, address, or phone number. When you use the Database Wizard to create a database, all the necessary tables and fields will be defined automatically, and you don't have to make any changes. But if you do want to include optional fields, or omit fields, here are the steps to follow:

1. Scroll to and click the name of the table you want to work with in the list of tables at the left side of the dialog box shown in Figure 18.2.

2. Look for the italicized field names on the list at the right side of the dialog box. These fields are optional. To include the field, check the box next to its name. To omit the field, clear the check mark from the box. As usual in Windows, clicking a checked box clears the check mark; clicking an empty check box puts a check mark in the box.

3. Repeat steps 1 and 2 as needed.

For these lessons, we'll assume you've chosen the fields that the Database Wizard suggested initially. That is, italicized fields are not checked, and nonitalicized fields are checked.

Choosing a Style for Forms

The third Database Wizard dialog box lets you choose a background color and general style for database forms (called *screen displays* in the Database Wizard dialog box). In Figure 18.3, we've selected the Standard style. To choose a style, click it in the list of styles. The left side of the dialog box will show a sample form that reflects your current choice. Preview any styles you wish and then choose Standard, which is the style used throughout this chapter. When you're ready to continue, click the Next button.

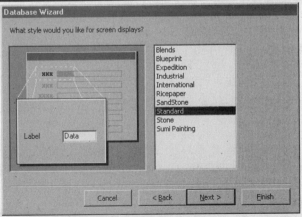

FIGURE 18.3: The third Database Wizard dialog box with the Standard style selected for forms

Choosing a Style for Printed Reports

In the fourth Database Wizard dialog box, you'll choose a general style for printed reports (see Figure 18.4). Again, you can click a style in the list and preview a sample until you find a style you like. Pick a style that appeals to you (or use the Formal style that we chose) and then click Next.

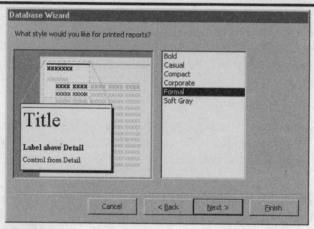

FIGURE 18.4: The fourth Database Wizard dialog box with the Formal report style selected.

NOTE

If you want to learn more about how to set up your own form and report styles and add them to the list of predefined styles, see Chapter 13 of *Mastering Access 2002 Premium Edition* by Celeste Robinson and Alan Simpson (Sybex, 2001). You'll also find out how to reformat an existing form or report with a different style.

Choosing a Database Title and Adding a Picture

In the fifth Database Wizard dialog box (see Figure 18.5), you can choose a different title for your database. This title will appear on the Main Switchboard form (which you'll see soon) and on all reports. For now, *Contact Management* is fine, so leave the title unchanged.

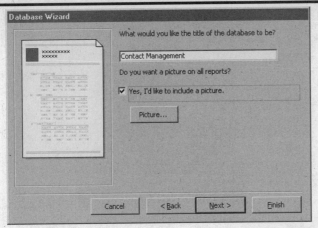

FIGURE 18.5: The fifth Database Wizard dialog box lets you choose a title and a picture to use for your database. In this example, we've used the suggested title and chosen the `contacts.gif` picture from the `\Program Files\Microsoft Office\OfficeXP\Bitmaps\Dbwiz` folder.

You can also include a picture on all reports. Just for grins, add a picture by following these steps:

1. Click Yes, I'd Like To Include A Picture to select that option and then click the Picture button.

2. Locate the folder named `\Program Files\Microsoft Office\Office10\Bitmaps\Dbwiz` in the Insert Picture dialog box (see Figure 18.6). Assuming you did a standard installation, you can just type **\Program Files\Microsoft Office\ Office10\Bitmaps\Dbwiz** in the File Name text box and press Enter.

3. Click a filename in the left side of the dialog box. Each time you click a filename, a preview of the picture it contains will appear in the preview area. If you don't see a preview area, click the drop-down arrow for the View button in the Insert Picture dialog box and choose Preview from the shortcut menu that pops up. The example in Figure 18.6 shows the `contacts.gif` filename and preview selected.

4. Click OK when you're satisfied with the picture you've selected. The sample picture will appear in the Database Wizard dialog box, next to the Picture button.

5. Click Next to continue to the next dialog box.

Part vi

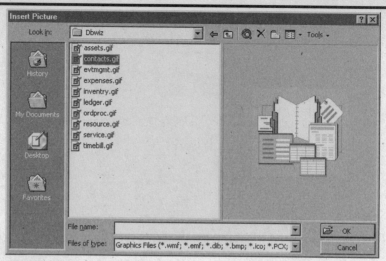

FIGURE 18.6: After clicking the Picture button in the dialog box shown in Figure 18.5, you can search for and preview pictures. The list of graphics will depend on which software you've installed and which folder you've chosen to search.

Finishing Up

That's all the information the wizard needs. In the final dialog box, you have two options:

Yes, Start The Database   Leave this option checked if you want to go to a switchboard form that lets you start working with your database immediately. Clear this option if you want to go directly to the Database window, bypassing the switchboard. For now, leave this option checked.

Display Help On Using A Database   Checking this option will display online help about using a database. Leaving this option unchecked won't display any extra help. Leave this option unchecked for now.

To create the database with all the choices you made, click the Finish button now. (If you need to revisit any of the previous Database Wizard dialog boxes, click the Back button as needed.)

Wait patiently for a few moments while the Database Wizard conjures up an entire database of tables, forms, reports, and other objects. (On-screen bars will keep you informed of the wizard's progress as it works.) When the wizard finishes its job, you'll see the Main Switchboard form for your database (see Figure 18.7).

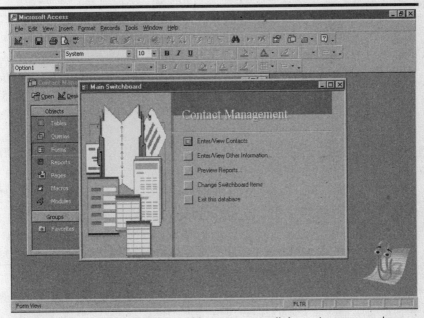

FIGURE 18.7: The Main Switchboard form gives you all the options you need to create and manage Contact Management data. Access creates a Main Switchboard form automatically any time you use the Database Wizard to create a nonblank database.

Congratulations! You've created your first Access database. Easy, wasn't it? In the following lessons, you'll learn how to work with and customize your new database.

At Your Leisure

To learn more about databases and tables, go to the Access Help Contents, open the *Creating And Working With Databases* book, and then peruse the subtopics. Or just skip all that and move on to Lesson 2.

If you want to take a break at the end of this or any other lesson, close your database as discussed next under "Taking a Break." Before you resume a lesson, reopen the Contact Management Lessons database (see "Returning from a Break").

Taking a Break

Any time you want to take a break at the end of a lesson, take one of these steps to save your work and close the database (*before* you turn off the computer):

- ▶ If you're viewing the Main Switchboard form, shown in Figure 18.7, click the button next to the last option, Exit This Database.

- ▶ If you're viewing the Database window (the one that lists *File-name*: Database at the top left of the window), choose File ➢ Close from the menu bar, press Ctrl+W, or click the Close button on the Database window.

If you're done using Access for a while, exit Access by choosing File ➢ Exit from the Access menu bar.

Returning from a Break

To resume with a new lesson after taking a break, you need to open the Contact Management Lessons database and its Main Switchboard form. Here's a summary of the steps necessary to accomplish this:

- ▶ If you're at the New File task pane and you see Contact Management Lessons in the list under Open A File, click that name.

- ▶ If you're at the New File task pane and Contact Management Lessons doesn't appear in the list, click More Files and then use the Open dialog box to find and open Contact Management Lessons.mdb.

- ▶ If you're at the Microsoft Access main menu, choose File from the Access menu bar. If Contact Management Lessons appears near the bottom of the File menu, click its name. If it doesn't appear, choose Open and then use the Open dialog box to find and open Contact Management Lessons.mdb.

- ▶ If you're at the Windows Desktop and you've used the Contact Management Lessons database recently, choose Start ➢ Documents ➢ Contact Management Lessons.mdb.

The Contact Management Lessons database will open, and the Main Switchboard form will appear (see Figure 18.7).

Some Important Switchboard and Database Window Tips

These tips are worth remembering as you work with the Contact Management Lessons database:

▶ To open the Contact Management Lessons: Database window without opening the Main Switchboard first, hold down the Shift key while you open the Contact Management Lessons database. You'll be taken directly to the Database window.

▶ To open the Main Switchboard form from the Database window, click the Forms tab on the Database window and then double-click the form named Switchboard.

▶ To open the Database window without closing the switchboard form first, press F11, click the Database Window toolbar button, or choose Window ➢ Contact Management Lessons: Database from the menu bar.

▶ To open the Database window when it's minimized on the Access Desktop, click the Database window's Restore button, double-click the window's title bar, or press F11.

Part vi

LESSON 2: EXPLORING THE CONTACT MANAGEMENT LESSONS DATABASE

Before you enter any data or print any reports, why not explore the Contact Management Lessons database and switchboard forms a little? You'll have plenty of places to investigate.

Exploring the Contact Management Form

Let's start with the first option on the Main Switchboard (refer back to Figure 18.7):

1. Click the button next to Enter/View Contacts. You'll see the Contacts form, which lets you review or change information

for each contact. Here's what you can do with the buttons at the bottom of this form:

▶ To log a call to the person whose record is shown on the form, click the Calls button. (For now, click the Close button for the Calls form.)

▶ To dial your contact's phone number with your computer's modem, click the box that contains the phone number you want to dial and then click the Dial button. An easy-to-use AutoDialer box appears. (For now, click Cancel if you've opened that dialog box.)

▶ To switch between page 1 and 2 of the Contacts form, click the command buttons labeled 1 and 2—or click the Page Up and Page Down buttons.

2. Click the Contacts form's Close button or press Ctrl+W to return to the Main Switchboard form when you are finished exploring the Contacts form.

NOTE

In Lesson 4, you'll learn how to add and change data and how to use navigation buttons to move from record to record. For now, just take a look at what's available and don't worry too much about adding any data.

Exploring the Contact Management Reports

The Main Switchboard's Preview Reports option lets you preview and print a variety of reports about your contacts. Here are some steps to try:

1. Click the button next to Preview Reports. A Reports Switchboard form will appear (see Figure 18.8).

2. Click a button to preview one of the reports (the Alphabetical Contact Listing, for example). Lesson 5 will show you how to work with reports.

3. Return to the Reports Switchboard form by clicking the Close button on the Preview window's toolbar or by pressing Ctrl+W.

4. Return to the Main Switchboard form by clicking the button next to Return To Main Switchboard.

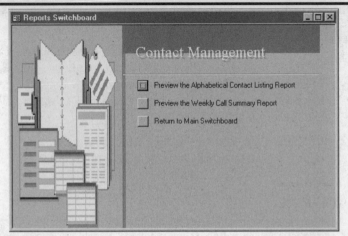

FIGURE 18.8: These options let you preview or print information about your contacts. The last option returns you to the Main Switchboard form.

Other Buttons on the Contact Management Main Switchboard

Figure 18.7 shows two more options on the Contact Management Main Switchboard form.

Change Switchboard Items   Enables you to add, change, and delete prompts on the switchboards and create new switchboards. We'll look briefly at ways to customize the switchboards in Lesson 8.

Exit This Database   Enables you to close the Main Switchboard form and the Contact Management Lessons: Database window in one step and return directly to the main Microsoft Access menu.

LESSON 3: CREATING AND CUSTOMIZING A FORM

An Access form is like a fill-in-the-blanks paper form, except that you fill it in using the keyboard rather than pencil or pen. Our Contact Management Lessons database already has a nice form. But let's go ahead and create a new one for practice:

1. Close the Contact Management Main Switchboard form and return to the Database window. To do so quickly, click the Close button in the upper-right corner of any Contact Management switchboard form, and press F11 to restore the Database window.

2. Click the Tables button in the Database window, and then click the Contacts table name to highlight it.

WARNING

The Switchboard Items table contains entries that control the switchboard forms for your database. Do not change items in this table, or your switchboards may stop working correctly. In Lesson 8, you'll learn how to use the Switchboard Manager to maintain this table in a safe manner.

 3. Click the drop-down arrow next to the New Object toolbar button (shown at left, and second-to-last on the toolbar) and then choose Form from the menu that appears. In the New Form dialog box, double-click AutoForm: Columnar. Wait a moment while Access creates an automatic form.

Access creates the form for entering and editing Contact Management data and names it *Contacts* (see Figure 18.9). The form contains one control for each field in your table. If you haven't added any data yet, the form will appear blank.

NOTE

A *control* is a graphical object that displays data, performs an action, or makes the form (or report) easier to read.

Modifying and Saving the Form Design

The new form is fairly usable as is. But chances are you'll want to tailor the wizard's instant form to your own personal tastes. We'll show you some basic skills for designing fancier forms. When you finish the next set of steps, your form will resemble Figure 18.10.

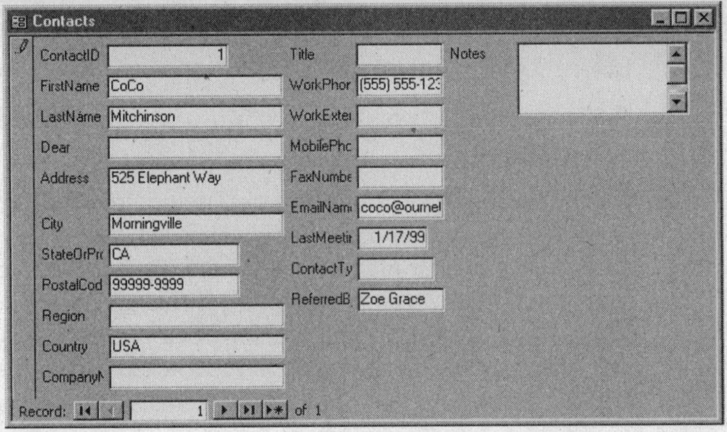

FIGURE 18.9: To create this form, choose the Form option from the toolbar's New Object drop-down button and then double-click AutoForm: Columnar in the New Form dialog box.

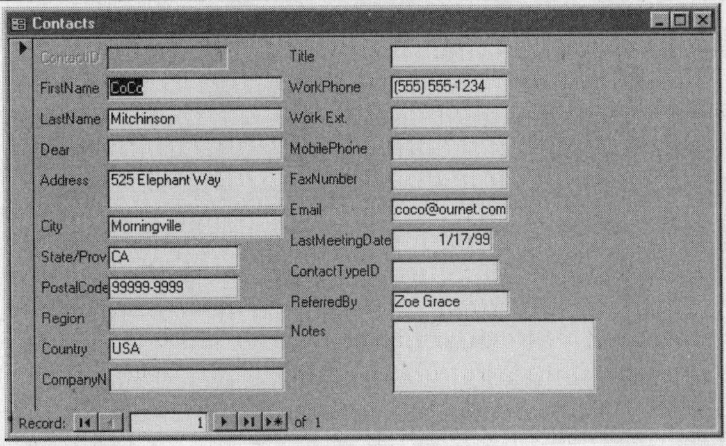

FIGURE 18.10: The Contacts form after changing some field labels, dragging fields to more convenient places on the form, and changing the ContactID field.

Whenever you want to change the look or behavior of something in Access, you must switch to Design view. In Design view, you'll see menu commands and toolbar buttons that help you make changes. You also may see a grid, which makes it easier for some people to size and align controls on the form. Let's switch to Design view now and move some controls around on the Contacts form.

1. To switch from Form view to Design view, click the Form View toolbar button (shown at left), or choose View ➤ Design View from the menu bar.

2. To give yourself lots of room to work, maximize the Design view window.

3. To hide or show the optional tools in Design view (if they are covering your form or are missing), choose the appropriate options on the View menu. For example, if the toolbox is in your way, choose View ➤ Toolbox. For this exercise, select (check) the Ruler and Form Header/Footer options on the View menu. Leave the other options unchecked to hide those other tools.

4. Scroll down until you can see the Notes control and then click the Notes control (the empty box in the right corner of the Design view window). When the control is selected, move and size handles appear on the control, as shown below.

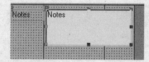

5. Keep your finger *off* the mouse button and move the mouse pointer to any edge of the control until the mouse pointer changes to a move icon (a hand with all five fingers showing), as shown at left.

6. Press the mouse button (without moving the mouse) and drag the Notes control down and to the left until it's underneath the ReferredBy control, as shown below.

NOTE

These mouse operations may take some practice. If you don't get them right the first time, repeat steps 5 and 6 until you do.

You've now moved the Notes control. You can use the same dragging technique to size controls and to move a label and/or text box independently. Always move the mouse pointer to an edge or corner of the control first until you see the mouse pointer change to the icon that best expresses what you want to do. The functions of the icons are summarized below:

Move all selected controls	
Move current control only	
Size diagonally	
Size horizontally	
Size vertically	

A Few Designer Tips

Here are some designer tips that might help you fine-tune the form. (You don't need to try them now.)

▶ To select several controls at once, hold down the Shift key as you select, or drag a "lasso" around them. To lasso those critters, start with no control selected and the mouse pointer on the grid or an empty part of the form, not on the control. Hold down your mouse button while you drag a frame around all the controls you want to select.

▶ To select all the controls at once, choose Edit ➢ Select All or press Ctrl+A.

▶ To deselect one selected control or all selected controls, click anywhere outside the selection area.

▶ To deselect only one of several selected controls, hold down the Shift key while clicking the control(s) you want to deselect.

▶ To size and align the selected controls, use the Format ➢ Align and Format ➢ Size commands from the menu bar.

▶ To make a label fit its text exactly, select the label, move your mouse pointer to any of the sizing handles, and then double-click the sizing handle. Alternately, select the labels you want to resize and then choose Format ➢ Size ➢ To Fit from the menus.

▶ To delete the selected control(s), press the Delete key.

▶ To undo a change you're not happy with, choose Edit ➤ Undo, press Ctrl+Z, or click the Undo toolbar button.

To change the text in a label (the part that appears to the left of a control), follow these steps:

1. Click the label text so that selection handles appear around the label.

2. Click inside the selection. An insertion point will appear, and the sizing handles will disappear temporarily.

3. Use normal Windows text-editing techniques, including the following, to change the text:

   ▶ To highlight (select) text, drag the mouse through that text or double-click a word.

   ▶ To position the blinking insertion point, click the mouse.

   ▶ To delete selected text or text at the insertion point, press Delete or Backspace.

   ▶ To add new text at the insertion point, simply type it.

4. Press Enter when you're done making changes. The selection handles will reappear around the label.

Try Some Hands-On Designing

Go ahead and try some more hands-on designing now. Don't worry if you don't get *exactly* the results we show—it's okay to make mistakes, and it's okay to experiment.

1. Change the label text for these controls, as follows:

   ▶ Change the label for the StateOrProvince control from State/Province to **State/Prov**.

   ▶ Change the label for the WorkExtension control from Work Extension to **Work Ext**.

   ▶ Change the label for the EmailName control from Email-Name to **Email**.

2. Resize all the labels on the form so they have a snug fit. The quickest way is to select all the controls (Ctrl+A) and then choose Format ➤ Size ➤ To Fit.

3. Click in an empty area of the form to deselect all the controls.

Next, resize the text controls that show field values on the right side of the form to make more room for their labels to be visible. First, hold down the Shift key and click each text control in turn, without selecting their labels, too. (You should see a handle at the upper-left corner of each label control, but no others except those around the text controls.) Then point to the handle in the middle of the left side of any selected text box and drag to the right, leaving enough room for the longest labels to show. Then point to a handle in the middle of the right side of any selected text control and drag to make the text controls wider.

TIP

To move a text control (one that shows a field value) closer to its label, make sure the text control is selected and then move the mouse pointer to the sizing handle at the upper-left corner of the text control (the pointer changes to a hand with one pointing finger). Drag to the left until the text control is closer to its label.

Preventing the Cursor from Landing in a Field

When you enter a new record, Access will assign a value to the ContactID field automatically. (You can't change this value.) The form will be more convenient to use if you prevent the cursor (also called the *insertion point* or *highlight*, depending on its shape) from landing in that field. To disable the ContactID control:

1. Click the ContactID control (the box to the right of the ContactID label) to select it.

2. Click the Properties toolbar button (shown at left) or choose View ➤ Properties. You'll see the Properties sheet on the screen.

3. Click the Data tab at the top of the Properties sheet and then double-click the Enabled property to change its setting from Yes to No (see Figure 18.11). The ContactID control will be dimmed on the screen.

4. Click the Close button on the Properties sheet (or click the Properties button or choose View ➢ Properties) to hide the Properties sheet again.

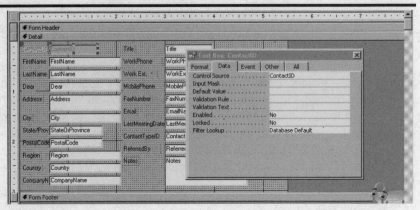

FIGURE 18.11: The Enabled property for the ContactID control is set to No to prevent the cursor from landing on that control when you use the form for data entry.

NOTE

Properties are characteristics of elements in your database, and you can change them any time.

Closing and Saving the Form

None of the design work you've done so far is saved yet, so saving is the next order of business. To save the form and close it:

1. Choose File ➢ Close or press Ctrl+W.

2. Click Yes when Access asks if you want to save your changes to the form.

3. Type **Contacts1** (or just accept the suggested form name) in the Save As dialog box and click OK.

4. (Optional) Click the Restore button on the Database window to restore the window to its previous size.

That's all there is to it! The form name will appear in the Database window whenever you're viewing form names (that is, after you've clicked the form's Objects tab on the Database window). In the next lesson, you'll open the form and start using it.

At Your Leisure

To reinforce what you've learned and explore forms in more depth, go to the Office Assistant, enter **Forms**, and explore any subtopics that intrigue you. You also may want to pick up a copy of *Mastering Access 2002 Premium Edition* by Celeste Robinson and Alan Simpson (Sybex, 2001) and refer to Chapters 11 and 13.

LESSON 4: ADDING, EDITING, SORTING, AND SEARCHING

Your database now contains several objects, including tables and forms. You can use the Contacts form created by the Database Wizard or the form you created in the last lesson to enter some data into the table.

Opening the Form

To open the Contacts1 form, follow these steps:

1. Start from the Database window and click the Forms button.

2. Double-click the Contacts1 form name, or highlight (click) the name and then click Open. Your form will appear in Form view (refer back to Figure 18.10). Notice that the ContactID field is dimmed and the cursor is positioned in the FirstName field. The cursor skips the ContactID field because you changed the Enabled property for that field to No in the previous lesson.

TIP

If you prefer to use the Contacts form that the Database Wizard created for you automatically, either double-click the Contacts form name on the Forms tab of the Database window or click the button next to the Enter/View Contacts option on the Main Switchboard form.

Part vi

Entering Data

If you have a Rolodex or little black book of contact names, addresses, and other vital statistics, grab it now. Or if you don't want to bother with real names and addresses, use the fake data shown in Figure 18.12. Either way, follow these general steps to add some names and addresses to your Contacts table via the Contacts1 (or Contacts) form. (If the table is currently empty, you can skip to step 2 and begin entering data immediately.)

1. Click the New Record button (shown at left) on the toolbar or the navigation bar to move to a new, blank record.

2. Type the person's first name into the FirstName field; then press Tab or Enter or click anywhere within the LastName field.

3. Type that person's surname into the LastName field; then press Tab or Enter or click within the Dear field.

4. Fill in each of the remaining fields, as shown in Figure 18.12. Here are some tips to help you enter the remaining data:

   ▸ To move forward from one field to the next, press Tab or use the mouse. You also can press Enter to move to the next field.

   ▸ To move from one line to the next in a field like Notes, press Ctrl+Enter.

   ▸ To leave a field empty, press Tab to skip it or click the field you want to type in next.

   ▸ To enter postal codes, type the numbers only. The form automatically displays a hyphen after the first five digits. Example: When you type **441471234** in the Postal-Code field, Access changes your entry to 44147-1234.

   ▸ To enter telephone numbers, type only the numbers. The form automatically displays parentheses around the area code and a hyphen after the exchange. Example: When you type **2165551225** in the WorkPhone field, Access changes your entry to (216) 555-1225 as you type.

   ▸ To enter dates, omit slashes between the numbers for the month and day if the numbers have two digits. If the numbers for the month and day have only one digit, type a slash to move to the next part of the date. Access will insert slashes in the field automatically. Example: When you type **121598** in the LastMeetingDate field, Access automatically changes your entry to 12/15/98 as you type. To enter the numbers for a January 5, 1999, meeting, type **1/5/99** or **010599**. (If you are entering dates before 1930—for example, a birth date in 1925—enter **04071925** to make sure Access knows you are entering a date in the 20th century. Otherwise, Access will store 04/07/2025. You will be able to do this only if the input mask on the field allows you to enter four digits for the year.)

NOTE
You can enter the punctuation in the postal code, telephone number, and date fields, but doing so requires extra work. Data entry shortcuts, such as automatically inserting parentheses and hyphens in telephone numbers, are controlled by input mask properties in the table or form design.

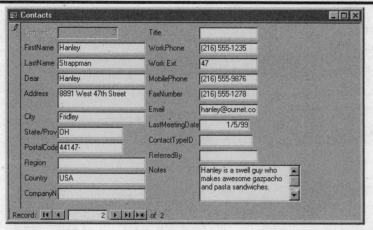

FIGURE 18.12: A new record added to the Contacts table via the Contacts1 form you created earlier

5.   Repeat steps 2 through 4 to fill in more names and addresses. For practice, make at least three entries. If possible, include some entries that have the same state/province.

Making Changes and Corrections

If you're an experienced Windows user, you'll find that editing text in an Access form (or the Datasheet view) is similar to typing and editing text in any other Windows program. If you're not experienced, these techniques can help you fix typing mistakes:

▶ To delete text at the highlight or insertion point position, use the Backspace and Delete keys.

▶ To move to the next field, press Tab. To move to the previous field, press Shift+Tab. To move to any field in the form, click that field.

▶ To switch between Navigation mode and Edit mode, press F2. You're in Navigation mode when you use the keyboard (Tab, Shift+Tab, and Enter) to move to another field; in this mode, the field's contents will be selected, and anything you type will *replace* what's already in the field. When you switch to Edit mode, you can *change* (rather than replace) what's already in the field; in this mode, the blinking insertion point replaces the selection highlight. You can press F2 any time you need to switch from one mode to the other.

▶ To move to other records, use the navigation bar at the bottom of the window (see Figure 18.13). Or press Page Up and Page Down to scroll up and down through existing records.

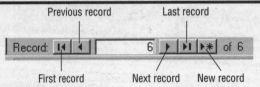

FIGURE 18.13: The navigation bar allows you to move through existing records and to add new records.

NOTE

In the Contacts form created by the Database Wizard, Page Up and Page Down display the first or second page of the Contacts form, respectively. Pressing Page Down when you're on the second page of the form takes you to the second page of the next record. Pressing Page Up when you're on the first page of the form takes you to the first page of the previous record (if any).

▶ To switch to Datasheet view, where you can see all the data that you've entered so far, click the drop-down arrow next to the Form View toolbar button (shown at left, and the first button on the toolbar) and then choose Datasheet View; or choose View ➤ Datasheet View. You can make changes and corrections in Datasheet view (shown in Figure 18.14), if you wish—it's not necessary to switch back to Form view.

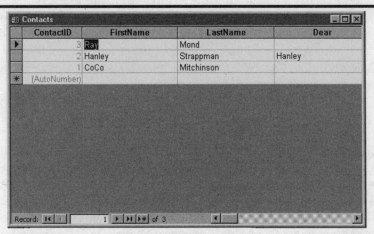

FIGURE 18.14: The sample table in Datasheet view.

▶ To resize columns in Datasheet view, move the mouse pointer to the vertical line at the right edge of the column header for the column you want to resize, and then drag the line to the left or right. For a snug fit, double-click the vertical line that's just to the right of the column name.

▶ To move an entire column in Datasheet view, move the mouse pointer to the column name in the header, click the mouse, and then drag the column to the left or right.

▶ To switch to Form view, click the drop-down arrow next to the Form View toolbar button and choose Form View; or choose View ➤ Form View.

NOTE

If you click the Form View toolbar button (instead of clicking the drop-down arrow next to that button), you'll switch to the view that's shown on the button. For example, clicking the Form View button when you're in Form view takes you to Design view and vice versa.

Part vi

TIP
You can't change the contents of the ContactID field, and there's no reason to. In fact, you can't even move the cursor into that field.

▶ To move to a new, blank record, click the New Record button on either the toolbar or the navigation bar.

▶ To delete a record, click the record selector at the left side of the record and press Delete. Or click anywhere in the record you want to delete and then click the Delete Record toolbar button (shown at left). When prompted, click Yes if you're sure you want to delete the record, or click No to retain the record. Warning: Once you click Yes to delete the record, it's gone for good.

Don't Save Each Record

In case you're paranoid about losing your work (which certainly is understandable), rest assured that as soon as you finish filling in (or changing) a record and move to another record, Access saves that record to disk. The only record that isn't saved is the one you're editing at the moment. (This unsaved record is marked with a pencil icon in the record selector that runs along the left side of the form window.)

Sorting and Filtering

After you've put a few records into your table, you can unleash Access's real power. Let's begin by sorting (alphabetizing) the records:

1. Switch to Datasheet view if necessary. To do so, choose View ➤ Datasheet View from the menu bar.

2. Click any person's surname to move the cursor into the Last-Name column.

3. Click the Sort Ascending toolbar button (shown at left), or choose Records ➤ Sort ➤ Sort Ascending. You can also right-click and then choose Sort Ascending from the shortcut menu.

Instantly your records are sorted (alphabetized) by surnames. You can follow steps 1 through 3 to sort on any field in your table. Try it and see.

Now suppose you want to see only contacts who live in Washington (or whichever state you want to look for). Here's a quick way to filter out those unwanted non-Washington contacts temporarily:

1. Put the cursor in any State/Prov field that contains *WA*—be sure not to highlight any text in the field.

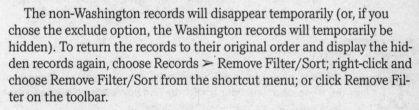

2. Click the Filter By Selection toolbar button (shown at left), choose Records ➤ Filter ➤ Filter By Selection, or right-click the field and then choose Filter By Selection from the shortcut menu. (If you prefer to see all records *except* those for your Washington contacts, right-click and choose Filter Excluding Selection instead.)

The non-Washington records will disappear temporarily (or, if you chose the exclude option, the Washington records will temporarily be hidden). To return the records to their original order and display the hidden records again, choose Records ➤ Remove Filter/Sort; right-click and choose Remove Filter/Sort from the shortcut menu; or click Remove Filter on the toolbar.

Filter By Input is another easy way to filter records. To see how Filter By Input works, point with your mouse anywhere in the State/Prov field (but not on the header) and right-click. In the Filter For text box, enter **WA** and press Enter. As with Filter By Selection, to display the hidden records again, choose Records ➤ Remove Filter/Sort; right-click and choose Remove Filter/Sort from the shortcut menu; or click Remove Filter on the toolbar.

TIP
You can sort and filter records in Form view or Datasheet view. However, we suggest using Datasheet view because the results are easier to see from there.

Finding a Record

Suppose you've added hundreds, or even thousands, of names and addresses to your Addresses table, and now you want to look up a particular contact's address or phone number. Here's the easy way to do a lookup:

1. Switch to Form view or Datasheet view. (Choose View ➤ Form View or View ➤ Datasheet View.)

Part vi

2. Click in the field you want to search. (In this example, click in any LastName field.)

3. Choose Edit ≻ Find, or press Ctrl+F, or click the Find toolbar button (shown at left). You'll see the Find And Replace dialog box.

4. Type *exactly* the last name you're looking for in the Find What text box. (Don't worry about upper- and lowercase, but do spell the name correctly.)

5. Click the Find Next button. The LastName field of the first record that has the requested name will appear highlighted on the screen. (If Access didn't find a match, a message will appear; click OK to clear the message.)

TIP

If several people in your table have the same last name and you want to find each one in turn, continue to click the Find Next button as needed. When Access tells you it has finished searching, click OK.

6. Click the Cancel button in the Find And Replace dialog box when you're done searching.

Remember: Computers Are Dumb!

If your search doesn't find what you were expecting, remember that the computer isn't smart and it can't read your mind. You must click the field you want to search *before* starting the Find command and typing the text you want to search for. For example, if you click the Address field and search for *Strappman,* you'll get no match.

The exception to this rule is when you want to search all the fields in a table for a value. When this is the case, click the Find button with any field selected. Then, when the Find And Replace dialog box opens, change the setting for Look In to the table name.

The computer is also bad at guessing alternate spellings. If you type a first name such as *Steven* into your table and then search for *Stephen,* Access won't find the correct record. *Steven* and *Stephen* are similar enough for you to say, "Yeah, that's a match." However, Access isn't smart enough to figure out that *Steven* and *Stephen* sound alike, and it certainly won't know if you want to match either name.

NOTE

Filter By Form, Advanced Filter/Sort, and queries let you use wildcards to search for text that's similar to text that you enter. For example, you can tell Access to find a first name like *St*en*. This statement will match records that contain Steven or Stephen in the FirstName field.

Closing the Form or Datasheet

When you're done playing with the data, close the Form or Datasheet view.

1. Choose File ➤ Close or press Ctrl+W. Access might ask you if you want to save your current work.

2. Click Yes if you want to save any filtering or other changes to the table or form; click No if you want to discard those changes.

Don't worry if you're not asked for permission to save your work—Access will ask only if you've altered the Form or Datasheet view. All the names and addresses you typed are stored safely on disk for future reference.

At Your Leisure

To explore the topics described in this lesson online, go to the Help Contents, open the books *Working With Data* and *Finding And Sorting Data*, and then investigate the subtopics shown. Or move ahead to the next lesson now.

LESSON 5: CREATING AND PRINTING REPORTS

In this lesson, you'll create, preview, and print a set of mailing labels. These mailing labels will be a nice addition to the reports that the Database Wizard created for you automatically.

Preparing Mailing Labels

Let's prepare a report that can print names and addresses on standard Avery mailing labels. Here are the steps:

1. Click the Tables button in the Database window and then click the Contacts table name.

Part vi

2. Click the drop-down arrow next to the New Object toolbar button (shown at left, and the second-to-last toolbar button) and then choose Report (or choose Insert ➢ Report from the menu).

3. Double-click Label Wizard in the New Report dialog box. In a moment, the Label Wizard dialog box will ask, What Label Size Would You Like?

NOTE

If you forget to choose a table (or query) in step 1, you'll need to choose one from the drop-down list in the New Report dialog box.

4. Choose Sheet Feed under Label Type if you are using a laser printer (or other sheet-fed printer) to print labels. Otherwise, choose Continuous (if you are using a dot-matrix printer to print labels).

5. Scroll to and click the appropriate Avery label size and then click Next.

TIP

The Avery label number and label dimensions are printed on the package of labels. If you don't have labels already, just pick Avery number 5095 or some other two-across size.

6. Choose any font and color options you want to use. The sample text at the left side of the dialog box will reflect your current choices. Click Next to continue.

7. Use the following techniques to fill in the Prototype Label box, making it look like the example shown in Figure 18.15.

   ▶ To add a field to the label, click in the Prototype Label box where you want the field to appear. Double-click the field in the Available Fields list, or click the field and then click the > button. The field will appear in the Prototype Label box.

   ▶ To add a space, punctuation mark, or other text, click where you want the space or text to appear (if the insertion point isn't there already) and then press the appropriate key(s) on your keyboard.

▶ To start a new line on the prototype label, click the next line in the Prototype Label box or press Enter.

▶ To delete a field or text, position the insertion point in the Prototype Label box where you want to start deleting and then press the Delete or Backspace key as needed. You can also select text with your mouse or keyboard and then press Delete or Backspace.

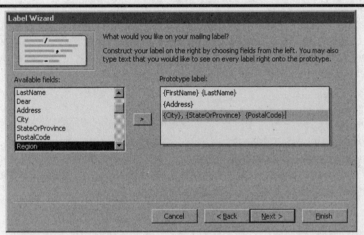

FIGURE 18.15: Fields from the Contacts table arranged for printing on a mailing label

8. Click Next when you're done filling in the Prototype Label box. Access will ask you which fields you want to sort by.

9. Scroll down to PostalCode in the Available Fields list and double-click that field name. (If you prefer to sort by Last-Name and FirstName, double-click those field names instead.) Click Next to continue.

TIP

If you accidentally double-click the wrong field(s), click the ‹‹ button to clear all the fields and then double-click the correct field(s). To clear just one field, click that field in the Sort By list, and then click the ‹ button.

10.   Click the Finish button in the last dialog box and wait a few seconds.

The Label Wizard will create a report with names and addresses formatted for the label size you specified. When the Label Wizard is done, you'll see a preview of the labels on-screen.

Closing and Saving the Report

You'll learn more about how to preview and print the report in a moment. But first, save the report and close the report preview window. To do so, choose File ➤ Close or press Ctrl+W. (If you click the Close toolbar button by accident, you'll be taken to Design view. Just press Ctrl+W to return to the Database window quickly.) Your report format is saved with the name *Labels Contacts*, as you can see by clicking the Reports button in the Database window.

Don't Reinvent the Wheel!

Keep in mind that Access has saved the report format, not its contents. So even if you add, change, or delete addresses in the future, you do not need to re-create the reports to print the data. Whenever you print a report, Access automatically puts the table's current data into the report's format.

Previewing and Printing a Report

Previewing and printing a formatted report is a snap. Here are the steps:

1.   Make sure your printer is ready. If you want to print on mailing labels, load the labels into the printer.

2.   To see the list of available reports, do one of the following:

   ▶ If you're starting from the Database window, click the Reports button. You should see the names of the reports the Database Wizard created, plus the one you created.

   ▶ If you're using the Main Switchboard form in your Contact Management application, click the button next to the Preview Reports option. You'll see options for printing reports created by the Database Wizard. (Later in this chapter, we'll show you how to add your new Labels Contacts report to this list of options.)

3. To preview the report, do one of the following:

   ▶ If you're starting from the Database window, click the name of the report you want to print (for example, Labels Contacts) and then click the Preview button on the Database window, or just double-click the report name. You also can choose File ➢ Print Preview from the menu bar.

   ▶ If you're starting from the list of reports on the Reports Switchboard form, click the button next to the report you want to view.

TIP

To print a report from the Database window without previewing it first, right-click the report name you want to print and choose Print from the shortcut menu that pops up.

4. The report will open in Print Preview mode with sample data shown. (Maximize the window if you wish.) Here are some tricks you can use to view your report:

   ▶ To zoom in and out between 100 percent magnification and a full-page view that fits on your screen, move the mouse pointer into the report area and click, then click the Zoom toolbar button (see Figure 18.16). Click the Zoom button again to return to the previous size.

FIGURE 18.16: The Print Preview mode toolbar

   ▶ To zoom to various magnifications, choose options from the toolbar's Zoom drop-down list. Or right-click in the report area and choose a Zoom setting using the shortcut menu. Or choose View ➢ Zoom from the menu bar and select the desired magnification.

   ▶ To display multiple pages at once, right-click in the report area, choose Multiple Pages, and then choose a page layout. Alternately, choose View ➢ Pages from the menu bar to change the layout. You can also click the toolbar's One Page, Two Pages, or Multiple Pages buttons.

5. Choose File ➤ Print (or press Ctrl+P) when you're ready to print the report, and then click OK in the Print dialog box that appears. Or to bypass the Print dialog box, click the Print toolbar button (shown at left).

NOTE

The Print dialog box lets you choose a printer, print the report to a file, select a range of pages to print, and specify the number of copies and collation method. The Setup button in that dialog box lets you change the margins and layout for the report.

6. Click the Close button on the Print Preview toolbar to return to the Database window or the Reports Switchboard form.

At Your Leisure

If you want to learn more about reports before moving on to the next lesson, go to the Access Help Contents, open the *Reports And Report Snapshots* book, and then explore the subtopics shown.

LESSON 6: CREATING A DATA ACCESS PAGE

Data access pages are similar to forms, in that you can use them to view and sometimes edit data, but they are actually web pages that can be opened from Access or Internet Explorer 5 (or later). Instead of being part of the database or project they belong to, data access pages are stored in their own HTML files, which makes them different from other types of Access objects you find in the Database window.

You can start from scratch and create a data access page on your own, or you can get the Page Wizard to do all the hard work for you. In this lesson, you'll see how to use the Page Wizard to create a data access page for the Calls table and then browse that data from Access or Internet Explorer.

Using the Page Wizard

Using the Page Wizard is similar to using the Form Wizard and the Label Wizard:

1. In the Database window, click the Tables button and highlight the Calls table.

2. Click the New Object drop-down arrow on the toolbar and choose Page.

3. When the New Data Access Page dialog box opens, double-click Page Wizard. The first step of the Page Wizard looks like this:

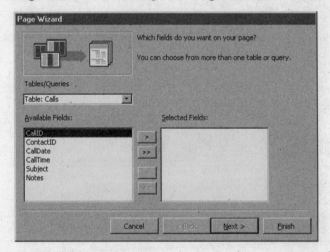

4. Make sure the Calls table is selected under Table/Queries and then click the >> button to move all the fields in the Calls table to the Selected Fields list. Click Next.

5. The next step enables you to optionally group the records that are shown on the page. When you group records on a page, you can expand or collapse the detail records in each group. For this example, leave the grouping set to ContactID and click Next.

6. When the next step opens, optionally select up to four fields for sorting records and click Next.

7. Leave the title for the page unchanged.

8. Click the check box for Do You Want To Apply A Theme To Your Page? Then click Finish to have the Page Wizard do its work.

9. After a moment, a new Data Access Page window will open, along with a Theme dialog box. Select the theme you want to use (you can preview it on the right side of the window) and click OK. The page will look something like the one below, depending on the theme you choose. The following page has the Blends theme:

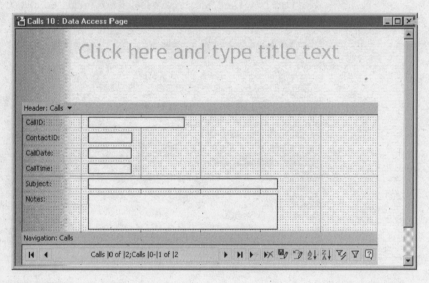

Unless you changed the setting for the open mode in the last step of the Page Wizard, the page will appear in Design view. Next you'll see how to browse data by opening the page from Access or Internet Explorer 5 (or later).

NOTE

The data access page we just created shows the ContactID for each person in the Calls table, instead of their names. To find out how to link in descriptive fields like names from related tables, as in the Contacts table for this example, check the Office Assistant, or refer to Chapter 14 of *Mastering Access 2002 Premium Edition* by Celeste Robinson and Alan Simpson (Sybex, 2001).

Browsing Your New Page

To browse a data access page, use any of the following techniques:

- ▶ If the page is open in Design view, click the Page View button on the toolbar.

- ▶ To open the page from the Database window and view it with Access, click the Pages button, right-click the page you want to view, and choose Open from the shortcut menu. The Calls page we just created looks like this when opened in Access with the detail records expanded:

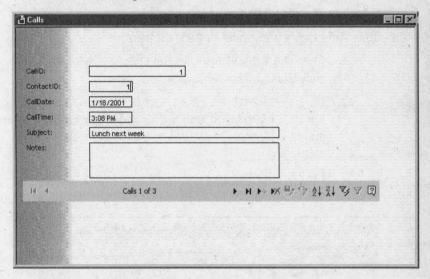

- ▶ To open the page in Internet Explorer from the Database window, click the Page button, right-click the page you want to browse, and choose Web Page Preview from the shortcut menu.

- ▶ To open the page from Internet Explorer, enter the full name of the page—for example, C:\My Documents\Calls.htm—in the Address box.

For more information on data access pages, use the Office Assistant to look for the relevant topics.

LESSON 7: USING QUERIES

You can use *queries* to isolate certain fields and records of data in a table, to sort data into alphabetical or numeric order, to combine data from several related tables, and to perform calculations on data in tables. In this lesson, you'll use queries to set up a simple list that shows specific fields and specific records in the Contacts table in sorted order by last name. Then you'll change the query to show records for everyone in the table.

Creating a Query

To create a query from your Contacts table:

1. Click the Tables button in the Database window and then click the Contacts table name.

2. Click the drop-down arrow next to the New Object toolbar button (shown at left, and the second-to-last toolbar button) and then choose Query (or choose Insert ➤ Query from the menu bar).

3. Double-click Design View in the New Query dialog box. Figure 18.17 shows the query design window that appears.

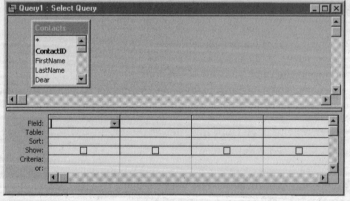

FIGURE 18.17: The query design window shows the field list for the Contacts table in the top pane and the design grid in the bottom pane.

NOTE

Using the Simple Query Wizard (and other query wizards) is often the easiest way to speed up the job of creating queries. However, for the query you'll be designing next, the from-scratch method is a little faster, and it gives you practice using the query design window.

Choosing Fields to View

To fill in the design grid, you first choose the fields you want to work with in the order you want them to appear. Follow these steps now to add the LastName, FirstName, City, StateOrProvince, and WorkPhone fields to the grid:

1. Maximize the query design window so you can see more columns in the design grid at once.

2. Add the LastName field to the design grid by double-clicking that field in the Contacts field list near the top of the window. The LastName field will appear in the first blank column of the design grid. The Table row in that column will show the name of the table the field comes from, and the Show row will include a check mark to tell Access to display that field when you run the query.

TIP

Here are two other ways to add a field to the query design grid: drag the field name from the field list in the top of the query window to the appropriate column in the design grid; or click the Field box in the appropriate column of the design grid, click the drop-down arrow that appears, and then choose the field name you want to use.

3. Add the FirstName field to the design grid by double-clicking that field in the Contacts field list. The field will appear in the next (second) column of the design grid.

4. Add the City field by scrolling down in the field list and double-clicking the City field name.

5. Use the same techniques described in step 3 to add the State-OrProvince and WorkPhone fields to the design grid.

Part vi

TIP

If you add the wrong field to a column of the design grid, click in the Field box for that column, click the drop-down arrow, and then choose the correct field name from the list. To delete a column in the design grid, move the mouse pointer just above the field name in that column (until the pointer changes), click the mouse to highlight the entire column, and then press Delete.

Figure 18.18 shows the five fields in the query design grid.

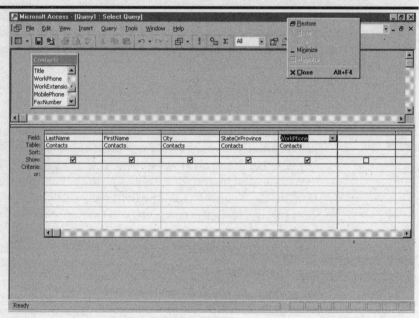

FIGURE 18.18: Five fields—LastName, FirstName, City, StateOrProvince, and WorkPhone—added to the query design grid

Choosing Records to View

Suppose you want to view the list only for people who live in California. To do so, type **ca** (or **CA**) into the Criteria row under the StateOrProvince column. Here's how:

1. Click in the Criteria box in the StateOrProvince column.

2. Type **ca**, or the abbreviation for any state that you've stored in the table (see Figure 18.19). Don't worry about typing exact uppercase and lowercase letters.

3. Press Enter. Access automatically adds quotation marks around the text you typed and moves the cursor to the next column.

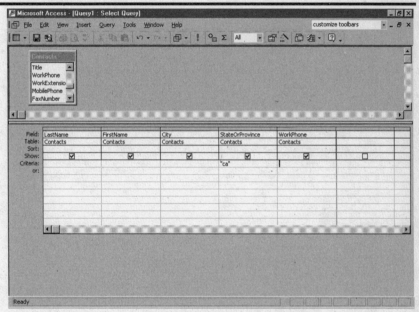

FIGURE 18.19: The query will display the LastName, FirstName, City, StateOr-Province, and WorkPhone fields of records that have California ("ca") in the State-OrProvince field.

Choosing the Sort Order

To sort the list by last name and then by first name within identical last names, tell Access which fields (columns) to sort by and whether you want to sort in ascending (A to Z) order or descending (Z to A) order. Here are the steps:

1. Use the horizontal scroll bar to scroll the design grid back to the LastName column, and click in the Sort box below the LastName column. Click the drop-down arrow that appears and choose Ascending from the list.

2. Click in the Sort box below the FirstName column, click the drop-down arrow, and then choose Ascending. Figure 18.20 shows the query design window after you complete this step.

TIP

If you chose the wrong column to sort by, click the Sort box below the appropriate column, click the drop-down arrow, and then choose *(Not Sorted)*.

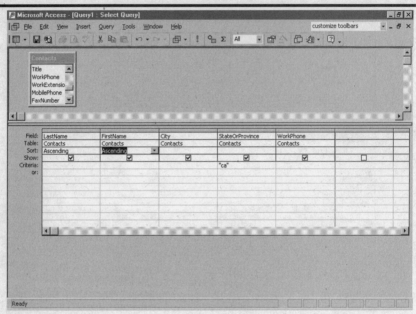

FIGURE 18.20: This query will sort the query results by last name and first name within identical last names. Because the StateOrProvince Criteria is set to "ca" (California), the query results will show data for people in California only.

Because the LastName column appears to the left of the FirstName column in the design grid, records will be alphabetized by people's last names. The FirstName field will act as a tiebreaker, meaning that records with identical last names will be alphabetized by first name.

Running the Query

Running the query is a snap. To try it, click the Run toolbar button (shown at left) or choose Query ➤ Run from the menu bar.

The query results will appear in Datasheet view and will show only the Last Name, First Name, City, State/Province, and Work Phone columns, and only the people in California, alphabetized by last name and first name (see Figure 18.21). All the data is *live,* and you can change it the same way you change any data in Datasheet view.

NOTE

You might have noticed that the column headings (or captions) shown in Figures 18.14 and 18.21 don't exactly match the field names. For example, the field name for a person's surname is *LastName*; however, the column heading shows *Last Name* (with a blank space between words). These column headings are controlled by the Caption property in the table or query design.

Last Name	First Name	City	State/Province	Work Phone
Mitchinson	CoCo	Morningville	CA	(555) 555-1234
Mond	Ray	San Francisco	CA	(415) 555-5050

Record: ◄ ◄ 1 ► ►► ►* of 2

FIGURE 18.21: The query results appear in Datasheet view.

Changing the Query

Changing the query to display an alphabetized list of all the records in the table is easy. Try it now:

1. Click the Query View toolbar button (shown at left, and the first button on the toolbar) or choose View ➤ Design View to switch back to the query design window. Maximize the query design window if necessary.

2. Delete "ca" in the Criteria box below the StateOrProvince column. To do this quickly, select (drag your mouse through) "ca" and then press Delete.

3. Run the query again. (Click the Run toolbar button.)

Now the Datasheet view resembles Figure 18.22. Because you removed the "ca" (California), the query results show all records in the table—not just the people from California.

Just for grins, print a quick copy of this list now by choosing File ➤ Print and clicking the OK button, or by clicking the Print toolbar button.

Part vi

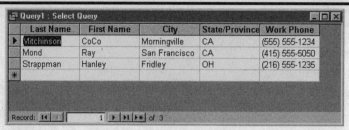

FIGURE 18.22: The datasheet after removing "ca" from the StateOrProvince field of the query design, running the query again, and restoring and resizing the window

Saving and Reusing the Query

You'll probably want to see an updated list sometime later, perhaps after you've added, deleted, or changed some records. Rather than re-creating this query each time, you can save it and reuse it any time. To save the query now:

1. Click the Save toolbar button or choose File ➢ Save.

2. Type a valid Access object name (such as **Contacts Phone List Query**) and then click OK.

3. Close the Select Query window (press Ctrl+W). The query design and datasheet will disappear, but your query will be saved.

TIP

You can save the query design from the design window or the datasheet window—the steps are the same. You also can save the design when you close the window. If you're asked about saving changes, click the Yes button and enter a query name if prompted to do so.

To run a saved query, go to the Database window (press F11 if necessary), click the Queries button, click the query you want to run (Contacts Phone List Query in this example), and then click the Open button on the Database window. Or just double-click the query name. The query will run on the latest data in your table. (If you want, close the datasheet window and return to the Database window.)

NOTE

To change the query design instead of running the query, click the Queries tab in the Database window, click the query you want to change, and then click the Design button in the Database window.

At Your Leisure

To learn more about queries, use the Office Assistant to search for the relevant help topics.

LESSON 8: CUSTOMIZING AN APPLICATION

Now you've created several database objects—a table, a form, a report, a data access page, and a query. But those objects aren't put together in a way that allows people who know nothing about those objects to use the database easily. To make your database extra easy to use, you can add these objects to the *turnkey* application that the Database Wizard created for you automatically. In this lesson, you'll learn some techniques for doing just that.

Adding a Hyperlink to a Form

Hyperlinks let you jump to other Access database objects or even to information on the Web. We'll step through a simple example here that shows you how to add a hyperlink to jump to the labels report from the Contacts1 form we created in Lesson 3. For more information on working with hyperlinks, use the Office Assistant.

1. Click the Forms button, click Contacts1, and then click the Design button in the Database window. You'll see the form design window, where you can modify the form.

2. Click the Insert Hyperlink toolbar button to open the Insert Hyperlink dialog box.

3. On the left side of the Insert Hyperlink dialog box, click the button for Object In This Database. Under Select An Object

Part vi

In This Database, click the expand button and make your selection.

4. A new underlined control will appear in the upper-left corner of the form design window. This control is the hyperlink. Drag the hyperlink to the place you want it to appear on the form.

5. To test the hyperlink, click the Form View toolbar button and then click the hyperlink to open the report. When you close the report window, you'll return to the form window.

Adding Command Buttons to a Form

Let's begin by adding command buttons, like those shown in Figure 18.23, to the Contacts1 form you created in Lesson 3.

1. Go to the Database window, click Forms, click Contacts1, and then click the Design button in the Database window. You'll see the form design window, where you can modify the form. Maximize the form design window to give yourself some room to work.

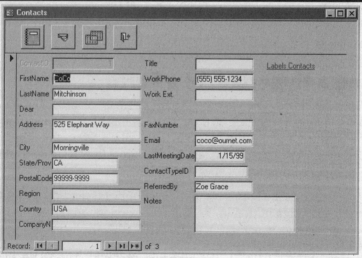

FIGURE 18.23: This Contacts1 form has four command buttons and a hyperlink in its form header. These buttons are similar to the Calls and Dial buttons on the Contacts form created by the Database Wizard.

2. Move the mouse pointer to the bottom of the Form Header section until the pointer changes to an up/down arrow crossed by a bar (shown below) and drag the horizontal line at the bottom of the section downward. This action increases the height of the Form Header section so that it is big enough to hold the command buttons. For this example, make the form header about .75 inches high. (Look at the vertical ruler, which is marked in .25-inch increments, as you resize the form header.)

3. Check to see if the *toolbox* (shown in Figure 18.24) is visible, because you will use it to create the command buttons. If the toolbox isn't visible, click the Toolbox toolbar button (shown at left) or choose View ➢ Toolbox.

4. Make sure the Control Wizards button (the one with the sparkling magic wand) is selected (pushed in). You can drag the toolbox anywhere you want it in the Access window.

NOTE

If the Properties sheet or another tool is blocking your view in the form design window, hide that tool by choosing its name from the View menu.

FIGURE 18.24: The toolbox lets you create new objects on a form.

Part vi

5. Create a command button by clicking the Command Button tool in the toolbox and then clicking where you want the upper-left corner of the button to appear on your form. In this example, click the left edge of the form header. The Command Button Wizard dialog box appears.

6. Click Report Operations in the Action Categories list (first column) and then click Preview Report in the Action list (second column).

7. Click the Next button to continue.

8. Click Alphabetical Contact Listing in the list of report names in the next dialog box. (The Database Wizard built this report automatically when it created the Contact Management Lessons database.) Click the Next button to display another dialog box.

9. Click Next to accept the suggested button picture. The Database Wizard asks you to name your button.

10. Type **Alphabetical Contact List** and click Finish.

The button appears on the form as shown below. You can't test the button yet because it works only when you're in Form view. (You're in Design view now.) Before testing that button, you'll add three more buttons.

TIP

To move a button, drag it to a new location. If you want to bypass *grid snap* while moving or sizing an object, hold down the Ctrl key while you're dragging.

Creating the Button for Mailing Labels

Follow these steps to add a second button to your form:

1. Click the Command Button tool in the toolbox, and then click slightly to the right of the command button you just created.

2. Click Report Operations and Preview Report in the two columns in the next wizard dialog box, and then click Next.

3. Click Labels Contacts in the list of available reports, and then click Next.

4. Select (check) Show All Pictures in the next wizard dialog box, scroll up to Mailbox (the pictures are listed in alphabetical order, by picture name), and then click that picture name. This step will put a picture of an envelope going through a mail slot on the button.

5. Click Next.

6. Type **Labels Preview Button** and click Finish.

Creating the Query Button

Follow these steps to add a button that will run the query named Contacts Phone List Query:

1. Click the Command Button tool in the toolbox, and then click slightly to the right of the Mailbox command button you just created.

2. Click Miscellaneous and Run Query in the two columns in the next wizard dialog box, and then click Next.

3. Click Contacts Phone List Query in the list of available queries, and then click Next.

4. Click Next to select the suggested picture in the next wizard dialog box.

5. Type **Contacts Phone List Query** and click Finish.

Creating the Close Button

The final button will make it easy to close the form. To create it:

1. Click the Command Button tool in the toolbox and then click just to the right of the last button at the top of the form.

2. Click Form Operations in the first column, click Close Form in the second column, and then click the Next button.

Part vi

3. Click Next to accept the default Exit picture in the next wizard dialog box.

4. Type **Exit Button** and click Finish in the next wizard dialog box.

5. Save your work by clicking the Save button on the toolbar or by pressing Ctrl+S.

TIP

To align buttons or other objects on the form, select the objects you want to align and then choose Format ➤ Align and an appropriate alignment option. To set equal horizontal spacing between objects, select the objects and choose Format ➤ Horizontal Spacing ➤ Make Equal.

Adding Visual Basic Code to a Form

Next you'll learn how to add some Visual Basic (VB) code to your form. Please don't think that programming is something you have to do in Access. You can create very powerful Access applications with no programming whatsoever. This little experiment with Visual Basic serves mainly as a way to get your hands dirty, so you can see how programming with VB works.

Follow these steps (carefully) to add some programming code to your form now:

1. Click the Properties toolbar button or choose View ➤ Properties to open the Properties sheet.

2. Choose Edit ➤ Select Form, or click the form selector (the box in the upper-left corner of the form window where the rulers would intersect). The Properties sheet displays the properties for the entire form.

3. Click the Event tab on the Properties sheet, and then scroll down to the OnOpen property. You'll add some code to maximize the Contacts1 form window any time you open the Contacts1 form.

4. Click in the OnOpen text box, click the Build button that appears, and then double-click Code Builder. A module-editing window will appear with the cursor positioned on the

blank line between the `Private Sub Form_Open` and `End Sub` statements.

5. Press the Tab key and then type the following *exactly:*

    `DoCmd.Maximize`

    Be careful to type the text correctly—there's no margin for error when you're writing program code.

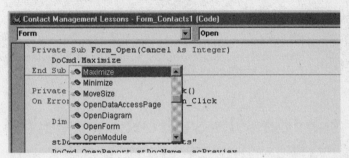

6. Click the Close button for the Microsoft Visual Basic window (the big window that holds the smaller code window), or choose File ➢ Close And Return To Microsoft Access (from the menu for the Visual Basic window) to return to the form design window. Notice that `[Event Procedure]` now appears as the OnOpen property.

7. Scroll down to the OnClose property of the Properties sheet. You'll add some code that restores the previously displayed window to its original size any time you close the Contacts form.

8. Click the OnClose text box, click the Build button that appears, and then double-click Code Builder. A module-editing window will appear with the cursor positioned on the blank line between the `Private Sub Form_Close` and `End Sub` statements.

9. Press the Tab key and then type *exactly:*

    `DoCmd.Restore`

NOTE

This `DoCmd.Restore` command restores a window to its previous size. For example, if you open the Contacts1 form from the Database window, the Database window will reappear at its previous size when you close Contacts1. Likewise, if you open Contacts1 from the Main Switchboard, the Main Switchboard form will reappear at its previous size.

10. Click the Close button for the Microsoft Visual Basic window (the big window that holds the smaller code window), or choose File ➤ Close And Return To Microsoft Access to return to the form design window.

11. Choose File ➤ Close ➤ Yes to save and close the modified form.

You'll return to the Database window (press F11 if necessary).

NOTE

When you're entering code in the Visual Basic window, the rules for editing are the same as when you're working with Word.

Customizing the Switchboard Form

The switchboard form that the Database Wizard created when you set up the Contact Management Lessons database provides buttons and options that make it easy to update and report information about your contacts. Since you've gone to the trouble of setting up some new forms and reports, you'll probably want to add them to the switchboard. You also might want to change the names of options that appear on the switchboard.

To begin, open the Main Switchboard form and then click the button next to Change Switchboard Items. Or choose Tools ➤ Database Utilities ➤ Switchboard Manager from the menu bar. You'll see the Switchboard Manager dialog box, shown in Figure 18.25.

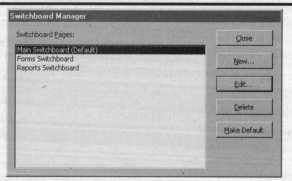

FIGURE 18.25: The Switchboard Manager enables you to create new switchboard pages, edit existing pages, delete pages, and choose a default switchboard page.

Adding the Contacts1 Form to the Main Switchboard

Follow these steps to add your new Contacts1 form to the Main Switchboard page:

1. Click Main Switchboard (Default) in the Switchboard Pages list and then click the Edit button in the Switchboard Manager dialog box. The Edit Switchboard Page dialog box will appear (see Figure 18.26 for a completed example).

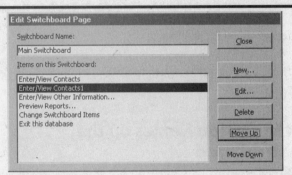

FIGURE 18.26: The Edit Switchboard Page dialog box after adding a new item and moving it to the top of the list

2. Click the New button to open the Edit Switchboard Item dialog box.

3. Type **Enter/View Contacts1** in the Text box.

4. Click the drop-down button next to the Command box, and choose Open Form In Edit Mode. A Form box will appear.

5. Click the drop-down button next to the Form box, and choose Contacts1. The completed Edit Switchboard Item dialog box looks like this:

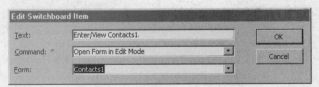

6. Click OK to return to the Edit Switchboard Page dialog box. Your new entry appears at the bottom of the Items On This Switchboard list.

7. Move your new item to the top of the list by clicking that item and then clicking the Move Up button four times. Figure 18.26 shows the completed Edit Switchboard Page dialog box.

TIP

If you want to remove the old Enter/View Contacts option from the list, click that item in the Items On This Switchboard list, click the Delete button, and then click Yes to confirm the deletion.

8. Click the Close button to return to the Switchboard Manager dialog box.

Changing the Option Names on the Reports Switchboard

We think the options for printing reports on the Reports Switchboard are a bit verbose and maybe even somewhat wordy. If you agree, follow these steps:

1. Click Reports Switchboard in the Switchboard Pages list and then click the Edit button. Here's what you'll see:

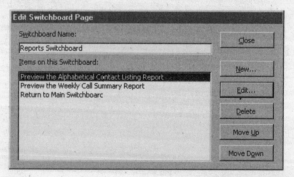

2. Click the first item in the Items On This Switchboard list and then click the Edit button. The option name will be highlighted in the Text box.

3. Replace the selected text with **Alphabetical Contact List**. To do this task quickly, select "Preview the " (including the space after *the*) and press Delete. Drag over "ing Report" at the end of the name, press Delete again, and then click OK.

4. Repeat steps 2 and 3 for the second item on the switchboard. Change the text to **Weekly Call Summary**.

Now add the new Labels Contacts report to the list of items on the Reports Switchboard:

1. Click the New button to open the Edit Switchboard Item dialog box.

2. Type **Mailing Labels** in the Text box.

3. Click the drop-down button next to the Command box, and choose Open Report. A Report box will appear.

4. Click the drop-down button next to the Report box, and choose Labels Contacts.

5. Click OK to return to the Edit Switchboard Page dialog box. Your new entry appears at the bottom of the Items On This Switchboard list.

6. Click the Mailing Labels item and then click the Move Up button once to move your new entry up a notch. The Edit Switchboard Page dialog box will resemble the example shown below:

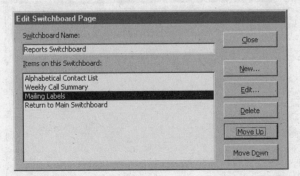

7. Click the Close button twice to return to the Database window.

Putting It All Together with Startup Commands

When you open a database, Access looks for certain startup commands and executes them automatically. You can customize your database by choosing startup commands that hide the Database window, go straight to a specific form, and more. The Database Wizard took care of setting up the essential startup commands for you automatically. But let's customize those startup commands just for practice:

1. Choose Tools ≻ Startup, or right-click any tab in the Database window and choose Startup from the shortcut menu. You'll see the Startup dialog box (a completed example appears in Figure 18.27).

2. Type **Contact Management Lessons** in the Application Title box. This title will appear on the Access title bar any time the database is open and on the Taskbar.

3. Make sure Switchboard appears in the box below Display Form/Page. You can use the Display Form/Page drop-down list to choose any form that's available for the Contact Management Lessons database; however, using Switchboard gives you the most flexibility.

4. Click OK. The new application title immediately replaces *Microsoft Access* in the window's title bar.

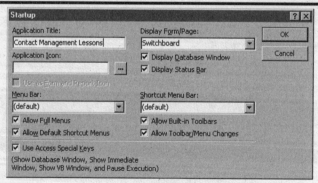

FIGURE 18.27: The Startup dialog box after we filled in the Application Title

NOTE

The Main Switchboard form automatically minimizes the Database window when you open the form; therefore, you don't need to clear the Display Database Window check box in the Startup dialog box.

Testing the Application

Now you're ready to test the whole thing. Follow these steps to close and then reopen the database:

1. Choose File ➢ Close, or press Ctrl+W, until the Main Switchboard form and Database window disappear.

2. Open the database you just closed by choosing File ➢ Contact Management Lessons from the menu bar.

The Main Switchboard form will open, and you'll see the text *Contact Management Lessons* in the Access window's title bar. Now you can explore the Contact Management switchboard form to your heart's content. When you're finished, do one of the following:

▶ To close the Main Switchboard form and the Database window, click the button next to Exit This Database on the Main Switchboard form.

▶ To close the switchboard form but leave the Database window open, click the Close button on the Main Switchboard or Reports Switchboard form (or press Ctrl+W) and then press F11 to display the Database window.

THERE'S MORE THAN ONE WAY TO CREATE TURNKEY APPLICATIONS

As you've seen, there's more than one way to automate your work and to create turnkey applications with Access. For example, you can use a switchboard form, which Access sets up any time you use the Database Wizard, to create a database. You also can add hyperlinks, command buttons, and Visual Basic programming to forms as you did for your Contacts1 form. Your application can be as simple or as sophisticated as you want, depending on your requirements and your expertise. It's all up to you!

Part vi

When you're done using Access, choose File ≻ Exit to return to Windows. Your database application will be stored safely on disk for future use. To use the application in the future, start Access and open the Contact Management Lessons database.

WHAT'S NEXT

Creating web pages to disseminate information is fast becoming nearly as popular as more traditional means, such as creating documents in Word or building a spreadsheet/worksheet using Excel.

In Part VII, web publishing with Office XP moves to the forefront of your continuing education.

The next chapter will show you how to use both Word and Excel to create web pages almost as easily as you would a document or workbook, as well as introduce you to website basics in preparation for working with FrontPage 2002 later in this final part.

PART VII
WEB PUBLISHING WITH OFFICE XP

Chapter 19

CREATING WEB PAGES WITH WORD AND EXCEL

The increasing emphasis on web-based publishing even in the workplace makes it necessary for you to be able to create web pages on the fly—either to publish on an Internet site or to share with co-workers on an intranet.

While FrontPage 2002 (which you'll learn more about in the next chapter) is a complete web page creation package, let's turn our attention first to how you can create web pages from more standard desktop applications such as Word and Excel. This is smart because it can save you a fairly time-consuming step—instead of creating a web page separately and then trying to fit Word or Excel information into it, you can create the page right from Word or Excel.

Adapted from *Mastering Microsoft Office XP Premium Edition* by Gini Courter and Annette Marquis with Karla Browning

ISBN 0-7821-4000-9   1392 pp $49.99

By itself, Word gives you three different ways to produce your web pages, including:

- ▸ Using the Web Page Wizard
- ▸ Applying a web template
- ▸ Converting an existing Word document

The Web Page Wizard creates not only web pages but also full *webs:* collections of pages with links between them. If the project you are undertaking involves multiple documents, the Web Page Wizard is generally the best choice, because it creates links for you and gives your pages a consistent look and feel. If you are providing content to your corporate intranet and you've been given a template to use, you may want to apply the template directly or convert an existing document without going through the wizard. However, after you use the wizard, you'll find it's a great tool whatever your goal.

Using Excel's web tools, you can publish static and interactive spreadsheets, charts, and pivot tables. Interactive web pages let users add formulas, sort and filter data, analyze data, and edit charts. In this chapter, we'll review Word's web tools and show you how to add Excel components to make your pages even more valuable.

NOTE
What's the difference between a web and a website? A web becomes a website once it's published and assigned a URL that others can access.

CREATING WEB PAGES USING THE WEB PAGE WIZARD

The Web Page Wizard can create single pages or webs that can be published as complete websites or appended to existing sites. If you want to create more than one page, it's a good idea to draw up the layout of your web before you start the wizard. You'll want to know the names of as many pages as possible so the wizard can create the links between them. If you have existing documents you want to include in the web, be sure to know their names and where to locate them.

When you are ready to create your web pages, choose File ≻ New from the Word menu. Select General Templates from the New Documents task pane. Select the Web Pages tab in the New dialog box and select Web Page Wizard. Click OK to start the wizard and Next to move on to the first step.

NOTE

The Web Page Wizard may not be already installed. If you try to open the wizard, you may be prompted to install it on demand, so make sure you have access to the CD or network drive that Office was installed from.

The Title And Location page, shown in Figure 19.1, determines the official title of your web. Although it can be changed later, it's important to give your web a descriptive title, because the various web search engines use the site's title when users search for a site on the Internet. A good title could mean the difference between someone finding your site or not.

By default, the wizard creates a new folder for your web, so if you change the location, be sure you change it to an empty folder. The wizard creates additional subfolders for storing graphics and other supporting files, but the main pages are stored in the folder you specify. If you don't designate a unique folder, your web files get mixed in with unrelated documents, making it difficult to manage the web effectively. Enter the title and location and click Next.

Part vii

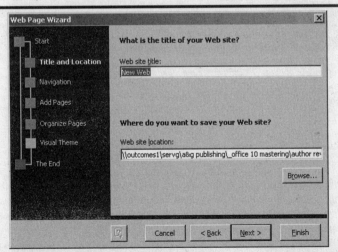

FIGURE 19.1: Enter a descriptive title and folder location for your web.

Using Frames for Navigation

The Web Page Wizard offers three choices for the layout of your pages, as shown in Figure 19.2:

> **Vertical Frame**   Runs down the left side of the page and contains links to the other pages in the web.
>
> **Horizontal Frame**   Positioned across the top of the page and contains links to the other pages in the web.
>
> **Separate Page**   Opens each page in a full window and does not use frames. Forward and Back buttons and appropriate links are added to the pages.

Choose the Navigation option you prefer and click Next.

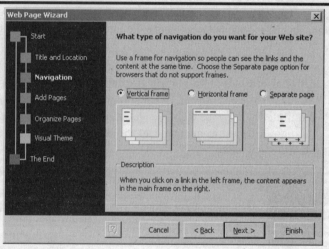

FIGURE 19.2: The Web Page Wizard automatically creates navigation links between pages.

NOTE

Not all browsers support frames, and text readers (used by people with vision impairments) don't work well with frames. Many web developers who use frames also offer visitors a no-frame alternative on the site's Welcome page, but if you can choose only one layout, choose the Separate Page option for the widest range of accessibility. For more information about making your websites accessible to people with disabilities, visit www.cast.org/bobby.

DIFFERENTIATING TEXT FRAMES FROM WEB FRAMES

You may already be familiar with text frames for positioning text on a page. *Text frames* are used extensively in PowerPoint and Publisher, and they can be used in Word and Excel to position a block of text outside of the normal paragraphs or cells. *Web frames* may contain text, but their primary purpose is to organize content on a web page. Web frames typically appear on the top or left of a page and include navigational links that remain visible even when the visitor moves to a different page of your web. See "Working with Frames" later in this chapter for more information.

Adding Pages

A web created by the Web Page Wizard comes with three pages: a Personal Web Page and two blank pages. The Personal Web Page is a template that includes sections for work information, favorite links, contact information, current projects, biographical information, and personal interests. If you are not creating a personal web with yourself as the focus, you can delete this page by selecting it and clicking Remove Page. The first blank page moves into position as the new home page for your web.

NOTE

The home page is typically the first page visitors see when they visit a website, but a Welcome page that gives visitors options such as no frames or no graphics may precede it.

If you want to add additional pages to your web, now is the best time to do so. As shown in Figure 19.3, you can add a new blank page, add a page based on a template, or insert an existing document into the web. To add a blank page, click the Add New Blank Page button, and the new page appears at the bottom of the list (you will be given the option to rename pages in the next step of the wizard).

Selecting a Template for Your Page

Word includes seven web page templates. Some of these templates include specific page layouts, such as the Left-Aligned Column and Right-Aligned Column templates. Others provide a structure for web content, such as the

Frequently Asked Questions and Table Of Contents templates. To review each of the templates, in the Add Pages step of the wizard, click the Add Template Page button. This opens the dialog box and preview window shown in Figure 19.4. Click any of the templates in the Web Page Templates dialog box to see a full-page view of the template. When you have chosen the template you want to include in your web, click OK. If you'd like to add another template page, click Add Template Page again and repeat the process.

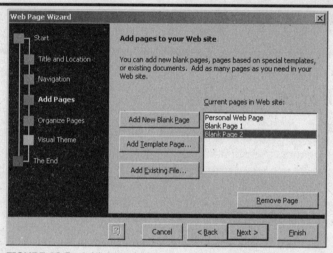

FIGURE 19.3: Add a new blank page, a template page, or an existing file to your web using the Add Pages step of the Web Page Wizard.

NOTE

The web page templates are also available outside of the wizard by choosing File ➤ New, selecting General Templates from the New Document task pane, and clicking the Web Pages tab.

Adding Existing Documents

If you would like to convert any existing documents and add them to your web, go to the Add Pages step and click the Add Existing File button. Locate and double-click the file you would like to include. The wizard saves a copy of the file as HTML and includes it in the web folder. Repeat the process to add additional documents.

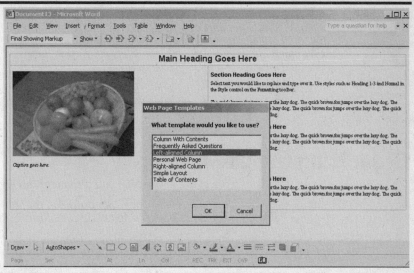

FIGURE 19.4: A selected template is displayed as a full page behind the Web Page Templates dialog box so you can see what elements it contains.

WHEN MULTIPLE WORD PAGES BECOME ONE WEB PAGE

When you insert a file in the wizard, it is added as a single page, even if it's a multipage document. If you have a document that you want to present as several individual pages, use copy-and-paste to create and save a separate Word document for each page before launching the wizard, and then insert each document.

If you need to convert a number of existing Word documents to the HTML format, you can use the Batch Conversion Wizard. Create a new folder, and then move or copy all the Word documents to the folder. Choose File ➢ New. Select General Templates from the New Document task pane and click the Other Documents tab. Double-click the Batch Conversion Wizard. (If the wizard isn't listed in the New dialog box, you need to install it from the Office XP CD or your network installation point.) The Batch Conversion Wizard can also be used to recover corrupt documents and to convert files to and from the Word format from applications such as Pocket Word, Inkwriter, WordPerfect, Works, Windows Write, and Excel.

WARNING

If you try to add an HTML page created in FrontPage 2002 or a page created in Excel or Access that uses the Office Web Components, it opens in its native application instead of being added in the wizard.

When you have finished adding pages, click Next to move on to the Organize Pages step of the wizard.

Organizing the Links

Now that you have the pages in your web, you can rename them and change their relative order, as shown in Figure 19.5. This order determines the order of the links. Use the Move Up and Move Down buttons to rearrange the pages and the Rename button to change a page's name. Click Next to move on to the next step.

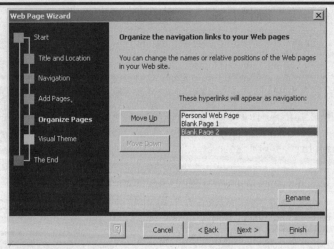

FIGURE 19.5: Putting the web pages in order and giving them useful names will make the web more organized.

Applying Themes

Themes were first introduced in FrontPage 98 and are now included in several Office XP applications. A *theme* is a collection of colors, fonts, graphics, backgrounds, bullet characters, and styles that fit together. Office includes over 65 themes that can be applied to print publications, online documents, and web pages. To select a theme, click the Browse Themes button in the Visual Theme step of the Web Page Wizard.

The Theme dialog box, shown in Figure 19.6, displays a preview of each theme listed on the left. Options for Active Graphics (typically appearing as animated bullets and horizontal lines) and Background Image are on by default. If you would also like to use Vivid Colors, click the check box. You can see the results of turning these options on or off in the preview window on the right, although you won't see active graphics actually move.

Once you decide on a theme (you can also choose No Theme from the top of the list), click OK. If you decide to use a theme, make sure Add A Visual Theme is selected in the Visual Theme step of the wizard.

Click Next to move to the last step of the wizard and click Finish. The wizard creates your web pages, adds the links you specified, and saves the pages to the folder you chose.

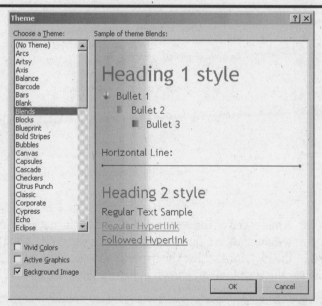

FIGURE 19.6: You can apply web themes to web and print documents to create a consistent look and feel for all your publications.

Exploring Your Web

After the Web Page Wizard finishes its job, it opens the home page in Word. If you used frames in your website, the Frames toolbar opens (see more about frames in "Working with Frames" later in this chapter), but you have to open the Web toolbar manually if you want it available. The home page contains navigation links to other pages in the web, either in frames—as shown in Figure 19.7—or at the top of the page if you chose the Separate Page option.

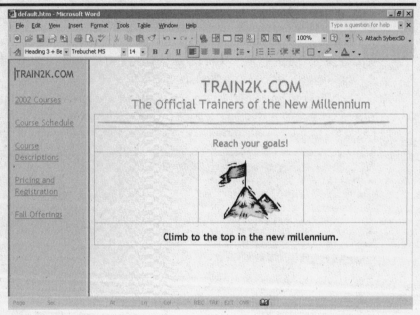

FIGURE 19.7: The Web Page Wizard creates your web pages and opens the home page.

To view the other pages of the web, point to any of the navigation links. The pointer changes to a hand and provides a screen tip about the file location of the hyperlink. Click the hyperlink to open the page. When the page opens, the Web toolbar, shown in Figure 19.8, also opens.

FIGURE 19.8: The Web toolbar

The Web toolbar is the standard Internet Explorer browser toolbar. Click the Back button to return to the home page.

TIP

To see the files the Web Page Wizard creates, open the folder in My Computer or Windows Explorer. You may notice a number of subfolders and files that you aren't familiar with. Default.htm —or index.htm if you are saving the web on hard disk as opposed to a web server—is the filename the wizard automatically assigns to the first or home page of the web. The wizard creates a subfolder for each page and uses it to house graphics and other objects related to the page. For example, when you insert a graphic on a page and save the page, Word automatically saves the graphic to the page's corresponding subfolder. Graphics and other objects are not saved as part of a web page but rather are saved separately and linked to the page. This is standard web design protocol and helps keep the myriad of individual files streamlined and organized.

ADDING CONTENT TO A WEB PAGE

Editing web pages in Word is not much different than editing other Word documents. You have access to all of Word's formatting and editing tools, including fonts, paragraph formatting, bullets, tables, and borders and shading. Web pages also include features that are not typically used in print documents: hyperlinks, frames, form controls, active graphics such as scrolling text boxes, and other special multimedia features. These tools are described in this section. If you learn to use these tools effectively, you'll be able to design web pages that are dynamic, attractive, and effective.

Saving and Reopening a Web

If you create a web using the Web Page Wizard, the wizard automatically saves the web pages and associated files. After you make changes to any of the pages, click Save or choose File ➢ Save to resave the files just as you would any other document.

When you reopen a web, you can choose to open individual pages for editing or the entire web. The frame at the left or top of your web pages is actually a separate page, so it will not open when you open individual pages. To make changes to the frames page, open the file TOC Frame.htm. To open the home page with the frame giving you access to the entire web, open the file called default.htm or index.htm.

Part vii

Creating Hyperlinks

Hyperlinks are what make the World Wide Web what it is. When Tim Berners-Lee, CERN researcher, developed HTML, his primary interest was in being able to access related documents easily—without regard to computer platform or operating system— by connecting the documents through a series of links. Hyperlinks allow readers to pursue their areas of interest without having to wade through tons of material searching for specific topics, and hyperlinks take readers down paths they might never have traveled without the ease of clicking a mouse. Adding hyperlinks to your documents moves information down off the shelf, dusts it off, and makes it a living, breathing instrument that people can really use.

Creating a hyperlink in an existing web page is easy. Just follow these steps:

1. Enter or select some descriptive text in the page to define the link; for example, you could either type **Click here to view new courses** or select existing text that says *New Courses*.

2. Select the text, right-click within it, and choose Hyperlink to open the Insert Hyperlink dialog box, as shown in Figure 19.9.

3. Type a file or web page name, or click the Existing File Or Web Page button to browse for the file. Click the Place In This Document button to create a link to another location in the same document, or click the E-Mail Address button to create a link to an e-mail message form.

4. If you want to change the hyperlink text, enter new text in the Text To Display box.

5. Add a screen tip to the hyperlink by clicking the ScreenTip button and entering the text you want to appear in a screen tip.

6. Click OK to create the link.

NOTE

Word automatically creates a hyperlink when you type an address it recognizes as an Internet or file path address. If, for example, you type www.train2k.com, Word creates a hyperlink to that address. To turn hyperlink automatic formatting on or off, choose Tools ➢ AutoCorrect. Click AutoFormat As You Type and check or clear the Internet And Network Paths With Hyperlinks check box.

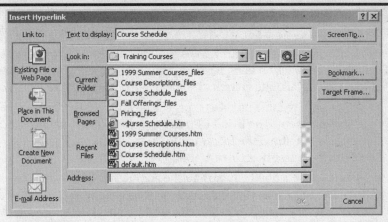

FIGURE 19.9: Create hyperlinks to other documents, web pages, e-mail addresses, and other places in the same document by using the Insert Hyperlink dialog box.

TROUBLESHOOTING HYPERLINKS

A hyperlink's effectiveness depends on its being able to locate the file or Internet address to which it is linked. If the file has moved or been renamed, or the address no longer exists, clicking the hyperlink returns an error message. It's important to regularly verify hyperlinks you've included in your site. If a link does not work, check the following:

1. Do you currently have access to the Internet or intranet site the link is calling? If not, check the link again when access has been restored.

2. Has the site or file moved? If so, right-click the link and choose Edit ➤ Hyperlink. Update the location of the linked file.

3. Does the file still exist? If not, right-click the link and choose Edit ➤ Hyperlink. Click Remove Link.

If the link still does not work after you have followed these steps, make sure the address is spelled correctly and there are no syntax errors in the address (for example, a comma instead of a dot).

If Edit Hyperlink does not appear on the shortcut menu when you right-click, it could be because the text contains a spelling or grammar error. Word displays the Spelling shortcut menu until the error is corrected.

Part vii

Inserting Graphics

Visitors to a website expect to see more than just text. Fast-loading graphics add impact to your web pages. The trick is to use small, attention-grabbing graphics on main pages and give visitors the option to view larger, more elaborate graphics by clicking to another page.

Inserting a graphic into a web page is no different than placing one in a Word document. The Insert Clip Art task pane opens when you select Pictures ➤ Clip from the Insert menu; from the task pane, you can choose art or any other clip art or photos you want to use.

Web browsers don't support all the graphics features available in Word. To ensure that your web pages look as good when viewed by a browser as they do in Word, features that are unsupported have been disabled. Only some of the wrapping styles available in Word documents, for example, are available for use in web pages. As a result, you may find that once you've inserted a graphic, you have difficulty positioning it where you want it. To change how text wraps around the picture so you can more easily place the graphic where you want it, right-click the graphic and choose Format Picture or choose Format ➤ Picture from the menu. Select the Layout tab and change the Wrapping Style, as shown in Figure 19.10.

FIGURE 19.10: By changing the Wrapping Style, you can more easily position graphics.

You can also access the wrapping styles from the Picture toolbar that opens when you select a picture. Click the Text Wrapping button and choose a wrapping style from the menu that opens.

Inserting Alternative Text

A number of other options are available in the Format Picture dialog box. Because not all browsers can display graphics and some people just don't have the patience to wait for your beautiful graphics to appear on a web page, it's possible to insert alternative text that describes the graphic. When the web page opens, the alternative text appears while the page is loading, allowing visitors to click when they find the text they want without waiting for the graphic. To specify alternative text, select the Web tab of the Format Picture dialog box.

MAKING GRAPHICS STAY WHERE YOU WANT THEM

If you are having trouble positioning graphics on a web page, you might want to try a web designer's trick. Insert a table into the page. Three columns are usually sufficient, but add more columns if you want to line up a series of graphics. Then, position the graphic inside a cell of the table and change the table properties so the table expands to fill the size of the screen. To do so, follow these steps:

1. Click inside the table and choose Table ➤ Table Properties.

2. Select the Table tab and change Preferred Width to 100% Measure In Percent. (Although this step is not necessary, it makes it easier if you aren't sure about precise placement and sizing.) Click OK.

3. Now place the graphic inside the cell of the table that corresponds to the position you would like for the graphic. Click the Center button on the Formatting toolbar to center the graphic in the cell.

Before publishing the web page, you can change the table's borders to No Borders. To do this, select the table, choose Format ➤ Borders And Shading, click the Borders tab, and click None. Your table won't be visible on the page, but the graphics will stay where you put them.

Using the Web Tools Toolbar

Word comes equipped with a Web Tools toolbar, shown in Figure 19.11, to help you add sounds and video, create forms, and add scrolling text. To turn on the Web Tools toolbar, choose View ➤ Toolbar and click Web Tools (be careful not to choose Web, or you'll get the browser toolbar).

FIGURE 19.11: The Web Tools toolbar can help you add sounds, video, forms, and scrolling text.

Adding Background Sounds and Movies

Even though we don't seem to mind being constantly barraged by sounds from radio and television, most of us have not yet developed a fondness for sounds from the Web. Only occasionally will you happen upon a website that opens with background music drawing you in—or turning you away, as the case may be. However, if you'd like to add background sounds to your site despite all the evidence to the contrary, Word makes it easy for you to do so.

To add a sound file to a page, follow these steps:

1. Check to see that you are in Web Layout view (View ➤ Web Layout).

2. Turn on the Web Tools toolbar by choosing View ➤ Toolbars ➤ Web Tools.

   3. Click the Design Mode button on the Web Tools toolbar.

4. Move the insertion point to any obvious place on the page—it doesn't matter where you insert it as long as the icon remains visible.

TIP

You can move into Design mode from any view, not just Web Layout view, but if you're working on a web page, it's best to begin in Web Layout view so you know what your finished product will look like.

5. Click the Sound button on the Web Tools toolbar.

6. Enter the name of a WAV file or click Browse and locate the file.

7. Click the Loop down arrow to choose the number of times you want the sound to play, either 1–5 or Infinite.

8. Click OK.

9. Click the Design Mode button to return to your previous view. The sound file should begin playing immediately and will play whenever you open the page, as many times as you instructed it to.

NOTE

Your browser (along with add-ins like RealPlayer—www.realplayer.com— and the Microsoft Windows Media Player) determines the types of sound files you can play. MIDI and WAV files are common, but MP3 files are becoming the most common. After you insert the file, test it in your browser and in browsers that your site's visitors would commonly use.

To add a movie file, click the Movie button on the Web Tools toolbar (remember to click the Design Mode button and position the insertion point first). Enter the settings in the Movie Clip dialog box, as shown in Figure 19.12. It's a good idea to include an alternative image to display in browsers that do not support movie clips, or you can put the clip on a page so that users can choose whether to download it. However, even if a browser does support movie clips, the image will be small and difficult to see on most systems. If possible, test the display on several machines with different browsers to see how the movie file looks before making it a permanent part of your web page.

To remove a sound or movie clip, switch to Design mode. Locate the Sound or Movie icon, like the ones shown here. Select the icon you want to delete and choose Edit ➢ Clear.

NOTE

Movie clips consume a lot of bandwidth, so be cautious about using movie clips if most of your visitors use a dial-up connection to reach your site.

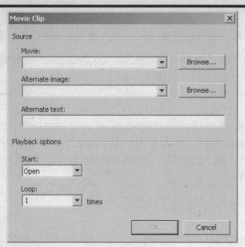

FIGURE 19.12: To display a movie clip on a web page, enter the settings for the clip you want to play and an alternative graphic for those browsers that do not support clips.

Adding Scrolling Text

Scrolling text is a way to grab your visitors' attention with a special announcement or notice. If you've used the Windows Scrolling Marquee screensaver, you're already familiar with the concept. To add scrolling text, follow these steps:

1. Click the Design Mode button on the Web Tools toolbar.

2. Position the insertion point where you want the scrolling text to appear.

3. Click the Scrolling Text button on the Web Tools toolbar.

4. Enter the text in the text box.

5. Set the options for Behavior, Direction, Background Color, Loop, and Speed.

6. Click OK to insert the scrolling text box.

7. Click the Design Mode button to exit Design mode; the text box doesn't scroll in Design mode.

You can resize or move the scrolling text box in Design mode as you would any text box in Word. To delete a scrolling text box, switch to Design mode, click the box to select it, and choose Edit ➢ Clear.

Viewing a Word Web Page in a Browser

If you are working on a website in Word, the easiest way to take a look at your work in a browser is to choose File ➢ Web Page Preview. You'll want to do this on a regular basis to make sure the page looks the same in the browser as it does in Word. You don't want any surprises after you've finished your work on the web. Use the navigation links on the page you preview to see other pages in the web.

If you have your browser open and the web you want to view is not open in Word, follow these steps to view the web in the browser:

1. Start the browser.

2. Choose File ➢ Open and locate the home page (`default` `.htm` or `index.htm`) for the website you want to view. Click OK.

3. Use navigation links to move from the home page of the website to the page you are working on.

CREATING WEB-BASED FORMS

To make the web truly interactive, information has to go in both directions. Web users need the ability to send information to the site owners, and web owners need to know who their visitors are and what they are looking for. *Web forms* provide a way for visitors to respond to surveys, register with a site, voice their opinions about issues, search your site, or submit feedback.

You can add a form to any web page. When you add a form control from the Web Tools toolbar, Word automatically adds Top Of Form and Bottom Of Form boundaries to the form, as shown here:

Top of Form

Bottom of Form

Word comes equipped with 11 built-in controls for you to use on forms. Here's a quick look at each one.

Check boxes   Use check boxes when users are allowed to select more than one option within a group. For example, you could have your check box say something like, "Send me more information about:" and then list various choices for the user to select from.

Option buttons   Option buttons indicate that a user can select only one item from a group of options, such as indicating that they would like to receive information Daily, Weekly, or Monthly.

Drop-down boxes   Drop-down boxes give users a list of specific options, from which they can choose one. For example, from a drop-down list of cities, you can pick yours to see its weather report.

List boxes   List boxes are similar to drop-down boxes in that they give users a list of options to choose from. However, instead of clicking an arrow to open a list, users use scroll buttons to scroll through the list. List boxes allow users to select multiple choices by using Shift or Ctrl while clicking.

Text boxes   Text boxes are fields where users can enter text, such as a name, address, or other specific information.

Text areas   Text areas are open text boxes with scroll bars where users can write a paragraph or more to give feedback, describe a problem, or provide other information.

Submit button   A Submit button is an essential element on a form, because a user must click the Submit button so that the data they entered is sent to the web server for processing.

Submit With Image control   The Submit With Image control lets you substitute an image for the standard Submit button. Make sure users know they have to click this button to submit their data—and that clicking the button submits the data. For example, don't use the same image for a Next Page button and a Submit button.

Reset button   Reset is a command button form control that clears the data in the current form so the user can start over.

Hidden   Hidden is a form field, invisible to the user, that passes data to the web server. For example, a hidden control could pass information about the user's operating system or web browser.

Password   In a Password control, typed text is replaced with asterisks so users can type passwords confidentially.

Laying Out a Form

Tables are a big help in laying out a form so that it looks organized. Create the table so it has twice the number of columns you would want to display in a single row. For example, in Figure 19.13, the third row contains three fields, so the table contains six columns. After you have inserted all the field names and form controls, save the page and open it in Internet Explorer or another browser to see how it looks.

NOTE

Because of the way different browsers display form fields, it is impossible to make every field line up perfectly with the fields above it unless you use tables.

FIGURE 19.13: Using a table to lay out form fields helps to align them in organized columns.

Setting Form Field Properties

All form controls have properties that determine how they behave. Some form controls require that you set the properties before the control can be used. For example, you must enter the values that you want to appear in a drop-down list so the user has options to choose from. To set or edit a control's properties, double-click the control to open the Properties dialog box, like the one in Figure 19.14.

If you haven't worked with control properties before, these dialog boxes can be a bit intimidating. Once you understand what you are looking at, you can choose which of the property settings to change and which to just leave alone. Each of the Properties dialog boxes has two tabs: Alphabetic and Categorized. They both contain the same properties in different order. The Alphabetic tab displays the properties in, you guessed it, alphabetical order. The Categorized tab groups the properties into various types: Appearance, Data, Miscellaneous, and so on.

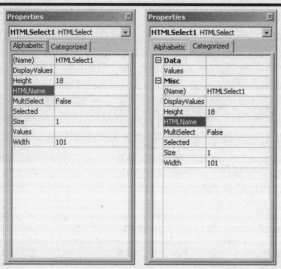

FIGURE 19.14: Set or edit form field properties on the Alphabetic tab of the Properties dialog box or view the same properties in collapsible and expandable groups on the Categorized tab.

To make changes, double-click any of the properties to enter Edit mode. One change you should always make is to rename the control from the default name to a name that describes the field—for example, change *HTMLText1* to *FirstName*. Control names cannot contain spaces, but they can contain numbers and both uppercase and lowercase letters.

Entering Values for Drop-Down Lists and List Boxes

To enter options for a drop-down list or a list box, type the first value in the DisplayValues property. Enter a semicolon and no space before entering the next value. Figure 19.15 shows you the values in the control properties and the end result in a drop-down list. As you can see, the values you type each appear on a separate line in the list. To test the drop-down list box, exit Design mode and click the down arrow on the form control.

For more information about form control properties, refer to the Word help topic "Form Controls You Can Use On A Web Page."

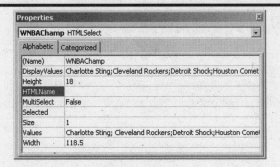

FIGURE 19.15: Enter values for a drop-down list in the DisplayValues property. When you view the page, the values you entered appear on separate lines in the drop-down list.

Adding Submit and Reset Buttons

After a user fills out your fabulous form, it would be nice if the data actually went somewhere. Every web form needs Submit and Reset buttons to complete the form's functionality. The Submit button must be tied to some action so that the data knows where to go. The Reset button clears the form when the user makes mistakes and wants to start over. To insert Submit and Reset buttons, move to the end of the form—stay above the

Part vii

Bottom Of Form marker—and click the Submit or Reset buttons on the Web Tools toolbar.

To make the Submit button really work, you may need the help of your web server administrator. Data can be stored in a comma-delimited text file, an Access table, or other database format. But first, it has to have a script, referred to as a *CGI script* or *form handler*, to tell it what to do with the data it collects. If you don't know how to write this script and you don't have a web server administrator to help you, consider taking your form into FrontPage. FrontPage makes it easy to create these scripts by just answering a few questions in a dialog box.

WORKING WITH FRAMES

A *frame* is a structure that displays a web page on every other page of the website. The page that displays the frames is called a *frames page*. Although the Web Page Wizard is the easiest way to create a simple navigational frame, Word offers you the option of adding and deleting frames manually.

TIP

There's a Frames toolbar that you can use to add, delete, and set the properties of frames. Right-click on any toolbar and choose Frames to display the toolbar.

To add a frame, choose Format ➢ Frames to open the Frames menu. If you want to add only a table of contents to the existing document, choose Table Of Contents In Frame. This option creates a table of contents for the displayed document based on heading styles used in the document. Figure 19.16 shows an example of a table of contents frame for a book chapter. A link is created for each heading formatted using a heading style.

To create a page that you can use with frames, choose Format ➢ Frames ➢ New Frames Page to create the frames page. Choose Format ➢ Frames again to choose the position of the frame you would like to add. You can choose from several options about where to place the frame on the page. New Frame Above creates a header frame, and New Frame Below creates a footer frame. If you plan to add horizontal and vertical frames, add header and footer frames first so they extend the width of the page. Resize frames by dragging the frame border in the direction you want. After adding a horizontal frame, click in the main body of the page before clicking New Frames Left to add a vertical frame. Otherwise, you divide the header into two sections. Click in each frame to add content.

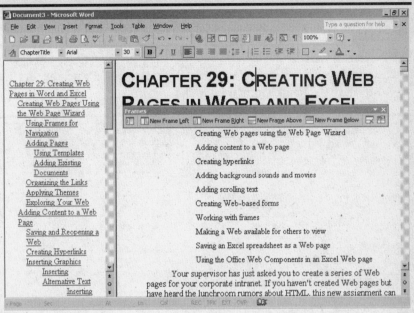

FIGURE 19.16: The Table Of Contents In Frame option creates a table of contents for the displayed document based on the heading styles.

Saving a Frames Page

If you save the frames page before adding any content, Word saves all three frames as a single document. Unlike with other web pages, however, Word doesn't give this document a title in the Save As dialog box. As soon as you add content to a frame, Word also saves the frame as an individual document. Because you are going to end up with several documents for each frames page you create, it's a good idea to create a folder to save in before saving a frames page. This keeps the main frames page and all the individual frames together in one easy-to-find place. Give the main frames page a name that reminds you it's a frames page. If it is the home page of the web you are creating, however, save it as default.htm.

If you add graphics or other objects to a frame, Word creates subfolders to house them in. The subfolder has the name of the page followed by an underscore and the word *files*. For example, let's say you insert a graphic on a frame that you saved as *Training Overview*. Word creates a folder called Training Overview_files to store the graphic. It also creates an XML document in the folder called filelist.xml that keeps a list of all the images in the document. Each frame gets its own subfolder to hold image files. The example in Figure 19.17 shows the results of creating a frames page with three frames and inserting text and graphics on each page. In saving the main page as TRAIN2K Registration.htm, Word also saved each frame as an individual document and created folders in which to store the images from each frame.

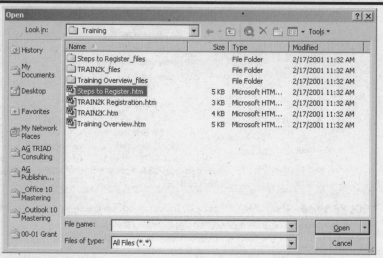

FIGURE 19.17: Word saves each frame individually and creates folders in which it saves image files.

Renaming Frames Pages

After Word creates folders in which to store images related to a frames page, the process of renaming a frame document is a little more complicated than renaming a normal document. To maintain the association between the document and the folder, you must first open the document you want to rename and resave it using File ➤ Save As to give it the new name. Word creates a new folder to store the image files. You must then choose File ➤ Open and delete the original document and associated *_files folder. It's an awkward process, but it works. The key thing is to remember to discard the old document and folder so it doesn't confuse you down the road.

Setting Frame Properties

 Right-click any frame, or select the frame and click the Frame Properties button on the Frames toolbar, to open the Frame Properties dialog box, shown in Figure 19.18. The initial page should be set to the frame that is open. However, you can change the page that opens in a frames page by selecting a different initial page from the drop-down list or clicking Browse to search for one. Give the frame a name by selecting or entering one in the Name box. Adjust the size of the frame by adjusting the Size controls. By default, frames are set to a relative size. You can change the relative size to a specific pixel size or a percentage of the screen display by changing the Measure In options.

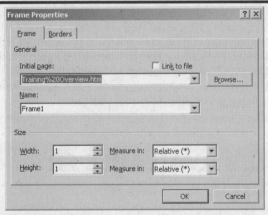

FIGURE 19.18: Use the Frame Properties dialog box to adjust the size of frames, borders, and other frame settings.

On the Borders tab of the Frame Properties dialog box, set whether you want to display frame borders and, if you do, what size and color you want them to be. You can determine whether users will be able to adjust the frame size by clearing or checking the Frame Is Resizable In Browser check box. Turn scroll bars on or off using the Show Scrollbars In Browsers setting.

WARNING

If you move a frames page to a different folder or drive location, you must copy all of the related frames documents to the same location.

Removing a Frame from a Frames Page

 If you decide you want to remove a frame from a frames page, click in the frame and choose Format ➤ Frames ➤ Delete Frame or click the Delete Frame button on the Frames toolbar. You may want to save the frame under a different name before you delete it in case you decide you want to use it at a later time. To save the frame under a different name, right-click in the frame and choose Save Current Frame As.

TIP

Although Word 2002 provides some exciting web page design options, creating a complex website requires some knowledge of HTML and other web-programming tools. While you are creating web pages in Word, Word is writing the HTML and XML code behind the scenes. You can view this code and even edit it directly by choosing View ➤ HTML Source. This opens the Microsoft Development Environment design window where you can edit HTML and active server page (ASP) files. If you are not a programmer, this is a good place to take a look at what it takes to produce the content you are creating and see HTML in actual application. If you are a programmer, you can edit the HTML file and add Microsoft Visual Basic, JScript, and VBScript to your files.

Making a Web Available for Others to View

When you have your web looking just the way you want, it's time to put it out there for others to use. In today's environment, you may be publishing a web to your company's intranet, an extranet, or the World Wide Web. If you are developing for your company's intranet, contact the web administrator to see how to proceed from here. It may be as simple as saving the files to a shared network folder.

If you want your web pages to be available for the whole world to see, you need to publish the site to a web server that others can access. The web server may be within your company or run by a web-hosting company. The cost of having a website hosted by an external company has come down dramatically, so unless you have a burning desire to run your own server, the smartest choice is to let a specialist do it. A good web-hosting company is sure to have fast equipment, T1 lines for fast connections, and multiple phone lines to handle the heavy traffic that will be generated by your site. The company you choose can give you instructions on how to publish the web to their server.

TIP

If you need to find a company to host your web, HostSearch.com (www .hostsearch.com) can help. HostSearch.com maintains an unbiased directory of web-hosting companies and lets you search for a host using a number of criteria including cost, space, and features. You can read reviews by actual users and compare up to five plans that meet your criteria.

CREATING WEB PAGES WITH EXCEL

Excel 2002 is well-equipped to work with the Web. Not only can you save Excel worksheets as web pages, you can open HTML files directly from Excel and drag and drop HTML tables from your browser directly into Excel worksheets. When you save or publish Excel 2002 worksheets as web pages, the pages you create are either interactive or noninteractive. *Noninteractive pages* are simply static pages that users can look at to examine data, like those you could publish in prior versions of Excel. With the interactive opportunities made available by using the Office Web Components, users can work with the data via the browser using some of the same tools they would in Excel 2002.

NOTE

Saving and *publishing* web pages in Office XP are not the same things. In Excel, for example, saving always creates noninteractive pages.

Excel 2002 includes three Office Web Components, and each one supports specific kinds of interactivity. The components are as follows:

▶ The Spreadsheet component inserts a spreadsheet where users can add formulas, sort and filter data, and format the worksheet.

▶ The Chart component is linked to data in the Spreadsheet component so that the chart can display changes when the data in the spreadsheet changes.

▶ The PivotTable component lets users analyze database information using most of the sorting, filtering, grouping, and subtotaling features of pivot table reports.

UNDERSTANDING OFFICE WEB COMPONENTS

The Office Web Components are based on the *Common Object Model (COM)*. With these components, you don't need to learn Java to create the slick interactive interface your users are asking for. The COM standard defines groups of functions called *interfaces*. Interfaces like the Office Web Components are grouped into component categories, which are in turn supported by applications like Excel, Access, and Internet Explorer 4 and 5. COM objects used in Office XP are interactive only if the user's browser supports COM. If a user has an older browser, they'll still see the spreadsheet, chart, or pivot table, but they will not be able to manipulate it in their browser.

To create either an interactive or noninteractive web page, open the spreadsheet you want to save to the web. Then choose File ➢ Save As Web Page from the menu to open the Save As dialog box.

You'll notice a couple of differences between this and the typical Save As dialog box. You can choose to save the entire worksheet or just the selected sheet. To create interactive pages that website visitors will be able to work with, enable the Add Interactivity check box to add Office Web Components to your page. You can save an entire workbook as a web page, complete with sheet tabs; however, the page cannot be interactive. To save an entire workbook, simply click Save to create the web page and close the dialog box.

NOTE

To have Chart functionality, you must first create a chart in the worksheet and select it before opening the Save As dialog box.

Publishing the Active Sheet

If you want to publish the active sheet in the open workbook to a web server, click Publish to open the Publish As Web Page dialog box, as shown in Figure 19.19.

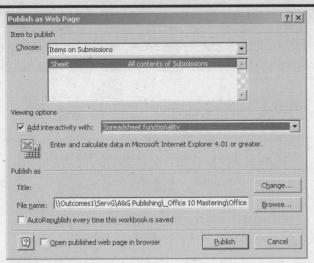

FIGURE 19.19: In the Publish As Web Page dialog box, you can select the parts of the sheet you want to publish, the viewing options, and where you want to publish it.

Choose what part of the workbook you want to publish. You can choose to publish the entire workbook without interactivity, you can choose a range of cells, or you can choose any of the sheets in the workbook.

If you have enabled interactivity, choose the component you wish to use from the drop-down list by selecting the kind of functionality you want users to have: spreadsheet or pivot table.

In the Publish As section of the Publish As Web Page dialog box, click the Change button if you want to designate a page title. Click Browse to find the web folder you want to publish to. In Excel 2002, you can select the AutoRepublish Every Time This Workbook Is Saved check box to take the hassle out of remembering to republish the worksheet every time you make a change.

If you want to immediately view your work in the web browser, select the Open Published Web Page In Browser check box before you click Publish. When you are ready to publish, click the Publish button. Excel creates the web page, including any interactivity you have specified. Figure 19.20 shows a web page that includes the Spreadsheet component.

Part vii

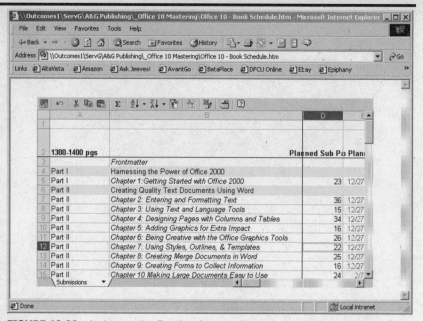

FIGURE 19.20: An interactive Excel web page that includes the Spreadsheet component

Most of the toolbar buttons on a published Excel worksheet are familiar Excel buttons. There are two additions: the Export To Excel button and the Commands And Options button. The Export To Excel button re-creates the Excel worksheet at a user-specified location. The Commands And Options button opens additional user tools, as shown in Figure 19.21. Use this dialog box to change the format of a worksheet, work with formulas in the sheet, find worksheet data, and change worksheet and workbook options.

In Figure 19.22, we've published the same data using the PivotTable component. The COM object works like the Excel pivot table report with areas for row data, column data, and page data (filter data).

The Chart component displays both the chart and the underlying data (see Figure 19.23). Users manipulate the data to change the chart, just as they would in Excel. They can't change the chart type or other chart features, so make sure you create a chart that's useful before saving it as an interactive page.

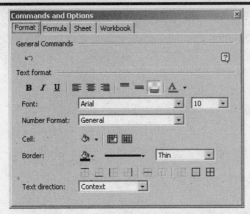

FIGURE 19.21: Users can change the properties of selected cells.

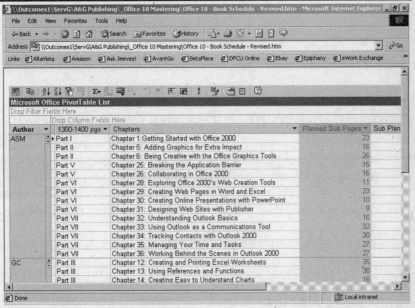

FIGURE 19.22: The PivotTable component lets users interactively analyze data.

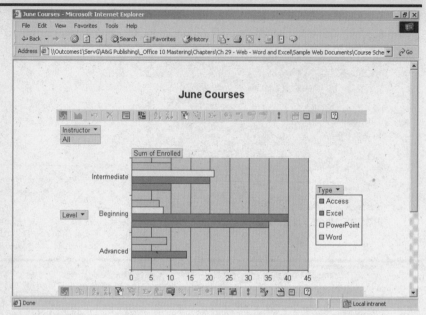

FIGURE 19.23: The Chart component reflects changes in the underlying data.

Appending to an Existing Web Page

If you already have a published spreadsheet and you'd like to add another web component such as a chart or a pivot table to it, you can append the data to the existing page. To place a second component on a single web page, choose File ➢ Save As Web Page and then click Publish to open the Publish As Web Page dialog box. Enter the existing HTML file in the File Name text box. When you click Publish, Excel prompts you to replace or add to the page. Choose Add To File to display more than one component on the page.

WHAT'S NEXT

Now that you understand the fundamentals of creating web pages using Word and Excel, we move to FrontPage 2002 in the next chapter. You will see what you can create and further develop using this web page creation package.

Chapter 20

CREATING A WEBSITE WITH FRONTPAGE 2002

FrontPage 2002 allows those with limited web page design experience to create, modify, and maintain full-featured, professional-looking pages without having to learn how to use all functions and features by coding them from scratch.

Part of FrontPage's power is that it is scalable, meaning its use can expand—or shrink—to fit. This means that if you do have some experience in creating web pages, you can use Front-Page 2002 to hasten as well as automate both the creation and publishing process. With FrontPage, you can create the basics you want, and then add your own code.

Adapted from *Mastering Microsoft FrontPage 2002 Premium Edition* by Peter Weverka and Molly E. Holzschlag

ISBN 0-7821-4003-3   1200 pp $49.99

Web Pages, Websites, and HTML

The Web sometimes seems like a vast and confusing place, and publishing a website can seem like a daunting task. It helps to realize that the Web isn't really a "place" at all, but rather files stored on computers called web servers, all of which are hooked together with phone lines and other types of network connections. When you surf the Web using a web browser such as Netscape Navigator or Microsoft Internet Explorer, you merely access files stored on the web servers.

The files themselves are called web pages. The text, pictures, and other elements that you see on your computer screen as you explore the Web are stored on web pages. A *website* is simply a collection of web pages that are linked together and offer information about the same topic. The first step in creating a website is to create the web pages. (Well, the first step is really to plan your website—ponder its look and feel and consider what you want it to communicate.)

Underneath the text-and-picture pages you see on your computer screen when you surf the Internet is the skeletal system of every web page: the Hypertext Markup Language (HTML). HTML is computer code that consists of tags. The tags define how web pages look. Web browsers interpret the tags so that you can see text, pictures, and whatever else on a web page. For example, one HTML tag (<B>) creates bold text; another HTML tag (<IMG>) inserts an image onto a page. When you view a web page using a web browser, the browser translates the HTML tags into attractive, clearly laid-out pages. Figure 20.1 shows the HTML tags that produce the web page shown in Figure 20.2.

TIP

Next time you are surfing the Web, take a peek at the HTML tags that produce the web page you are looking at. To see the tags, choose View ➤ Source in your browser.

HTML tags can be kind of scary. Not so long ago, web page creation was reserved for individuals with a technical background who understood HTML tags. For that reason, many people shied away from learning HTML and relied on professionals to build web pages. Fortunately, you no longer need to learn HTML in detail to create web pages, because FrontPage can help you build a website even if you know nothing about HTML and don't care to learn it.

TIP

A working knowledge of HTML can be a great asset, especially when you are troubleshooting a web page and you have to "get under the hood" and correct problems. At its most basic, HTML is not difficult to understand, but becoming fluent in HTML takes time.

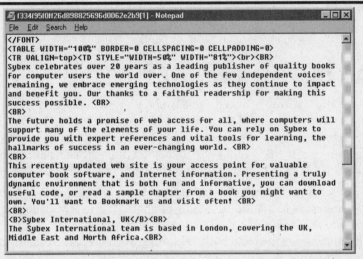

FIGURE 20.1: Behind every web page is the skeletal system of the Web: HTML.

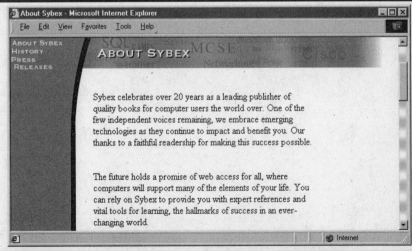

FIGURE 20.2: The Web browser translates HTML tags into text and images.

You can create a great website right now without learning a single HTML tag. You've got everything you need already—good concepts regarding design and an excellent tool to work with. You're ready to go to work! Soon, you'll have a complete website to call your very own.

TIP

For a good HTML authoring reference, see www.htmlhelp.com.

WHAT IS FRONTPAGE?

So, there's the Web, which is full of websites, which are made up of web pages, which are created using HTML. Where does FrontPage fit in? FrontPage is a *web-authoring* or *web-publishing* program. Web-publishing programs put the power of website creation in everyone's hands—including those who don't want or don't have the time to learn HTML.

In FrontPage, you create web pages in much the same way as you create documents in a word processing program. The following illustration, for example, shows how similar FrontPage and Word really are. By using the FrontPage menus and toolbar buttons, you enter and format text, pictures, and other page elements in much the same way as you enter and format these items in Word.

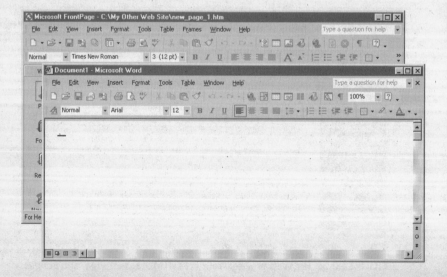

FrontPage generates the HTML tags in the background. You need never concern yourself with them. However, if you want to go into the HTML view and make changes, you can do that as well.

FrontPage Builds Websites Big and Small

You can use FrontPage to build many different kinds of websites:

A personal website   A popular type of public Internet site, the personal website is all about *you*. It can describe your interests, your friends, and your family, or offer hyperlinks to your favorite websites. Many web development professionals got their start by creating a personal website. The personal website is a chance to be creative. Being a user-friendly program, FrontPage is a good choice for this small but exciting type of website.

A small business website   If you have a home-based or small business and your advertising budget is small, a website is a great way to spread the news about your product. FrontPage can help you create a website for a small business. By making use of the FrontPage templates, you can set up a professional storefront without having to spend months learning techniques and technologies.

A corporate website   Large companies want their websites to provide product information, customer support, consumer relations information, and even online shopping. FrontPage is useful in a corporate setting because its powerful tracking features make it possible for more than one person to make changes and updates to website pages. And FrontPage is compatible with and can be integrated with many other software products.

A corporate intranet   A corporate intranet is an internal company network that employees can surf in the same way that they surf the Internet. A website on an intranet is like a website on the Internet except for the fact that it is available only to employees who can access the company network. Because an intranet is protected from curious web surfers, internal company information such as sales figures, human resources communications, and department resources can be transmitted company wide. FrontPage has tools for creating customized intranets.

FrontPage Is a Collaborative Software Program

You can use FrontPage in collaboration with these Microsoft applications:

Microsoft Office XP   FrontPage 2002 shares menus and toolbars with Office XP. Files that were created in Word, Excel, and PowerPoint can be made into web pages. What's more, users of Office products can export their work from other Office programs to a FrontPage website.

Visual InterDev   Visual InterDev is a high-powered management and programming tool for database applications. High-end developers use Visual InterDev to manage sites.

Microsoft Internet Explorer   Use the Internet Explorer web browser to surf the Web and to preview your site before it goes live.

FINDING INFORMATION ONLINE

You can find detailed information and news about the products discussed previously at the following websites:

▶ Microsoft Office: www.microsoft.com/office

▶ Visual InterDev: msdn.microsoft.com/vinterdev

▶ Microsoft Internet Explorer: www.microsoft.com/ie

FRONTPAGE WEB-BUILDING BASICS

The best way to learn a new skill is to just do it. Because you already have a fair idea of how the Web works and you understand what a powerful tool FrontPage is, you are ready to jump in feet first.

On the following pages, you will start FrontPage and create a new website. Along the way, you'll become familiar with the FrontPage interface and learn how to add new pages to a website.

Starting FrontPage

Starting FrontPage requires the same steps as starting most other Windows programs. To start FrontPage in one easy step, from the Windows Start menu, select Programs ➤ Microsoft FrontPage. FrontPage starts (see Figure 20.3).

FIGURE 20.3: FrontPage, ready to go

HOW TO GET HELP WITHIN FRONTPAGE

For quick FrontPage assistance, turn to the FrontPage help system. The help system identifies unfamiliar menu items and toolbar buttons, and provides general overviews and step-by-step instructions for FrontPage operations. To access FrontPage help, select Help ➤ Microsoft FrontPage Help. To get context-sensitive help, click the Help button available in many FrontPage dialog boxes, or press Shift+F11 and then click the item of interest.

Like most computer programs, FrontPage includes a main menu and toolbars for completing tasks. Where it differs, however, is the *Views bar* along the left side of the window. As "FrontPage Views" explains later in this chapter, you can click an icon in the Views bar to embark on tasks or discover something new about your website.

Creating a Website with Templates

If you're not sure how to begin building a website or you need a complete website fast, FrontPage gives you plenty of help in the form of templates. A template is a ready-made website where all that is required of you is entering text where the placeholder text is and, if you wish, inserting new graphics where the placeholder graphics are now. The idea is for you to customize the ready-made pages with your own text and designs.

WARNING

Sometimes creating a website from a template falls into the "more trouble than it's worth" department. Yes, the template takes care of much of the formatting. And the pages in the website are linked together very nicely. The problems start when you make the website your own. After you enter your own text and the graphics, the web pages often need tweaking. You have to reformat pages and move text around. You end up having to do the same tasks that you would do if you created the website without a template.

FrontPage provides templates for many different purposes—a Customer Support website, a Personal website, and a Project website. There's also the One Page website for creating a website that comprises a single page and an Empty website for creating the structure of a website but nothing more.

TIP

You can create your own templates by either modifying an existing template or creating one from scratch.

Choose File ➢ New to create a new folder in which to store each new website you create. Doing so makes organizing the different files in the website easier. After you create a new folder, follow these steps to create a website from a template:

1. Choose File ➢ New ➢ Page Or Web. As shown in Figure 20.4, the New Page Or Web task pane appears on the right side of the screen.

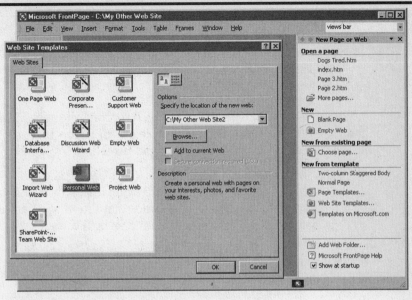

FIGURE 20.4: Creating a website from a template

2. Look under New From Template in the task pane, and click the Web Site Templates hyperlink. As shown in Figure 20.4, the Web Site Templates dialog box appears. It lists templates that are available to you. You also see one or two wizards, but we'll get to those in a bit. For the sake of an example, Personal Web is a good choice. Using that template, you can create a website to describe your personal interests.

3. Click to highlight the Personal Web icon.

4. On the right side of the dialog box, enter the folder where you want to store your new website. To do so, type the path to the folder (or click the Browse button, locate and select the folder in the New Web Location dialog box, and click the Open button). If you intend to store your website on a company intranet, get the URL from the network administrator and enter it in the text box.

5. Click OK. FrontPage does a bit of thinking, and in a moment or two, your new website is ready.

TIP

When you create a new website, FrontPage generates a local URL for it (URL stands for Uniform Resource Locator, another name for a website address). The URL points to an address on your computer. The address is a stand-in for the Internet address to which you will eventually upload your website.

The name of the folder where you stored your website appears in the FrontPage title bar. But where are the web pages? Follow these steps to view the home page of the website you just created:

1. Click the Folders button in the Views bar. As shown in Figure 20.5, you see the name of the folder where you stored your website in the Folder List. Notice that FrontPage created a handful of subfolders to store the many files that make up your website.

2. Double-click the file named index.htm. The home page of your new website loads into the main window.

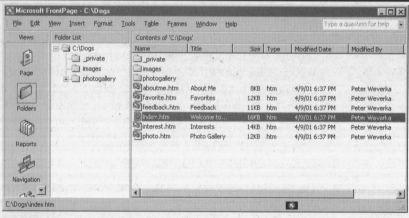

FIGURE 20.5: Opening a website in Folders view

Later in this chapter, "FrontPage Views" introduces you to the different ways of viewing websites. Each view is meant to help you with a different aspect of website creation, management, and maintenance. For now, just look at the Views bar in the FrontPage window to see the different views you can use—Page, Folders, Reports, Navigation, Hyperlinks, and Tasks. For example, select Navigation to see the view shown in Figure 20.6.

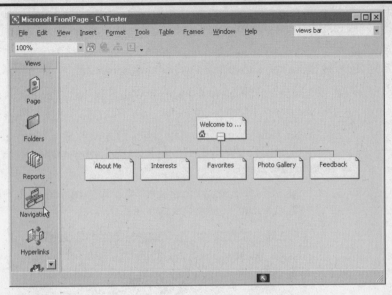

FIGURE 20.6: Navigation view of a personal website

You'll be doing a whole lot more with this down the road, but let's move on to learning other ways to view and create websites in FrontPage 2002.

Creating a Site with a Wizard

FrontPage provides wizards for creating its two most complex templates, the Corporate Presence website and the Discussion website. A wizard is a series of dialog boxes that ask you questions about something you want to create—in this case, a website. After you tell the wizard what you want, the wizard generates the website.

FrontPage offers these wizards:

- ▶ The Corporate Presence Web Wizard builds an entire corporate site by asking you what kind of information you want to present on the site.

- ▶ The Discussion Web Wizard creates a FrontPage *discussion group*, a website that hosts a public forum where visitors can post articles and respond to articles that others have posted.

- ▶ The Import Web Wizard is for gathering files and documents for a website.

▶ The Database Interface Wizard is for creating a website that enables visitors to query, sort, and add records to a database table.

Follow these steps to create a website with a wizard:

1. Choose File ➢ New ➢ Page Or Web. The New Page Or Web task pane opens.

2. Under New From Template, click the Web Site Templates hyperlink. The Web Site Templates dialog box appears (refer to Figure 20.4).

3. Choose the Corporate Presence Web Wizard and click OK. The first wizard dialog box appears.

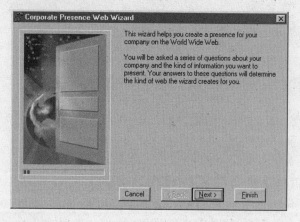

4. Read the introduction and click the Next button to advance to the next panel, where you can specify which pages you'd like to have included in your website. Customize these by removing or adding a check mark next to the page description. When you're ready, click Next.

5. You'll now be asked for a descriptive title for your website. Make it a sensible title—something that relates to the subject you're working on.

6. In each subsequent panel, read and follow the wizard's directions. To proceed to the next panel, click Next. To go back to a previous panel, click Back.

7. When you reach the final panel, the Next button appears grayed out. To finish creating the website, click the Finish button. The wizard uses the information you provided to generate the website.

When the website is complete, you can open and view it by clicking Folders in the Views bar and then double-clicking the `index.htm` file (refer to Figure 20.5). Now you can open the pages and start customizing.

WARNING

Websites created using FrontPage templates and wizards contain all sorts of unique FrontPage features. A few of these features—for example, keyword site searches and discussion groups—work only if the site is published on a web server.

Creating an Empty Website

If you're not sure where to begin, or if you'd like to see examples of how typical websites are structured, FrontPage templates and wizards are the way to go. But if you know your way around FrontPage and you want to start from scratch, more power to you. You can start with a single blank website and take it from there.

Follow these steps to create a website from scratch:

1. Choose File ≻ New ≻ Page Or Web. The New Page Or Web task pane appears.

2. Under New in the task pane, click the Empty Web hyperlink. You see the Web Site Templates dialog box. The Empty Web template is highlighted.

3. In the Specify The Location Of The New Web text box, either type the path to the folder where you want to store your new website or click the Browse button and select the folder in the New Web Location dialog box.

4. Click OK.

The next step is to start adding the web pages. See "Adding Pages to a Website" later in this chapter.

Importing an Existing Website into FrontPage

Suppose you created a website with another software program and now you want to do your web work in FrontPage. It can be done. You can import the website into FrontPage and thereby transform the site into a FrontPage website. To do the trick, you use the Import Web Wizard, which can import any website file that is stored on your computer, on a network that your computer is connected to, or on the World Wide Web itself.

TIP

When you import a website into FrontPage, the website is unchanged. You copy the website into a new folder and place it under the auspices of FrontPage when you import a website.

Take note of where the website is located and follow these steps to import it:

1. Chose File ➤ Import. The Import dialog box appears.

2. Click the From Web button. You see the Import Web Wizard dialog box (see Figure 20.7). It asks where you want to import the web pages from.

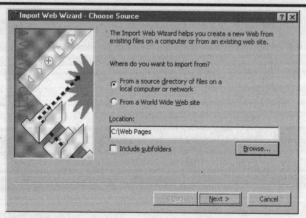

FIGURE 20.7: Here you specify the location from which a website will be imported.

3. Specify the location of the website you want to import. If the site is currently stored in a folder on your computer or local network, click the From A Source Directory Of Files On A Local Computer Or Network button. In the Location text box, type the path to that folder, or click the Browse button to select a folder from a list of folders on your computer and local network. To import files stored in the site's subfolders, click the Include Subfolders check box.

   If the site is available on the World Wide Web, click the button labeled From A World Wide Web Site, and in the Location text box, type the site's URL.

4. Click Next. Which dialog box appears next depends on the location of the website files. If the site is stored on your computer or network, the Import Web Wizard – Edit File List dialog box appears. If the site is stored on the Web, the Import Web Wizard – Choose Download Amount dialog box appears.

5. In the Import Web Wizard – Edit File List dialog box, the Files list box lists all the website files contained in the location you specified. To exclude one or more files, press the Ctrl key while clicking the names of the file(s), and then click the Exclude button. To start over with a complete file list, click the Refresh button.

   Or, in the Import Web Wizard – Choose Download Amount dialog box, specify the download options you want the wizard to use. The dialog box enables you to control the number of levels (the successive depth of subfolders) to import and the total file size of the imported files. You can also choose to import only the site's web pages and its image files.

6. In either dialog box, click Next. The Import Web Wizard – Finish dialog box appears.

7. Click the Finish button. The Import Web Wizard imports the files you selected into your website (this may take a moment, especially if you're importing a big website).

You can now use FrontPage to update and maintain your website. When you're ready to start working on your website, skip ahead to the section "Titling a Web Page" and work through the rest of the chapter.

KEEPING IT CONTAINED

For the Import Web Wizard to properly import a website, the site's files must be contained within a single main folder (it's okay if the main folder contains subfolders). If the site's pages are not contained in one folder, you need to import the pages by using the Import Web Wizard, and then import the rest of the pages individually (you'll see how in the section "Importing Web Pages for Your Website" later in this chapter). Because the imported site's filesystem will no longer fit the site's original structure, importing a site in this manner risks creating broken hyperlinks. (Hyperlinks are bits of highlighted text or images in a web page. You click these to jump to different locations.) You'll learn how hyperlinks work later in this chapter.

FRONTPAGE VIEWS

Like other programs, FrontPage has a main menu and toolbars along the top of the screen for giving commands. And, also like most programs, you will find a status bar along the bottom of the screen that provides helpful information. Where FrontPage differs from other programs, however, is the Views bar. Use it to change views of the website you are working on. To change views, click an icon in the Views bar.

Each view presents a different type of information about the website you are working on and enables you to work with the site in a different way. This section looks at each view in detail.

TIP

You can also change views by choosing an option on the View menu.

Page View

Think of *Page view* as the "editor" view. In Page view, you see one page—the one you're working on (see Figure 20.8). You can make changes or adjustments to the items on a page in Page view.

One of the most powerful aspects of Page view is that you can click a tab—Normal, HTML, or Preview—along the bottom of the screen to switch modes. Page view offers these modes:

Normal This is the standard mode, the one in which you enter text and graphics. The view shows roughly what the page will look like in a web browser. Dotted lines show where page elements begin and end.

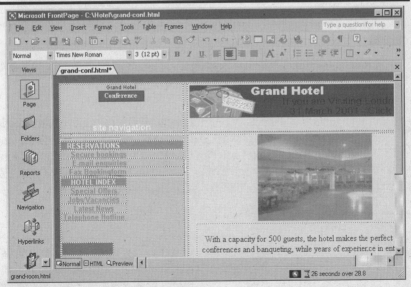

FIGURE 20.8: Page view in Normal mode

HTML In this mode, you can actually get to the heart of the matter: the HTML code. You can make changes directly to the code or see how the code has been altered by changes made in the visual editor. (See Figure 20.9.)

Preview Preview mode is where you see what your page will look like after it is published on the Internet. Here, you see the final results of the page, with no code or editing marks. (See Figure 20.10.)

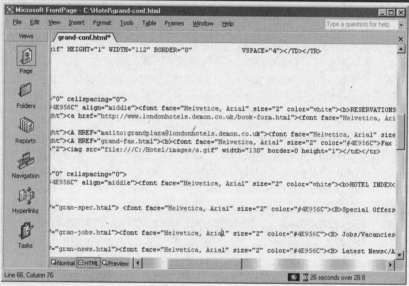

FIGURE 20.9: FrontPage's Page view in HTML mode

Page view is especially helpful because you can not only make visual alterations but can also work behind the scenes with the HTML code. And when you're done, you can check out the way the page will look in Preview mode. Page view is also where you'll spend most of your Front-Page time. Get well acquainted with this view.

TIP

Yet another way to see what your web page will look like in a browser is to open it in a browser window. FrontPage offers a command for doing just that, File ➤ Preview In Browser. Choose that command, and your default browser will open and you'll see the web page there.

FIGURE 20.10: FrontPage's Page view in Preview mode

Folders View

In *Folders view* (shown in Figure 20.11), the screen is split in two panes. The Folder List pane shows a hierarchical list of folders inside the website you are working on. The Contents pane shows a detailed list of pages and files in the folder that you selected in the Folder List pane.

The Folder List side of the window works much like Windows Explorer. Click the plus sign (+) next to a folder to see its subfolders. To collapse a folder and make its subfolders disappear, click a minus sign (–). Use Folders view to manage and rename files, create new folders, and move web pages to different subfolders (you'll see how shortly).

TIP

When you change the name or location of a file, FrontPage automatically updates all hyperlinks to the file. Therefore, you don't have to worry about links becoming inoperative when you move files.

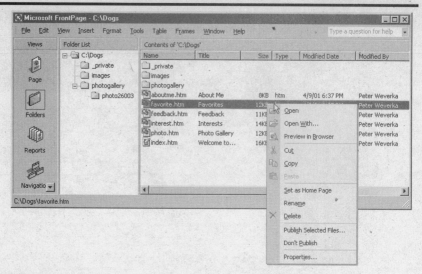

FIGURE 20.11: Folders view is for managing the files in a website.

Each FrontPage website is equipped with two standard folders: the _private folder and the images folder. The _private folder (note the underscore character before the word *private*) is a good place to store pages you don't want other people to see—for example, in-progress work—because visitors to your website can't see or access it. And you can use the _private folder to shield web pages from the FrontPage text-indexing component, the component by which visitors can search your website. (FrontPage *components* are prepackaged interactive elements you can add to your site without having to do any programming.)

TIP
Another way to keep a file in your website from actually being published on the Internet is to right-click it in Folders view and choose Don't Publish on the short-cut menu.

The images folder is the best place to store web graphics. Keeping web pages and graphic files in separate locations makes managing the elements of a website a little easier. Adding images (graphics) to your website is the topic of Chapter 21, "Adding Images to Your Web Pages."

Here is a rundown of the file management tasks you can do in Folders view:

Opening a file   Double-click the filename. The file opens in Page view.

Seeing the contents of a folder   Double-click the folder's name. Its contents appear—where else?—in the Contents pane of the window.

Renaming a file   In the Contents pane, right-click the file and select Rename on the shortcut menu. Then type a new name where the old name was and press Enter.

Creating a new folder   From the FrontPage menu, choose File ➤ New ➤ Folder. A new folder appears in both panes. Type a new folder name in the space provided and press Enter. You now have a new folder, ready to use.

Moving a page into a folder   Click and drag the page to the target folder (in either pane). The page moves to its new location. You can also right-click a page, choose Cut on the shortcut menu, right-click a folder, and choose Paste.

Sorting the file list in the Contents pane   Click one of the header labels at the top of the pane. For example, to sort the list alphabetically by name, click the Name label.

Deleting a file   Click the filename and press the Delete key. The Confirm Delete dialog box appears. Click Yes and your file is history.

View a file's properties   Right-click the filename and choose Properties from the shortcut menu. The Properties dialog box appears. From there, you can change the title of a web page (on the General tab), enter a comment (on the Summary tab), and assign categories (on the Workgroup tab). Categories make finding a file easier. Comments can be read in Folders view.

Reports View

Switch to *Reports view* when you want to get statistics or learn more about your website. When you first switch to Reports view, you land on the Site Summary screen (see Figure 20.12), a screen that presents hyperlinks that you can click to generate reports. Do one of the following to generate a report:

▶ Click a hyperlink on the Site Summary screen.

▶ Choose View ➤ Reports, select a submenu name, and choose a report on the submenu that appears.

▶ Click the Reports button, choose an option from the drop-down menu, and choose a report name from the submenu (refer to Figure 20.12).

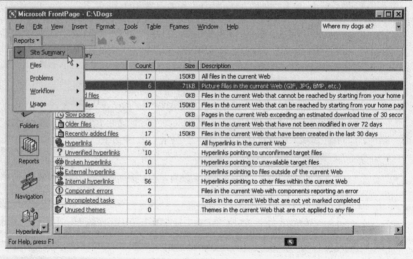

FIGURE 20.12: Switch to Reports view to learn more about your website.

The Description column on the Site Summary screen tells you what each report does. To return to the Site Summary screen, click the Reports button and choose Site Summary on the drop-down menu.

Navigation View

In *Navigation view* (shown in Figure 20.13), you can see at a glance how visitors will find their way around your website. What's more, by building a *navigational structure* in Navigation view, you also create *navigation bars,* the rows of text hyperlinks or buttons that visitors click to move from web page to web page.

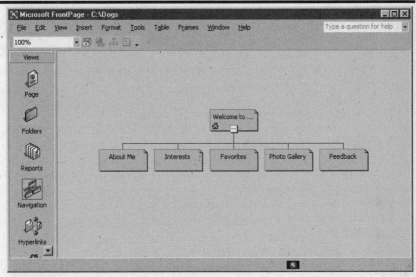

FIGURE 20.13: Navigation view shows the structure of your website.

TIP

If you're ever asked to create a site map for a client, you can use Navigation view to generate the map. Simply import the site into FrontPage using the Import Web Wizard and switch to Navigation view. You can print a site map when in Navigation view. To do so, choose File ➢ Print.

Hyperlinks View

In *Hyperlinks view* (shown in Figure 20.14), you can see which pages in your website a certain page is linked to. Being able to see hyperlinks is very convenient when you want to examine hyperlinks to see how the pages in your website are linked together.

To choose which web page to examine in Hyperlinks view, start by choosing View ➢ Folder List to display the Folder List pane (see Figure 20.14). From there, select the web page whose hyperlinks you want to examine.

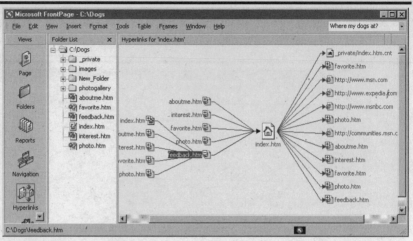

FIGURE 20.14: In Hyperlinks view, you can see very clearly how pages are linked.

TIP

A fast way to open the Folder List pane is to click the Toggle Pane button on the Standard toolbar. If the Navigation pane, not the Folder List pane, appears, open the drop-down menu on the Toggle Pane button and choose Folder List.

The left side of the window shows links to the page; the right side shows links from the page to other pages in your website. Pages with hyperlinks show a plus sign (+). By clicking the plus sign, you can branch out and examine more links.

Right-click the screen in Hyperlinks view and choose options from the shortcut menu to examine links in different ways:

See page titles instead of filenames   Choose Show Page Titles on the shortcut menu. Sometimes identifying pages by title is easier than identifying them by filename.

See links to graphics as well as other pages   Choose Hyperlinks To Pictures on the shortcut menu.

Examine hyperlinks with the same target page   Choose Repeated Hyperlinks to find out when hyperlinks go to the same website.

TIP

If you came to Hyperlinks view to look for broken hyperlinks, you came to the wrong place. Switch to Reports view and choose View ➣ Reports ➣ Problems ➣ Broken Hyperlinks to generate a Broken Hyperlinks report.

Tasks View

In *Tasks view*, you can maintain a to-do list of items that need doing for your website to be complete. Tasks view is especially useful when more than one person is working on a website, because the entire team can maintain the list.

Tasks						
Status	Task	Assigned To	Prio...	Associated ...	Modified Date	Description
● Not Started	Hurry Up	Peter Wev...	High		4/10/01 8:49:3...	The Cats page has to be done by Th...
● Completed	Investigate th...	Roger Ra...	Low		4/10/01 8:51:0...	Case links need investigating

ADDING PAGES TO A WEBSITE

After you create a FrontPage website (especially if it is only one page long), the next step is to start adding more web pages. To create a new page, you can rely on a template or simply attach a blank page to your website. For that matter, you can import a web page from another website. Keep reading.

Creating a Blank Web Page

Create a new blank page when you want to start from scratch and do all the layout work yourself. Follow these steps to attach a blank web page to your template:

1. Switch to Folders view. To do so, click the Folders button in the Views bar.

2. Click the New Page button or press Ctrl+N. A placeholder filename is highlighted on the Contents tab in Folders view. The filename is new_page_1, unless you are starting from a blank website. In that case, the placeholder file is called index.

Part vii

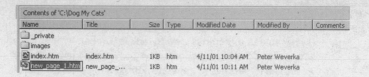

Contents of 'C:\Dog My Cats'						
Name	Title	Size	Type	Modified Date	Modified By	Comments
☐ _private						
☐ images						
🗎 index.htm	index.htm	1KB	htm	4/11/01 10:04 AM	Peter Weverka	
🗎 new_page_1.htm	new_page_...	1KB	htm	4/11/01 10:11 AM	Peter Weverka	

3. Type a filename for your new page. The filename should be short, descriptive, and easy to remember, and should have the .htm or .html extension.

4. Press Enter.

WARNING

After you finish creating a new web page, be sure to select it, choose File ➢ Properties, and enter a title for the page on the General tab of the Properties dialog box. When you view a web page in a browser, the page's title appears on the title bar at the top of the screen. Unless you enter a title, people who visit the web page you created will see its filename, not a title, in the title bar of their browser windows.

Creating a Web Page from a Template

By creating a web page from a template, you save yourself from doing some of the layout work. You get a web page that was laid out and developed by a professional. All you have to do is enter your own text and graphics where the placeholder text and graphics are on the page.

Follow these steps to create a new web page from a template:

1. Choose File ➢ New ➢ Page Or Web. The New Page Or Web task pane opens.

2. Under New From Template, click the Page Templates hyperlink. The Page Templates dialog box appears (see Figure 20.15).

3. Select a page. The Preview box shows roughly what each page looks like.

4. Click OK.

Pages created with a template come with placeholder text and, in some cases, sample graphics to help you get an idea what a completed page is supposed to look like. Replace the generic text with your own words of wisdom and make other layout changes as you see fit.

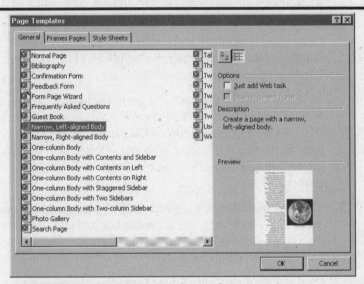

FIGURE 20.15: Creating a new web page from a template

The dotted gridlines that surround the text in most templates are the boundaries of *invisible tables* (tables without any border specifications). Invisible tables form the framework in which the table is laid out.

Importing Web Pages for Your Website

Import a web page if you've already created (or have access to) a finished web page and you want to attach it to the website you are working on. For that matter, you can import more than one page at a time or import an entire folder. Pages you import can be stored on your computer, a local network, or the World Wide Web.

TIP

You can actually import any type of file from a website into your FrontPage website—not just HTML files, but also graphics files, sound files, text files, and so on. Earlier in this chapter, "Importing an Existing Website into FrontPage" explained how to import a website you created with another software program.

Part vii

Follow these steps to import a web page into your website:

1. Choose File ➤ Import. You see the Import dialog box.

2. To import a file or files that are stored on your computer or local network, click the Add File button. The Add File To Import List dialog box appears.

   Or, to import an entire folder that's stored on your computer or local network, click the Add Folder button. The File Open dialog box appears.

   To import a file or folder that is currently located on the World Wide Web, click the From Web button. The Import Web Wizard – Choose Source dialog box appears. (For help with using the Import Web Wizard, refer to "Importing an Existing Website into FrontPage" earlier in this chapter.)

3. If you are importing files, select the files you want to import in the Add File To Import List dialog box and click the Open button. Back in the Import dialog box, the files you selected appear in the Import list.

   Or, if you are importing a folder, select the folder you want to import and click the Open button. Back in the Import dialog box, files in the folder you selected appear in the File list.

TIP

In the File list, the local URL of each file you want to import appears in the URL column. To change where FrontPage stores a file, select the file and click the Modify button. In the Edit URL dialog box, enter a new location for the file. For example, if you are importing an image named face.gif and you want the image to be stored in the images folder, type **images/face.gif** in the text box. Click OK to close the dialog box. The new URL appears in the Import list.

4. In the Import dialog box, click OK. FrontPage imports the file(s) you chose. When the import process is finished, the dialog box closes.

FIXING IMPORTED FILES

It goes without saying that importing a web page into the website you are working on saves work. But, sad to say, not all web pages land flawlessly in FrontPage after you import them. FrontPage is very picky about HTML. For your web page to work properly, certain HTML tags have to be present. If you import a web page, switch to Page view, and discover that the page isn't displaying properly (if you see a blank page, for example, when you know there is supposed to be information on it), investigate the page's HTML source code. To do so, click the HTML tab at the bottom of the Page view window and do the following:

▶ Verify that the first and last tags of the file are, respectively, <HTML> and </HTML>.

▶ Verify that the <TITLE> tag is between the <HEAD> and </HEAD> tags.

▶ Verify that the body of the page is between the <BODY> and </BODY> tags.

If you notice that one of these tags is missing or out of place, go ahead and make corrections. Then switch back to the Page view and see if that fixes the problem.

OPENING A FRONTPAGE WEBSITE YOU CREATED

When you start FrontPage, the program opens the website that was open when you last closed the program. Follow these steps, if need be, to open a website you created:

1. From the FrontPage menu bar, select File ➤ Open Web. The Open Web dialog box appears. Folders where websites are kept are marked with a circle.

2. Locate and select the folder where you keep the website you want to open.

3. Click the Open button.

TIP

The fastest way to open a website is to choose File ➢ Recent Webs, and then, on the submenu, select a website. The submenu lists the last four websites you worked on. You will find the same list of websites at the top of the New Page Or Web task pane.

DELETING A WEBSITE

Suppose you need to delete a website. It can be done, but before you do it, remember that a website can't be recovered after you delete it. You can't visit the Recycle Bin and resuscitate it, for example. If the website you want to delete is worth anything whatsoever, make a backup copy before you delete it.

Follow these steps to delete a website you created in FrontPage:

1. Open the condemned website and switch to Folders view.

2. Find the topmost folder, right-click it, and choose Delete on the shortcut menu. You see the Confirm Delete dialog box.

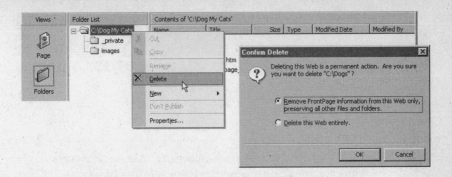

3. Choose an option button and click OK:

    Remove FrontPage Information From This Web Only
    Deletes the website, but preserves the files. In other words,
    the website as an entity is gone, but the graphics and web
    pages with which it was made remain on your computer.

    Delete This Web Entirely   Removes all files in the web-
    site from your hard disk.

WARNING

After you delete a website, it is gone for good. FrontPage does not include an
Undelete or Undo command in case you change your mind. If you nix a website
by mistake, you'll just have to start over.

TITLING A WEB PAGE

In web page parlance, the *title* of a page has nothing to do with what
appears at the top of the page itself. No, the title is what appears *in the
title bar* of the browser window, as shown in the following illustration.
This title also appears on the Forward and Back drop-down menus (in
Internet Explorer) and the Go drop-down menu (in Netscape Navigator)—the menus that web surfers make use of when they want to jump to
web pages they visited before. Most search engines index pages by giving
weight to the title of a web page, so choosing a good title for pages is
important if you want your pages to be found in web searches.

Part vii

TIP

Giving a web page a clear, descriptive title is very smart. Many search engines give special credence to words in the title, so the accuracy of a title helps users to find your web pages. The title also appears in the search engine's *hit list* (the index of search results a user gets), and even in bookmark lists.

Giving your page a title is easiest to do when you save it. The first time you save a web page, the Save As dialog box appears (see Figure 20.16), and you are prompted to give your web page a name as well as a title. Click the Change Title button and enter a title in the Set Page Title dialog box.

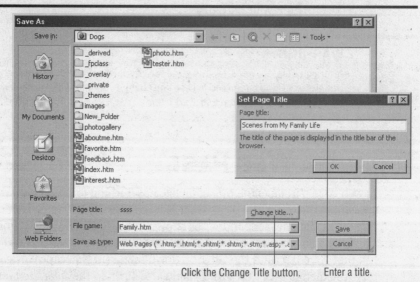

Click the Change Title button.   Enter a title.

FIGURE 20.16: You can give a web page a title when you save it for the first time.

No matter what title a web page has, you can change it by following these steps:

1. Open the Page Properties dialog box (see Figure 20.17). To open it in Page view, choose File ➢ Properties. In the Folders

or Navigation view, select the page and choose File ➤ Properties. If you start in Folders or Navigation view, you get a simplified version of the Page Properties dialog box (see the right side of Figure 20.17). No matter—you can title a web page starting either place.

2. On the General tab, enter a title in the Title text box.

3. Click OK.

Your page now has a distinguishable title.

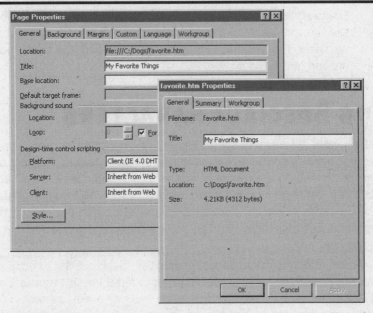

FIGURE 20.17: Which Page Properties dialog box you see depends on whether you are in Page view (left) or Folders or Navigation view (right).

ENTERING TEXT ON A WEB PAGE

To enter text on a web page, open the web page and begin typing in Page view. Entering text on a web page is very much like entering text in a word processing document. You can also copy or cut text from a text file, a Microsoft Word file, an e-mail message, or another web page, and then paste it into the page you're working on (just as you did earlier in Word 2002).

Of course, entering text is one thing, and arranging it on the page is another. Besides typing it straight in, consider these strategies for entering text on a web page:

Entering text in text boxes   A text box is like a miniature page inside another page. After you enter text in a box, you can drag the text box wherever you want on the page and in so doing position the text where you want it to be.

Using tables to lay out text   You can make text land on web pages where you want it to land by entering the text in tables.

Using styles to make pages consistent with one another   By assigning styles to text, you can make sure, from web page to web page, that headings and paragraph text look the same and are laid out the same way.

USING SPECIAL CHARACTERS

A few symbols, known as *special characters*, are commonly used in day-to-day editing. The registered symbol (®), for example, denotes a type of trademark; the copyright symbol (©) denotes ownership. Letters such as è and ñ are required if you decide to sprinkle a foreign language word or two in the text. These symbols and letters don't appear on the keyboard. To enter them, word processors provide a special menu or dialog box.

Unfortunately, you can't simply enter a special character or unusual letter in FrontPage because the character or letter doesn't translate into HTML. Therefore, it doesn't show up on web pages. Fortunately, HTML provides special codes called *escape characters* for generating special characters and letters that are not found on the keyboard. These aren't tags, precisely, but bits of code that tell a web browser what to display.

FrontPage makes entering special characters and oddball characters fairly easy by way of the Insert ➢ Symbol menu command. Follow these steps to enter a special character:

1. In Page view, click where you want the character to go.

2. Choose Insert ➢ Symbol. The Symbol dialog box appears.

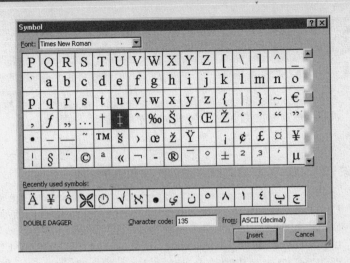

3. Locate the symbol you want to insert, click it, and then click the Insert button. The symbol appears in your document.

4. Click Close to close the dialog box and return to the Page view window when you're done.

MAKING PARAGRAPHS WORK

Words turn into sentences, and sentences have a habit of turning into paragraphs. When you reach the end of one line, text *wraps,* or moves down to continue on the next line. Press Enter to create a new paragraph.

In HTML, the language of the Web, paragraph breaks don't mean quite the same thing that they do on the printed page. Short of entering a few blank spaces, for example, indenting the first line of a paragraph is impossible. On most web pages, white space marks the end of one paragraph and the beginning of the next. Fastidious designers sometimes create the illusion of indents and other conventions of the printed page. The next few pages explain how fastidious designers do it.

By the way, a *paragraph* in FrontPage is simply all the text that comes before a paragraph break. A heading is a paragraph. So is a single line of text. Why do you need to know this? Because when you give a paragraph-formatting command, your command applies to all the text in the paragraph.

TIP

Paragraphs wrap from one line to the next, but where one line ends and the next begins usually has to do with browser settings and screen settings. Unless you press the Enter key or use another technique for breaking lines, lines break according to viewers' screen resolution and browser settings. Keep that in mind as you enter paragraphs on your web pages.

Inserting a Paragraph Break

In Page view, inserting a paragraph break is as simple as pressing the Enter key. FrontPage inserts a paragraph break, which is then marked in HTML by the <P> tag. If you click the HTML tab in Page view and examine the source code of your web page, you will see a <P> at the end of each paragraph where you pressed the Enter key. The <P> tag inserts a blank line and enters a line of blank space between one page element and the next.

Breaking a Line

Line breaks, represented as <BR> in HTML, can be used to format text when you want to end one line and continue it on the following line, without inserting a blank line between the items you're delineating. For example, suppose you are formatting the text of a poem, a recipe, a masthead, or a table of contents and you want a break but not a chasm of white space to appear between lines. Figure 20.18 shows a poem in Preview mode formatted with paragraph breaks, and the same poem below it, formatted with line breaks.

To insert a line break, follow these steps:

1. In Page view, click where you want the line break to appear.
2. Choose Insert ➤ Break. The Break dialog box appears.

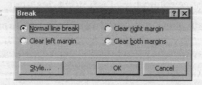

3. Select the Normal Line Break option button.
4. Click OK.

Paragraph breaks

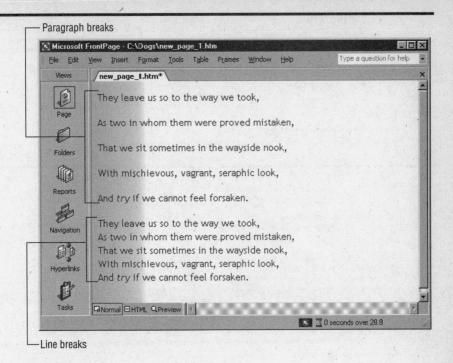

Line breaks

FIGURE 20.18: Paragraph breaks insert a line of white space between units of text, but line breaks simply break lines.

TIP

You can insert a line break quickly by holding down the Shift key and pressing Enter.

As a glance at the Break dialog box shows, you can break a line in several different ways. Figure 20.19, for example, shows an image with a caption. The first example is a normal line break, the second clears the left margin, the third clears the right margin, and the last example clears both margins. To format line breaks around images, choose Insert ➤ Break and select one of these options in the Break dialog box:

Select This...	To Do This...
Normal Line Break	Insert a regular line break between the image and the text.

Select This...	To Do This...
Clear Left Margin	Move the next line of text down until it clears the left margin of the image.
Clear Right Margin	Move the next line of text down until it clears the right margin of the image.
Clear Both Margins	Move the next line of text down until it clears both margins of the image.

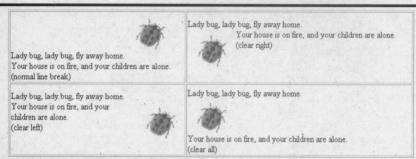

FIGURE 20.19: FrontPage offers more than one way to break a line.

Aligning Paragraphs

Figure 20.20 demonstrates the different ways that you can align text. Starting in Page view, follow these steps to tell FrontPage how you want to align the text:

1. To align a single paragraph, click the paragraph. To align multiple consecutive paragraphs, highlight all or part of the paragraphs to be aligned.

2. Click an Alignment button on the Standard toolbar or choose Format ➢ Paragraph and, in the Paragraph dialog box, select an option on the Alignment drop-down list.

TIP

Most, but not all, browsers can display justified text. A browser that can't display justified text left-aligns the text instead.

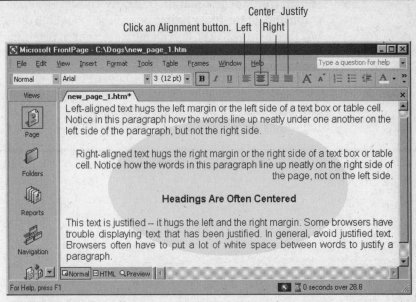

FIGURE 20.20: The different ways to align text on a web page

Indenting Paragraphs

Yes, it is possible to indent a paragraph from the left margin or right margin of a web page. Remember: A *paragraph* in FrontPage means any amount of text—a word, a heading, a Faulkneresque 500-word strung-together sentence. To indent a paragraph or paragraphs, follow these steps:

1. Click the paragraph if you want to indent it; to indent more than one paragraph, select all or part of each one.

2. Do one of the following:

    Indent from the left margin by clicking the Increase Indent button   You will find this button on the Formatting toolbar. Click it (or press Ctrl+M) and the paragraph(s) indent by 50 pixels from the left margin. You can click the button as many times as necessary to increase the amount of the indentation. To unindent a paragraph, click the Decrease Indent button (or press Ctrl+Shift+M).

Part vii

Indent from the left margin   Choose Format ➤ Paragraph and, in the Indentation area of the Paragraph dialog box (see Figure 20.21), enter a measurement in pixels in the Before Text text box.

Indent from the right margin   Choose Format ➤ Paragraph and, in the Indentation area of the Paragraph dialog box (see Figure 20.21), enter a measurement in pixels in the After Text text box.

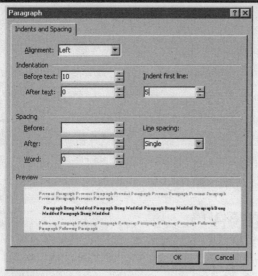

FIGURE 20.21: The Paragraph dialog box presents one way to handle paragraph indentations.

TIP

Centered paragraphs can't be indented. If you want a paragraph to be off-center, change its alignment to either left- or right-aligned (see the previous section, "Aligning Paragraphs") and then indent it.

The Paragraph dialog box (refer to Figure 20.21) calls for you to enter measurements in pixels. A pixel (the term stands for *picture element*) is a tiny dot that, together with thousands of other tiny dots, makes up the images you see on the computer screen. Most people's computer screens are either 640×480 or 800×600 pixels. If you indent by 50 pixels on a

640 × 480 screen, you indent by about one-twelfth the width of the screen; indent by 50 pixels on a 800 × 600 screen and you indent by about one-sixteenth the width of the screen.

TIP

Style sheets afford you much more control over the alignment and indentation of paragraphs.

Entering Nonbreaking Spaces

Plain spaces that you enter by pressing the spacebar are considered extraneous by most web browsers. If you put in a bunch of blank spaces one after another to try to format text, only one blank space will show up. Therefore, if you are serious about entering blank space, enter a *nonbreaking space*. FrontPage enters the HTML code   in your document, and that code tells the browser to indeed display blank spaces on-screen.

TIP

Like word processors, web browsers wrap text from one line to the next at spaces. They do not, however, wrap text at nonbreaking spaces; that's why they're called *nonbreaking*.

Suppose you work for ABC Computers and the company prefers that lines never break between "ABC" and "Computers." Type **ABC Computers** on a web page and the words may fall on one line, but if you enter a nonbreaking space between the words, "ABC Computers" will always appear on the same line. Similarly, phone numbers look bad if they are broken across two lines, but you can prevent that from happening with a nonbreaking space.

To insert a nonbreaking space, start in Page view and follow these steps:

1. Click to place the insertion point at the spot in the text where you want the nonbreaking space to be.

2. Click the HTML tab to see the HTML code in the web page.

3. Type the following: ** **.

Part vii

MAKING MULTIPLE PARAGRAPH BREAKS

Although you can stack line breaks (<br>), you can't stack paragraphs (<P>). Place several <P> tags in a row, and most web browsers will ignore everything after the first single <P> tag. If you need to enter a lot of blank space on a web page, use one of these methods:

▶ Combine one <P> tag and several <br> tags:

```
<P>
<br>
<br>
```

▶ Stack as many <br> tags as you want:

```
<br>
<br>
<br>
```

▶ Press Enter several times in a row in Page view to produce code that looks like this:

```
<P> </P>
<P> </P>
<P> </P>
<P> </P>
```

This code tells the web browser to leave several lines of white space, by creating a paragraph whose only character is a nonbreaking space.

This last method is particular only to WYSIWYG editors like FrontPage.

UNDERSTANDING THE HTML BEHIND YOUR WEB PAGE

So you have a website and at least one web page. You're ready to begin placing images on web pages, and eventually you'll be manipulating those images. But before we show you how to do those things, we feel you need to be able to view and understand the *way* your text and images are put on the page.

Besides showing you what your pages will look like, Page view allows you to work directly with the underlying HTML code—the code that tells the browser where to put text, images, and other media. Besides viewing pages, you can also peek under the virtual hood and enter HTML code yourself. What's more, you can enter HTML code that is not directly supported by FrontPage, check your work, and even make changes to a page's code.

To view the HTML code and perhaps edit it, switch to Page view and then click the HTML tab. The HTML source code for the document appears (see Figure 20.22). Now you can make changes by typing new or modified HTML directly into the page. You can also delete extraneous or unwanted HTML by highlighting the unwanted code and pressing the Delete key.

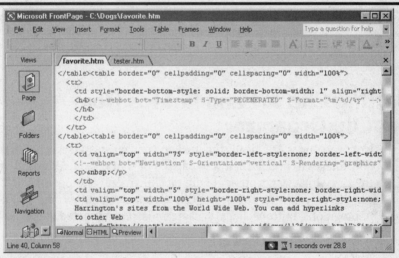

FIGURE 20.22: Looking under the hood at the HTML code

WARNING

Be careful: It is very easy to turn your functioning web page into a nonfunctioning page by deleting necessary code. This can result from something as simple as removing just one tag that you don't realize is required by FrontPage. This is why it's good to get some background in HTML. If you're interested in doing more hands-on work, check out *Mastering HTML 4, Premium Edition* by Deborah S. Ray, Eric J. Ray (Sybex, 1999).

When you are done and want to switch back to Normal view, simply click the Normal tab at the bottom of the Page view window. The contents of the window change to reflect the HTML editing you did.

WORKING WITH GRAPHICS

The Web consists of much more than just text. Today's website is designed to have a handful of graphics. To make web pages more compelling, you can include a clip art image from the Microsoft Clip Organizer, a graphic stored on your computer, or a graphic from the Internet. Better keep reading.

TIP

Graphics must be in the GIF or JPEG format to be viewed using most web browsers. If the images you want to use aren't in one of these two formats, use your favorite image editor to convert them to GIF or JPEG files.

Getting Clip Art and Photos from the Clip Organizer

Not everyone is artistically inclined and can create, or scan and manipulate, images to put on their web pages. For that reason, Microsoft offers the Clip Organizer, a library of digital clip art and photographs that you can use on your web pages. The Clip Organizer contains clip art images, photographs, buttons, lines, backgrounds, and animated graphics.

Follow these steps to place a clip art image or photograph on a web page:

1. In Page view, click where you want the graphic to go.

2. Choose Insert ➢ Picture ➢ Clip Art or click the Insert Clip Art button on the Drawing toolbar. The Insert Clip Art task pane appears (see Figure 20.23).

3. In the Search Text box, enter a keyword that describes the kind of graphic you want.

Enter a keyword.

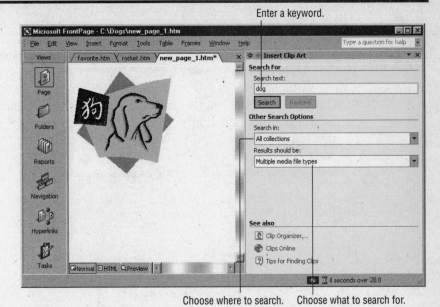

Choose where to search.   Choose what to search for.

FIGURE 20.23: Inserting a clip art image or photograph on a web page

4. Open the Search In drop-down list and check or uncheck boxes to tell FrontPage where to search for graphics.

My Collections   Graphics you have placed in the Favorites folder and any other folder you created.

Office Collections   Folders with graphics you installed when you installed FrontPage.

Web Collections   Folders on the Design Gallery Live website, a website that Microsoft maintains. You must be connected to the Internet to search web collections.

TIP

To search a folder and all its subfolders, double-click the folder's check box. You can tell when all the subfolders will be searched because three overlapping boxes appear where normally you see one check box.

5. Open the Results Should Be drop-down list and choose what kind of graphic (or multimedia file) you want. By clicking the plus sign (+) next to Clip Art, Photographs, Movies, or Sound, you can be more selective and choose what kind of file you want. Here, GIF and JPEG graphics are being sought.

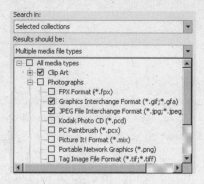

6. Click the Search button.

7. Scroll to and click an image to insert it on the web page.

If the graphic you need doesn't show up in the Insert Clip Art task pane, click the Modify button and start all over.

TIP

If you really like a piece of clip art and anticipate using it again, open its drop-down menu in the Insert Clip Art task pane and choose Copy To Collection on the drop-down menu. Then, in the Copy To Collection dialog box, select the Favorites folder or another folder of your choice and click OK.

After a graphic has landed on the page, you can drag it to a new location. To delete an image if you decide that you don't want it, click to select it and then press the Delete key.

TIP
If you can't drag an image and it stubbornly stays in the same place, display the Pictures toolbar and click the Position Absolutely button.

Putting Your Own Clip Art and Photographs on a Web Page

Chances are, you keep more than a few clip art images and photographs on your computer or on the network that your computer is connected to (if your computer is connected to a network). Remembering that GIF and JPEG graphics are the best choice for a web page because all browsers can display them easily, follow these steps to place an image of your own on a web page:

1. In Page view, click where you want the graphic to go.

2. Choose Insert ➤ Picture ➤ From File. The Picture dialog box appears.

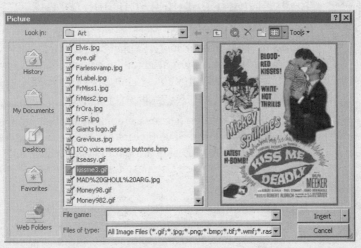

TIP
In the Picture dialog box, open the drop-down menu on the Views button and choose Preview. That way, the dialog box shows you what the images look like.

3. Select the graphic you want to place on your web page.

4. Click the Insert button.

Your image is there, displayed in the Page view window. You can drag it to a new location if you so desire. And if the image refuses to be dragged elsewhere, display the Pictures toolbar and click the Position Absolutely button.

WARNING

Grabbing images from other people's web pages is easy enough, but the legal ramifications of doing so aren't so simple. If the images are clearly marked as being public domain, and you are very confident that this is true, feel free to use them as you like. Otherwise, the author of the image holds copyright on it—and there are no exceptions to this rule of intellectual property. If you can't live without an image, send its owner an e-mail message and ask permission to use it.

BORROWING GRAPHICS YOU FIND ON THE INTERNET

You can copy a graphic you discover on the Internet to your computer and use it on your own web pages—provided, of course, that the graphic is not copyrighted and does not belong to someone else. Follow these instructions to borrow a graphic you discover in the course of your adventures as a web surfer:

► In Internet Explorer: To copy a graphic in Internet Explorer, right-click it and choose Save Picture As. You see the Save Picture dialog box. Find and select the folder where you want to save the graphic (and give it a new name, if you so desire). Then click the Save button.

► In Netscape Navigator: To copy a graphic in Netscape Navigator, right-click it and choose Save Image As. You see the Save File dialog box. Find and select the folder where you want to store the graphic file, and click the Save button.

The next section in this chapter explains how to copy a graphic to the images folder in your website. From there, you can make it a part of your website very easily.

Importing Many Graphics for Use in Your Website

Importing a graphic means to move it to a website folder so you can use it later on—not that you will use the graphic necessarily, but you will have easy access to it if you do decide to put it on a web page.

Follow these steps to import a graphic or graphics so you can use them later on:

1. In the Views bar, click the Folders icon to switch to Folders view. Now you can see the folders and files in your website.

TIP

When you create a website, FrontPage gives you a folder called *images*. Storing graphics there is a good idea. That way, you know where the graphics you want to use are located. You can, however, import graphics into any folder by selecting the folder in step 2.

2. In the Folder List, click the images folder to display its contents. The files in the images folder appear on the Contents side of the window.

3. Choose File ➤ Import. The Import dialog box appears.

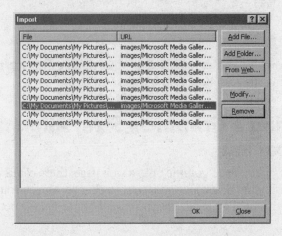

4. To add a single file to the images folder, click the Add File button. The Add File To Import List dialog box appears. Use it just like any other Open dialog box to locate and select the

graphic you want to import. When you're done, click Open to return to the Import dialog box, where you see the name of the file you just selected.

Or, to copy the entire contents of a folder to the images folder, click the Add Folder button. The File Open dialog box appears. Locate the folder on your hard drive or local network and select its icon. When you're done, click Open to return to the Import dialog box, where you'll see the names of all the files in the folder you just selected.

To add files from a website, click the From Web button. The Import Web Wizard appears. Simply follow the wizard through the necessary steps to import the file(s) you want right off the Web.

5. Repeat step 4 as often as you like until you've selected all the images you need.

TIP

The Import dialog box is for importing all kinds of documents, not just graphics. When you import the contents of a folder, for example, you get all its files, whether or not they are graphic files. In the Import dialog box, you can select a file and click the Remove button if it isn't a graphic file and you don't care to import it.

6. In the Import dialog box, click OK.

Now that you've imported all your graphic files into the images folder, putting the graphics on web pages will be a snap.

Changing a Graphic's Size, Alignment, and Spacing

After you insert a graphic onto a web page, there could very well be something about the graphic you want to change. Maybe you'd like to change its size or realign it. Maybe you would like to place a border around it.

To tinker with a graphic's properties, click to select the graphic and then open the Picture Properties dialog box (see Figure 20.24). Front-Page offers no fewer than four different ways to open the Picture Properties dialog box:

▶ Choose Format ➤ Properties.

▶ Double-click the graphic.

▶ Right-click and choose Picture Properties.

▶ Press Alt+Enter.

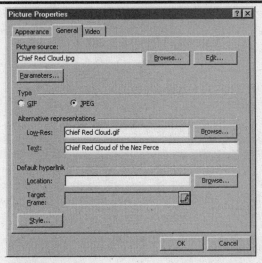

FIGURE 20.24: Go to the Picture Properties dialog box to tinker with a graphic's properties.

The General tab of the Picture Properties dialog box offers the following commands:

Type   Change the graphic type from GIF to JPEG or vice versa.

Low-Res   Some people configure their browsers to show low-resolution, black-and-white graphics in place of normal ones. To satisfy these users, click the Browse button under Type and choose a low-resolution or black-and-white graphic in the Select Alternate Picture dialog box.

Text   In the Text box, enter a description of the graphic. Someone who visits your web page and moves the mouse over the graphic will see the text you enter.

WARNING

It's very important to include alternate text for any image that will be visibly displayed. The reason for this is that many people accessing the Web cannot see or choose not to see images. Individuals in remote areas are often at the mercy of restricted bandwidth or older computer systems, necessitating text-only browsing, or browsing without images. Still others prefer fast access to information, so they will browse with the automatic image-loading feature in their browser turned off.

Default Hyperlink   These options (Location and Target Frame) have to do with frames.

Style button   Modify any sheet information included with the text by clicking the Style button. A new dialog box pops up, and you can make changes to the styles there.

Click the Appearance tab of the Picture Properties dialog box to tell FrontPage where you want the graphic to be on the page. Here are your options:

Wrapping Style   Choose the None, Left, or Right option to tell FrontPage what to do when text runs up against the graphic. Text can run around its left or right side. The None option leaves white space on either side of the graphic.

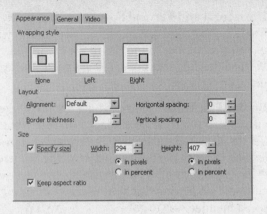

Layout Alignment   Choose alignment for the graphic. You can align the image according to the browser's default behavior (most browsers use Baseline as the default), in which case choose the Default setting. To choose another alignment, however, open the Alignment drop-down list and choose an option. Table 20.1 explains the options.

TABLE 20.1:   Layout Alignment Options in the Picture Properties Dialog Box

OPTION	WHAT IT DOES
Left	Places the graphic on the left side of the browser window, with text or other elements wrapped around the right side of the graphic.
Right	Places the graphic on the right side of the browser window, with text or other elements wrapped around the left side of the graphic.
Top	Aligns the top of the graphic with the top of the tallest element on the same line.
Texttop	Aligns the top of the graphic with the top of the tallest character on the same line.
Middle	Aligns the middle of the graphic with the middle of the surrounding text.
Absmiddle	Aligns the middle of the graphic with the middle of the largest item on the current line (stands for *absolute middle*).
Baseline	Aligns the bottom of the graphic with the imaginary line on which the surrounding text rests. Use this option to place a small image on a line of text.
Bottom	Aligns the bottom of the graphic with the bottom of the surrounding text (this is another name for *baseline*).
Absbottom	Aligns the bottom of the graphic with the bottom of the current line of text (stands for *absolute bottom*).
Center	Centers the graphic horizontally in the browser window.

Part VII

Horizontal and Vertical Spacing   You specify that the browser leave a margin of white space around your graphic by entering a number (in pixels) in the Horizontal Spacing and Vertical Spacing text boxes (10 is a good start; you can experiment from there).

Border Thickness   You can have a solid border appear around an image. If you'd like your image to include a border, type a number (in pixels) in the Border Thickness text box. Entering 0 (or leaving the text box empty) prevents the border from appearing at all. Borders around images can make a page look tight and cluttered, so leaving this setting empty or specifying 0 is the recommended way to go.

TIP

If you're concerned about the visual appearance of your pages (as well you should be!), be sure to place white space around your graphics. This is especially true when the surrounding text wraps around a graphic. If the text is too close to the graphic, the page will appear cramped and be difficult to read.

Size   Specifying the size of an image allows the browser to load the page more efficiently, because it can draw a placeholder while it is fetching the image itself. FrontPage automatically sets the image size when you first insert it, but if you want to resize the image, you can do so.

WARNING

Changing the size of a graphic in the Picture Properties dialog box is unwise. If you want to make a graphic larger or smaller, change the physical size of the image in an image editor before you place it on a web page. You can do this in almost any image editor. One of the rare exceptions to this good rule of thumb is when using single-pixel GIFs to fix table widths or create visual rules.

USING RULED LINES

Horizontal rules are pretty much what they sound like: horizontal lines that separate one part of a web page from another. You can insert ruled lines beneath document heads, between parts of a memo or article, or anywhere else you please. There are basically two kinds of ruled lines: horizontal rules created through the <HR> tag in HTML, and graphics that look like lines (and act to divide space) but don't share their HTML properties. Many of the decorative ruled lines that you have seen on the Web are probably graphics. Figure 20.25 shows several different ruled lines; the two at the bottom are graphic images.

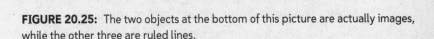

FIGURE 20.25: The two objects at the bottom of this picture are actually images, while the other three are ruled lines.

Standard HTML-based horizontal rules include a line of white space before and after the line itself, and their properties include height, width, and the option of 3D shading. When you insert a horizontal rule, you get an engraved line that's centered on the page and occupies 100 percent of the width of the window. You can then change the look and properties of this line; additional lines you create after adjusting the properties of that line will continue to look like it until you reset their properties.

Drawing a ruled line in Page view is quite easy. In the following pages, you find out how to draw a line, adjust the properties of a line and in so doing alter its appearance, and use a graphic image as a ruled line.

Inserting a Ruled Line

Follow these steps to drop a ruled line onto a web page:

1.   In Page view, click where you want the ruled line to appear.

2.   Choose Insert ➢ Horizontal Line. A horizontal line appears across the page.

That's easy enough, isn't it?

TOO MANY LINES SPOIL THE WEB PAGE

You might be tempted to put fancy, flashy, engraved, colorful, beveled dividing lines all over your web pages. Don't do it!

Dropping ruled lines onto a page is easy, but many a website developer forgets the purpose of ruled lines: helping people read and comprehend the message of the website. Instead of using ruled lines, try a few other tricks. Generally, white space works as well as a ruled line when it comes to dividing one part of a web page from another. When working with blocks of text, you might also try using different alignments (left, right, and center) in combination. Consider using different text colors to make one paragraph stand out. Or indent text and tables to help distinguish different parts of a page.

Ruled lines are fine, but use them sparingly.

Changing the Look of a Ruled Line

In our opinion, the plain, engraved, ruled line you get by default breaks up a page too dramatically. To soften the line, change its thickness, give it a different color, or change its properties. Follow these steps to do so:

1. Either double-click the line or right-click it and choose Horizontal Line Properties. You see the Horizontal Line Properties dialog box.

WARNING

If you selected a theme for your website, you can't change the look of a ruled line. Sorry. The line is part of the theme and can't be changed.

2. Enter new measurements in the Width and Height text boxes to change the length and height of the line. Make these choices as well:

   ▶ To enter a measurement relative to the window, click the In Percent option button.

   ▶ To enter a measurement in pixels, click the In Pixels option button.

3. By default, ruled lines appear in the center of the page, but you can make them run to the left or right margin by selecting the Left or Right option button under Alignment.

4. If you want the line to stand out more, choose a new color from the Color drop-down menu.

5. If you'd like to remove the beveling (the 3D shading) from your line, place a check mark in the Solid Line (No Shading) check box.

6. For advanced users who are using style sheets, you can modify the rule with style information. Click the Style button to open the Modify Style dialog box. Use this dialog box to change the rule.

7. Click OK.

ABOUT PIXELS AND PERCENTAGES

When you're choosing the size for a web page element, you're often given two choices for the unit of measure: percentage or pixels. *Percentage* means that the measurement is drawn to occupy a certain portion of the available screen size—usually the screen's width.

Pixels are actually (and generally) a unit of projected light. There's no precise size for pixels; a pixel is just a dot of light on a screen. Televisions and computer screens both use pixels as their basic unit of measure, although the pixels on a TV screen are generally much bigger than those on computer screens. The higher the resolution of the medium, the smaller the pixels are.

When you're using pixels as your unit of measure, you should realize two things: One pixel is pretty small, but it's not invisible; and pixels are different sizes when viewed on screens of different sizes or resolutions. The lowest-resolution screens these days are 640 pixels by 480 pixels (640 × 480). In recent years, screens with a resolution of 800 × 600 and even 1024 × 768 pixels have become more common. Some high-end computers come with screens of much higher resolution; they'll have lots more pixels.

In designing web pages, you ought to consider the size of screen you'll generally design for (this goes back to what sorts of machines you expect your audience to have). You'll also want to consider this in choosing a pixel size for elements that appear on your pages.

Using a Graphic as a Ruled Line

As you know, when you create web pages, you are actually creating HTML codes; you just don't see it that way while you're doing the deed. Instead of typing in the code—the HTML instructions for how a page should look—you create the text, images, and other objects, making them look as you want them to appear to users. All the while, little HTML elves work behind the scenes to write the code that allows those instructions to be carried out by the user's browser software. A simple ruled line is just that—simple. It does not show up as a string of teddy bears holding hands, a multicolored zigzag line, or anything very fancy at all. You might wonder how to create such nifty effects. The answer is simple: These are not really ruled lines, but graphics masquerading as ruled lines.

Using graphics for ruled lines involves different HTML. Horizontal rules in HTML are represented by the <HR> tag, which can include other attributes (such as height and color—we described creating and modifying a ruled line like this in the previous sections).

You can insert an image that *acts* and *looks* like a ruled line quite easily. In fact, the Clip Organizer comes with an assortment of images intended for this purpose. It's best to start with an image that's pretty long and narrow, but even that's not a prerequisite. You can use an image of your own or a line from the Clip Organizer.

Getting a Ruled Line from the Clip Organizer

Follow these steps to get a ruled line from the Clip Organizer:

1. In Page view, click where you want the line to appear.

2. Choose Insert ➤ Picture ➤ Clip Art, or click the Insert Clip Art button on the Drawing toolbar. The Insert Clip Art task pane appears. To search for ruled lines, leave the Search Text box blank and look in categories instead.

3. Open the Search In drop-down menu and, by choosing categories, tell FrontPage that you want to look for ruled lines. Web Collections offers ruled lines in these categories: Dividers & Decorations and Web Dividers.

TIP

Earlier in this chapter, "Getting Clip Art and Photos from the Clip Organizer" explained in detail how to search in the Insert Clip Art task pane.

4. Open the Results Should Be drop-down menu and select Clip Art in the All Media Types folder.

5. Click the Search button. Ruled lines and other decorations appear in the task pane (see Figure 20.26).

6. Click a ruled line to enter it on the web page.

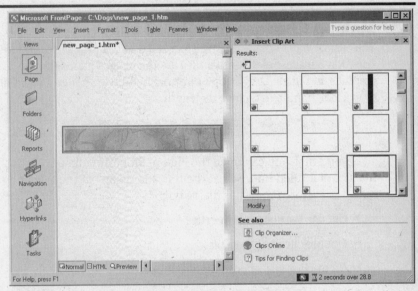

FIGURE 20.26: Getting a ruled line from the Clip Organizer

Using a Ruled Line of Your Own

You can create your own images to use as graphical lines. For that matter, you can find them in clip art collections on the Web. Either way, you can insert a ruled line you've stored on your computer onto a web page by following these steps:

1. In Page view, choose Insert ➤ Picture ➤ From File or click the Insert Picture From File button on the Drawing toolbar. The Picture dialog box appears.

2. Locate and select the ruled-line graphic. Be sure to open the drop-down menu on the Views button and choose Preview to get a good look at the lines.

3. Click the Insert button.

TIP

Earlier in this chapter, "Importing Many Graphics for Use in Your Website" explained how to keep graphics on hand in the images folder so you can find them easily when you need them for a website. Try putting a few ruled lines in the images folder and using them as you need them. You'll save time that way.

Making Changes to a Ruled Line

The easiest way to make changes to a ruled line is to select it and drag a selection handle. Selection handles are the black squares that appear on graphics and lines. Drag a top or bottom handle to change a line's height; drag a side handle to change its length.

Beyond that, you can open the Picture Properties dialog box to change the size of a ruled line. Select the line and do any of the following to open the Picture Properties dialog box:

▶ Choose Format ➤ Properties.

▶ Double-click the graphic.

▶ Right-click and choose Picture Properties.

▶ Press Alt+Enter.

On the Appearance tab, enter Width and Height settings to change the size of the ruled line. For example, if you'd like your graphical line to take up 90 percent of the width of the window, click the In Percent option button (under Width), and then type **90** in the Width text box. If you'd like the line to be a certain number of pixels wide, click the In Pixels option button, and then type a number in the Width text box. You can adjust the height of your image in the same way.

If your image looks a little funny or is not what you had in mind, keep playing with it by repeating the steps above until you get it right.

TIP

To quickly change the alignment of a ruled line, select it and click one of these alignment buttons on the Formatting toolbar: Align Left or Align Right.

CREATING BACKGROUNDS FOR WEB PAGES

The background of a web page really sets the tone. A subdued background, a flashy background, a bright background—and let's not forgot no background at all—tell you a lot about a website or a web page. Read on to find out how to choose background color for a web page, use a graphic in the background, and decorate a page or website with a theme, a ready-made design from Microsoft.

Choosing a Background Color

Being able to choose a single background color for a web page is great—but it's also a potential design pitfall. Take care when designing pages that you choose simple, harmonious color schemes. Not many people, for example, bother to read a web page with orange text superimposed over a bright-green golf course.

WARNING

If you chose a theme for your website, you can't change the background color.

Follow these steps to choose a background color for a web page:

1. In Page view, choose Format ➢ Background or right-click and choose Page Properties. You see the Background tab of the Page Properties dialog box (see Figure 20.27).

2. Open the Colors/Background drop-down menu and choose a color. To choose a color apart from the default colors, select More Colors at the bottom of the drop-down menu. The More Colors dialog box appears. Choose a color there and click OK.

WARNING

Choosing a color from outside the default range can be problematic for older browsers. The default color palette in FrontPage is made up of a series of colors referred to as *browser-safe* or *web-safe* colors. These colors are well suited to different browsers, computer platforms, and hardware types. It's always best to stick with a browser-safe color selection.

3. Click OK to apply the background color you just chose.

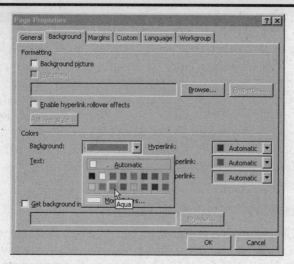

FIGURE 20.27: Use the Background tab of the Page Properties dialog box to change the color of your pages.

Choosing a Background Graphic for Web Pages

Choosing a background graphic is quite similar to specifying a background color. The graphic you choose should be subtle and serve the purpose its name suggests—a background for the text on the page. Web browsers that can display background images *tile* the graphic. As shown in Figure 20.28, the graphic is repeated over and over until it fills the browser window completely (no matter what size the user's browser window is). If you've ever changed your Windows Desktop wallpaper, you're probably familiar with the concept of tiled images.

Follow these steps to choose a background graphic for a web page:

1. In Page view, choose Format ➤ Background or right-click and choose Page Properties. The Background tab of the Page Properties dialog box appears (refer back to Figure 20.27).

2. Click to enter a check mark in the Background Picture check box.

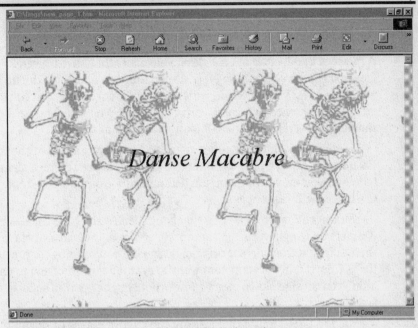

FIGURE 20.28: Example of a tiled background graphic

3. In the Background Image text box, type the full path name of the location for the background image you want to use, or click the Browse button and select the graphic you want to see in the Select Background Picture dialog box.

4. If you're using a large image for your background (an image that takes up a screenful or so of page real estate), consider placing a check mark in the Watermark check box to make the graphic stationary. Watermarks don't scroll along with any text or other page elements in the latest browsers; instead, they remain anchored on the page while everything else scrolls by.

5. Click OK.

Double-check the graphic to make sure it is a suitable background for the page. To do so, save your web page and click the Preview tab in Page view. While you're at it, choose File ➢ Preview In Browser to see what the page looks like in a genuine web browser.

Part vii

Choosing a Theme for Web Pages and Websites

A *theme* is a collection of page design elements that have a given look and feel. You can save yourself a lot of design time by choosing a theme for a web page or for your entire website. The professional artists at Microsoft created the themes that come with FrontPage. When you choose a theme, you get a professional-looking web page or website.

Themed pages have a banner image and a navigation bar at the top. Each has an attractive background. To get you started, themes include labels so you know what you are dealing with. Your job is to replace the labels with genuine text.

You can choose from among the many themes and base the design of your site on whichever seems appropriate. The only disadvantage to themes is that they are not original designs. If you're going for practical, that's fine, but if you want your website to stand out, you need to use or refine your design skills, or get a professional to help with the look and feel of your site.

You don't *have* to use themes. You can change horses in the middle of the theme, or you can start with a theme or two or more and then do away with themes on your pages altogether. Furthermore, you can select a theme for an entire website or a single page.

Follow these steps to apply a theme to a single web page or an entire website:

1. If your goal is to apply a theme to a single page, open that page (if you want to apply a theme to the whole site, go straight to step 2).

2. In Page view, choose Format ➤ Theme. The Themes dialog appears (see Figure 20.29).

3. Under Apply Theme To, choose the All Pages option button to apply the theme throughout your website; choose Selected Page(s) to apply a theme to a single page.

4. Browse the list of themes that appears along the left side of the dialog box and select one you like. A preview of that theme appears in the window's right side so you can see what you're in for.

5. Make sure the All Pages option button is selected.

Choose a theme.

Apply a theme to the website or to a single page.

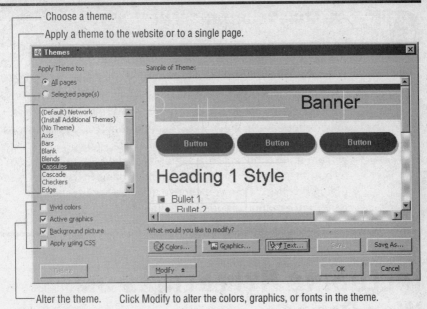

Alter the theme.   Click Modify to alter the colors, graphics, or fonts in the theme.

FIGURE 20.29: The Themes dialog box allows you to select and modify themes.

TIP

You can modify the look of any given theme to include a background color instead of a background image, to include colors that are more vivid or less vivid, or to use animated (*active*) buttons and images. To adjust these properties, select (or deselect) the check boxes marked Vivid Colors, Active Graphics, or Background Picture. Advanced users interested in adding style sheet information to control the appearance of the page can check the Apply Using CSS check box, too.

6. Click OK when you are ready to apply a theme to the entire website.

If you regret applying a theme, follow the same procedure for applying the theme, but in step 4, instead of choosing a theme, select No Theme.

If you'd like to remove the banners and buttons and such that are on your page and start with more or less a clean slate, just select the bits you want to remove with your mouse and then press the Delete key.

CREATING YOUR OWN THEME

To create your own theme, open the Themes dialog box (see Figure 20.29) and select the theme that most resembles one you want to create. Then click the Modify button. Five new buttons appear in the Themes dialog box—Colors, Graphics, Text, Save, and Save As.

Click the Colors, Graphics, or Text button and a Modify Theme dialog box appears. In the Modify Theme dialog box, you can choose a new color for part of a theme, new graphics, and new fonts. When you are done choosing colors, graphics, and fonts, click the Save As button and enter a name for your new theme in the Save Theme dialog box. Next time you choose a theme for a website or web page, you can choose your new theme in the Theme list.

INCLUDING HYPERLINKS ON WEB PAGES

Hyperlinks, or just plain *links*, probably constitute the biggest difference between the Web and other media. You can't click a map on TV, an author's name in a magazine, or a song title in a book and expect to go anyplace.

As you're undoubtedly aware if you've been on the Web for even 15 minutes, a link can point to any address on the Internet. Click a link and you go to another web page, another place on the same web page, or another website altogether. Sometimes you click a link to download a file, hear a sound, or play a video. Click certain links and your e-mail software opens so you can send an e-mail message.

The following pages explain how to create hyperlinks to these places:

▶ A different page in your website (that is, to the top of the page)

▶ A specific location on a different page in your website (for example, the middle of the page)

▶ A different place on the same web page (for example, somewhere further down the page)

- Another web page on the Internet

- A *mail-to hyperlink* (a hyperlink that opens the clicker's default e-mail program so he or she can send you an e-mail message)

First, however, a few basic instructions for creating hyperlinks.

Creating a Hyperlink: the Basics

No matter what kind of hyperlink you want to create, follow these basic steps:

1. In Page view, select the item that will serve to launch the hyperlink. You can select a word, a phrase, or a graphic.

2. Choose Insert ➤ Hyperlink, click the Hyperlink button on the Standard toolbar, or press Ctrl+K. The Insert Hyperlink dialog box appears (see Figure 20.30).

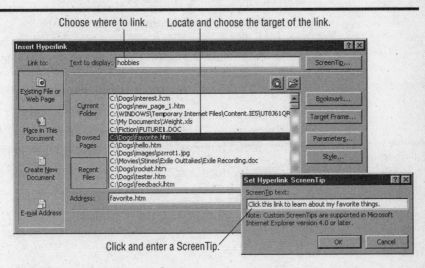

FIGURE 20.30: Creating a hyperlink

3. Click the ScreenTip button and enter a phrase or a short sentence in the Set Hyperlink ScreenTip dialog box that describes the who, the what, or the where of your hyperlink. When a visitor moves the pointer over your completed hyperlink, he

or she will see the text you enter and decide whether to click the link.

where you will find a list of my favorite things.

Click this link to learn about my favorite things.

4. Under Link To, choose what kind of hyperlink you want to create:

Different page in your website   Click the Existing File Or Web Page icon under Link To, and then locate the web page you want to link to. See "Linking to a Different Page in Your Website" later in this chapter for details.

Different place on the same web page   Click the Bookmark button. In the Select Place In Document dialog box, select a bookmark. See "Linking to a Different Place on the Same Web Page" later in this chapter for details.

Specific location on a different page in your site
Locate the web page you want to link to, and then click the Bookmark button. In the Select Place In Document dialog box, select a bookmark. See "Linking to a Specific Place on a Different Web Page" later in this chapter for details.

Another web page on the Internet   Enter the address of the web page in the Address text box. See "Linking to a Web Page on the Internet" later in this chapter for details.

Mail-to link   Under Link To, click the E-Mail Address icon. Fill in the Edit Hyperlink dialog box and click OK. See "Creating Links to E-Mail Addresses" later in this chapter for details.

5. Click OK.

After you create a hyperlink, be sure to test it. To do so, click the Preview tab in Page view, and then click the link. If it doesn't work or if it goes to the wrong location, click the Normal tab in Page view, then right-click the link and choose Hyperlink Properties on the shortcut menu. You see the Edit Hyperlink dialog box, where you can alter the link (it works exactly like the Insert Hyperlink dialog box shown in Figure 20.30). To remove a link, click the Remove Link button in the Edit Hyperlink dialog box.

Linking to a Different Page in Your Website

Read "Creating a Hyperlink: the Basics," the previous section in this chapter, to get a general idea of how to create a hyperlink. In the Insert Hyperlink dialog box (refer back to Figure 20.30), do the following to create a link to a different page in your website:

- ▶ Click the Existing File Or Web Page icon under Link To.

- ▶ Click the Current Folder button, locate the web page you want to link to, and select it. As long as the Current Folder button is selected, the Insert Hyperlink dialog box works like an Open dialog box. You can click the Up One Folder button, open the Look In drop-down menu, or click the Browse For File button to navigate on your hard drive and locate the web page.

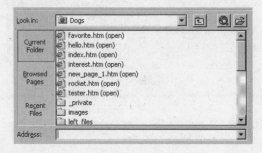

TIP

If you opened the web page recently, try clicking the Recent Files button to see a list of files and select the web page there.

Creating a Bookmark so You Can Link to a Specific Place

Suppose you want to create a hyperlink, not to the top of a web page, but to a place in the middle of a web page. To link to a specific location, either on the page where the hyperlink is located or on a different page in your website, you have to mark the target of the hyperlink with a bookmark. Later, when you create the link, FrontPage gives you the opportunity to choose a bookmark to link to. Someone who clicks the link will go, not to the top of the page, but to the bookmark you created in the middle of the page.

Follow these steps to create a bookmark that can be used to create a hyperlink:

1. Open the web page where you want to place a bookmark and click the location where you want others to go when they click the hyperlink. In other words, click the spot that others will see when they activate a hyperlink.

2. Choose Insert ➤ Bookmark or press Ctrl+G. The Bookmark dialog box appears.

3. Enter a name for your bookmark in the Bookmark Name text box and click OK.

A small flag appears next to the text you selected in step 1, indicating that this text has been bookmarked.

TIP

To delete a bookmark, select Insert ➤ Bookmark. In the Bookmark dialog box, select the bookmark you want to delete and click the Clear button. Click the Goto button to go to a bookmark on your web page.

Linking to a Different Place on the Same Web Page

To link to a different place on the same web page, read "Creating a Hyperlink: the Basics," earlier in this chapter, to get a general idea of how to create a hyperlink. If necessary, read "Creating a Bookmark so You Can Link to a Specific Place" as well. It explains bookmarks and how to mark the target of a hyperlink with a bookmark.

Knowing that the place to which you want to link has been book-marked, select the hyperlink text or graphic, click the Bookmark button, or choose Insert ➤ Hyperlink and, in the Insert Hyperlink dialog box (refer back to Figure 20.30), click the Place In This Document icon under Link To. You see a list of the bookmarks on the web page. Select the bookmark that marks the target of your hyperlink and click OK.

Linking to a Specific Place on a Different Web Page

Before you can link to a place on the middle or bottom of a different page in your website, you must mark the place with a bookmark. (See "Creating a Bookmark so You Can Link to a Specific Place," earlier in this chapter. Read as well "Creating a Hyperlink: the Basics," earlier in this chapter, if you need instructions about hyperlinks and how to open the Insert Hyperlink dialog box.)

In the Insert Hyperlink dialog box (refer back to Figure 20.30), do the following to create a hyperlink to a specific place on a different web page:

1. Click the Existing File Or Web Page icon under Link To.

2. Click the Current Folder button. Using the tools in the dialog box, locate the web page with the bookmark you want to link to.

3. Click the Bookmark button. The Select Place In Document dialog box opens. It lists the names of bookmarks on the web page you selected.

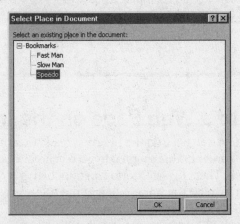

4. Select a bookmark and click OK.

Part vii

RELATIVE VS. ABSOLUTE HYPERLINK ADDRESSES

Not that you have to be too concerned about it, because FrontPage handles hyperlinks in the background, but there are only two kinds of hyperlink addresses: relative and absolute.

Relative addresses contain only a filename, its extension, and possibly its location within the file directory. The URL of a relative address points to a file that resides on the same web server as your website. For example, when you're linking from one page to another within the same folder on your website, you can simply point to its filename: figs.html. If you're in your main folder and you want to link to a graphic in the images folder, you can point to that with a relative address, too. It would look like this: images/figs.gif.

Using relative addresses is a good practice when you're linking items on the same website, because relative addresses make it much easier for you to maintain a website. If you've used relative addresses, you can move files from one folder on a web server to another without having to make major changes to your HTML.

On the other hand, if you were to spell out the entire URL, such as http://www.mysite.com/figs.html, you'd be using an absolute address instead. *Absolute* addresses start with http://, ftp://, or another protocol type. (A protocol is an agreed-upon way of doing things. HTTP is the name of the protocol for web pages, for example.) The protocol is then followed by the rest of a full URL. The term *absolute* indicates that not only the name of the document on a server is given, but the full, exact, honest-to-goodness location of the entire server itself is also spelled out.

Generally, links that point to *local* resources—items on the same server—use relative links, while links that point out into cyberspace use absolute links.

Linking to a Web Page on the Internet

To link to a web page on the Internet, read "Creating a Hyperlink: the Basics," earlier in this chapter, to get a general idea of how to create a hyperlink. Then, in the Insert Hyperlink dialog box, enter the URL of the page with which you want to link in the Address text box. FrontPage offers these shortcuts for entering the URL:

▶ Click the Browse The Web button to open your web browser, and then go to the web page you want to link to. When you return to the Insert Hyperlink dialog box, the address of the web page appears in the Address text box. The Browse The Web button is the small button with a picture of a globe on it.

▶ Choose a URL from the Address drop-down menu.

▶ Click the Browsed Pages button to see a list of pages you visited in the last 90 days, and select the page if you can remember it.

Creating Links to E-Mail Addresses

After web addresses, the most common type of address you'll want to provide a link to is your e-mail address. When someone clicks the link, his or her default e-mail software opens. Your e-mail address is entered automatically in an e-mail message, as is a subject for the message.

Follow these steps to create a link to an e-mail address:

1. In Page view, type something to indicate that the link will lead to you—your name, or the words *webmaster*, *mail me*, *feedback*, or whatever you like. Type it wherever you want it to appear on the page, and then highlight it.

2. Choose Insert ➢ Hyperlink, press Ctrl+K, or click the Insert Hyperlink button. The Insert Hyperlink dialog box appears.

3. Under Link To, click the E-Mail Address icon. As shown in Figure 20.31, the Insert Hyperlink dialog box offers new options for creating a mail-to link.

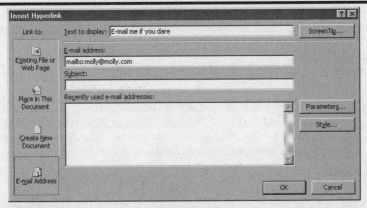

FIGURE 20.31: Creating a mail-to hyperlink

4. In the E-Mail Address text box, type your full e-mail address, which should look like this: *user@site.com*. FrontPage places the word *mailto:* before the address.

5. In the Subject text box, enter a subject for the message.

TIP

You don't have to enter a subject, but by doing so, you spare others the trouble of entering it. What's more, when others send you e-mail messages, you will recognize the subject and know what the messages are about.

6. Click OK.

Now, when your page is loaded onto the Web and someone clicks the link to your e-mail address, they'll be able to send you a message and tell you how cool you are.

QUITTING FRONTPAGE

More than one website can be open at the same time. When more than one is open, each has a button on the Taskbar. Click a Taskbar button to switch from one website to another. To close a website, either click its Close button (the *X* in the upper-right corner of the FrontPage window) or choose File ➢ Close Web.

Follow these steps to close FrontPage and call it a day:

1. Choose File ➢ Exit or press Alt+F4.

2. If you didn't save your work before giving the Exit command, a dialog box asks whether to save your work. Click Yes or No.

TIP

As mentioned earlier, the last website you worked on appears on-screen when you start FrontPage, but if you prefer not to see the last one you worked on, choose Tools ➢ Options, select the General tab in the Options dialog box, and uncheck the Open Last Web Automatically When FrontPage Starts check box.

Part vi

What's Next

In the upcoming chapter, you'll advance your web page development skills further by learning how to add images to your web pages.

Adding such images requires the ability to manipulate those images before they are included and to control how they appear on your pages. You'll learn about this, too.

Chapter 21

ADDING IMAGES TO YOUR WEB PAGES

A dding images to web pages can be very effective and also sounds like an easy task—and it can be just that.

However, even professionally designed websites sometimes don't always utilize images to optimize results. As a consequence, precious space on a page may be lost if an image isn't properly cropped or sized to fit, and the page may take too long to load through a slower Internet connection if one very large graphic or multiple large graphics (large, in terms of file size) are used. Images also don't always look through a browser the way they did through your desktop viewer. All these factors must be considered in the process of adding images to your web pages.

Read on to learn more.

Adapted from *Mastering HTML 4, Premium Edition*
by Deborah S. Ray, Eric J. Ray

ISBN 0-7821-2524-7   1216 pp $49.99

DEVELOPING IMAGES

Although images add life to your web pages, they can become a liability if not developed properly. For example, images can take F-O-R-E-V-E-R to load, becoming an obstacle for your visitors. Likewise, images can unnecessarily hog page space (or disk space), perhaps obscuring important content. So, your goal in using images is to develop them properly by considering three things:

- ▶ File size
- ▶ Physical dimensions
- ▶ File type

Determining File Size

Think of image files as being three-dimensional, having height and width as well as a number of colors. For example, a 16-color image not only has height and width, which you can see on the screen, but it also has 16 *layers*, one for each color. Therefore, the image's basic file size equals width × height × color depth.

You can reduce file size and, therefore, make your images as efficient as possible, with the following techniques:

- ▶ Reduce the number of colors. For example, you can reduce the color depth of an image that has millions of colors to only 256 colors with surprisingly little degradation in quality.

- ▶ Reduce the physical image size. For example, you can reduce an image from 600 × 400 pixels to 300 × 200 pixels. The resulting smaller image includes the details and clarity of the larger size, yet it occupies significantly less disk space. (You'll find guidelines for sizing images in the following section, "Dealing with Physical Size.")

- ▶ Use a format that *compresses* the file to cram more data into less space. (You'll find more details about suitable image formats in the section "Understanding Image Formats," later in this chapter.)

Dealing with Physical Size

The physical size of an image is its height and width and affects not only how it appears in a browser, but also how quickly it loads. Just how big should images be? Well, that depends. Many sites use itty-bitty images, such as buttons and icons, that effectively add color or dimension to a web page. Other sites use larger graphics for logos or button bars, which are also effective. There's no "right" size for images; instead, the key is to consider the following:

▶ The image's purpose

▶ The overall page design

▶ Your visitors' computer settings

Considering Image Purpose

Every time you add an image to a page, you need a good reason for doing so—to illustrate a point, to show a person or a location, to outline a process, or simply to add some color and zest to an otherwise humdrum document. Be sure that every image enhances content, design, or both.

When determining the size of an image, consider its importance. For example, if your visitors need an image to understand a concept, the image should be larger. On the other hand, an image that merely adds a splash of color should probably be a bit smaller. If you're not sure how important an image is, lean toward smaller. Remember, images add to loading time and can affect how easily a visitor can access your pages.

Considering Page Design

Images are visually "weighty" objects—that is, they attract attention faster than other page elements. Images that are too large often over-whelm page contents and obscure the message. When determining image size, in particular, consider how the image will appear relative to other page elements. Here are some questions to ask yourself:

▶ Will the page include multiple graphics?

▶ Will the page incorporate borders and shading, which are also weightier than text?

▶ Will the page contain a substantive amount of text or only a few words? Text can make up in volume what it lacks in visual weight. A lot of text balances a graphic more effectively than a small amount of text.

Considering Visitors' Computer Settings

Your visitors' computer settings will also affect how images appear on-screen. An image that's 600 × 400 pixels will take up practically the entire screen at a resolution of 640 × 480. But that same image will take up much less screen space on a computer set to 1280 × 1040. A good rule of thumb is to limit image size to no more than 600 × 400 pixels. An image of this size will fit completely within the browser window on Windows computers using the lowest (and, unfortunately, still quite common) screen resolution of 640 × 480 pixels. And, of course, if you can make images smaller, do so to help speed loading time.

TIP

To convey content adequately, few images need to be larger than 600 × 400. Something in the 300 × 200 pixels range is usually a good size for photographs, and buttons are generally 50 × 50 pixels or smaller.

Understanding Image Formats

When developing images, you should also consider your format options. Basically, you can use GIF, JPG, or PNG formats, depending on what you want to do.

Understanding GIF

The most common image format is GIF (pronounced with a *j* sound, as in *jiffy*), which is an acronym formed from Graphics Interchange Format, developed by CompuServe for online use. If you're browsing in your image-editing software's Save As options, you'll notice that the GIF file format has two versions: 87a and 89a. You'll want to choose version 89a, which includes the following features.

GIF Supports Transparency

Transparency sets an image's background color to the browser's background color, thereby making the image appear as if it has no background. For example, the ASR Outfitters logo shown in Figure 21.1 is a transparent image—the corner areas are a different color and set to be transparent. Figure 21.1 shows this image as it appears in an image-editing program (Paint Shop Pro); even if you set the background as transparent, you can still see it. Figure 21.2 shows this image as it appears in a browser (Internet Explorer).

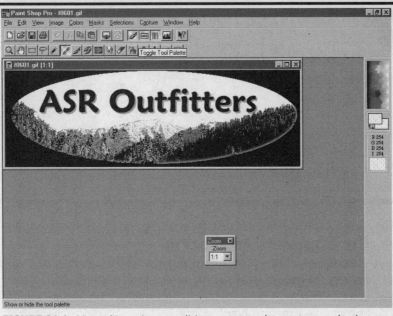

FIGURE 21.1: Viewed in an image-editing program, the transparent background is still visible.

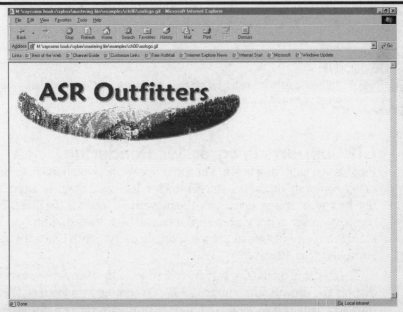

FIGURE 21.2: Viewed in a browser, the transparent background is not visible.

Part vii

ABOUT THESE IMAGES

First, the image shown in Figures 21.1 and 21.2 is about 600 pixels wide, and it is almost overwhelming when viewed in a browser at common resolutions.

Second, the background of the image is pure white, and the visible area within the oval is almost, but not quite, white. We had to change the background color to make transparency apparent on the printed page. When you create transparent images, you might find it useful to set the transparent color to an unusual color, thus making it easier to see at a glance what is supposed to be transparent.

GIF Supports Animation

Some image-editing programs and specialized programs can combine several GIF images into a single file, which then displays each image or panel in turn. The effect is rather like that in cartoon flip books—you flip the pages and see an illusion of motion.

Not all browsers display animated GIFs, although most commonly used browsers support them. Using animated GIFs is a simple way to provide animation without resorting to Java applets or to more sophisticated plug-ins.

TIP

Animated GIFs are much larger than nonanimated GIFs, containing the equivalent of an additional image for each panel of animation.

GIF Supports Progressive Rendering

Progressive rendering is also known as *interlacing*, which refers to how an image comes up on the screen. A browser displays a noninterlaced image line by line, as it is received over the network or loaded off a disk. The complete image is not visible until it has all been loaded. A browser displays interlaced images in passes, filling in every eighth line until the entire image is displayed.

The effects of interlacing vary from browser to browser. Some browsers display the downloading image as slowly coming into focus. Other browsers display it as venetian blinds slowly being opened until the entire image is displayed. Either way, interlaced images begin to appear on the screen faster than noninterlaced images and allow visitors who are familiar with the image to get the gist before the whole image appears.

GIF Supports Lossless Compression

Lossless compression is an efficient way to save files without losing image details. When GIFs are saved, they are compressed to take less space on the disk and less time to download. With lossless compression, the compression algorithm notices broad expanses of single colors, and, instead of recording the color for each individual pixel, it indicates the color and the number of times to repeat the color. The image is not changed; it is simply saved more efficiently. Because GIF compression is lossless, GIF images are best for line art, icons, and drawings.

NOTE

GIFs do have one significant disadvantage—they can include only 256 colors, which is not sufficient for true photographic quality. Although for many purposes 256 colors is adequate, you may want to use the JPG file format for images requiring higher quality.

Understanding JPG/JPEG

JPG, which is pronounced *jay-peg*, is an acronym formed from Joint Photographic Experts Group. This image format (often written as JPEG) is the second most popular for images on the Web. As a whole, JPG images are less flexible than GIF images, and most significantly, they do not support the variety of rendering options that GIFs support.

TIP

Although JPG supports progressive rendering, the most common browsers do not take advantage of this feature.

The most significant advantage of JPG is that it supports millions of colors, thereby providing much more realistic photographic reproduction. Additionally, because JPG images use a more effective—but lossy—compression algorithm, they are much smaller and download faster. *Lossy compression* discards some details of the image to decrease the file size. JPG images are best for photographs because the loss of detail is less noticeable with photographs than with line art; plus, the compression ratio and resulting quality are much better with photographs.

Setting JPG options in your image-editing program helps control both the eventual file size and the quality. In many image-editing programs, you can set the number of dots per inch (dpi) and the level of JPG compression. If the images are only for web use—they won't be used for print publications—a dpi of 100 is more than adequate. Depending on the image, the application, and the eventual purpose for the image, you can often increase the compression substantially without losing much detail.

Understanding PNG

PNG, pronounced *ping*, stands for Portable Network Graphics. This new image file format is supported by only fairly recent browser versions (Microsoft Internet Explorer 4 or later and Netscape Navigator 4.04 or later); however, PNG images combine most of the advantages of GIF, including transparency and interlacing, plus the ability to accommodate millions of colors and a tight, lossless compression technique.

NOTE

PNG was developed to replace the use of GIF graphics on websites because GIF is a copyright-protected format, and, if the rules were strictly enforced, you would owe a usage royalty to CompuServe, the owner/developer of the GIF graphics format. The historical problem has been that the GIF format became popular and few paid attention to whether they had the right to create images stored in this format. PNG doesn't come with these usage limitations.

Which Image Format Is Right for You?

Which image format you choose depends on the features you want to include. Table 21.1 compares the features of the three graphic formats examined.

TABLE 21.1:   Features of GIF, JPG, and PNG

FEATURES	GIF	JPG	PNG
Transparency	Yes	No	Yes
Interlacing/progressive rendering	Yes	Qualified Yes	Yes
Millions of colors	No	Yes	Yes

TABLE 21.1 CONTINUED: Features of GIF, JPG, and PNG

FEATURES	GIF	JPG	PNG
Lossless compression	Yes	No	Yes
Good for line art	Yes	No	Yes
Good for photographs	No	Yes	Yes
Accepted on most browsers	Yes	Yes	No

As you can see, GIF and JPG have complementary advantages and disadvantages. As more browsers support PNG, however, it will probably become the first choice.

ADDING IMAGES

In this section, you're going to create some web pages for ASR Outfitters, a mountaineering and hiking supply company that is a mythical, miniature version of REI, the recreation equipment retailer. In the process, you'll learn how to include images in an HTML document. Although this may seem like putting the cart before the horse, knowing how to include images makes learning to develop them easier.

Table 21.2 shows the main image tags and attributes used to insert images in web pages.

TABLE 21.2:   Image Tags and Attributes

TAG	USE
<IMG>	Marks an image within an HTML document
ALT="..."	Specifies alternative text to display if an image is not displayed
SRC="..."	Points to an image file (URL) to include
HEIGHT=n	Specifies the final height of an image in pixels
WIDTH=n	Specifies the final width of an image in pixels
BORDER=n	Specifies the width of a border around an image in pixels
ALIGN="..."	Specifies image alignment as TOP, MIDDLE, BOTTOM, LEFT, or RIGHT

Adding an Image

Adding an image is similar to adding tags and attributes. You use the <IMG> tag, which specifies an image, plus the SRC= attribute to specify the image filename or URL. For example, if you're including an image that's located within the same folder as your document, your code might look like this:

```
<IMG SRC="logo.gif">
```

Or, if you're including an image located on the Web, you would include an absolute URL, like this:

```
<IMG SRC="http://www.asroutfitters.com/gifs/asrlogo.gif">
```

A URL used in the SRC= attribute is called a *remote reference*. Referencing logos and images remotely has certain advantages and some significant drawbacks. One advantage is that remote references to images ensure that you're always using the current logo. For example, if ASR Outfitters hires a graphic design company to change its corporate image, a franchisee's site that uses remote references to the main site will reflect the changes as soon as the main site changes. Additionally, remote references lighten the load on your server and reduce the number of files you must manage and manipulate.

On the downside, changes that are out of your control can easily break links from your site. If the ASR Outfitters webmaster decides to move the images from a GIFs subdirectory into an images subdirectory, the franchisee's images will no longer work, because the SRC= attribute points to the subdirectory that no longer contains the image files. From the visitor's perspective, the franchisee simply has a nonfunctional site—the visitor really doesn't know or care about the reason.

COPYRIGHT LAWS APPLY TO IMAGES

Be careful about linking to remote images, as you may be using copyrighted material. For example, if Bad Karma Hiking Equipment decided that the ASR Outfitters images were cool and incorporated those cool images in a site design by using remote links without permission, they would be infringing on ASR Outfitters' copyrighted material. This also applies to background images (covered later in this chapter) and any other content in any document. Be careful!

Additionally, network glitches or server problems can render your images inoperative if you link to them remotely. If the load on your own site is significant and you use remote images, the other site may be swamped with the demand and not even know why. Overall, you're probably better off copying the images to your local folder or at least to a different folder on your server, rather than relying on remote servers.

To add images to your document, start with a basic HTML document that, along with content, includes the following tags:

```
!DOCTYPE
<HTML>
<HEAD>
<BODY>
```

We used this basic document for ASR Outfitters:

```
<!DOCTYPE HTML PUBLIC "-//W3C//DTD HTML 4.0//EN">
<HTML>
<HEAD>
<TITLE>ASR Outfitters</TITLE>
</HEAD>
<BODY>
<H1 ALIGN=CENTER>ASR Outfitters</H1>
<P>We provide mountaineering and hiking equipment
    nationwide via mail order as well as through our stores
    in the Rocky Mountains.</P>
<HR WIDTH=70% SIZE=8 NOSHADE>
<P>Please select from the following links:</P>
<UL>
<LI><A HREF="camping.html">Camping News</A>
<LI><A HREF="catalog.html">Catalog</A>
<LI><A HREF="clubs.html">Clubs</A>
<LI><A HREF="contact.html">Contact Us</A>
<LI><A HREF="weather.html">Check Weather</A>
</UL>
<HR WIDTH=70% SIZE=8 NOSHADE>
<CENTER>
<ADDRESS ALIGN=CENTER>ASR Outfitters<BR>
```

Part vii

```
<A
    HREF="mailto:info@asroutfitters.com">info@asroutfitters
    .com</A><BR>
4700 N. Center<BR>
South Logan, UT 87654<BR>
801-555-3422<BR>
</ADDRESS>
</CENTER>
</BODY>
</HTML>
```

To add an image to this basic document, follow these steps:

1. Insert an <IMG> tag where you want the image to appear.

   ```
   <H1 ALIGN=CENTER>ASR Outfitters</H1>
   <IMG>
   <P>We provide mountaineering and hiking equipment
       nationwide via mail order as well as through our
       stores in the Rocky Mountains.</P>
   ```

2. Add an SRC="..." attribute pointing to the image filename. In this example, the filename is asrlogo.gif, and it's in the same folder as the document.

   ```
   <IMG SRC="asrlogo.gif">
   ```

3. In this case, add a line break tag, <BR>, after the <IMG> tag so that the next text starts on the following line (and not in any available space behind the image).

   ```
   <IMG SRC="asrlogo.gif"><BR>
   ```

4. Because the image duplicates the content of the first-level heading, consider removing the first-level heading.

5. The first-level heading was centered, so consider adding a <CENTER> tag around the logo to center it.

   ```
   <CENTER><IMG SRC="asrlogo.gif"><BR></CENTER>
   ```

NOTE

The <IMG> tag supports ALIGN= attributes with values of TOP, MIDDLE, BOTTOM, LEFT, and RIGHT, but does not support horizontal centering. If you want to use horizontal centering, use the <CENTER> tag. See the "Aligning the Image" section, later in this chapter, for more information.

You can see the resulting image on the ASR web page shown in Figure 21.3.

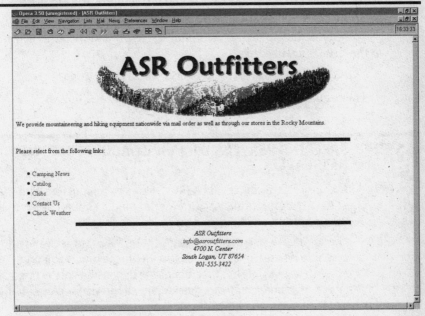

FIGURE 21.3: An image on the ASR web page

Including Alternative Text

Alternative text describes an image that you have inserted. You include alternative text for the following reasons:

- ▶ Some of your visitors may be using text-only browsers.
- ▶ A visitor may have turned off images so that a file will load faster.
- ▶ Sometimes browsers don't display images correctly.
- ▶ Sometimes images don't display because the links aren't working properly.
- ▶ Sometimes browsers display alternative text while images load.

Alternative text should be clear and concise. Provide your visitors with enough information so that they can understand the image content without viewing it. For example, alternative text for a logo can be as simple as the company name and the word *logo*. Even text as simple as "ASR Sample Photograph" or "ASR Content-Free Image" is helpful to visitors. If they see only the word *Image* (as they would if you omit the ALT= attribute), they'll have to load the images to see the content.

To add alternative text to your images, simply add the ALT= attribute to the <IMG> tag, like this:

```
<IMG SRC="asrlogo.gif" ALT="ASR Outfitters Logo">
```

The resulting alternative text is shown in Figure 21.4.

SPEEDING PERCEIVED IMAGE-LOADING TIME WITH NETSCAPE

A Netscape-specific tag, LOWSRC=, works in conjunction with the SRC= attribute; it tells the browser to load a smaller version of the image first and then load the full image.

The idea is to use a small image (in terms of file size) for the LOWSRC= image. For example, use a JPG image that is compressed as much as possible but that retains the dimensions of the original image. This image appears quickly, and, if the visitor stays on the page long enough, the full image then loads.

This attribute, although not universally recognized, causes no adverse effects in browsers that don't support it—they simply ignore it.

Specifying Height and Width

You can speed the loading time of images by specifying an image's height and width. As the browser loads the page, it notes the height and width attributes and leaves that much space for the image. Next, it lays out the remaining text, and then it goes back and fills in the image. If you do not include these attributes, the browser has to load enough of the image to get the dimensions before it can lay out the rest of the text, thereby slowing the display of other page elements.

To specify image height and width, add the HEIGHT= and WIDTH= attributes in the <IMG> tag, like this:

```
<IMG SRC="asrlogo.gif" ALT="ASR Outfitters Logo"
    HEIGHT="192" WIDTH="604">
```

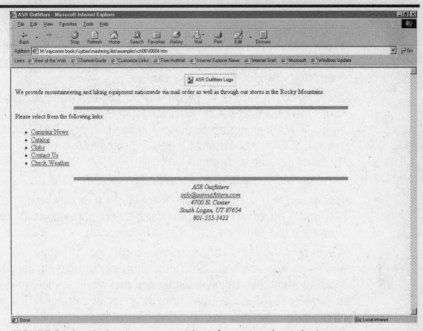

FIGURE 21.4: Alternative text provides information about the image.

As a rule, use the actual height and width of the image. To get the dimensions, open the image in an image-editing program, and look at the status bar. You will see something like "604 × 192 × 256," which indicates, in this example, that the asrlogo.gif image is 604 pixels wide, 192 pixels high, and 256 colors deep. With this information, you can then add the width (604) and height (192) attributes to the <IMG> tag.

FORMATTING USING THE TRANSPARENT GIF TRICK

You can use transparent images to help force specific spacing in your documents. Suppose you want a blank space between two paragraphs. Because you can't insert a carriage return like you would in a word processor, you have to put in the blank space some other way—inserting a transparent GIF works really well in this case. A transparent GIF could also ensure that text appears a specific distance from the left margin.

CONTINUED →

Part vii

To add spacing in a document with a transparent GIF, simply create a 1×1 pixel transparent GIF in your image-editing software and then insert that GIF into your HTML document.

Does the space have to be 1 pixel wide or 1 pixel high? Not necessarily. You can insert the itty-bitty (and thus very fast to download) image in the document and specify the size in which it will appear in a web browser by adding the HEIGHT= and WIDTH= attributes. For example, your code might look like this:

```
<IMG SRC="trans.gif" HEIGHT="10" WIDTH="1">
```

This example results in a blank space that's 10 pixels high and 1 pixel wide—ideal for ensuring spacing between paragraphs. Or, set the height to 1 and the width to 10 to indent text.

We present this option to you because, well, lots of people use it, and if you have really specific formatting needs, it works. Keep in mind, though, that it's not standard and that we don't recommend it. HTML doesn't pretend to provide exact layout control, and attempting to get it is likely to prove frustrating.

If you really need to control the formatting exactly and your visitors have fairly new browsers, your best bet is to try style sheets, which is the up-and-coming way to format your pages.

Aligning the Image

HTML provides several image alignment options:

- ▶ Three vertical options align the image with respect to a line of text.

- ▶ Two options align the image to the left or to the right of the window (with corresponding text wrap).

The alignment options within the <IMG> tag override other alignment settings within the HTML document (for example, the <CENTER> tags surrounding the <IMG> tag).

By default, images align on the left, with a single line of accompanying text appearing on the same line; however, long text wraps to the following line. To ensure that accompanying text appears beside the image, specify ALIGN="LEFT" in the <IMG> tag, like this:

```
<IMG SRC="asrlogo.gif" ALT="ASR Outfitters Logo"
    WIDTH="604" HEIGHT="192" ALIGN="LEFT">
```

The text appears to the right of the left-aligned image, as shown in Figure 21.5.

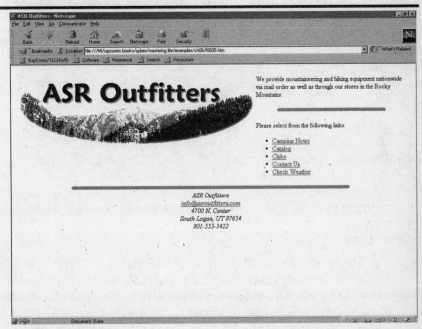

FIGURE 21.5: Specifying left alignment ensures that accompanying text appears to the right of the image.

You can create attractive effects by combining image alignment and text alignment. For example, setting an image to ALIGN="RIGHT" and then setting the accompanying text to ALIGN="RIGHT" forces the text to be flush against the image with a ragged left margin, as shown in Figure 21.6.

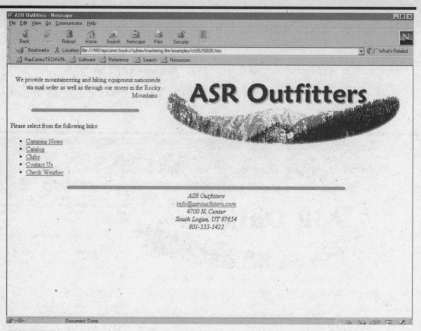

FIGURE 21.6: Specifying right alignment for the image and text produces appealing results.

The remaining alignment options—TOP, MIDDLE, and BOTTOM—offer more in the context of small images. You use them to align the image within the text. For example, using ALIGN="TOP" aligns the top of the image with the top of the surrounding text, and the remainder of the image hangs below the text line. Using ALIGN="MIDDLE" places the middle of an image at the baseline of surrounding text. Similarly, using ALIGN="BOTTOM" places the bottom of an image on the same line as the text, and the remainder of the image extends considerably higher than the surrounding text. The effect of these options is shown in Figure 21.7.

HTML 4 OPPORTUNITIES

Though any of these image-formatting tags will appear fine in browsers that comply with HTML 3.2 or 4, you might consider using style sheets for your formatting needs—including image formatting.

The HTML 4 specification deprecates formatting tags, including alignment options, in favor of style sheets.

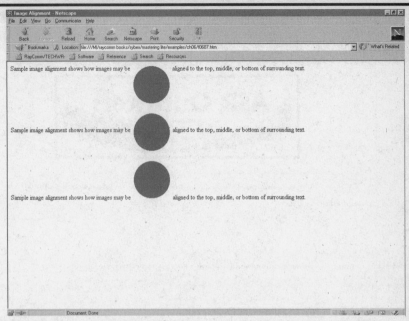

FIGURE 21.7: Top, middle, and bottom alignment float the image differently in relation to the surrounding text.

Controlling the Border

You control the border around an image with the BORDER= attribute. In most browsers, by default, the border is visible only on images that are used as links. To turn the border off for all images, add the BORDER="0" attribute to the <IMG> tag, resulting in a complete image tag:

```
<IMG SRC="asrlogo.gif" ALT="ASR Outfitters Logo"
    WIDTH="604"  HEIGHT="192" BORDER="0">
```

TIP

Remember, placing quotes around numeric values—such as 0, 192, or 604—is optional in attributes.

Likewise, you can increase the border width around an image by increasing the value in the BORDER= attribute, like this:

```
<IMG SRC="asrlogo.gif" ALT="ASR Outfitters Logo"
    WIDTH="604"  HEIGHT="192" BORDER="7">
```

The resulting border looks like that in Figure 21.8.

Part vii

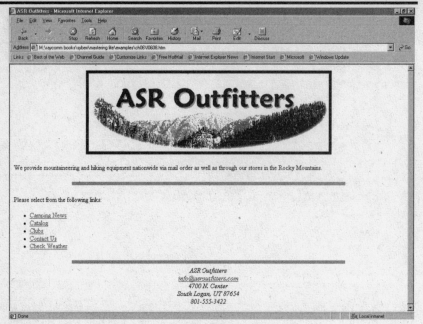

FIGURE 21.8: Setting a large border width frames your images.

Choosing Suitable Colors

When creating your own images—or choosing colors for web page or table backgrounds—you want to choose colors that look good in most browsers, most of the time. If you're selecting colors for text or for small swatches, choose anything that appeals to you. However, if you're selecting a background color or a color that will appear in broad expanses of your HTML documents, be careful.

If you choose a color that is not available on a viewer's system, the browser will dither the color to approximate its appearance. *Dithering* is the technical term for substituting other colors, partially or wholly, to minimize the impact of not having the correct color. Dithering in photographs or small images is rarely noticeable, but dithering in large single-color areas results in blotchy or mottled appearances.

Now, consider that a large number of your visitors—or, at least, a large number of web users in general—have computers set to display 256 colors. Sounds like the solution is to choose one of those 256 colors, doesn't it? Not quite. Macintosh, Unix, and Windows each use a different set of colors for system functions, and those colors—up to 40—are taken from the available 256, leaving only 216 colors for general use. If you choose one of these 216 colors, however, you can be fairly certain that the colors will look as good as they can in all browsers on all platforms. These remaining 216 colors are evenly distributed over the color spectrum, giving you a wide range from which to choose.

In computer-speak, colors are represented as proportions of red, green, and blue (RGB) and are specified by an RGB number. These RGB numbers combine to produce all available colors.

To specify a color, you provide numeric values to represent the proportions of red, green, and blue. In most image-editing programs, you can provide values in decimal numbers. However, when you're specifying colors in some image-editing programs and for colors within a web page, you use hexadecimal numbers.

What are these numbers? They are the decimal values 0, 51, 102, 153, 204, and 255 for each color. That is, a good (preferred) color might be 51, 51, 51 for the red, green, and blue values. In hexadecimal, the good values are 00, 33, 66, 99, CC, FF, so the corresponding sample color would be #333333. Where do these good values come from?

Table 21.3 lists the preferred (good) RGB values using hexadecimal numbers; Table 21.4 lists the values using decimal numbers. To create a safe (nondithering) color, choose one value from each column. For example, choose 66 from the first column, 33 from the second, and 00 from the third to create an RGB color of 663300.

TABLE 21.3: Preferred RGB Values in Hexadecimal

RED	GREEN	BLUE
00	00	00
33	33	33
66	66	66
99	99	99
CC	CC	CC
FF	FF	FF

TABLE 21.4:   Preferred RGB Values in Decimal

RED	GREEN	BLUE
0	0	0
51	51	51
102	102	102
153	153	153
204	204	204
255	255	255

As a rule, colors close to these colors will also not dither, but there's no hard-and-fast rule on how *close* is close enough. For example, we tried 000001 and found that it didn't visibly dither on our computers... this time.

Using Images as Links

Using images as links offers two distinct advantages to both you and your visitors. First, images really can be as good as a thousand words. Often, including an image link can replace several words or lines of text, leaving valuable space for other page elements.

Second, you can also use *thumbnails*, which are smaller images that link to a larger one. By doing so, you can let visitors get the gist of an image and choose whether they want to load the larger version. (You'll find details about thumbnails in the section "Creating Thumbnails," later in this chapter.)

Creating Image Links

To add an image as a link, start by adding an image tag. In this example, we are adding a fancy button to the ASR Outfitters page to replace the more prosaic *Camping News* bulleted list item. The name of the image is camping.gif, and the file it should link to is camping.html.

NOTE

When you use images as links, alternative text is critical. If clicking the image is the only way visitors can connect to the other page, the alternative text is their only clue if the image is not displayed (because of technical difficulties, because they've turned off images, because they have a text-only browser, because they use a screen-reading program for the visually impaired, and so on).

Here are the steps for adding an image link:

1. Add an image tag and an SRC= attribute to the document.

   ```
   <IMG SRC="camping.gif">
   ```

2. Include alternative text using the ALT= attribute.

   ```
   <IMG SRC="camping.gif" ALT="Camping News">
   ```

3. Add the remaining attributes you want to include, like the HEIGHT=, WIDTH=, and BORDER= attributes. If you choose to use BORDER=0 and turn off the border completely, be sure that the image is visually identified as a link. Otherwise, your visitors might not know it's a link unless they pass their mouse over it and see the pointing-hand cursor.

   ```
   <IMG SRC="camping.gif" WIDTH="300" HEIGHT="82"
       BORDER="0"  ALT="Camping News">
   ```

4. Add the link anchor tag, <A>, before and after the image.

   ```
   <A><IMG SRC="camping.gif" WIDTH="300" HEIGHT="82"
       BORDER="0" ALT="Camping News"></A>
   ```

5. Add the HREF= attribute to the opening anchor tag to spec-ify the image filename.

   ```
   <A HREF="camping.html"><IMG SRC="camping.gif"
       WIDTH="300" HEIGHT="82" BORDER="0" ALT="Camping
       News"></A>
   ```

Now you have an image that acts as a link to the camping.html file. After adding a couple more images and surrounding them all with the <CENTER> tags, the ASR Outfitters page is similar to Figure 21.9.

Creating Thumbnails

As we mentioned earlier, a thumbnail is a smaller version of an image, but it is also a link to the larger version. Thumbnails can also link to mul-timedia applets or to other content that is time-consuming to download or not universally accessible.

Part vii

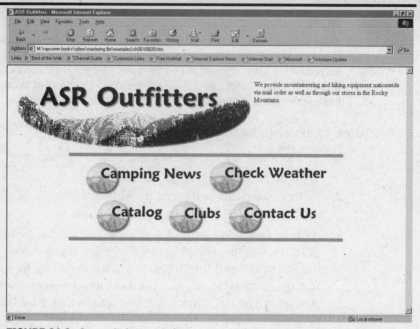

FIGURE 21.9: Image links can make a page much more attractive (and slower to load).

For example, ASR Outfitters could include a thumbnail of the original photograph that inspired its logo. This thumbnail would link to the original photograph, a larger image.

To add a thumbnail image, start by having both images—the thumbnail and the larger version—available. Make a thumbnail by starting with the full-size version (scanned from your private collection or from any other source). Then, use your image-editing software to resize or resample the image to a much smaller size—as small as possible while still retaining the gist of the image. Save this second image under a different name. Then follow these steps:

1. Include the thumbnail image in your document as you'd include any other image. For example, the code might look like this:

```
<IMG SRC="photo-thumbnail.jpg" HEIGHT="78"
    WIDTH="193" ALIGN="RIGHT" BORDER="1" ALT="Thumbnail
    of Original Photo">
```

2.   Add a link from the thumbnail to the larger image.

```
<A HREF="photo.jpg"><IMG SRC="photo-thumbnail.jpg"
    HEIGHT="78" WIDTH="193" ALIGN="RIGHT" BORDER="1"
    ALT="Thumbnail of Original Photo"></A>
```

If you set the border to 0, be sure that the supporting text or other cues in the HTML document make it clear that the image is, in fact, a link to a larger photograph. Alternatively, do as we did and simply set BORDER=1 to make clear that an image is a link. Here's the result from the bottom corner of the ASR Outfitters home page:

Although you can achieve the same visual effect in your document by using the original image and setting a smaller display size with the HEIGHT= and WIDTH= attributes, this technique defeats the purpose of thumbnails. Even if you reset the display size with HEIGHT= and WIDTH=, the entire (full-size) image will have to be downloaded to your computer. The trick to effective thumbnails is to reduce both the dimensions and the actual file size to the smallest possible value so the page will load quickly.

CREATING IMAGE MAPS

An *image map*, also called a *clickable image*, is a single image that contains multiple links. In your web travels, you may have used image maps without knowing it. Clicking on a portion of an image map takes you to the link connected with that part of the visual presentation. For example, a physician might present an image map of the human body to a patient, with instructions for the patient to "click where it hurts." Another good use replaces individual images (that browsers could realign depending on the window width) with a single *graphical menu*. Figure 21.10 shows a sample image map from the ASR Outfitters website. (Visitors can click on each area for weather conditions—weather at the high peaks and lower elevations—and even the ultraviolet index.)

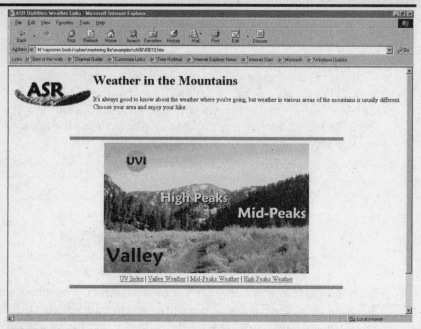

FIGURE 21.10: Image maps are single images with multiple links to other information or graphics.

Understanding Image Map Types

The two types of image maps are as follows:

- ▸ Server-side
- ▸ Client-side

The feature distinguishing the two types is where the processing takes place (where a visitor's mouse-click is translated into a link to another document). The processing can occur either on the server (hence, *server-side image map*) or on the visitor's computer (hence, *client-side image map*).

Server-Side Image Maps

In a server-side image map, the coordinates of the click are transmitted to the server computer, which determines the instructions that apply to that click. The server then sends that information back to the client, which then sends a request for the appropriate document. The server computer does the calculating and tells the client what to do.

The advantages to using server-side image maps are that they have been around longer than client-side maps and that they are widely supported. The disadvantages to using server-side image maps include the following:

▶ Because a server-side image map requires input from the server, it generally responds slower than a client-side image map, depending on network traffic.

▶ The server may need supplemental software to process the image map.

▶ The server administrator may have to specify how the image map is processed.

Client-Side Image Maps

Generally, you'll want to use client-side image maps for several reasons. To start with, they're faster (because there's no need for back-and-forth communication between client and server to process the map) and more reliable, for those browsers that support client-side maps (and most do). For example, if a document with a client-side image map comes from server A and points to a document on server B, the client can do the calculations and request the document directly from server B.

Client-side image maps are more user-friendly than server-side image maps. When a visitor moves the cursor over an image map link within a document, the status bar generally displays the URL of the link. Newer browsers, including the latest versions of Netscape Navigator and Internet Explorer, also show information about the link in a small pop-up window. In contrast, when a visitor places the cursor over a server-side image map link, the status bar displays only the coordinates of the cursor.

Finally, client-side image maps are better for you, the web author, because you can use and test them before you put the image map on the server. In contrast, server-side maps do not work until they have been installed on the server, making testing much more difficult.

TIP

If your visitors might be using particularly old browsers, consider using both client-side and server-side image maps. If browsers see a client-side map, they'll use it. If they don't recognize the client-side image map, they'll revert to the server-side map. The only disadvantage to this approach is that you have to do twice as much work.

Part vii

Making Appropriate Image Maps

Poorly constructed or carelessly selected image maps can be much worse than no image map at all. The inherent disadvantages of images (for example, their download time and their inaccessibility for text-only browsers) apply in spades to image maps. When determining whether an image map is appropriate for your needs, ask the following questions:

Is the image map linking to a stable navigational structure? If the links will be changing or if the overall site navigation structure isn't completely worked out, it's not time for an image map. Revising image maps is possible, but generally a real hassle. Often it's easier to completely redo an image map than to update it.

Is the image final? If the image hasn't passed all levels of review and isn't polished, you're not ready to make an image map. Changes as trivial as cropping the image slightly or rescaling the image by a few percentage points can completely break your map.

Is the image function appropriate to an image map? Flashy images on a home page are good candidates for image maps, particularly if the design reflects the corporate image. In many cases, an intricate design must be a single image—browsers cannot always accurately assemble individual images into the arrangement the designer intends. However, pages buried within an intranet site or that have a technical and practical focus are less likely to benefit from an image map.

Is the image content appropriate to an image map? Artificial or gratuitous use of image maps can be a real drawback to otherwise fine web pages. Is clicking certain spots in an image really the best way for your visitors to link to the information they need? For example, in a website about automobile repair and diagnosis for the layperson, a picture of a car and the instructions to click where the funny sound seems to originate is completely appropriate. In a site directed at experienced mechanics, however, a list of parts (hood, trunk, dashboard, tire) would be much faster and more appropriate.

Does the function or content merit an image map? If both do, that's great. If one does, you can probably proceed with an image map. If, however, the links on a page don't need to be flashy and the content is not substantially clarified with an image map, omit the image map entirely.

Can the image map be completely reused?   If you are planning to use an image map on several pages (you will use exactly the same image and code), its value increases. In this case, it's more likely to be worth the download time than if it's a one-time use.

If you answered *no* to one or more of these questions, consider using traditional, individual images or navigation aids. For example, if you can easily break the content or image into multiple smaller images with no significant problems, strongly consider doing so. Remember that image maps are time-consuming to develop and may not be available to all your visitors, so be sure an image map is right for your needs before developing one.

Selecting an Image

When you select a suitable image to use as an image map, follow the same guidelines as you would for choosing other images:

- ▶ Be sure that the image supports the content.
- ▶ Be sure that the physical size is as small as possible, but large enough to convey the content.
- ▶ Be sure that the file size is as small as possible.

For example, if you are creating an auto repair image map for laypersons, use a simple drawing or schematic. At the other extreme, however, is the ASR Outfitters image map, which is primarily a visual attraction with only a tangential function. The image map shown in Figure 21.10, earlier in this chapter, is part of a localized weather page. Visitors can click an area to get the weather for that region.

Setting Alternate Navigation

Unless you know beyond a doubt that *all* your visitors have graphical browsers and will choose to view images, you must provide alternate navigation options. Those who don't see the images—for whatever reason—won't be able to link to the information via your image, so provide text-based alternatives. An easy solution is to create a list of links. For example, alternate navigation for the image shown in Figure 21.10, earlier in this chapter, might look like the following code:

```
<BR>
<A HREF="uvi.html">UV Index</A> |
<A HREF="valley.html">Valley Weather</A> |
<A HREF="midpeaks.html">Mid-Peaks Weather</A> |
<A HREF="highpeaks.html">High Peaks Weather</A>
```

In this code, the vertical line (|) separates the links and creates the menu effect, as shown at the bottom of Figure 21.10.

TIP

Creating the alternate navigation before you develop the image map helps remind you of the links to include.

Creating Client-Side Image Maps

Creating a client-side image map involves three steps:

1. Defining the image area
2. Creating the image map
3. Activating the image map

Defining Image Areas

All image maps are simply a combination of three shapes:

- ▶ Circles
- ▶ Rectangles
- ▶ Polygons (any shapes other than circles and rectangles)

You can create almost any image by combining these shapes. Figure 21.11 shows the ASR Outfitters image map from within a map-editing program. The UVI link is a circle, the valley-temperatures link is a rectangle, and the mid- and high-peak links are polygons.

TIP

You don't have to be precise with most map definitions. You can assume that most visitors will click somewhere in the middle of the link area; if not, they're likely to try again.

The next three sections show you how to define these three shapes. Before you get started, open an image in an image-editing or -mapping program.

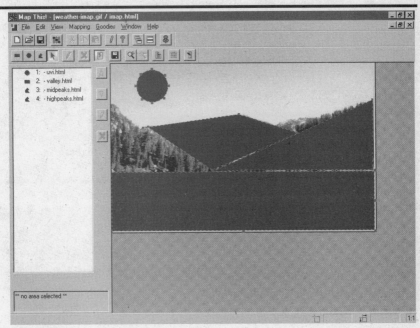

FIGURE 21.11: This image map includes a circle, a rectangle, and two polygons.

TIP

If you'll be developing several image maps, we recommend installing and using image-mapping software available on the Internet. If you're creating simple maps or if you're doing only a few, however, creating them manually is almost as easy.

Defining Circles

To define a circle, follow these steps:

1. Identify the center and the radius. Use the cursor to point at the center of the circle, and note the coordinates in the status bar of your paint program. For example, in Paint Shop Pro, the cursor looks like a magnifying glass, and the x,y coordinates are at the bottom of the window. The *x* is the number of pixels from the edge of the image, and the *y* is the number of pixels from the top.

2. Move the cursor horizontally to the edge of the circle, and note the coordinates.

3. Subtract the first *x* coordinate from the second *x* coordinate to get the radius of the circle.

4. Make a note of these coordinates.

Defining Rectangles

To define a rectangle, follow these steps:

1. Identify the upper-left corner and the lower-right corner. Point your mouse at the upper-left corner of the rectangle

and record the coordinates; then point at the lower-right corner and record the coordinates.

2. Make a note of these coordinates.

Defining Polygons

To define a polygon, follow these steps:

1. Identify each point on the shape, moving in order around the shape. You can start at any point on the perimeter and proceed clockwise or counterclockwise, as long as you don't skip points. For example, in the ASR Outfitters map, the Mid-Peaks area can be defined with three points—making a right triangle with the long side running between the Mid-Peaks and High Peaks areas. The High Peaks area might include several points across the top of the mountains, or it might be as simple as another triangle.

2. Make a note of these coordinates.

Creating the Image Map

When you create an image map, you include tags and attributes that tell a browser what to do when a visitor clicks the defined map areas. You can include this information within the HTML document that contains the image map, or you can include it in a separate document. The first is more common, but if you'll be using the image map (say, as a navigation aid) in several documents, consider storing it in a separate file and referencing it from each of the documents.

You can place the map definition block anywhere within the body of your HTML document, but it is easier to update and maintain if you place it either immediately after the opening <BODY> tag or immediately before the closing </BODY> tag. Table 21.5 explains image map tags and attributes.

TABLE 21.5:   Image Map Tags and Attributes

Tag/Attribute	Use
USEMAP="..."	Names the client-side map definition to use. Attribute of <IMG> tag.
ISMAP	Specifies that the image uses a server-side image map. Attribute of <IMG> tag.

TABLE 21.5 CONTINUED: Image Map Tags and Attributes

Tag/Attribute	Use
<MAP>	Marks the map definition block within the HTML document.
NAME="..."	Provides a name for the map definition block.
<AREA>	Defines an area within the map.
SHAPE="..."	Identifies the shape of an area as RECT, CIRCLE, or POLY.
HREF="..."	Specifies a target for an area. A click in the area links to this URL.
NOHREF	Specifies that a click in this area will not link anywhere.
COORDS="x,y,x1,y1,x2,y2"	Identifies the shape of an area.
ALT="..."	Provides alternate text (or pop-up text) describing each link.

To include a client-side image map, follow these steps (we'll use the ASR Outfitters page in this example):

1. Within your HTML document, add opening and closing <MAP> tags.

   <MAP>
   </MAP>
   </BODY>

2. Give the map a clear, descriptive name with a NAME= attribute. This name is comparable to the NAME= attribute of the <A> tag. It provides an internal anchor of sorts that you can link to from either the same document or other documents.

   <MAP **NAME="weather_zones"**>

3. Add an <AREA> tag for one of the shapes.

   <MAP NAME="weather_zones">
   <AREA>

4. Add a SHAPE= attribute to the <AREA> tag. In this example, CIRCLE represents the UVI area in the ASR example map.

   <AREA **SHAPE=CIRCLE**>

5. Add the COORDS= attribute with the x,y coordinates of the center of the circle and with the radius of the circle.

   <AREA SHAPE=CIRCLE **COORDS="82,43,30"**>

6. Add an HREF= attribute pointing to the target file. You can use relative or absolute URLs in client-side image maps, but, as with other links, using relative URLs is a good idea. In this case, the area links to a file called uvi.html in the same folder.

```
<AREA SHAPE=CIRCLE COORDS="82,43,30" HREF="uvi.html">
```

7. Add the ALT= attribute describing the link for use in pop-ups.

```
<AREA SHAPE=CIRCLE COORDS="82,43,30" HREF="uvi.html"
    ALT="UV Index">
```

NOTE

As you add areas, some may overlap others. The first area defined overrides overlapping areas.

8. Add additional <AREA> tags, one at a time. In this example, the next <AREA> tag is for the Valley area, so it is a RECT. The coordinates for the top left and lower right are required to link to valley.html.

```
<AREA SHAPE=CIRCLE COORDS="82,43,30" HREF="uvi.html"
    ALT="UV Index">
<AREA SHAPE=RECT COORDS="1,209,516,320"
    HREF="valley.html" ALT="Valley Weather">
```

9. For the Mid-Peaks area, a triangle will suffice to define the area; so the shape is a POLY with three pairs of coordinates. This links to midpeaks.html.

```
<AREA SHAPE=CIRCLE COORDS="82,43,30" HREF="uvi.html"
    ALT="UV Index">
<AREA SHAPE=RECT COORDS="1,209,516,320"
    HREF="valley.html" ALT="Valley Weather">
<AREA SHAPE=POLY COORDS="199,207,513,205,514,71"
    HREF="midpeaks.html" ALT="Mid-Peaks Weather">
```

10. The High Peaks area is easily defined with a figure containing four corners—vaguely diamond shaped, as in the following example.

```
<AREA SHAPE=CIRCLE COORDS="82,43,30" HREF="uvi.html"
    ALT="UV Index">
<AREA SHAPE=RECT COORDS="1,209,516,320"
    HREF="valley.html" ALT="Valley Weather">
<AREA SHAPE=POLY COORDS="199,207,513,205,514,71"
    HREF="midpeaks.html" ALT="Mid-Peaks Weather">
```

Part vii

```
<AREA SHAPE=POLY COORDS="63,123,251,98,365,134,198,
204,73,121"
   HREF="highpeaks.html" ALT="High Peaks Weather">
```

Refer back to Figure 21.11 for a reminder of what this shape looks like.

11. Set the HREF= attribute for the remaining areas. You could set the remaining area so that nothing at all will happen when a visitor clicks there.

```
<AREA SHAPE=default NOHREF>
```

That's all there is to it. The final map looks something like the following code:

```
<MAP NAME="weather_zones">
<AREA SHAPE=CIRCLE COORDS="82,43,30" HREF="uvi.html"
   ALT="UV Index">
<AREA SHAPE=RECT COORDS="1,209,516,320" HREF="valley.html"
   ALT="Valley Weather">
<AREA SHAPE=POLY COORDS="199,207,513,205,514,71"
   HREF="midpeaks.html" ALT="Mid-Peaks Weather">
<AREA SHAPE=POLY
   COORDS="63,123,251,98,365,134,198,204,73,121"
   HREF="highpeaks.html" ALT="High Peaks Weather">
<AREA SHAPE=default NOHREF>
</MAP>
```

Activating the Image Map

Before you can activate the map, you must place the map image in your document. The image tag (in a new document) looks like this:

```
<CENTER>
<IMG SRC="weather-imap.gif" ALIGN="" WIDTH="516"
   HEIGHT="320" BORDER="0" ALT="Weather Zones in the
   Mountains">
</CENTER>
```

To connect the image to the map definition created in the previous section, simply add the USEMAP= attribute, as in the following example.

```
<IMG SRC="weather-imap.gif" ALIGN="" WIDTH="516"
   HEIGHT="320" BORDER="0" ALT="Weather Zones in the
   Mountains" USEMAP="#weather_zones">
```

TIP

The USEMAP= attribute requires a pound sign (#) in the value to indicate that the link goes to a place within a document.

If you want to link to a map definition in another document, add an absolute URL to the USEMAP= attribute. If you do this, test thoroughly because not all browsers support this feature. The final map looks like that shown in Figure 21.12.

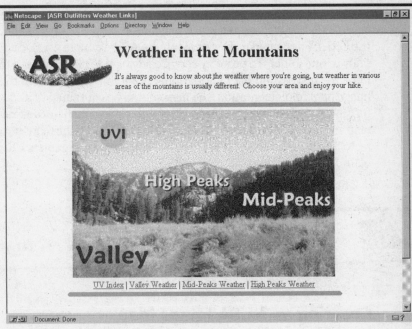

FIGURE 21.12: The ASR Outfitters image map

Creating Server-Side Image Maps

The process for making server-side image maps is virtually identical to that of making client-side image maps. The only real difference is in the map file format. Each type of server can have a different type of image map configuration.

In practice, however, only two main server-side map formats exist: National Center for Supercomputing Applications (NCSA) and Centre Europeen pour la Recherche Nucleaire (CERN). They function in similar ways, but each requires a slightly different format for map definitions. Each format represents an implementation of server-side image maps from the earliest server software these organizations produced.

NOTE

Ask your server administrator which image map format you'll need to use for a server-side image map. Additionally, check on what the URL is for using a server-side image map.

The only real issue with converting your client-side image map to a server-side image map is that you must know more about (and be sure of) the URLs. For example, everything in the ASR example was located initially in one folder. To properly set up a server-side map, we need to determine the full path to the information. Because of limitations in the NCSA image map implementation, the map should be contained in a subdirectory, not in the server root. ASR will put the image map document, the map file, and the associated (linked) files together in the weather subdirectory on www.asroutfitters.com. Therefore, the complete URL to the main file is as follows:

```
http://www.asroutfitters.com/weather/asrweather-imap.html
```

NOTE

You must use server-relative URLs or absolute URLs to ensure that everything works properly.

Creating an NCSA Image Map

In general, the NCSA image map format is as follows:

```
method URL coordinates
```

The code for the sample client-side image map looks like this:

```
<MAP NAME="weather_zones">
<AREA SHAPE=CIRCLE COORDS="82,43,30" HREF="uvi.html"
    ALT="UV Index">
<AREA SHAPE=RECT COORDS="1,209,516,320" HREF="valley.html"
    ALT="Valley Weather">
<AREA SHAPE=POLY COORDS="199,207,513,205,514,71"
    HREF="midpeaks.html" ALT="Mid-Peaks Weather">
```

```
<AREA SHAPE=POLY
    COORDS="63,123,251,98,365,134,198,204,73,121"
    HREF="highpeaks.html" ALT="High Peaks Weather">
<AREA SHAPE=default NOHREF>
</MAP>
```

You use an NCSA server-side map file like this:

```
default /weather/asrweather-imap.html
circle /weather/uvi.html 82,43,30
rect /weather/valley.html 1,209,516,320
poly /weather/midpeaks.html 199,207,513,205,514,71
poly /weather/highpeaks.html
    63,123,251,98,365,134,198,204,73,121
```

The default item points explicitly back to the file containing the map, so clicks outside active areas will not link to other pages. The remaining lines include the shape, URL, and coordinates, just as the client-side map definition file did, but using a slightly different format.

NOTE

The NCSA server-side format also supports a *point* shape (in addition to the circle, rectangle, and polygon) with a single pair of coordinates. A click near the point takes a visitor to that URL. If you provide multiple points, the server chooses the closest one to the click. Because other image map formats do not support the point, we recommend using only the existing shapes.

After you create this map file, save it with a .map extension. ASR places the map file in the same folder as the rest of the files—that is, in the /weather folder, just below the server root.

Activating NCSA-Style Server-Side Image Maps

Activating the server-side image map makes much more sense if you think of it as making the image a link (though one with an added level of complexity). Follow these steps:

1. Start with the map in your document (the client-side map, if you choose).

```
<IMG SRC="weather-imap.gif" ALIGN="" WIDTH="516"
    HEIGHT="320" BORDER="0" ALT="Weather Zones in the
    Mountains" USEMAP="#weather_zones">
```

Part vii

2. Add the ISMAP attribute to the <IMG> tag, as shown here:

```
<IMG SRC="weather-imap.gif" ALIGN="" WIDTH="516"
    HEIGHT="320" BORDER="0" ALT="Weather Zones in the
    Mountains" USEMAP="#weather_zones" ISMAP>
```

3. Add a link around the image.

```
<A>
<IMG SRC="weather-imap.gif" ALIGN="" WIDTH="516"
    HEIGHT="320" BORDER="0" ALT="Weather Zones in the
    Mountains" USEMAP="#weather_zones" ISMAP>
</A>
```

4. Add the HREF= attribute specified by the network administrator. In all probability, it will look something like this:

```
<A HREF="http://www.asroutfitters.com/cgi-
    bin/imagemap/weather/weather-imap.map">
<IMG SRC="weather-imap.gif" ALIGN="" WIDTH="516"
    HEIGHT="320" BORDER="0" ALT="Weather Zones in the
    Mountains" USEMAP="#weather_zones" ISMAP>
</A>
```

If the client recognizes a client-side image map, it disregards the
server-side map. If the client cannot recognize the client-side map, it uses
the server-side map.

TIP

When you've finished creating the map, be sure to upload the map file at the
same time you upload the rest of your files. That's an easy one to forget.

Implementing CERN-Style Image Maps

CERN-style maps are considerably less common than NCSA-style maps.
Again, the same basic information is included, but slightly reshuffled.
The original client-side map format is as follows:

```
<MAP NAME="weather_zones">
<AREA SHAPE=CIRCLE COORDS="82,43,30" HREF="uvi.html"
    ALT="UV Index">
<AREA SHAPE=RECT COORDS="1,209,516,320" HREF="valley.html"
    ALT="Valley Weather">
```

```
<AREA SHAPE=POLY COORDS="199,207,513,205,514,71"
    HREF="midpeaks.html" ALT="Mid-Peaks Weather">
<AREA SHAPE=POLY
    COORDS="63,123,251,98,365,134,198,204,73,121"
    HREF="highpeaks.html" ALT="High Peaks Weather">
<AREA SHAPE=default NOHREF>
</MAP>
```

After converting it, you end up with a CERN map file like the following:

```
default /weather/asrweather-imap.html

circle (82,43) 30 /weather/uvi.html
rect (1,209) (516,320) /weather/valley.html
poly (199,207) (513,205) (514,71) /weather/midpeaks.html
poly (63,123) (251,98) (365,134) (198,204) (73,121)
    /weather/highpeaks.html
```

The major differences are that the coordinate pairs are enclosed in parentheses, the coordinates go before the URLs, and the rectangle can use any two opposite coordinates, rather than just the top left and lower right. The URLs can be either absolute or server-relative.

TIP

Other types of servers exist, and administrators configure their servers differently. Asking up front how to implement a server-side image map will reduce frustration.

USING BACKGROUND IMAGES

Most browsers support background images, the patterns or images behind the text in HTML documents. As a rule, background images are *tiled* throughout the available space, meaning that they are multiple copies of one image placed side by side to fill the screen.

Tiling offers two main advantages. First, you can produce a *seamless background,* meaning that the casual viewer cannot see where individual images start and stop. Figure 21.13 shows a seamless background.

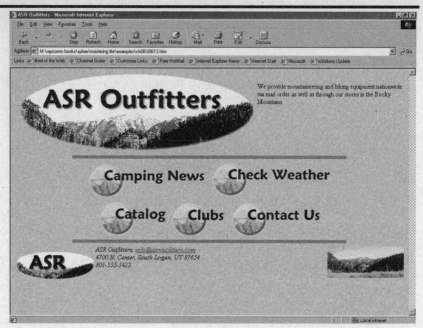

FIGURE 21.13: In seamless backgrounds, the tiled images blend together.

Second, you can develop more visually interesting backgrounds by ensuring that background images tile either horizontally or vertically. For example, an image that is only 10 pixels high and 1280 pixels wide is as wide or wider than any browser window is likely to be. Therefore, the image will repeat vertically, but not horizontally. This can produce a vertical band, as shown in Figure 21.14.

TIP

The magic number *1280* ensures that no browser can be wider than the image. If you use a narrower image, you might have an attractive image when viewed at 800 × 600 resolution, but with two vertical bands (on the left and near the right) at 1024 × 768 resolution, for example.

Similarly, you can use a tall image to produce a tiled horizontal band, as shown in Figure 21.15. Pay careful attention to making the image taller than your page could possibly be; otherwise, the background will repeat. A good technique is also to make the image fade into the background color of the document.

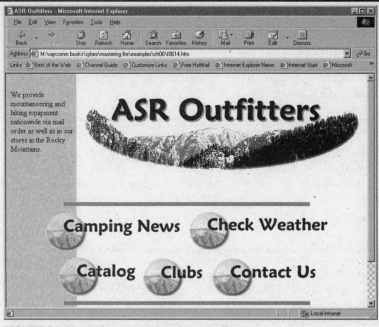

FIGURE 21.14: Wide images tile only vertically.

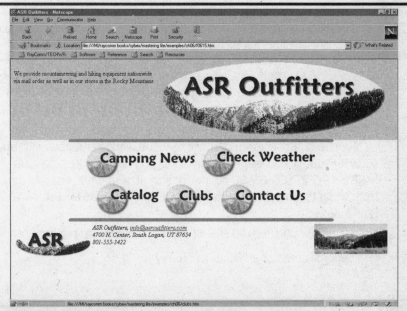

FIGURE 21.15: A horizontal band looks like this in a browser.

If you use background images in your document and the color of the image does not adequately contrast with the text color, reset your document colors. You might also want to set the colors to complement your background image.

To add a background image, use the attributes in Table 21.6 in the opening <BODY> tag.

TABLE 21.6: Background Attributes

Tag	Use
BACKGROUND="..."	Uses URL to identify an image for the background of an HTML document
BGPROPERTIES=FIXED	Sets the background image as nontiled, nonscrolling for use with Internet Explorer

To specify a background image, add the BACKGROUND= attribute to your opening <BODY> tag.

```
<BODY BACKGROUND="asrback.jpg">
```

TIP

You can use style sheets to include background images behind individual page elements, rather than placing a background image behind the entire page.

When you develop background images, you will find that creating a seamless image is difficult. Although some programs, such as Paint Shop Pro, offer a menu option to create a seamless image, you still often see a vague repeating pattern.

If you have a background image that you want to use as a watermark of sorts for your pages—and if your visitors will use Internet Explorer—add the BGPROPERTIES=FIXED attribute. This attribute prevents the image from tiling throughout the background. The full code for the <BODY> tag is as follows:

```
<BODY BACKGROUND="asrbackfull.jpg" BGPROPERTIES=FIXED>
```

This produces the effect shown in Figure 21.16.

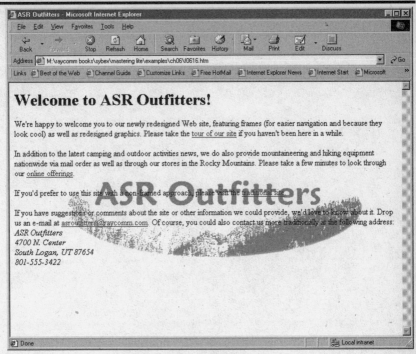

FIGURE 21.16: A fixed background acts as a watermark.

What's Next

In the next and final chapter, you'll further develop your understanding of HTML while focusing on a powerful new extension of it called Extensible HTML (XHTML), specifically designed to allow documents in HTML to include video, animations, graphics, and even sound.

Chapter 22

INTRODUCING XHTML

I n the previous chapters, you learned how to create web pages in Word and Excel as well as in FrontPage. You also learned how to add images to these web pages to help illustrate them.

In this final chapter, you're going to learn more about HTML, the basic web page creation language. You'll gain a great deal more control and flexibility in posting documents to the Web using a powerful extension to HTML called Extensible HTML (XHTML). As a side benefit, you'll also learn how web page language standards are established and how they develop in capability.

Adapted from *Mastering XHTML* by Ed Tittel, Chelsea Valentine, Lucinda Dykes, Mary Burmeister

ISBN 0-7821-2820-3   1056 pp $39.99

WHAT ARE HTML AND XHTML?

XHTML is a *markup language:* a system of codes that identify parts and characteristics of documents. As Figure 22.1 shows, XHTML documents are plain text files. They contain no images, no sounds, no videos, and no animations; however, they can include *pointers*, or links, to these file types, which is how web pages end up looking as if they contain nontext elements.

```
file-upload[1] - Notepad                                         _ □ ×
File  Edit  Format  Help  Send
<!DOCTYPE html PUBLIC "-//W3C//DTD XHTML 1.0 Transitional//EN"
   "http://www.w3.org/TR/xhtml1/DTD/xhtml1-transitional.dtd">
<html xmlns="http://www.w3.org/1999/xhtml">
<head>
  <title>W3C HTML Validation Service: Upload files</title>
</head>
<body>
  <p>
    <a href="http://www.w3.org/">
    <img align="left" src="http://www.w3.org/Icons/www/w3c_home"
         height="48" border="0" alt="W3C" /></a>
  </p>

  <p align="right" class="navbar">
    <a href="./">Validator home</a> |
    <a href="about.html">About this service</a> |
    <a href="feedback.html">Feedback</a><br clear="all" />
  </p>
  <h1>HTML Validation Service</h1>
  <p>
    This form allows you upload files from your computer to have
    them validated.
  </p>
  <form method="post" enctype="multipart/form-data" action="/check">
    File: <input type="file" name="uploaded_file" size="50" />
    <table cellpadding="0" cellspacing="0">
      <tr>
        <td>
          <input name="ss" type="checkbox" value="" /> Show source input
        </td>
        <td>
          <input name="outline" type="checkbox" value="" /> Show an outline of this
          document<br />
        </td>
      </tr>
      <tr>
        <td>
          <input name="sp" type="checkbox" value="" /> Show parse tree
        </td>
        <td>
          <input name="noatt" type="checkbox" value="" /> exclude
          attributes from the parse tree<br />
        </td>
      </tr>
    </table>
    <input type="submit" value="Validate this document" />
    <input type="reset" value="Reset this form" />
  </form>
</body>
</html>
```

FIGURE 22.1: XHTML documents are just text files, containing the code and content you provide.

As you can see, XHTML documents look nothing like the web pages you have likely seen before. Instead, XHTML is made up of elements, tags, and attributes (which will all be defined later in the chapter) that work together to identify document parts and tell browsers how to display them. Figure 22.2 shows how the tags and attributes of Figure 22.1 work together to create a web page.

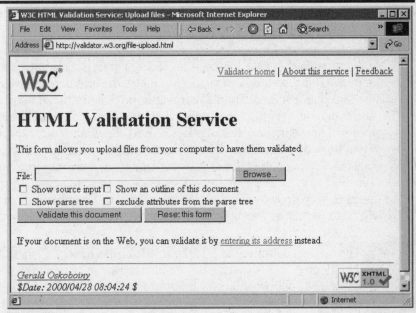

FIGURE 22.2: Browsers interpret the code to determine how to display XHTML documents.

The roots of HTML (which is the predecessor to XHTML) go back to the late 1980s and early 1990s. That's when Tim Berners-Lee first developed HTML to provide a simple way for scientists at CERN (a particle physics laboratory in Geneva, Switzerland) to exchange reports and research results on the Web. HTML is based, in turn, on a formal definition created using a powerful *meta-language*—a language used to create other languages—called the *Standard Generalized Markup Language (SGML)*. SGML is an International Organization for Standardization (ISO) standard tool designed to create markup languages of many kinds.

By 1993, the power and reach of the World Wide Web was becoming well known, and CERN released HTML for unrestricted public use. CERN eventually turned HTML over to an industry group called the World Wide Web Consortium (W3C), which continues to govern HTML and related markup language specifications. Public release of HTML (and its companion protocol, the *Hypertext Transfer Protocol [HTTP]*, which is what browsers use to request web pages and what web servers use to respond to such requests) launched the Web revolution that has changed the face of computing and the Internet forever.

In the intervening years since the early 1990s when HTML became a public standard, HTML has been the focus of great interest, attention, and use. Today, web-related traffic dominates the Internet, and websites have become a standard part of corporate and organizational information access and delivery. Unfortunately, HTML is a *closed* language, which means that the markup it recognizes is fixed and immutable, except when its underlying SGML-based formal definition is altered. Because of this characteristic, HTML has gone through many versions—from version 1 in 1993 to version 4.01 in December 1999—as the language definition seeks to keep up with new, but nonstandard, language elements introduced in particular web browsers such as Microsoft Internet Explorer and Netscape Navigator.

The original definition of HTML provided a mechanism to identify and mark up *content*—specific information judged to be of sufficient importance to deliver online—without worrying too much about how that information looked or how it was presented and formatted on the user's computer display. But as commercial interest in the Web exploded, graphic designers and typographers involved in web design found themselves wishing for the kind of presentation and layout controls that they received from software such as PageMaker and QuarkXPress. HTML was never designed as a full-fledged presentation tool, but it was being pulled strongly in that direction, often by browser vendors who sought market share for their software by accommodating the desires of their audience.

Unfortunately, these browser-specific implementations resulted in variations in the HTML language definitions that weren't supported in all browsers, and in functionality that wasn't part of any official HTML language definition. Web designers found themselves in a pickle—forced either to build web pages for the lowest common denominator that all browsers could support, or to build web pages that targeted specific browsers that not all users could necessarily view or appreciate.

Basically, XHTML was created as a way to clean up this mess. XHTML provides a way to take advantage of a newer, more compact underlying meta-language called XML that is inherently extensible and, therefore, open-ended. XHTML 1.1 was recommended for approval by the W3C in early 2001, making it the most current standard. More importantly, XHTML helps rationalize and consolidate a web markup landscape that had become highly fragmented (a result of different and incompatible implementations of HTML). There are many other good reasons for using XHTML instead of HTML, and you'll learn more about them later in this chapter. But first, some coverage of the basic concepts and terminology that make XHTML work!

Understanding Elements and Tags

Because XHTML uses XML-based terminology, it identifies the markup text that signals the placement of document controls and content containers as *elements*. XHTML elements serve two primary functions. First, they identify logical document parts—that is, major structural components in documents, such as headings (h1, for example), numbered lists (ol, also called *ordered lists*), and paragraphs (p). Therefore, if you want to include a component in an XHTML document, you type the text and apply the appropriate elements to that text. (We'll show you how in the following sections.) That's pretty much all there is to it.

TIP

If you're familiar with HTML, you're probably used to hearing the word *tag* to describe HTML markup—for example, a single tag such as <br> and a tag pair such as <title>...</title>. However, in XML, both are called elements; an element can be either a single instance of markup or a matched pair of markup instances.

Also, some elements in XHTML documents also refer to other things—that is, elements can include pointers and links to other documents, images, sound files, video files, multimedia applications, animations, applets, and so on. For example, if you want to include an image of your company's product in your XHTML document, rather than pasting an image directly into the document (as you might in a word processing file), you include an element (tag) that identifies the filename for that image, as shown here:

```
<img src="logo.gif" alt="corporate logo" />
```

In this example, the img (image) element points to a logo file (logo.gif) that the browser should display. This illustrates that browsers rely on information within an XHTML document to tell them what to display, as well as how to display it.

In this chapter, when we refer to an XTHML element in the text, we will omit the opening and closing angle brackets (and other markup, where appropriate) and simply use the element name to refer to an element in general. On the other hand, when we identify a specific tag, we will reproduce it exactly as it should appear in an XHTML document. Thus, we would refer to the element that identifies a document's title as the title element, but we would produce the following snippet of code to specify an actual document title that includes the opening <title> and closing </title> tags (which are the markup items that create the title element):

```
<title>A Title Identifies a Document's Purpose or Primary
Content</title>
```

In the preceding example, the <title> and </title> tags enclose the actual content related to the title element. When the XHTML document appears within a web browser, the string "A Title Identifies a Document's Purpose or Primary Content" appears in the title bar for the window in which it appears, as shown in Figure 22.3.

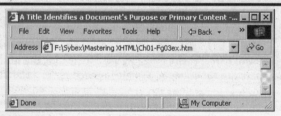

FIGURE 22.3: The title element's content appears in the browser window's title bar.

XHTML tags come in one of two forms:

▶ A singleton tag, such as <br /> or <img />, is formally called an *empty element* because it includes no actual text content. In XHTML, such tags must end with a space and a slash before the closing right angle bracket. (The space is a little trick that allows older browsers—ones that may not recognize XHTML—to treat such tags as HTML and therefore recognize them. Without the space before those closing characters, older browsers may ignore such tags altogether.)

▶ A pair of related tags, such as `<title>...</title>` or `<head>... </head>`, enclose and identify document content. In such cases, the first tag in a pair (for example, `<head>`) is called an *opening tag* because it opens a content container. The second tag in a pair (for example, `</head>`) is called a *closing tag* because it closes the content container opened by the opening tag.

Unlike HTML, which allows great latitude in how markup is included or omitted from documents, XHTML is persnickety about the markup it's willing to recognize. In any XHTML document, all tag text must appear in lowercase; every empty element must end with the closing `/>` string; and every opening tag must be followed by a corresponding closing tag at an appropriate point. Understanding the details of these general rules is important.

Understanding Element Components

As our examples so far should illustrate, XHTML elements, and the tags that represent them in XHTML documents, are reasonably intuitive. Although markup can occasionally be cryptic, you can usually get some idea of an element's function from its name. Let's take a look at the components that go into building tags for XHTML elements.

First, all tags are composed of *element names* that are contained within *angle brackets* (`< >`). The angle brackets simply tell browsers that the text between them represents XHTML markup rather than ordinary text content. Some sample tags look like these:

▶ `<h2>` (for heading level 2)

▶ `<p>` (for document paragraph)

▶ `<strong>` (to emphasize a particular section of content strongly)

Second, many elements are designed to contain content; they use a pair of tags, where actual content occurs between the opening tag (for example, `<h1>`) and the corresponding closing tag (`</h1>`). Both tags look alike, except the closing tag includes a forward slash (`/`) to denote the end of the element container. To apply tags to something in your document, place an opening tag before the content that should be associated with the element you wish to use, and place the closing tag after it, as follows:

```
<h1>Information to which the tags apply.</h1>
```

When creating XHTML markup by hand, you can make life easier on yourself by entering both the opening and closing tags at the same time. That way, you won't forget the closing tag. If you do forget a closing tag, most elements will treat all subsequent content after the opening tag as content for the opening element until the browser finds a matching closing tag. On the other hand, if you use an XHTML or HTML editor, most of these tools will create content tags in pairs to absolve you of this responsibility.

To apply more than one element to a particular piece of content, you nest the tags. *Nesting* means placing one set of tags inside another set. For example, to apply strong emphasis to a word within a paragraph, you nest the strong element within the paragraph (p) element, as follows:

```
<p>The <strong>right</strong> way to use strong emphasis is to
    enclose only those words you wish to emphasize inside a
    strong element</p>
```

TIP

Throughout the book, because of the width limits of the printed page, we wrap and indent code lines that are meant to be written all on one line. This doesn't mean you have to; you should type these long lines without a return in your code. (A little later, in the section "Improving XHTML Readability," we'll explain when and why you should type code on multiple lines.)

When you nest elements, the first opening tag must be matched by a corresponding closing tag at the end of the outside block of content, and the second opening tag must be closed with a corresponding closing tag immediately after the internal content block that it relates to. XHTML is quite insistent that you can't use tags out of order; therefore, a block of text like this:

```
<p>The last word gets strong <strong>emphasis.</p></strong>
```

is invalid because it closes the outside p element before closing the nested (or inside) strong element.

Typing Tags Correctly

When typing tags, be particularly careful not to include extra spaces within the tag itself. If you do this, a browser may not recognize the tag and may not display the content associated with the corresponding XHTML element correctly. Sometimes, a browser might display the markup itself because it's unable to distinguish improperly formed markup from normal element content.

For example, a `title` element should look like this:

```
<title>Correctly Formed Title</title>
```

Do *not* include spaces within tags for nonempty elements, as in this erroneous example:

```
< title >Incorrectly Formed Title< /title >
```

This explains the strange appearance of the browser view of this markup shown in Figure 22.4.

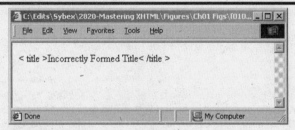

FIGURE 22.4: An incorrectly formed `title` element's content appears inside the browser window, not in the title bar.

Of course, the exception to this rule is empty elements, which need a space before the closing `/>`. Type an empty element's tag like this:

```
<img src="picture.jpg" alt="A picture of us" />
```

Improving XHTML Readability

You'll find it easier to read and use tags if you follow a few conventions. In particular, use hard returns between elements to create shorter lines. This does not affect how browsers display an XHTML document; it just makes that document easier for you to read when you're editing its contents.

The following two examples show you how hard returns and indents can improve readability.

```
<!DOCTYPE html PUBLIC "-//W3C//DTD XHTML 1.0 Transitional//EN"
"http://www.w3.org/TR/xhtml1/DTD/xhtml1-transitional.dtd">
<html xmlns="http://www.w3.org/1999/xhtml"><head><title>
Mastering HTML Document Title</title></head><body>Mastering
HTML Document Body</body></html>
```

The preceding code produces exactly the same display as this:

```
<!DOCTYPE html PUBLIC "-//W3C//DTD XHTML 1.0 Transitional//EN"
    "http://www.w3.org/TR/xhtml1/DTD/xhtml1-transitional.dtd">
<html xmlns="http://www.w3.org/1999/xhtml">
    <head>
        <title>Mastering HTML Document Title</title>
    </head>
    <body>
        Mastering HTML Document Body
    </body>
</html>
```

No question which one's easier to read or follow, right?

TIP

Those of you who are already familiar with HTML may be wondering why all XHTML element names appear exclusively in lowercase. Perhaps some of you even know that HTML is indifferent to case for tag text. That's not true for XHTML, however: All tag text—except attribute values (covered in the next section) and DOCTYPE declarations—must be lowercase. This is to match how the tags that correspond to XHTML elements are defined formally in the document type definition (DTD).

Understanding XHTML Attributes

Some XHTML elements take modifying values called *attributes*, which provide additional information about these elements, such as:

- ▶ What other files should be accessed, such as an image file

- ▶ What language is used for an element's content

- ▶ Whether an element's content should read right to left or left to right

Attributes are also used to uniquely identify an element instance within a document and to apply some presentation style to an element. Normally, attributes take the form *attribute*="*value*"; they always follow the tag name within the opening tag of a nonempty element or within an empty element's tag.

Let's assume you want to center a heading 1 in the browser window. You'd start with your heading and tags, like this:

```
<h1>A heading goes here</h1>
```

Next, add the `style` and `type` attributes to the opening tag, like this:

```
<h1 type="text/css" style="align:center">
    A centered heading goes here</h1>
```

All attributes are separated from other attributes and the tag itself by spaces. In XHTML, *all* attributes require quotes. As our example illustrates, you can include multiple attributes in a single tag by placing a space between each attribute/value pair.

TIP

Within opening tags, or the tags that correspond to empty elements, attributes can appear in any order after the element name, but the element name must always appear first.

WHAT CAN YOU DO WITH XHTML?

You're likely most familiar with HTML, or XHTML, because it's used to create web pages; but either of these markup languages may be put to many other uses:

Developing intranet or extranet sites   XHTML is commonly used to develop intranet websites—sites accessed by people within a company or organization from one or more locations— or extranet sites, used by people from a specific group of companies or organizations that routinely share information among themselves.

Developing help files   XHTML can also be used to develop online help files that are accessible on any platform. Online help files allow developers to produce documentation inexpensively.

Developing network applications   XHTML is particularly suitable for creating entire applications, such as training programs, interactive chats, or databases that are available through web pages.

Part vii

Developing kiosk applications   XHTML can also be used to create kiosk applications—those stand-alone computers with the neat touch-screen capabilities.

Delivering content for web-enabled phones, personal digital assistants (PDAs), or handheld computers   In March 2001, a consortium of wireless device manufacturers—including Nokia, Ericsson, Motorola, 3Com, and Handspring—announced that they were adopting XHTML as their standard markup language. This is because XHTML includes special facilities that make it easy to transform and filter XHTML documents for display on wireless devices.

WHAT TOOLS DO YOU NEED?

For your first XHTML documents, you need only the following basic tools:

- A plain-vanilla text editor, which you will use to create and save your XHTML documents (see the sidebar "HTML Editors" for an explanation as to why we can't currently recommend any XHTML editors)

- An XHTML validator, which you will use to check the syntax and structure of your XHTML documents

- A web browser, which you will use to view and test your XHTML documents

Text Editors

Although there are dozens of excellent HTML *What-You-See-Is-What-You-Get (WYSIWYG)* editors available, you should learn to code XHTML using a standard text editor. Text editors force you to *hand-code*, meaning that you, not the software, enter tags and attributes. Hand-coding helps you learn XHTML elements, attributes, and structures, and lets you see exactly where you've made mistakes. Also, with hand-coding, you can easily include the newest XHTML enhancements into your documents. Some good text editors are Notepad for all Windows versions, vi or pico for Unix, and TeachText or SimpleText for Macintosh.

TIP

Learning to hand-code is essential for using the latest and greatest XHTML effects—whether it's the current XHTML 1.1 or a future version. Most new XHTML versions are not supported by WYSIWYG editors yet, so you need to hand-code new elements and attributes in your documents anyway, even when using an HTML- or XHTML-savvy tool.

HTML EDITORS

As we write this chapter, few editors are available that produce native XHTML code. However, it's possible to use an HTML editor, instead of a simple text editor, to create an initial version of your XHTML documents and then to make use of a special-purpose tool, such as HTML Tidy or HTML-Kit, to transform your HTML into equivalent, properly formatted XHTML. Because this requires a bit more savvy than we assume from our general readership, this material is aimed only at those more experienced readers to whom this kind of approach makes sense.

In general, HTML editors fall into two categories:

▶ Text- or code-based, which show you the HTML code as you're creating documents

▶ WYSIWYG, which show the results of code, similar to the way it will appear in a browser, as you're formatting your document

Simple WYSIWYG editors, such as Netscape Composer and Microsoft FrontPage Express, are good for quickly generating HTML documents. These editors only give you a close approximation of page layout, design, and colors, but are good for viewing the general arrangement of features. However, they do not give you, the author, as much control over the final appearance of your document as code-based editors do.

After you've developed a few HTML documents and understand basic HTML principles, you may choose to use both a WYSIWYG editor and a code-based editor. For example, you can get a good start on your document using a WYSIWYG HTML editor and then polish it (or fix it) using a code-based one. For now, though, we recommend that you hand-code XHTML using a standard text editor.

WARNING

Using a word processing program such as Word, WordPerfect, or even WordPad to create HTML documents often introduces unwanted formatting and control characters, which can cause problems. XHTML requires plain text with no formatting controls, so either make a special effort to save all documents as plain text within such applications or take our advice and use a text editor instead.

The W3C Validator

One of the primary benefits that XHTML confers to its users is the ability to mechanically—or at least, programmatically—*validate* XHTML documents. In plain terms, this means that after you've created an XHTML document, you can submit it to an online syntax-checking tool for analysis. This tool will tell you whether the document follows the rules for some specific, well-known form of XHTML syntax; if it finds errors, it will identify them by their location in the document. This means you can check whether your documents follow one or more sets of XHTML syntax rules, and keep working through them until you achieve the XHTML equivalent of nirvana: a clean bill of health from the validator!

Using this tool is incredibly simple. You need only visit http://validator.w3.org/file-upload.html, browse your local hard disk, and upload the file you want validated through the nearly mindless interface. If you're in luck, what you get back looks like what's shown in Figure 22.5. If you're not in luck, you will need to find out how to read and interpret the validator's sometimes cryptic error messages.

Our main point is that you should make validation part of your standard XHTML-authoring process. That way, you'll get the best possible guarantee that most browsers will be able to view and display the contents of your XHTML documents.

Web Browsers

If you've ever surfed the Web, you've used a web browser to view HTML or XHTML documents. The most common browsers are Microsoft Internet Explorer (IE) and Netscape Navigator; however, many other browsers are also available for virtually all computer platforms and online services. We're especially fond of Opera (available free from www.opera.com) and Amaya (available free at www.w3.org/Amaya) because they often support advanced features and functions sooner than the more popular IE and Netscape browsers do.

Exactly how your documents appear, though, varies from browser to browser and from computer to computer. For example, most browsers in use today are *graphical* browsers: They can display elements other than text. A *text-only* browser can display—you guessed it—only text. How your XHTML documents appear in each of these types of browsers differs significantly, as shown in Figures 22.6 and 22.7.

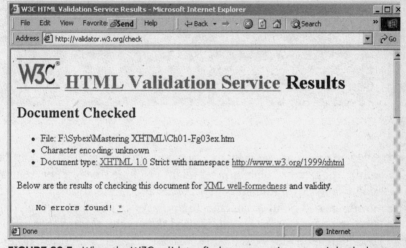

FIGURE 22.5: When the W3C validator finds no errors, its output is both short and very sweet!

FIGURE 22.6: An HTML document displayed in Netscape Navigator

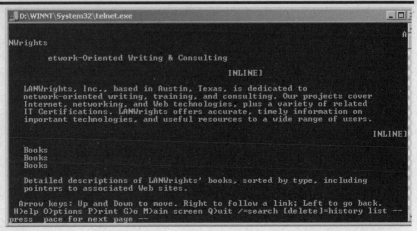

FIGURE 22.7: The same HTML document viewed in Lynx, a text-only browser

Even different graphical browsers tend to display things a bit differently. For example, one browser might display a first-level heading as 15 point Times New Roman bold, whereas another might display the same heading as 14 point Arial italic. In both cases, the browser displays the heading bigger and more emphasized than regular text, but the specific text characteristics vary. Figures 22.8 and 22.9 show how two other browsers display the same XHTML document.

Finally, your user's computer settings can also make a big difference in how your HTML or XHTML documents appear. For example, the computer's resolution and specific browser settings can alter a document's appearance.

So, as you're developing and viewing your XHTML documents, remember that what you see may look a bit different to your users. If possible, test your documents in as many different browsers, at as many different resolutions and color settings, on as many different computers as possible. You won't be able to test for all possible variations, but you should be able to get a good idea of what your users might see.

FIGURE 22.8: The W3C Amaya browser has its own unique look and feel.

FIGURE 22.9: The Opera browser shows the same document with slightly different formatting.

What Other Resources Can Help?

You can find information, resources, and specifications on the Web. In particular, the W3C site, as well as several product-specific websites, will help you learn, use, and keep up with changes in XHTML.

Visit the W3C

The W3C was created in 1994 at the Massachusetts Institute of Technology (MIT), home of many computer innovations, to oversee the development of web standards, eventually including the XHTML standard. This consortium defines and publishes XHTML and numerous other web-related standards, along with information about the elements and attributes that may legally appear within XHTML documents. So, an excellent way to monitor XHTML changes is to visit the W3C site at www.w3.org/MarkUp. There you'll find new releases of XHTML standards and information about HTML standards.

For more information on proposed standards and other developments in web-related specifications, such as Cascading Style Sheets (CSS) and XML specifications, visit the W3C's home page at www.w3.org.

Can you use new elements and attributes as they become available? For the most part, yes. By the time many popular elements and attributes become part of a standard, they already work with many or most browsers. However, some elements and attributes (including some that were introduced with XHTML 1.0 and continued in 1.1) did not have wide or stable browser support when the specification was released and, to this day, do not have nearly the breadth of support that some other elements and attributes enjoy.

Monitor Netscape and Microsoft Sites

When HTML was the prevailing web markup standard, each time Netscape or Microsoft released a new browser version, they would also add new markup *extensions*, which are browser-specific, nonstandard elements and attributes. Some of these extensions were useful, some less so. However, as a whole, any nonstandard elements introduced into HTML caused problems both for web developers and for users.

Fortunately, fewer extensions seem to be introduced now that XHTML has made the scene, but you should still be aware of what's added with each new browser release.

If you're considering using extensions in your XHTML documents, keep in mind that they're not standard and that the W3C validator will not recognize or validate nonstandard markup. Also, extensions that are specific to a particular browser (for example, Netscape) will probably not work in other browsers (such as Internet Explorer or Opera). For this reason, we strongly recommend that you refrain from using extensions and use only standard XHTML elements and attributes. This way, you'll not only be able to validate your documents to make sure they're syntactically correct, but you can also be reasonably sure that all your users can access the information you provide therein.

TIP

As of early 2001, about 75 percent of web surfers used Internet Explorer, about 18 percent used Netscape Navigator, and the remaining 7 percent used a variety of other browsers. Realistically, about 80 to 90 percent of web users can access most sites that use standard XHTML markup.

You can find Netscape's elements and attributes at `http://developer.netscape.com/docs/manuals/htmlguid/index.htm`.

And you will find Microsoft's elements and attributes at `http://msdn.microsoft.com/workshop/author/default.asp`.

Monitor Other Sites

Although definitive information comes from the W3C, Microsoft, and Netscape, you can check other reliable resources. Here's a list of sites to check regularly:

Organization	URL
Web Design Group	`www.htmlhelp.com`
Web Developer's Virtual Library	`www.wdvl.com`
HTML Writer's Guild	`www.hwg.org`
C|Net's Builder.com	`www.builder.com`
Zvon	`www.zvon.org`

Part vii

Appendix A

INSTALLING MICROSOFT OFFICE XP

Installing Microsoft Office XP is relatively easy, if you do the necessary preparation. Before you put the Office XP CD in your drive, you'll want to make sure you have enough memory and hard-disk capacity to use Office XP. The Microsoft-recommended system configuration is Microsoft Windows 2000 Professional on a computer with a Pentium III processor and 128 megabytes (MB) of RAM. Table A.1 lists Microsoft's minimum hardware/software requirements as well as our comments.

Adapted from *Mastering Microsoft Office XP Premium Edition* by Gini Courter and Annette Marquis with Karla Browning

ISBN 0-7821-4000-9   1392 pp $49.99

TABLE A.1: Minimum and Recommended Hardware/Software Requirements for Office XP

HARDWARE/ SOFTWARE	MINIMUM REQUIREMENTS	COMMENTS
Computer/processor	Computer with a Pentium 133 megahertz (MHz) or higher processor.	
Memory	RAM requirements depend on the operating system used.	You need at least 128MB for speech recognition.
	Windows 98 or Windows 98 Second Edition: 24MB of RAM plus an additional 8MB of RAM for each Office application (such as Microsoft Word) running simultaneously.	
	Windows Me or Windows NT: 32MB of RAM plus an additional 8MB of RAM for each Office application (such as Microsoft Word) running simultaneously.	
	Windows 2000 Professional: 64MB of RAM plus an additional 8MB of RAM for each Office application (such as Microsoft Word) running simultaneously.	
Hard disk	Hard-disk space requirements will vary depending on configuration; custom installation choices may require more or less hard-disk space.	Microsoft identifies the need for an additional 100MB of hard-disk space if you plan to install the Office XP Media Content and an additional 50MB for each language interface you install.
	245MB of available hard-disk space with 115MB on the hard disk where the operating system is installed.	
	Users without Windows 2000, Windows Me, or Office 2000 Service Release 1 (SR-1) require an extra 50MB of hard-disk space for System Files Update.	
Operating system	Windows 98, Windows 98 Second Edition, Windows Me, Windows NT 4 with Service Pack 6 (SP-6) or later, or Windows 2000 or later.	
Drive	CD-ROM drive.	
Display	Super VGA (800 × 600) or higher resolution monitor with 256 colors.	
Peripherals	Microsoft Mouse, Microsoft IntelliMouse, or compatible pointing device.	

In addition to these requirements, you may want to install speech and handwriting recognition. For speech recognition, you minimally need the following:

▶ A high-quality, close-talk (headset) microphone. A Universal Serial Bus (USB) microphone with gain adjustment support is recommended. Gain adjustment is a feature that modifies microphone amplification so that the input sound level is appropriate for use by the system.

▶ 400 megahertz (MHz) or faster computer

▶ 128 megabytes (MB) or more of RAM

▶ Microsoft Windows 98 or later, or Microsoft Windows NT 4 or later

▶ Microsoft Internet Explorer 5 or later

For handwriting, you will want to have a graphics tablet, although it is not required if you are talented with the mouse!

There are a number of different versions of Office XP, but each is supplied on one or more CDs. To begin the installation, close any open applications, and then insert CD 1 in your CD-ROM drive. The CD should run automatically. If you've disabled the Windows AutoRun feature, open My Computer or Explorer; then locate and double-click the `setup.exe` file on the CD-ROM to begin installation. The Windows Installer loads and checks your computer system, and the message "Preparing to Install..." appears in the Microsoft Office XP Setup dialog box on the screen.

In the first step of Office XP Setup, shown in Figure A.1, verify your name. Setup gets your name from your computer system; if it is incorrect, select and type over your name. Enter your initials and the 25-character key for the Office XP CD. Generally, you can find the key on the CD case, but it may be included on a separate license packaged with your CD. Click Next to continue.

The end-user license agreement (EULA) appears on the second page. You didn't really buy Office XP from Microsoft—you're licensing it. Take a minute and scroll through the terms of the agreement so you understand your rights and responsibilities with the software. (If you don't indicate that you agree with the terms, you cannot install Office XP.) When you've finished reading, click the I Accept The Terms In The License Agreement option and click Next.

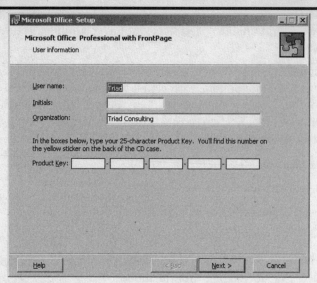

FIGURE A.1: Enter your name, initials, and CD key to begin installation.

The third step of installation is to choose the type of installation you want to do. You can choose Upgrade Now if you want to install Office based on your current configuration. It removes any previous versions of Office. You can choose from four other types:

- ▶ Typical installs the standard Office XP features.

- ▶ Complete installs all of the XP features—be forewarned that you need a boatload of disk space.

- ▶ Custom allows you to choose the applications and features you want to install.

- ▶ Minimal installs only the basic Office features without all the bells and whistles. Choose this option if you have limited hard-disk space.

We generally recommend that you choose Custom even if you don't want to make any changes to the Typical installation. Customizing is the only way you can see which features you are installing. Click Next.

In the fourth step, choose a location for the Office XP files. The default location is the Program Files directory on your boot disk (the hard disk that also has Windows installed). Office XP installs about 115MB of files on your boot disk, even if you choose to install on another hard disk; the remaining files will be put in the disk and folder you designate here. Click Next to continue.

Windows Installer searches your computer to see if you have any previous versions of Office applications installed. The applications are listed, as shown in Figure A.2, and you can choose to retain or remove them when Office XP is installed. If you are not sure you want to remove the applications right away, you can retain any of them except Outlook. You can't run Outlook 2002 and previous versions of Outlook. Either choose to remove earlier versions of Outlook or don't install Outlook 2002. You can always remove the earlier Office versions later using Add/Remove Programs in Windows Control Panel.

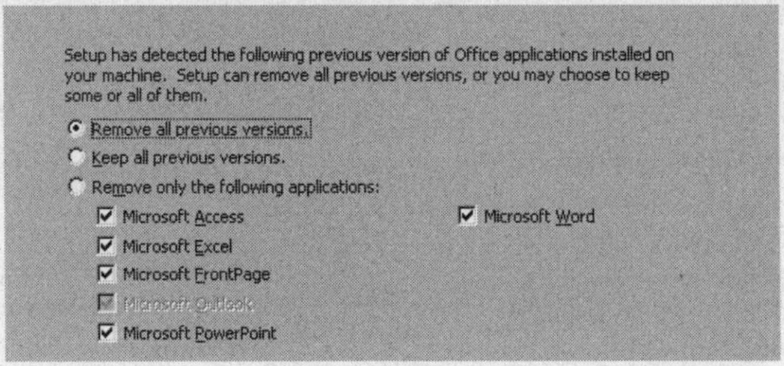

Setup has detected the following previous version of Office applications installed on your machine. Setup can remove all previous versions, or you may choose to keep some or all of them.

- ● Remove all previous versions.
- ○ Keep all previous versions.
- ○ Remove only the following applications:
  - ☑ Microsoft Access   ☑ Microsoft Word
  - ☑ Microsoft Excel
  - ☑ Microsoft FrontPage
  - ☑ Microsoft Outlook
  - ☑ Microsoft PowerPoint

FIGURE A.2: You can choose which previous Office versions you want to retain.

The last version of an application installed is the default Windows version, so double-clicking, for example, an Excel file in the Explorer launches the most recently installed version of Excel. This is a problem only with Access, which uses different file types in the 97 and 2000 versions. If you'd like Access 97 to be your default version, reinstall Access 97 after installing Office XP.

If you chose a Custom installation, you'll now have an opportunity to select which applications you would like to install, as shown in Figure A.3. You can choose the typical options for the applications selected or elect to review detailed installation options for each application. We recommend this second choice.

The Office XP applications are listed in an Explorer-like tree. Click a feature to see its description below the list. To see the options for an application, click the Expand button (the plus sign in front of the icon) to expand the view. In Figure A.4, Excel has been expanded.

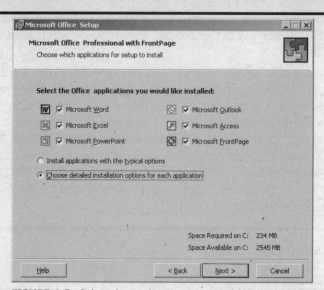

FIGURE A.3: Select the applications you would like to install, and then choose to review the detailed installation options for each application.

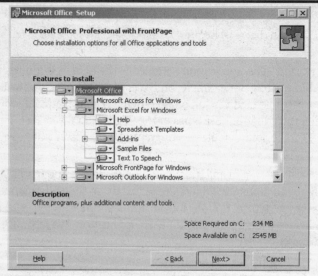

FIGURE A.4: Click the plus sign to view options for an application.

The Installer shows you the features that would have been installed if you had chosen the Typical installation. With earlier versions of Office, you had an unappealing choice: Either waste disk space on components you might not use, or rerun Setup to add components you did not install initially. With Office XP, you don't have to waste disk space or reinstall. A feature introduced in Office 2000 called *Install On Demand* lets you choose to install a component or feature the first time you try to use it. If there are features that you think might be needed at some point, you can make them available in the Setup program's Select Features window.

TIP

The downside of Install On Demand is that you need access to the installation point—network drive or CD—to install the feature when you need it. If you think you'll use an application feature, install it now. Save Install On Demand for features you're less likely to use.

Click a feature's icon and select how, where, and when you want the feature installed from the menu:

Run From My Computer   Installs the feature on your computer now.

Run All From My Computer   Installs the feature and any related subfeatures on your computer now.

Run From Network   Installs the feature on your network.

Run All From Network   Installs the feature and any related subfeatures on your network.

Installed On First Use   Opens a message box to verify that you want to install the feature on your computer the first time you attempt to use it in the application. This option is the default on some but not all features. For example, additional templates are by default installed on first use.

Not Available   Indicates a feature that is not installed; to install the feature, you must run Office XP Setup again.

The required disk space and total free space available on the disk you selected earlier are displayed at the bottom of the dialog box (see Figure A.4); as you add or remove features from the installation list, these numbers change. You won't be allowed to select additional features after you exceed the free disk space. If you have only one hard disk and are installing features on your computer, make sure you still have 50–100MB free after all the features are selected, or you'll create problems for the Windows virtual memory manager.

TIP

If you work in a mixed-platform office with colleagues who use other computers and other applications, pay particular attention to the Office Tools and Converters And Filters features. If you don't know what applications your colleagues use, you can hedge by installing all the filters and converters or indicating that they should be installed on demand.

When you have finished specifying which features should be installed, click the Install Now button to begin installing Office XP. Depending on the features you selected and your computer's system speed, installation may take up to 50 minutes. A progress meter appears in the Setup dialog box to indicate how much of the installation is completed. At times, the meter may stop completely for several minutes. Don't assume that this is a problem. If installation stops for more than 10 minutes with no disk activity, press Ctrl+Alt+Del to open the Close Program dialog box and see if Setup is shown as *Not Responding*. If it is, select Setup and click End Task (you may have to do this two or three times) to exit Setup. Exit Windows completely, restart Windows, and then launch Office XP Setup again from the CD.

When the first CD is finished, the Installer prompts you to reboot your computer; click Yes.

TIP

Although Microsoft's installation instructions indicate that you do not have to reboot until you have installed all of the Office XP CDs, we recommend rebooting after each CD to avoid known problems with the installation process.

After you reboot your computer, the Installer requires a few more minutes to complete the installation before you are ready to use your new Office XP applications. Each application is added individually to the Programs menu, so you can launch all of the applications from there, from the Office Shortcut bar (if you chose to install it), or by choosing New Office Document or Open Office Document from the Start menu.

If you ever want to add features you didn't install or remove features you don't want, choose Add/Remove Programs from Windows Control Panel or just insert the Office XP CD in your CD drive.

Appendix B

SPEECH AND HANDWRITING RECOGNITION IN OFFICE XP

This appendix is designed to give you more information for working with the speech and handwriting recognition capabilities included in Office XP.

Adapted from *Mastering Microsoft Office XP Premium Edition* by Gini Courter and Annette Marquis with Karla Browning

ISBN 0-7821-4000-9   1392 pp $49.99

PREPARING TO USE OFFICE XP'S SPEECH RECOGNITION TOOLS

Speech recognition has come a long way in the last six years. Certainly, software developments have played a part in its moving into the mainstream. But it's hardware advancements that have really tipped the scales. The availability of more memory, faster processors, better microphones, and larger hard drives are all players in the speech recognition equation. Before deciding whether you want to delve into this new technology, take a look at the following hardware and software requirements recommended by Microsoft:

- A high-quality, close-talk (headset) microphone with gain adjustment support (USB preferred)

- A 400MHz or faster computer

- 128MB or more of memory

- Windows 98 or later or Windows NT 4 or later

- Microsoft Internet Explorer 5 or later

NOTE

Gain adjustment support is a feature in microphones that amplifies your input for use by the speech recognition software.

Although not indicated by Microsoft, you also need a good-quality sound card—read the sidebar "Can a Different Microphone Help Me Improve Recognition Accuracy?" for suggestions. Most sound cards are designed primarily for quality output. Only recently have sound cards been designed to handle input to complement speech and voice recognition software.

NOTE

Speech recognition software is software that translates spoken words into typed text. *Voice recognition* hardware and software identify individual voice patterns and are primarily designed for security purposes.

Be aware that the hardware requirements for processor speed and RAM are minimum requirements. Although we have used speech recognition on 128MB of RAM and a slower processor, it is less than ideal. In fact, you may even find it interfering with your ability to run other software without crashing. If you can afford to upgrade to 196MB of RAM, you'll find it makes a drastic difference.

After you've selected and installed the sound card and microphone, you're just two short steps away from speaking your text and commands:

1. Set up your microphone with the Microphone Wizard (less than 5 minutes).

2. Create speech files with the Voice Training Wizard (less than 20 minutes).

WHY WON'T SPEECH RUN RIGHT ON MY SYSTEM?

Speech recognition has some special requirements depending on the operating system you are using and exactly what you want to do with it. If you would like to use Speech to make Office as hands-free as possible, consider the following requirements:

▶ If you are running Windows 98 (not Microsoft Windows 98 Second Edition) and you want to dictate into dialog boxes, you should download the Microsoft Active Accessibility Redistribution Kit (RDK). Although we recommend upgrading to Windows 98 Second Edition if at all possible, you can download the RDK from Microsoft at www.microsoft.com/enable/msaa/download.htm#RDK.

▶ If you are running Windows NT 4, be sure you are using Internet Explorer 5.5.

▶ If you are using HTML format for your e-mail messages and you are running Microsoft Windows 2000 with Microsoft Internet Explorer 5.5, you need Internet Explorer 5.5 Service Pack 1 (SP1).

Setting Up Your Microphone

Locate the microphone and headphone jacks on your computer and plug in your microphone. If you have a USB microphone, plug it into the USB port. You can run the Microphone Wizard from any Office application. Choose Tools ➤ Speech from the menu bar. The Language bar appears, floating somewhere over the application window:

| 🖋 Correction | 🎤 Microphone 🖳 Tools | ✍ Handwriting | ⬍ |

CAN A DIFFERENT MICROPHONE HELP ME IMPROVE RECOGNITION ACCURACY?

Before you even attempt to use the speech recognition tools, Microsoft recommends a minimum of a 400MHz processor and 128MB of RAM. As with any recommended minimum, you will not see optimal performance at this level. You need 192MB to 256MB to give you more stability and improve the software's accuracy. If you meet these requirements and are still having problems with accuracy, it could be your microphone.

At the time of this writing, Microsoft recommends only one microphone for use with its Speech tools, the Microsoft SideWinder Game Voice, which also lets you control games with voice commands. We have tried several other headset-style microphones with varying degrees of success. USB microphones with gain adjustment support are clearly the best choice. You can choose from desktop, headset, collar, and digital microphones. If you go with a headset or collar, choose one that fits you well and is comfortable so that the microphone stays positioned near your mouth at all times—off to the side of your mouth is usually best. Microphones with a swivel arm such as the Labtec Axis 501 make it easy to move it out of the way and return it to the same position when you are ready to dictate. If you choose a desktop model, be sure you keep it in the same place each time you dictate. Moving it around could affect accuracy, especially if the distance changes. Finding quality microphones for under $50 that are especially designed for speech recognition is becoming easier. The key is to not just settle for the microphone that came with your computer. Chances are it will not do the job for you. Invest a few dollars and you'll have a lot more fun with Speech.

NOTE

Options on the Language bar may vary depending on the options you've installed and what is active at the current time. For more about Language bar options, see "Working with the Language Bar" later in this chapter.

If the microphone has not been previously set up, you are prompted to run the Microphone Wizard. The wizard adjusts the volume from your microphone so that it works well with the Office applications. Even if the microphone has been set up before, we recommend running it again to adjust its settings to your preferences. If you are not prompted for the Microphone Wizard, choose Tools ➤ Options from the Language bar to open the Speech Properties dialog box.

Click the Configure Microphone button in the Speech Properties dialog box to start the Microphone Wizard. Follow the instructions in the wizard to configure your microphone for optimal use with Microsoft Office XP.

NOTE

If you're using your headset microphone and laptop in a hotel room rather than your office, it's a good idea to invest a few minutes and run the wizard again to ensure the best recognition.

Training the Speech Recognition System

After the microphone is configured, you will use the microphone to train the Speech Recognition System. Train the system in the environment where you intend to use it: If you're going to use it in your office, train the system in your office with the normal level of office noise.

The first time you set up your microphone, the voice-training process starts automatically as soon as your microphone is configured. If you need to start it manually, choose Tools ➤ Training on the Language bar to create a user profile and begin training the system to recognize the way you pronounce words. You read the text that's displayed in the dialog box, and the Speech Recognition System highlights each word as it recognizes it, as shown in Figure B.1. Your first training session will probably take around 20 minutes. You can pause at any point and continue later, but we don't recommend it. If you stop prior to the end of the session, you need to start at the beginning the next time you wish to train.

When you've completed the introductory training session, your speech settings are saved in a speech profile. The system keeps a separate profile for each user. After you've worked with the Speech Recognition System in Office XP applications for a little while, we suggest going back for more training using other materials to increase recognition. Just choose Tools ➤ Training on the Language bar and choose one of the sessions from the list.

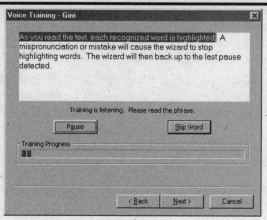

FIGURE B.1: As you read the session text, each recognized word is highlighted by the Speech Recognition System.

NOTE

When you complete training, Office plays a short training video to help you get started. It's worth seeing just to learn how Microsoft suggests using the tools.

USING THE SPEECH RECOGNITION SYSTEM

You can use the Speech Recognition System in Office XP in three ways:

- ▶ Dictate or correct text.
- ▶ Issue voice commands to activate buttons, menu commands, and dialog boxes.
- ▶ Play back printed text from a document.

Dictating in Office XP

To use the dictation or voice command features of Office XP, open the Tools menu on any application and choose Speech. This activates the Language bar.

NOTE

If you've never used speech recognition software before, we suggest you start dictating in the application where you feel most comfortable. For most people, that is Word.

Click the Microphone button on the Language bar to turn the microphone on. When the microphone is active, you can see additional options on the Language bar for Dictation and Voice Command. To the right of Voice Command is a yellow balloon that displays messages as you dictate. Some messages, such as Too Soft, let you know to speak up. When you are in Voice Command mode, this message box displays the last recognized command or what you could have said rather than using the mouse or keyboard.

Correction	Microphone	Dictation	Voice Command	Too soft	Tools	Handwriting

To begin dictating text, make sure the Dictation button is blue. If it is not, click it and then begin speaking to enter text in your document. Speak each word clearly, and speak the names of the punctuation marks (comma, period, question mark). When you want a new paragraph, say **New Paragraph**. When you first begin, don't worry about making corrections. Just keep dictating and get comfortable with developing an appropriate speed and rhythm. If you are getting good recognition, keep going and worry about editing later. Don't forget to speak punctuation marks.

In addition to using punctuation marks, you can also use the commands listed in Table B.1 in Dictation mode.

TABLE B.1:   Commands You Can Say in Dictation Mode

TO COMPLETE THIS TASK...	YOU SAY...
Start text on the next line.	**New Line**
Start a new paragraph.	**New Paragraph**
Turn the microphone off.	**Mic Off**
Press the Tab key once.	**Tab**
Backspace a Tab.	**Shift Tab**
Press the Enter key once.	**Enter**

TABLE B.1 CONTINUED: Commands You Can Say in Dictation Mode

To Complete This Task...	You Say...
Spell out the next word. You have to pause for a second after spelling out the word to switch back to normal Dictation mode.	**Spelling Mode**
Enter a number or symbol instead of spelling it out such as *2* instead of *two*. Pause for a second after using this command to revert to normal Dictation mode.	**Forcenum**

TIP

If you want to enter several numbers, dictate the numbers without the Forcenum command. Speech recognizes strings of numbers and enters them as numbers rather than text. It even formats phone numbers for you automatically.

You can dictate in any Office XP application. In Outlook, select the text box in an open form before you begin speaking. In Excel, cell navigation is part of dictation: Precede the direction with the words **Go To**, **Go Up**, **Go Down**, **Go Left**, or **Go Right** and then indicate how many cells—**One Cell**, **Two Cells**, and so on.

When you are finished dictating or need to take a break, click the Microphone button again to turn Speech off or click Voice Command and say **Microphone**.

Making Corrections and Enhancing Recognition

| 📋 Correction | If the Speech Recognition System does not accurately recognize a word or string of words, select the words and |

click the Correction button to hear a recording of your dictation of the word or phrase. Choose the correct words from the list of suggestions, or select and respeak the words. Remember, you can always use the mouse and keyboard to make corrections if the words you want are not in the list.

If you would like to add words to the speech dictionary to aid in recognition, you can add them individually, or you can use the Speech tools to review a document and identify any words it does not know. This second option is particularly valuable if you have a document that contains a lot of words that are unique to your business. To add words individually, follow these steps:

1.   Click Tools on the Language bar.

2. Click Add/Delete Words to open the Add/Delete Words dialog box.

3. Select a word from the list or enter your own word.

4. Click Record Pronunciation and say the word correctly.

5. Repeat steps 3 and 4 until you have added all the words you want to add.

6. You may also want to delete a word that was automatically added to the list from your documents. Select the word and click Delete.

7. Click Cancel when you are finished adding and deleting words.

To review an entire document for words that are not in the speech dictionary, choose Tools ➢ Learn From Document. When the document has been reviewed, a Learn From Document dialog box appears with the list of words it identified. Select and delete words you don't want to add. Click Add All to add the rest of the words. If you'd like to add pronunciation, follow the steps listed above to access the Add/Delete Words dialog box.

Giving Voice Commands in Office XP

You can switch from dictating text that you want recognized to giving voice commands to operate the application by clicking the Voice Command button on the Language bar. You can use voice commands to move the insertion point within a document, to activate a toolbar button or a menu, and to input responses in a dialog box.

For example, suppose you want to designate specific page setup options for a document. You want your document to have landscape orientation with 1" left and right margins on 11" × 8.5" paper with a different first page header. Use your voice to make these setting changes:

1. Say **Voice Command** to switch to Voice Command mode.

2. Say **File** to open the File menu.

3. Say **Page Setup** to open the Page Setup dialog box.

4. Say **Margins** to select the Margins tab.

5. Say **Tab**, **Tab**, **Tab** to set the left margin—the insertion point should move into the Left Margin text box.

6. Say **Down Arrow**, **Down Arrow**, **Down Arrow** to reduce the left margin to 1.0".

7. Say **Tab** to move the insertion point to the Right Margin text box.

8. Say **Down Arrow**, **Down Arrow**, **Down Arrow** to reduce the margin to 1.0".

9. Say **Paper** to switch to the Paper tab.

10. Say **Paper Size** to open the Paper Size drop-down list.

11. Say **Legal** to select Legal from the drop-down list.

12. Say **Layout** to switch to the Layout tab.

13. Say **Different First Page** to select the Different First Page check box.

14. Say **OK** to accept the changes and close the dialog box.

When you are dictating or entering text, you can use voice commands to move the insertion point around your document. Table B.2 shows voice commands that are available throughout Office XP.

NOTE

If you are having trouble using a particular voice command, minimize the application you are working in or switch to another application and then switch back to the application and try it again. Chances are it will work better after this little kick.

TABLE B.2:   Office XP Voice Navigation Commands

TO COMPLETE THIS TASK...	YOU SAY...
Press Enter	Return
	Enter
Press Backspace	Backspace
	Delete
Press the spacebar	Space
	Space Bar
Press Esc	Escape
	Cancel
Right-click for a context menu	Right Click
	Right Click Menu
	Show Right Click Menu
	Show Context Menu
Press Tab	Tab
Press Ctrl+Tab	Control Tab
Press Shift+Tab	Shift Tab
Press End	End
	Go End
Press Home	Home
	Go Home
Press Up arrow	Up
	Go Up
	Up Arrow
	Arrow Up
Press Down arrow	Down
	Go Down
	Down Arrow
	Arrow Down
Press Left arrow	Left
	Go Left

TABLE B.2 CONTINUED: Office XP Voice Navigation Commands

To Complete This Task...	You Say...
Press Left arrow	**Left Arrow**
	Arrow Left
Press Right arrow	**Right**
	Go Right
	Right Arrow
	Arrow Right
Press Page Down	**Next Page**
	Page Down
Press Page Up	**Previous Page**
	Page Up

For a list of the voice commands that are available in each specific application, refer to "Speech Recognition Commands Available throughout Office XP," later in this chapter.

NOTE

Some people think that speech and handwriting recognition tools are ways to avoid learning how to use applications. However, to use these tools effectively in Office, you must first know how to use the application you want to work in, or you will not know how to use the voice commands. Speech and handwriting will help people who don't know how or are unable to type, but those users still have to learn how an application works before they can use it.

Tweaking the Speech Recognition System

Speech recognition is a trade-off between recognition and accuracy. Words are recognized in context; the more surrounding words the system has to examine, the more likely it is to determine which word you actually spoke. The more words the system examines, the longer it takes to display your dictated text on-screen.

If the lag between dictation and display is too long, or if the percentage of incorrectly recognized words is too high, you can change the Recognition/Accuracy settings to improve recognition or speed. You can also adjust the Rejection Rate setting if the system frequently ignores menu commands in Voice Command mode.

To access the Speech Recognition System settings, choose Tools ➢ Options from the Language bar menu. In the Speech Properties dialog box (see Figure B.2), select your profile, and then click the Settings button to open the Recognition Profile Settings dialog box, shown in Figure B.3. Here you can adjust Pronunciation Sensitivity and the Accuracy vs. Recognition Response Time. If you set the sensitivity too high, you may find that it's trying to translate all of your *ums* and mumbles, so keep this setting toward the center. If you have a fast processor and lots of memory, increase the accuracy levels for the best recognition. To have the system automatically adjust and learn from your speech patterns as you are dictating, make sure the Background Adaptation check box is selected.

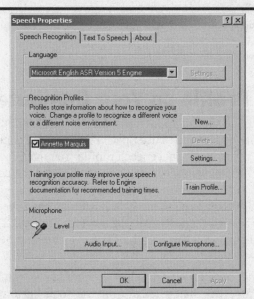

FIGURE B.2: In the Speech Properties dialog box, you can create new profiles and augment your speech training.

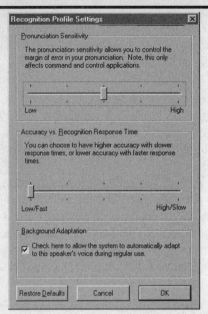

FIGURE B.3: Use the settings in the Recognition Profile Settings dialog box to tweak the performance of the Speech Recognition System.

Creating a New Profile on Your Computer

Speech recognition files are specific to each person's voice and should not be shared. If another user wants to use Speech on the same computer, they need to set up an additional speech profile. You may also find it useful to have a different profile at work and at home if the noise level is drastically different. To set up a user profile, choose Tools ➤ Options on the Language bar and click the New button on the Speech Recognition tab of the Speech Properties dialog box (see Figure B.2). The Profile Wizard will guide you through the steps to create another user profile.

After you create a user profile, you can select the profile you want to use from the Speech Properties dialog box or from the Tools button on the Language bar. Choose Current User to verify the current user or select a different one.

Removing Speech Recognition Services

If you've given Speech a fair trial and you decide that it just isn't for you (or for your computer), you can remove the text service from Office XP without uninstalling the entire feature from your computer. To remove the service, right-click the Language bar and choose Settings to open the Text Services dialog box, shown in Figure B.4. Select the speech service you have installed in the Installed Services list and click Remove (the speech service is the one with the microphone in front of it). After it is removed, it no longer loads with your software and as a result frees up any memory it was using. If you decide you want the speech service back, just reverse the process, clicking Add in the Installed Services list.

To uninstall the speech recognition service completely from your computer, use Add/Remove Programs in the Control Panel.

NOTE

If you have text services installed for more than one language, select the language first from the Default Input Language drop-down list and then remove the speech text service.

FIGURE B.4: Remove the text service from Office XP with the Text Services dialog box.

Working with the Language Bar

The Language bar is a completely new kind of Office toolbar. Rather than docking in the application window, the Language bar floats above it. You can move the Language bar around the application window by pointing to the left edge—the pointer becomes a four-header arrow so you can drag the bar where you want it.

To control the Language bar, right-click anywhere on it for a shortcut menu of options.

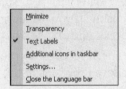

Minimize   Positions the Language bar as an icon on the Windows system tray—just to the left of the clock. Click the icon and select Show The Language Bar to activate it for use.

Transparency   Makes the Language bar turn clear when not in use so as not to disrupt whatever is beneath it. Can be toggled on and off.

Text Labels   Toggles between showing text and icons on the Language bar buttons.

Additional Icons In Taskbar   Adds a microphone and handwriting icon to the Taskbar when the Language bar is minimized. You can activate Dictation or Handwriting mode by clicking the Taskbar button.

Settings   Takes you to the Text Services dialog box.

Close The Language Bar   Shuts down the Language bar completely. To reactivate, choose Text Services in the Windows Control Panel and choose to show the Language bar from the Language Bar Preferences.

You can also control which buttons appear on the Language bar by clicking the Options button (the small downward-pointing arrow on the right end of the bar). Select the buttons you would like to have available on the Language bar from the list of Correction, Speech Tools, and Help.

USING *TEXT TO SPEECH* WITH EXCEL

Text To Speech is a feature that reads back to you text you have entered into a document. Designed as one of Microsoft's new Accessibility features, Text To Speech is available, at this point, only in Excel. Microsoft is working hard to develop software that is accessible to people with disabilities, so we expect that this feature will be expanded in future releases.

Before using the Text To Speech feature, you first want to visit the Speech Engine settings in the Windows Control Panel, available by clicking the Speech icon. On the Text To Speech tab, you can choose whether you'd like to have Michael or Michelle reading to you. Be sure to have your headset on so you can preview both of the voices before making this momentous choice. You can also adjust the speed at which your choice speaks to you, so if you're from New York you can have it read faster, and if you're from New Orleans you can slow it down. You are now ready to activate Text To Speech. To use the feature, start Excel and choose Tools ➤ Speech ➤ Show Text To Speech Toolbar.

To start reading from a particular position on the worksheet, click that cell and then click the Speak Cells button on the Text To Speech toolbar. By default, Michelle (or Michael) reads across the rows until she comes to the last cell of the worksheet and then returns to column A. Click the Stop Speaking button to stop the operation. To change directions and have her read down the column rather than across the row, click the By Columns button. If you'd like Michelle to speak entries as you enter them, click the Speak On Enter button. Just close the toolbar when you are finished with the Text To Speech tools.

HANDWRITING RECOGNITION

Handwriting recognition offers a wealth of opportunity for new types of computers. No longer tied to a keyboard, new computing devices will offer the same freedom that legal pads and steno books have given us for years. Already personal digital assistants (PDAs) and handheld computers such as Palms and Pocket PCs offer handwriting recognition as the primary input method. Tablet computers are beginning to show up in the catalogs of computer hardware resellers. The inclusion of handwriting recognition in Office XP brings us one step closer to throwing out our keyboards and giving users more natural and flexible computing options.

The Handwriting tools in Office XP, which are not part of the standard installation, include soft keyboards, on-screen drawing, and actual handwriting recognition. If you would like to use them, run the Office XP Setup program and add Handwriting in the Office Shared Features folder under Alternative User Input.

Using Soft Keyboards

As part of the set of Handwriting tools, Office XP offers two on-screen keyboards: Standard and Symbol. The Standard keyboard, shown in Figure B.5, is a traditional QWERTY keyboard that floats on the screen. The Symbol keyboard, shown in Figure B.6, is a collection of language symbols for written languages other than English.

The Standard keyboard option offers little advantage to the desktop or laptop user—it is designed primarily for the handheld computer market. The Symbol keyboard, however, used in conjunction with a traditional keyboard, can be an effective shortcut for users who have to type in languages that require keys not readily available on the QWERTY keyboard.

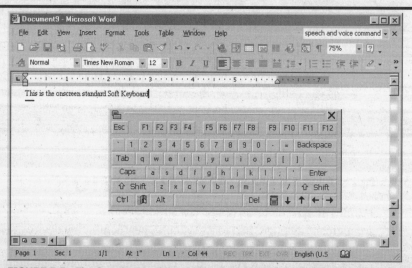

FIGURE B.5: The Standard keyboard offers handheld computer users a familiar input method.

FIGURE B.6: The Symbol keyboard gives ready access to characters that are not available on the QWERTY keyboard.

To activate either the Standard or Symbol soft keyboards, click the Handwriting button on the Language bar to select the keyboard you want to use.

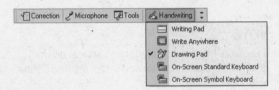

If you would like to add the keyboard to the Language bar so you can easily turn it on and off, click the Options button at the right end of the Language bar (the small black arrow) and choose Microsoft Handwriting Item from the menu. With this option turned on, whatever handwriting item you select in the Handwriting menu appears on the toolbar.

Click the keys on the soft keyboard to enter text on the screen. When you want to turn the keyboard off, click the Close button on the keyboard (or the Handwriting button on the Language bar).

Drawing On-Screen

The Drawing Pad is designed to make it easy to insert a quick drawing into a document. Although you have many more tools available using the Drawing toolbar, the Drawing Pad offers simplicity and flexibility for alternative computer devices. To activate the Drawing Pad, click Handwriting on the Language bar and choose Drawing Pad. This opens the Drawing Pad, shown in Figure B.7.

FIGURE B.7: Use the Drawing Pad to create simple drawings and insert them into a document.

NOTE

If the Drawing Pad button doesn't appear on the Language bar, click the Language bar's Option button and select Microsoft Handwriting Item from the list of button choices.

To use the Drawing Pad, just point and draw. You don't have any pen or brush choices, but you can change the width and color of the lines you draw. Click the Options button in the title bar of the Drawing Pad to open the Draw Options dialog box, shown in Figure B.8. You must return to the Draw Options dialog box every time you want to change pen color or width.

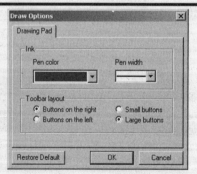

FIGURE B.8: Change the pen color and width and also the toolbar layout of the Drawing Pad in the Draw Options dialog box.

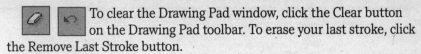 To clear the Drawing Pad window, click the Clear button on the Drawing Pad toolbar. To erase your last stroke, click the Remove Last Stroke button.

When you are ready to insert your masterpiece into your document, click the Insert Drawing button. If you decide it needs a little more work in another application, click the Copy To Clipboard button.

Using Handwriting to Input Text

Handwriting recognition in Office XP is amazingly accurate even if all you have available to you is your trustworthy mouse. Obviously, handwriting tablets will become more common as more people experience the ease with which Office converts even the most illegible scrawl into typed text. Figure B.9 shows how accurately Office XP converts handwriting.

To activate handwriting, choose Lined Paper from the Write menu on the Language bar and then click the Lined Paper button. This opens the Lined Paper Writing Pad, shown in Figure B.9.

You have the option of writing so that it is automatically converted into text. You can also leave it as handwriting if, for example, you want to sign a letter.

 To use automatic handwriting recognition, click the Text button on the Writing Pad. If you print on the Lined Paper writing surface, your letters are immediately transcribed. If you write cursive style, your writing is automatically transcribed when you pause for more than a second or two.

To write using the mouse, hold the mouse button down to write; release it to move to the next word. It definitely takes a little work to get used to writing this way, but with a little practice, you'll do fine.

NOTE

If you have access to a graphics tablet (as you might use with 3D or Computer-Aided Drafting software), you will find handwriting a much more pleasant experience. You will also find new tablet-PCs and handwriting tablets available in your local or online computer store. If you have a laptop with a touchpad, you can purchase a pack of PDA styluses or a stylus pen and use the touchpad as your writing surface—depress the left touchpad button as you write. As far as tablets go, we've been impressed with the WACOM Graphire (www.wacom.com). The tablet comes with a cordless pen and mouse—you must use the mouse on the tablet—and a bunch of bundled software. Some of the software is unnecessary with the handwriting and drawing features in Office XP, but they still give you some cool toys to play with and a solid, well-made tablet, all for under $100.

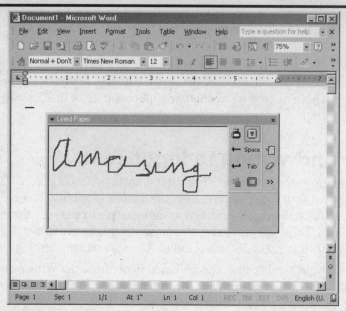

FIGURE B.9: Office XP can accurately convert even this scrawl into typed text—it truly is amazing!

If you would prefer to transfer your handwriting without having it transcribed, click the Ink button on the Writing Pad. Be sure to write directly above the line on the Writing Pad to have your writing appear inline with the text. Use this option to add a real signature to an e-mail or letter.

The text you write appears in whatever size font you have selected. If you're working in a 10 point font, then the handwriting appears very small. If you would like to format the handwriting, select it just as you would any other text and change the text size, color, and alignment or even add bold, italics, and underline.

Correcting Your Handwriting

Whether you are using the Ink or Text tools to enter handwriting, you can correct mistakes that Office or you make in the text. To correct transcribed text, right-click any word and select the correct word from the list of choices just as you would if the word were misspelled.

You can also select the erroneous word and click the Correction button on the Writing Pad to see a list of word alternatives.

If you want to correct handwriting itself, right-click the word and choose Ink Object and then choose either Alternate List or Recognize. Either way, Office converts the handwriting into typed text. If you want to make a correction and keep the handwriting, the only option is to rewrite it.

FINDING HELP FOR SPEECH AND HANDWRITING RECOGNITION

Although you'll find some help files in each application, the general help files on speech and handwriting recognition are available on the Language bar. Click the yellow-question-mark Help button on the Language bar and choose Language Bar Help. Choose Use Speech on the Contents tab to get help for speech and handwriting recognition.

You can also find extensive help on the Microsoft Office Update site at www.officeupdate.microsoft.com.

NOTE

When using Speech to control dialog boxes, you must switch to Dictation mode (say **Dictation**) before entering text in a text box. Switch back to Voice Commands (say **Voice Commands**) before proceeding.

SPEECH RECOGNITION COMMANDS AVAILABLE THROUGHOUT OFFICE XP

TABLE B.3:   To Access Menus, Dialog Boxes, and Task Panes

TO COMPLETE THIS TASK...	YOU SAY...
Display all the commands on a menu	**Expand**
	More Buttons
In a dialog box, move to the next option or option group	**Tab**
In a dialog box, move to the previous option or option group	**Shift Tab**
Close a dialog box without saving any changes and close menus	**Escape**
	Cancel

TABLE B.3 CONTINUED: To Access Menus, Dialog Boxes, and
Task Panes

To Complete This Task...	You Say...
Display the right-click menu	**Right Click**
	Right Click Menu
	Show Right Click Menu
	Context Menu
	Show Context Menu
If the AutoCorrect Options button is visible, display the Auto-Correct Options button menu	**AutoCorrect Options**
	Options Button
If the Paste Options button is visible, display the Paste Options button menu	**Paste Options**
	Options Button
If the Smart Tag Actions button is visible, display the Smart Tag Actions button menu	**Smart Tag Actions**
	Actions Button
Show the task pane	**Task Pane**
	Show Task Pane
	View Task Pane
Hide the task pane	**Hide Task Pane**

TABLE B.4:   To Move the Insertion Point (Except in Excel and Access)

To Complete This Task...	You Say...
Enter a new paragraph	**New Paragraph**
Go to the end of a line	**Go End**
Go to the beginning of a line	**Home**
	Go Home
Enter a backspace	**Backspace**
Enter a space	**Space**
	Spacebar

TABLE B.4 CONTINUED: To Move the Insertion Point (Except in Excel and Access)

To Complete This Task...	You Say...
Move the insertion point one space to the left	Left
	Left Arrow
	Arrow Left
	Go Left
Move the insertion point one space to the right	Right
	Go Right
	Right Arrow
	Arrow Right
Move the insertion point one word to the right	Right One Word
	Forward Word
	Forward One Word
	Go Forward One Word
	Next Word
	Go Right Word
	Control Right
Move the insertion point one word to the left	Left One Word
	Back Word
	Back One Word
	Go Back One Word
	Last Word
	Control Left
Go up one line	Up
	Go Up
	Up Arrow
	Arrow Up
Go down one line	Down
	Go Down
	Down Arrow
	Arrow Down

TABLE B.4 CONTINUED: To Move the Insertion Point (Except in Excel and Access)

TO COMPLETE THIS TASK...	YOU SAY...
Scroll up	**Page Up**
	Previous Page
Scroll down	**Scroll Down**
	Page Down
	Next Page

TABLE B.5:   To Select Text

TO COMPLETE THIS TASK...	YOU SAY...
Select the next word	**Shift Control Right**
	Select Next Word
Select the previous word	**Shift Control Left**
	Select Last Word
Select text going backward	**Shift Control Up**
	Select Last Line
Select text going forward	**Shift Control Down**
	Select Next Line
Select all	**Select All**

TABLE B.6:   To Edit Text

TO COMPLETE THIS TASK...	YOU SAY...
Cut selected text	**Cut**
Copy	**Copy**
Paste	**Paste**
Undo	**Undo**

TABLE B.6 CONTINUED: To Edit Text

TO COMPLETE THIS TASK...	YOU SAY...
Redo	Redo
	Repeat
	Same As Before
Show the Office Clipboard	Office Clipboard
	Show Clipboard
	Show Office Clipboard
Hide the Office Clipboard	Hide Clipboard
	Hide Office Clipboard

TABLE B.7:   To Format Text and Paragraphs

TO COMPLETE THIS TASK...	YOU SAY...
Bold	Turn On Bold
	On Bold
	Begin Bolding
Remove bold	Turn Off Bold
	Remove Bold
	Off Bold
	Unbold
	Stop Bolding
Italicize and remove italics	Italicize
	Italic
Left justify	Left Justify
	Left Justified
	Justify Left
Right justify	Right Justify
	Right Justified
	Justify Right

TABLE B.7 CONTINUED: To Format Text and Paragraphs

TO COMPLETE THIS TASK...	YOU SAY...
Center justify	Centered
	Center Justify
	Center Justified
Capitalize selected text	Capital
	Capitalize

TABLE B.8: To Manage Files

TO COMPLETE THIS TASK...	YOU SAY...
Open a file	Open
	File Open
	Open File
Open a new document	New Document
	New Blank Document
Close a document	Close Document
	File Exit
Open a file	File Open
Save	Save
Print preview	Print Preview
Print document	Print

TABLE B.9: To Ask for Help

TO COMPLETE THIS TASK...	YOU SAY...
Move the insertion point to the Ask A Question box	Ask A Question
	Type A Question For Help
Hide the Office Assistant	Hide The Assistant

SPEECH RECOGNITION COMMANDS UNIQUE TO EXCEL 2002

TABLE B.10: To Use Smart Tag Options

To Complete This Task...	You Say...
If the Insert Options button is visible, display the Insert Options button menu	Insert Options
	Options Button
If the AutoFill Options button is visible, display the AutoFill Options button menu	AutoFill Options
	Options Button

TABLE B.11: To Navigate in a Worksheet

To Complete This Task...	You Say...
Go to the end of a row	End
	Go End
Go to the beginning of a row	Home
	Go Home
Move one cell to the left	Left
	Left Arrow
	Arrow Left
	Go Left
Move one cell to the right	Right
	Go Right
	Right Arrow
	Arrow Right
Move up one cell	Up
	Go Up
	Up Arrow
	Arrow Up

TABLE B.11 CONTINUED: To Navigate in a Worksheet

To Complete This Task...	You Say...
Move down one cell	**Down**
	Go Down
	Down Arrow
	Arrow Down
Move down one row	**Return**
	Enter
	New Line
	Next Line
	New Paragraph
Move to the previous sheet in the workbook	**Previous Page**
Move to the next sheet in the workbook	**Next Page**
When you're editing in a cell, move the insertion point one word to the right within the cell	**Right One Word**
	Forward Word
	Forward One Word
	Go Forward One Word
	Next Word
	Go Right Word
	Control Right
When you're editing in a cell, move the insertion point one word to the left within the cell	**Left One Word**
	Back Word
	Back One Word
	Go Back One Word
	Last Word
	Control Left
When you're editing in a cell, select the next word on the right in a cell	**Shift Control Right**
	Select Next Word
When you're editing in a cell, select the last word on the left in a cell	**Shift Control Left**
	Select Last Word

TABLE B12:   To Select Cells

To Complete This Task...	You Say...
Select a set of cells going up in the worksheet	**Shift Control Up**
	Select Last Line
Select a set of cells going down in the worksheet	**Shift Control Down**
	Select Next Line

TABLE B.13:   To Format Cells

To Complete This Task...	You Say...
Add a decimal place to a selected cell	**Decimal Up**
Decrease a decimal place from a selected cell	**Decimal Down**
Increase the size of a selected cell to fit text	**Auto Fit**
	Auto Fit Selection

Speech Recognition Commands Unique to Outlook 2002

TABLE B.14:   To Manage Outlook Items

To Complete This Task...	You Say...
Open the selected item	**Open**
Create a new message	**New Mail**
	New Message
	New Mail Message
	New E-Mail Message
Create a new appointment	**New Meeting Request**
	New S Plus
Post in folder	**New Post**
	New Post In This Folder

TABLE B.15: To Manage Outlook Folders

TO COMPLETE THIS TASK...	YOU SAY...
Display the folder list	**Folder List**
	Show Folder List
Hide the folder list	**Hide Folder List**
Create a new folder	**New Folder**
Create a new distribution list	**New Distribution List**
Open Outlook Today folder	**Outlook Today**
	Open Outlook Today
	Go To Outlook Today
Open Inbox folder	**Inbox**
	Open Inbox
	Go To Inbox
Open Calendar folder	**Calendar**
	Open Calendar
	Go To Calendar
Open Contacts folder	**Contacts**
	Open Contacts
	Go To Contacts
Open Drafts folder	**Drafts**
	Open Drafts
	Go To Drafts
Open Tasks folder	**Tasks**
	Open Tasks
	Go To Tasks
Open Notes folder	**Notes**
	Open Notes
	Go To Notes
Open Outbox folder	**Outbox**
	Open Outbox
	Go To Outbox

TABLE B.15 CONTINUED: To Manage Outlook Folders

To Complete This Task...	You Say...
Open My Documents folder	**My Documents**
	Open My Documents
	Go To My Documents
Open Journal folder	**Journal**
	Open Journal
	Go To Journal
Open Deleted Items folder	**Deleted Items**
	Open Deleted Items
	Go To Deleted Items
Open Sent Items folder	**Sent Items**
	Open Sent Items
	Go To Sent Items
Open My Computer folder	**My Computer**
	Open My Computer
	Go To My Computer

SPEECH RECOGNITION COMMANDS UNIQUE TO POWERPOINT 2002

TABLE B.16: To Access Smart Tag Options

To Complete This Task...	You Say...
If the AutoFit Options button is visible, display the AutoFit Options button menu	**AutoFit Options**
	Options Button
If the Automatic Layout Options button is visible, display the Automatic Layout Options button menu	**Automatic Layout Options**
	Options Button

TABLE B.17:   To Navigate through Slides and Views

TO COMPLETE THIS TASK...	YOU SAY...
Scroll up through the slides in a presentation	**Page Up**
Scroll down through the slides in a presentation	**Page Down**
Switch to the next slide	**Next Page**
Switch to the last slide	**Previous Page**
View the slide show	**View Show**
	Begin Slide Show
	Start Slide Show
	Slide Show View
Switch to Normal view	**Normal**
	Normal View
Switch to Slide Sorter view	**Slide Sorter**
View the Slides tab	**Slides**
View the Outline tab	**Outline**
Close a presentation	**Close Presentation**

TABLE B.18:   To Add Slides

TO COMPLETE THIS TASK...	YOU SAY...
Insert a new slide	**New Slide**
	Insert New Slide

SPEECH RECOGNITION COMMANDS UNIQUE TO ACCESS 2002

TABLE B.19:   To Navigate in an Access Object

TO COMPLETE THIS TASK...	YOU SAY...
Go to the end of text or row	**End**
	Go End

TABLE B.19 CONTINUED: To Navigate in an Access Object

To Complete This Task...	You Say...
Go to the beginning of text or row	Home
	Go Home
Move one space to the left	Left
	Left Arrow
	Arrow Left
	Go Left
Move one space to the right	Right
	Go Right
	Right Arrow
	Arrow Right
Go up	Up
	Go Up
	Up Arrow
	Arrow Up
Go down	Down
	Go Down
	Down Arrow
	Arrow Down
Press Enter	Return
	Enter
Scroll up	Page Up
	Previous Page
Scroll down	Page Down
	Next Page
Move to the right where text exists	Right One Word
	Forward Word
	Forward One Word
	Go Forward One Word
	Next Word
	Go Right Word
	Control Right
Move to the left where text exists	Left One Word
	Back Word

TABLE B.19 CONTINUED: To Navigate in an Access Object

TO COMPLETE THIS TASK...	YOU SAY...
Move to the left where text exists	Back One Word
	Go Back One Word
	Last Word
	Control Left

TABLE B.20:   To Manage Database Files and Objects

TO COMPLETE THIS TASK...	YOU SAY...
Close a database	File Exit
	Close Database
Select an item under Objects	Tables
	Queries
	Forms
	Reports
	Pages
	Macros
	Modules
	Favorites

SPEECH RECOGNITION COMMANDS UNIQUE TO PUBLISHER 2002

TABLE B.21:   To Navigate in the Workspace

TO COMPLETE THIS TASK...	YOU SAY...
Move the page up in the window	Page Up
Move the page down in the window	Page Down

SPEECH RECOGNITION COMMANDS UNIQUE TO FRONTPAGE 2002

TABLE B.22:   To Navigate between FrontPage Views

TO COMPLETE THIS TASK...	YOU SAY...
Display the Navigation pane	**Navigation Pane**
	Show Navigation Pane
Hide the Navigation pane	**Hide Navigation Pane**
Switch tab view going forward (for example, switch from Normal view to HTML view)	**Next Page**
Switch tab view going backward (for example, switch from HTML view to Normal view)	**Previous Page**
Select an option under Views	**Page**
	Folders
	Reports
	Navigation
	Hyperlinks
	Tasks

TABLE B.23:   To Manage Files

TO COMPLETE THIS TASK...	YOU SAY...
Display the folder list	**Folder List**
	Show Folder List
Hide the folder list	**Hide Folder List**

Appendix C

TROUBLESHOOTING PC PROBLEMS

This appendix is intended to help you diagnose and resolve common problems related to your PC that may impact your ability to work.

To learn much more about PC troubleshooting, get a copy of *The Complete PC Upgrade & Maintenance Guide (12th Edition)* by Mark Minasi (Sybex, 2001).

Adapted from *The Complete PC Upgrade & Maintenance Guide (12th Edition)* by Mark Minasi

ISBN 0-7821-2990-0   1488 pp $59.99

PRELIMINARIES

Before you start, there are some things you may need on hand. These include:

- ▶ Documentation for your PC and/or its separate components (including warranty information)
- ▶ Container for placing screws between removal and reinstallation
- ▶ Appropriate screwdriver(s), such as a Phillips-head
- ▶ Antistatic wrist strap
- ▶ Boot disk and operating system installation CD (just in case)
- ▶ Connector cleaner or hard, white artist's eraser
- ▶ Diagnostic utilities

GENERAL TROUBLESHOOTING RULES

These rules have kept me out of trouble for a long time. I know they'll be of use to you.

PC TECHNICIAN'S CREED

Although some of these suggestions are a bit tongue-in-cheek, there's a nugget of advice in every one, and they're all part of the philosophy of troubleshooting.

- ▶ Remember: "Don't Panic" and "I Will Win"
- ▶ Wait...and Repeat
- ▶ Write Everything Down
- ▶ Do the Easy Stuff First
- ▶ Reboot and Try Again
- ▶ Simplify, Simplify, Simplify!
- ▶ Draw a Picture, Separate into Components, and Test
- ▶ Never Assume
- ▶ Trust No One: The Documentation Sometimes Lies
- ▶ Observe like Sherlock Holmes

Remember: "Don't Panic" and "I Will Win"

You need to have confidence in yourself as a troubleshooter. Look, this stuff isn't that hard. My technical training is as a Ph.D. economist rather than as a computer scientist or engineer, I have 10 thumbs, and people pay *me* to fix machines. If I can do it, you can do it, too. There's not that much to these machines. When it comes right down to it, the only thing that you really can't replace for (at most) a hundred dollars or so is your data, and you can protect that with frequent backups.

If you don't go in there *knowing* that you're going to win, you're going to get beaten—these machines can *smell* fear. A former girlfriend, a black belt in tae kwon do, told me once that an important tenet of tae kwon do is to "have an indomitable spirit." Sounds good to me—practice some *tech* kwon do, and don't forget that indomitable spirit.

Wait...and Repeat

It's a simple fact that the vast majority of "computer" problems are actually caused by human error. (That means you, bub!) If something goes wrong when you're using your PC, stop what you're doing, take a few deep breaths, and then try it again. Chances are you hit the wrong key, clicked the wrong button, or just plain zigged when you meant to zag. There's a lot to be gained by having a little patience and perhaps going a little slower so you don't repeat your mistakes.

Write Everything Down

Documenting what you do with your PC can be very helpful in the troubleshooting process. I tend not to write things down when I'm pretty sure that the operation will be simple (it almost never is), or when it's sufficiently traumatic that I'm certain that I couldn't forget (there's always another, bigger trauma waiting). I've found that I'm more likely to write down important notes if I keep my notebook—the paper kind—handy. These notes might include, for example, special location information or notations about a problem, such as a bent pin or the actual layout being the reverse of how it appears in the manufacturer's diagram. As a bonus, writing things in your notebook means that you'll be able to find them later.

Do the Easy Stuff First

I am, by nature, a lazy person. That's why I got interested in computers: They were machines that could free me from some drudgery. The *inexperienced* and lazy troubleshooter tries to save time by not making notes, by acting before thinking, and by *swapping* components or configuration information when he ought to be *stopping*...stopping to consider his next move.

What I've eventually figured out is that well-planned laziness is a virtue. An *experienced* lazy person looks ahead and says, "Oh, heck, what if I *can't* fix this thing? I don't want to create any more trouble for myself than necessary." And so the lazy person keeps diagrams and writes down everything that she does so she doesn't have to tear out her hair trying to put the PC back together.

The *experienced* lazy person does the easy stuff first; if it's a video problem, and it's not software, then four things could be swapped: the motherboard, the video board, the cable, or the monitor. What gets swapped first? The easy thing: the cable.

Reboot and Try Again

Your computer is affected by fluctuations in the power supply of as brief a duration as 4 milliseconds. This means that if your power disappeared for only 1/200 of a second, you wouldn't see the lights flicker, the microwave would still work, and the TV wouldn't skip a beat—even the digital clocks wouldn't start blinking. But several bytes of your computer's memory (not a lot of the memory, or you'd see a memory error message of some kind) get randomized. The result is that a program that has always worked pretty well all of a sudden stops dead. You'll never find out why it locked up that one time in a thousand. Maybe everybody in the building was running their photocopiers at the same time. Maybe radiation from a solar storm assaulted your memory chips (yes, that can happen, although it's unlikely; when a technician blames something on "cosmic rays," she's being facetious). It doesn't matter; the quick answer to this problem is just to start over and reboot the machine.

Now, don't get too trigger-happy with the reboot if you're in the middle of an application. It's usually a really bad idea to do a hard reboot (the Ctrl+Alt+Delete kind) out of Windows—try everything you can to get the machine to respond and let you do a graceful shutdown. If you reboot in the middle of an application, the application may leave files open, and those files will be lost. (Such half-finished files lead to a phenomenon you may have seen called *lost clusters*.)

Simplify, Simplify, Simplify!

The average PC has about a bazillion screensavers, applications, background communications programs (such as fax receive programs), and of course driver programs for sound boards, network cards, video boards, and the mouse—to name just a few. Determining the source of a problem is really hard when there are innumerable interactions between hardware and software.

This means that it's a good idea to eliminate as much as you can from a PC before trying to diagnose it. For example, boot without the network. If you're running Windows 95/98/Me, wait for the "Starting Windows..." message and press F8. That gives you the chance to boot Windows in Safe mode. In Windows NT/2000/XP, you can choose a configuration with a simple video driver at startup and then use the Control Panel, under Services, to stop the loading of any unnecessary drivers or programs.

I've seen this happen over and over again. Programs or drivers or *whatever* that get loaded into your computer's memory—often without your knowledge—bump into other programs or drivers or whatever, causing a major conflict that can freeze up your entire system. Check out *everything* that gets loaded when Windows launches (and don't forget to look in the Startup program group) and eliminate those things that don't need to be there. Software troubleshooting is just like hardware troubleshooting: Divide and conquer. Each piece of software that you're running is a piece of the system, and you want to minimize the number of pieces that you have to deal with.

Draw a Picture, Separate into Components, and Test

This is a true story: A friend was once a PC troubleshooter-type for a county government in Virginia, where I live. She tells this story about another PC troubleshooter-type—let's call him Ignatz. One day, their help desk got a phone call.

"Ignatz," the caller said, "Microsoft Word isn't printing with the new laser printer!"

Now, an experienced lazy person listens and says, "Gosh—how can I fix this without leaving my chair?" Many of us would probably zero in on that word *new*. As in "*new* laser printer." The next questions might be something like, "What kind of printer did you have before the new laser printer?" "Have you ever seen Word print on this laser printer before?" (Probably not.) "Have you reconfigured Windows for the laser printer?" (A confused "What?" is the probable answer.)

Ignatz, on the other hand, attacked the problem by first swapping the motherboard on the PC that was attached to the laser printer.

Yes, that's right—you read that correctly. It even kind of fixed the problem, as Iggie figured that he would reload the user's software while he was at it. Yeah, we can observe that Ignatz is, umm, shall we say, "a couple sandwiches short of a picnic" when it comes to troubleshooting. But I see people do less extreme (but just as unnecessary) things all the time. Heck, I still do a lot of dumb things myself, playing Macho Man With A Screwdriver. But I hope to get better at remembering to be lazy when troubleshooting.

Now, if old Ig had stopped to think, then he could have diagrammed the whole system. Simplified, you could say that the laser printer is attached to a cable, which attaches to a parallel port, which is connected to the motherboard, which runs the software. That kind of divides the problem into: laser printer, cable, parallel port, motherboard, and software. Each of those components can then be isolated and tested. *Testing* most hardware just means swapping it, as most of us lack the expensive equipment needed to test hardware. But software can be played with in many ways, the most fruitful of which is usually in its setup and configuration. I'd look at the software first. I always look at the software before I go after the hardware. Why? Simple: I have a much better chance of finding the answer in software.

Never Assume

It's far too easy to assume that something is blameless. "How could the problem be the new version of PowerQuick? It's been clean for the last five versions!" Subject everything to your scrutiny, *including* the documentation. And while I'm on the subject...

Trust No One: The Documentation Sometimes Lies

Many years ago, I bought my first Video Graphics Adapter (VGA) board. It was made by Compaq Computer Corporation, and it wasn't cheap, but I bought it from Compaq because I knew that they made a compatible, high-quality product. Since it was in the early days of the VGA, many clones were kinda wobbly compatibility-wise, so I was playing it safe.

When I went to install the board, I took the time to read the documentation. About half of the booklet that came with the board discussed installation. In particular, several pages outlined how to properly set the three jumpers that were clearly marked and even illustrated in black-and-white photos. Before even removing the board from its antistatic bag, I studied the documentation and figured out how to set the three jumpers. Donning my antistatic wrist strap, I removed the board from its bag.

But it had only one jumper on it.

I looked and looked and *looked*, but there was only one jumper on the %$#@! thing. I picked up the manual again—and a lone piece of paper fluttered from between its pages. It basically said, "Your VGA is a new and improved model. It has only one jumper. Set it like this." Frustrating, yes, but at least Compaq provided the right documentation, albeit hidden. I've often wondered if the documentation's author didn't have a sense of humor, however: This 3-by-8-inch piece of paper was *copyrighted*.

Jumpers are usually not the real nightmare, however; the documentation is. Almost every one of these manuals is badly translated from some Pacific Rim nation's language to English, and, worst of all, it's usually wrong. The jumper setting for the parallel port is usually off, and I've seen incorrect documentation for the serial port jumpers as well. If you're wondering, by the way, how I figure out the correct settings when the documentation is wrong, then I'm afraid that there's no single trick that I can share with you. When I run into one of these boards, I check my notes to see whether I've run into this particular model before. If I have, great; if not, all I can do is work by trial and error.

Today, more and more information about PC hardware (and software) is available from the manufacturers' online websites.

Observe like Sherlock Holmes

In Arthur Conan Doyle's tales of the Great Detective, Sherlock Holmes sometimes exclaims about some new piece of evidence. He's obviously excited about it, but when Dr. Watson asks him *why* he's excited, Holmes gives nothing away. "Not yet, Watson," he demurs. "It's too early for theories."

What Holmes knew was that problem solving entails making theories, and then proving or disproving the theories with facts. But suppose Holmes had advanced an early theory aloud, perhaps in the company of the beleaguered Inspector Lestrade? Lestrade would like nothing better than to witness his harasser Holmes brought down by a faulty theory. Now, Holmes also knows that, so he has a subconscious aversion to finding any facts that disprove this ill-uttered supposition. By keeping his mouth shut until he has enough facts, he can offer a theory that he feels confident about.

You'll see this in your everyday troubleshooting life. Someone stands over your shoulder as you peer inside a disemboweled PC carcass. "What do you think it is?" he asks.

This is a crucial moment. Learn to say automatically, "I don't know—there's not enough information yet." Otherwise, you'll find that now the game you're playing is no longer *fix the machine;* unconsciously, you're now playing a game called *prove you're right.* So hang onto the theories until you have the facts.

When you open up a machine, you expose the machine to a certain risk that you'll do something dumb to it. PC troubleshooting differs from, say, automotive troubleshooting, in that the thing that's most commonly broken is the user. If you separate out the "user is broken" stuff (they forgot to turn it on, for example), software is the next most common problem. Honest-to-goodness hardware problems are actually quite uncommon compared to user and software problems. That leads me to the six specific troubleshooting steps.

SIX STEPS TO TROUBLESHOOTING SUCCESS

The smart troubleshooter makes the troubleshooting job tractable by breaking down problems into individual steps. Don't panic, and remember to be methodical; otherwise, you will thrash helplessly about and get frustrated. Once you are frustrated, you are *lost*, and you start creating new problems.

Following is the method that I use. It looks a lot like methods suggested by other people, but it's not the only method. You certainly don't have to use *my* method, but find one you like and stick to it—even for the small or seemingly easy jobs. It's the "this'll take only 5 minutes" repairs that get me in trouble. (You know—like when someone gives you directions, saying, "You can't miss it." I *know* I'm in trouble then.) I'll assume for this discussion that you are interacting with someone else (the person with the PC problem), but you can just as easily interview yourself.

Before opening up the computer, do the following:

1. Check for operator errors—commands or configurations that you may have done wrong, software or hardware that you may have set up incorrectly, or instructions that you may have reversed (for example, literally reversing a cable or putting a jumper on exactly opposite from the way it needs to go).

2. Check to make certain that everything that should be plugged into either a direct power source or the PC itself is plugged in correctly, and that the connection is secure.

3. Check the software, including program files and drivers, to make sure you have the most current versions installed—and configured properly.

4. Check for external signs of trouble, such as flickering LED power indicators or those that don't come on at all, strange sounds or lack of sound, and lack of display.

5. Run appropriate diagnostic programs.

6. Only when all else fails, disassemble the PC. Shut it down, disconnect all power, remove the case, ground yourself, and go inside to check cable and power connections, the proper seating of expansion boards and memory modules, and anything out of the ordinary.

Notice that the first five steps *aren't* hardware steps; let's take a closer look at all six.

TIP

If you're running Windows Me and experience a problem after installing a new piece of software or hardware, consider using the new System Restore feature to effectively "undo" the installation and return your system to its previous (that is, working) condition. Once your system is back up and working properly, you can analyze what went wrong—and consider trying the installation again.

Check for Operator Error

Operator error is responsible for 93.3 percent of PC failures. (That's a made-up statistic. But it got your attention and probably isn't far from the truth.) There are lots of things that an operator can do wrong. But one real statistic from the PC retail industry is that up to 75 percent of hardware purchases returned as defective aren't defective and work fine on retesting.

Regardless of how inflated that statistic may or may not be, that means a lot of folks aren't installing their hardware properly. Sure, some of it can be blamed on bad instructions, but many people flat-out admit that they never look at any documentation packed with the device they're trying to install—or read it after the first three to four times a device won't install instantly.

And since the accompanying paperwork often ends up in the trash can with the packaging from the hardware, you can end up feeling isolated and uninformed a few months later, when the device stops working. Remember the old saying about how desperate people do desperate things?

There are three main sources of problems for PCs: hardware, software, and users. Guess which one is the most likely? Users. Software's second. Hardware is a distant third.

That begs the question of why the computer industry has so many people problems. In my opinion, it's mainly because the user interfaces still stink—even the "good" ones.

Frequently, people will ask me how to prepare a new hard disk to use in their PCs. I'll go through all the steps, and usually point them to a website or two that spells out the steps again for them, so they have something in print they can stare at. All too many times, however, one of these folks will come back to tell me, "It didn't work."

"What didn't work?" I'll ask.

The answer will come back, "I can't access my CD-ROM drive to install Windows" or "I followed all the instructions but the hard drive won't boot up!!!"

Invariably, I find that they didn't follow one—or more—of the steps. They either didn't FDISK or FORMAT (necessary to prep the drive) so it's not really ready for use, or they decided they didn't need to go to the trouble of installing a DOS CD-ROM driver on their boot disk, so they can't access their CD-ROM drive to install their operating system.

You see, computers are made up of hardware, and hardware for the most part is a pretty logical beast. Turn something one way, and a device becomes available for use. Turn it another way, and a device doesn't respond to you. You can't see a list of 10 steps and decide which 5 you might like to follow, because all 10 steps are likely required to get the result you want.

Still, the language of computers confuses people. You've heard the stories about users doing goofy things; well, they're true. I've seen them. Back in the old days of personal computing, I once watched a user follow the dBASE III installation instructions: "Insert System Disk 1 in drive A and close the door." He inserted the disk in the drive, then got up (looking a little puzzled, I'll give him that), and closed the door to his office. If I hadn't been there to see it, I probably wouldn't have believed it. But before you giggle too loudly, consider: Where was the "door?" Have you seen a door on a floppy drive lately? No, there's never been one, really—although old 5¼-inch drives did have a little latch across the drive opening. I mean, if you hired me to put a door on your house, and instead I installed a little plastic latch, then you'd sue me, and you'd *win*.

I teach quite a few computer classes, and now and then I've had some guy staring at the keyboard in puzzlement.

"What's wrong?" I'd ask.

"I'm looking for a key," he'd reply.

"Which one? I'll point it out," I would offer.

"The Any key," he'd say, still puzzled. I would look at the screen, where the software program was prompting "Press any key to continue...." I had just finished with my "pay attention to what the computer is doing" lecture, and so this poor soul was trying his hardest to follow my directions. (Nowadays, there is an answer for the Any key searchers. You can buy an Any key kit: It's a keytop sticker that says, "ANY KEY." You install it on...well, any key.)

I've seen users "copy a floppy" with a photocopier. I once saw a bank organize their backup floppies by punching holes in them so they would fit into a small binder. True stories, all of them.

A friend at Microsoft tells the story of being called by someone who couldn't get Windows to do anything. "I've got my foot on the pedal," he said, "and it's not doing anything!" Well, mice are often found on the floor, but still...

Even worse, sometimes users will (horrors!) prevaricate slightly. "I didn't do anything. It just stopped working." Please note: I'm not one of those techie types whose motto is, "Assume that the user is lying," but sometimes it happens. More often, it's not that they lie. It's just that they don't know what's important, or they're embarrassed to tell you what they really did.

People feel defensive calling a support person (such as you). You want to collect as much information as possible. If you make them feel defensive, they'll misremember, or withhold information. Here's a trick that telemarketers are told: Smile when you're on the phone with someone. It works. (As the late Sam Kinison once said, "It creates the illusion that you care.") Being a support person can be wearing. There's a tendency to feel like "these people must get up early in the morning to think up dumb things to ask," but you can't let it get you down. Remember, these folks can't be too dumb—after all, the same company that hired them hired you, too. (Heh, heh.)

Again, think *lazy*. How can you collect enough information while on the phone to fix the problem right over the phone? The key is to not act like so many support people, the ones who don't even let you get your question out before they break in with, "Are you sure your computer is plugged in?" Stop and think about how idiotic this phrasing is. Who's going to answer "No"? It's roughly equivalent to saying, "Oh! Look at that. It's not plugged in. I *am* an idiot. Sorry to bother you."

Now, don't get me wrong: You have to ask the question—that's why it's step two in my six steps. But there's a right way and a wrong way. One right way is the "bureaucracy" approach: "I'm sorry that's happening to you. That must be really frustrating; I'll do whatever I can for you. But first, you know how it is here at XYZ Corp.; we have a form for everything. Forgive me, but I have to ask some dumb-sounding questions. Can you just double-check for me that the PC is plugged in...." Another good approach is to couch it in a self-deprecating way: "My asking you if the PC is plugged in reminded me of something dumb I did the other day.

The PC was plugged into the surge protector, and the surge protector was plugged into the wall. It took me 15 minutes to figure out that the surge protector was turned off! Can you believe that I did something that stupid?" If the next sound you hear is, "Umm, can I call you back? Someone just walked into my office," then you can be pretty sure you've just engineered another fixed PC.

Best of all, however, is that your *user* just fixed that PC. He's now had a success, so he'll remember that particular problem/solution combination. (Psychology tells us that people learn better with positive reinforcement than with negative reinforcement.) He'll probably end up feeling more capable, more likely to tackle the problem himself next time. "Success is a habit," said Vince Lombardi.

Another source of operator error stems from inexperienced operators. The PC isn't exactly the simplest thing in the world to master. The author of a book titled *Computer Wimp: 166 Things I Wish I Had Known before I Bought My First Computer* observes in that book that learning to use a computer system may be the most difficult learning endeavor that a person will undertake in their post-school life. (Things like raising kids are undoubtedly tougher, but they're different kinds of learning experiences.) It doesn't take a genius to recognize that most PC hardware and software manuals aren't the easiest things to comprehend. The answer? Good education. There are tons of good books, videos, college courses, and professional seminars on PCs—one for every budget. "If you think education is expensive," they say, "try ignorance."

Make Sure Everything Is Plugged In— Correctly

I know this sounds stupid, but we've all done it. A friend bought a modem and couldn't get it to work. It accepted commands all right, but could not dial out. The phone line was tested with a regular phone and worked fine. He was quite puzzled until he realized that he'd plugged the phone line into the *out* jack in the modem instead of the *in* jack. (The out jack is intended to be connected to the phone itself—not the phone line—so that the line can be shared between the modem and the phone.)

As I just said, when you ask the user, "Is it plugged in?" be diplomatic. (Don't you hate it when tech support people ask *you* that question?) But don't be afraid to ask for firm answers to the following questions:

- Is the PC plugged into some kind of multi-outlet strip?

- Is the strip on? Did the user kick off the power switch?

- Can the user actually see that the power strip is plugged into the wall?

- Are the other devices that are plugged into the power strip working? Try having the user plug a desk lamp or fan into the power strip to see whether it works.

- If the PC or peripheral is plugged into an outlet controlled by a wall switch, is the switch turned on?

- Are the peripherals plugged in? Are they plugged *into the computer?* Are they plugged into the proper ports or connectors on the computer?

I know of a large communications company that kept sending technicians to try to determine why a LAN server kept dying at strange hours of the night. They'd set up the software at the user site, leave it running, and then eventually get called back to the site because after a day or two all kinds of files had been trashed. The techs would always ask, "Has this been turned off in the middle of an operation?" The users would solemnly (and annoyingly—this tech guy wasn't going to weasel out of fixing his company's buggy software *that* easily, they thought) shake their heads no. Finally, this large company sent their SuperTech—the guy who'd seen it all. He looked over the server and listened to the users' stories.

Now, this guy *knew* from the symptoms that the server was getting shut down improperly. (Remember that indomitable spirit. On the other hand, save the spirit for the machine—don't get snotty with the users.) So he looked for easy ways to turn off the machine accidentally. Noticing two light switches on the wall and only one fluorescent ceiling panel, he flipped both switches. You guessed it—the server was plugged into a switched outlet. The security staff, in making the rounds each night, would shut off the lights.

When you are checking whether peripherals are plugged in, you also need to make sure that they are in *tight*. Multiple-pin connectors slowly bend under gravity unless the mounting screws are tightened. As someone stretches their legs under the desk, a loose power cord could be moved enough to disconnect it, or disconnect and reconnect it. Connectors on the floor take a lot of abuse.

I think that people don't properly secure connectors because it often can't be done without one of those small straight-slot screwdrivers that are smaller than the one you have in the kitchen tool drawer, but larger than the one you use to adjust the screws in your glasses. (Of course, we true PC repair warriors are never without our small screwdriver with the pocket clip and the logo of some company on its side, but normal humans...) Nowadays, you can find a remedy: Many cables are sold with big plastic screws that are easily hand-turnable. (Many folks call those screws *thumbscrews*, and I guess it's as good a term as any, but I find it a bit medieval.) Whenever possible, get cables with hand-turnable screws. They'll pay for themselves in the long run.

I'm one of the worst offenders in the cable screws department. As I install and reinstall various PC components a lot, I tend to just push my serial and video cables into their sockets, not bothering with the screwdriver. (I don't have the little screwdriver with the pocket clip when I don't happen to have my pocket protector around. You know, sometimes I want to work undercover, so I leave the pocket protector behind.)

A few years ago, I had myself convinced that my serial port or modem was fried, because I was getting terrible error rates on my communications sessions all of a sudden. As I'd just finished giving a lecture on lightning damage to serial ports, and it was T-storm season in Washington, I figured ruefully that I'd just lost a serial port. "But," I thought, "Who knows? Maybe when lightning toasted the port, it burned up some chips—I can at least take some pictures." So I got ready to take my PC apart. Of course, one of the first things I did was to remove the cables, and that's when I noticed that the serial cable just about fell off the back of the PC when I touched it. So I returned the cables to their interfaces—making sure they were secured tightly—and, as you've already guessed, the problems went away.

Check the Software

Remember I said that more problems are software problems than hardware problems? Software problems arrive in several guises:

- ► Operator error
- ► Keyboard/screen/disk/timer conflicts with memory resident software
- ► Software that doesn't clean up after itself
- ► Software that requires hardware that isn't connected or activated
- ► Buggy applications
- ► Buggy driver programs

Software troubleshooting could be a book in itself. In fact, most of the books out there on supporting Windows, Linux, Novell NetWare, and the like are software-troubleshooting books. But let's tackle some of the broad causes of software problems.

Virtual Device Drivers and Dynamic-Link Libraries

Modern operating systems, such as Windows, are built in a kind of layer-cake fashion. The application programs (such as word processing, e-mail, and spreadsheet programs) sit atop the cake—they're the frosting. Your applications are supported by layers of cake and filling, layers that they need in order to work—heck, frosting all by itself is a bit much, right?

The bottom layer of the cake is the hardware. Application programs need services (such as printing, communicating with a network server, or saving files) done for them by the hardware (the printer, the network card, or the hard disk). How do applications communicate with hardware? How does your system prioritize and handle multiple requests without exploding?

Enter the operating system. If every application tries to use a piece of hardware at the same time, nothing works. What you need is a kind of traffic cop between the apps and the hardware. The OS is that cop, the piece that routes hardware requests between applications and hardware, keeping traffic jams to a minimum and crashes nonexistent (well, in theory, anyway). The OS acts as a "traffic cop" layer between your hardware and your applications.

Also in between your hardware and applications are two components that applications rely on to operate correctly. They are called *virtual device drivers* (VxDs) and *dynamic-link libraries* (DLLs). Both act as filling between the layers, hidden from exterior view but key to the structure of the cake. I will discuss DLLs in a minute, but first let's consider drivers.

The lowest level of system software is the set of programs called *drivers*, which are customized to particular pieces of hardware. Drivers attach in a modular fashion to the main body of the OS (called the *kernel*). For example, in order to get Windows to recognize and use your Hewlett-Packard LaserJet model 5P, you must load a driver for that printer, adding it to the Windows system software.

Drivers can pose a bit of a problem for software stability. Most of the operating system is designed by a close-knit software development team; for example, most of the code in Windows 2000 was written by a handful of individuals working together at Microsoft. But most Windows drivers aren't written by Microsoft. Instead, the burden of writing driver programs usually falls to the hardware vendors: Diamond Multimedia writes drivers for its video boards, Hewlett-Packard (HP) writes drivers for its laser printers, and so on. Programmers working at these companies don't get the same kind of support (in terms of information, resources, and time) that they'd have if they were working at Microsoft, and so as a result they can't always write driver programs that are well integrated into an operating system. This is not a slap at programmers at Diamond, Hewlett-Packard, or any other hardware vendor; it's just a reality that the guy on Microsoft's Windows programming team who writes the Calculator code probably plays softball on the same team as the woman who writes the Windows kernel code. And that has to mean that he'll get better answers to sticky programming questions than would someone from outside Microsoft.

Because of the way that drivers work in modern operating systems, they're usually called *virtual* device drivers. In the Windows world, the acronym for that is *VxD*. VxDs are sometimes designed to plug into a particular operating system (which means, for example, that you might not want to waste your time trying to use a Windows 95 VxD under Windows Me or Windows NT, unless you know that the driver will work in both of those operating systems).

The bottom line is that driver programs are often a weak link in an operating system. Windows may run fine for weeks, and then you install a new version of the driver for your ATI Mach 64 video card. You try to enter Print Preview mode from your favorite word processor, and something happens, whether it's an outright lockup or some garbage on the screen. The problem is most likely to be that new driver.

While this isn't gospel, most operating system designers do much of their initial development on "lowest common denominator" hardware, such as VGA for video. Keep those plain-Jane drivers around and use them when possible as a kind of "known good" baseline configuration.

And a final tip about device drivers: When a new version comes along, *keep the old one around for a while!* "Latest" isn't always "greatest" when it comes to drivers.

TIP

If you're running Windows Me, you can use the System Restore feature to return your system to its previous state after you install a bad or incorrect driver.

I recommend that you do what a friend of mine does, and use the baby food method of testing new drivers. The first time she mentioned this to me, I was puzzled.

"The *baby food* method?" I asked her. (I'm an excellent straight man.)

"Sure," she replied. "When a baby starts eating solid food, you don't know what he's going to be allergic to. So, suppose you want to see if he's allergic to carrots. You start feeding him carrots; if a few days go by and he hasn't swollen up, then carrots are probably okay."

"I do that with device drivers. I just pop 'em into the system, try out all my applications to make sure that none of them break, and then just live with the thing for a week to see if anything new and unpleasant happens to my system. If not, I keep the driver. If I get troubles, then I document the troubles, restore the old device driver, and see if those troubles go away."

Good advice. But I'd add one thing to it. When you swap drivers on a piece of hardware, be sure to power down the system completely before restarting it. Some video drivers in particular don't work quite right unless you shut down the PC and restart after installing them

Another term you'll see turn up when troubleshooting software is *DLL*, short for *dynamic-link library*. A *library* is a file containing a bunch of small programs that get a particular task done. It's called a library for two reasons: First, there are usually many of those small programs in a particular library, and, second, the library file resembles a library in that it is publicly available; the programs in it are available to any application. For example, the program that tells Windows how to change the color of a part of the screen is almost certainly part of a library.

Now, the way a program finds a library is called *linking*. For most of the history of computer programming, libraries have become linked when a program called the *link editor* makes a copy of the desired library routines and incorporates those routines directly into the program. This is called *static linking*. Static linking is bad because, first, if you are running three programs that all know how to print (for example), then you're wasting RAM because you now have three copies of the print routine resident in memory; and, second, if the way that the OS wants an application to print (to continue the example) changes, then every application would have to be rebuilt.

Operating systems in use since the early '80s incorporate a different kind of linking, called *dynamic linking*. Under dynamic linking, a dynamic-link library is relinked every time the application calls for one of its library routines. Taking the example of printing, a program using static linking gets the whole library program inserted into it. A program linked dynamically to a library contains only a note that says, in essence, "When you need this routine, go out to PRINT.DLL, load it up, and link the routine before going any further." A DLL can also be shared; once one program has PRINT.DLL in memory, any other program needing PRINT.DLL gets the one copy that's already in memory, rather than loading another one.

What's this got to do with troubleshooting? Well, sometimes an incorrectly installed program may crash, complaining of a lack of a DLL. That may be fixable by reinstalling the program, or by editing the Windows Registry to include the correct path for the DLL. Or the DLL may have been accidentally erased. Or it could have been replaced.

Whenever you select File ➤ Open in any Windows program, your program calls up a DLL that contains a routine that knows how to put an Open dialog box on the screen. (In Windows, the DLL is called COMMDLG .DLL.) Now and then, I've installed programs that replaced the "comes in the Windows box" version of COMMDLG.DLL with their own, "improved" versions.

How do you find out whether you have a cowbird DLL in the nest? One simple way is to just compare the dates of the *other* DLLs that shipped with the OS to the suspect one. Or, as is more frequently the solution, you can simply reinstall the OS; it often saves more time than poking through DLLs looking for the "pretender."

Ill-Behaved Software

A number of mysteries can be linked to software that doesn't recover well from disabled or nonexistent hardware. Here are some common problems:

- ▶ Trying to print to a nonexistent printer

- ▶ Trying to print a non-PostScript formatted file to a PostScript printer—or vice versa

- ▶ Trying to print to a printer that is offline

- ▶ Trying to display high-resolution graphics data on a low-resolution monitor

- ▶ Trying to run a program that needs more memory than the PC contains

▶ Trying to install a program that insists on using your modem to dial into the mothership to register itself before it finalizes the installation—even if you don't have a modem connected to your system

These aren't really problems with the software—the problems all have something to do with the hardware—but the real issues arise because the software doesn't deal well with the hardware problem. The easy fix, however, is on the hardware side; you can't recode the program, but you *can* make simple hardware fixes.

Faulty Software

Sometimes the problem *is* just plain buggy software. Even the most popular programs can misbehave when faced with a full disk, insufficient memory, or some situation that the designer didn't anticipate or didn't test.

If you experience a problem with software, try to note exactly when the behavior occurs. Perhaps it always fails when trying to save to a network drive, but not to a local hard drive. Or maybe the software always crashes when system resources on the desktop run below 50 percent. Or maybe the software will run on any PC except one with a Cyrix CPU. Any behavior like this that you can reproduce can be very helpful to a team trying to debug a program.

If you have some experience with software and compiler/decompilers, you can sometimes check out the source code used to design the program and spot where an error might be (such as a wrong command issued). Normal human beings can dismiss this possibility.

Finally, you can try uninstalling the suspect program to see whether that sorts things out. It always amazes me how often an uninstall/reinstall will fix even the most persnickety problems.

Check External Signs

If the computer has indicator lights, what do they indicate? Are all the lights glowing on the modem? Does the printer indicate "ready"? Is the hard disk squealing or grinding? Does the monitor image look bent? Your drives and other peripherals produce hums, whirrs, and clicks. After a while, these noises become familiar, and any variation in them signals a problem. Pay attention to these signs.

The first step in successful troubleshooting is to isolate the problem component. These external signs can point the way.

It is important to document any signs here. Write down what lights are on and off, the positions of switches, etc.

Run a Diagnostic Utility

There is lots of help out there for your hardware problems—in the form of diagnostic software. Some computers ship with diagnostic programs that can help pinpoint various problems. Windows itself comes with a variety of diagnostic utilities, and other diagnostic programs are available from third parties or via downloading from freeware/shareware software archives.

Diagnostic programs can be quite valuable in helping to track down and fix both hardware and software problems—but only if your computer is up and running. If your computer is dead as a doornail, having a copy of the latest and greatest diagnostic program won't do you a lick of good, unless you want to use the CD as a drink coaster. (And by this point, having a good stiff drink might seem very appealing!)

Of course, if your computer is up and running, you might question the value of running a diagnostic program. After all, what must be functioning for you to run one of these programs? Well, the system board must be running, the video must be running so you can see the screen, the keyboard must be active to accept commands, and the floppy disk or CD drive must be working so the program can load. Merely loading the diagnostic program (or any other program, for that matter) tells you some things about your system.

Then there's the additional bonus that most diagnostic programs are visually impressive—they look technical as heck. My friend Dave Stang says that if nothing else, running a diagnostic on a customer's machine buys you a few minutes to think about what's actually wrong.

A Diagnostic Wish List

When assembling a set of tools to help you diagnose and fix hardware-related problems, you should consider the following types of utilities:

System inventory These programs display and inventory what they can detect in your system. That can be useful not as inventory in and of itself; its greater value is in cataloging what the system can *see*. If you know darn well that you installed the mouse interface, but it doesn't show up on the system inventory, then you have a problem. Before looking *too* hard for the answer, however, ask yourself first: Is the driver for the mouse loaded? Diagnostic programs, like the operating system itself, usually can't detect an unusual piece of hardware unless the driver for that program is loaded.

Burn-in   When you first get a computer, it's a good idea to *burn it in*. This means to run it continuously for at least three days, running some kind of diagnostic software over and over again. Some PC manufacturers even offer a burn-in when buying a new PC.

Simple diagnostics are no good for this kind of process—for two reasons. First, most simple diagnostics insist on informing you of any errors, then *requiring* you to press a key to acknowledge that you've seen the error message. Higher-quality diagnostic programs allow you to run the diagnostic in a *logging* mode, whereby any error messages are saved to a file, and do not require confirmation of an error. Second, simple diagnostics tend to be of the "run once" variety; good diagnostics let you run the diagnostic in a *continuous* mode, meaning it runs over and over and over until you tell it to stop.

Burn-in is an important step, so don't ignore it! Of the last 10 computers I've installed, 2 didn't fail until after four days of continuous testing. If I'd not done a burn-in on them, I probably would have ended up with a mysterious error appearing at a no-doubt inopportune time (Mr. Murphy and his law seem to have taken up residence in my office).

Interrupt/DMA/input/output address summary   The hardest thing about installing a new circuit board is adjusting some things called the input/output port address, the DMA channel, the IRQ level, and the ROM address. The reason that you adjust these settings is to make sure that they don't conflict with the port/DMA/IRQ/ROM of any other boards. For example, if you're putting a board in the system and that board must use either interrupt number 5 or interrupt number 7, but there's already a board in your system that uses interrupt 7, then you can't let the new board use interrupt 7. But the question arises, how do you find out what interrupts are in use on your system? Diagnostic procedures *try* to report this information. I say "try" because they unfortunately can't be trusted in this task, not due to inadequacies on the part of their programmers, but because of a simple fact: There's no way to reliably detect ports, DMAs, IRQs, or ROM addresses. How *do* you find out this information? You can look at the devices in your system by launching the System applet in the Windows Control Panel.

Hardware testing   A good diagnostic program should provide your hardware a workout. It will test your computer's memory thoroughly, test every possible data pattern on your hard disk, run your serial port at its maximum speed—in short, a good diagnostic program should be a sort of cybernetic boot camp for your computer.

Setup   Some of these programs do things associated more with setup responsibilities than diagnostic ones. For example, most of these programs will low-level format a hard disk, an important step in setting up an older type of hard disk. Others may have a built-in system setup program that sets up the CMOS chip in a computer.

If you read these items carefully, you no doubt noticed a lot of *shoulds*, as in "a good diagnostic program should...." All this equivocation has a purpose, believe me: Most diagnostic programs are junk. Look carefully before you spend the ton of money that you can easily spend on a diagnostic package.

TIP

One word of advice when running a diagnostic: Although I told you to load all drivers before running the diagnostics, don't run your memory manager; it just confuses a memory test.

Third-Party Diagnostic Software

There's an entire subset of the computer software industry dedicated to providing software and hardware diagnostic utilities. Between the commercial publishers and the freeware/shareware publishers, you can find literally dozens of utilities, each designed to provide a variety of diagnostic functions.

It is said that one time the science fiction author Theodore Sturgeon was approached by a literary critic who said, "Ted, you write such good stuff; why do you waste your time writing science fiction?" Sturgeon asked, "What's wrong with science fiction?" The critic answered, "90 percent of science fiction is crap." (Well, he didn't actually say "crap," but this book is rated for general audiences.) Sturgeon is reported to have replied archly, "90 percent of *everything* is crap." I'm afraid that this truism, dubbed *Sturgeon's Law* by generations of science fiction fans, applies well to the diagnostics world. Let me then not waste ink beating up on this chaff; let's look at the wheat.

Technical Hardware-Only Diagnostics

The first class of diagnostics to consider is those that focus exclusively on hardware-related problems. These are often quite technical in nature, and sometimes include hardware (such as loopback plugs) to facilitate the testing of various hardware components. (Some of them are also quite expensive—the most comprehensive packages will cost you anywhere from $200–$400.)

CheckIt   A fairly useful, extremely comprehensive set of hardware diagnostics from Smith Micro Software (formerly Touchstone Software). Actually, there are several different versions of CheckIt; for the most detailed diagnostics, you want the Professional Edition. Note that CheckIt does not include some of the hardware accessories that you need to do a thorough system check, such as loopback plugs for external port testing. (Smith Micro does have loopback plugs available as an extra-cost option, however.) That's not meant as a negative assessment; I like CheckIt and use it quite a bit. It has a good set of motherboard checkout routines (DMA, timer, IRQ, and the rest) as well as one of the better memory testers out there. See www .smithmicro.com/checkit/ for more information.

PC-Technician   An industrial-strength package from Windsor Technologies. I first looked at PC-Technician back in 1988, and I must truthfully say that I didn't think much of it then. But it's matured into a decent, general, inventory/setup/deep diagnostic routine. The full package includes the test disks, the loopbacks, a nice manual, and a carrying case for your tools. (Just make sure you don't put any magnetic screwdrivers next to the disks in the case!) Windsor also sells a program that will put your PC printer through its paces, as well as a plug-in BIOS POST code. The features that I like best about PC-Technician are the memory test—again, a good one in the same league as CheckIt's—and the serial and parallel tests. All in all, PC-Technician is the best all-in-one tester, but it's pricey. See www.windsortech.com/pctech.html for more information.

DisplayMate   A utility from DisplayMate Technologies (formerly Sonera Technologies) that checks only one thing—your display. But it does an extremely thorough job, testing aspects of your monitor that you probably didn't know were testable—*pincushioning*, for example. The accompanying manual is a tutorial on monitor problems and solutions. It won't test your memory or your printer, but it deserves a place on your diagnostics shelf. See www.displaymate.com for more information.

General Hardware/Software Diagnostics

The second class of utilities to consider includes those that perform both hardware and software diagnostics. These programs typically aren't as technical as the hardware-only diagnostics and therefore aren't as rigorous in their testing. They are, however, more consumer-friendly and thus easier for the average user to use.

WARNING

Some diagnostic programs—such as McAfee's First Aid and Norton Crash-Guard—are promoted as crash-prevention tools, meant to help prevent problems with your PC or with Windows. However, these programs require you to run them all the time; they attempt to create a buffer, or a shield, between the errors you might make and the machine itself. Although this type of software can keep you from making a fatal mistake, it also may interfere as you troubleshoot PC problems—the software may not allow you to make the changes that you need to make. Over time, you may also find that the rescue program isn't working as effectively—perhaps because it's configured wrong, or perhaps because you overrode it when it suggested you do or not do something. When this happens, whole new sets of problems can crop up that may affect booting your PC or Windows' proper operation. Thus, using this protection software may leave you needing protection from it. Use judiciously.

As I've suggested, you can spend a *lot* of money on diagnostic programs, so it's a good idea to take advantage of the option that many computer dealers provide today whereby you can buy software and return it within a few weeks if it fails to live up to expectations or doesn't work properly with your PC setup. Better yet, check to see if there's a free 30- or 45-day trial of the program you can download and try, and then buy the full package if it works well for you.

Windows Diagnostics

While not focused exclusively on hardware issues, all versions of Windows from Windows 98 on include a set of diagnostic system tools (accessed via Start ➤ Programs ➤ Accessories ➤ System Tools) that can help you track down many types of system problems. For example, ScanDisk enables you to perform either a surface or thorough scan of your drives and tries to fix errors it finds; Disk Defragmenter defragments and reorganizes your hard drive to make it run more efficiently.

Microsoft's System Information tool provides a host of indispensable data about various components of your system, and (via its Tools menu) serves as a gateway for several more "hidden" utilities. These utilities include the Dr. Watson logging tool, which keeps track of operations performed and error messages generated; System File Checker, which seeks out missing or damaged essential files and attempts to replace them; and System Information Utility (a.k.a. MSCONFIG), which enables you to set up a troubleshooting bootup mode and select which items you really want to load at Windows startup.

These diagnostics are not available directly within Windows 95 or Windows NT 4. Windows 95 (as well as all later versions) does include Device Manager, one of the tabs available under the System icon in Control Panel. Although it's not a diagnostic checker, vital information gets reported there that you need to check when you're having a problem. You may see an exclamation mark or red X on a device, indicating a device in conflict or disabled entirely. Or you may find a needed device driver not present at all when it should be. Or you may find a note on your hard drive indicating that the drive is running in MS-DOS compatibility mode (meaning Windows feels the drive isn't set to run properly in Windows, so it's running in a slower mode compatible with MS-DOS).

Look Under the Hood

Assuming that you've worked through steps one through five—and especially availed yourself of the appropriate troubleshooting utilities built into the Windows operating system—it's possible, if your troubles persist, that you may actually have a problem inside your PC's system unit.

Fortunately, many internal hardware problems can be handled simply and without any fancy equipment. Step six just says the following:

- ▶ Take the PC apart.

- ▶ Clean any connectors with an artist's eraser or connector cleaner.

- ▶ Push all socketed chips back into their sockets.

- ▶ Reassemble the PC.

Edge connectors get dirty and make circuit boards fail. Sometimes "dead" boards will do the Lazarus trick if you clean their edge connectors.

If you examine most circuit boards, you'll see that most chips are soldered right onto the board. *Soldering* is a process whereby the chip is bonded to the printed circuits on the board by heating a mixture of tin and lead to the point that it is molten, then allowing the tin/lead mixture to flow over the printed circuit and chip leg, and finally solidify. Soldering is a great technique for mass-producing electronic components. The downside is that when you must fix soldered components, you must *first* de-solder the components. This isn't much fun, and most people don't have soldering skills.

Not all chips are soldered to boards, however. Some are put in *sockets*. A typical board might have 30 soldered chips and 4 socketed ones. Chips are socketed because they've been voted "most likely to fail," because the designer wanted to put off a decision until the last minute, or because the chip will likely have to be replaced periodically because it contains software that changes over time—remember ROM? So socketing chips makes our jobs as troubleshooters easier.

On the other hand, heating and cooling of systems make these socketed chips creep out of their sockets. That's why you should push socketed chips back into their sockets when inspecting a board for whatever reason. One particularly persnickety tech whom I know takes the socketed chips out of their sockets, cleans their chip legs with connector cleaner, *then* puts the chips back in the sockets.

This should be obvious, but let me point it out anyway: Don't push *soldered* chips. The best that it can do is nothing. The worst that it can do is damage a board and maybe a chip. When you push socketed chips back into a board, be sure that you are supporting the *back* of the board. If you just put a board on a table, then push down on the chips, you can end up bending and damaging the board.

I know that this kind of advice—"take it apart, clean the connectors, push the chips back in the sockets, and reassemble"—doesn't sound very dazzling. But, darn it, *it works!* Buying a board to replace a defective one is a pretty rare event for me as a troubleshooter, and I don't do much soldering. And besides, it impresses the people whose machines you're fixing—all they see you do is basically touch the boards. Eventually, you get the reputation as a person who can just "lay hands upon the board...and make it *whole!*" (With apologies to the evangelists in the crowd.)

When All Else Fails

Don't feel ashamed if you can't diagnose every single problem you encounter. Even the best of us get stumped from time to time. When you've checked all your cables, run all the diagnostics, and disassembled/reassembled your entire system—and the darn thing *still* doesn't work!—it's time to turn to the experts for help.

One level of expert, of course, can be found on the Internet. There are a number of tech support sites on the Web, and most hardware and software vendors maintain tech support sections on their official websites. It's likely that your problem has already been reported and documented *somewhere*, and the information available online might keep you from reinventing the wheel.

If the online help isn't any help, then you need to drop back 10 and punt—and call the vendor's official technical support line. This might cost you bit, but at least you'll be getting advice from the horse's mouth. (Know that while some vendors still offer toll-free—and fee-free—tech support, others have eliminated 800-number lines and even make you pay them a fixed amount per call.) While e-mail support might be preferred by many vendors—and, in fact, may be just as effective—sometimes there's nothing like talking to a real human being in your quest to get your system back up and running.

Before you call tech support, make sure you've done your homework and have the following in front of you:

- ▶ The vendor's tech support phone number. (Don't laugh—you can't look it up on their website if you can't start your PC!)

- ▶ The make and model number of your PC, along with other pertinent information—processor speed, amount of RAM installed, other peripherals attached, etc.

- A detailed description of your problem, including what operations you were performing just before the problem occurred.

- A list of what other steps you've taken to track down the problem (no sense doing the same thing twice).

- A good book or a big, thick magazine—because you'll probably be on hold for a long, long time!

When you finally get through to a support technician, keep calm, cool, and collected, and be as polite as possible. As frustrated as you may be with your particular problem, the guy (or gal) on the other end of the phone has already listened to dozens of complaining customers already today. If you're nice to them, they'll be nice to you—and do whatever they can to help you find and fix your problem.

COMMON PROBLEMS—AND SOLUTIONS

Enough with the theory and advice—let's get down to practical matters! This section looks at some of the more common hardware-related problems you may be unfortunate enough to encounter, and offers up the most-likely causes of those problems.

Your Computer Won't Start

This is perhaps the scariest problem you can encounter. Either nothing at all happens, or you hear a few familiar or unfamiliar sounds, or even see a blinking light or two, but it all leads to a big fat zero. What can cause your entire system not to work? Here are some things to look for:

- Make sure the power cable is connected, both to your PC and to either a power strip/surge suppressor or wall outlet. If connected to a power strip/surge suppressor, make sure the strip is turned on—and that other devices plugged into the strip are working. (The strip itself could be bad.) Make sure that the wall outlet has power. (Flip that wall switch—and check that circuit breaker—just to be sure.)

- Check to see whether the power cable itself is bad. If you have a spare cable or one from another PC, try swapping it for the current cable.

- If your system unit lights up and makes noise but nothing appears on-screen, make sure that the computer monitor is turned on and getting power, and that it is connected properly and securely to the monitor output on your system unit. If you suspect you actually have a monitor problem rather than a system unit problem, try connecting your PC to a different monitor.

▶ If your computer starts up but you receive an error message telling you that you have a nonbootable, invalid, or nonsystem disk, you've accidentally left a floppy in drive A. Remove the floppy.

▶ If your system *tries* to start but then locks up, it's possible you have some type of damage to your main hard disk. You could have a damaged boot sector, or an internal connection may have worked loose, or your key system files might have become corrupted. Try restarting with an emergency boot disk (or the Windows Startup disk) and then use ScanDisk to check for hard-disk errors.

▶ If your system appears to start but then generates a series of beeps (with nothing showing on your video display), it's possible that you have a problem with your video card. (Consider this a *probability* if you've just installed a new video card!) Make sure the video card is seated firmly in its slot, and that you've switched the appropriate switches on your motherboard (if necessary) to recognize the new card. Try uninstalling the new card and reinstalling your old one—it's possible the new card is defective.

▶ A beeping-and-not-starting scenario can also be caused by incorrect settings in your system's CMOS setup. Check the video and memory settings, specifically. Another possible cause is a bad memory chip, or faulty memory installation. A weak or dead CMOS battery can also cause this problem.

▶ If nothing turns on—no power lights light, no disk drives whirr, nothing—it's possible that the power supply transformer in your system unit is bad.

Your Computer Locks Up

In terms of causing extreme user panic, a frozen system is second only to a completely dead system. What can cause your system to freeze up? Here are some of the most likely causes:

▶ It's possible that it's not your entire system that's locked up—it could be your keyboard or mouse. Check the connections for both these devices, and make sure both cables are firmly plugged into the appropriate ports. If you're using a wireless keyboard or mouse, replace your batteries.

▶ Misbehaving software is, perhaps, the greatest cause of frozen systems. If a program is stalled, try switching to another open program, either from the Windows Taskbar or by pressing Alt+Tab to shuttle through all open programs. If things are still frozen, press Ctrl+Alt+Delete (the old "three-fingered salute") to display the Close Program dialog box; highlight the program that isn't responding and click the End Task button. If, after trying all these actions, your system is *still* frozen, you'll have to reboot completely—press Ctrl+Alt+Delete *twice* to shut down and then restart your entire system. If even this doesn't shut things down, you'll have to use the Power button on your system unit—or, in the worst of all possible cases, unplug the system unit from its power source.

WARNING

Shutting down your PC by any method other than the standard Windows shutdown procedure runs the risk of damaging any currently open files—and, under some circumstances, of altering some of your system's display and operational settings.

▶ Many computer lockups are caused by too many programs trying to use more memory than is available. It's possible that you'll get a kind of warning before a total lockup; if your computer starts to slow down in the middle of an operating session, it's a sure sign of an upcoming memory-related failure. If the problem recurs, try closing a program or two to free up system memory—or upgrade the amount of memory in your system unit.

▶ Since Windows uses free hard-disk space to augment random access memory, too little disk space can also cause your system to slow down or freeze. Make sure you've gone through your folders and deleted any nonessential or unused files—especially TMP files in the \WINDOWS\TEMP\ directory.

Finally, any time something weird happens with your system, consider whether the problem could have been caused by a computer virus. Make sure you're running some sort of antivirus program—especially when downloading files from the Internet or opening e-mail attachments—and run a full system sweep if you start experiencing performance problems.

A New Piece of Hardware Won't Work—or Messes Up Your System

It happens to the best of us. You install a new card or external peripheral, and all of a sudden your system either starts working funny or stops working completely. Obviously, something in the new installation caused the problem—but what?

- ▶ Make sure that the new hardware is properly installed. If you installed a new internal board, make sure the board is fitted properly in its slot, that any additional wires or cables are connected properly, and that any switches are set appropriately. If you installed a new external peripheral, make sure that it's plugged into the right port, that the cable is firmly connected, and that the device is hooked up to and is receiving external power (if that's required).

- ▶ Some new devices require you to reset specific jumpers or switches on your system's motherboard. Check the item's installation instructions and make sure you've performed this vital step.

- ▶ Check your system configuration. It's possible that Windows Plug and Play didn't recognize your new device, didn't recognize it properly, or installed the wrong driver. Try uninstalling both the hardware and its associated software, and then reinstalling. Use the Add New Hardware Wizard to override the standard Plug and Play operation.

- ▶ Make sure you have the latest version of the item's device drivers. Go to the vendor's website and download updated drivers, if necessary. (While you're there, check the online support facilities to see whether there are any documented problems between this peripheral and your specific system.)

- ▶ Look for an interrupt conflict, which could occur if the new device tries to use the same IRQ as an older device. This happens a lot with COM ports—not only is sharing the same port a problem, but some devices (such as mice and modems) don't like to share even- or odd-numbered ports. (Meaning that you may have a conflict between COM1 and COM3 that could be fixed by moving one of the devices to COM2 or COM4.) If worse comes to worst, try reassigning the IRQ for your new piece of hardware.

- ▶ It's possible that your system's CMOS settings need to be changed. This is most common when you upgrade or change memory or disk drives. Enter the CMOS configuration utility on system startup and change the settings appropriate to the new hardware you added.

Your Hard Disk Crashes

Any problem you may encounter with your hard disk is a major problem. That's because everything—from your system files to your program files to your data files—resides on your hard disk. If you can't access your hard disk, your multi-thousand dollar computer system is just that much more junk.

What are the most common causes of hard-disk problems? Here are a few to look for:

▶ If your system can't access your hard disk at all, you'll need to reboot using a system disk or the Windows Startup disk. Run ScanDisk from a floppy (it's built into the Windows Startup disk) to check drive C for defects, and then fix any found damage.

▶ If ScanDisk or some similar hard-disk utility doesn't get your hard disk spinning again, call in an expert. Even if your hard disk is seriously damaged, it may be possible for a professional technician to rescue the data on the damaged hard drive and transfer it to another disk.

▶ If you encounter frequent disk write errors, it's possible that you have some physical damage on your hard disk. Run ScanDisk or some other hard-disk utility to check and fix any defects.

▶ If your disk is working but running slower than normal, it probably needs to be defragmented. Run a good disk defrag program (such as Windows' Disk Defragmenter) to get all those noncontiguous clusters lined up properly.

▶ If you experience a lot of disk write errors or your system runs much slower than normal, and if you're using DriveSpace for disk compression, the problem is probably in DriveSpace. DriveSpace gives your system a pretty good workout and can cause lots of different types of problems. You may find that disk compression is more trouble than it's worth; if so, uncompress the drive! (In these days of cheap hard drives, you're probably better off to install a second hard-disk drive than you are to use DriveSpace or some similar disk compression utility.)

To avoid catastrophic hard-disk crashes, make sure you perform preventive maintenance. I know it's a cliché, but an ounce of prevention is certainly worth a pound of cure, especially where the valuable data on your hard disk is concerned.

Your Monitor Doesn't Display Properly

If your computer is working but your monitor isn't, look for these possible causes:

▶ Make sure the monitor is plugged in, turned on, and firmly connected to your PC.

▶ Try to determine whether it's a monitor problem or a video card problem. If you have a spare one handy, plug a different monitor into your PC; if it works, your old monitor has a problem. If it doesn't, the problem is most likely in your video card.

▶ Make sure that your system is configured properly for your video card/monitor combination. Right-click anywhere on the Desktop and select Properties to display the Display Properties window; use the Settings tab to select the correct hardware and configuration settings.

▶ If your monitor suddenly goes blank and emits a high-pitched whine, turn off your monitor—*immediately!* Leaving the monitor on in this condition could damage it. Now check the settings on your video card (or in Windows' Display Properties window); chances are the configuration is set to a higher resolution than your monitor is capable of displaying. Reconfigure the settings for a lower-resolution display, and you should be fine.

▶ If your monitor pops and crackles and maybe even starts to smell (like something's burning), turn it off and go check the credit line on your nearest charge card. While it's possible that all this hubbub is caused by dirt building up inside your monitor, it's more likely that something major—like the power supply—has gone bad, and that it's time to invest in a new monitor.

Your Modem Won't Connect

In this interconnected world, we all need the Internet to survive. What do you do if your modem won't let you connect?

▶ Check your cables! If you're using an external modem, make sure it's firmly connected to the correct port on your PC, and that it's plugged into and receiving power from a power strip or wall outlet. If you're using an internal modem, make sure the card is firmly seated. For all modems, make sure that it's connected to a working phone line—and that you have the cable connected to the *in* jack on the modem, not the *out* jack!

▶ Make sure your modem is configured correctly. If you're using Windows 98 or Windows Me, use the Modem Troubleshooter to track down potential problems. Otherwise, go to the Control Panel and start the Modems applet, then run the diagnostics in the Modem Properties window. If problems persist, try uninstalling and then reinstalling the modem on your system—and then check whether an updated driver is available from the modem vendor.

▶ Check your dial-up configuration. Make sure you have the right phone numbers listed, that you've entered the right username and password, and that any ISP-specific information (such as DNS numbers) is entered correctly.

▶ Check your system network or TCP/IP settings. This isn't so much a problem with Windows 98/Me/2000/XP, but it can be an issue with Windows 95/NT and other operating systems.

Also, remember that just because you can't connect to your Internet Service Provider doesn't mean that you have a modem problem. Many ISPs try to connect too many users through too few phone lines, resulting in busy signals, slow connections, dropped connections, or similar problems. See whether your connection problems ease up at different times of the day (the after-dinner period is a typical "rush hour" for most ISPs), or if your ISP has different numbers that you can use to connect. If the problem persists, consider changing ISPs.

Your Printer Won't Print

Printer problems are quite common—especially after you've just hooked up a new printer to your old system. Here are a few things to look for:

▶ It sounds so simple as to be insulting, but make sure that your printer is plugged in and has power, and that it is connected properly to your PC. A loose printer cable can cause all sorts of bizarre problems.

- ▶ Along the same lines, make sure that your printer isn't out of paper, and that it's online and not experiencing any type of paper jam.

- ▶ Make sure that Windows recognizes your printer—and that it recognizes the *correct* printer. (Recognizing a similar model from the same manufacturer doesn't cut it.) Make sure that Windows has the correct printer driver installed. You may even want to check with the manufacturer to make sure you have the latest and greatest version of the printer driver.

- ▶ If you have more than one printer installed on your system or network (including faxes and devices that your system sees as printers), make sure you have the correct printer selected.

- ▶ Check for device conflicts. Fax machines and printers frequently interfere with each other, but any two devices, if not configured properly, can cause conflicts.

- ▶ Make sure you have enough free disk space to print. Windows will use temporary hard-disk space (called a *cache*) to store data while a print job is in process. Try deleting old and unused files (including TMP files in the \WINDOWS\TEMP\ folder) to free up additional disk space.

TROUBLESHOOTING TIPS FOR AN EMERGENCY

There really is a reason why I caution you to stay calm and not do anything desperate when you hit a snag. When people get scared, they do things they wouldn't even think about doing when their minds are more clear. If you lose your cool, you could end up having to fix several problems you created when trying to fix the first one.

Try to remember these considerations when troubleshooting a PC emergency:

- ▶ Have an emergency kit handy: a good screwdriver, a good flashlight, a boot disk or two (including the Windows Startup disk, if you're running Windows), a floppy-based copy of a virus scanner, and some key diagnostic utilities.

▶ Have your operating system installation CD ready. Many problems—both hardware and software—require you to have the installation CD to reinstall or fix components. This is especially true with Windows operating systems, though not entirely unique to them.

▶ When you see the problem, stop! You need to take a moment to shift gears from working to troubleshooting.

▶ Ask yourself, "What's the last thing I did?" Understanding the steps you just took to get you into the problem can help you identify the steps necessary to get you back out of it.

▶ Do a first analysis of the damage before you try to change anything. The first thing you spot wrong might not be the only thing wrong, and you need all the information you can gather to make a smart choice about how to proceed.

▶ If you find yourself getting frustrated, take a break. That doesn't mean have a stiff drink (though you may feel like it), because you need your wits about you when you return to the computer.

▶ When you finally put your hands on the PC to begin correcting the problem, take it one step at a time. Try one procedure and see whether it fixes the problem. If not, undo it, and try the next. Do too many things at once, and you'll start to forget what you tried or what your results were.

▶ If you have another PC available, get on the Internet and use web-based resources to look for help.

▶ Ask yourself why you have no backup system in place (and apologies extended if you're one of the statistical minority who regularly backs up their files...or even thinks about doing so until they've lost data they sorely need). Then ask yourself whether the time you're going to waste doing work over again is better than the time you thought you'd waste making a backup. If backups are taking too long, the answer isn't fewer backups, but faster, more capable backup hardware.

▶ Make sure you have the tech support number of your hardware manufacturer handy—just in case everything else you try fails!

Appendix D

TROUBLESHOOTING PRINTERS

This appendix contains information on troubleshooting problems with your printer that might appear when you're trying to print Office XP files—or at any other time.

Adapted from *The Complete PC Upgrade & Maintenance Guide (12th Edition)* by Mark Minasi

ISBN 0-7821-2990-0   1488 pp $59.99

CONNECTING AND TESTING A PARALLEL PRINTER

Before you start, there are some things you may need on hand. These include:

- ▶ Printer's manual
- ▶ Computer's manual
- ▶ Printer's setup software, if you're running Windows
- ▶ (Optional) Extra parallel cable to swap with, in case there is any doubt whether the current one is working

Before you connect a printer to a PC, make sure that:

- ▶ The computer is turned off
- ▶ The printer is turned off

Here are the basic steps for connecting a printer. For in-depth coverage on printers and how to troubleshoot printer problems, refer to the rest of this appendix.

1. Set up the printer and turn it on. Run its self-test to confirm that it's working properly.

2. Turn the printer off. Then connect the printer to the computer with a parallel cable. If you want to use ECP or EPP, make sure you have a parallel cable that is capable of that.

3. Turn on the PC. If needed, enter the PC's BIOS setup program and make sure the parallel port type is set correctly (ECP, EPP, Bidirectional, etc.).

4. If you're using Windows, run the setup software that came with the printer to install its printer driver.

   Or, if you're using a DOS-based program, configure the program to use the printer.

5. Print a self-test using the printer's Windows driver or utility program.

   Or, in a DOS program, create a simple document or drawing and print it as a test.

Printer Maintenance

Keeping your printer in top condition means giving it a little maintenance attention now and then. Printer maintenance varies depending on the type of printer, so let's look at the upkeep for some of the most common printer types.

Dot-Matrix Printers

If you're still using a dot-matrix printer, either you are seriously strapped for cash or you need to print multipart forms. I'll assume the latter. Because dot-matrix printers strike the page with the print head (printers that use this type of technology are known as *impact* printers), they can print through multiple layers of carbon (or carbonless) copies, and some businesses need that capability.

NOTE

The only kind of impact printer you'll find for sale these days is a dot-matrix printer. Daisy-wheel printers, which used to rule the marketplace 10 to 15 years ago, are all but extinct. (Okay, you might find a daisy-wheel printer at an estate sale, or in a mysterious forgotten crate in a government warehouse.) And even dot-matrix printers are over the hill.

To clean a dot-matrix printer, use a dry, soft cloth to clean both the paper path and the ribbon path. Most manufacturers suggest cleaning every six months, as the ribbon path can build up a film of inky glop that causes the ribbon to jam. Before doing this, go to a drug store and buy a dispenser box of 100 clear latex gloves. Use them when working on the printer so that you don't have to wash your hands for hours to remove the ink (but don't use them when you're working on chips and boards—that latex can build up some mean static).

TIP

When working on a printer, it's easy to get ink on yourself and your clothes. Here's a tip that will help you clean up. A friend once told me that hairspray will remove ink from fabric. So another friend and I experimented with her hair mousse stuff—you know, the spray that you use to make your hair defy gravity? It did nothing. Then we tried some Aqua Net, a hairspray that hasn't changed since Jackie Kennedy used it in the White House. The result? We found that cheap hairspray works a lot better than the expensive stuff. Spray it on the fabric and rinse with cold water. A little soap will pick up the rest.

You can also vacuum out the paper chaff periodically from the inside of the printer. The continuous-feed paper used in impact printers is somewhat more prone to leaving dust behind than single sheet paper. You may find it unwieldy to use the same vacuum on the printer as you use on the living-room carpet. Purchasing a tech vacuum of some sort may be best because it is smaller and easier to use in tight areas, and it won't suck keytops right off your keyboards.

On an impact printer, the print head moves back and forth across the page, which means there is probably a drive belt. Determine if there is a belt-tightening mechanism for the printer and find the correct tension values. Keep a replacement belt on hand. (Believe me, they're no picnic to find in a hurry.)

WARNING

Some dot-matrix printers have ribbon cables that are used to carry the data to the print head. They often look like drive belts, but they are definitely not. Tighten these, and they'll usually break. If they do, you can say goodbye to your printer.

Most impact printers never need to be lubricated. In fact, oil can do considerable damage if applied to the wrong places. If you thoroughly disassemble the printer, you will probably have to lubricate various points as you reassemble it. If you intend to do this, I strongly recommend that you get a maintenance manual from the manufacturer.

Here's a tip that will extend the life of both the ribbon and the print head: Put some WD-40 lubricant on a used ink ribbon. Let it soak overnight. It'll produce good output the next day, and you won't damage the print head—WD-40 is a good lubricant for print heads. Let me stress, however, that this applies only to ink ribbons. If you have any other type of printer, this will not work. So don't go soaking that laser toner cartridge in anything, okay?

The expensive part of a dot-matrix printer that dies is the print head. Luckily, almost all dot-matrix printers these days have a thermistor (basically, a temperature sensor) that detects when the print head is getting too hot and shuts the printer down until it cools off. To avoid excess heat buildup around a dot-matrix printer, avoid stacking things around it— leave a clear path for airflow on all sides.

Replacing the print head is not economical on many printers because of the high price that manufacturers charge for replacements. For example, the print head replacement for a good-quality wide-carriage dot-matrix printer might cost $100 or more. Fact is, in almost every case, it makes no sense to replace a dot-matrix print head unless you have one of the very expensive high-speed dot-matrix printers. You can buy a brand-new printer for about the cost of a replacement dot-matrix print head.

Ink-Jet Printers

Ink-jet printers have come a long way since their introduction back in the '70s. At one time, ink-jet printers clogged pretty regularly because the ink would dry in the tiny holes in the heads. Today, the jets are designed to resist drying, and the heads are generally protected by a rubber boot that keeps the holes from drying out. Also, on some models, the heads are built into the ink tanks so that when you replace an empty tank, you're also getting new jets. This keeps the print on these printers looking like new.

Still, if you let an ink-jet printer sit too long without using it, the ink in the jets (and/or in the ink cartridges) will dry out, and one or more colors won't print. This can result in some odd-looking printouts with amusing (but definitely not lifelike!) colored stripes. If this happens, run the printer's built-in head-cleaning utility. You can do this by pressing certain buttons on the printer itself, or in most cases through the printer's driver in Windows 95/98/Me/2000. (Select Start ➤ Settings ➤ Printers, or choose Printers from the Control Panel, then right-click the printer in the Printers window and choose Properties. Look for the cleaning command, usually on the Utilities tab.) After cleaning the heads, run a nozzle test, which you can also do through the printer's buttons or its Properties dialog box in Windows. The nozzle test prints some basic geometrical pattern of lines on the page in each of its colors, so you can see which color, if any, is failing to print. Sometimes several cycles of cleaning followed by testing are required to clear out the dried-up ink residue.

You may see advertisements for refilled ink cartridges, or even kits that promise to let you refill the cartridges yourself, but this is seldom a good idea. True, it can save you money, but on many models, as I mentioned, the heads are built into the ink cartridges, so that you get new heads when you get new ink. This is by design. If you continue to print with the old heads tankful after tankful, the print quality will definitely suffer, and you may harm your printer.

NOTE

On some ink-jet printers, moving the ink cartridges into view so you can replace them can be a real exercise in coordination. On certain Epson models, for example, you have to hold down two little tiny buttons simultaneously for several seconds, then press another button. Check the printer's manual to find out the procedure for your specific model—that's usually the only way to find out (other than visiting the manufacturer's website and searching for the info).

TIP

Using Draft or a lower output quality mode for printing all files that don't need to be professionally distributed will increase the life of a standard ink cartridge.

All-in-One Combos

If space is a luxury to you but you need printing, faxing, copying, and scanning capabilities, you may have already considered an all-in-one combo. Some products that fall into this category are the Hewlett-Packard Office-Jet series, the Brother Multi-Function printers, and the Canon MultiPass series. Here, many options are available. Most of these combos come with ink-jet printers (either black-and-white or color), but some of the more expensive models come with laser printers. Maintenance on the printer portion is similar to the methods discussed in the preceding section on ink-jet printers, or in the following section on laser printers.

The all-in-ones also come with either a sheet-fed or flat-top scanner that also serves as a copier and fax input device. Some of the combos are designed to work with the fax modem on your PC, while others connect to the phone line directly so that you can receive faxes while your PC is off.

Although all-in-ones provide a space-saving advantage, there is one drawback. If you experience trouble with one of the components (printer, scanner, or fax) and need to send it in for repair, you also lose the ability to use the other features during that time. Still, all-in-ones are a convenient and cost-effective alternative to purchasing each component individually.

Thermal-Transfer Printers

When you were a kid, did you ever make pictures by coloring with crayons onto a piece of heavy paper and then using an iron to transfer the colored wax to another piece of paper? (If not, just nod politely and keep reading—I'll get past the "when you were a kid" stories in a minute.) Thermal-transfer printing works something like that. Very hot pins are pressed onto a wax- or wax/resin-coated ribbon, and the wax or resin melts and is transferred to the paper beneath it. The difference is that the paper has to go through the process four times, once for each color (typically cyan, yellow, magenta, and black). This kind of printer produces excellent quality color images—better than an ink-jet, and arguably better than color lasers—but is rather expensive in terms of consumables. You won't find them for sale in the typical office supply store—they're a specialty item. (Refills for them are also generally not available at your regular retail outlets.) Some of these also require special thermal paper, which of course is a lot more expensive than standard paper.

The issues involved with thermal-transfer printers are much like those with other printers: Keep them cool and keep them plugged in. If you're having problems with print quality, such as smearing, you might try using another manufacturer's paper or ribbons.

Laser Printers

The laser printer is very similar to a copy machine. Having said that, it's amazing that they are as reliable as they are.

You may be surprised to learn that many different brands of laser printers operate using the same basic innards. The most common laser engine is made by Canon. Many of the HP LaserJets, Apple LaserWriters, and Canons (obviously), as well as the older QMS Kiss and others, are built around the Canon engine. These need very little maintenance except for a new cartridge every few thousand copies or so. The cartridges cost in the neighborhood of $70 to $120, and, according to HP, contain all that is needed for routine maintenance. So, every time that you change your cartridge, you'll perform routine maintenance like cleaning the corona wires and paper pickup pawls.

It's okay to buy recycled toner cartridges, but make sure your refill company completely rebuilds the insides, including replacing the photo-electric drum. Avoid the "drill and fill" vendors, as they don't replace the insides, and using that kind of refill will lead to a lower-quality print image and may damage the laser printer. If you don't refill them, many of the cartridge manufacturers provide a way to mail in the used ones for recycling (and sometimes a rebate).

Laser printers require proper ventilation and a fair amount of power. Other than that, don't pour any Cokes in them and they last a long time. Never ship a laser with a toner cartridge in place. It can open up and cover the inside of the laser with toner. And don't take the toner cartridge out and wave it around, or toner might spill out and make a mess. You will also want to wipe out any stray toner in the printer's insides every time you change the toner cartridge.

TIP

To get the last little bit of life out of a toner cartridge, you can take it out and shake it gently from side to side. But don't turn it on end, and don't shake it up and down, or toner might spill out.

On some models, a new toner cartridge comes with a long, thin felt strip mounted on a piece of plastic. You drop this into some slot or other on the printer, replacing the old and cruddy strip that was there before. Not all laser printers have this, though.

PRINTER INTERFACES

The parallel port is far and away the most common type of interface between printer and computer, so it's important that you understand its basics. But it's also important that you're aware of the other ways that a PC can communicate data to a printer.

Parallel Ports

The vast majority of printers connect to a PC via the *parallel port*, a female 25-pin connector that's typically built right into the PC. In an ATX design, it's a built-in part of the motherboard that sticks out of the back of the PC; in an AT design (the older standard), it's a connector attached to the motherboard with a ribbon cable. As with other peripheral troubleshooting, you should start your diagnosis by checking this connection at all junctures. Is the parallel port functioning? Is the printer cable connected firmly at both ends? If it's an AT system, is the little ribbon cable inside the PC from the connector to the motherboard snugly plugged in?

The History of Parallel

The parallel port was originally devised as a high-speed, low-cost alternative to a serial port for printer interfaces.

Until 1976, serial ports were the established way of hooking up a printer to a computer. The problem was that serial port hardware was expensive. Adding a serial port to a computer could raise the computer's price by anywhere from $250 to $1000. That got in the way of selling printers, and so a printer company, Centronics, decided to do something about it—they created the Centronics parallel interface, which is essentially the parallel interface that PCs still use today.

There were some drawbacks to the parallel interface, however (and there still are today). While RS-232 (another term for serial cables) allows cables of more than 50 feet in length, the Centronics interface is reliable for only 15 feet—actually, less for modern ports. RS-232 is bidirectional and quite flexible as to the kind of things it can support. Originally, the Centronics parallel interface was designed to be unidirectional and was aimed only at printers. RS-232 is serial, employing only two wires for data; Centronics is an eight-bit parallel interface, with eight wires for data. The circuitry required to implement a parallel port, however, is much simpler than that required to implement a serial port because data in your computer is also parallel. The computer simply transmits the data as it is, so the cost of making a parallel port is much lower. The result was a Centronics interface that was easy to cobble together for just a few dollars and offered terrific throughput, as much as 500,000 bits per second (bps) compared to RS-232's 20,000bps.

Today's Parallel Ports

Since then, the parallel port has continued to evolve. First, some laptops offered bidirectional parallel ports. Then those bidirectional parallel ports were further modified to become *enhanced parallel ports (EPP)* and *extended capabilities ports (ECP)*. ECP is more commonly used for printers, while EPP is more common for other parallel devices such as scanners. These newer port types let you print with the speed of the wind, between 500,000 and 1,000,000bps. They also let printers form a lasting relationship with computers based on communication—the printer not only listens to the computer but also communicates its own problems, like being out of paper or having a paper jam. Using an ECP port, you don't need to go to the printer to discover that it didn't do its job—a message will pop up on your monitor telling you so.

To use an ECP port, you need four things: an ECP or EPP/ECP port, an ECP-capable printer, an IEEE 1284–compliant parallel cable, and Windows 95/98/Me/2000/XP. Once you have installed these features, you will begin to print with unparalleled speed (excuse the pun). If your parallel port's controller is built into the motherboard (as almost all are these days), you can set its mode in the BIOS setup program. Normally, the BIOS lets you choose a parallel port mode, such as Output Only (the old, unidirectional mode), Bidirectional (a simple bidirectional mode), ECP, or EPP.

The expanded capabilities of the parallel port have led to the parallel port's use in more areas than just printers. The parallel port now sees use as a file transfer interface (for removable media drives or external CD-ROMs), as a connection to a local area network adapter, or as a connection to an input device such as a scanner. Trouble is, you have only one parallel port on most systems, so how can you have more than one parallel device at once? Well, you can continually switch cables, or you can attempt to share the port among the devices. Some nonprinter parallel devices, such as scanners, have a built-in pass-through that lets you connect the parallel devices in a sort of daisy chain, like SCSI. This works on some systems better than others. Generally speaking, ink-jet printers have a harder time sharing a parallel port than do other printer types, and different BIOS settings for the parallel port can sometimes make the difference between sharing success and failure.

Windows 95/98/Me/2000/NT/XP have support for up to three parallel ports, LPT1 through LPT3. Parallel port addresses are hex 3BC, 378, and 278. The PC has a peculiar process for relating I/O addresses to LPT addresses. First, it looks for address 3BC. If there is a port at that address, it assigns it LPT1. If not, it looks for 378 and, if it exists, assigns *that* to LPT1. If that's not available, it finally tries for 278. Once LPT1 is assigned, it looks (in the same order) for LPT2 and LPT3. This means that if you put a first parallel port into a machine and the port has address 278, you'll end up with an LPT1, even though 278 is intended for LPT3. But install a second port at 378, and the next time you boot up, the 278 port will become LPT2. Most systems have only the one port, LPT1, but you can easily add expansion boards with extra ports (both parallel and serial).

USB Ports

Some newer printers will attach to your computer by a Universal Serial Bus (USB) port. To use a USB printer with your PC, you need two things. First, verify that your PC has USB ports. Most Pentium II and III motherboards support USB, and you may find one USB port on your Pentium II or III laptop or two USB ports on the back of your Pentium II/III desktop or tower case. If your motherboard doesn't support USB, you can also get a PCI USB adapter card. Second, you need an operating system that supports the USB interface. Windows 98/Me/2000/XP offer USB support, while Windows NT does not. USB supports Plug and Play installation, and you can hot-plug the USB cable from the printer to the PC while your PC is on. Typically, the first time you plug the printer into your PC's USB port, Windows 98/Me/2000/XP will automatically detect the connection and prompt you to install the printer drivers and related software. As a result, installing a USB printer is virtually painless. You have no IRQ settings to worry about, and you can be up and running in no time.

USB devices have some distinct advantages over serial or parallel ports, and it is expected that the latter two types of ports will be completely replaced by USB in the near future. Theoretically, you can connect up to 127 peripheral devices such as mice, modems, keyboards, and printers on a single USB port, and most newer PCs have two USB ports. However, there is a slight catch. Let's say you have a USB keyboard connected to one of your USB ports, and a USB mouse connected to the other. Now you want to add a USB printer. Each USB device that you connect to your PC has to get power from somewhere. So you'll need to purchase a USB hub to connect additional peripherals.

Serial Ports

The original printers connected to computers via serial (RS-232) ports. It's still possible to connect printers serially today, provided the printer has a serial interface (not all do). But I don't recommend it. Serial port printing can be very slow, and with today's graphics-heavy print jobs, that can mean frustration and waiting around.

Some printers have both a parallel and a serial interface, so, in theory, you could hook up two PCs to the same printer, each through a different interface. However, because of the speed issue with serial, I recommend instead that you share the printer through some other means—perhaps using a switch box or a network.

Infrared Ports

For members of the "virtual office" who have no desk but only a laptop to carry around and plug in as needed, there's a way to eliminate at least one of the cables you need to plug in: Printers with infrared ports are available. Rather than requiring a parallel cable to connect the printer to your computer, a ray of infrared light shines between a transceiver on the computer and one on the printer.

Data travels between the computer and printer via an infrared connection. Light and electric impulses all pulse at a certain rate per second; this rate is called the *frequency*–the more pulses, the higher the frequency. Signals with higher frequencies can transmit data more quickly (each pulse can carry a bit of data). However, they have a shorter range and are more prone to interference than lower-frequency signals because anything that interferes with the signal will affect more data than it would if there were fewer pulses per second. Infrared light has a high frequency. Thus, the computer sends a beam of infrared light to the receiver on the printer. The devices have a pretty good range, but it is usually limited to line of sight. (You can't print from an office around the corner.)

If you're having trouble with a wireless printer, check the following:

▶ Are the infrared ports on the printer and computer both clean and unblocked?

▶ Does it help to move the printer/computer to one side?

▶ Did someone stand between your printer and computer during the print job?

Other than that, troubleshooting an infrared printer is much like troubleshooting any other printer. The tricky thing about wireless printers is making the connections.

Network Printing

Most businesses today don't want to be tied down to providing a printer for every single PC–or, conversely, limiting each PC to printing on only one printer. Thus was born the network printer.

There are two ways to use your LAN to print. One is to connect the printer to a PC and then share that printer on the LAN. Although the printer "belongs" to the person using that PC, anyone on the network can send printer jobs to it. The other way to share a printer is to hook it directly into the network. This requires a network-capable printer. Some printers come network-ready; others can be made ready by installing an upgrade card in them. (This capability varies among manufacturers, but HP offers a JetDirect card for some models that makes them network-capable.)

There are, however, a few caveats to using these marvels of technology. As with any network device, you must be using the same protocols on your server that you use on the printer's network interface, because the printer driver is installed on a server and then shared. Standard protocols supported are TCP/IP, IPX/SPX, EtherTalk, and DLC. Unlike other protocols, DLC (which stands for Data Link Control) is used only for printing and mainframe access in the Windows environment, so you may not have it installed. You must also be sure that the protocols are configured correctly—if you are using TCP/IP, for example, you must have an IP address and a subnet mask for the printer. It is also a very good idea to be sure that your network cable is securely plugged into the card and hub.

COMMON PROBLEMS AND SOLUTIONS

It's hard to discuss printer problems and troubleshooting them without delving too deeply into the specifics of the thousands of models out there. I haven't got the space to do that (or, truthfully, the time to get to know all those printers), but there are some generic pieces of advice that I can pass along.

Isolate the Problem

As always, try to isolate the problem. Something in the computer or its software? The printer interface? The cable? The printer? Is the printer plugged in, cabled, and online?

The steps I use are as follows:

1. Check whether the printer is online, is plugged in, has paper, and is turned on.

2. Turn the printer off and then on again. Reboot the computer, and try it again.

3. If it is a network printer, check the network configuration (such as the IP address and subnet mask on TCP/IP).

4. Use the printer self-test to see whether the test page prints correctly. The printer's manual usually tells how to do this.

5. Check that the software is configured for the printer and that the correct drivers are loaded for it in Windows (if used).

6. Swap the printer cable to make sure your cable isn't faulty.

7. If it is a network printer, try printing from another computer.

8. Swap the printer with a different one of the same model, if possible.

Some other things to check right off the bat:

▸ Do a DIR from the command prompt, then try a screen print using the Print Screen key.

▸ If you are troubleshooting a network printer, check the queue at the server to be certain there are no stuck jobs. If there are, then purge the queue.

▸ Check the printer manufacturer's website to see whether an updated driver is available for your version of Windows or for the particular DOS-based program you want to print from.

Check Cable Lengths

The role of cable lengths in noise and interference is one issue. But another problem is overly long cables. Serial cables aren't supposed to be longer than 50 feet, and older parallel cables should not exceed 6 feet. Newer IEEE 1284 (ECP and EPP)–compliant cable can go to 15 feet. If you're using long cables and getting mysterious errors, the cables may be the culprits.

There are parallel port extenders—check Black Box (www.blackbox.com) to find them. An extender will let you run your parallel cable up to a kilometer.

Something I've noticed in recent years is that modern parallel port chips don't put out all that much power. I used to be able to share a printer between two computers with an A/B switch, but now it's often the case that it won't work unless the A/B switch has amplification power. The moral seems to be to keep those parallel port cables as short as possible. It is also not recommended to use an A/B switch with laser printers unless you have a powered switch.

Set Emulation Options Correctly

A more and more common problem is emulation mode. Many printers nowadays will emulate a Hewlett-Packard LaserJet of some kind. Unfortunately, some vendors' idea of "Hewlett-Packard compatible" is a blend of fact and fantasy. Anyway, if you've got your Acme Laser Printer set up for HP emulation, don't tell your software you've got an Acme—tell it you've got an HP. This sounds simple, but you'd be surprised at the number of people who get tripped up on that one.

Another emulation option is international capability—that is, the ability to specify what country the output is being prepared for distribution in. Many printers speak foreign languages. If you set up your printer for British, you may get the pounds sterling sign rather than the dollar sign. Oh, and by the way, most printers nowadays don't have DIP switches; they support some kind of software setup. Many of the newer printers not only support multiple emulation modes, but they know enough to automatically switch modes based on the driver being used to print. Check the printer's documentation to see how your printer handles it.

Check Ports, Their Settings, and Connections

As you know, printers can have a serial or parallel interface. On the PC, the only visible difference between the two is that the parallel port has a female connector and the serial port has a male connector.

Electronically, they are radically different, however. The parallel interface uses different voltages and handshakes from the serial interface. Most printers today come with only parallel, or, less commonly, with both parallel and serial. As I mentioned before, given the choice, use parallel. It's a cleaner and faster interface.

As laser printers get faster and, more particularly, support higher resolution, more high-speed interfaces will appear. For example, Apple uses an AppleTalk 230,000bps interface to an Apple LaserWriter. Some printers interface with SCSI, and some use proprietary CPU-to-printer interfaces.

Some printer cables fasten with clips; others fasten with screws. You should tighten the screws if your cable uses them; don't just plug it in and hope nobody comes along to bump it. I once saw an Okidata printer that was printing consistently incorrect characters. I tried to understand the problem by comparing the ASCII codes of the desired characters to the codes actually printed. I found in each case that bit 6 was always *1*. It turned out that the wire for line 6 was not fully seated. Securing the connector did the job.

I found a similar problem with a broken wire in a cable. Here's an example. Suppose I try to print *Hello* but get *Iekko*. Compare the codes of the desired and actual characters in Table D.1.

TABLE D.1:   A Sample Printer Cable Problem

DESIRED CHARACTER	CODE	ACTUAL CHARACTER	CODE
H	01001000	I	01001001
E	01100101	E	01100101
L	01101100	K	01101101
L	01101100	K	01101101
O	01101111	O	01101111

The *E* and *O* aren't affected, but *H* and *L* are. Notice that in all cases the low bit is *1*.

The serial port, being the versatile interface that it is, allows you to set several communication settings for it:

- Speed (1200, 2400, 4800, 9600, 14400, or 19200)
- Parity (Even, Odd, or None)
- Number of data bits (7 or 8)
- Number of stop bits (usually 1 or 2)

You can set these settings in the Properties dialog box for the port (from the Device Manager) in Windows. However, you are more likely to find a serial printer used in a very old system that doesn't have Windows 9*x*. In that case, you can modify the settings at the command prompt, like so:

```
MODE COM1: speed,parity,data bits,stop bits,p
MODE LPT1:=COM1:
```

In the first case, an example would be the following:

```
MODE COM1:9600,N,8,1,P
MODE LPT1:=COM1:
```

Meaning: 9600 bits per second, no parity, 8 data bits, 1 stop bit. The P means that it's a printer.

If you are using one of those newfangled ECP parallel ports for your printing needs, you may run into problems like garbled text or graphics. This is because some printers on the market haven't quite reached IEEE nirvana yet and therefore don't work so well with ECP. There are two things to do in this instance: In Windows, change the printer-spooling properties from EMF to RAW; if that doesn't work, change the port back to Bidirectional or Output Only mode in your BIOS setup program.

If you're having other port problems, did you install something recently? Could something be conflicting with the printer port?

Consider the Weather

Everyone talks about it, but...

A printer repairman told me about a day that he'd had the previous October. He said that all over town a particular model of printer was failing left and right. He couldn't figure it out. We thought about it. Around the middle of October, we turn on the heat in Washington. That dries out the air and, in turn, the items in the work area. Chips don't mind being dried, but what about capacitors? Could a paper-type capacitor be malfunctioning because it was drying beyond a certain point?

A repair memo came around from the manufacturer a couple of months later. Sure enough, a particular capacitor didn't like it too dry. The answer: Either put a humidifier near the printer, or change the capacitor to a similar, less dry-sensitive replacement. Moral: Be suspicious when the seasons change.

TROUBLESHOOTING TIPS

Like a bad cable TV connection on the night of the big pay-per-view fight, printers are notorious for going on the fritz when you've got 2 minutes to print and fax vitally important documents. Here are some additional troubleshooting tips to help you avoid resorting to the ultimate show of frustration: whacking your printer upside its paper tray as if it were a vending machine gone bad.

Printer Won't Print at All

If the printer won't print at all:

- ▸ Check that the printer is getting power, is online (check the Online button), and is connected to the PC.
- ▸ Turn the printer off and then on again. The same for the computer.
- ▸ Look on the printer for any error codes or flashing lights that could give a clue as to the problem.
- ▸ See that the printer has ink, toner, or ribbon, and that it's installed correctly.
- ▸ Turn off the computer and run the printer's self-test to see if it can print as a separate entity from the computer.
- ▸ Check to make sure the correct driver is installed on the PC.
- ▸ Check the printer queue and purge any print jobs that appear to be hung up.
- ▸ Turn the printer off, let it sit for 10 minutes, and try again. Overheating can shut down a printer temporarily.
- ▸ Try a different printer cable.
- ▸ Try hooking up the printer to a different computer to determine whether the problem is with the printer, the computer, or the software.

Printout Has Quality Problems

If the printout isn't all it should be:

- ▸ Ensure that the correct printer driver has been installed.
- ▸ Check the printer to make sure it is using the right print emulation mode if it has more than one available.
- ▸ On a dot-matrix printer, ensure that the belt is adjusted properly.

▶ Replace the ink, ribbon, or toner cartridge if needed, along with any other replacement parts, such as the felt pad in some laser models.

▶ Clean the printer according to the instructions in its manual.

▶ On an ink-jet, clean the nozzles by using the printer's built-in utility for that purpose.

Reference

DISCOVER WINDOWS XP: COMMAND AND FEATURE REFERENCE

In this reference, we provide you with an alphabetical listing of the Windows XP commands and features that are apt to be most useful as you work with Office XP and its many components.

Adapted from *Windows XP Home and Professional Editions Instant Reference* by Denise Tyler

ISBN 0-7821-2986-2   512 pp $24.99

BACKUP

 Backup Allows you to safeguard the data stored on your computer, or on network drives to which you have access, by copying the data to a data storage device, such as a tape drive or additional hard disk. Should there be a problem with your live data (such as disk failure, accidental deletion of files, or file corruption), you can restore data from a backup.

> **NOTE**
> Supported filesystems include FAT and NTFS. You must have administrative privileges to perform backup- and restore-related functions.

Choose Start ➤ All Programs (or Start ➤ Programs in the Classic Start menu) ➤ Accessories ➤ System Tools ➤ Backup to open the backup utility.

By default, the Backup Or Restore Wizard appears when you choose the Backup command. To switch to the advanced backup utility, click the Advanced Mode link on the first screen of the wizard. To return to the wizard, click the Wizard Mode link on the Welcome tab of the advanced backup utility.

> **NOTE**
> Windows XP Professional Backup is a feature of Windows XP Professional only.

Backup Or Restore Wizard

The Backup Or Restore Wizard guides you through the process of configuring the parameters for backup jobs. You can then run these backup jobs to back up files.

Backing Up Files

To create a backup with the Backup Or Restore Wizard, follow these steps:

1. On the Welcome screen, click Next.

2. On the Backup Or Restore screen, choose Back Up Files And Settings. Click Next.

3. On the What To Back Up screen, choose one of the backup options. If you select the Let Me Choose What To Back Up option, click Next; the wizard will let you check or uncheck files and folders from various folders and drives. You can expand or collapse the hierarchy tree to select files, or double-click a folder in the tree to display its contents on the right. After you select your backup option and any files and folders, click Next.

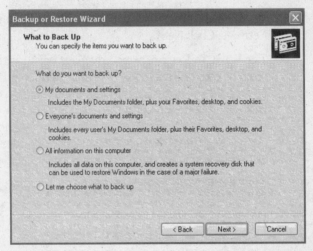

4. Select the drive to which you want to perform the backup. Floppy drives and removable drives appear in the list by default. Choose Browse to back up the files to a location that you specify. Enter a name for the backup and click Next.

5. The Backup Or Restore Wizard applies several default settings about the type of backup, verification, compression, and job scheduling. If you want to tailor these settings yourself, click Advanced and make your choices on the appropriate screens. When you're finished, click Next to continue.

6. Verify that the information on the Summary screen is correct and click Finish. Your backup job starts either immediately or at the scheduled time.

The Backup Progress dialog box will inform you when the backup is complete. It also displays additional information, such as the media name, status of the backup job, time elapsed during the backup, and the number of files and bytes processed. Click Close to close the dialog box, or click Report to see more detailed information about this backup job.

Restoring Files

To restore files that have previously been backed up with the Backup Or Restore Wizard, follow these steps:

1. On the Welcome screen, click Next.

2. On the Backup Or Restore screen, choose Restore Files And Settings. Click Next.

3. The What To Restore screen displays backups that you previously created with the wizard. Navigate the available backup sets by using the plus and minus signs or double-click the available media and folder names. The left pane shows you the entire folder structure; the right pane shows only the contents of the currently selected drive or folder. Select files or folders from either pane. Click Next.

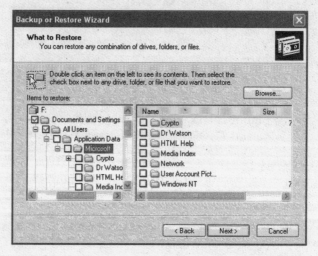

4. By default, files are restored to their original locations, but the utility does not replace files that already exist. If you want to change these and other settings, click Advanced. When you're finished, click Next to continue.

5. Read the Summary screen and click Finish to start the restore operation.

Follow any additional prompts, which may vary depending on your backup media. When the restore begins, you'll see the Restore Progress dialog box with the same information as the Backup Progress dialog box. When the restore is complete, click Report if you wish to see more detailed information about the process, or click Close to dismiss the dialog box.

BROWSE

Browse... Used to find files and directories on the computer or in the network. This button appears in many dialog boxes where you need to provide the name and path of a file or folder or specify an Internet or intranet address.

Click Browse to open the Browse dialog box. The left side of the dialog box displays shortcuts to various locations on the computer or network where you can look for the files you want. Click one of these shortcuts or enter a folder name in the Look In text box. The contents of the selected folder appear in the window below. Double-click folders in the window to move further down the directory structure.

Use the Files Of Type drop-down list to specify the type of files you want to display in the Browse window, or choose to see all files of all types.

Select a file to display it in the File Name field, then click Open. You return to the dialog box from where you were browsing, and the name and path to the file appear in the appropriate field.

CAPTURING IMAGES

Windows XP allows you to capture screen images to the Clipboard, which you can then paste into a document. To capture and paste an image, follow these steps:

1. To capture the entire screen, press Shift+Print Screen (often abbreviated as *PrtSc*). To capture an active window, press Alt+Print Screen.

NOTE
You won't see anything happen on the screen when you capture a screen or window with Print Screen.

2. Place the cursor where you want to insert the image in your document.

3. Press Ctrl+V or choose Edit ➤ Paste. Windows pastes the image into your document.

CD WRITING WIZARD

Windows XP allows you to write files and folders to your CD-R recorder or CD-RW rewriteable drive. After you copy files, you can *burn* them to a CD.

1. In Windows Explorer, copy the desired files and folders to your CD drive.

2. Insert a blank, writeable CD (or even a partly written CD-RW disk) into your CD-R or CD-RW drive.

3. After you copy files, the notification area displays a message that there are files waiting to be written to the CD. Click the message to display the files and folders, or select the drive in Explorer. They appear in a temporary staging area named Files Ready To Be Written To The CD. Verify the list of items to copy.

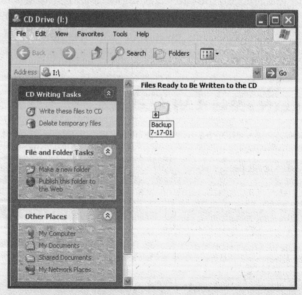

NOTE

When you insert a CD into a CD-R or CD-RW drive, Windows XP prompts you to open the writeable CD folder or take no action. You can make either of these choices the default option.

4. From the CD Writing Tasks area, select Write These Files To CD. The CD Writing Wizard appears. If the CD does not have enough space to hold all the files, the wizard prompts you to reduce the amount of files before you continue.

5. Assign a name to the CD, or accept the default (the date). Check or uncheck the option to close the wizard after you write the CD. Then click Next to continue. The wizard copies the files to your CD writer. A progress bar displays the amount of time remaining while the files are written to the CD.

6. After Windows XP writes the files to the CD, it ejects the CD from your CD recorder. If you elected to keep the wizard open, the wizard displays a message that the CD is complete. The option Write These Files To Another CD lets you burn another copy; if you're done, click Finish. Review the contents of the CD that you burned to confirm that all of the files were copied.

NOTE

If you chose to close the wizard after burning the CD, Windows XP automatically deletes the files that were copied from the staging area and closes the CD Writing Wizard.

CLIPBOARD

Temporary holding place for data. When you use the Cut or Copy command in programs running on a Windows XP computer, the selected data is placed into the Clipboard. Use the Paste command to retrieve the contents of the Clipboard. To view the contents of the Clipboard, use the ClipBook Viewer.

WARNING

The Clipboard stores only one item at any time. When you cut or copy a new item, it replaces the contents currently in the Clipboard. You can use ClipBook Viewer to save Clipboard contents into your local ClipBook.

ClipBook Viewer

ClipBook Viewer allows you to view and save the contents of the Windows XP Clipboard. To open ClipBook Viewer, choose Start ➤ Run, then type **clipbrd** and click OK. ClipBook Viewer has two windows: the Local ClipBook and the Clipboard. Maximize or resize the Clipboard to view its contents.

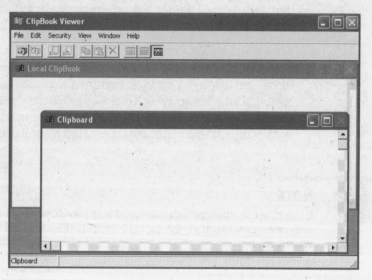

You can save the contents of the Clipboard either to a file or to the local ClipBook.

Saving the Clipboard Contents to a File

To save the contents of the Clipboard to a file (with a `.clp` extension), open ClipBook Viewer and click somewhere in the Clipboard window to activate it. Choose File ➤ Save As, browse to the folder where you want to save the file, enter a name for the file, and click Save.

Saving the Clipboard Contents in the Local ClipBook

When you save the Clipboard contents to your local ClipBook, you can share ClipBook pages with other users. You can also set up permissions and auditing for each ClipBook page (for remote user access after you share a page) and take ownership of a page, via the options on the Security menu.

After you place pages in your local ClipBook, you can display them using the Table Of Contents view (the default), Thumbnail view, or Full Page view (which displays the contents of the selected page). Access the views either from the View menu or by clicking a toolbar button.

To save the contents of the Clipboard to a page in the local ClipBook, perform the following steps:

1. Click inside the ClipBook window to activate it.

2. Choose Edit ➢ Paste. The Paste dialog box appears.

3. Enter a name for the ClipBook page you're creating. Select Share Item Now if you want to share the page.

4. Click OK. The page is added to the ClipBook. If you selected the Share Item Now option, provide the necessary information in the Share ClipBook Page dialog box (see following section).

Sharing a ClipBook Page

To share ClipBook pages with other users, follow these steps:

1. In the local ClipBook, select the page you want to share.

2. Choose File ➢ Share or click the Share button on the toolbar. The Share ClipBook Page dialog box appears.

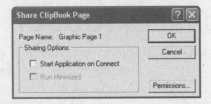

3. Select Start Application On Connect to automatically open the application that was used to create the contents of the page when another user accesses the page. Choose Run Minimized to run the application in a minimized window.

4. Click Permissions to configure the users and groups that are allowed to access the page, and the type of access they should have. Click OK to return to the Share ClipBook Page dialog box.

5. Click OK to share the page. A hand appears at the bottom of the page's icon to indicate that the page is shared.

To stop sharing a page, select the page in the local ClipBook and choose File ➢ Stop Sharing, or click the Stop Sharing button on the toolbar.

Accessing Pages in Another User's ClipBook

To access pages in another user's shared ClipBook, choose File ➢ Connect or click the Connect button on the toolbar. In the Select Computer dialog box, browse to and select the computer to which you want to connect, then click OK. A list of all shared ClipBook pages appears; double-click the ClipBook page you want to open.

To disconnect from the remote computer, choose File ➢ Disconnect or click the Disconnect button on the toolbar.

COMMUNICATIONS

Communications Predefined program group from which you access the following communication-related program groups: Network Setup Wizard, HyperTerminal, New Connection Wizard, NetMeeting, Network Connections, Phone Dialer, Remote Desktop Connection, and Fax. Choose Start ➢ All Programs (or Start ➢ Programs in the Classic Start menu) ➢ Accessories ➢ Communications to access the Communications program group.

DATA SOURCES (ODBC)

 Data Sources (ODBC) Shortcut 2 KB Allows you to configure and store information that determines how users connect to data sources such as dBase, Excel, and Access files. Use the ODBC Data Source Administrator dialog box to configure your ODBC connections. To open this dialog box, choose Start ➢ Control Panel (or Start ➢ Settings ➢ Control Panel in the Classic Start menu) ➢ Performance And Maintenance ➢ Administrative Tools, then double-click Data Sources (ODBC).

The ODBC Data Source Administrator dialog box consists of seven tabs: User DSN, System DSN, File DSN, Drivers, Tracing, Connection Pooling, and About. Each of these tabs includes several buttons in common:

▶ Click the OK button to accept changes on the current tab and to close the ODBC Data Source Administrator dialog box.

▶ Click the Cancel button to close the ODBC Data Source Administrator dialog box without applying the changes you made on the current tab (changes you made on other tabs will apply).

▶ Click the Apply button to accept changes on the current tab and to keep the dialog box open.

▶ Click the Help button to obtain help on the features included on the current tab.

User DSN Tab

The User DSN tab allows you to add, delete, or configure data sources with user data source names (DSNs). The data sources that you configure in this dialog box are accessible only by the current user of the local computer.

The User Data Sources list contains user DSNs that the current user can access on the local computer. Double-click an item in the list, or highlight an entry and click Configure, to configure the data source name, description, database version, and directory and index information.

Click Add to add a new data source; select a driver in the following dialog box and click Finish to configure the data source information. To remove a DSN from the list, highlight an entry and click Remove.

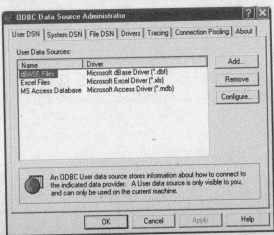

System DSN Tab

The System DSN tab allows you to add, delete, or configure data sources with system data source names (DSNs). The data sources that you configure in this dialog box are accessible by any user who has user privileges on the local computer.

The System Data Sources list displays a list of system DSNs that users can access on the local computer. Double-click an item in the list, or highlight an entry and click Configure, to configure the data source name, description, database version, and directory and index information.

Click Add to add a new data source; select a driver in the following dialog box and click Finish to configure the data source information. To remove a DSN from the list, highlight its entry and click Remove.

File DSN Tab

The File DSN tab allows you to add, delete, or configure data sources that are accessible by any user who has the same drivers installed. The data sources do not have to be user-dedicated or local to the computer.

The Look In box initially displays the default directory that stores database drivers. Click the down arrow to select any directory from the entire directory structure. Click the Up One Level button to replace the directory shown in the Look In box with the directory that is one level above. Click the Set Directory button to use the directory that appears in the Look In box as the new default directory.

When you select a folder in the Look In box, the tab displays a list of DSNs and subdirectories in that folder. Double-click an item in the list, or highlight an entry and click Configure, to configure the data source name, description, database version, and directory and index information.

Click Add to add a new data source. The following dialog box prompts you to select a driver for the current data source. After you select the driver, click Finish to configure the data source information. To remove a DSN from the list, highlight its entry and click Remove.

Drivers Tab

The Drivers tab displays information about ODBC drivers that appear on the local computer. To install ODBC drivers, use the driver setup program that is specific to the data source to which you want to connect. After you install your drivers, the tab displays the driver name, version, company, filename, and creation date of each ODBC driver on the computer.

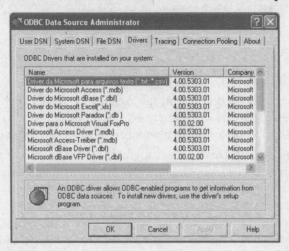

Tracing Tab

The Tracing tab specifies how the ODBC driver manager traces any calls to ODBC functions. The driver manager can trace calls continuously, or for one connection only. It can also perform dynamic tracing, or you can assign a custom DLL file.

By default, Windows XP stores the trace log in a file named sql.log. Enter a new filename and path in the Log File Path field, or use the Browse button to select another location or file.

Windows XP uses the odbctrac.dll file (shipped with the MDAC SDK) by default to perform tracing. To specify a different trace DLL file, enter the path and filename in the Custom Trace DLL field, or click the Select DLL button to select a folder and file.

To start continuous dynamic tracing, click the Start Tracing Now button. Windows XP establishes a connection to the data source and traces the connections until you click Stop Tracing Now.

You can also enable or disable the Visual Studio Analyzer to debug and analyze your distributed application. Click Start Visual Studio Analyzer to use this feature, or click Stop Visual Studio Analyzer to turn the feature off.

NOTE

Additional information about the Visual Studio Analyzer appears in the MSDN Library, which is available on CD-ROM or at `http://msdn.microsoft.com/library`.

Connection Pooling Tab

Use the Connection Pooling tab to configure connection retry wait times and time-out periods when you use connection pooling. You can also enable and disable performance monitoring to record a number of statistics.

The ODBC Drivers list displays the name of each driver and the associated connection-pooling time-out option. To configure a time-out option, double-click a driver in the list, or highlight a driver in the list and click Connection Pooling Timeout, to open the Set Connection Pooling Attributes dialog box. This dialog box allows you to enable or disable pooling and to specify the number of seconds that unused connections remain in the pool. After you configure the pooling options, click OK to return to the Connection Pooling tab.

Click the Enable radio button to enable performance-monitoring counters for connection pooling, or the Disable radio button to disable them. Use the Retry Wait Time field to enter the number of seconds (six or fewer numerals) that the OBDC driver will wait before it tries again to make a connection to the database server.

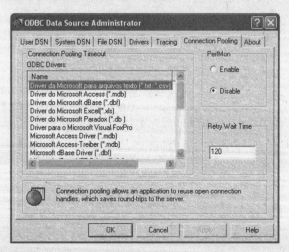

About Tab

The About tab displays information about the ODBC core components. These components include the Driver Manager, cursor library, installer DLL, and other core component files. The files appear in the About The ODBC Core Components list and include information such as the file description, version, filename, and location.

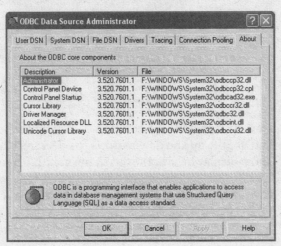

DATE/TIME

 Settings used by Windows XP to assign dates to files when you create or modify them. It is important to set the correct date, time, and time zone on your system clock. To do so, choose Start ➤ Control Panel (or Start ➤ Settings ➤ Control Panel in the Classic Start menu). Click Date, Time, Language, And Regional Options, and then click the Date And Time icon to open the Date And Time Properties dialog box. This dialog box includes three tabs: Date & Time, Time Zone, and Internet Time.

TIP

Double-click the system clock in the notification area of your Taskbar to quickly open the Date And Time Properties dialog box.

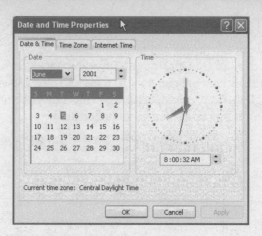

Date & Time tab   Select the month from the drop-down list, and use the up and down arrows to select the year. Use the calendar display to click the day of the month. To set the time, click to select the hour, minutes, seconds, or AM/PM. Enter the correct value, or use the up and down arrows to change the value. Your current time zone appears at the bottom of the dialog box.

Time Zone tab   Select the correct time zone from the drop-down list. If daylight saving changes apply to your time zone, check the Automatically Adjust Clock For Daylight Saving Changes option; Windows XP will automatically reset your clock for daylight saving time when appropriate.

Internet Time tab   Use this tab to synchronize the clock on your computer with a time server on the Internet. Synchronization occurs only when your computer is connected to the Internet. You may not be able to use this feature if you connect to the Internet through a proxy server or firewall.

To enable this feature, check the Automatically Synchronize With An Internet Time Server option. Use the drop-down list to select an Internet time server.

Click Apply to apply any changes you make without closing the dialog box, or click OK to save changes and close the dialog box.

Use Regional And Language Options in Control Panel to change the format in which short and long dates and times display in the Taskbar, as well as in the Date And Time Properties dialog box.

DEVICE MANAGER

Device Manager   MMC snap-in that displays a list of all hardware installed in the computer and provides information about this hardware. Use Device Manager to verify that your hardware is working properly after you install new hardware. You can also use Device Manager to enable, disable, configure, and check the status of devices and to view and update device drivers.

TIP

You must log on as a computer administrator to make certain changes to devices in Device Manager.

To access Device Manager, choose Start ➤ Control Panel (or Start ➤ Settings ➤ Control Panel in the Classic Start menu) ➤ Performance And Maintenance. Next, click the System icon to open the System Properties dialog box. Select the Hardware tab, and click the Device Manager button.

Device Manager lists the hardware on your computer in several different classes (for example, Display Adapters or System Devices). To view the devices in each class, click the plus sign at the left of the class name. Each device appears in the list with an icon, followed by the name of the class or device.

NOTE

If the device icon contains a yellow question mark, the device is unknown. Unknown devices are typically non–Plug and Play devices for which you must install drivers that came with your hardware. If the device icon contains a yellow exclamation point, a hardware or software problem exists for the device. Double-click the problem device to open the Properties dialog box. Click the Troubleshoot button on the General tab to open the Hardware Troubleshooter.

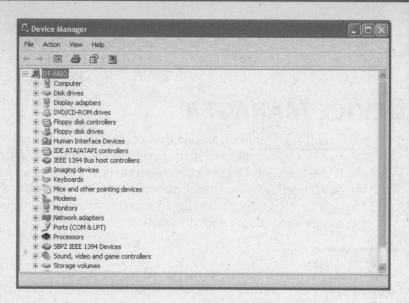

As with all MMC consoles and snap-ins, Device Manager has Action and View menus that contain options specific to the currently active MMC snap-in.

Action Menu

Action   Select a device in Device Manager, and then use commands in the Action menu to perform device-related actions. Commands unique to this menu include Update Driver, Disable (which toggles to Enable), Uninstall, and Scan For Hardware Changes.

TIP

An alternative method for accessing the options available under Action is to select a device and right-click. If you select a device class, only the Scan For Hardware Changes and Properties options are available. If you select the workstation itself, the Disable option won't be available.

Disable and Enable

Disable   The Disable option temporarily disables a Plug and Play device. When you disable a device, you do not have to physically remove it from the computer to avoid having Windows XP load drivers for the device.

Use this feature to set up different hardware profiles—for example, one profile to attach your laptop to a docking station and another to use when your laptop is not docked. When your laptop is docked, you might use a network adapter to connect to the Internet and to your company network. When the laptop is not docked, you might use a modem instead.

NOTE

The Disable and Enable options appear only if you have administrative privileges.

After you choose Disable, Windows XP informs you that your device will not function after you disable it, and prompts you to confirm your selection. A red *X* appears over the device icon when it is disabled.

To enable the device later, right-click the device and choose Enable, or use the Action ➢ Enable command. The red *X* disappears, indicating that the device is enabled again.

Uninstall

Uninstall Allows you to remove a device driver from your Windows XP computer. After you uninstall a device driver, you need to physically remove the hardware device from your computer; otherwise, Windows XP will reinstall the drivers the next time you start up.

When you uninstall a device driver, Windows XP asks you to confirm your action. Click OK to uninstall the device from Device Manager. Then, turn your computer off and physically remove the device.

If you later need to reinstall the device and the device driver, install the hardware in your computer according to the manufacturer's recommendations. Windows XP automatically installs device drivers for Plug and Play devices when you restart your computer. Use the Add New Hardware Wizard to install non–Plug and Play devices.

NOTE

The Uninstall option is available only when you log on as a computer administrator.

TIP

Another way to uninstall a Plug and Play device is to shut down the computer (necessary for most devices), physically remove the device, and then start Windows again. Windows XP automatically removes the device.

Scan For Hardware Changes

Scan for hardware changes Allows you to manually scan your computer to see whether hardware changes have occurred, such as a device being removed from or added to the computer.

If Windows XP detects changes in your hardware, it takes appropriate action. Windows XP may remove or add devices to the list, and may display messages about the changes it makes. For example, when you remove or unplug a device before you disable the service, Windows XP displays the Unsafe Removal Of Device dialog box.

WARNING

You should always disable a device before you remove it from the computer; otherwise, serious problems may result. Many devices also require that you power off the computer before you remove the device. Consult your hardware documentation for more information.

Print

Print Allows you to print a hard copy of your system summary, information on a selected class or device, or all devices and a system summary. Select the items you want to print (choose Computer from the Device Driver list to print all items), and select report options from the Report Type section of the Print dialog box. Then click Print to send the report to your printer.

Properties

Properties Allows you to view and change properties of the selected device. To display the Properties dialog box, highlight a device in Device Manager and choose Action ➤ Properties, or right-click the device and choose Properties from the menu that appears. The tabs and settings that appear in the Properties dialog box vary depending on the device you select. The most common tabs are General, Driver, and Resources.

TIP
You can also click the Properties button on the Device Manager toolbar to display properties for a device.

General tab   Displays general information about the device, such as device type, manufacturer, location of the device, and the device status. If the device status indicates that the device is not working properly, click the Troubleshoot button to open the appropriate Windows XP Troubleshooter. Use options in the Device Usage drop-down list to enable or disable the device.

Driver tab   Displays information about the device driver used for the selected device. Information may include driver provider, date, and version, and digital signer. Four buttons appear on the Driver tab:

Driver Details   Opens a dialog box that displays the paths to the driver files that are installed for the device.

The information that you see on the Driver tab is repeated in the lower portion of the Driver File Details dialog box.

Update Driver   Opens the Hardware Update Wizard, which allows you to install software for your device. You can install software automatically or select devices from a list or specific location.

Roll Back Driver   Allows you to revert to a previous version of a device driver when you experience trouble with your computer after you change a device driver. If no previous driver files are backed up for the device, Windows XP asks whether you want to launch the Troubleshooter. If one or more previous versions of the driver exist on your system, follow the prompts to select the version of the driver that you want to revert to.

Uninstall   Allows you to uninstall the device driver. Windows XP asks you to confirm the removal.

Resources tab   Displays information about the system resources the device is using. Device information includes the I/O (input/output) port address range, IRQ (interrupt request), DMA (Direct Memory Access) channel, and memory address range. Windows XP automatically assigns resources for Plug and Play devices. For non–Plug and Play devices, you may have to manually configure resource settings.

If a conflict exists, the Conflicting Device List displays the device with which your current device conflicts. You will need to select different settings to resolve the conflict. To select different settings, deselect the Use Automatic Settings check box. Then, select a different hardware configuration from the Setting Based On drop-down list, until you locate a setting that does not conflict with other devices or drivers. Alternatively, deselect the Use Automatic Settings check box and select a resource from the Resource Settings list. Then, click the Change Setting button to manually change a resource setting. You cannot change some resource settings.

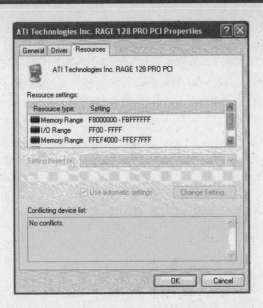

WARNING

Change resource settings only if you are very comfortable with device hardware settings. Otherwise, the device or other devices may no longer function properly after you make a change.

View Menu

View The View menu in Device Manager allows you to display devices and resources by using various sorting methods. It also allows you to display hidden devices and customize the view.

Devices By Type Displays hardware devices in alphabetical order by device type (the default setting).

Devices By Connection Displays hardware devices in alphabetical order by device connection. The devices are listed in relation to the interface or bus to which they connect.

Resources By Type Displays the devices by the type of resources they use. Devices are arranged by the DMA, I/O, IRQ, and memory resources that they use.

Resources By Connection   Displays the devices in a combination of the types of resources they use (DMA, I/O, IRQ, or memory) and the interface or bus to which they connect.

Show Hidden Devices   Displays devices that are not visible by default. They can include items such as non–Plug and Play drivers, printers, and other (unknown) devices.

Customize   Opens the Customize View dialog box, which allows you to show or hide items in Device Manager. Check or uncheck options to show or hide the console tree, standard menus (Action and View), standard toolbar, status bar, description bar, and taskpad navigation tabs. You can also show or hide other Device Manager menus and toolbars.

Additional Toolbar Buttons

The Device Manager MMC snap-in toolbar contains some of the buttons commonly found on MMC consoles, such as Back, Forward, Up One Level, Show/Hide Console Tree/Favorites, and Help. It can also contain various buttons depending on whether you selected the workstation, a device class, or a device, and whether a device is disabled or enabled; these are self-explanatory, except that the Update Driver button opens the Hardware Update Wizard, which allows you to update the driver for the selected device.

DRAG-AND-DROP

Functionality you can use to copy, move, and delete files and folders in many application programs and on the Desktop. To drag and drop a selection, place the mouse pointer over any item (or items). Press and hold the left mouse button while you move the mouse to drag the selection to another folder or drive, your Desktop, or another destination. Place the pointer over the destination to highlight it, and then release the left mouse button.

The result of the drag-and-drop operation can differ, as outlined below:

▶ If you drag a file or folder to a folder on the same disk, Windows moves the item. To copy the item instead, press the Ctrl key while you drag and drop the selection.

- ► If you drag a file or folder to a folder on a different disk, Windows copies the item. To move the item instead, press the Shift key while you drag and drop the selection.

- ► If you drag a file or folder to the Recycle Bin, Windows deletes the item (this is not permanent until you empty the Recycle Bin).

- ► If you drag a file to a printer shortcut on the Desktop, Windows prints the file.

FOLDER OPTIONS

Folder Options: Controls the appearance and use of files and folders, and configures file associations. Any settings you make determine how folders are displayed and used in Windows Explorer, My Documents, My Network Places, My Computer, and Control Panel.

To open the Folder Options dialog box, choose Start ➢ Control Panel (or Start ➢ Settings ➢ Control Panel in the Classic Start menu) ➢ Appearance And Themes ➢ Folder Options. The Folder Options dialog box contains four tabs—General, View, File Types, and Offline Files.

TIP

You can also access Folder Options from the Tools menu of any Windows Explorer window.

General Tab

Controls how folders appear and work. The tab is divided into three sections:

Tasks   Allows you to display common tasks in folders (default), or to use Windows classic folders.

Browse Folders   Allows you to open a new folder in the same window (default) or in its own window.

Click Items As Follows   Allows you to open items with a single click or a double-click (default). You can also choose to underline icon titles as configured in your web browser, or only when you point at them.

TIP

If single-clicking is specified, move the mouse pointer over an item to select it.

You can return to default values by clicking Restore Defaults.

View Tab

Controls the appearance and advanced settings for folders. Click the Apply To All Folders button to apply the View tab settings from the current folder to all other folders. This button is available only when you access the Folder Options dialog box from the Tools menu of Windows Explorer. You can reset the view of all folders to the default setting (Large Icons) by clicking Reset All Folders.

In the Advanced Settings list box, select check boxes for the settings you want to apply, such as displaying the full path in the title bar, hiding file extensions for known file types, and showing hidden files and folders.

File Types Tab

Controls which file types are associated with which file extension, and
the default application used to open a file type. The Registered File Types
list displays all registered file types and their extensions. The following
buttons are available on the File Types tab:

New   Allows you to create a new file extension. Click the
Advanced button to associate a new or existing file type with
the new extension. You can also enter an existing file extension
and then change the file type associated with the extension.

Delete   Allows you to delete an existing file extension and
associated file type.

Change   Allows you to change the default application that Windows uses to open files of the selected extension and file type.

Advanced   Allows you to change the selected file type's associated icon and actions. Any configured actions appear in the
File menu and shortcut menu for the item. You can configure a
new action by clicking New and then specifying the action as
well as the application that is supposed to perform that action.
You can also edit or remove existing actions, and you can specify whether you want files to open immediately after they have
finished downloading. Finally, you can choose to always show
file extensions and to enable browsing in the same window.

Offline Files Tab

Used to configure whether files on the network are available when you
are not connected to the network. On this tab, you can choose to enable
or disable offline files, synchronize files when you log on or before you log
off, display reminders at regular intervals when you are working offline,
encrypt these files to secure data, and adjust the amount of space to store
offline files.

The following three buttons appear on the Offline Files tab:

Delete Files   Allows you to delete temporary offline files or all
offline files.

View Files   Displays files that are in the Offline Files folder.

Advanced Allows you to choose events that occur when you lose connection to the network. You can request notification and continue to work offline, or you can choose to never allow the computer to go offline. You can also configure exceptions for specific computers.

FONTS

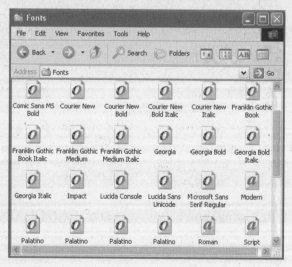

Folder used to view and manage the fonts (type styles) that are used by Windows XP and Windows applications. To open the Fonts folder in an Explorer window, choose Start ➤ Control Panel (or Start ➤ Settings ➤ Control Panel in the Classic Start menu) ➤ Appearance And Themes.

From the See Also list in the left pane, click Fonts to open the Fonts window. All fonts that are currently installed appear in this window.

Windows XP supports TrueType fonts, Open Type fonts (an extension of TrueType), Type 1 fonts (by Adobe Systems), vector fonts, and raster fonts. The icon in the Fonts folder displays an indicator for each font type. For example, Open Type fonts show an *O* in the font icon; TrueType fonts show two *T*s; and Type 1 fonts display an *A* (for Adobe).

Viewing Font Examples

Double-click a font icon to open a window that contains examples of the font in different sizes. You'll also see information such as font type, typeface name, file size, version, and copyright information. Click Print to print the font example.

If you have many fonts installed on your system, it can get difficult to keep track of what fonts you have available and what they look like. The View menu of the Fonts folder includes two options that make it easier to keep track of your fonts:

List Fonts By Similarity   Produces a drop-down list from which you choose a font that you are familiar with. Fonts are then listed by name, arranged by similarity to the font you selected. You can also click the Similarity button on the toolbar to display this view.

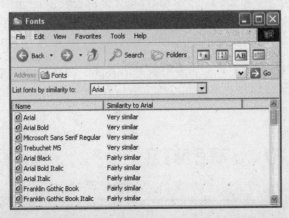

Hide Variations (Bold, Italic, etc.)   Lists only main fonts and does not show the variations of the font (such as bold or italic). This reduces the number of items in the list and makes it easier to find or choose a font you're looking for.

Adding New Fonts

You can add new fonts to your computer at any time by following these steps:

1. Choose File ➤ Install New Font.

2. Browse for the location of the new fonts.

3. Select one or more fonts from the List Of Fonts list box, and check or uncheck the option to copy the fonts to your Fonts folder.

4. Click OK. Windows installs the fonts and returns you to the Fonts folder.

HELP AND SUPPORT CENTER

Help and Support   The Windows XP help system includes extensive explanations and step-by-step instructions for Windows XP. You can access the information contained in the system by browsing its contents, querying the index, searching by keyword, or bookmarking and checking favorite areas of help. The help system pages are written in HTML, and as a result, if you're connected to the Internet, you can also follow links that point to pages on the Internet.

For a broad introduction to Windows XP, select the "What's New In Windows XP" help topic that appears in the left portion of the Help And Support Center home page. This link allows you to read *What's New* topics; take tours, tutorials, or walk-throughs of Windows XP; obtain help on activation, licensing, and registration; and learn more about Windows components.

MY DOCUMENTS

 My Documents   Default folder where Windows XP stores documents created in such applications as WordPad and Paint. My

Documents allows any user who is logged on to the computer to organize and quickly access his or her own personal documents.

To open the My Documents folder, choose Start ➤ My Documents, or navigate to it using the Folders pane or Address bar in any Explorer window.

TIP

To change the location of the My Documents folder, right-click the My Documents shortcut on the Start menu and choose Properties. On the Target tab, enter a new path in the Target text box and click OK, or click Move and then browse to the new target folder.

By default, the My Documents folder contains folders such as My Music, My Pictures, My eBooks, My Received Files, and My Videos. Single-click any folder to display details in the left pane. Windows XP may create additional My Documents subfolders automatically as you work with applications; for example, the Fax Cover Page Editor creates a Fax subfolder. The left pane also allows you to create new folders, publish selected folders to the Web, and share folders over the network.

MY MUSIC

 My Music Default folder (within the My Documents folder) that stores music files that you copy from a CD or download from the Internet.

The right pane in the My Music folder displays large icons for each music folder in your music library. If you have ripped songs from a CD, a small picture of the CD cover appears on the folder. The left pane displays a list of music tasks that changes, depending on the selections you make in the main pane. When no folder is selected, click Play All to play all songs from the My Music folder in Windows Media Player.

When you select a folder from the main pane, details about it appear in the left pane. Additional options appear in the Music Tasks list, depending on the type of folder you select. Choose Play Selection to play all music in a selected folder. Choose Copy To Audio CD to burn the contents of a selected folder to CD.

MY RECENT DOCUMENTS

My Recent Documents Start menu option that provides a list of shortcuts to the 15 most recently accessed documents so that you can quickly access them again when necessary. The list remains after you shut down and restart Windows XP. To use the My Recent Documents list, choose Start ➤ My Recent Documents, and click any item in the list to open the document in the appropriate application.

NOTE
The submenu also contains a shortcut to My Documents and My Pictures, which are default folders that Windows XP uses to save documents or images from many Windows XP applications.

NETMEETING

NetMeeting Allows you to use voice and video to communicate with other people over the Internet. To run NetMeeting, your computer must have speakers or headphones, a microphone, and a video camera installed.

NetMeeting enables you to engage in real-time chats, work together in shared applications, send files, and create drawings together on a shared whiteboard. Voice, video, and images display on the screen while you participate in online conferences.

The first time you run NetMeeting, a wizard helps you configure NetMeeting and tune your audio settings. Subsequently, you will be brought directly to Microsoft NetMeeting.

OFFLINE FILES

✓ Make available offline   Allow you to use network or shared files or folders when you're not connected to the network. From Windows Explorer, right-click a file or folder and choose Make Available Offline.

TIP

To display this menu option in Windows Explorer, choose Tools ➤ Folder Options, and check Enable Offline Files on the Offline Files tab.

WARNING

You cannot make files available offline when Fast User Switching is enabled.

The *first* time you choose the Make Available Offline command, the Offline Files Wizard appears. Complete it as follows:

1. On the Welcome screen, click Next.

2. If you don't want files to synchronize automatically when you log on and off the computer, uncheck the Automatically Synchronize option. Click Next.

3. Check Enable Reminders to receive a periodic message that reminds you that you're working offline. It is also strongly recommended that you check the option Create A Shortcut To The Offline Files Folder On My Desktop.

4. Click Finish. The wizard synchronizes the file or folder to the Offline Files folder, and you return to Windows Explorer.

Thereafter, whenever you choose the Make Available Offline command, Windows Explorer automatically synchronizes the selected file or folder to the Offline Files folder. Two opposite-facing arrows appear in the bottom-left portion of the icon for an offline file or folder.

TIP

To remove a file from the Offline Files folder, right-click the file and select Make Available Offline. This removes the check mark on the menu item.

When you are offline, you can access your offline files or folders as though you were connected to the network. Click the computer icon in the notification area of the Taskbar to see your current offline file status. If you have reminders set up, a pop-up message periodically tells you that you're working offline. Choose Folder Options from Control Panel to further configure reminders.

Offline Files Folder

Offline files are also accessible through the Offline Files folder. Double-click the shortcut on your Desktop (if you created one) to open the Offline Files folder. This folder displays the names of all offline files, the synchronization status, the availability, and the access rights you have to each file. If you delete a file from the Offline Files folder, the network version of the file remains.

TIP

You can also browse to offline files or folders with Windows Explorer or My Network Places. The left side of Explorer displays a message that tells you when a folder is offline.

To work on a file offline, select it from the Offline Files folder. Open it and make any changes you need. Synchronization occurs automatically when you connect to the network (unless you change default settings in Synchronization or in the Offline Files Wizard).

To synchronize manually, open the Offline Files folder. Choose View ➢ Details if necessary. The Synchronization column indicates local files that have been modified. To synchronize files, close any offline files that are opened. To synchronize all files, choose Tools ➢ Synchronize, then click Synchronize. To synchronize an individual file, select the file and choose File ➢ Synchronize, or right-click the file and choose Synchronize.

PICTURE AND FAX VIEWER

Allows you to view, rotate, and add category information to images on your computer. To open the Picture And Fax Viewer application, double-click any image in any folder.

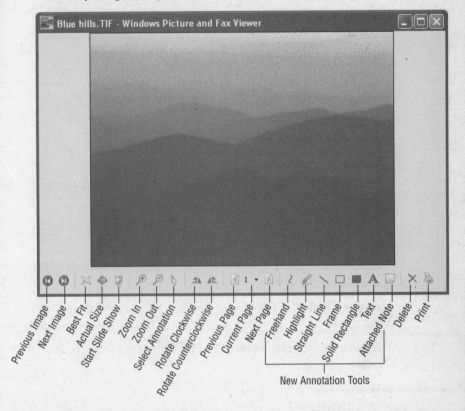

New Annotation Tools

Right-click the Picture And Fax Viewer icon that appears in the upper-left corner of the title bar; a menu appears. In addition to using the commands that are available with the toolbar buttons described next, you can set the image as wallpaper or open the image in another application. Use the Send To command to send your image to a compressed folder; create a shortcut on your Desktop; send your image by e-mail; copy the image to your floppy drive or to your My Documents folder; or publish your image on the Internet.

The Picture And Fax Viewer window displays a toolbar at the bottom of the page. The available toolbar buttons vary, depending on the type of image you select. When you select a TIFF image, you see a toolbar with the following buttons (some listed with the corresponding keyboard shortcuts in parentheses):

Previous Image (Left arrow)   Displays the previous image in the folder, based on the sort order

Next Image (Right arrow)   Displays the next image in the folder, based on the sort order

Best Fit (Ctrl+B)   Sizes the image so that you view the entire image in the preview window

Actual Size (Ctrl+A)   Displays the image in its actual size, which may be larger or smaller than the preview window

Start Slide Show (F11)   Displays a full-screen slide show of each image in the folder, based on the sort order

Zoom In (+)   Zooms in closer to the image to display more detail

Zoom Out (–)   Zooms out to display more of the image in the preview window

Select Annotation   Selects an annotation that you previously added to the image

Rotate Clockwise (Ctrl+K)   Rotates the image 90 degrees to the right

Rotate Counterclockwise (Ctrl+L)   Rotates the image 90 degrees to the left

WARNING

Rotating an image might reduce its quality.

Previous Page (Page Up)   Displays the previous page in a multipage TIFF document or fax

Current Page   Displays the current page number, and allows you to choose a specific page in a multipage TIFF document or fax

Next Page (Page Down)   Displays the next page in a multi-page TIFF document or fax

New Annotation Tools Allow you to draw or type on your image

> **Freehand** Draws a red freehand shape

> **Highlight** Highlights a yellow rectangular area

> **Straight Line** Draws a straight red line

> **Frame** Draws a red rectangular outline around an area

> **Solid Rectangle** Draws a solid (opaque) yellow box

> **Text** Adds text with a transparent background—first, draw a rectangle, then click the rectangle to add text

> **Attached Note** Adds text with a yellow background—first, draw a rectangle, then click the rectangle to add text

NOTE

The annotation buttons appear when you open a TIFF image. After you add annotations to your image, you can move, resize, or delete them at any time.

Delete (Delete) Deletes the image from the current folder

Print (Ctrl+P) Allows you to print your image

NOTE

When you install third-party Windows image-editing software on your computer, images might open in your third-party application instead of the Picture And Fax Viewer window, due to file associations installed during your program setup.

PRINTERS AND FAXES

 Used to manage all aspects of printing. Allows you to add, remove, and share printers; assign permissions; set the default printer; change printer properties; set, view, and manage job queues; and pause or cancel printing. You can also set print server properties.

To open the Printers And Faxes folder, choose Start ➢ Control Panel ➢ Printers And Other Hardware ➢ Printers And Faxes. (From the Classic

Start menu, choose Start ➢ Settings ➢ Printers And Faxes.) Alternatively, you can access the Printers And Faxes folder through My Computer, Windows Explorer, or Control Panel.

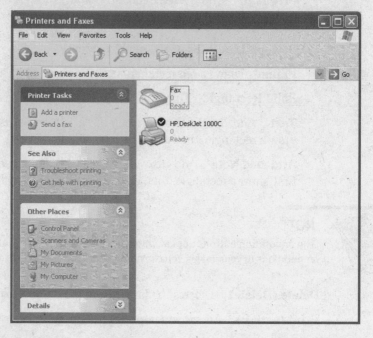

You configure the majority of your printer options through printer properties. You can also use File menu commands or right-click any printer icon to perform some printing-related actions or access configuration pages. For example, you can:

- ▶ Set a printer to be the default printer
- ▶ Access the printing preferences pages
- ▶ Pause printing
- ▶ Cancel printing of all documents
- ▶ Share a printer
- ▶ Use a printer offline
- ▶ Create a shortcut to the printer
- ▶ Delete or rename the printer
- ▶ Access the printer Properties sheet

▶ Access the print server Properties sheet (available only on the File menu)

Open

Printing Preferences...

Pause Printing

Sharing...
Use Printer Offline

Add Printer
Server Properties
Send Fax

Create Shortcut
Delete
Rename
Properties

Close

Adding a New Local Printer

To add a new local printer, follow these steps:

1. From the Printer Tasks list in the left pane, click Add A Printer. The Add Printer Wizard appears. Click Next to continue.

2. Choose the Local Printer radio button, and check or uncheck the option to specify whether you want Windows to automatically detect a Plug and Play printer. If you check the option, click Next and proceed with step 3. If you do not check the option, click Next and proceed to step 4.

3. If you selected Automatically Detect And Install My Plug And Play Printer, Windows XP tries to find the printer.

   ▶ If Windows finds the printer, it adds the printer automatically and returns you to the Printers And Faxes folder. You can now customize printer settings.

   ▶ If Windows cannot find your printer, it prompts you to click Next to install the printer manually. Click Next to continue.

4. Select the printer port to which your printer connects, or create a new port. Click Next.

5. Select your printer manufacturer and model, then click Next.

NOTE

If your printer does not appear in the list, click Have Disk to install the Windows XP–compatible drivers that came with your printer, or click Windows Update to find a list of drivers that are available online.

6. Enter a name for the printer, and check or uncheck the option to use the printer as your default printer for Windows applications. Click Next.

NOTE

When you assign a name to your printer, or to a print server that shares printers, limit the name to 31 characters or less. This ensures compatibility with clients and software applications that cannot recognize longer printer names.

7. Specify whether you want to share the printer. If you share the printer, enter a shared printer name, using eight characters or less, followed by a period and three-letter extension if you need to provide Windows 3.*x* or MS-DOS client compatibility. Click Next. If you chose not to share the printer, skip to step 9.

8. If you share the printer, enter a location for the printer (such as the name of a building or office). You can also add a comment that further identifies the printer (such as *Creative Dept.* or *Executives' Printer*). Click Next.

9. Specify whether you want to print a test page. Click Next.

10. Review your choices and settings and click Finish to close the Add Printer Wizard. Windows XP adds the printer to the Printers And Faxes folder.

TIP

In the Printers And Faxes folder, a check mark appears at the top of the default printer's icon.

Connecting to a Network Printer on Another Computer

To connect to a printer on another computer on your network, follow these steps:

1. From the Printer Tasks list in the left pane, click Add A Printer to start the Add Printer Wizard. Click Next.

2. Click the A Network Printer, Or A Printer Attached To Another Computer option button. Click Next.

3. You can find the printer in one of three ways: Browse for the printer in your network folder; enter the qualified name of the printer (such as `\\server-1\hp_laserjet`); or enter the URL for a printer that is located on the Internet or your company or home network. Enter any necessary information, and click Next. If you specified the printer's name or URL, skip to step 5.

4. If you chose to browse for the printer, the Browse For Printers screen appears. Select the printer you want to use from the list of shared printers, or enter the printer name in the text box. When you select the printer, information in the lower portion of the window displays the comments for the printer, the printer status, and the number of documents that are waiting to be printed. After you select the printer, click Next.

5. Specify whether you want this printer to be the default printer for Windows programs. Click Next.

6. Review your choices, then click Finish to close the Add Printer Wizard.

Printer Properties

Right-click the appropriate printer icon and choose Properties. The Properties dialog box has seven tabs for configuring different aspects of the printer: General, Sharing, Ports, Advanced, Color Management, Device Settings, and Services. Because each printer has different features and functionality, the options available and features you see on some of these tabs differ from printer to printer.

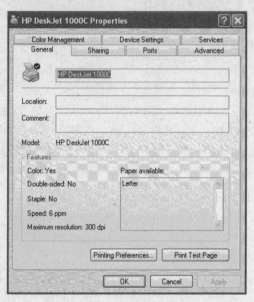

General tab   Allows you to specify the printer name and location. You can also add comments, such as who typically uses the printer and whom to contact if there's a problem. The General tab displays the printer features, which differ for each printer type and model.

Click the Printing Preferences button to configure settings for page layout and paper source and quality. Click Advanced to configure other advanced printing features. Click the Print Test Page button to verify that the printer is connected and functioning properly. If the test page doesn't print, click the Troubleshoot button to open the Windows XP Help And Support Center Printing Troubleshooter.

Sharing tab   Allows you to configure the printer as a local computer (not shared) or to share the printer with other users in the network. You can also specify additional printer drivers for those who use different hardware and/or operating system platforms. The correct drivers download automatically when a computer connects to the printer.

WARNING

You can share a printer only if you log on as a member of the Administrators group or if you have Manage Printers permissions.

Ports tab   Allows you to specify, delete, and configure the port to which the printer is attached. You can also enable bidirectional support and printer pooling.

Advanced tab   Allows you to configure advanced options, such as printer availability, logical printer priority, printer drivers, spooling settings, printing defaults, print processor options, and separator pages.

Color Management tab   Allows you to automatically or manually select a color profile to use when you print images. You can add or remove color profiles from the list and select a default color profile.

Device Settings tab   The options available on this tab depend on the capabilities and functions of your printer. Use this tab to view and manage printer-specific settings. Some examples include:

- ▶ Assigning forms to specific paper trays
- ▶ Substituting unavailable fonts with available fonts
- ▶ Setting printer-specific installation options, such as the amount of installed memory

Refer to your printer documentation for specific settings and their values.

Services tab   The availability of this tab depends on the printer you have installed. This tab can include service options such as aligning or cleaning print cartridges on ink-jet printers.

NOTE

To change printer properties, you must be the creator of the printer; log on as a computer administrator or member of the Administrators or Power Users group; or have Manage Printers permissions.

Sharing a Printer

You must share a computer in order for the printer to be accessible to other users on your network. To share a printer, right-click it in the Printer And Faxes window and choose Properties. Then select the Sharing tab in the Properties dialog box.

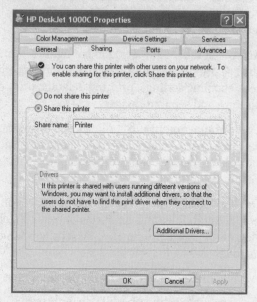

To share the printer, click the Share This Printer option button and enter a name for the shared printer in the Share Name text box (this can be different from the printer name). The name should consist of no more than eight characters, followed by a period and three-letter extension if you need to provide Windows 3.x or MS-DOS client compatibility. The name you enter appears when other users browse the network in My Network Places and Windows Explorer.

If you need to provide support for older versions of Windows (such as Windows NT 3.5 or 4, or Windows 95 or 98) or for different hardware platforms, click the Additional Drivers button. Select the appropriate hardware and OS version, and click OK to install the drivers. When users connect to the printer, their workstation downloads the correct drivers.

TIP

Windows 95 and 98 workstations download the driver only when the workstation connects to the printer the first time. You need to manually install newer drivers on these platforms when you update your printer driver. Windows 3.*x*, NT 4, and 2000 clients automatically download driver updates.

Printing Documents

There are several ways to print documents with Windows XP. To send a print job to your default printer, use one of the following methods:

▶ Open the document in any Windows application and click the Print button.

▶ In Windows Explorer, My Documents, My Computer, or My Network Places, select a file or files. Right-click the selection and choose Print, or choose File ➢ Print.

▶ Drag and drop one or more selected files to a printer in the Printers And Faxes folder, or to a printer shortcut on the Desktop.

To print a document to a printer that is not your default printer, open the document in the applicable Windows application (for example, open Microsoft Word to open a Word document). Choose File ➢ Print in the application to open the Print dialog box. Select the printer that you want to print to, and click the Print button to print.

Once you click the Print button to print your document, Windows XP sends it to a print queue on your local computer or on the print server. The document stays in the queue until it is printed.

Print Dialog Box

The tabs in the Print dialog box vary depending on your printer's capabilities (specified through the printer driver). What follows are examples of tabs and settings you commonly see in the Print dialog box. Other printer-specific tabs and settings may be available for your printer. Click Apply to save any changes you make on these tabs without closing the dialog box.

Choose the printer you want to print to and whether you want to print to a file (the default is printing to a printer). You can search for printers and view the status of the currently selected printer. You can print the entire document, the selected portion of a document, the current page, or a specific range of pages. You can also specify the number of copies you want to print and whether the printer should collate the copies.

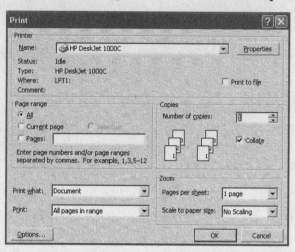

Click the Properties button in the Print dialog box to configure layout and paper options for your document. The Properties dialog box displays two tabs: Layout and Paper/Quality. On either tab, click the Advanced button to open the Advanced Options dialog box; the settings you find in this dialog box are printer specific.

Layout tab   Used to make document layout choices. Examples are orientation, print order, and pages per sheet.

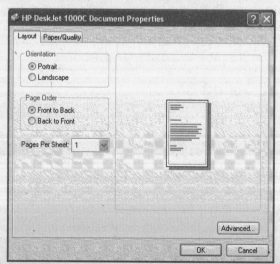

Paper/Quality tab Allows you to select the paper source and media type. Options vary depending on the capabilities of your printer. Refer to your printer documentation for more information about specific settings.

TIP
You can also access printing preference tabs using one of these other methods: Right-click any printer icon and choose Printing Preferences; or click the Printing Preferences button on the General tab of the Properties dialog box.

Using the Print Queue

The print queue stores print jobs from the time a user sends a document to the printer until after it has printed. You can use the print queue to manage and view the status of print jobs. Double-click a printer icon in the Printers And Faxes folder to access the print queue for the selected printer.

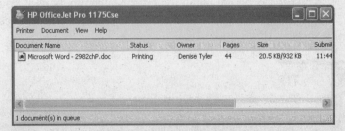

The print queue dialog box displays the following information for every print job in the queue:

Document Name   The name of the document that is currently printing or waiting to be printed

Status   The status of the document (printing, spooling, paused, or error)

Owner   The username of the person who sent the print job

Pages   The total number of pages in the document (for print jobs that are waiting in the queue), or the number of pages printed and total number of pages for jobs that are currently printing

Size   Total and printed document size in kilobytes

Submitted   The time and date when the document was sent to the printer

Port   The port the printer uses

The status bar at the bottom of the print queue dialog box displays the number of print jobs in the queue.

Use the Printer menu to connect to the printer, set the printer as the default printer, set up printing preferences, pause printing, cancel all documents, configure printer-sharing options, use the printer offline, access printer properties, and perform other functions. Most of these functions are also available on the File menu of the Printers And Faxes folder when you select a printer.

TIP
If you choose to use a printer offline, the printer icon is gray (disabled) in the Printers And Faxes folder.

Use the Document menu to perform such functions as pausing, resuming, restarting, and canceling the print job and to access document properties.

TIP
You can pause, resume, restart, cancel, and access properties for more than one print job at a time by selecting multiple print jobs and then making your choice from the Document menu.

NOTE

By default, only the creator of a job can manage his or her own print jobs. A user needs Manage Documents permission or administrative privileges in order to manage other people's print jobs.

Document Properties

Contains settings related to the document to be printed. Select a print job in the queue and choose Document ➤ Properties.

The General tab displays the name of the document, its size, number of pages, data type, processor, owner, and the date and time the job was submitted. By default, Windows notifies the owner of the document when the print job is complete, but you can specify that Windows notify a different user by typing the name in the Notify text box. You can move a slider left or right to change the priority of the print job in relation to other print jobs in the queue. Finally, you can specify a time range in which to print the job.

You can also access other printing preference tabs, such as the Layout and Paper/Quality tabs, from the Document Properties dialog box.

REGIONAL AND LANGUAGE OPTIONS

Enables you to customize the display of fractional or large numbers, currencies, dates, and times as used in your geographical location. Windows XP also supports the use of multiple languages. You can view or change the languages and methods available to enter text, and allow non-Unicode programs to display menus and dialog boxes in your native language.

To display the Regional And Language Options dialog box, choose Start ➤ Control Panel (or Start ➤ Settings ➤ Control Panel in the Classic Start menu) ➤ Date, Time, Language, And Regional Options. Next, select the Regional And Language Options icon. The Regional And Language Options dialog box opens, containing three tabs: Regional Options, Languages, and Advanced.

Regional Options Tab

Select your geographical region here and choose how to format numbers, currencies, times, and short or long dates. You can also select a region for local information such as news and weather.

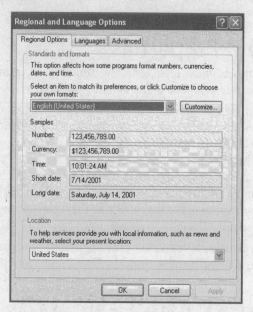

In the Standards And Formats area, there is a drop-down list where you choose the geographical region that you want to use. By default, this field displays the language option that you selected during Windows XP installation. When you choose another option from the drop-down list, the Samples fields display noneditable examples to show how numbers, currency, time, short date, and long date are formatted in that region. The Location drop-down list, at the bottom of the tab, allows you to select a region for local information such as news and weather.

Customizing Regional Options

To customize your regional options, click the Customize button on the Regional Options tab. This opens the Customize Regional Options dialog box, which features four tabs: Numbers, Currency, Time, and Date.

Numbers tab   Adjust the display of decimal symbols, the number of decimal digits, the digit grouping symbol, digit grouping, the negative sign symbol, the negative number format, the display of leading zeros, list separators, and the measurement system. As you enter or select new values for each field, the Sample area displays examples for positive and negative numbers.

Currency tab   Adjust the display of the currency symbol, the positive and negative currency formats, the decimal symbol, the number of digits after the decimal, and the digit grouping and digit grouping symbol options. As you enter or select new values for each field, the Sample area displays examples for positive and negative currency values.

Time tab   Adjust the display of times on the clock that appears in the notification area of your Taskbar and in related dialog boxes. These times appear in hours (*h*, *hh*, *H*, or *HH*), minutes (*mm*), and seconds (*ss*). Use *h* or *hh* to display time in 12-hour format, and *tt* to display AM or PM. Use *H* or *HH* to display time in 24-hour format. This dialog box also allows you to enter or select symbols for the time separator, as well as for the AM and PM symbols. As you enter or select new values for each field, the Sample area displays an example of your customized time values.

Date tab   Adjust the display of dates in dialog boxes and in documents that you create with applications such as Microsoft Word. When you enter a two-digit number for a year (such as *02* for 2002) in any dialog box or application that recognizes dates, Windows XP automatically interprets any value starting at 1930 and ending with the value you specify in the Ending Year field of the Calendar area. In the Short Date area, you can customize the format and separator used to display short dates; the Short Date Sample box displays an example of your customized short date format. In the Long Date area, you can specify how long dates are displayed and see a sample of your customized format.

Languages Tab

Allows you to view or change the languages and methods you use to enter text. The Supplemental Language Support section contains two options:

▸ Select the Install Files For Complex Script And Right-To-Left Languages check box if you want to install Arabic, Armenian, Georgian, Hebrew, Indic, Thai, and Vietnamese language files on your computer. These additional files use approximately 10MB of disk space.

▶ Select the Install Files For East Asian Languages check box to install additional files for Chinese, Japanese, and Korean language files. These files use approximately 230MB of disk space.

To configure language services, click the Details button to open the Text Services And Input Languages dialog box.

Text Services And Input Languages Dialog Box

The drop-down list in the Default Input Language area allows you to specify the default language that you use to enter text. This language is used when you start up or log on to your computer.

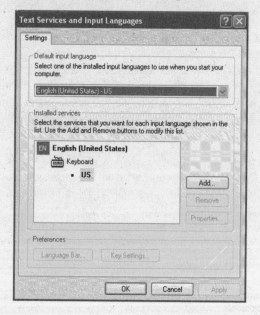

The Installed Services area displays all language and text services that are installed and loaded into memory when you start your computer. The text services you can select for each language installed on your computer include keyboard layouts, input method editors, and handwriting and speech recognition options. Use this area to add, remove, or check properties for additional language services.

To install additional language services, follow these steps:

1. From the Text Services And Input Languages dialog box, click Add. The Add Input Language dialog box appears.

2. Use the Input Language drop-down box to select the input language that you want to add.

3. The Keyboard Layout/IME field displays a keyboard layout to correspond with the selection you made in step 2. You can choose another keyboard layout if you desire.

4. Click OK to return to the Text Services And Input Languages dialog box. The new service appears in the Installed Services list.

Language services require computer memory and can affect performance.

NOTE
When you install a new language service, Windows XP may prompt you to insert your Windows XP CD to install additional files, and to reboot your computer for settings to take effect.

To remove an installed language service, highlight the service you want to remove, and click Remove.

The Preferences area at the bottom of the Text Services And Input Languages dialog box allows you to specify options for the Language bar. If you have speech recognition, handwriting recognition, or an input method editor installed as a text service, the Language Bar button is available; it opens a dialog box that allows you to change the look and behavior of the Language bar.

Click the Key Settings button to open the Advanced Key Settings dialog box. This dialog box allows you to configure the hot-key settings that you use to switch between your installed language services and to turn off the Caps Lock function. The default hot key to switch languages is Left Alt+Shift.

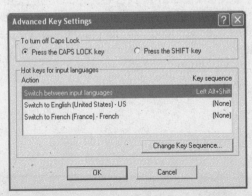

RUN

 Used to open programs, folders, documents, and Internet resources. Most frequently used to run installation programs. To use this function, follow these steps:

1. Choose Start ➤ Run. The Run dialog box appears.

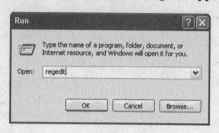

2. In the Open text box, enter the full path and name of the resource you want to open, or use the Browse button to locate the resource on your hard drive. You can also use the drop-down list to select a resource that you previously opened.

3. Click OK to open the resource.

SCANNERS AND CAMERAS

 Lets you configure scanners and cameras that are installed on the Windows XP computer.

Choose Start ➤ Control Panel (or Start ➤ Settings ➤ Control Panel in the Classic Start menu) ➤ Printers And Other Hardware. Next, click the Scanners And Cameras icon to display the Scanners And Cameras folder. This folder contains icons for the scanners and cameras that are installed on your system. The Add An Imaging Device task, in the left pane, allows you to install cameras and scanners that Windows XP does not automatically detect.

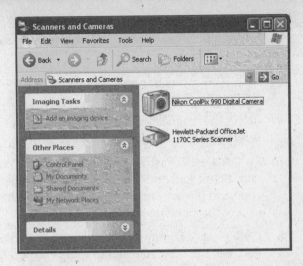

When you right-click a scanner or camera, a pop-up menu displays several options for the device. These allow you to delete or rename the device, or to get pictures using the Scanner And Camera Wizard. To view or modify the properties of a scanner or camera, right-click it in the list and choose Properties. The properties you see vary depending on your hardware but may include such items as port settings used for the device and color management. The Properties dialog box also includes options to test and troubleshoot problems with your scanner or camera and to configure color management profiles.

Scanner And Camera Installation Wizard

In most cases, Windows XP automatically detects your imaging device when you connect it to your computer and prompts you to install the drivers and any third-party software that came with your device. In the event that Windows XP does not detect your hardware, you can use the Scanner And Camera Installation Wizard to install your hardware.

To use the Scanner And Camera Installation Wizard, follow these steps:

1. Choose Start ≻ Control Panel (or Start ≻ Settings ≻ Control Panel in the Classic Start menu) ≻ Printers And Other Hardware. Next, click the Scanners And Cameras icon to display the Scanners And Cameras folder.

2. From the Imaging Tasks list in the left pane, choose Add An Imaging Device. The Scanner And Camera Installation Wizard appears.

3. Click Next. A dialog box prompts you to select the device driver to install for your hardware.

4. Select the manufacturer of your device from the Manufacturers list in the left portion of the dialog box.

5. The Models list (on the right) displays a list of available products. Select your device from the list. If your device does not appear in the list, click Have Disk to install the drivers that came with your hardware device.

6. Click Next to continue. You are prompted to connect your device to the computer, and to select the port to which it is connected. Choose Automatic Port Detection to detect the port automatically, or manually select the port from the list of available ports.

7. Click Next to continue. The wizard prompts you to choose automatic port detection, or to select from a list of ports.

8. Click Next to continue. Enter a name for your device. Edit the name if desired.

9. Click Next to display the final wizard screen. To complete the installation, click Finish.

Send To

Send To ▸ Lets you send a file or folder directly to a compressed folder; your Desktop (as a shortcut); a mail recipient; a floppy disk, Zip disk, or CD; or your My Documents folder—or to publish to the Internet.

To send an item to a destination using Send To, perform these steps:

1. In any Explorer window, right-click a file or folder and choose Send To from the menu that appears.

2. Select the destination:

   ▶ Choose Compressed (Zipped) Folder to create a ZIP file that contains the item(s) you selected.

   ▶ Choose Desktop (Create Shortcut) to create a shortcut on your Desktop that opens the selected item.

   ▶ Choose Mail Recipient to send the file to a contact from your address book, or to the e-mail address you enter.

   ▶ Choose 3-½ Floppy to copy the selection to a floppy disk.

   ▶ Choose My Documents to send the document to your My Documents folder.

   ▶ Choose CD-Drive to write the selected file(s) to CD.

SHARING

Sharing and Security... Lets you share folders, disks, printers, and other resources on your computer with other users on a network. When you share a folder or disk, you can specify which users have access to the resource and configure the permissions for them. Sharing settings are configured on the Sharing tab of the resource's Properties sheet. Users can see and access your shared resources through My Network Places.

Sharing a Folder or Disk

To share a folder or disk with users of the network, perform the following steps:

1. In any Explorer window, right-click the folder or disk you want to share and select Sharing And Security. The Properties dialog box opens to the Sharing tab.

TIP
Alternatively, you can right-click the folder or disk, select Properties, and then select the Sharing tab.

2. Select Share This Folder On The Network and enter a name for the share.

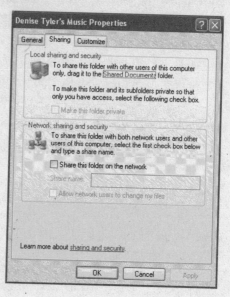

3. Check or uncheck the option to allow network users to change the files.

4. Click OK to apply your selections.

WINDOWS COMPONENTS

Add/Remove
Windows
Components

Windows XP Home and Professional install many Windows components on your computer, and also provide many other components to suit your specific needs. The default options installed with Home and Professional are not identical.

Examples of Windows components installed by default include WordPad, Calculator, HyperTerminal, Phone Dialer, Media Player, and Volume Control. Additional Windows components include Component Services, Data Sources, Event Viewer, Remote Storage, and so on.

To add additional components that Windows XP does not install by default, choose Start ➤ Control Panel (or Start ➤ Settings ➤ Control Panel in the Classic Start menu) ➤ Add Or Remove Programs. Select Add/Remove Windows Components from the left pane. For information

about each of the available components, use the Windows XP Help And
Support Center.

WINDOWS UPDATE

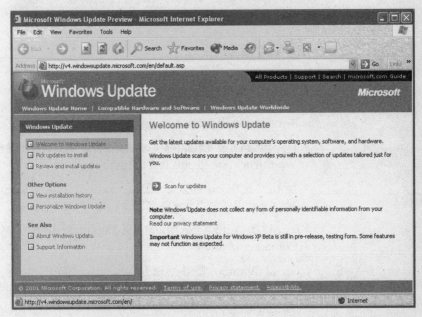 Windows Update   Choose Start ➢ All Programs (or Start ➢ Programs in
the Classic Start menu) ➢ Windows Update to connect
to the Microsoft Windows Update home page. Windows Update scans
your computer and provides you with a list of the latest updates that help
keep your Windows XP operating system, hardware, and software running at peak performance. Windows Update also tracks the updates you
have already installed so that you do not have to download them again.
Click the appropriate links to find the information you're looking for,
such as critical updates, recommended updates, top picks, device drivers,
additional Windows features, and help on using the site.

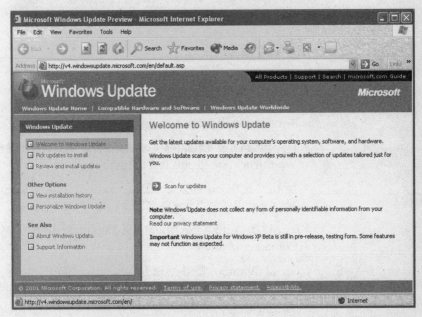

You can also configure Windows XP to automatically notify you when
updates are available. To configure update notification, follow these steps:

1. Choose Start ➢ Control Panel (or Start ➢ Settings ➢ Control
    Panel in the Classic Start menu) ➢ Performance And
    Maintenance.

2. Click the System icon to open the System Properties dialog box.

3. Select the Automatic Updates tab.

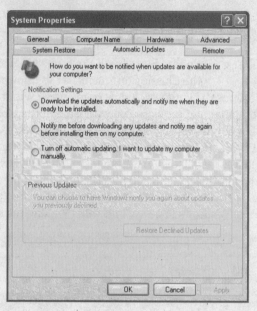

4. Choose one of the following self-explanatory options from the Notification Settings section of the dialog box:

- ▶ Download The Updates Automatically And Notify Me When They Are Ready To Be Installed.

- ▶ Notify Me Before Downloading Any Updates And Notify Me Again Before Installing Them On My Computer.

- ▶ Turn Off Automatic Updating. I Want To Update My Computer Manually.

5. By default, Windows Update hides update notification items that you previously declined. To make these updates available again, click the Restore Declined Updates button.

6. Click OK to apply your settings and exit the System Properties dialog box.

INDEX

Note to the Reader: Page numbers in **bold** indicate the principle discussion of a topic or the definition of a term. Page numbers in *italic* indicate illustrations.

A

Access databases, **547–614**, *See also* Office XP
changing storage folders, 559
creating
adding pictures to reports, 563, *564*
adding titles, 562, *563*
bypassing switchboard, 564
choosing fields, 560–561, *560*
choosing form styles, 561, *561*
choosing report styles, 562, *562*
displaying help, 564
finishing up, 564–565, *565*
navigating wizard, 560
overview of, 553, 558–559, *559*
customizing
adding close buttons, 605–606
adding command buttons, 602–604, *602–603*
adding hyperlinks, 601–602
adding mailing label buttons, 604–605
adding query buttons, 605
adding Visual Basic code, 606–608
and closing, 613
overview of, 601, 613
startup commands, 612–613, *612*
switchboard forms, 608–611, *608–609*
and testing, 613–614

customizing forms
aligning form objects, 573, 606
and closing, 576, 585
controls in, defined, **570**
creating and, 569–570, *571*
deleting controls, 574
in Design view, 570–575, *571*
disabling cursor landings, 575–576, *576*
editing label text, 574
mouse operation icons in, 572–573
moving controls, 572–573, 575
resizing labels, 573, 575
resizing text controls, 575
and saving, 576
selecting controls, 573
sizing controls, 572–573
undoing changes, 574
data access web pages
browsing, 593
creating, 590–592
defined, **28**, **590**
defined, **551**
entering data using forms
and closing, 585
in Datasheet view, 581, *581*
in Edit mode, 580
and editing, 580–582, *580*
and filtering, 583
and finding, 583–585
in Form view, 572, 581

P

ABOUT THE CONTRIBUTORS

Some of the best—and best-selling—authors have contributed chapte from their books to *Microsoft Office XP Complete*.

Karla Browning is the Training and Project Manager for TRIAD Consult LLC. She holds teaching credentials for both Michigan and California. Sl the primary trainer and developer of TRIAD's Microsoft in the Classroom series and coauthor of the *Word 2000 MOUS Study Guide* with Courter a Marquis.

Mary Burmeister is a project manager, editor, and writer at LANWrights Inc. She has helped produce books on markup languages, including *HTM For Dummies, Hip Pocket Guide to HTML 4.01, XML For Dummies*, and *XHTML For Dummies*.

Gini Courter and **Annette Marquis** are co-owners of TRIAD Consulting, LLC, a firm specializing in computer applications training and database development, including customized solutions using Microsoft Outlook an Microsoft Exchange Server. Courter and Marquis are the authors of nume ous books, including *Mastering Microsoft Office 2000, Mastering Microso Outlook 2000*, and *Office 2000 User Specialist Study Guide*, all from Sybex.

Lucinda Dykes is the principal at Zero G Web Design in Santa Fe, New Mexico. She has been developing websites and writing code since 1994 an teaches web-related classes at Santa Fe Community College.

Molly E. Holzschlag is an author, instructor, and designer honored as one of the "Top 25 Most Influential Women on the Web." Her popular column "Integrated Design" appears monthly in *Web Techniques* magazine, and she contributes regularly to numerous web developer sites.

Mark Minasi is a noted educator and author in the fields of PC computing, data communications, and operating systems. His best-selling books include *Mastering Windows 2000 Server, Mastering Windows 2000 Professional, Mastering TCP/IP for NT, The Hard Disk Survival Kit*, and *Troubleshooting Windows*, all from Sybex. Mark also serves as CNN's resident computer expert.

Perspection, Inc. have been writing and editing software training books since 1991. They have written more than 60 books, with several best-sellers to their credit, and sold over 3.5 million books.

Deborah S. Ray and **Eric J. Ray** are owners of RayComm, Inc., a technical communications consulting firm that specializes in cutting-edge Internet and computing technologies. Together they have coauthored more than 10 computer books, including the first and second editions of *Mastering HTML 4* from Sybex. They also write a syndicated computer column, which is available in newspapers across North America, and serve as Technology Review Editors for *Technical Communication*, the Journal of the Society for Technical Communication.

Celeste Robinson has worked as a systems engineer, small business consultant, technical trainer, and database developer in a computing career that spans more than 20 years. She has coauthored (with Alan Simpson) *Mastering Access 97*, *Mastering WordPerfect Office 2000*, and *Mastering Access 2000*, all from Sybex.

Alan Simpson is a software consultant, best-selling author, and teacher, who has been active in the computer industry for over two decades. His books include dozens of popularly, critically, and technically acclaimed titles.

Ed Tittel is a principal at LANWrights, Inc., where he writes, consults, and teaches on a variety of networking and web-related topics. He has written or coauthored more than 100 computer books and hundreds of magazine articles.

Denise Tyler is a technical writer with more than eight years of experience writing books on Windows applications and Internet-related topics. She has served as a consulting and training specialist for a software company that develops Windows multimedia applications.

Chelsea Valentine is a webmaster, writer, and trainer at LANWrights, Inc., developing sites and teaching others how to do the same.

Peter Weverka is the author of 33 computer books. As a website developer, he has worked for Clorox, VISA, and other companies.

Mastering Microsoft Outlook 2002

by Gini Courter and Annette Marquis

752 pages; $39.99
ISBN 0-7821-4001-7

The latest release of Outlook is more about business productity than ever before, and this comprehensive guide provides wealth of information on the techniques you need to know to make Outlook work just right for your team—from customization to collaboration. With coverage of everything from the basics of Outlook to topics like forms creation, security, VBA programming, and troubleshooting, this is the Outlook book users will want.

Mastering Access 2002 Premium Edition

by Celeste Robinson and Alan Simpson

1224 pages; $49.99
ISBN 0-7821-4008-4

This comprehensive reference covers the entire range of Acce 2002 functionality, from basic to advanced. Special attention paid to new features, making the transition from an earlier ve sion quick and painless, and 200 pages of bonus macro mate teach you ways to customize and automate Access. You'll als find expanded coverage of such hot topics as enhanced XML support, integration with Microsoft's .NET and SQL Server 20 and web security. The CD contains all the sample databases from the book, plus a variety of custom Visual Basic functions and a searchable electronic edition of the book.

MASTERING MICROSOFT FRONTPAGE 2002 PREMIUM EDITION

BY PETER WEVERKA AND MOLLY E. HOLZSCHLAG

1200 pages; $49.99
ISBN 0-7821-4003-3

In this definitive reference to FrontPage 2002, readers planning, building, promoting, and maintaining professional websites will find complete coverage of FrontPage features—from basic to advanced—so they can tackle web projects with confidence. Seasoned web developer and columnist Molly Holzschlag shows you the key design principles that contribute to a successful site, and popular author and Microsoft applications expert Peter Weverka guides you through the FrontPage techniques that will enable you to realize your design objectives quickly and easily. The CD contains a 30-day fully functional version of Microsoft's FrontPage 2002, demos of tools covered in the book, and more.

MASTERING HTML 4 PREMIUM EDITION

BY DEBORAH S. RAY AND ERIC J. RAY

1216 pages; $49.99
ISBN 0-7821-2524-7

Here's an unbeatable value: everything in *Mastering HTML 4*, plus 200 entirely new pages and a CD packed with code, a searchable HTML reference, and powerful web utilities—all for $49.99! Special topics available only in the Premium Edition include XML and DOM, expanded DHTML coverage, an update on HTML development tools, and productivity-enhancement tips. Enjoy both print and electronic versions of the popular Master's Reference to HTML tags, style sheets, JavaScript, HTML special characters, and HTML color codes. This is as comprehensive as it gets!

THE COMPLETE PC UPGRADE & MAINTENANCE GUIDE (TWELFTH EDITION)

BY MARK MINASI

1488 pages; $59.99
ISBN 0-7821-2990-0

This extensively revised and updated twelfth edition of the best-selling guide to PC upgrading and maintenance include updated information on memory, modems, sound boards, di drives, printing problems, operating system upgrades, vide capture, digital audio, networking, combo printers, vendor guides, memory, and more. Loaded with more than 1400 pag of hard-core information, this is the one book no profession student, or serious home user can afford to be without!

MICROSOFT EXCEL 2002 SIMPLY VISUAL

BY PERSPECTION, INC.

288 pages; $24.99
ISBN 0-7821-4006-8

A must-have for anyone new to Excel 2002, this easy-to-read visual guide introduces users to the most essential features o Microsoft's premier spreadsheet program. Using illustrations and to-the-point explanations, this book takes you step by st through the program's interface, key features, and tools, and shows you the fundamentals you need to create professional-quality spreadsheets.